Visual Basic® .NET:
The Complete Reference

About the Author

Jeffrey R. Shapiro is a software architect and IT specialist who has written several books on software development and technology, including *SQL Server 2000: The Complete Reference*.

Visual Basic® .NET:
The Complete Reference

Jeffrey R. Shapiro

McGraw-Hill/Osborne

New York   Chicago   San Francisco
Lisbon   London   Madrid   Mexico City
Milan   New Delhi   San Juan
Seoul   Singapore   Sydney   Toronto

McGraw-Hill/Osborne
2600 Tenth Street
Berkeley, California 94710
U.S.A.

To arrange bulk purchase discounts for sales promotions, premiums, or fund-raisers, please contact **McGraw-Hill**/Osborne at the above address. For information on translations or book distributors outside the U.S.A., please see the International Contact Information page immediately following the index of this book.

Visual Basic .NET®: The Complete Reference

1234567890 DOC DOC 0198765432

ISBN: 0-07-213381-3

Publisher	**Copy Editors**
Brandon A. Nordin	Mandy Erickson, Bill McManus
Vice President & Associate Publisher	**Proofreader**
Scott Rogers	Pat Mannion
Acquisitions Editor	**Indexer**
Ann Sellers	Valerie Perry
Project Editor	**Computer Designers**
Elizabeth Seymour	George Toma Charbak, Melinda Moore Lytle
Acquisitions Coordinator	
Timothy Madrid	**Illustrators**
	Michael Mueller, Lyssa Wald
Technical Editors	
Lou Boni, Amir Liberman	**Series Design**
	Peter Hancik

This book was composed with Corel VENTURA™ Publisher.

This book is dedicated to the late Sabas (Saby) Blanco
November 13, 1975 to October 7, 2001

Contents at a Glance

Contents

Part I

Introduction to Visual Basic .NET

Part IV

Writing Software with VB .NET

Foreword

This book started over a burger in a downtown Seattle café in late 2001. I was reflecting with my editor, Ann Sellers, about the discussions we had just had with the Microsoft .NET protagonists. We came to the conclusion that if Microsoft could pull off the .NET Framework, it would change software development—at least for the Windows operating systems—forever. This book's publication is testimony to the achievement that is the .NET Framework and, in particular, Visual Basic .NET.

Visual Basic .NET and the .NET Framework and I go back almost five years when I was an aggressive Java programmer (of course, the framework was just a nameless, mysterious OO project at MS then). While I worked with several flavors of Java, all my customers needed stuff for the Windows platform. Visual J++ was my tool of choice (especially after programming Delphi for a few years). Then, delegates (those so-called object-oriented function pointers) and other things that Microsoft was doing with Java hit a nerve center at the house of Sun. The result was the Intifada between the two software makers that stopped VJ++ in its tracks.

For the next couple of years the Visual J++ Web site at Microsoft.com and "VJ" remained unchanged. The Java world moved on with newer stuff from Sun, and VJ and Windows Foundation Classes (WFC) languished in the lawsuits. I and tens of thousands of Windows VJ programmers lost a lot of faith in the software development business.

Many of us felt passionate enough, and were hurt enough, to get some answers directly from Microsoft on where they were heading. At the end of 1998 I was told "if you can wait for our new object-oriented software to arrive you will really be pleased." My reply to that was "What should I do in the meantime?" "Go and develop with Visual Basic and we'll call you when it's ready." Not knowing what they were baking, I took their advice, and that's exactly what I did for the next few years. I went on to use VB for a number of major projects.

While I developed some sophisticated stuff in VB, I also kept current with Java (not VJ). So it did not take me long to finally "get" what had "set" so many VB programmers to refusing to use anything else to develop their software (no matter how much certain technology lacking affected them).

When Visual Basic .NET emerged I realized I had the best of both worlds—everything I loved about VJ and VB in one package. Sure, I still have an affinity for curly braces, but no other language in the world is as productive as Visual Basic .NET, not even C#. And I tell you that as a programmer who has coded in more than just Java, Delphi, and Visual Basic . . . and C#.

Well, it is finally here, and it's the best thing since strawberry-flavored cranberries.

While chewing on my burger, I also reflected on what Microsoft had said to us earlier that day about how they would like us to write about the .NET Framework. The one statement that stood out was that they were keen to see books that did not simply rehash the tons of information that were going to be put out, or compete with the online material (which is excellent). They were looking for books that would help people understand not only the fundamentals of the framework and its many languages, but also how to use the extremely powerful and complex constructs and technologies they were going to unleash.

It became apparent to me how different .NET in general and Visual Basic .NET in particular was going to be from the current version of the language (VB 6) and the current Windows software development paradigms and object models, such as COM and ActiveX. I was both surprised and amused at how familiar Visual Basic .NET and the .NET Framework now looked to Java, Visual J++ and Delphi.

I found myself in a unique position, having arrived at Visual Basic (I skipped the earlier versions and cut my teeth on VB 5 and 6) via C++, Delphi, and Java. I at once felt that Visual Basic .NET would appeal not only to existing VB developers (or scare some of them half to death) but to the many Java and Delphi programmers. The latter are of special interest to me because, like me, they are not only dedicated to the Windows platform, but they have been programming in true object-oriented languages for almost a decade now. After all, I learned Delphi back in the early 1990s, Java in 1995. Much of what's new to Visual Basic, like true OO and free threading, has been part of the Delphi and Java arsenal for many years. You will see that I talk not only to VB programmers (for the most part) but also to VJ and Delphi programmers.

What you now have in Visual Basic .NET is the marvelous utility and simplicity of Visual Basic coupled with the incredible power of OO and Visual J++ (ten-fold). To put it in a nutshell: You can now do with Visual Basic .NET what you once only dreamed was possible, and do it faster than with any other language. In many cases, once you get up to speed with the syntax and semantics, you *can* just about write the software in your sleep.

I have written a number of computer books, but it was a challenge to write a really good software development book. The proverbial hat goes off to all those guys and gals who have penned something for software developers.

Having my own library of software development books, I know that you need to strike a balance between talking and showing. If you talk too much and don't provide enough examples, you lose your audience. If you show too much you end up alienating everyone and might as well be writing in hieroglyphics. I especially dislike books that provide a page of narrative and then throw 15 pages of unexplained code at you. I must admit I have never learned much about writing software from any of those tomes.

It's also difficult to provide meaningful examples and enough of them. I believe the examples should be plucked from live code in functioning products. They should not be examples knocked up in Notepad that were obviously never compiled. While I have taken some shortcuts here and there to provide a quick and dirty example, every line of code written in this book has been written and compiled in Visual Studio .NET and then tested.

You will also find that there is more narrative than code in many places. I have gone to great lengths to explore all the various facets of the constructs and technologies you will encounter as a .NET programmer. The reason is simple. Computer books don't seem to get thinner, and this is compounded by there being so much to talk about or explain. I decided that instead of publishing 1500 pages with hundreds of examples that cannot be compiled from wood pulp, or compiled on the train to work, that it would be better to put as much extra code as possible into the various projects that were created with this book.

A giant Visual Studio .NET solution, Vb7cr, is included with this book that by publication will have been culled from more than 50 projects, some of them implemented for commercial applications. You will find a lot in the projects, from the linked list classes to a full-blown ASP.NET application that implements a sophisticated search facility, and more. They have all been compiled and tested with the released version of Visual Studio and the .NET Framework. You can download the software from www.osborne.com and www.sdamag.com. It's just code and downloads easily on a 56K connection, so Osborne and I deemed it unnecessary to come out with a CD.

Of particular interest in the solution is a complete binary tree example, which extends the linked list project covered in the book. Rather than publishing the 50 pages this particular project took, the code has been fully tested and is available in the first version of the solution. Not only will you find the classes useful for building sophisticated data structures, but the project provides an excellent learning tool for object-oriented enthusiasts. It at once provides grounding in OO, inheritance, aggregation, composition, and polymorphism, and discusses how to use interfaces, delegates, exception handling, and some sophisticated algorithms. There are a number of interesting killer methods in the classes (like recursing the tree nodes and using delegates to speed up binary search), so you get to work at a high level of abstraction on the one hand and a very low level on the other.

This book assumes you have some idea how to program. But it will also work for you if you have never so much as written a **While** statement before and you are willing to learn. I have provided some grounding on software development practices for newcomers, like what constitutes good method writing or class construction. Experts will no doubt gloss over these areas, although those experts new to Visual Basic .NET will do well to refresh themselves with the practices that can help them become very efficient OO practitioners.

If you don't know the Unified Modeling Language (UML), you should get a guide to bring yourself up to speed. I express many concepts using UML class diagrams. Visual Studio .NET for Enterprise Architects ships with a version of Visio 2002 specifically geared for architecting .NET software using UML. For all sizable software development projects, completing the model (as discussed in Chapter 9) is the first thing you must do before you hack out a single method.

You will find that I spend an enormous amount of time in object-oriented aspects of Visual Basic .NET. I believe to the credit of the book some chapters are more about OO software development than Visual Basic .NET (hence the reason for the number of UML diagrams in the book). However, every general discussion about OO software development is backed up by an example in Visual Basic .NET.

I cannot stress enough, especially to my learned comrades, how important it is to fully understand and use Visual Basic .NET to write correct *object-oriented* software. If you are going to live in the OO house you need know what's in the ceiling, what the walls are made of, and what's lurking in the basement. If you take it all in and not just cook spaghetti on the stove, I promise you will be richly rewarded with an ability to write software in any .NET language you want (J# included).

I am incredibly impressed by how Microsoft has gone to great lengths to reduce the complexity involved in writing good software, while at the same time providing constructs that allow you to create the most incredible facilities. While you get advanced constructs like a free-threading model, which can add to complexity, they have taken away the need for you to manage every ounce of memory on a computer. I once had the unfortunate job of creating a high-end mail server, which needed to manage numerous threads. Having to manage memory on every thread at the same time made that task unforgettable.

This book in no way covers everything about Visual Basic .NET and the .NET Framework. Just because the title says "Complete Reference" does not mean we need to cover every class and every method in .NET, although many readers expect exactly that. I remember a reader chewing on me about not covering ISAPI in my *SQL Server 2000: The Complete Reference*." You call this a complete reference?" he said. "Where's the stuff on using ISAPI to connect SQL Server to the Web?" I wrote the guy back and said "Perhaps I'll add some stuff about herbal remedies as well," only to be told he would hold me to that statement.

To cover everything you need several volumes. However, I am fortunate to have a publisher and a great editorial team that has been willing to allow me to write more than one book. Otherwise, we would probably have been looking at around 2000 pages.

This book is my second on Visual Basic .NET. The first book, *Visual Basic .NET Developer's Headstart,* is an introduction to Visual Basic .NET. It's designed as a quick read to place you on familiar footing with Visual Basic .NET. It's especially useful if you come from the world of Java and Delphi, and want to be sure Visual Basic .NET is for you.

The book you are holding is aimed at core material and fundamentals. The Introduction will fill you in with that aspect of it.

I encourage you to send me your contributions, comments, and any suggestions on fixing or enhancing the material presented in this book. You can write me at jshapiro@sdamag.com or visit www.sdamag.com. Any contribution you wish to make will be considered and you'll be asked permission to include it in future editions or in the solutions.

I sincerely hope you will enjoy reading this book and gain the enrichment that I have garnered from writing it.

Acknowledgments

M any people made this book possible. Besides editors and production people and writers, authors, testers, and reviewers, a great many people who did not have a direct involvement in this book nevertheless provided contributions which were indispensable. I would like to thank these dear friends first.

During the early stages of this book, I relied heavily on my coworker and assistant, Saby Blanco, who was sadly taken from us without warning in late 2001. (I know God had a reason for recalling Saby in a heartbeat; I just wish I knew what that reason was). I have dedicated this book to his memory and to thank him for his friendship and help. He is sadly missed by many. He was a terrific person.

My wife and dear friend, Kim, has certainly had it rough in recent years, but without her unfaltering commitment and support it would have been very difficult to reach this stage in the life of not only this book but in my other books as well.

A special thank you to my sister, Lesley Kalish, for her assumption of many of my family responsibilities that made it possible for me to dedicate the time I did to this project. I owe the same level of appreciation to my uncle, Charlie Frank, for his support, love, and friendship.

I also owe more that a few words of thanks to my wife's family, the Zagnoevs, and in particular to my father-in-law and mother-in-law, Barney and Entha Zagnoev, whose support in this "venture" and several others in the not-too-distant past, has meant a great deal to me.

Many coworkers and collegues in the past years made it possible for me to put the words and code in these pages between book covers. They include Steven Cohen at TempArt who always happens to call just when you think it's time to give him a shout; Armando Blanco for his support in various technical fields over the years and for his friendship; and Mike Costolo at C&L Insurance, Inc., who deserves a special thank you for his support, especially during the weeks and months this book had me deep in living in an alternate reality.

Two people deserve special thanks for the effort and support they have given me over the past eight years—especially with respect to my career. They are Stephen Kain, of the law firm Polatsek and Sclafani, and my book agent, David Fugate, of Waterside Productions, Inc.

No author can boast that he or she did a book single-handedly. And no matter how much effort goes into the creative side, without the help and dedication of editors and production people a good book can very quickly go bad. On that note, I would first like to thank the Production Editor at Osborne, Elizabeth Seymour, for going more than the extra mile for me. Besides the hard work and commitment to the publishing task, her support, understanding, and tolerance (of me) are greatly appreciated.

I also would like to thank my publishers and the all the production and editorial staff that helped keep this book on track. In particular, I owe my publisher McGraw-Hill/Osborne for support and patience during the long haul. Special thanks and appreciation are due to my editor, Ann Sellers, for her commitment and support, during the approximately 18 months it took to publish this book, from conception to reality. I am especially indebted to Ann for the opportunity she has given me in this venture.

My technical reviewers, Lou Boni and Amir Liberman, of Ziphex Consulting, Inc. (www.ziphex.com), and Jared Kalish all deserve a special thank you for the extra effort each made to not only read my chapters but also to test my code. I am especially indebted to my nephew, math whiz Jared Kalish, for his direct help in reviewing many of the pages I thought I had lost my way with. His blunt "Am I supposed to understand what this means?" style of editorial critique and review is directly responsible for a lot of polish.

I have received a lot of help from Microsoft over the past five or so years that I greatly appreciate. I especially feel a debt of gratitude to Stacey Giard (.NET Developer Support Group PM) for her commitment, and to Eric Foster at Waggener Edstrom (Wagged) for the help he has given me with all my books.

Introduction

Before I introduce the chapters I want to tell you what this book is not. It is not a book that caters to migrating from the earlier versions of VB to Visual Basic .NET. There are several reasons for not talking about what was and what now is. In many cases, the effort to migrate is not worth your time; you might as well start from scratch. Besides, you must learn the new language. Also, anything written in classic VB is unlikely to carry over well from the design and architecture points of view (especially the much earlier versions of VB). While I don't know VB prior to VB 5 and 6 very well, I know enough about the latest versions to tell you that there is a huge difference between classic VB and Visual Basic .NET. You will undergo a shift in psyche, from being a VB programmer to being a Visual Basic .NET programmer. You have to change the way you think—thinking in objects—not only change the way you write software. Now is a good time to rebuild your VB application from ground level and put it on a solid object-oriented foundation.

While I have made a few notes in places about the differences, it is only to reflect on interesting points and anomalies. I believe that if you are an expert in "classic" VB you will know exactly where to look to find the differences; you'll adapt both personally and with the software with relative ease. I work with VB 6 every day. I also work with VB programmers every day, some of them with one leg in VB 6 and the other in .NET. We don't run to find a book that explains the differences between interfaces and arrays, for example. We get into it and find out the differences at the moment we are most disposed to encounter them.

If, however, you need to understand how involved migration will be you can simply open your VB apps in Visual Studio .NET and let the upgrade tool tell you what you are in for.

If you are not an expert in classic VB and come from Delphi or Java, any discussion about the differences is a waste of time. And if you are new to programming I strongly urge you not to dilly-dally in classic VB because that will cause frustration when you do change to Visual Basic .NET. Just come on in and get started . . . the OO water is just fine.

The book you are holding aims to impart as much information as it can to allow you to become familiar with key concepts as quickly as possible. I believe in the cliché that if you give a poor person ten bucks you feed him or her for a day, but if you give the person a fishing rod then perhaps they will go off and start a fishing factory that turns out the world's finest lox.

Once you understand the core constructs and fundamentals, like control-flow, iteration, operators, methods, and properties, and then the advanced, yet still core, object-oriented concepts like inheritance and polymorphism, you will be ready to take on anything in Visual Basic .NET.

The marvel of the .NET Framework is that once you have a grasp of these core concepts, using the classes and the facilities in the base class libraries and the advanced libraries is relatively straightforward. I liken it to learning how to drive a car. Once you know how to change gears, park, accelerate, and so forth, you have what it takes to get into any car and drive away.

This became very clear to me during the writing of this book when I was assigned to create an ASP-based application and decided to do it in ASP.NET instead. There was no mode change or gear shift for me at all. Sure, the Web-related elements, which apply to all languages, are a different matter. This book would not be doing justice to its cause or readership if it suddenly started going into XML basics or HTML layout. The so-called code behind the Web-based application is the same code you write for standard Windows applications and services. That's the marvel of .NET.

When it came to ASP.NET related code, like instantiating session objects, I found that everything I knew about core Visual Basic applied to these ASP related constructs. It was as if they were simply objects you use in standard Windows applications.

You will also *not* find much more than passing references about ADO.NET, GDI+, ASP.NET, and the network libraries in this book. I took this course for a number of reasons. The first is that I don't consider the discussion core reference material. Giving you a book of 50 chapters averaging 20 pages a chapter, just to say ADO.NET does this and ASP.NET does that is not a book I consider any help toward achieving the fundamental understanding of how .NET and Visual Basic .NET works. For this reason, many of the chapters are long and complex. I have made every effort to cover the concepts as thoroughly as possible.

Another reason is that once you have mastered the fundamentals, and learned to think in object semantics and the construct syntax, you will be able to incorporate these technologies with your eyes closed. This is why some of these technologies only feature

The chapter takes you through ages of procedural and structured programming, and into the object-oriented paradigm. We will discuss modularity, class cohesion, and related topics.

The largest section in this chapter goes into what makes a pure object-oriented language. It discusses the so-called "three corners of OO": inheritance, polymorphism, and encapsulation. It also points out how many constructs, like encapsulation, are rooted in programming models, pre-OO. Most important is that you'll see how Visual Basic now fits the bill as an extremely powerful and pure OO language.

The chapter covers the differences between object-oriented programming (OOP) and object-based programming (OBD). There is also a discussion about frameworks.

The concept of patterns in software development is a very important subject. The subject of patterns is introduced in this chapter. Several chapters go into key structural and behavioral patterns in detail; these include Composite, State, Bridge, and Singleton. You will see how many patterns that have been used for years in OO software development lay the foundations for many sophisticated technologies in .NET. Delegates are a case in point.

Chapter 2

It is important to get up to speed with the .NET Framework and the common language runtime (CLR) as soon as possible. While it is true you can install the CLR and forget it for many applications, there are a lot of things you need to be aware of when it comes to how your code is executed. This chapter goes into Microsoft intermediate language, how your application code gets packaged into assemblies, and how the runtime locates and runs your code.

When I first started this book I thought it would not be necessary to go into the CLR in any detail; maybe give the subject a few paragraphs. Then I tried to deploy an application for a client to the production servers, only to discover the code was unable to run due to some obscure security condition. While this chapter presents the basics of security (the runtime environment and the CLR), the information I gained from learning about the CLR made all the difference. A few tweaks here and there, and the code was up and running.

You need to know about the assembly cache, side-by-side execution, the Common Language Specification, and .NET security. While you do not need to become a guru on all the subject matter covered in Chapter 2, you'll have the confidence to move your software off your development workstation and know what it needs to run with in the world at large.

Chapter 3

This chapter aims at making you productive with Visual Studio .NET as quickly as possible. The chapter has been designed to have you learning important points from

in places in the code examples—because they were needed in the code exam[p]
you know how to access an array and iterate through its elements, accessing a
and iterating through its elements is practically the same thing. The only differe
in one case you reference classes at **System.Array** and in the latter case you refere
classes at **System.Data**.

So sophisticated is Visual Basic .NET, the common language runtime, and the .l
Framework, that even cryptic and hard to understand COM or ActiveX technology
melts away when wrapped inside .NET. I have imported dozens of COM objects,
fearing pain worse that root canal, to find myself up and running with them within
minutes as if they were simply another bunch of .NET objects.

I also chewed long and hard on whether to get into reflection, garbage collection,
attributes, and the like but felt, based on my experience with Visual J++, that you'll
hardly need to deal with these concepts for most of your applications, especially in a
book that boasts core coverage. You might, however, find yourself calling on reflect
methods, or trying to do something odd with the garbage collector, on very few
occasions or when you need to start working on sophisticated applications, such as
those that need to invoke methods remotely

The same is true for threading, although I felt it important to discuss the basic
concepts in a small part of the book dealing with Windows Forms and user interfaces.

Now to what this book *is* about. It's certainly about the fundamentals—Parts I and
II deal with the core constructs of the language, of Visual Basic .NET, and of using
Visual Studio .NET. By the time you are well into Chapter 7 you will be writing Visual
Basic .NET code like a pro.

Part III chapters take you through higher-level concepts like inheritance,
composition, encapsulation, and interfaces. The chapters progress from providing a
grounding in OO concepts in Chapters 8 through 11, to advanced OO and code
construction concepts covered in the remaining chapters.

I decided to exclude a glossary because there are many fine general programming
books in the world that supply that need. Apart from delegates, which have been given
special coverage in this book, Visual Basic .NET and the .NET Framework does not
stray from the standard procedural and object-oriented programming concepts and
constructs in any way that would require a glossary of terms and concepts.

While I have designed the book to be tackled logically from the first chapter to the
last, here is a brief description of the chapters to help you pinpoint parts you may wish
tackle first.

Chapter 1

The first chapter is not so much about Visual Basic .NET as it is about programming in
general and programming in .NET in particular. Experienced programmers will likely
skim over this chapter, but newcomers would benefit from the background to
programming in general, and from finding out what Visual Basic .NET and the .NET
Framework have to offer.

the get-go, so that you'll be able to have code compiled and running before you reach the end of the chapter.

You'll learn about the important features, windows, and tools in Visual Studio, and how to load the Visual Studio solution and projects that partner this book. The chapter also includes a small application—not exactly a killer version of "hello world"—but enough to get your feet wet.

Chapter 4

There's a lot of ground to cover in this book and Chapter 4 gives you the lay of the land. The first part tells you which chapters to turn to for coverage of certain constructs. It also provides information on .NET code writing style, such as whether to use Hungarian notation (which is discouraged), what should be cased in camel casing, and what should be cased in Pascal casing.

The chapter also goes into the various declaration spaces and contexts of a .NET program. For example, it covers the compiler options (**Option Explicit**, **Option Strict**, and **Option Compare**), namespace declarations and the concept of namespaces, class characteristics, and the class members. This chapter covers variables, constants, important keywords, conversion, scope, and lifetimes.

Chapter 5

I got somewhat carried away with this chapter. It started as a big section in Chapter 4 and then grew to a point where it deserved to be its own chapter. This chapter is unique for a number or reasons—not only have I gone over every operator bit for bit, but I have also covered some stuff that is not currently in Visual Basic .NET at all: operator overloading.

There is a good reason for why I did this. Operator overloading is important for a lot of reasons and there has been quite a debate over whether Visual Basic .NET, unlike C# but like Java, should have supported it. I decided to get into the subject for the sake of providing Visual Basic programmers with an understanding of what operator overloading is useful for and if it is necessary to have in Visual Basic .NET. Once you have read this chapter you will be able to fathom if the subject is worth pursuing with Microsoft or whether you would prefer they spent their time on more important issues.

I delved into the subject of shift operations and the shift operators in Visual Basic .NET. The problem you have here is that there are no shift operators in Visual Basic. Only C# has them. I decided to show them anyway—only I had to write the examples in C#. Surprised? You should be. The C# section is important for two reasons. It shows you what you can do with shift operators (which may make you envious of C# programmers), and at the same time it shows you how you can incorporate another .NET language into a VB project with relative ease.

Do not be surprised to find a number of tables and lists in various places that include some C# items alongside the Visual Basic ones. There are two reasons I did this. First, the framework classes are written in C# so it helps when you encounter terms like **sealed** and **static** that you know what they mean to your Visual Basic code. Second, switching out to C# to knock up something you need to incorporate in a Visual Basic application is not to be discouraged.

The chapter also looks at short-circuiting in operators. It includes a section on numbering systems, which we all need to be sharp about.

Chapter 6

This chapter deals exclusively with flow-control, iteration, and the conditional constructs. Without these fundamental facilities we cannot program any logic into our software. We would not be able to provide choice or make selection.

The chapter covers all constructs, and touches a little on the legacy ones that I have never been enamored with as a VB 6 programmer. I found it very hard to cater to error handling with the **On Error** construct, and after having coded with exception handlers for years, it was difficult getting used to the very un-object oriented way VB error handling had to be dealt with.

I also got into so much trouble with **Goto** in my early programming days (with **Dbase** and the like) that I now hate this facility with a passion. While I cover **Goto** in this chapter, I have made it clear that it is not needed in .NET at all. Apart from the single example of **Goto** in this chapter, the construct is not covered anywhere else in the book nor is it used in any of the software projects.

Chapter 7

Methods are what make your objects work. They come in two flavors: functions and sub-routines. The latter is known as a **Sub** in Visual Basic. **Function**s return values while **Sub**s do not. This chapter deals with everything you need to know about methods. It deals with method characteristics, parameter lists, return values, pass-by-value, and pass by reference.

This chapter also covers the polymorphic facilities of methods, such as overloading, overriding and shadowing. It explains the difference between static or shared methods, and instance methods, and it explains the purpose of abstract, virtual, and final methods.

I also decided to cover several general method topics in this chapter: Recursion, and method performance and analysis. If you are up for some teeth-grinding, you can tackle some computer science in a section that introduces O-notation and the running-time analysis of methods.

This chapter also introduces exception handling, a precursor to Chapter 11, which covers exception handling exclusively and in much more depth.

Chapter 8

Visual Basic .NET and the .NET Framework provide outstanding support for value types, structures or structs, and enumerated types (enumerations or enums). This chapter covers the object reference model, the difference between the objects that live on the stack (a more efficient region of memory), and the objects that live in heap memory.

The chapter explains the concept of boxing, how objects get moved between the stack and the heap.

Chapter 9

Understanding the basics of object-oriented software development is a prerequisite to comprehending the more advanced chapters. This chapter covers all aspects of classes and objects, from class characteristics and how classes are constructed and relate to each other, to how classes become objects.

I also cover modeling in depth in this chapter and provide a small introduction to UML. This section includes a guide to the UML symbols used in a number of class diagrams throughout the book.

The chapter also covers inheritance in detail, and explains the differences between inheritance, aggregation, and composition. We investigate how to construct base classes, abstract classes, and how to decide how classes should relate to each other. The chapter also covers static classes and how to seal a class.

Chapter 10

Interfaces probably underpin the entire .NET Framework and I devote an entire chapter to the subject so that you fully understand what interfaces are, how they are used, and why they are so important.

The chapter details how interfaces provide the polymorphism so important to object-oriented software. It not only goes into interface factoring, how interfaces are constructed and so on, but it sets you up to understand the more complex programming concepts, like method indirection, delegation and **Delegate**s, wrapping, and varying implementation.

The chapter covers everything you need to know about working with interfaces from declaration and definition to implementation, instantiation, and bridging.

Chapter 11

I consider exception-handling so important that it deserves a chapter of its own as well. This chapter follows up on the short introduction to exception handling introduced in

Chapter 7. It not only covers the ins and out of using exception handling in your code, guarding code in **Try ...Catch ...Finally** constructs, but also shows you how to create custom exception handling objects.

Chapter 12

Data structures and collections are where you store the data you work with in your programs. They include arrays, lists, stacks, and queues. This chapter is extensive and deals with the specifics of the most important data structures. The first part of the chapter deals with declaring and using the likes of stack objects and queues. It also introduces the key interfaces that are implemented in collection classes, which provide the support for iteration and framework wide constructs.

The chapter then delves into arrays. It looks at how to fill arrays, access array elements, iterate over arrays, and how to pass arrays to methods. Later in this chapter, we look at sorting and investigate how to write sorting algorithms like quicksort, bubble sort, and so on. There are two motives behind the work with sorting algorithms. First, they cover important method construction issues, like method decomposition and how to divide units of work in your algorithms. Second, these sections bring us down from the lofty abstractions of object and classes in the previous chapters. In short, the chapter lets us get down to some gritty code writing.

Chapter 13

Patterns are as critical to object oriented software as blueprints are to architects. This chapter investigates several of the most important patterns in OO. These include the Singleton pattern, the Bridge and Strategy patterns (which make extensive use of interfaces), and the State pattern.

The chapter specializes in the Composite pattern and looks at composition and aggregation in some detail. It covers the creation, from design and specification, of a full-blown linked list class, that you can emulate and incorporate in your code. To iterate the list I show you how to implement the collection interfaces, **IList**, **ICollection**, and **IEnumerable**. You will also learn how to build a collection class and an iterator for traversing it by implementing the **IEnumerator** interface.

Chapter 14

If you don't understand delegates, then this is the chapter to turn to. It tackles the subject of **Delegate** objects, **Adapter**s and delegation head-on. This subject has its roots in Visual J++ and is one that gives programmers a lot of trouble. Few constructs create as much confusion and debate as the **Delegate** class and how to use it.

Chapter 14 is closely tied to Chapter 13, covering patterns, and Chapter 10, which covers interfaces. Apart from implementation inheritance discussed in Chapter 9, I believe that unless you understand polymorphism as well as you understand your mother tongue, you will struggle with everything from services to user interfaces to multithreaded applications. I may have gone overboard on the polymorphism subject, but there is a very good reason for it. If you don't understand or know how to use or program against interfaces and delegates, then you can't move up to the more intense and more complex technologies you need to master. And you can practically forget about getting into building controls and components, let alone how to build sophisticated event-driven programming.

This chapter also looks at the debate between using interfaces and adapter class for event-driven software vs. the **Delegate**. We examine how **Delegate**s are used as object-oriented function pointers. While I touch on the subject of callbacks and asynchronous programming, this chapter deals mainly with simple method pointing. It takes recursion used with the sort methods in Chapter 13 and shows how to replace it with **Delegate**s.

Chapter 15

Manipulating data and getting data into and out of your application are other core requirements for you to master. Chapter 15 covers string handling and I/O, and several important namespaces and classes that cater to I/O.

After discussing string manipulation and regular expressions, the chapter goes into an extensive investigation of all the file, directory, and I/O classes. These include the various stream classes, and text readers and writers.

The chapter wraps up with a discussion of using the XML reader and writer classes, and a discussion of object serialization using XML. It will show you how to provide serialization supports for the linked list class built in Chapter 13 so that you can persist the data in the lists nodes to disk.

Chapter 16

This book introduces user interface constructs and logic very late; you'll find out why in the introduction in the chapter. The chapter presents an introduction to user interfaces, how to create a multiple document interface (MDI) application, and more. It also presents some simple threading concepts.

Chapter 17

The last chapter deals with debugging and tracing. It can be argued that this chapter should have come much sooner, but I believe that if you are just starting out programming, using the debugging tools and facilities is not going to be easy. After all, using the **Debug** class, performance counters, trace listeners, the **Trace** class, and numerous other complex classes in the **System.Diagnostics** namespace is not straightforward without a basic understanding of the core language. Once you are up to speed with the concepts presented in the earlier chapters you'll find Chapter 17 a cinch to read, and the debugging aids like breakpoints and code step-through features and the classes, a matter of course.

Conventions

Many of the conventions used in this book are self-evident. However, I have added a number of symbols in many tables that differentiate between properties, methods, fields, static methods, and instance methods. These symbols are listed in the following table.

Symbol	Explanation
(a)	Denotes an abstract class or method
(d)	Denotes a **Delegate** object
(fi)	Denotes a field
(fl)	Denotes final
(i)	Denotes an instance method
(m)	Denotes a method
(p)	Denotes a property
(s)	Denotes a static method

A number of tables provide lists of class members. These tables will give you an idea of what constructs are available to the class and may or may not correspond to an element further explained in the text. However, in most of the cases the tables are abridged. They especially do not list the members that are always inherited from the root **Object**. Defer to the .NET SDK for the full picture.

The Complete Reference

Part I

Introduction to Visual Basic .NET

Chapter 1

Software Development
and Visual Basic .NET

3

Visual Basic .NET is a radical departure from the previous versions of Visual Basic, the world's most popular programming language. If you have had experience with *Object-Oriented* (OO) languages like Java or Delphi you will probably take to Visual Basic .NET fairly quickly. After you have spent a few months using Visual Basic .NET, you'll find it hard to return to an earlier version (unless you really must).

You have probably also read or heard that support for the *common language runtime* (CLR) and the .NET Framework transforms Visual Basic .NET into a "pure" or "true" object-oriented language. To decide how true this claim is, let's first understand what a "pure" and "true" OO language is.

If you are new to object-oriented software development, this chapter will introduce you to the OO concepts that all Visual Basic programmers need to know. This chapter introduces these software developments and OO concepts early on, to help you derive the most benefit from this book and from Visual Basic .NET.

We begin by reviewing the evolution of software development over the past few decades. Then we shall see how Visual Basic .NET—hereon referred to as Visual Basic—has risen to meet the challenges of a demanding industry, answering the world's thirst for software.

Visual Basic and the Difficulty of Developing Software

Whether silicone- or carbon-based, what makes computers tick is simply the groupings of the numbers 1 and 0, combined in sequences to form instructions. This is known as *software*—how it is created and used is what drives technology.

The essence of software is the ability to marshal and control bits of data in order to communicate; to control devices; to display, project, and render images; to model, design and manufacture widgets; to move objects; to perform highly complex computations and calculations, and so on.

Software is an extremely complex science. At the same time it is an art form—the software developer must be creative in designing and writing software that simulates and addresses real world scenarios. Developers are required to do much more than just write code for complex mathematical algorithms or to simply transfer information from point A to point B.

Software development is time-consuming: The combination of both time and complexity makes it a very costly process. Unless a software engineer knows practically everything there is to know about the *core language* syntax and grammar and has experience using it, a development process can rapidly expand beyond the range of affordability. "Core language" doesn't mean peripheral or collateral technologies, or libraries like the database libraries (ADO.NET) or the Internet communications libraries, or the Web development technologies (ASP.NET), but the foundation used to create all these collateral technologies. This does not mean that these collateral technologies are not important—they are very important—it means that you cannot hope to use or even create the collateral technologies or components unless you first understand the foundations, processes, and facilities used to build them.

Reducing Complexity and Time-to-Market with Reuse

There have been many horror stories of how a miscalculated value caused a machine to explode, or how a bank lost millions due to a single errant statement in an algorithm, or how a product had to be recalled because of an incorrect quality control constant.

An experienced programmer knows to use well-written and proven software components to avoid having to rewrite and retest the product. We in the software industry know that software is an iterative process. It is also a refining process. Without the ability to reuse what has been refined or what currently works well for the task at hand, we will not advance as quickly as we need to in the coming decades. If we had not been able to reuse what so many have done before us we would not be where we are today.

Take C.A.R. Hoare's famous sorting algorithm, *quicksort.* He invented this sort in 1960; it is used today in every modern language (we will cover this algorithm in Chapter 12, "Arrays and Other Data Structures," along with *bubble sort,* and in Chapter 14 in the discussion of delegates). Many software geniuses have chosen to share their efforts. Bruce Schneier's *blowfish* encryption algorithm springs to mind, as does the emergence of formally cataloged patterns for software design. (There are also a number of algorithms that are patented and that we can't use. The sirens of the data compression wars are still ringing in many companies.)

Software development has certainly changed over the past few decades. The demand for reusable code, and the ever-increasing demands on software writers to turn out better code, have resulted in improved software design and implementation techniques that facilitate today's software-engineering principles and requirements. Had not Visual Basic been adapted for the need, had it not risen to the challenge, it would have been replaced by something else.

Software Development and Software Engineering

Software engineering is not easy to define; indeed, many argue that it is not a form of engineering at all and that its designers are not really engineers. But software developers *are* engineers and include in their ranks many professionals with formal training and experience. According to Webster's dictionary, "[software] engineering is the application of mathematical and scientific principles to practical ends, as the design, construction, and operation of efficient structures, equipment, and systems."

Declared an engineering discipline by NATO in 1968, software design also "provides the equipment, systems, and tools to facilitate all forms of engineering practice" (this author's words). Modern software development has also borrowed greatly from other related disciplines such as civil, electrical, mechanical, and structural engineering—

especially in the fields of analysis, design, and construction. Even the concept of patterns, discussed later in this chapter, is borrowed from civil engineering.

Note *While many excellent software engineers are graduates of computer science schools, programmers with an engineering background have the benefit of forward training in design and construction.*

The software industry emerged in the mid-20th century with the advent of the modern computer and has progressed through three distinct "ages" since then:

■ **The Procedure-Oriented Age**   Procedure-oriented programming was largely concerned with computational results rather than data—the focus being on procedures, or just code, as islands of functionality. Software systems were not organized in any meaningful structure and were merely collections of files containing huge functions and procedures that were processed as required for discrete calculations. Data was external to the function—a black box—and easily accessible because it was global. Because the systems were fixated on a result, a value, they could be *adequately* managed by the very dedicated individuals that wrote them. Examples of such languages include Assembly Language, C, generic BASIC, generic Pascal, Ada, COBOL and so forth. Most languages today have evolved to accommodate the modern programming practices, yet many programmers still work in a flat, linear procedure-oriented style. Current Web development has not helped this situation, either. The following example, while extreme, is simple BASIC in all its procedural glory. (Think of thousands of lines focused on one result, computing the speed of a spacecraft relative to the forces imposed on it in space.) This type of programming is now as foreign as English in a Dead Sea Scroll:

```
...
60 FOR TOPSP%=10 TO 100:
70 VOERC=TOPSP%/100
80 GOSUB 180:REM calculate top speed
90 THETA5$=STRS$(FIX((THETA5+.005)*100))
...
```

■ **The Structure-Oriented Age**   As software systems grew, programmers needed to manage and maintain them more efficiently. The structure-oriented age introduced a paradigm in which the functions were organized in structures— a module containing procedures and data. In other words, the unit or level of abstraction became the module rather than the individual procedure. Structural programming lends itself to encapsulation, data-centric programming, collections of like routines, and object-like programming.

■ **The Object-Oriented Age**   By the end of the 1960s it became apparent that the ever-growing complexity of software systems would necessitate a new model, one that was more humanly manageable and comprehensible. Now almost half a century after the first object-oriented software language, Simula, was created, the OO age has finally taken hold in response to this complexity. OO lets us model and design software systems around familiar concepts (objects) behind which complexity is hidden through abstraction, much like the abstraction found in nature. The focus of programming is mostly on attributes and data rather than computations or calculations. Encapsulation and other features have been refined, and continue to be refined, to better serve the OO model.

Note   *Simula-1, the first OO language, arrived in 1966 and introduced the first attempt to focus on behavior and data in objects rather than procedures. If you are new to OO I would jump to Chapter 9, which kicks off discussing classes and Chapter 10 which delves into the subject of abstraction and interfaces.*

The remainder of this chapter will explore how and why object-oriented technology has gained critical acceptance in the software-development community today and how this model of programming can now be utilized by any modern software language.

The Classic Programming Models

Computer programming as we know it today began in the late 1950s and burgeoned in the 1960s. In those days, writing code was not considered an engineering profession. Computers could do very little, and people could usually calculate mathematical problems more quickly. There were many stories from that time concerning public institutions that spent millions on computers, only to learn that their staff could outperform the machines.

At first the effort involved in programming a computer was not worthwhile. The first useful programs were nothing more than reams of sequential instructions. After processing the steps, the computation would be complete and the computer would be ready to start again.

This process worked for simple programs, but as computers became more powerful and sophisticated, the complexity and effort required to program them became barriers to their usefulness. According to one industry maxim, "Program complexity grows until it exceeds the capability of the programmer to maintain it." Then chaos takes over.

Identifying structure in computer programs became a popular crusade for many scientists and teachers in the early years of the profession. By the end of the 1960s, it culminated in a movement called *structured programming,* a software engineering discipline that is still widely taught in first-year computer science and software engineering courses. Many colleges require it as a prerequisite to learning object-oriented programming (OOP). As you will see, Visual Basic .NET and the .NET Framework present a highly structured programming framework.

Structured Programming

This is essentially the technique of organizing programs into a collection of small stand-alone modules. The modules can be grouped into a hierarchy or a network, and each unit has a single entry and a single exit point. Processing the lines of code in the module occurs from the top down, and the control structure usually forbids unconditional branching.

Specific techniques let us divide algorithms into small functional units so that one or more programmers can work on each unit, refine it, test it, debug it, and share it with the rest of the team. Fellow programmers then debug and check each other's code. In a process similar to modern manufacturing, all the units are then combined to produce the larger application or system. This is a highly efficient method that works both for teams and individuals.

Modules are not special "objects" or language-specific containers, and as long as a language can compile and link multiple source-code files it can be structured along modular lines. It is important to note an important distinction here: Structured programming divides the engineering practice into two categories—design and construction (or implementation).

Note   *Software maintenance includes not only debugging and fixing faulty software, but also adding required features, improving performance, and more.*

On the one hand, software-design engineers use structural techniques to analyze the problems, determine a solution path, and create a system to meet several objectives, which include satisfying the customer and maintaining the software.

On the other hand, software-construction engineers use their code-writing skills to implement the code. They provide the necessary implementation at the functional level of the module with regard to the specific methods or algorithms. In many shops, assigning engineers to specific design and implementation roles can provide huge dividends.

Many programmers hate modeling and design at the higher levels of abstraction and are more productive devising code, in which the radius of focus is only a few millimeters. In fact, this is the age that coined the slogan "code is king." To quote Paul C. Clements:

> "While 'top-down programming' and 'structural programming' were all the rage in 1974, both referred to practices in which getting to code was clearly the end game. (Contrast this to the current object- or component-oriented world in which we concentrate on services provided, not statement executed.)"
> *from Paul C. Clements' Introduction to David Parnas' famous paper*
> *"On a 'Buzzword': Hierarchial Structure"*

Gifted engineers are versatile enough to produce at both the macro- and microlevels. A number of important benefits emerged from the structure-oriented programming paradigm, as the next few sections will illustrate.

Bug-Reduced Code

The boundaries of buggy code are within the confines of a module, which is usually the responsibility of one programmer. It is much easier to detect a bug in a module through isolation than in a file containing a single mega-procedure. Once the bugs are dispatched from the modules, the pest-free code can then be reused in other parts of the application.

 A number of studies suggest a small procedure, a method, is not necessarily more bug-free than a gargantuan method of 500 lines.

Divide and Conquer

The strongest Roman emperors realized that the solution to conquering their enemies was to divide the armies of resisters and then conquer the smaller units. Modern analytical problem- solving techniques teach the same approach, as do many successful algorithm masters. The best way to solve a problem is to restate it in as many ways as you possibly can; this helps identify the "real" problem, which you then break down into smaller components. I teach this technique in designing algorithms and will discuss it in later chapters.

For now, let's imagine you are hired to build an accounting system that will debit an account in one process and credit an account in another. Would it not be best to create discrete **Debtor** and **Creditor** modules with clearly defined interfaces to accomplish these tasks? The **Debtor** module would first deduct an amount from an account and then convey the number deducted to the **Creditor** module. These modules can be in the same code file or in different files, as long as they remain separate entities. This ensures that if a bug arises in the creditor part of the code, the debtor part will not collapse as well.

Reuse

Contrary to what many OO purists claim, reuse became the battle cry of software professionals long before the rise of object-orientation. The idea even predates the industrial revolution, which heralded the effort to make better products through faster and cheaper means.

Here's an excellent example of reuse. During World War II, the United States government ordered car manufacturers to help build bombers such as the Avenger, a small aircraft that was capable of dropping a torpedo, bomb, or mine on the enemy. The companies were ordered to build the components exactly according to specifications so that parts made by one manufacturer could be used or replaced with the parts of another. The result was that by the end of the war many Avengers were flying with transplanted components made from several manufacturers.

Software reuse allows us to build better programs faster and with fewer programmers. Over the years, many libraries have been built and sold to thousands of companies using identical code in many different products. The code in these components has been tested countless times and reused in the many different circumstances.

Teaming

Structured programming allows us to build a software product in teams. As with the Avenger, various programmers, grouped into designers and implementers, can work independently on different parts of a product. Structured programming also lets us delegate according to skill sets, which include writing the stored procedures; driving the code on the web site; sorting the data structures; and controlling specifications, class diagrams, use cases, and documentation.

Structural Nada?

Despite the progress made since the advent of structure-oriented programming, many designers still do not program in a "structured way." They program without regard for the interrelationships of modules, organization for reuse, overall structure, or protection of data. Software project managers often talk in terms of the "number of function points" in an application or system, so as to express the extent or size of the project. But talking about so-called function points is meaningless if there is no way to express the architecture of that system, its components, their interrelationships, and its various structures.

As I said earlier, many courses in OOP first teach structured programming, because a good OO program is also a well-structured one. Many first-year programming courses that begin with C++ or Java require you to learn structured programming in these languages before you learn to "objectify" your code.

Object-Based Programming

As structured programming methods became more refined, it became apparent to the engineers that modules of code could be related to as objects. Many languages gradually become more object-based, especially as compilers emerged that could enforce encapsulation and cater to the compiling, linking, and binding of numerous modules into complete applications.

A good example of object-based programming plots the transformation of C into C++. Today C++ is what you would call a *hybrid* language because it allows you to code standard C modules, to add objects and do object-based programming, or to invoke the object-oriented features of the language such as inheritance and polymorphism.

Visual Basic is an excellent example of the evolution of a language. It was born in May 1991, the child of a shapeless language parent, BASIC. Then it grew into its structured programming and module-based programming stages (all the way to VB 6). Now it has matured into a true object-oriented language, Visual Basic .NET. Today the language has pure, compiler-enforced support for inheritance, polymorphism, and all the great features that pure OO languages support.

Object-Oriented Software Development

Computer specifications are advancing at a record pace while prices for these systems are falling rapidly. As computer hardware gets cheaper, software is getting more and more expensive. In order to create machines that will address bigger and more complex problems, we need software that is more complex and thus more expensive. There is also new hardware such as mobile devices, super fast processors, cheap memory, and tiny hard disks that require sophisticated new software. The problem is further compounded by our desire for ever-faster and more powerful computers.

In the early 1990s, servers cost far more than the software running them. Today, you can buy many powerful servers for the same price as the operating system and application suite that will be used by a team of people.

While structured programming helps flatten the complexity curve of programming, it is still difficult to manage large software development projects with structure-oriented practice alone.

Ten years ago, a text-based word processor consisted of fewer than 30,000 lines of code and probably required fewer than five people to build and maintain it. It was easy to write the modules to its easily defined structure. Fifteen years ago, word-processing software merely displayed characters, saved text files, and at best provided spell checking.

Today, an average word processor comprises millions of lines of code, highly complex data structures, and algorithms—not to mention all the complexities of the underlying operating system. Today's system caters to writing, linguistics, semantics, grammar, design, layout, typography, printing, production, imaging, word recognition, and so much more.

As soon as a structured-programming project becomes large and complex, your ability to manage and maintain the application begins to break down. Couple this with the demand for artificial intelligence, highly advanced and complex algorithms, specialized graphics and effects, sophisticated business systems, and so on, and you end up with software too complex to comprehend.

The main problem in building such software is that our human abilities to design, organize, manage, and maintain it have not evolved much. In fact, we are less able to take control of our software today than we were 10 or 20 years ago. It would be safe to say that any sizable application is beyond the ability of any one person to comprehend.

Thus, the founders of OOP realized that if software modules were managed according to the objects they represented instead of the collective sums of their functions, however well organized, then the development process would undergo a major paradigm shift.

While both structure-oriented and object-based programming focus on design practice, object-oriented development pushes this process to the level of attributes, services, properties, and concepts. OO allows us to design, understand, and maintain highly complex software by hiding the complexity of the code behind familiar objects.

Large structured-programming projects are very difficult to manage. Even with a small team of designers, it becomes very hard for each member to understand what the others have written and why. Furthermore, the extreme amount of detail can easily obscure the larger picture.

Despite the fact that OOP is not a new idea (it was introduced at about the same time that structured programming began to take hold), many experienced programmers still struggle with the concepts underlying it, principally due to the fixation on code. To fully understand OO requires a mental shift away from code construction/implementation, toward design/metaphorical thought. In many ways you have to lose some of the mathematician/rocket-scientist mentality. To fully appreciate and understand OOP, you need to become an artist, a choreographer, and a biologist.

Not long ago I had two "experienced engineers" write to me: one responding to a statement in my Java newsletter and another trying to understand Visual Basic .NET. The former said, "OOP sounds revolutionary, but really modularity has been part of a structured programming for decades." The latter said, "Well, if all that Visual Basic .NET adds to VB is inheritance, then I have been programming in an OO language for years already, so I don't see what the big ideal is."

In the next few sections we will talk about the concepts of OOP, but just enough for you to take the OO test and judge Visual Basic. I believe you need an unshakable understanding of OOP to get the best out of .NET development and Visual Basic programming. Thus, several chapters in the book are directly about OOP concepts in Visual Basic and every chapter touches on OO concepts in one form or another.

Real-World Reflections

In recent years, object-oriented development has gained enormous popularity because it helps us decompose extensive software systems from a high viewpoint. It takes abstraction to the highest levels above the code because it allows the software designers to model and design their system as collections of objects that can be associated with real-world situations or as objects in the real world.

Take a look at your hand. What do you see? Do you first see a hand or its anatomy? Even an orthopedic surgeon, who is trained to see the anatomy, still does not focus on the molecules that make up the anatomical parts of the hand. If we were unable to mentally encapsulate all anatomical or molecular ingredients at these lower-levels, we would not last ten seconds in the world.

OO provides the same benefits. It lets us collect the anatomical and molecular low-level routines of our software in objects that are then grouped together to make the system. Thus, we could say that an application is a collection of 250 objects, or we could choke on the statement that "our system is 100,000 lines of code, 4,000 functions, 200 variables, and so forth."

How do the objects integrate and interoperate to form the application and perform its collective duties? In the real world, objects in a biological system accomplish this through a complex network of messages. *Sender* objects send messages to *Receiver* objects, which act on the requirements contained therein. If the receiver does not process the input correctly, or the sender falters in its delivery, or the messaging system itself is faulty, the entire "organism" might be affected. For example, when we get hungry and pick up a sandwich, our mouth receives the message to open and to process the food. If the neurological pathways begin to break down, as in the case of multiple sclerosis sufferers, the objects that make up the organism are unable to act and the organism dies.

We use object-oriented design techniques and tools to help us develop object-oriented systems. The engineering of OO software is similar to other engineering disciplines; an OO system is built in the same way a structural engineer constructs a bridge or an architect designs a house.

An architect starts by sketching and then transfers the design to a computer so that it can be properly scaled and organized into its respective system of objects (hence my attestation that software engineering facilitates all forms of engineering). The house may be modeled so that it can be viewed in its physical form, albeit much scaled down. When the house is ready to be built, the various objects of the house are *constructed.* We software developers prefer to use the term *implemented,* but the idea is the same.

Our modeling and design tools have become very advanced in recent years. With Unified Modeling Language (UML) as the principal [modeling] language, tools like Rational Rose and Visio 2002 (to mention two premier products) enable us to design and model the most complex systems effortlessly. If our customers can imagine it, we can build it; the only limitation is their budget.

Note	*The concept of pattern languages is beginning to take root and will be part of mainstream software engineering, like UML, within a few years.*

What Makes a Pure Object-Oriented Language

While OO allows us to apply abstract concepts to the design of our systems, the closer we get to the implementation, or code, the less we begin to care about OO. In fact, once the source code is compiled, the "OO-ness" is completely gone, because the processors do not care about objects and their attributes. They care about what operations need to be performed, what instructions need to be processed, and how much memory it takes to do the computations or process the data. At the method—or routine—level, we are programming the objects; the logic and practice at this level are the same for object-oriented languages as they are for structured-oriented languages.

However, if OO were nothing more than a design technique, it would not be as useful as we would like. We can design according to real-world problems, scenarios, and objects, and we can also implement the functionality along real-world lines, as far as possible. So there are a number of additional traits or features of OO languages that allow us to extend the object model to the lower levels, which allows the objects to interoperate on the outside and the methods to interoperate on the inside.

A "pure" or "true" object-oriented language thus comprises the following traits:

1. Modularity is achieved in modules called *classes,* the unit of encapsulation.

2. Related classes are grouped in hierarchies. The classes are related by descent—*inheritance.*

3. The classes can be instantiated at runtime as *objects,* and their functionality and data dynamically accessed. (Class functionality can also be statically accessed without instantiation.)

4. Objects access one another's data and implementation using *messages* passed between them.

5. Objects are able to dynamically respond in different ways and serve up variations in functionality in response to the same message—*polymorphism.* Through the employment of interfaces, polymorphism is achieved because different implementations can exist behind the same interface used in more than one place.

If you expected to find *encapsulation* on the list, you might be surprised. Let's consider some of the points made earlier. Encapsulation is often cited as one of the three most important tenets of an OO language (*inheritance* and *polymorphism* are the other two). But while it is vital to OO, encapsulation is really a trait of all modern programming methodology, adopted without question by OOP from both object-based programming and structured programming practice. Encapsulation was certainly supported in the earlier versions of Visual Basic. Therefore, *inheritance* and *polymorphism* are the two critical enabling features of all true OO languages. Visual Basic now supports both.

Having said that, just because a language supports both *inheritance* and *polymorphism* does not mean that it is 100 percent object-oriented. Let's review the five essential traits and then investigate implementation according to real-world analogies.

Just Classes

In an OO environment, all code is written in a class structure. The attributes of the structure, compiler directives, class declaration, references and directives in the implementation code, direct compilation and the transformation of the class into a member unit of an application, or as part of a dynamically linked library that can be accessed by other applications.

The .NET Framework classes comprise the built-in types, base classes, objects, interfaces, attributes, enumerators, events, and so forth, which cater to the fundamental object-oriented software principles of modularity, abstraction, encapsulation, and classification.

Classes for Modularity, Cohesion, and Coupling

The principle of modularity in software systems (which, as we discussed already, predates OOP) requires that classes be organized into highly *cohesive,* but *loosely coupled* units. Figure 1-1 illustrates the concept. The *cohesion* in the classes relates to the collection of methods and data that are organized to serve the *common purpose* of the class.

In order to define common purpose, let's consider the cells in the human body. Different cells have specialized jobs to do, and their contents are highly cohesive

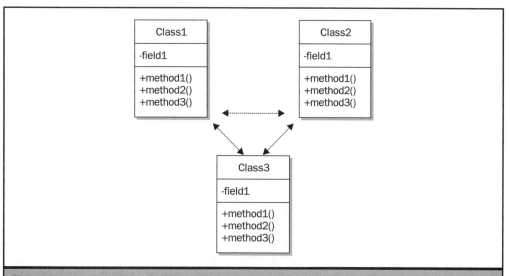

Figure 1-1.   *Cohesive, loosely coupled units send messages to each other*

properties that serve a common purpose. Brain cells, for example, do not have the same properties and methods—ways of doing something for an organism—that blood cells do. They're only composed of elements that enable brain functions, such as memory retention. Similarly, our white blood cells contain only the highly cohesive assortment of components that fulfill their role of protecting against bacterial infection. The properties of divergent types of cells may look the same, but they do different things for varying reasons. Each cell's contents are isolated from other cells—nature does not store the functions of brain cells in blood cells.

Likewise, you would not put the elements required for file operations in a class catering to encryption. When you need to use methods for file operations, however, the **File** class should be accessible to all other classes. This is where loose coupling comes into the picture.

The loose coupling of classes relates to their interdependency. In other words, classes can interact with each other—an activity that is achieved through the messaging network (method calls) we discussed earlier. (Incidentally, this loose coupling is also very similar to the interdependencies of living cells. Figure 1-2 shows how forms are used to present the user interface and how they need only provide implementation for user input and information. Access to data and functionality is derived from a framework of classes and objects in which the form is merely a central object for presentation and input (a very different focus from the form-centric model in older versions of Visual Basic).

Conversely, classes can also be *tightly coupled* when they need to be. Inheritance, composition, aggregation, interfaces, and other coupling techniques provide proven methods of interaction among classes that depend on each other.

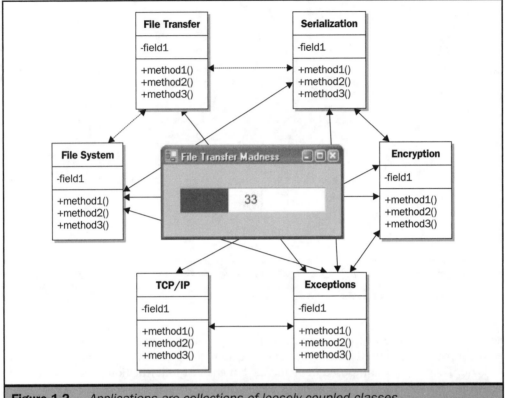

Figure 1-2.   *Applications are collections of loosely coupled classes*

Classes for Abstraction

We encounter abstraction every day of our lives. Complex systems are presented to us with their intricacies separated from the essential components required to understand them. Software engineers and information technology experts work with this reality all the time. Whites Papers, for example, aim to present a technology through abstraction and are nothing more than distillations of extremely complex subjects. Chapter 2, albeit lengthy, is an abstract of the *common language runtime*. Its coverage of the subject should be sufficient for programmers who don't have plans to build a new compiler or a new .NET language. (See Introduction about White Papers.)

Abstraction in OOP is a central principle dictating that programmers do not need to grasp the complexities of various implementations in order to use them. For example, there is little reason to know how a method executes the *heapsort* algorithm if you only need to sort and not to implement a better heapsort.

Classes for Encapsulation

Encapsulation and abstraction go hand in hand. Classes abstract the complexities of their functionality but make that capacity available through simple interfaces. This is the essence of encapsulation.

Interfaces are a central tenet in OOP and a very important feature of the .NET Framework. Interfaces and implementation are separated from each other. The latter is provided as standard class members.

But the framework also allows you to provide abstract classes as the foundation for class hierarchies. These base classes are able to provide abstract methods without implementation and allow you to inherit such interfaces for implementation in descendant classes. The framework also supports formal interface classes. Later we'll examine how they facilitate polymorphism. Interfaces are discussed at length in Chapter 10, "Interfaces"

Classes for Hiding Information

Encapsulation hides information, implementation, and data from parties that don't need to access them. You only need to know how to pass data to the class's sorting methods, what the impact of the sort may be on system resources, and how the sorted data is returned to you. It's similar to taking your shirts to the cleaners. It doesn't matter what machinery they use as long as the shirts are cleaned well.

Why is it so important to hide certain data and procedures? (You'll see notes and references to hiding in many places in this book.) In understanding the benefits and differences of loose coupling, tight coupling, and cohesion in classes, you'll quickly comprehend why publicly accessible data detracts from these traits.

As soon as loosely coupled classes begin to access each other's data directly via publicly accessible fields they begin to depend on each other. For example, if class B contains methods that depend on data residing in class A, it would be better to merge the two classes, or have class B inherit from class A because you might not be able to easily change the interface to the data without damaging the dependent class's interest. The classes have thus become tightly coupled through bad design . . . and the coupling may be the opposite of what we want to happen.

Shared information and data makes software maintenance much more costly and time-consuming, as illustrated in Figure 1-3. Several classes that can directly access the public variable of a single class will do so. And if they do, they will all have to be updated every time the shared data field is changed or the interface to the class is altered or discontinued. You may only have one publicly exposed field, but if a thousand classes depend on the field, changing it affects all one thousand classes.

In highly complex systems involving many programmers, it becomes difficult to chart which class is dependent on the data in another class without formal coupling techniques such as inheritance and aggregation. Sharing information per se is generally not wise, even if you have no formal specification or requirement in place for accessing the public data.

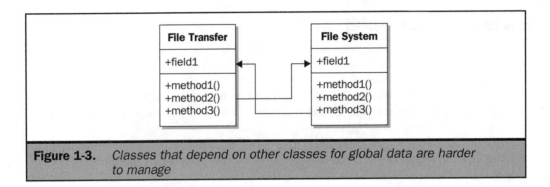

Figure 1-3.   *Classes that depend on other classes for global data are harder to manage*

It is also much easier to trace sources of bugs and defects when elements and methods are encapsulated because you know that no other class, except a nested class, is dependent on them. So when changes are made, they only affect that class's members, which also makes this group less prone to causing problems in the application.

There are suitable techniques for sharing information when this is a requirement. In the chapters to come, we will explore explicit design techniques and patterns that accomplish this. For the most part, access to data occurs through strictly controlled interfaces and protocols. If you remember that the contents of your class are secret and only available on a need-to-know basis, you'll have far fewer problems with your code down the line.

Code that is open to public variables is also vulnerable to security breaches. When multiple threads access public variables, the code becomes less reentrant and more apt to suffer corruption and data loss.

Classes for Classification

We know that if a module of structured code can be organized as objects, then those objects can be grouped into classes that share functionality and mirror real-life scenarios. Further, these can be aggregated into libraries, allowing classes that have similar traits to share and reuse data and implementation.

The test for classification is a simple one. If a conglomerate of classes belongs to a hierarchy, or the components are logically derived from each other, then they belong together. The same is true for animals: It's easy to differentiate between canine and feline, for example. It's not difficult to determine if classes already belong to a certain group. You simply ask "What is it?" The answer will take the form *"it is an x"* or *"it is a kind of"* and you have the collection of classes to which it belongs. If you cannot identify what your class *is* and the design calls for more classes of the same "thing" then you have the makings for a new class collection.

Sometimes its harder to determine what your class *is* a member of. For example, a cheetah has all the signs of being *a kind of* cat, but it does not have retractable claws. So you would have to decide whether the cheetah *"is a kind of cat"* or *"is a kind of dog."*

Class that Beget Classes: Inheritance

Now that you can aggregate your classes in hierarchies and collections, it becomes much easier to reuse the classes or couple them in various ways. A feature of OOP is inheritance—modeled on nature, it lets classes share common functionality and data in a formal framework. In nature, descendants receive many attributes from their parents. We never derive 100 percent from them because then we would lose our uniqueness.

A file manipulation class at the base level, for example, requires the fundamental ability of providing the essential file manipulation functionality: create, open, delete, move, and save files. It makes sense that once a class with these basic functions is established, new classes performing some type of input/output (I/O) might inherit this functionality.

This is what code reuse means: It involves using the exact same code provided in the base class everywhere you need a basic-file I/O routine, not reusing legacy code written 40 years ago by cutting and pasting it into a new class. In other words, even if a mega-application has 150 different classes that need access to file manipulation routines, there is only one file-manipulating class that the entire application has access to.

In properly designed applications, reuse can achieve as much as a 70 percent reduction in the introduction of new code.

Classes for Objects: Instantiation

Classes are represented at runtime by their objects. You can think of a class as the blueprint for the object. At design time, the class is nothing more than a unit of implementation—the equivalent of the module in structured programming. At runtime, the classes become objects through a process called instantiation, instance creation, or instance activation.

Once an object is created and represented in memory, it can enjoy relationships with other objects through the messages distributed around the application. Objects occupy heap space or stack space, so they need to be managed as part of the software/computer "eco-system." If they take up space and are no longer needed, then they need to be disposed of so that other objects can be created and allowed to do their work.

Classes for Association, Aggregation, and Composition

Objects are related to each other and interact with each other in ways that make sense and mirror nature. For starters, if objects become too big they can be broken down into smaller objects, which can then share associative relationships. For example, with an **Employee** class that provides an authentication facility by verifying presented credentials against a database, it may make sense to break it down into two classes—one to specialize in authentication and one to handle **Employee** data. This will yield a smaller **Employee** object that processes data and communicates with the user interface on one hand and the smaller **Authenticate** object on the other. The two objects will be associated by the need for an employee to authenticate. The associative relationship will be from **Employee** requesting authentication from **Authenticate,** which receives the data and presents it for verification against a database, and not the other way around. The buzzword for this relationship is "delegation."

When an object is required to take on more than one role, we say that the object has an *association* relationship to another object. For example, **Employee** objects need to *associate* with **Company** objects for various reasons, such as signing non-disclosure agreements. But it is also possible for the **Employee** to interact with the **Company** object as a shareholder, director, or executive officer. Composition is similar to aggregation, but it exists for the exclusive relationship that one object has with another. An example of composition is a linked list which is constructed from two types of classes: a class that represents the list object as a unit and a composite node class that is instantiated as nodes belonging only to the list object in which it resides.

We will delve into various relationships further in Chapters 9 and 13.

Classes for Events

OOP is the key enabling technology for event-driven programming. If one object changes the state of its data or a variable and another object needs to know about the event, a message can be passed that allows independent objects to act on input from the first one. Thus, entities can make control-flow decisions or take action according to changes in the system as a whole. The .NET Framework event-model is discussed mainly in Chapter 14, but also in the chapters in part IV.

Classes for Message Passing

In pure object-oriented systems, objects interoperate by passing messages as described earlier. Objects issue messages to invoke functionality, send or receive data, and so on. In the .NET languages, this is known as the *method call*. In order to reference methods, properties, and other components of classes, the method calls need to conform to a format. This format is known as the *message signature*.

How do you send a message to an object? First your code needs to reference the name of the object and its method. Consider the following method:

```
MyPhone.Dial(PhoneNumber)
```

This is a message communicating to a phone object named **MyPhone** and telling it (the method call message) to phone the number passed in the message to the parameter called **PhoneNumber. "MyPhone"** is the name of the *receiver* and the object that sends the "dial" message is called the *sender*.

Classes for Polymorphism

Polymorphism means "many forms" in Greek. It is one of the foundational tenets of object-orientation and is usually one of the hardest traits to grasp in OO development. It allows the implementation behind an interface to change without affecting the client or the value of the service expected by the client. It is also the process that allows entities to act in different ways depending on the message they receive.

If you are new to programming, polymorphism might be an easier concept to master than if you were trained in classic Visual Basic and had never been exposed to the idea. Polymorphism is nonexistent in the procedural-structural or object-based programming worlds where functions and procedures do not hide inside objects that interact with their environment through a system of messages.

The public-switched telephone network (PSTN) is a good example of polymorphism at work. Ever since the invention of the telephone, the user experience has hardly changed. Except for a few adjustments in the way you request a telephone number, the process of dialing and speaking has remained unchanged for more than a century—you pick up the phone, dial the number (dials are actually obsolete), and speak.

It all started with two tin cans and a piece of string (which was the model). But once electrical current was introduced and voice was carried over the circuit, or the loop, our lives changed forever. Behind the interface, however, there have been many updates to the processes involved in making the connections, converting the signals, switching, and so on.

No matter what implementation technology is behind the interface, or telephone—tone detection, voice recognition, pulse detection, digital or analog transmission, wire or fiber optics, landlines, the Internet—the user remains unaffected and obtains the service expected.

Classes for Interfaces

The .NET Framework provides for the incorporation and employment of interfaces, which are key to integrating method polymorphism in an OO framework. The concept of pure interfaces that provide no implementation may be difficult to comprehend. But if you understand the meaning of polymorphism, the reason we have interface classes becomes clear.

Polymorphism implies that you can have many different implementations (code) of a method behind a single interface. Methods are defined in interfaces by providing only the signature, which consists of the method's identifier (its name) and formal parameter list. The interface and the definition become part of a contract between the implementor and the interface provider for the purpose of enabling polymorphism at the method level.

Thus, wherever the interface is *implemented* it provides the additional *forms* in which a method definition can be implemented. In the end, you have a single interface and a method definition, but many forms of implementation. Once the implementing classes are coupled with other components in the .NET Framework, or with private or third party collections, the entire framework is extended and advanced.

Frameworks

Frameworks are collections of reusable classes that present software designs and code that can be recycled for various application domains. A framework can be a small collection of classes or it can be a massive collection of libraries and technologies composed of thousands of reusable classes, and millions of lines of code, organized in namespaces and packaged in assemblies, as in the .NET Framework.

The .NET Framework caters to the complexity problem associated with extensive class libraries, components, and various interoperable layers. In short, it is a massive and deep foundation on which to build software economically. It would have been extremely difficult, time-consuming, and expensive for us to have to write the code that exists in the framework, to deal with the various operating systems, the networks, the hardware, and so on, in addition to writing the software our clients require.

> **Note** *You could argue that the .NET Framework tries to solve a problem that feeds on its solution. The bigger and more complex the operating system and the bolder the application- and problem-domains, the more we depend on the framework.*

.NET's object-oriented design facilitates the reuse and extends the code base through OO development features, such as inheritance and polymorphism. Frameworks are discussed further in Chapter 2, which introduces the *common language runtime*.

Patterns

Patterns drive frameworks and encourage not only code reuse but design reuse. Code reuse relates to the sharing of classes and code. For example, a method, which may be inherited, can be deployed unchanged in many different places. At a higher level, the .NET Framework becomes a natural facility for the incorporation of patterns.

The use of patterns is a fascinating trend that has emerged from the many features of OO software creation. Patterns prescribe, through *design* and *architecture,* how reusing various solutions and techniques can solve any software problem. This represents a higher level of abstraction.

To understand design patterns in software development, you should understand the model behind the concept. The idea of pattern use is not new. It is borrowed from the works of architectural genius Christopher Alexander who described how for thousands of years people's design and construction techniques remained unchanged. In three books and numerous papers on building patterns, Alexander illuminated timeless building practices that can be distilled into 253 patterns.

See The Timeless Way of Building *by Christopher Alexander (1979)*, A Pattern Language— Towns, Buildings, Construction *by Christopher Alexander et al., (1977)*, *and* The Oregon Experiment *by Christopher Alexander et al. (1975).*

According to Alexander, "Each pattern describes a *problem* which occurs over and over again in our environment, and then describes the core of the *solution* to that problem, in such a way that you can use this solution a million times over, without ever doing it the same way twice."

Over the years OO developers have found parallel concepts for software-design patterns. In 1995, Erich Gamma and three of his colleagues published one of the first software-pattern catalogs called "Design Patterns", which was based on the findings of Alexander. See *Design Patterns: Elements of Reusable Object-Oriented Software by* Erich Gamma, Richard Helm, Ralph Johnson, and John Vlissides (Addison-Wesley, 1995).

Gamma's work contained a collection of 23 of the most commonly used general-purpose software-design patterns that are application- and problem-domain independent. The book classifies the patterns as follows:

- **Creational Patterns**   Deal with the creation of objects
- **Structural Patterns**   Deal with the static composition and structure of classes and objects
- **Behavioral Patterns**   Deal with the dynamic interaction among classes and objects

Pattern use has been widely adopted by large developer communities. It is as much a part of the Java developer's arsenal as are code-reuse concepts like inheritance and composition. Developers of .NET find themselves poised to exploit not only a framework but also a vast collection of proven patterns from which to begin software construction.

You will find pattern references being repeated many times in this book: These include ones for static classes, object creation, inheritance, aggregation, association, delegation, and more. The text will encourage you to develop and refine your own patterns and contribute them to the efforts of the developer community.

Note

There is now alternative thought that patterns are outmoded in the new world of Web services, XML, and the Simple Object Access Protocol (SOAP). But just because client and server processes can be split over wide areas and across disparate platforms and networks does not make the implementation on each side any less object-oriented. On the contrary, I believe formal pattern use among .NET developers is set to explode. See Chapters 4 and 9.

Observations

Albert Einstein was quoted as saying: "Everything should be made as simple as possible, but no simpler." In many respects, Visual Basic .NET and the .NET Framework should be viewed in the essence of that remark. It is going to take a lot of effort to fully understand all the features and implications of using the new "version," but in the end, software engineering will become much easier.

It should be very easy for you now to understand what Visual Basic .NET is and that it supports all the tenets and principles of a pure OO software-development language, such as inheritance and polymorphism.

However, Visual Basic also supports many other desirable features of a pure OO language, and these include structured-exception handling (the application of objects to trap and handle errors), free threading for concurrency, and so on. The extensive framework does not only support Visual Basic like all .NET languages, but a common-language managed-code runtime environment that takes care of the economics and housekeeping.

Hopefully it is now clear that this book is a reference manual for both the construction and implementation abilities of Visual Basic as well as its design, structuring, modeling, and maintenance abilities. Many chapters are devoted to using the OO features and the design-level aspects of software engineering; others focus lower down in the class "ranks" of the framework where we deal with services, functionality, and code.

It should also be clear to you as an experienced Visual Basic programmer that Visual Basic .NET introduces a significant paradigm shift in the development of applications. It replaces the concept of developing with forms, which is an outdated model that harks back to an over-hyped era of "visual" programming. As discussed earlier in this chapter, our focus is on classes, objects, and new concepts, not on how to "drop" controls on forms. This is the reason that the main discussion on Windows forms and user interfaces is reserved for the latter part of the book.

However, before we can tackle either the design or the construction subjects, we first have to get familiar with the framework and the runtime that support the language. This and more are the subjects of Chapter 2.

The Complete Reference

Chapter 2

Visual Basic .NET and the .NET Framework

C hapter 1 introduced you to the .NET Framework and hinted at what's possible in the .NET runtime environment.

This chapter focuses on the common language runtime, the CLR. In tackling this subject we will be able to design and code applications with the runtime in mind; in particular, the issue of memory management represents the biggest change in the way we write applications. Knowing about the runtime is crucial for programming with the correct security model, implementing exception handling, referencing the correct assemblies to target namespaces, debugging assemblies, and otherwise managing assemblies (deployment and maintenance).

Acquiring background on how the runtime operates and executes your code will allow you to become fully proficient in .NET programming. It's admirable being an expert in software design and construction—and this book is mainly about that—but the best-written applications are useless if they get "trampled" in the runtime environment.

However, we don't need to cover everything about the CLR. We will focus primarily on the concerns of Visual Basic developers—deploying assemblies, programming for security, and performance—and less on the needs of framework developers—writing their own .NET runtimes, compilers, and languages. You'll want to closely examine the discussion on assemblies and intermediate-language (IL) code, because in later chapters we will evaluate the IL with respect to performance and debugging issues.

This chapter deals with theory. Here we examine the following key components of the .NET Framework:

- **The common type system (CTS)**   This system provides the type architecture of the framework and guarantees type safety.

- **The Common Language Specification (CLS)**   The specification that all .NET language adopters and compiler-makers employ so that their languages integrate seamlessly into the .NET Framework.

- **The common language runtime (CLR)**   The runtime and managed-execution environment in which all .NET applications are allowed to process.

We will then break down the common language runtime into several components to be discussed as follows:

- **Managed execution**   We define it and discuss how it differs from other execution environments, such as VBRUN, Smalltalk's runtime, and the Java Virtual Machine. We also introduce the garbage collector.

- **Runtime environment**   We discuss how the CLR uses metadata and Microsoft intermediate language (MSIL) to execute code. We also investigate the just-in-time compilation architecture and look briefly at the relevance of application domains vis-à-vis your deployment requirements.

- **Understanding Assemblies** We delve deeply into assemblies, examining how .NET applications, class libraries, and components are packaged. We also touch on the subject of attributes—a facility for increasing the programmer's control over the execution and management of code in the runtime environment.

- **The .NET Security Model** We introduce the security architecture of the CLR and how it affects your code and your ability to deploy.

Getting to Know the Framework's Runtime

A common language runtime, managed execution, and automatic memory management will now be the dominant features for most Windows applications. Programming to the CLR represents a major paradigm shift for Visual Basic designers—especially the notion of a garbage collector doing the memory housekeeping for objects on the heap. Yet, the classic VB runtime provided a similar degree of automation, so the paradigm shift is not as radical as it appears to be.

Many classic VB applications do not require the same level of memory management as those of C++ or Delphi. For the most part, you don't need to free an object explicitly, because the old VB runtime supposedly handles this. The .NET Framework accomplishes a lot for you. The architecture providing the foundation for managed execution is known as the *common type system* (CTS). For information on where objects live in memory, see Chapter 8.

The Common Type System

The common type system is the formal definition of how all types in the .NET Framework are constructed, declared, used, and managed. The CTS ground rules protect the integrity of executing code. Generally, we refer to *object models* in object-oriented programming, but the common type system is more than an object model.

The CTS specifies how types—classes—are referenced, and how applications and class libraries are packaged for execution on the CLR. This entire book is, in fact, about the common type system. It defines class declaration, inheritance, referencing, and type management as .NET Framework idioms, not as Visual Basic idioms. In other words, all .NET development environments must coincide, if they hope to be tightly integrated with the platform.

Each language's architects have the freedom to interpret the CTS requirements and be flexible in their usage. Small differences between C# and Visual Basic evidence this; we anticipate that over time C# and Visual Basic will focus more on the needs of their respective developer communities (or followers), thus increasing their differences.

In particular, the common type system provides the following foundations for the .NET Framework:

- CTS provides a first-class, pure object-oriented model supported by all programming languages that have adopted the .NET Framework. In this regard it is responsible for the common language specification and its implementation by .NET adherents.

■ CTS establishes the foundations and reference framework for cross-language integration, interoperation, type safety, security, and high-performance code execution.

■ CTS defines rules that languages must follow, which helps ensure that objects written in different languages can interact with each other.

You could consider that the CTS also encompasses the subjects of assemblies and namespaces, discussed later in this chapter and in Chapter 4, respectively. Let's look at the CTS object model to gain perspective.

Throughout this book, you will encounter references to the root of the object model, **Object,** and how it functions as the so-called ultimate object of the framework.

All the classes shown in Figure 2-1 are discussed in this book: Value types are introduced in Chapter 4, in the discussion of fundamental types, and discussed in depth in Chapter 8; reference types are discussed in Chapters 9 and 10.

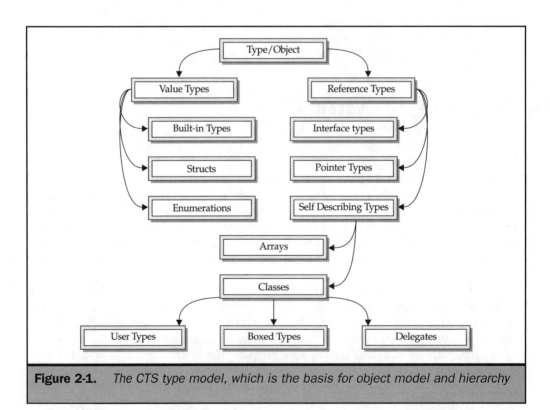

Figure 2-1.   *The CTS type model, which is the basis for object model and hierarchy*

The Common Language Specification

Language interoperability, or *interop,* is considered to be one of the Holy Grails of software development—and the .NET Framework has risen to the challenge admirably. Opinions about the Common Language Specification (CLS) vary. One that is accurate, but not intended to be complimentary, calls .NET "many languages for one platform" (while Java is "one language for many platforms"). For now it may be true that Windows is the only operating system, but for the programmers of the many languages that support .NET, the CLS is a major breakthrough.

By writing "CLS-compliant code," you construct classes and components that can be used by any language and its respective IDEs and development tools, without the need for complex COM and ActiveX interfaces and registration details. To achieve the magic, the CLS requires that class and component providers expose to consumers only the features that are common to all the .NET languages.

The CLS is really a subset of the common type system, as mentioned earlier. All the rules specified by the common type system in the runtime environment, such as type safety, determine how the CLS governs compliance at the code-construction and compilation levels. The CTS protects the integrity of code by ensuring *type safety*; code constructs that risk type safety are excluded from the CLS. As long as you produce CLS-compliant code, it will be verified by the CTS.

The cliché that says rules are made to be broken is likely to be echoed in various far-flung shops. When you program against the specs in the CLS, you ensure language interoperability for your intended audience and for others. CLS compliance warrants that third parties can rely on your code and that the facilities you want exposed are available to the entire spectrum of developers.

Table 2-1 provides an abridged list of software-development features that must meet CLS compliance rules and indicates whether the feature applies to both developers and compilers (All) or only to compilers.

Feature	Applies to	What Must Be CLS Compliant
General	All	Visibility and exposure; types that are exposed need to be compliant, but global static fields and methods do not.
Naming	All	Characters and casing (see Chapter 4). Keywords (compilers must prevent clashing; see Chapter 4 for use of escape characters); names must be unique, and signatures must ensure that return and parameter types are compliant.

Table 2-1. *Abridged Version of the CLS*

Feature	Applies to	What Must Be CLS Compliant
Types	All	Fundamental types such as **Integer**, **Boolean**, **Double**, and so on. (Primitive types, like Java's primitives, are not compliant. Visibility, interface methods, closure, and constructor invocation must be compliant.)
Type members	All	Overloading, uniqueness, and conversion operations.
Methods	All	Accessibility and calling conventions and parameter lists.
Properties	All	Accessor metadata, accessibility, modification, naming, and parameters (see Properties in Chapters 4, 7, 8, 9, and 10).
Events	All	Event methods and metadata, accessibility, modification, naming, and parameters.
Pointers	All	Pointers are not compliant.
Interfaces	All	Signatures and modification.
Reference types (objects)	All	Construction and invocation.
Class types	All	Inheritance (all classes must inherit) from at least one compliant class.
Arrays	All	Elements, dimensions, and bounds.
Enumerations	All	Underlying types, the **FlagsAttribute**, and field members.
Exceptions	All	Must derive from the base **System.Exception** class.
Custom attributes	All	Value encoding.
Metadata	Compilers	Compliance marking.

Table 2-1.   *Abridged Version of the CLS* (continued)

The CLS includes the language constructs that are needed by developers of all .NET languages. That may seem impossible, but the specification is not too big or complex for a .NET language to support. After all, many of the languages at the source-code level are as different from each other as fish are from birds. For instance, compare Smalltalk to Pascal, or C#, or the managed extensions of C++ to Visual Basic.

Visual Basic does things in its own peculiar way. So writing Visual Basic .NET code to achieve a particular end may produce strange nuances when packaged and accessed in C#. A good example—Visual Basic and C# implement properties in very different ways.

The advent of the CLS also brings an end to the C++ days of writing components for Visual Basic (and other languages). For many VB programmers, .NET reverses this role: you can now create components and class libraries that can be targeted to other CLS-compliant platforms, such as Visual C++ .NET and Visual C#. I predict that most .NET components will now be written in Visual Basic rather than C++ (for managed components). You may still have to test and document your classes and components in the target environments, however, because a particular bit of code might mean one thing to you and something else to the C# consumer. Yet, many immediate benefits are apparent:

- Classes produced in one language can be inherited by ones used in other languages.

- Objects instantiated from the classes of a sender written in one language can be passed to the methods of receiver objects whose classes were created in other languages. The receiving objects accept your arguments and process them as if they were written in the same language as the receiver.

- Exception handling, tracing, and profiling are language agnostic; you can debug across languages and even across processes. Exceptions can be raised in an object from one language and understood by an object created in another language.

Language interop helps maximize code reuse, which is one of the founding principles of all object-oriented languages, as we'll see in Chapters 9 and 10. Interoperability is achieved through metadata—in executables and class assemblies—that describes the makeup of assemblies and the intermediate-stage code that is understood across the entire framework.

Note   *Components that adhere to the CLS rules and use only the features included in the CLS may be labeled as CLS-compliant components.*

While the members of most types defined in the .NET Framework class library are CLS-compliant, some may have one or more members that are not; nonetheless, they're included to enable support for non-CLS compliant features, such as function pointers (a subject we touch upon in Chapter 7 and Chapter 14).

C#, for example, can be used to access these so-called unsafe features, but the architects of Visual Basic have decided to avoid unsafe code. The non-compliant types and members are identified and discussed in the .NET Framework Reference. In all cases, a CLS-compliant alternative is available.

> **Note**   *If you want your classes and components to be totally language agnostic, they need to conform to the CLS and be free of elements not supported by all CLS languages.*

The Common Language Runtime

Your Visual Basic .NET applications, class libraries, and components live in two realities. The design-time reality is where you write source code, create classes and objects, design applications, debug, and compile your code. The runtime reality is an external environment and for .NET managed-code applications, this environment is the common language runtime, better known as the CLR (not commonly referred to as just the runtime environment by the .NET architects).

Code that targets the CLR is called managed code, indicating that its execution in the runtime environment is *managed* by the CLR. We will soon discuss what exactly the CLR *manages.*

The CLR is a *hosted-execution* environment—before it can be bootstrapped on a target platform, the CLR's host must be supported on that platform. Microsoft has already released several hosts, including Windows 2000, Windows XP, .NET Server (I consider the operating system to be the host on .NET Server), Internet Information Services (IIS), and SQL Server 2000. A number of small device hosts are also due, and the industry expects a non-Windows host that could be installed on operating systems like Linux. A subset of the CLR, called the *Common Language Infrastructure (CLI)*, has already entered the international standardization process (see Figure 2-2.)

> **Note**   *For more comprehensive details, see the specification for the Common Language Infrastructure in the .NET Framework SDK.*

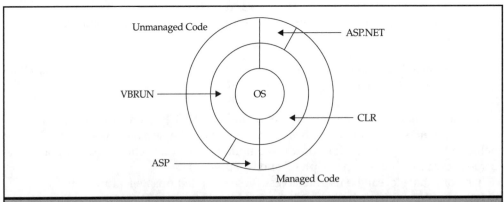

Figure 2-2.   *The CLR and its relationship to other runtime environments*

The CLR is like a proxy service that sits between your application and the operating system. The illustration shows the CLR sitting atop its host, a thin veneer of binary support, and interacting with the operating system via the host.

Services and Forms
Data and XML
Base Classes

CLR

HOST

OS

In order to understand the common language runtime, consider it an enhanced version of the classic Visual Basic runtime (VBRUN) that has evolved over time—lots of time. You may feel perplexed by the need to pay so much attention to the runtime environment. Executing the simplest application involves gathering all the runtime elements and making sure they are properly installed first. A Delphi programmer, by contrast, doesn't need to ensure that a runtime layer on the target operating system supports their application, because Delphi compiles to native code like C++. However, the big Delphi applications produce large executables and DLL files tend to be either very large or very numerous.

Historically, VB and Java required many megabytes of supporting libraries just to run a tiny executable of no more than, say, 100K. Ensuring the support of the correct VM in Java was a painful chore. (In writing Windows applications, I learned to program against the Java components of Internet Explorer, to be sure that my Visual J++ apps would work. And of course this had a lot to do with the first user interface libraries for Java—which were miserable.) Testing for IE's JVM was actually the easiest way to deploy VJ++ apps back in 1997 or 1998. And this is still true if you are only providing applications to the legacy Windows operating systems.

After a few years, however, it became clear that the target operating systems many clients were using already had the supporting runtime environment. This was more the case with the JVM than VBRUN, because virtually everyone had the latest versions of Internet Explorer. In the new Millennium, as long as your operating systems are well patched and service-pack supported by your IT staff, you will no longer need to concern yourself with the runtime for both classic VB apps and Java apps.

This is not yet true for .NET applications; but, with time, it will be. For a number of years, most of the machines in use will likely have the CLR and the .NET Framework installed on them, and for each first-time installation you are going to need to install this support for your .NET apps. Over time, you will take it for granted that the CLR is installed on your clients' machines, just as you now know that most of them accommodate the VBRUN libraries or the JVM. Most Windows 2000, Windows XP, and .NET Server products will be .NET ready. Also, .NET Server ships with the CLR built-in.

Microsoft Intermediate Language

When you compile your Visual Basic .NET source code, it is changed to an intermediate language (IL) that the CLR and all other .NET development environments understand. All .NET languages compile code to this IL, which is known as Microsoft Intermediate Language, MSIL, or IL. We use all of these terms in this book. At the IL level, all .NET code is the same—regardless of whether it came from C++, Oberon, or Visual Basic. The idea of compiling to an IL is not new. As you know, two popular languages compile to an intermediate language (or level) that runs on a so-called virtual machine: Java and Smalltalk.

Java compilers produce bytecode, which can be executed on the JVM or after further just-in-time (JIT) compilation to machine code. Smalltalk's IL code is similar in concept to the Java and Smalltalk bytecode. Smalltalk's IL is so versatile that some versions have been ported to various Java virtual machines. Thus, Smalltalk support for .NET was a given. Surprisingly, core Java can also be easily ported to the CLR—if you rid it of its C/C++ leftovers—hence the advent of J#.

There are many advantages to IL (and several disadvantages we will discuss shortly). For starters, compilation is much quicker because you don't have to compile to machine code just to run debug builds. Furthermore, the development environments of the other .NET languages can consume components and class libraries from the other languages because at the IL level all .NET code is the same.

Note	*MSIL represents a major paradigm shift in the compilation of code for the Windows platform. Vendors no longer need to tout compiler speeds or robustness of linkers. Today, thanks to languages like Java, Smalltalk, and .NET most of the code we write is first compiled to IL, and effortlessly converted to the machine-code when needed.*

Cross-language debugging and profiling is also possible as long as the CLR is the code management authority end-to-end. Exceptions caused by code that was originally written in Visual Basic can be handled by a C# application, and vice versa. Specifically, IL ensures the following benefits:

- It offers cross-language integration, including cross-language inheritance, which allows you to create a new class by deriving it from a base class written in another language.

- It facilitates automatic memory management, fondly known as garbage collection. Garbage collection manages object lifetimes, rendering reference-counting obsolete and delivering you from the task of explicitly freeing memory.

- It incorporates self-describing objects—complex APIs, like those requiring Interface Definition Language (IDL) for COM components, are now unnecessary.

- It allows you to compile code once and then run it on any CPU and operating system that supports the runtime.

On the other hand, IL also has some disadvantages:

- IL is not compiled to machine code like native code produced by Delphi or Visual C++ compilers, so it can more easily be reverse engineered. Defense mechanisms for handling this are likely to follow shortly after the .NET Framework is officially released.

- While IL is further compiled to machine code, a tiny percentage of algorithms will require a direct unwrapped access to system resources and hardware. Java and other runtime or abstract machine-dependent environments are in the same league. C, C++ and the like will probably dominate this extremely small market (one to three percent of applications) forever.

Note *The Java community has learned through its bytecode that decompiling intermediate code is not worth the effort. Obfuscating technology that will make IL code harder to decompile is available. So if you plan to email your class libraries or to allow them to be downloaded by your customers, they must be signed and then encrypted for travel. The security layers piled onto .NET code also ensure files that have been tampered with will not be used.*

Figure 2-3 (on the next page) shows what happens to your code from its inception in Visual Studio to execution.

Metadata

Once you have built and compiled an application, a class library, or a component, the IL code produced is packaged with its metadata in an *assembly*. These assemblies will have either .exe or .DLL as an extension, depending on whether they are executables or class libraries.

The code cannot be executed yet. Before the CLR can compile it to machine code, it needs to decide how to work with the assembly. The metadata in the IL directs how all the objects in your code are laid out and determines what gets loaded, how it is stored, which methods get called, control-flow, and exception handling.

The metadata also describes the classes used, signatures of methods, and the referencing required at runtime (which is what gives you such powerful features as reflection). Free threading is another feature afforded to Visual Basic programmers by the CLR.

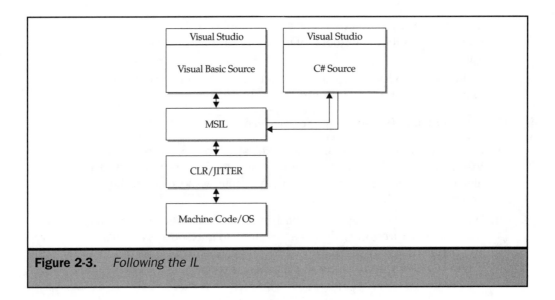

Figure 2-3. *Following the IL*

The metadata also describes the assembly by exposing these aspects of its IL code:

- The identity of the assembly (name, version, public key, culture context)
- Dependencies, or other assemblies this one depends on
- Security permissions, which are set by an administrator
- Visibility of the type
- The parent of the type, or what it inherits from
- Type membership (methods, fields, properties, events)
- Attributes, which are additional elements used on types and their members at runtime

All this data is embedded in the metadata, which allows the assembly contents to be self-describing to the CLR: This eliminates the hassles of application registration, type library registration, and the Interface Definition Language (IDL) required for ActiveX components.

In addition, self-describing containers of code do not need to be identified or registered with the operating system. By packaging metadata within the executable file itself, the assembly is able to describe itself to the CLR as soon as you try to execute it. (The idea is similar to that of carrying a magnetic card with all your personal information, instead of having to access it from an unwieldy database.) This is known as just-in-time execution. You click or launch the application and it immediately tells the CLR, "Here I am, this is what I need, I have permission to look in this directory, I want to call a certain method, I need this much RAM . . .". This may sound like a slow and cumbersome process, but as you will later see, it's not.

Assemblies and their metadata are better for security. You can trust self-describing components more implicitly than you can a file that publicizes itself in the registry—these entries date rapidly and their integrity can be easily compromised; they and their implementation counterparts (the DLLs and executables installed on the system) can also become easily separated.

Executable Code

Assemblies do not have *carte blanche* within the CLR. Code is not always passed directly to the JIT compiler. First, the IL code may undergo a thorough inspection if deemed necessary by the platform administrator. The code is given a verification test that is carried out according to the wishes of the network administrator, who might have specified that all .NET code on the machine must be executed according to a certain security policy. The IL code is also checked to make sure nothing malicious has been included. See the section "The .NET Security Model" later in this chapter for details how these checks are carried out. As always, it is crucial to be aware of all this when you get deployment.

 MSIL is first converted to CPU-specific code by a just-in-time (JIT) compiler specific to a flavor of the Windows operating system. The same set of MSIL, however, can be JIT-compiled and executed on any supported architecture.

The code is also checked to determine that it is type safe, that it doesn't try to access restricted memory locations, and that it references correctly. Objects have to meet stringent safety checks to ensure that they are properly isolated from one another and do not access each other's data. In short, if the verification process discovers that the IL code is not what it claims to be, it is terminated and security exceptions are thrown.

Managed Execution

The .NET just-in-time compiler has been engineered to conserve both memory and resources while giving maximum throughput. Via the code inspection process and self-learning, it can determine what code needs to be compiled immediately and when the rest will be needed. This function is known as JIT compilation—the code is compiled as soon as we need it. When we need machine code "yesterday," we can force compile it and have it ready for action.

Furthermore, the JIT compiler and the CLR manage resources and process "bandwidth" such that tests show CLR code has the potential of running even faster on the managed heap than it does on the unmanaged heap. At this writing, the next version of the CLR is already being upgraded in shop.

How does such a runtime do its job? The CLR is able to manage access to CPU-stack registers of the fundamental-type and the reference-type heaps in such a way that objects are accessed and processed quickly. Exception objects are also disposed of more rapidly under the CLR than on the unmanaged heap. And value types, which live on the stack, are eliminated as soon as they are no longer needed. Value types are not garbage-collected, as you will see in Chapter 8.

Applications and services may appear to be slow on first start-up, but subsequent execution obviates the need to send the code through the "JIT'er" again. For the most part, or at least until you have a substantial .NET project underway, you will not need to concern yourself with the JIT compiler.

Managed execution is also not a single process but a stack of many operations. The following list is an abridged stack that represents the birth-to-death course of a .NET application:

1. Code is generated by the developer.

2. Code is "compiled" to Microsoft Intermediate Language.

3. Code is described with metadata and gathered into an assembly.

4. Code is checked prior to execution and marked as "kosher" (or not).

5. Code is just-in-time (JIT) compiled if it *is* kosher.

6. Code is executed.

7. Code execution is managed.

8. Code is terminated and resources are freed.

Visual Basic .NET programmers focus on the top of the execution stack. As the illustration suggests, they are less concerned about what happens to their code further down the stack. Smart programmers, the architects, will do well to master the lower rungs, as this chapter suggests.

Programmer Writes Code	
Compiled to MSIL	
Code Described with Metadata	
Code is Verified	
Code is JIT Compiled	
Execution	
Management (GC)	
Termination	

■ Programer Interest Scale (highest is black)

Managed execution also entails a lot more than reading IL, verification, and JIT compilation. It also describes what the CLR does once it has loaded and executed an application. Three sophisticated operations of the CLR that will influence your application design and construction are *side-by-side execution, garbage collection,* and isolation of applications and services into *application domains.*

Side-by-Side Execution

The CLR is able to manage multiple versions of the same assembly simultaneously because the nature and makeup (metadata) of the assembly isolate it from the processing space of all other assemblies, even mutually dependent ones. This is a phenomenon known as side-by-side execution. This is not a new concept, but it has never been done as successfully as it is on the CLR.

Side-by-side execution has delivered us from complications associated with "DLL hell", because you no longer have to maintain backward compatibility of libraries and components when new applications and assemblies are installed on a machine.

In the past, applications that depended on a particular version of a component would break because a new application overwrote their component. But with .NET, as long as you keep the old component around, the application can still reference it. Newer versions of the component can be installed to the machine as needed by the newer applications. This is possible because, as mentioned earlier, you don't need to register the DLLs and components. When you are ready to eliminate the older ones, you can delete them.

Side-by-side execution is possible because an executable assembly expresses a dependence on a particular support assembly, which is versioned by the metadata. The executable will always use the correct code, by design. Versioning on .NET is more intelligent than simpler models based on version numbers and files that can be easily erased. Version policy can specifically force an application to upgrade to the new version of any dependent assemblies.

Despite the relief from DLL registration problems conflicts can still arise. You need good application design and proven patterns of software development to ensure that applications are safe and reentrant. Application domains, discussed next, make that possible.

Application Domains

Well-written applications with properly encapsulated data usually provide a certain level of isolation from others in legacy-processing environments. In some cases, two applications or algorithms that are closely related risk accessing the same resources and data, or spawning threads that can collide. Code processed from Web sites is particularly susceptible to such disasters.

For instance, two or more high-end mail servers working on the same machine need to be properly isolated from each other—though this can severely hamper scalability. In the past, we had to engineer such applications to run in separate, isolated processes, often requiring layers of proxy code to manage cross-application data exchange and task synchronization—a resource-intensive and risky proposition that could result in clashing and corruption. The CLR provides a higher degree of application isolation through the code verification process and type checking. The CLR can further protect the violation of processing space through creating and deploying applications in their own domains.

The runtime host creates these domains, which set up a safe execution environment around a CLR; a target application will run within this. Think of this architecture as a form of partitioning on a common operating system. A domain is created before the CLR is bootstrapped to accommodate application execution. Multiple domains can be spawned in the same process, which dramatically increases processing bandwidth and thus scalability. The SQL Server runtime CLR host would be a suitable target to run server-side functionality in application domains.

Application domains are extremely lightweight, so you could engineer a service that spawns a multiplicity of them in a single browser process; further, you could design it so that you prevent controls operating in the browser from trespassing into each other's backyards.

By using these domains, you protect your group of applications from the shortcomings of any individual one. It is feasible to keep an application running in one domain and maintain a standby application in an isolated "instance," where it would be ready to take over processing—like a form of software fault-tolerance. You cannot execute applications in the domains until the assemblies have been loaded there.

Automatic Memory Management

Automatic memory management is a boon for developers coding to .NET. A sophisticated memory-management algorithm called a garbage collector (GC) has enabled this. Many garbage collection algorithms have been tested and proven before the .NET version. CLR architects have been fortunate to implement one with much hindsight.

If you have programmed for Java, you are already familiar with garbage collection, because Java also manages memory for you. The GC, and how it is controlled, is investigated in Chapter 17.

In VB 6.0 and earlier versions of VB, objects that go out of scope, get lost, or become unnecessary had to be explicitly removed (remember **Terminate events** [VB], **Destroy Free** [Delphi], and **DeleteRef** [C++]). In manual memory management, problems arise because you have many objects—you might lose track of them or forget to discard them, allowing for a slow "memory leak." The .NET GC does not let this happen, because it removes these "lost" objects and automatically frees the memory they occupied. The specifics of memory allocation and how the GC works with it are discussed in Chapter 17.

Does automatic memory management imply that you can write code without worrying about freeing objects? The answer is a cautious "yes"—for most of your applications. But if you think you will never have to concern yourself with memory management—think again. It's untrue for the .NET languages, untrue for Java, and for all other automatic memory-management development projects.

First, so much legacy code exists that it will be five to ten years before most of our code will be using managed-execution runtimes with automatic memory management. If you build applications for the CLR that need to interoperate with legacy code (such as COM and COM+), you will need to free memory manually—implement **Dispose** methods in your .NET code to free resources running in the unmanaged space.

Second, it's not difficult to implement poorly designed software that uses a heap (no pun intended) more memory than it should. Automatic memory management only frees resources held by obsolete objects; it doesn't concern itself with object economics.

Here's an example: You create an application under the management of the CLR that has to open up sockets out to the Internet. It requires 10 threads, each running in its own little "slice" on the system. Such an application, like a mail server, would be rapidly activating objects.

The threads spawned in the application create objects, work with them, and then dump them. For the example's sake, let's say that the thread cannot reuse the objects. In this case, you will probably run out of memory despite having a garbage collector, because the GC can not clean up your wasteful threads quickly enough. Instead, you might have to rethink your design if you have critical applications that need to activate many objects and dispose of them quickly.

You cannot call **Finalize** or **Dispose** each time an object needs discarding. GC algorithms do not work that way. The finalization of objects in the GC world of automatic memory management is *non-deterministic*—you cannot predict exactly when an object will be removed from memory. Objects aren't removed chronologically; thus, the order in which they became obsolete is irrelevant.

Also, garbage collection can be a bottleneck. The boon of not having to set objects free has this trade-off: the CLR controls the GC, and when the collector stops to take out the garbage, your threads have to mark time. "Time leaks" may have replaced "memory leaks." But all is not lost. (See Chapter 17.)

The CLR allows you some management over the GC. A collection of GC classes and methods are at your bidding, though you still cannot force collection or make the cleanup *deterministic*. Rather, you can design your applications and algorithms such that you have some control over resource cleanup.

Having the benefit of garbage collection does not mean you can ignore application design and common sense. If you are coding applications that lose or nix objects indiscriminately, the GC is not going to work for you. Your design should be using the main objects you create until the application or service shuts down. The objects that have to be removed and restarted often should be lightweight structures (as discussed in Chapter 8).

Despite these caveats, the GC is very fast. For most applications you'll see no difference between how quickly the CLR disposes of an object and frees its resources, and the memory reclamation of your unmanaged apps. The time you might lose to collection is measured in microseconds in the life of the average application on a fast machine. In addition, the GC can be deployed on multiprocessor machines, allowing its threads to be allocated to one processor while yours run on the other. How the GC accomplishes this is beyond the scope of this book.

Just-in-Time Deployment

Application or service deployment no longer requires intricate installation procedures that infest the registry with keys and values like a swarm of bees invading an empty hive (perhaps that's why we refer to the partitions of the registry as the *hives*). You can now distribute applications to target runtimes in several ways. You can simply place your compiled assemblies (.DLL and .EXE files and any multi-file assembly members) into a private folder that you set up for your installation. Your user can then simply double-click the target's icon and it loads whatever it needs to run.

It used to be this way when all we had to worry about was a directory and a .INI file. What happened in between—along came Windows 95, the registry, and ActiveX; for the past seven years, installation and deployment have been getting increasingly tougher.

The following list shows the available deployment scenarios:

- Explicitly install into the global assembly.

- **XCOPY** your files—or just drag and drop them—into a folder or the GAC.

- Use the Windows Installer (version 2.0).

- Download (into the ASP.NET runtime).

- Use just-in-time (also known as on-the-fly) deployment.

From the start, you can keep things simple by creating a script that just drops your .NET apps onto the target machine and installs the icons.

Even uninstall nightmares are now a thing of the past. Simply copy the new versions to the target computer, delete the old one, or move them into a "legacy folder" in case the end user decides to roll back or something goes awry with the new version.

For global access to your files, you only need to drop them into the Global Assembly Cache (see the next section). Each computer that carries the CLR is endowed with a GAC (pronounced like *whack*). This "repository" for assemblies is a machine-wide code cache that stores assemblies that have been designated for sharing by more than one application on the machine.

Note	*The GAC is usually created in the root of your operating system folders. For example, on Windows .NET Server this might be* **C:\Winnt\assembly**.

The purpose of the GAC is to expose the assemblies placed in it—to applications and services that depend on them. When the CLR needs the assembly required by the application, it will go to the GAC.

Note	*COM interop code does not have to be installed in the GAC.*

If assemblies do not need to be shared among applications, you should store them with their "friends" in private locations. Administrators can then protect the folders if need be, and some of them can be placed entirely off limits to anything but the assemblies that depend on them.

You can use the Windows Installer, or any other .NET-compliant commercial installer, to deploy into the GAC or private folders. The .NET SDK also provides a utility called the Global Assembly Cache tool (GACUTIL.EXE), which you can use for inserting into the cache.

Note *Assemblies placed in the GAC must have strong names. See the section on security later in this chapter.*

When you are ready to deploy assemblies for ASP.NET applications simply XCOPY or FTP them to the server. When you allow Windows forms or Web service assemblies to be downloaded, they can be packed as either DLL files or compressed .CAB files. You can simply hook up the source via FTP or HTTP and allow the client to download the file through the link.

The benefit of using the Windows Installer, which generates .MSI packages, is you can integrate .NET installation with the Add/Remove Programs option in the Control Panel. You can accomplish installation, removal, and repair in this way.

Understanding Assemblies

The assembly is a "physical" container for at least one built (compiled) executable or class file, module, component, or icon. If the assembly is a library, then the class or classes it harbors are referenced by the fully qualified namespace described in Chapter 4. You still need to reference the assembly in the IDE to gain access to the namespace, so the two are connected at the hip.

If the assembly is an executable file, an application, you reference it by the name of the physical file, which needs an entry point to allow the operating system to initiate its execution. In the next chapter we will create a small application called "Welcome" to demonstrate this. The **welcome.exe** file we produce in that demo is the assembly.

Note *Assembly names and namespace names should not be confused. The two are often similar and sometimes identical, but have very little to do with each other, aside from their shared need to "register" an assembly so that Visual Studio can find its way to the namespace.*

At the physical level, an assembly is many things, and the organization of its contents—Microsoft Intermediate Language code and metadata—is quite complex. While you don't need to know the ins and outs of the contents of the assembly, you need to fully understand what it is, how to build it, name it, distribute it, and manage it in order to be effective in your development efforts. This section will help you achieve an understanding so that you can navigate your software development results and this book more easily.

You will understand assemblies better if we separate them into the four types that the Visual Basic compiler can produce:

- **Console Executable**   This assembly is a standard, GUIless, console Window which we have been referencing so far in this chapter. Console assemblies have the **.exe** extension. OS entry into the executable is through **Main.**

- **Windows Executable**   This is the standard .NET Windows executable file. The assemblies are also given the **.exe** extension. OS entry is through **WinMain.**

- **Class Library**   This is your standard .NET class library, which can be dynamically linked. These assemblies are given the **.DLL** extension. They can contain one class or many. OS entry into the library is via **DLLMain** (which is not a construct you need to concern yourself with).

- **Class Module**   This is your standard class module, which is used as a container for compiled classes that still need to be linked into a project or as part of a formal class library before it can be used. These assemblies are given the **.netmodule** extension. No entry into this file is required because entry is via the **DLLMain** of the assembly it is linked to.

It is wise in .NET programming to name an assembly according to its purpose and the purposes of the classes inside it. Be sure to give your assembly a name that does not "clash" with the root namespace name. The **System.DLL** file that ships with the framework is a good example. Naming the assembly "System" tends to blur the distinction between the assembly name and the namespace name (such as **System.Data,** which refers to both the namespace and the assembly name).

Before we further discuss the four types of output files and how they are produced, let's take a closer look at how assemblies are located by the runtime, their actual make-up, and the roles they play in your software development.

Locating Assemblies, Anytime

Usually the assemblies you create—executable applications, functionality, or resources—reside in a folder you establish via an installation routine or utility. The default location when you are building assemblies is the project folders for Visual Studio .NET.

The assemblies can be stored in the root folder of your application or in sub-folders. You have a lot of flexibility in choosing a location and routing them to their folders. The other location for your assemblies is the Global Assembly Cache, or GAC. Libraries placed in the GAC must be shared and given strong names (described later in this section)—these assemblies would typically be used by more than one application or user, even concurrently. The concept of "registering" with the GAC mirrors that of the registry, but is less fragile a process and is easier to maintain. There are ways of overriding the default methods for locating assemblies. Likewise, you can redirect the path to it. Assemblies can also interoperate with the COM and COM+ world and are accessible from unmanaged clients.

Microsoft suggests keeping assemblies private, thus out of the GAC, if they do not need to be shared. When you build the assemblies with the code provided in this book, you can leave them in their respective project folders.

What's in an Assembly

In the early days of developing for the Microsoft operating systems (usually one of the early shades of Windows), compilers produced a file that was compliant with two standards, the Microsoft Portable Executable (PE) Format and the Microsoft Common Object File Format (COFF). The two standards were created to enable the operating system to load and execute your applications, or link in the dynamic libraries.

The formats specified how the compiled files were laid out, permitting the OS to load files and execute accurately. The .NET assemblies have adopted the PE/COFF combination, enabling the runtime to process your files as it does your standard executables.

Tip   *You can ignore this section if are exclusively writing Visual Basic .NET code. However, knowing how assemblies are composed and processed is essential if you are in charge of quality control, debugging, performance issues, deployment, packaging, and security.*

The IL code in the PE/COFF file is not executable machine code, and it will not be able to process the application you develop in Visual Studio. Consider this Star Trek analogy: IL code is like the product of the universal translator that allows Klingons, Ferengi, Cardasians, Vulcans, and Humans to communicate. The CLR, wherever it may be, knows what to do with this new quasi-compiled, intermediate language.

The CLR scans the .NET PE file for metadata so it can interpret the IL code in the PE/COFF file. Microsoft has newly added this metadata section to the standard PE/COFF combination—it not only helps the CLR interpret what to do with the file, but the file itself publishes metadata to describe itself to the rest of the .NET "dominion." The .NET adaptation of the PE/COFF file also contains a native image section, as it did in the old era (see the illustration).

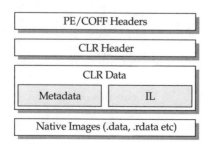

Finally, Microsoft chose the name *assembly* for its new conglomerate of data in the PE/COFF file. It might have considered the word *package,* but that was already taken by Borland, Sun (for use by Delphi and Java respectively), and several other competitors.

Although we often think of assemblies as *executables,* they are not executable outside the CLR. Whether you have built a collection of classes compiled as a DLL or an application with a .exe extension, in the CLR the *assembly* still has to be compiled.

Before we go further into developing with Visual Basic .NET, think about the following with respect to assemblies:

- Learn what goes into the assembly—although you don't need to know how to read or generate the assembly itself, unless you are keen to develop a compiler for .NET. Our quest begins with the sample code and figures in the section "The Nature of the Assembly." In later chapters, we'll interpret sequential IL code in the assembly. This knowledge is crucial for properly configuring compiler options or understanding why an application is moving slowly.

- More important, understand how assemblies are used, distributed, and deployed as your application or class library.

Metadata

The metadata that assemblies carry in order to describe themselves to the runtime environment (the CLR) communicates code and class data, text, images, resources (such as icons), and other information. Unlike their counterparts, .NET assemblies are compiled to MSIL, not to machine code, when they leave the IDE.

Metadata provides a streamlined programming model. We no longer need to work with complex and finicky Interface Definition Files (IDL), dozens of cryptic header files that are so tedious and time-consuming to prepare, and external dependencies for code and components alike.

When a .NET (PE) file is executed or loaded, the CLR scans the assembly for the metadata manifest that will allow it to interpret, process, just-in-time (JIT) compile (down to machine code), and then run the file. The metadata is not only for the benefit of the CLR; it also identifies the assembly—allowing it to describe itself—to the entire .NET environment or framework on a machine, and even across process boundaries.

The illustration demonstrates how the contents of the PE/COFF file are assembled.

Assembly Metadata
Type Metadata
MSIL (your code)
Resources (images etc)

More about Metadata

When you execute an application and a class is referenced, the CLR loads the metadata of the respective assembly and studies this payload to successfully accommodate the assembly, its resources, and the requests of the contents. The metadata describes the following:

- **Description of the Assembly**   Its identity, including name, version, culture, and public key. It also holds references to types that are exported, the assembly's dependencies, and security permissions.

- **Description of the Assembly's Types**   Includes the name, visibility of the class, the base class, and any interfaces implemented. It also describes class members, such as methods, data fields, properties, events, and type composition or nesting.

- **Description of Attributes**   Relates the additional descriptive modifiers for types and their members.

The metadata is a sophisticated mechanism that conveys everything the CLR needs to know about a module, its execution, and its interaction with other modules in the CLR. Since the assemblies do not require explicit registration to the operating system, application reliability is increased exponentially.

The metadata also facilitates language interoperability and allows component code to be accessed equally by any CLS-compliant language. You can inherit from classes written in other languages (demonstrated in several places in this book, and by virtue of the BCL (the base class library), which is mostly written in C#).

The PE file is divided into two sections, one for metadata and one for the MSIL code. The metadata portion references the MSIL via a collection of tables and heap structures that point to tokens embedded in the MSIL code.

As a result, you cannot change the contents of the assemblies or "fix" the MSIL code without the assembly metadata knowing about it. This helps ensure that the integrity of the assembly contents has not been compromised.

The metadata token is a four-byte number that identifies what the token references in the MSIL—a method, a field, or other constructs.

The Nature of the Assembly

In addition to the logical types described earlier, assemblies can be either static or dynamic, private or shared:

- **Static Assembly**   This is the .NET PE file you create whenever you compile and build a class library or some type of application. The namespaces we discussed earlier are typically partitioned across them—either in one assembly or across many.

- **Dynamic Assembly**   This is a memory resident module that gets loaded at runtime to provide specific services—for instance, the **Reflection** class collection, which allows you to reference and access runtime type information (see Chapter 13).

■ **Private Assembly**   This is a static version that can only be accessed by a specific application. It is visible only to the application or other assemblies in its private folder or sub-folder.

■ **Shared Assembly**   This assembly is given a strong name and public key data so that it can be uniquely identified by the CLR. Any application can use it. A dynamic assembly can also be a shared one.

Let's now take a closer look at the contents of an assembly—and among other things its IL code. The quickest way to do that (besides reading this book) is to run the IL disassembler application that ships with the .NET Framework Software Development Kit (SDK). The file is called ILDASM.EXE and you'll usually find it in the \\..\Microsoft.NET\ FrameworkSDK\Bin folder. Double click the application and the illustration provided in Figure 2-4 will load.

Go to File, Open and aim the application at any assembly you might have already created. The one we build in the next chapter is an excellent choice for your study, because it is a bare-bones console executable.

The Assembly Manifest

The manifest is the critical requirement of the assembly because it contains the assembly metadata. However, you can compile an assembly to MSIL without a

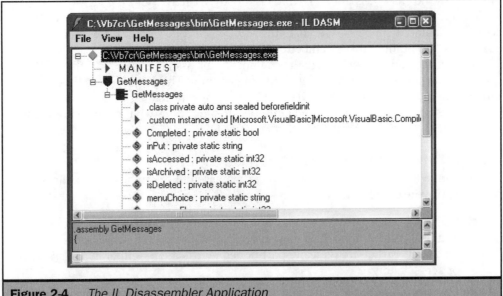

Figure 2-4.   *The IL Disassembler Application*

manifest, to produce a netmodule. Assembly manifests can be stored in single-file or multi-file assemblies, or in stand-alone files. Figure 2-5 illustrates the collection of files that can make up an assembly "unit."

The assembly manifest's metadata satisfies the CLR's version requirements and security identity requirements, the scope of the assembly, and resolution of resources and types.

The assembly manifest provides metadata that does the following:

- Identifies the assembly, which includes the name, version number, culture (language and culture), public key, and digital signature.

- Delineates all the files that comprise the assembly, as a single file or as many that form a logical unit.

- Resolves the assembly's types, their declarations, and implementations.

- Resolves dependencies (other assemblies on which this one depends).

- Allows the assembly to describe itself to the runtime environment.

The manifest code in the assembly is exposed as follows:

```
.module Vb7cr.dll
// MVID: {8A49956F-353C-4C11-9F7E-6C46EF6AF2FD}
.imagebase 0x11000000
.subsystem 0x00000002
.file alignment 512
.corflags 0x00000001
// Image base: 0x03680000
.namespace Vb7cr
{
  .class /*02000002*/ private auto ansi sealed Welcome
  extends [mscorlib/* 23000001 */]System.Object/* 01000001 */
{
 .custom /*0C000001:0A000003*/ instance void
[Microsoft.VisualBasic/* 23000002
*/]Microsoft.VisualBasic.Globals/* 01000003
*//StandardModuleAttribute/* 01000004 */::.ctor() /*
0A000003 */ = ( 01 00 00 00 )

.method /*06000001*/ public static void Main() cil managed
// SIG: 00 00 01
{
// Method begins at RVA 0x2050
```

```
// Code size       20 (0x14)
.maxstack  8
 .language '{3A12D0B8-C26C-11D0-B442-00A0244A1DD2}',
 '{994B45C4-E6E9-11D2-903F-00C04FA302A1}',
'{00000000-0000-0000-0000-
   00000000000}'
```

In the above IL sample, we have highlighted the assembly name **Vb7cr.dll**—which you can download from the Web-based sources listed in the Introduction to this book— the root namespace **Vb7cr** and the entry point of the class.

The Roles of the Assembly

Let's now investigate the essential roles of an assembly, which can provide:

- A type boundary
- A reference-scope boundary
- A unit of deployment
- A unit of execution
- A version boundary
- A security boundary

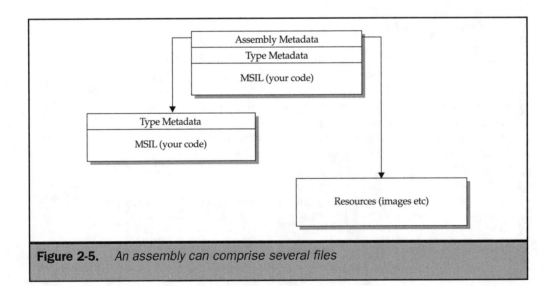

Figure 2-5.   *An assembly can comprise several files*

Assemblies as Type Boundaries

On the file system, the assembly looks like any other dynamic link library. It usually carries the DLL extension, although it can also be a cabinet file (with the .CAB extension). You can build a class and make its source code available to any application. But you would mostly do that for your own use, and maybe for your development-team members. However, we suggest you don't provide "raw" classes to your team members, because with access to the actual Visual Basic source code, multiple problems can be introduced. You would only supply the raw source files if your user specifically requested or needed them—such as readers of this book, or your customers who have opted to buy the source code of your components (usually as a safeguard against your going out of business).

The best examples of assemblies are the ones that contain the base-class libraries encompassing the .NET Framework. To compile a class to IL and package it into an assembly is very straightforward. You simply build the class and specify the assembly and its namespace for the compiler.

Classes (known as types once they have been reduced to IL) are separated by the assembly in which they reside—hence the term *type boundary*. In other words, two types can be placed onto the same namespace but they can exist in individual assemblies. The problem arises when you try to reference the type in the IDE because you can only Import to one fully qualified namespace. The IDE will not let you reference the second class twice and will notify you of your previous reference.

Assemblies as Reference-Scope Boundaries

The manifest metadata specifies the level of exposure a type and its resources have outside the assembly, the dependencies, or other assemblies on which it relies, and how types are resolved and resource requests satisfied.

If there are statically linked dependencies, the manifest includes metadata detailing information such as name and version.

The manifest also lists reference scopes of the types. The types can be accessed outside the assembly; this process lets you reference them by their FQNS or gives them friend access, implying that are hidden from the outside world—only accessible to those within the same assembly in which the friend resides.

Assemblies as Units of Deployment

When you execute an application, the application assembly calls into its dependencies, which are either visible to the exe file in the same folder or in sub-folders, or they are visible in the runtime environment because they have been installed in the GAC.

Assemblies installed in the GAC are shared, which exposes them to others that may need access to their internals. You might also have utility classes, culture and localization classes, or components, and these can be loaded into the installation folder or the GAC. These assemblies let you build very thin application assemblies and keep successive deployments small—where you just need to change the outdated assembly.

Versioning in .NET lets you or your users set up new variations on your assemblies without breaking those installed previously.

Assemblies as Units of Execution

The CLR lets all shared assemblies execute or be accessed side-by-side. Thus, as long as you create a shared assembly with a strong identity and a unique version number, and you register it into the GAC, the CLR will be able to execute it alongside another assembly. The DLL conflicts of the past are abolished under the CLR, because only the version number and unique public key data allow the CLR to distinguish between the assemblies.

As a Version Boundary

The assembly is the smallest versionable unit in the CLR; the types and other resources it encapsulates are versioned with the assembly as a unit. A class cannot stand alone and be accessed outside of the assembly architecture because there is no way to reference it. The class or type can either be part of the application assembly or stand alone in its own assembly, which provides the version data for it.

The version number is encapsulated in the assembly manifest, as shown earlier. The CLR uses the version number and the assembly's public key data to find the exact assembly it needs to execute, and any assemblies that may be dependent on the specific version.

In addition, the CLR provides the infrastructure to allow you to enforce specific version rules.

As a Security Boundary

The assembly is a security unit that facilitates access control to the data, type functionality, and resources it encapsulates. As a class provider, the CLR allows you to control access to your assembly's objects by allowing you to specify a collection of permissions on an assembly. The client process—rich clients, thin-clients, Web forms, or otherwise—must have the permission you specify in order to access the object in the assembly.

This level of security is known as *code access security*. When an assembly is called up, the CLR quickly determines the level of code access allowed on the assembly. You only get code if you have authorization. The idea of controlling code access is fairly new and in line with the model of distributed functionality that is becoming so widespread. Code access security also employs a *role-based security* model, which specifies to the CLR what a client is allowed to do with the code it can access.

The security identifier of an assembly is its *strong name,* which is discussed in the next section.

System resources also require protection from assemblies. The ASP.NET Web Application Security protects access to system resources by comparing credentials and proxies of credentials to Windows NT file system's security architecture.

Chapter 11 discusses techniques for handling exceptions and error conditions that may arise as a result of security-access violations.

Attributes, Reflection, and Assemblies

A critical facility of assemblies is the provision of runtime type information (RTTI) through a process known as reflection. As with most OO languages, basic RTTI is built into all classes with the **GetType** method and the **Is** operator (see Chapter 4 and Chapter 9); yet, reflection in the .NET Framework is especially sophisticated thanks to the assembly, its metadata, and the provision of attributes.

An attribute is an object containing information and runtime instructions defined in an attribute class and then compiled with the class it has been appended to. Attributes can be applied globally, at both the class and class-member levels.

The .NET Framework's reflection architecture lets you access the targeted attributes at runtime, through standard class instantiation. However, the runtime knows about the beneficiary of the attributes, because they are embedded in the assemblies of the beneficiaries. When you affix attributes to target classes or their members, the attribute class gets compiled along with the beneficiary. Then the metadata—of both attribute and beneficiary—ends up in the same assembly.

With some imagination, you can see that at one end of the sophistication scale attributes let the runtime have important information about an object it has instantiated. For example, the runtime learns from attributes whether or not it can honor a request to serialize an object to disk or to an XML stream, and it discovers what fields in the target objects are allowed to be persisted. You can even look up object authorship, version, and security information at runtime.

At the other end of the sophistication scale, entering the realm that was once thought to be science fiction, attributes can be used to reflect on, and reference, objects that are running in the processing space of another computer somewhere else on the Internet. With reflection we can reference the objects and determine their methods, accessible fields, constructors, and other elements in these other processes. Reflection is not an easy subject to grasp. It is also a subject at the center of much debate, particularly about its impact on performance. Chapter 4 introduces some attribute fundamentals but the subject is best left to an advanced treatise.

Strong Names

Assemblies can be given strong names, which will guarantee their uniqueness and provide security attributes. The strong name is made up of the assembly's standard name (such as **Vb7cr**), its version number, culture, public key data, and a digital signature. The strong name is generated from all this data, which is stored in the assembly manifest. If the CLR encountered two assemblies with the same strong name, it would know that the two files were identical. Strong names are issued by Visual Studio .NET and by development tools that ship with the .NET SDK. The idea behind strong names is to primarily protect the version lineage of an assembly, because the guaranteed uniqueness ensures that no one else can substitute their assembly for yours.

The strong name also protects your consumers and allows them to use the types and resources of your assemblies with the knowledge that the integrity of their system is intact. Combined with supporting certificates, you have the ultimate security system for the protection of enterprise and distributed code.

The .NET Security Model

Ever since the advent of the LAN, application security extended to the access rights and trust provided to a user by his or her administrator. Even applications that do not directly interface with humans have operated under the auspices of and in the context of user accounts. Most server side applications work this way, operating under the authority of the Administrator account. This model of security is known as the *user authentication* model.

In the mid 1990s, the *sandbox* security model became popular—at about the same time we discovered Java applets could be made to do all sorts of nasty things behind your Web browser. The idea behind the sandbox is to isolate applications in safe environments where they cannot go rouge and start looking for credit card numbers, passwords, and the like whenever you log onto a Web site.

.NET security combines both of these: the *user authority* model *and* the *sandbox* model. However, the security levels and rules are enforced by the CLR. Through a process known as code verification, the managed code is verified to ensure type safety. For example, if a method declares a parameter that takes a 4-byte argument, you won't get into the method with an 8-byte argument.

Execution flow-control is also "watched." Your code will be able to access only the locations allowed by the administrator. This is an important consideration when you are writing your code. While you might not have a malicious design in your application, if your code is infiltrated, the administrator will need to block access to the off-limit areas of your code. In the event of mistakes, lockdowns, and unintentional lockouts, you need to write code that can gracefully accept that the world is not its oyster.

The verification process also catches damaging errors that may not have originated due to hostile intention. The old sticklers like buffer overruns, overwriting memory locations, and arbitrary transfer-of-control are about as outdated as horn-rimmed spectacles.

Verification is performed by the CLR's verification algorithm when you attempt to run your applications or your application needs to access types. It is part of the JIT compilation process. At that point the MSIL code is classified as follows:

■ **Invalid** The verification algorithm has determined that the MSIL code cannot be JIT compiled by the CLR, which essentially means that something in the code prevented the MSIL from being converted into machine or native code. The code is promptly repudiated.

- **Valid** The MSIL code was found to be acceptable to the CLR and could thus be compiled into native code. The CLR accepts MSIL as being valid even if it might not be type-safe, a determination it still has to make.

- **Type-safe** The next stage of the verification process after code is declared valid is the type-safety check. Here the algorithm tests to see if types are "legally" accessed through the proper interfaces. Code that tries to circumvent the interfaces and tries to access the private members of a type, which is considered illegal, is considered not type-safe.

- **Verifiable** Once code passes the type-safety check the CLR accepts that code is both valid and type-safe and allows it to be executed or referenced. When code is classifed as verifiable by the algorithm it means that it is both valid and type-safe.

The CLR does not need to verify code every time it is executed or referenced by an application. It is smart enough to know to skip the process when code that has been previously verified is loaded. The CLR may also make this determination to skip the verification process if it trusts the code sufficiently. Code loaded from the Internet or a remote computer, for example, is not implicitly trusted and must be verified.

When is an assembly secure enough to earn the trust of the CLR? A number of mechanisms are in place to secure resources and assemblies from unauthorized users, hostile code, and viruses. Here are the basic security levels and models of .NET Security:

- **ASP.NET Web Application Security** This mechanism provides the means for controlling access to a Web or Internet site through authentication. Credentials are compared against the NT file system or against an XML file that contains lists of authorized users, authorized roles, and HTTP verbs.

- **Code Access Security, Authentication, and Authorization** This mechanism uses permissions to control assembly access to resources and operations. By setting permissions, you can protect the system from malicious code and simultaneously allow bona fide code to run safely. This form of *evidence based security* is managed by administrators.

- **Role-Based Security** This mechanism provides access to assemblies based on what it, as the impersonator of the user, is allowed to do. This is determined by user identity, role membership (like those you have in SQL Server 2000), or both. Business rules play a large part in the formulation of role-based security.

- **Evidence-Based Security** This refers to input to the security policy that describes the code. The input provides information about the site an assembly came from, the URL it slid in on, what particular zone it may have come from, and information gleaned from the assembly's strong name.

- **Isolated Storage**   Isolated storage is a special place set aside for data access when a .NET process precludes file or database access. This concept extends the sandbox model admirably by allocating a protected portion of hard-disk space to a specific assembly. Isolated storage is program driven—driven from your code.

- **Cryptography**   A variety of interfaces support the implementation of cryptographic services in the .NET Framework.

As a .NET developer, you need to consider security on a number of levels— determine how your code will run in the target environment, how it will resist attack, and how you can handle security exceptions that are raised when your code is blocked. You can do this in one of two ways: through *declarative* or *imperative* specifications.

Declarative specifications enable you to directly enumerate security requirements for an assembly in its metadata via attributes. You can then cater to the declarations in your code, which you accomplish through the attribute architecture we discussed earlier.

Imperative security is the practice of writing security support directly in your code. When a method calls a file object, you can set conditional steps to determine if the CLR will permit the call.

Unfortunately, developers with malicious intent may be reviewing the .NET security model to determine how to get their assemblies onto the .NET runtime. You can protect your assemblies from invasion through the techniques of *strong naming* or *digital signing*; I recommend you employ both if your assemblies will be in the public domain. A strong name is a unique name that is generated from the contents of an assembly, such as version numbers, simple names, digital signatures, or culture information. You should fully investigate both strong-naming techniques and digital signing of the assembly—which is achieved through public key encryption technology (PKI).

But even if you don't do anything special to your code after you have completed a project and released a version to the user, or deployed it to a Web site, the CLR remains the final authority. This means that there is a possibility that the CLR will reject your application's attempt to run because it has insufficient evidence that your code can be trusted.

During the development of the .NET Framework, code developed and deployed with the beta versions of Visual Studio and the framework was given a certain amount of leeway. ASP.NET and Web applications were fully trusted, specifically because the framework was not in its final version. However, just before final release Microsoft significantly tightened security and any code you deploy now must have sufficient security credentials before the CLR will allow it to run.

In the final release of the framework many classes in the various namespaces were decorated with stringent security attributes that might shut you out. The lock down was done to specifically protect customers moving their applications and services into production—to prevent attack from both private intranets and the Internet.

The new security attributes center around the code access security paradigm. In particular the CLR needs to know where the code comes from and various other factors before it allows it to run and possibly access system services like the registry, directories, and the file system. In fact ASP.NET and Web forms code is delegated to a controlled execution environment (a sandbox surrounded by barbed wire, minefields, and a crocodile infested moat) no matter where it comes from. Your apps, if allowed to run, are also delegated isolated storage units for their persistent storage needs.

This is a policy that is very different from the security policy that was in effect under the beta programs where Web apps had much more liberal access (policies demanded by Microsoft's customers). So don't be surprised when you discover that the neat stuff you were doing back at the lab gets blocked on your customer's Web site.

You can proceed to develop and test your applications, especially the code in this book, without concern for the code access security conditions. The chapters that follow focus on the core language, and further discussion of the security requirements for deployment of release builds, or what imperative constructs you need to introduce, is beyond the scope of this book. There is, however, a substantial amount of related material in the SDK and in the released version of Visual Studio that will point you, or your deployment team, in the right direction. A thorough understanding of why code needs to be properly trusted and verified is imperative for your good and that of your customers.

Observations

Why is such coverage of the .NET Framework's runtime environment so important in this book? Many programmers ask, "Why do I need to know about the CLR, assemblies, and metadata if I only want to write software? It seems like a waste of time."

In addition to questions such as these, I noticed in many news groups since June 2000 that very few questions were aimed at the CLR or runtime. When this book was first conceived I did not plan to cover the runtime environment.

Yet, over time it seemed that many programmers were wrestling with issues thought to be related to or caused by code, when, in fact, they were runtime related or solved through enlistment of runtime services and facilities. Many questions and problems thought to be related to code construction could have easily been solved with a basic understanding of what goes on in the runtime. Furthermore, subjects like debugging, deployment, security (so critical), and reflection all require you to have at least a basic understanding of how the CLR works.

While you certainly *can* write software without knowing any of the details mentioned in this chapter—and you may even be an excellent programmer—you will not necessarily be a highly productive .NET programmer. After all, you still have to get your classes and methods into your user's hands; for this you need to know how your software is going to be delivered and executed.

Therefore, it was decided to be highly worthwhile to cover the CLR and how it works. I hope this chapter provides you with the minimum foundation needed to be successful as a .NET Framework programmer. If you want to go further, you can access the many books that specialize in the subject, or get onto the beta program for the next version of the CLR. It will pay generous dividends.

The Complete Reference

Visual Basic .NET

Part II

Visual Basic .NET Fundamentals

The
Complete
Reference

Visual
Basic
.NET

Chapter 3

The Visual Basic .NET
Development
Environment

Y ou have three choices for quickly becoming *au fait* with the Integrated Development Environment (IDE) and the compiler. First option: You could go through all the dialog boxes to try to figure out what each option or setting does. (Some computer books might do that for you, but not this one. My focus is on showing you the code.) Second option: Get a book dedicated to the subject of Visual Studio .NET—and delay writing code until you know the IDE inside out. By the time you are done, you'll be ready to go into shrimp farming. Third option: start writing code.

The best option is the last one. You won't be an expert with Visual Studio (VS), even after some weeks, but you'll be productive from the get-go. I started working with Visual Studio after PDC 2000, when the release was so buggy it crashed the moment it opened. There was no documentation to help learn about its many aspects; but thankfully I had experience with Visual J++, the predecessor of this marvelous tool. Let's begin by helping you start a project or load up the example solutions that were developed for this book.

If you have not installed Visual Studio yet, do so now. It is straightforward and if you plan to set up in a team environment or on an application server you are accessing via terminal services, consult the Visual Studio installation instructions that shipped with the retail product packaging.

Once you've completed this, you'll notice that it has created program icons only for the MSDN Library of Visual Studio .NET and for Visual Studio .NET itself. What happened to all the options for Visual Basic, C#, or C++ that you chose during installation? All the languages are bundled into the same IDE. You will see how you can choose the language you need once you start up the IDE.

The primary objective in this chapter is to get you up and running with the demo solution as quickly as possible. To this end, we'll take a short tour of the IDE and Visual Studio .NET; then we'll examine the dialog boxes and options you'll need to know about. If you have not had any experience designing a Visual Basic .NET application, you will gain the necessary information to begin writing, compiling, and executing one by the end of this chapter.

Working with the Visual Studio IDE

Let's now start up the IDE and take that Visual Studio .NET tour. This will get you set up with projects you can apply to the sample code and with techniques for developing software and solving complex problems. To begin, start Visual Studio .NET. You will see the default layout of the IDE, which is illustrated in Figure 3-1 and represents the default settings. As usual, you can move and dock windows as you like.

Look first at the extensive environmental settings—ergonomic and workflow features—you can control from Visual Studio. To access these settings, go to Tools, Options and select the Environment folder. You can change the window layout from the default Tabbed Documents to MDI. This setting can be accessed from the General Section of the Environment folder.

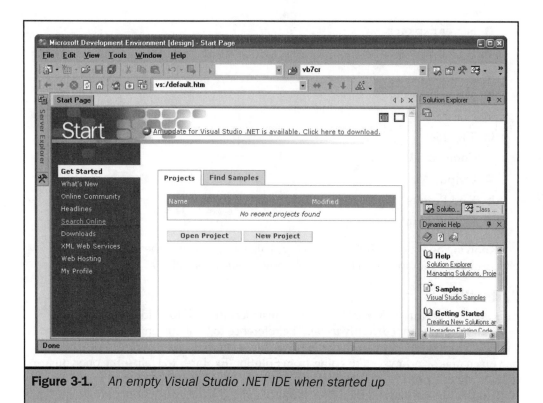

Figure 3-1.   *An empty Visual Studio .NET IDE when started up*

I suggest you only make the change to MDI if you are coming from an IDE that is MDI layout and the tabbed documents are making life hard for you. In general, the tabbed documents present a much more productive layout for this version of Visual Studio.

We'll return to the folder options in various chapters in this book. In the meantime, let's look at a minimal collection of elements provided by the IDE that you will be dealing with from the first line of code.

Navigating the IDE

Set a screen resolution of about 1024x768 to get as much IDE real estate as you can without reducing the icons and other elements beyond recognition. The following list provides the key IDE resources you should first learn about to help you develop in a manner and style that is comfortable for you.

- Auto Hide
- Dockable Windows
- Explorer Menu Bar

- Server Explorer
- Resource View
- Toolbox
- Macro Explorer
- Object Browser
- Task List
- Command Window
- Output Window
- Find Results
- Dynamic Help

Knowing about these IDE resources will also let you tackle the examples in this chapter before moving on to the more complex issues that follow.

Auto Hide

This is a new feature in Visual Studio that instructs the IDE to "hide away" the windows you are not currently *using*. The reference to "not currently *using*" suggests that the windows or panels are not in focus; however, they are not closed down. Thus, as you change windows—like going from Solution Explorer to Help—the one you are leaving slides closed.

This feature provides a lot more elbowroom for code construction and other tasks like debugging. When you need them, they're back in a jiffy. In my opinion, Auto Hide is one of the most sophisticated features you could want in an IDE, especially one that is the Swiss Army knife of development environments.

Auto Hide is not a permanent feature and if you want to keep a window exposed, simply toggle the feature off. To toggle Auto Hide on or off, simply click the pushpin (drawing pin) button next to the close button (x) of each window. As soon as the window hides away, its tab peeks out from the edge of the screen by about 20 pixels. Getting the window back requires only sliding your mouse pointer over the tab or right-clicking in the white space under the tabs and selecting the correct tab from the pop-up menu. Figure 3-2 shows the entire IDE with all non-essential windows hiding.

The standard toolbar also contains a collection of buttons that can "kiss" the hidden windows. If you can't find the correct tab hanging down in the viewable area, click the corresponding button on the toolbar to bring back the window. These buttons are stowed on the far right of the toolbar.

Dockable or Floating Windows

You can dock all windows in Visual Studio to any edge of the main IDE window. The Auto Hide toggle also serves to lock the window in place so you must first un-Auto Hide before you can move the window. Undocking a window is as simple as yanking the

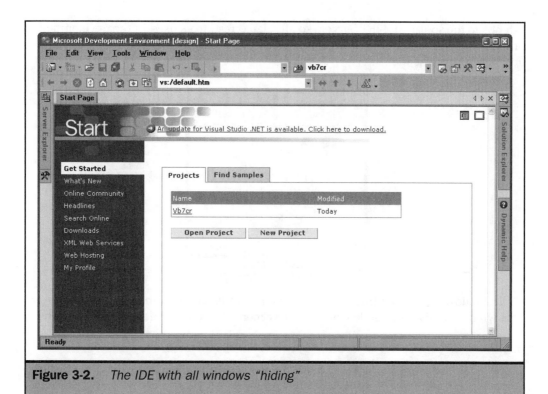

Figure 3-2.   *The IDE with all windows "hiding"*

window off the side of the IDE. You can also double-click the title bar to dock or undock a window once Auto Hide is off.

Internet Explorer Menu Bar

As you've probably noticed, the IDE provides a full-featured version of Internet Explorer (modestly named "Web Browser"). This browser is fully integrated with the main Internet facilities, so any folders created or favorites added will show up in the main Explorer browser.

Adding favorite URLs to the IDE, as you do with your main Internet Explorer (or whatever Web browser you prefer to use), is a prime feature. You will likely use this option a lot to store any help document, resource, or source file you need to access regularly. The help system for .NET is so vast that it's very easy to lose track of a page's location. We discuss the browser in detail in the "Start Page" section in this chapter.

Server Explorer

The Server Explorer window lets you access server-side resources, such as databases, email servers, event logs, and message queues. As you know, the entire .NET Framework extends to the so-called .NET Servers so all related resources used in the development process are accessible from within the IDE. The Server Explorer window is illustrated un-docked from the IDE.

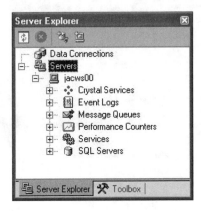

The following list identifies and explains the top-level nodes in the Server Explorer. This window is also accessible from the View menu and the standard toolbar buttons.

- **Crystal Services**   Installed Crystal Report options.

- **Event Logs**   Your standard Application, Security, and System Event Logs for the attached server. You will still need the necessary permissions, however, to access the logs.

- **Loaded Modules**   Lists the processes and loaded DLL's on the target server. Note that we can expose the properties of the processes running on the server by referencing the **System.Diagnostics.Process** namespace. See Chapter 17.

- **Management Data**   Enumerates the interfaces available through Windows Management Instrumentation (WMI) and gives you direct access to server management choices. For example, if you have the authorization, you can drill into Win32_Server, Logical Disk Manager, on down to your target server, where you make management selections.

- **Message Queues**   Provides the available message queues and their corresponding messages on the target server. Obviously you first need to install Message Queue. You get the same view of the message queues afforded by the Computer Management snap in.

- **Performance Counters**   Lists the Performance Counters for the target server. You will notice the massive amount of available performance counters— hundreds of new ones for .NET Server alone. The options to manage the built-in CLR on .NET Server are particularly useful.

- **Processes**   Lets you check the running processes on the target server.
- **Services**   Lets you check the running services on the target server.
- **SQL Server Databases**   Shows databases on the target SQL Server. This option is similar to the Data View window on the classic Visual Studio versions; it reminds me of Enterprise Manager. You don't need to have Enterprise Manager opened or installed in order to work with the databases. You can do everything directly from the IDE—such as add, edit, and delete tables, views, stored procedures, database diagrams, and functions.
- **Web Services**   Lists the Web Services according to the Project and File they were published with on the selected server.
- **Data Connections**   Lets you add connections to any database or server-provider that has an installed OLE DB provider. From here you can connect to servers such as Oracle, DB2, Exchange, and Active Directory.

Resource View

This window will be empty for a good reason. You can't open resources in the Resource View window for Visual Basic, C#, or any other managed development. To open resources in Visual Studio go to Solution Explorer and double-click the resource which appears in the drop-down list.

Toolbox

The Toolbox contains the components and controls that can be added to Windows Forms applications and Web Forms applications. The components of the Toolbox become available to you only when you have forms open, as illustrated. Chapter 16 covers the Toolbox, the standard controls available to you, and Windows Forms more extensively.

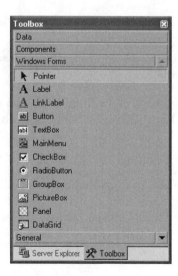

VB .NET FUNDAMENTALS

The Toolbox is divided into several sections as a tabbed layout that lets you navigate quickly and intelligently among the different types of objects or controls you may wish to add to your forms and classes.

The default Toolbox divisions are as follows:

- **Data**   Contains data controls such as **DataSet** and **DataView.**
- **Components**   Offers specialized components you can place on forms, such as timers, message queues, and processes.
- **Windows Forms**   Composed of visual (and some non-visual) controls used with Windows Forms, especially for building user interfaces.
- **Clipboard Ring**   Provides a scratch pad for copying frequently needed code snippets.
- **General**   To show all Toolbox tabs, right-click on General and select the Show All Tabs option. This will display non-default tabs. You will find many tabs, ranging from HTML options to Web controls. The full complement of tabs shows until you toggle the Show All Tabs options to its unchecked state.

To place a Toolbox item onto a form, simply drag the selected component to the location of the form where you want the control to reside. You can also double-click on a control to place it in or at the last focus position on the form. Once the control is on the form, use the mouse to drag/move it.

The Clipboard Ring is one of the most useful features of Visual Studio .NET. If you have code snippets that you use across many projects—even something as simple as a **Sub** method's base definition, which in its base form is five words—then the Clipboard Ring is the place to keep it. To add your code snippets to the Toolbox, perform the following two easy steps:

1. Select the code you wish to add to the ring, right-click on the selected region and click copy.
2. Right-click on the code snippet and select **Rename** to give the newly added code a meaningful name.

The Toolbox is also very customizable. Right-click on a tab and choose an option available to you. "Clipboard Ring" doesn't tell me much about the purpose of the tab so I renamed it "Scratch Pad."

Macro Explorer

Macros let you customize the IDE in ways that cater to your programming habits, style, and comfort. Macros and the Macro Editor are new to Visual Studio and give you more control over the IDE than the Tools/Options facility. The entire IDE is customizable through macros.

Macro Explorer, illustrated here, provides a few macros you can edit or use as a base. Unfortunately, an in-depth discussion of macros and the Microsoft Visual Studio Macros editing utility is beyond the scope of this book.

Object Browser

The Object Browser is one of the most important windows you will access during the lifetime of a development project. It lets you look at all the classes provided by the .NET Framework as well as any custom classes and types you are working on. It identifies the various namespaces and the assemblies within which they are packaged. Further, it reveals the classes and all their respective members, such as methods, properties, and fields.

The Object Browser is divided into three window panes: The left is called the Objects Pane and displays the hierarchical list of all objects available to your solution, including all custom classes, interfaces, structures, fundamental types, and namespaces. The right is called the Members Pane and shows you the class members, as well as enumerated items, variables, and constants. Both panes are illustrated in Figure 3-3.

The Description Pane, a third anchor pane in the Object Browser, provides details and further information about the selected class or members. It describes the various components and even displays the method signatures for you. Depending on the class, it may offer examples of the syntax you will use for certain members, including any dependencies, variables, and additional help description that may have been compiled with the object.

Note *Object Browser opens as a default tab; however, I recommend you convert it into a dockable window and activate Auto Hide, since you will rely on it constantly.*

A drop-down combo-box (Browse) at the top of the Object Browser lets you filter the classes and members pertaining to the objects in your project. You can also customize the browser with buttons that allow you to add additional components to the Object Browser's toolbar. We will return to this in more detail in Chapter 8 and in a number of other chapters.

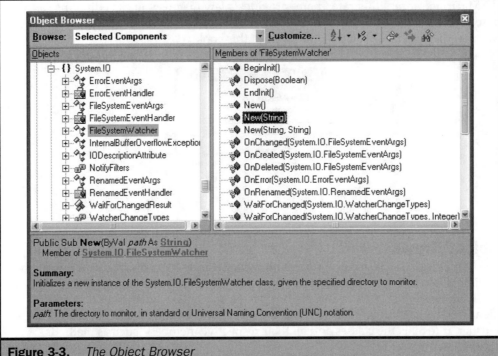

Figure 3-3.   *The Object Browser*

Task List

Once you become productive, the Task List will be another indispensable tool. This utility helps you manage tasks within the solution; but most importantly, it displays the compile-time errors and their causes. (See the illustration.)

The class units can contain several predefined tokens, which you can link to from the Task List. These include **TODO**, **UPGRADE_TODO**, and **UPGRADE_WARNING**. As you can see, these tokens have a lot to do with *trying* to migrate classic Visual Basic code.

You can access them by entering the name of your chosen token after the comment symbol (the single quote). The task is automatically added to the Task List. When you need to access the task again, just double-click the item and the appropriate section of code is brought up in the target unit, which moves to the front of all the tabbed documents. Connecting to the errors in your code works the same way. Simply double-click the Task List item and the IDE brings the error to the foreground.

To add your own tokens, a truly terrific feature, go to the Tool menu and select Options. You can then choose the Task List option from the Environment folder.

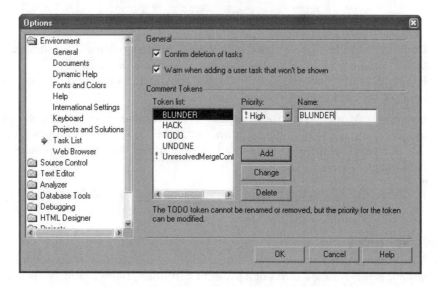

The default only shows build errors, but if you right-click on the Task List you will receive a Show Tasks option that can present the following views: All, Comment, Build Errors, User, Shortcut, Modeling, Policy, Current File, Checked, and Unchecked.

You might be tempted to choose "All," but if there are a lot of comments and errors in the code, the list tends to explode.

The Options dialog box can be accessed from the Tools, Options menu. It's worthwhile investigating the Options dialog box because we'll be returning to it in a number of future chapters.

Command Window

The Command Window is another imperative feature of the new Visual Studio .NET IDE. The Command Window has two views, **Command** and **Immediate**.

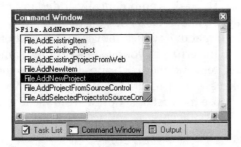

- **Command Mode**   Lets you execute Visual Studio Commands without using the IDE menu system. (The illustration shows execution of the **File.AddNewProject** command, which is the command behind the File menu item New, Project.)
- **Immediate Mode**   Used for debugging, expression evaluation, and variable modification. If you are familiar with Visual Studio 6, then you'll recognize that this window includes the same functionality as the VS 6 Immediate debugger window.

Both views in the Command Window support Intellisense and Autocomplete. Chapter 17 addresses the use of Immediate Mode for debugging.

Output Window

The Output Window displays build/compiler or diagnostic information depending on the mode it is in. During a build of a project or solution, the window is used to communicate build and compile information. In Debug mode, during processing, the Output Window displays libraries loaded, return codes, and various details being emitted from running code. For example, a special diagnostics **Debug** class—discussed later in this chapter and in depth in Chapter 17—lets you write debug information to the Output Window, shown here.

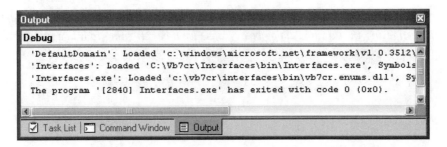

A third mode this window can switch to, Visio UML, kicks in as soon as you reverse-engineer classes to the UML for loading into Visio (Visio for Enterprise Architects). Selecting Visio UML, Reverse Engineer from the Project menu will achieve this.

Find Results

The Find Results windows (primary and secondary ones) display the results for "search and rescue" operations launched from the sophisticated Find and Replace dialog box. Find and Replace is accessed from the Edit, Find and Replace menu option. From here you can search for tokens, symbols, character strings with standard pattern-matching, regular expressions, and wildcards.

The results of your searches are displayed in the two Find Results dialog boxes and you can search in various places for your target—open documents, projects, and folders.

Dynamic Help and Search

Dynamic Help is one of the most useful features of this IDE (see Figure 3-1). Simply place your cursor on an element of your code (such as a class name or a method) and Dynamic Help finds and displays a link to the resource in the Visual Studio help system.

Another important feature is the help system's Search facility, which comes equipped with a Help Filter. It will save both time and resources, filtering your help material to just Visual Basic and related information.

Starting from the Start Page

When you first start Visual Studio .NET, the IDE loads up the Start Page, which is the built-in browser's "home page." This HTML page sports a menu of links on the left that provides several options you can choose to "surf to," such as updates and news from Microsoft. Figure 3-1 shows the IDE at its starting position, without any solutions to load. This is how the Start Page should look after a fresh installation.

You can toggle to the Start Page's beginning position from the icon to the right in the top right-hand corner of the IDE. The icon to the left tells the Web browser to load Web links, either within or outside of the browser.

It does not take long to lose the Web browser so remember that selecting Web Browser, Home from the View menu brings it back. The Help menu also returns you to the Start Page. The Web Browser option displays the Web Browser window in the main workspace. The default page that is displayed as your home page *is* the Start Page, the same one that appears when we fire up Visual Studio .NET.

The Start Page provides the following links, and you'll find it worthwhile to discover where they take you.

- Get Started
- What's New

- Online Community
- Headlines
- Search Online
- Downloads
- XML Web Services
- Web Hosting
- My Profile

Get Started

Any projects and solutions you have ready to roll will be listed in the center of the page, to the right of itemized links, under Get Started. Each solution contains the projects that comprise your applications, but we will see the solutions appearing later when we create these applications. If for some reason your most current application is not on the list, click on the Open Project or New Project links to go to the respective dialog boxes. We will see these boxes later when we access them in the traditional way, from the menu items.

What's New

What's New takes you to a list of links that connect to news and updates for the Microsoft .NET tools and technologies. Clicking a link in the center of the browser may connect to the MSDN files for this information, or to the internet for Web surfing if you are online. The other side of the What's New tab is illustrated in Figure 3-4.

The MSDN files are stored on your hard disks. You may alternatively have opted to access them from the CDs. The latter approach works better if you are diligent about replacing the CDs with every update of the MSDN disks and if you have a decent carousel to make it easy to change the CDs (or you can put in a single DVD version of the MSDN). What's New also looks for service packs and other late-breaking goodies from Microsoft.

 To reduce clutter, make your Start Page dockable, set Auto Hide on, and toss it out of the way. It will rush out when you need it.

Online Community

The link for the Online Community connects your IDE to the largest development community in the world. You can access the MSDN Web site, the sites for Microsoft's technology partners, and all the Microsoft newsgroups, .NET and classic.

Headlines

The Headlines tab connects you to the MSDN pages for Features, New, Technical Articles, and the MSDN knowledge base.

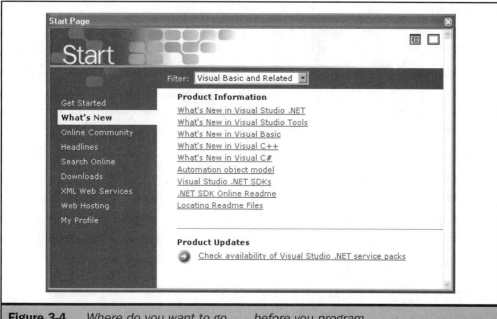

Figure 3-4.   *Where do you want to go . . . before you program*

Search Online

This page takes you to the MSDN search page, often the source of information updates since the disks were released to manufacturing. By integrating the MSDN home page directly into the IDE, you have all of the latest technical articles, news, and training information.

Downloads

This page connects to the MSDN options for code that you can download, sample applications, demos, and "how to" information.

XML Web Services

The XML Web Services page takes you to Microsoft's Universal Description Discovery and Integration (UDDI) facility for Web services. From this page you can learn about Web services, locate them, and register them with your applications.

Web Hosting

The Web Hosting page connects you to a number of commercial sites for standard and ASP.NET hosting facilities and for Web service hosting facilities.

My Profile

This tab provides for customizing the IDE in the way that best suits you, the individual programmer. The configuration options are Profile, which lets you choose the environment you write code in, such as Visual Basic or C#; Legacy Keyboard Schemes, relating to Version 6 of all the previous languages and compilers; the Window Layout; and the Help Filters. If you are a Visual Basic 6 developer, you may want to choose the Visual Basic Developer profile. And if you herald from Visual J++, the Visual Studio profile will be familiar. The following are the settings I have chosen for this book.

- Profile: (Custom)
- Keyboard Scheme: Visual Basic 6
- Window Layout: Visual Studio Default
- Help Filter: Visual Basic Documentation
- Show Help: Internal
- At Startup Show: Start Page

When you make changes, the settings are stored in the (custom) profile. You may find yourself wishing the tab could store more than one custom profile.

As you work with various documents, units, help files, and Web pages, you will begin to accumulate a collection of tabs in the main "viewing" area. You can right-click each tab to manage the underlying document or unit. You can also access the tabs from the View menu and the Window menu. Close them when finished, because too many open tabs clutter the IDE.

Now that our tour is over, we are ready to load some code.

Creating a Visual Basic .NET Solution

I have learned through experience that it is best to place a blank solution folder into a hierarchy of development folders on the local workstation or server. Using the "My Documents" folder setup is highly inconvenient when you need to search folders with the various .NET tools and the command-line compiler, which we will be working with in Chapter 17. Creating solutions and projects all over the place is chaotic and presents problems when you check your code into version control.

Creating a new solution is straightforward. Go to the File menu and select New, Blank Solution… from the menus. The dialog box illustrated in Figure 3-5 pops up and allows you to create a blank solution.

If you have just started Visual Studio for the first time, you've noticed the empty Solution Explorer on the right-hand side of the IDE. You manage your so-called development solution here. A solution is a container, a logical means of organizing your project's classes and resources; it is not part of any application nor is it

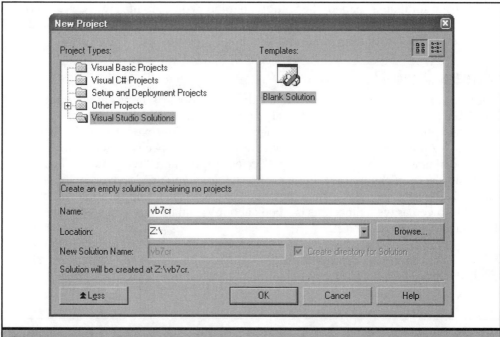

Figure 3-5.   *The dialog box for creating a blank solution*

understood by the compiler. You can add any projects or miscellaneous files you wish to collect within a solution space.

Another approach is to open an already existing solution; this is described in the next section.

Loading the Vb7cr Solution

To work with the examples in this book, load the demo solution called Vb7cr from www.osborne.com or from www.sdamag.com. You can follow along with this and try out the code examples in the later chapters. By the time you complete these chapters, you'll have seen a lot of code compiled and will gradually incorporate some of the more advanced features of the IDE, while learning "on-the-job."

As explained in the introduction, we opted not to publish a CD because there are so many paths to downloading the demo projects included with this book. Also, the file is rather small without the assemblies; you will produce them when you build the solution for the first time. You don't need to create a folder for the demo code. Simply unzip it into the root folder or drive of your choice. You can then open the solution into Visual Studio from the File, Open, Project menu items. Browse for the file where you unzipped everything (the root of Vb7cr) and click Open.

Once the solution is loaded, the Solution Explorer comes to life and you can access and open existing projects or create new ones. You can also review its configuration by right-clicking on the solution name and selecting Properties. (See Figure 3-6.)

Creating a New Project

When you are ready to add a project to the demo solution, right-click on it in the Solution Explorer and select Add, New Project. (You can perform the same step from the menu option that hangs off the File menu, but this is less expedient.) The dialog box in Figure 3-7 pops up and lets you name your project and specify its location.

The dialog is divided into two parts, "Project Types" and "Templates." The Project Types side lets you choose the language or technology you need to work with. If you installed C# with Visual Basic, then the option of creating a C# application will be available to you as well. Since this is a book about Visual Basic, we suggest you develop a Visual Basic project.

You can create a new project in another solution if you access the Add New Project dialog box from the File menu.

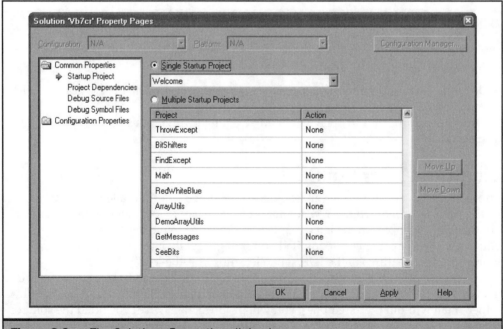

Figure 3-6.   *The Solutions Properties dialog box*

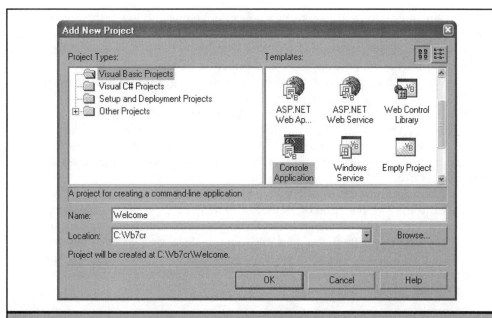

Figure 3-7.   *Creating a new project container in an existing Solution Container*

The Visual Basic projects you can create are as follows:

- **Windows Application**   Windows standard thick client applications based on forms (EXE)
- **Class Library**   For individual classes or collections of classes (DLL)
- **Windows Control Library**   Controls and components for Windows Forms (classic)
- **ASP.NET Web Application**   ASP.NET-based application composed of static or dynamic HTML pages
- **ASP.NET Web Service**   For Web services to be used by clients communicating over the HTTP protocol
- **Web Control Library**   Web-based controls for ASP.NET applications
- **Console Application**   Your standard Console application
- **Windows Service**   Create Windows services
- **Empty Project**   Empty Windows application project
- **Empty Web Project**   Empty Web server-based application

Choose the option to create a console application; name and locate the project in the Vb7cr solution folder. Install the project folder under the solution's root directory. In other words, the folder's namespace will be something like e:\Devshares\Vb7cr\ Welcome, and the name of the application should also be Welcome.

As soon as you have created the project, you can configure it via the Properties dialog box (don't confuse this dialog box with the Properties Editor discussed earlier). This box lets you specify the configuration for the project as a whole, which includes its strong name, namespace name, assembly name, build options, and options settings. The Configuration section in this dialog box includes the pages that let you specify debug and build options, optimization settings and deployment, and the class it represents at startup.

The Solution Explorer usually sits above the Properties Editor/Explorer. The Properties Editor is a vital section of the IDE: it manages the properties for everything that has to do with your solutions or project's resources. If your kitchen sink's software has a part in your project, then you'll be able to navigate its properties in this window. You can move the window wherever you want. Experience and testing have shown that it should live under the Solution Explorer, which is its default home and the standard Visual Studio .NET layout.

The Properties Editor confirms the location of your project files under our configured solution as shown on the next page.

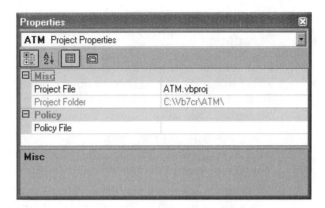

As I recommended in the introduction, stay clear of GUI elements and forms-based projects until you have completed up to Chapter 16 of this book. User-interface applications will only clutter the learning process. We'll look at forms briefly in Chapter 9, when we study inheritance, but everything else about forms is discussed in Chapter 16.

Until very recently classic VB revolved around the form, thanks to the less-than-pure OO technology it employed. I am not disparaging user interface programmers; some Visual Basic 6 UI designers and developers are among the best engineers in the industry. Yet for many VBers, it's time to shake the "form-painting" mentality and get down to programming classes, because most importantly, Visual Basic is a first-class OO language.

You can learn everything there is to know about .NET programming from a simple class. It is imperative to think in terms of objects and classes, not just forms. The J# and C# programmers are going to laugh at you every time you load a button and a form just to "see" what a few lines of code are going to do. By all means, when you are ready to build a user interface, reach for the forms and Chapter 16 and have a field day.

By the time you get to Chapter 17, you will have learned to observe what goes on under the hood with watch windows, the output window, breakpoints, and the disassembler utility. Each new chapter we tackle in this book will introduce you to more elements as it gets you progressively involved with the IDE tools and features.

Solution Directory Structure

Wherever you choose to place your projects, the solution creates a special collection of folders for the various files that make up the application. Table 3-1 lists the most important files and folders and describes their functions.

File Extensions

You should be aware of various file extensions for Visual Basic .NET applications. For starters, there are no more form (FRM) files that represented VB 6 forms. Now that forms in .NET are class files, the unit containing your form source is given the .vb

File/Directory	Description
Vb7cr.**sln**	Your solution file, which contains details about the individual projects and their locations in the solution. The file is text and can be manually edited so you can point to new project file paths.
Vb7cr.**vbproj**	Visual Basic project file. Contains information about all of the files connected with a specific project within a solution. Not recommended to open manually with Notepad.
Vb7cr.**suo**	The solution user-options file, which stores all your custom settings. It is hidden in the root folder of your solution. Make sure you back it up because the solution reads from this file whenever you open it. VS writes to the file as you make changes.
*.**vb**	This is the extension of source-code units. The files hold source code for classes, forms, and components. The data in a file is in plain text and can be edited with any text editor.
*.**resx**	Your assembly resource files (see Chapter 17) used for the definition of application resources.
Bin directory	The folder that builds are loaded from. During debug, builds VS will load files from this folder and pull files over from the **Obj** folder as well. Written to during builds.
Obj directory	Used for the output of specific configurations and builds. Written to during builds which store information is a special Program Debug Database (*.PDB).

Table 3-1.   *The Solution Folder Hierarchy for Each Project the Solution Contains*

extension. Also, most files prefixed or suffixed with an "x" harbor XML-compliant code. Table 3-2 describes each file extension.

Working with the Base-Class Library

The .NET Framework provides a huge number of reference types, static or shared classes, interfaces, and value types—built-in fundamental data types, such as ordinal, point, and character types—that allow you to build functionality and develop solid applications and services. The framework comprises so many elements that complete coverage of all its classes, members, and sample code would require many volumes.

File Extension	Description
XML	An XML Document
XSD	An XML Schema File without generated classes
TDL	Your Template Description Language File
VB	Standard source files for Windows forms, controls, classes, and miscellaneous code
RPT	Your Crystal Reports Designer files
HTML	Your HTML Source Files
XSLT	The XML files containing transformation instructions for XML and XSD documents
CSS	The Cascading Style Sheets used for HTML pages to apply styles
VBS	VB Script source files
WSF	Windows Scripting source file
JS	JScript .NET source file
ASPX	Web Application form
ASP	Active Server Page source file
ASMX	Web Service source file
DISCO	The Dynamic Discovery document source file that enumerates Web services and schema in a Web services project
WEB	The ASP.NET Configuration file
ASAX	ASP.NET Configuration File that handles Session_OnStart, Session_OnEnd, Application_OnStart, and Application_OnEnd script. This file is similar to Global.ASA files used for the legacy ASP applications that we loaded into Visual Interdev 6.0.

Table 3-2.   *Common File Extensions Used with the Visual Basic Projects*

The section will thus be devoted to a brief description of how to access the class libraries and assemblies they are packaged in, how to target individual classes in each respective namespace, and how to target methods and other elements in the structures. Not knowing how to find namespaces and objects in Visual Studio .NET affects many newcomers. To facilitate interoperability, the .NET classes and types are 99.9 percent CLS compliant. As mentioned in Chapter 2, some classes support non-CLS compliant features for very special purposes, and some of your objectives might only be achieved using another language, such as C#. Thus, we will occasionally employ C# code as a language secondary to Visual Basic .NET.

The .NET Framework classes provide an extensive array of functionality related to I/O, threading, networking, security, data access, forms, Web services, and much more. You can use the classes and data types to build sophisticated applications, services, components, or controls that can simply be plugged into any .NET-compliant environment. Later chapters delve into advanced usage of the class libraries for components and other elements.

You can either derive from the .NET classes and extend functionality where permitted, or you can implement an interface defined in the base class library directly in your class. The .NET Framework types are named using dot notation that defines an interface you can send messages to. The interface comprises the identifier of the static class or object and a method or property identifier—both are discerned in the interface with dot notation. This is illustrated with the following code, in which a message is sent to the **Debug** class.

```
Public Sub WriteSomething()
  Debug.WriteLine("something")
End Sub
```

Note *The **Debug** class is used extensively as a debugging tool, which is why I have introduced it so early. Also, the class and method emphasized in bold are shown encapsulated in a method. All calls or messages and other method operations must be declared within the context of a method, not outside the method declaration. Chapter 17 covers the Debug class in some depth.*

Referencing the object by its identifier is simple, but locating the class in question is another matter. As you learned, all the .NET types are referenced via the namespaces to which they belong. The **Debug** class belongs to the collection of diagnostic classes buried somewhere with the thousands of classes in the library. If Visual Studio complains that it cannot find the **Debug** class, as shown in the illustration, then you are either not referencing the correct namespace or not referencing the namespace correctly.

```
Sub DoSomething()
    Debug.WriteLine("something")
End Sub 'Debug' is not declared. Debug object functionality is available in 'System.Diagn
```

Let's first assume you are not referencing the namespace at all. You read about the **Debug** class but do not know where it is. How do you find it? Answer: Bring on the OB, the Object Browser.

Use the Find facility to look for the object in the OB. Click the Find Symbol icon (the binoculars button) on the OB toolbar, as demonstrated earlier in this chapter, and search for the symbol. The Find Symbol Results dialog box lists the hits, as demonstrated in this illustration.

Double-click on the line that represents the found symbol and the OB will pop up with the class you requested. Crawl up the namespace in the OB until you expose its entire range. Try referencing the object by declaring the entire namespace as follows:

```
Public Sub WriteSomething()
   System.Debug.WriteLine("something")
End Sub
```

You might still be told that **Debug** is not a member of **System**. The reason is simple: Visual Studio cannot find the assembly that packages the system namespace. Could it be that you are not referencing the assembly, the assembly is missing or not installed on the system, or there is something else wrong with it? Most likely, System—the assembly—is not referenced in your project.

As the message in the preceding illustration indicates, the **Debug** object "is not declared," and the object is located in the **System.Diagnostics.Debug** namespace. This also tells you that the namespace is packaged in the **System** assembly. If you are unsure of the assembly name, you can follow the namespace in the OB all the way up the hierarchy until you locate it. In this case, the *assembly* is called System—don't confuse it with the **System** namespace.

Expand the References folder in your project to check if System is in there; if not, you need to add it (even though you may see it in the OB). To add an assembly reference, right-click on the project name or References folder in Solution Explorer and select the Add Reference option—its dialog box will now load. (See Figure 3-8.)

The first tab lists all the assemblies provided in the Global Assembly Cache, including all of those within the framework libraries. Search for System.DLL in the list and double-click this file, which will be placed in the Selected Components. If it appears in this list, click OK. The System.DLL assembly will now be present in the References section of your project in Solution Explorer, and the error message in your code will vanish.

The good news is this: whenever you create a new project, Visual Studio automatically adds the System, System.Data, and System.XML assemblies to the

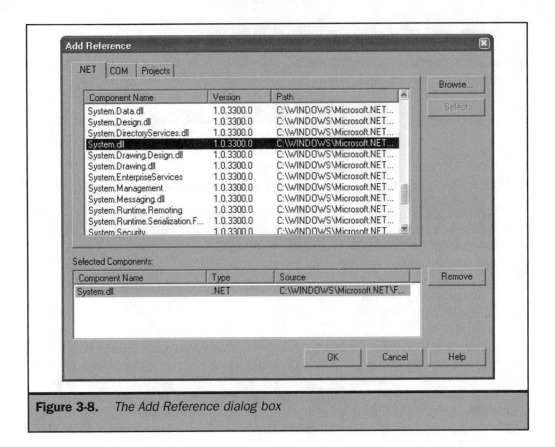

Figure 3-8. *The Add Reference dialog box*

References section because they contain the base classes you'll need for a minimal application. (These are not bolded here because they are assemblies [DLL files], not classes or namespaces.)

This is important to note since it's not always the case. All custom assemblies and many others that ship with the .NET Framework must first be accessed in this way before you can reference the namespaces and types in your code. Only after your project sees the DLL file containing the namespaces will you be able to reference the namespaces and the object you seek. Don't confuse the process of referencing the assembly with that of denoting the namespace, as show in the next section.

Looking at your code, you are probably wondering how Visual Studio knows where and what namespaces to select since it's the assemblies that are referenced. It's easy to find out. Right-click on your project and select the Properties options. The Properties dialog box loads. Drill into the Common Properties, Imports folder as illustrated.

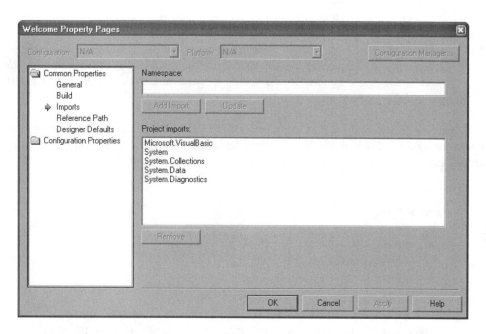

You can also select Properties from the Project menu. Go to the Imports sections and add your references there. Word of warning—this box does not check the correctness of your reference so make sure to type the correct class identifiers names and the correct notation.

  You also did not need to reference the MSCORLIB assembly, which hosts the console classes, because the compiler always does this for you.

A Minimal Visual Basic .NET Application

The actual namespace-naming notation is not unlike the notation used by Java, by the Internet Domain Name System, or by the Active Directory namespace. For example, the **System.Data.ADO** namespace refers to the hierarchy of classes that represent the functionality of the ActiveX Data Object technology. You would need to reference **System.Data.ADO** in order to directly access the ADO class, which is the last name in the namespace "chain" of classes. If you were to cite only **System.Data,** you would reference not only ADO but all other classes on the **System.Data** namespace as well. If you do not need any other data class in your application, you would be wasting a lot of resources.

The dot notation syntax has no effect on the visibility and access characteristics of classes and their members. It also has no influence on inheritance or binding or the interfaces available. In fact, the namespaces can also be partitioned across assemblies and a single assembly may contain multiple class namespaces as demonstrated throughout this book and the .NET Framework.

If you have already been playing around with Visual Studio .NET, then save your experiments, close down the IDE, and open Notepad. Using the IDE would be a little cumbersome here as we create the following seven-line application:

1. In Notepad, type the following code:

```
Module Welcome
   Sub Main()
     Console.WriteLine("Welcome")
     Console.ReadLine()
   End Sub
End Module
```

2. Save the file in the project folder—in the C:\Vb7cr\Welcome folder or anywhere on your computer. You can save the file as welcome.txt or as welcome.vb. (The **.vb** extension is recognized by the IDE as the official Visual Basic .NET extension for class files, so it's better to use this extension.)

3. Now find the Visual Basic .NET command-line compiler. If you installed the SDK and the Visual Basic .NET support in Visual Studio, then the compiler will be on your computer. It goes by the name of VBC.EXE and resides in your C:\Windows\Microsoft.NET\Framework\v1.0.3512 folder or in a similar one.

A list of compiler directives is provided in Chapter 17.

4. Compile the file from the command line as follows, substituting C for your drive letter and ensuring that VBC is on your execution path:

```
VBC C:\Vb7cr\Welcome\welcome.vb
```

5. The executable is compiled and the compiler puts the little application into the folder you used to execute VBC. You can now run it by double-clicking the file from Windows Explorer or running it from the command line. The console window illustrated here loads. It displays the message "Welcome" and then waits for some user input. Hit return to close the console application.

That's all there is to writing and creating a Visual Basic .NET executable (it takes all of five minutes). So what's so incredibly special about this code? Let's look at it again—notice the comments this time:

```
'This little app demonstrates
'referencing the System namespace
Module Welcome
  Sub Main()
    System.Console.WriteLine("Welcome")
    System.Console.ReadLine()
  End Sub
End Module
```

Note   *The use of a single quote mark denotes a comment in a Visual Basic .NET class file. The compiler ignores the entire line after the quote. While the comments here may not seem worth the screen space, it is good programming practice to comment on every application like this. See Chapter 4, Elements of Visual Basic .NET.*

The above code is identical to the earlier code, as well as the **Debug** example. We have bolded only the two lines of code that tell the runtime in which namespace (**System**) and which class (**Console**) to find the functionality that will let you create the console window, display a line of text, and wait for user input. This brings us to one of the most important concepts in the .NET Framework: class functionality is accessed by referencing the fully qualified class name on a partitioned dot notation (name.partition-n). In the above code, the **WriteLine** and **ReadLine** methods for the **Console** class are resolved on the **System.Console** namespace. You can think of this namespace as an address where you send messages to objects and access functionality.

> *QualifiedIdentifier ::=*
> *Identifier |*
> *QualifiedIdentifier . IdentifierOrKeyword*

Referencing the classes and namespaces in this way is very tedious for anything bigger than a seven-line application. So the alternative syntax you will use lets you specify the namespace at the top of every class file. This reference then exposes the namespace and the classes to the entire class; it is made possible with the **Imports** keyword. Here is an example:

```
'This little app demonstrates using
'the Imports keyword
```

```
Imports System
Module Welcome
  Sub Main()
    Console.WriteLine("Welcome")
    Console.ReadLine()
  End Sub
End Module
```

Note that you no longer need the namespace's root name to be tagged onto the **Console** class. For all intents and purposes, all .NET applications start out like this. In the above case, we have written a little code to access the "canned" functionality in a class belonging to the base-class library (BCL).

Note   *The fully qualified namespace is also an address for an object, as discussed in Chapters 8 and 9. If you are new to Visual Basic and unfamiliar with the peculiarities of the language, do not worry. We will not be covering any complex code in this chapter—but the code will be back in full force in Chapter 4.*

Observations

You now see that it's not difficult to start developing applications with Visual Basic .NET, although there is a myriad of options and elements to consider, even from the outset. Visual Studio is an extremely flexible environment, however, so do not hesitate to experiment and make changes. You can always restore things to their default settings or reinstall the demo code, especially if you back up your .suo file. This chapter also highlighted the importance of understanding how to correctly reference assemblies and namespaces. Visual Studio offers you a full-blown Integrated Development Environment, as well as the ability to compile code from the command line.

By now you should have sufficient grounding for the task ahead—designing and creating Visual Basic .NET applications. Our next objective is to learn the elements of our chosen .NET development language as quickly as possible. This task begins in Chapter 4.

The
Complete
Reference

Visual
Basic
.NET

Chapter 4

The Elements of Visual Basic .NET

This chapter introduces you to the lexical elements, grammar, building blocks, concepts, and foundation code that will start you on the road to writing software with Visual Basic .NET. If you are new to Visual Basic, set aside some time to fully review the elements.

Visual Basic syntax is rich, extensive, and very different from most other languages (with the exception of classic Visual Basic and the original BASIC language itself—the latter now a very distant ancestor). Visual Basic .NET is a radical departure from its predecessors, so even if you are a VB guru, you need to review the information in this chapter to be up to speed with Visual Basic .NET. You will get a view of the language, its idioms, its syntactical and lexical layout, its integration with the .NET Framework, and more. You will delve into the philosophy, metaphors, and concepts in Visual Basic programming. The concepts introduced in this chapter are fully treated in later chapters.

You will use Visual Studio .NET in this chapter, too. By now, you should have installed the IDE and the .NET Framework SDK on your development computer. If not, please do so as soon as possible. (At least install the SDK.) In following chapters, we are going to move rapidly from introductory material to "aggressive" code—application-ready examples for which you will need the CLR, the compiler, and the IDE.

Visual Basic .NET: The Foundation

This section is an abridged reference to the lexical and idiomatic elements of Visual Basic .NET. The foundation elements are discussed, along with related concepts. Some elements are discussed in depth in later sections in this chapter; others are discussed in the chapters that specialize in the concepts and how the idiomatic elements cater to them.

Lexical Elements

The lexical elements—the so-called "grammar" of the language—refer to the structure that makes up the layout of the source code within a Visual Basic unit. The layout is aided by the representation of characters, lines, line terminators, white space, comments, operators, and so on. Table 4-1 lists these elements and refers to where in the book they are principally discussed.

The lexical makeup of a language is represented by the many keywords it has. These include keywords like **Dim**, **ReDim**, **As**, **GetType**, **Nothing**, and others. Some of the

Lexical Elements	Principally Discussed in:
Characters and lines	Chapter 4
Line terminators	Chapter 4
Line continuation	Chapter 4
White space	Chapter 4
Comments	Chapter 4
Type characters	Chapter 4
Literal	Chapter 4
Nothing	Chapter 4
Separators	Chapter 4
Operator symbol	Chapter 5
Identifiers	Chapters 4, 8-10
Keywords	All chapters

Table 4-1.   *Lexical Elements and Grammar*

first keywords you will use are introduced in this chapter. Some of the more advanced keywords, such as **AddressOf**, will be covered in the chapters that deal with elements that use them the most, such as Chapter 14, which deals with **Delegates**, and Chapter 16, which introduces threading.

Preprocessing Directives

The preprocessing directives are the commands and keywords you use to specify how the compiler should compile your code. These directives are placed in the code and instruct the compiler to compile different regions or versions of the code depending on conditions you specify. Table 4-2 lists the preprocessing directives and the principal locations where they are discussed.

Preprocessing Directives	Principally Discussed in:
Conditional compilation directives	Chapter 17
Conditional constants	Chapter 17
Conditional compilation statements	Chapter 17
External source directives	Chapter 17
Region directives	Chapter 17

Table 4-2. *Preprocessing Directives*

General Concepts

The general concepts, which deal with accessibility and visibility, referencing (name spaces and type names), and so on, are covered in several chapters. Table 4-3 lists the principal locations where general concepts are introduced or covered in detail.
Namespaces and type names are generally covered in all chapters.

Option, Imports, and Namespaces Directives

The **Option** directives (**Option Compare, Option Strict**, and **Option Explicit**) govern the semantic and type-safety strictness applied during code construction. The **Imports** directives reference the source namespaces for referencing external classes used in code construction. Both are introduced in this chapter and then referenced throughout the book.

General Concepts	Principally Discussed in:
Accessibility (access modifiers)	Chapters 4, 7-10
Namespace and type names	Chapters 4, 8-10
Attribute constructs	All chapters

Table 4-3. *General Concepts*

Option, Imports, and Namespace Directives	Principally Discussed in:
Option Compare, **Option Strict**, and **Option Explicit**	Chapter 4
Imports, import aliases, regular imports	Chapter 4
Namespace declaration, namespace members	Chapters 4, 9

Table 4-4.   *Option, Imports, and Namespace Directives*

The namespace declaration space in the Visual Basic unit is used to scope the current class or classes, in the .vb unit, to a namespace.

Types

This section discusses the types that make up all .NET applications. The fundamental (or so-called *primitive*) types are principally introduced in this chapter (see Table 4-5) and are used and further discussed in all chapters in this book.

Types	Principally Discussed in:
Built-in Value types	Chapters 4, 8
Arrays and Collections	Chapter 12
Standard classes and modifiers	Chapter 9
Standard modules and modifiers	Chapter 9
Interfaces	Chapter 10
Enumerations and their members	Chapter 8
Custom Structures (value types)	Chapter 8
Delegates	Chapter 14

Table 4-5.   *Types of .NET Applications*

The declaration syntax for any type not discussed in this chapter is presented in the chapter in which the type is principally discussed.

Type Members

The type members represent the "action" or functionality in a Visual Basic class file. Chapter 7, for example, is devoted to the subject of methods, which comprise constructors, accessor methods, modification or regular methods, and properties. The present chapter covers variable and constant declaration, scope, lifetime, and so on. Table 4-6 tells you where to look for discussion of type members.

Statements and Statement Blocks

The Visual Basic .NET language contains a number of statement constructs used in the construction of code, many of which have been inherited from the earlier versions of VB, such as **With** statement blocks.

The statement block is a statement that encapsulates code within the class itself, to a local scope, such as **If**…**Then**…**Else** constructs and so on. Table 4-7 leads you to various discussions of statement and statement blocks.

Type Members	Principally Discussed in:
Constants	Chapter 4
Variables	Chapter 4
Methods	Chapter 7
External methods	Chapter 7
Constructors	Chapters 7, 8, 9
Properties	Chapters 7, 9
Interface method implementation	Chapter 10
Events and event handling	Chapter 14
Inner or composite types	Chapters 9, 13, 14

Table 4-6.   *Type Members*

Statements and Statement Blocks	Principally Discussed in:
Standard block	Chapter 4
Local declaration statements	Chapter 4
With statement blocks	Chapter 4
SyncLock statement blocks	Chapter 7, 16
Event statements and event handler statements	Chapter 14
RaiseEvent statements	Chapter 14
Interface method implementation	Chaptesr 10, 12, 13, 14
Assignment statements	Chapter 4
Compound assignment	Chapters 4, 5
Invocation statements	Chapter 7
Conditional statement blocks	Chapter 6
Loop and iteration statement blocks	Chapter 6
Control-flow statements	Chapter 6
Structured exception handling (SEH) statement blocks	Chapter 11
Unstructured exception handling statement blocks	Chapter 11
Array handling statements	Chapter 12

Table 4-7.   *Statements and Statement Blocks*

Expressions

Expressions are sequences of operators and operands that specify a computation and return a value. Table 4-8 directs you toward information on expressions.

Typically, an expression always evaluates to a value at run time, but the compiler may warn you that an expression you are trying to write does not constitute a

Expressions	Principally Discussed in:
Constant expressions	Chapter 4
Variable expressions	Chapter 4
Simple expressions	Chapter 4 and throughout
Literal expressions	Chapter 4
Parenthesized expressions	Chapter 4
New expressions	Chapters 4, 9
Cast and convert expressions	Chapter 4
Me expressions	Chapter 4
GetType expressions	Chapter 9
Is expressions	Chapters 4, 9
Invocation expressions	Chapter 7
Argument and parameter expressions	Chapter 7
Delegate expressions	Chapter 14
Event expressions	Chapter 14
Dictionary expressions	Chapters 12
Index expressions	Chapters 12

Table 4-8.   *Expressions*

legitimate expression. For example, the following code does produce a valuable expression:

```
Dim iAm As Boolean = True
Dim jDoo As Integer
Public Shadows Sub ShadowMethod(ByVal argS As String)
  Convert.ToInt32(iAm) = jDoo 'no good, cannot assign right to left
  jDoo = Convert.ToInt32(iAm) 'better
End Sub
```

Operators

Operators are covered everywhere (see Table 4-9), even in this chapter, but each operator is fully defined, and presented with examples of recommended usage and application, in Chapter 5.

Visual Basic .NET Mini Style Guide

Visual Basic .NET is a modern, pure object-oriented programming language. How you use it is up to you. You also have discretion in how you design, document, write pseudocode, collate specifications, and construct code. This book doesn't cover what constitute good programming practices in any depth, because this topic applies to all programming languages. Many good books have been written on the practice of software design and construction, and I will recommend several of the best ones as we progress through this book.

However, the .NET Framework architects have suggested some guidelines with respect to style and usage. Some are discussed here, while many others are discussed in the chapters in which the guidelines address the principal subject matter. You don't

Operators	Principally Discussed in:
Unary operators	Chapter 5
Logical operators	Chapter 5
Arithmetic operators	Chapter 5
Mod operator	Chapter 5
Exponentiation operators	Chapter 5
Relational operators	Chapter 5
Logical operators	Chapter 5
Is operator	Chapters 8, 9
Like operator	Chapters 7, 8, 9
TypeOf, TypeOf . . . Is operators	Chapters 7, 8, 9

Table 4-9. *Operators*

have to follow these guidelines, but they are intended to make your code easier to read and to promote consistency within the entire .NET programming community.

Naming and Notation

Maintain a consistent naming pattern across all of your classes. If you are managing a team, make sure the entire team adheres to a consistent naming pattern. The guidelines for naming are also provided to assist with language interoperability. It's especially important for you to maintain uniformity, especially if you plan to contribute classes or components and controls to the .NET community, whether for profit or to stroke your ego.

Capitalization

The .NET languages have adopted a particular capitalization style that sets them apart from, for example, Smalltalk or C++. The two main styles are *PascalCase* and *camelCase*. The Pascal casing convention capitalizes the first character of each word, even if the two words are conjoined. The following is an example of Pascal casing usage:

```
Public Class PascalClass
```

The camel casing convention capitalizes each new word, *except* for the first word of the identifier. Camel case usage is as follows:

```
Dim camelCase As New String
```

However, if an identifier is no more than two characters, such as an abbreviation, then use uppercase for both characters. Here are some examples:

```
Public Class UI
Namespace Vb7cr.CD
Imports System.IO
```

Table 4-10 lists the capitalization rules for the different identifiers.

Hungarian Notation

The .NET gurus at Microsoft would prefer that you not use Hungarian notation. This advice has some merit, considering that .NET comprises more than 20 languages—and the list is growing.

In order for Hungarian notation to succeed in the .NET Framework, it would need to be consistently used across the entire spectrum of CLS-compliant languages. That's unlikely to be the case; many of the languages that have adopted .NET specifically steer away from Hungarian notation (especially the Java-like languages, such as JScript, C#,

Identifier	Capitalization Rules	Example
Classes	PascalCase	**Class MyClass**
Enumerator values	PascalCase	**BackColors**
Enumerator types	PascalCase	**ColBlack**
Exception classes	PascalCase and should end with "Exception"	**MyKindOfException**
Final and read-only static fields	PascalCase	**MyValue**
Interfaces	PascalCase (prefix with I)	**ITreeIterator**
Methods	PascalCase	**GetSound**
Namespaces	PascalCase	**Vb7cr.ArrayUtils**
Properties	PascalCase	**Color.Black**
Public instance fields	PascalCase	**BaseAmount**
Protected instance fields	camelCase	**WarpSpeed**
Parameters	camelCase	**WarpValue**

Table 4-10.   *Capitalization Rules*

and J#). The notation is widely used with C++ programmers, however, especially Windows programmers.

If you are not familiar with the notation, it comprises three parts: type name, prefixes, and qualifiers. The prefix, for example, denotes the type of variable. An array is prefixed with *a*; thus, wherever a variable prefixed with an *a* is used, it is implied that the variable refers to an array. The following are examples:

```
Dim aAlarms(5) As Integer
'...
aAlarms(5) = 0
```

or

```
Dim a_alarms(5) As Integer
'...
a_alarms(5) = 0
```

The suffix *e* is used for element, *h* for handle, *i* for index, and so on. But why not just use the following equivalent; after all, the subscript notation (5) makes it clear enough that you are looking at a variable:

```
Dim alarms(5) As Integer
'...
alarms(5) = 0
```

The other problem with Hungarian notation is that it encourages uninformative variable identifiers (among lazy programmers) and thus makes code hard to read and work with. Here is an example:

```
Dim myhwnd As New hwnd
```

So what does this refer to: a window handle, a hot window, a wand, heavy wind? Who knows? Better to use the following notation:

```
Dim hWindow As New Window
Dim myWandHandle As New WandHandle
```

If you decide to use Hungarian notation, stick to consistent prefixes and qualifiers if your team possesses sufficient discipline to enforce consistent and uniform adoption. However, remember that names should describe the semantics, not the type.

Word Choice

There are no restrictions on word choice, but you cannot use words that are reserved as keywords in the languages. There is no need to present a table of all the keywords, because you will very quickly learn which ones they are, and the compiler will politely tell you to shove off when you choose a word it is already using, such as **Byte**, **Integer**, or **Event**.

If you must use a keyword, enclose it in the escape characters—the square brackets—to avoid a compiler error. Here's an example:

```
Dim [False] As Boolean = False
```

However, this practice is definitely not recommended because it makes code hard to read. More on this subject appears later in the chapter.

Spell out all words used in a field name and don't be too shy to use long names. Use abbreviations only if developers generally understand them, like "url," or "dir." You can make a field name all lowercase (as opposed to camelCase), especially if the names are short. My rule is lowercase for the entire word if it is five characters or less. I cap the letters in long names first at the syllabic breaks and second at the logical breaks (camelCase or PascalCase). The following is an example of correctly named fields:

```
Class SampleClass
   Private url As String
   Private destinationUrl As String
End Class
```

Getting Started

When the compiler parses the code you have written, it first translates the raw stream of Unicode characters into a series of logical lines. The compiler recognizes the logical line according to an ordered set of lexical tokens. The logical line in a class unit spans from either the start of the stream or a line terminator through to the next line terminator that is not preceded by a line continuation or through to the end of the stream. This syntax demonstrates what the compiler "considers" a logical line:

Start ::= [*LogicalLine+*]

LogicalLine ::= [*LogicalLineElement+*] [*Comment*] *LineTerminator*

LogicalLineElement ::= *WhiteSpace* | *Token*

Token ::= *Identifier* | *Keyword* | *Literal* | *Separator* | *Operator*

In other words, Visual Basic considers the following code to be a logical line, even though it is literally two lines in a unit:

```
Private Function GetPrice(ByVal price As Integer, ByVal discount As Double) _
   As Double
```

The preceding method represents a logical line, albeit broken into two actual lines with the line-continuation character. But the compiler will choke on the following representation of the same method if you write it as follows:

```
Private Function GetPrice(
   ByVal price As Integer,
   ByVal discount As Double) As Double
```

This representation causes a syntax error. To fix the error, use the line-continuation character (discussed shortly).

Character and Lines

The characters in your lines of code are drawn from the Unicode character set, which is the character set that all Visual Basic .NET programs are written in. A character is thus any Unicode character except the characters that represent line terminators.

Line Terminators

Unicode line-break characters are used to separate out the lines in your unit. Visual Basic .NET is not a free-format language, so line terminators are an essential part of the syntactic grammar. The following syntax represents the Unicode characters for line termination:

LineTerminator ::=
< Unicode carriage return character (0x000D) > |
< Unicode line feed character (0x000A) > |
< Unicode carriage return character > < Unicode line feed character > |
< Unicode line separator character (0x2028) > |
< Unicode paragraph separator character (0x2029) >

Line Continuation

The line-continuation character is represented by a single underscore or underline character, as shown earlier, which must appear as the last character of the actual line (other than white space). It must be preceded by at least one white-space character, as shown in the following example:

```
Private Function GetPrice(_ 'wrong no white space between characters
   ByVal price As Integer, _ 'correct
   ByVal discount As Double) As Double
```

Line continuations are treated as white space and do not mark the end of logical lines, as demonstrated with this syntax:

LineContinuation ::= WhiteSpace _ [WhiteSpace+] LineTerminator

White Space

White space separates tokens and serves no other function. Logical lines containing only white space are ignored. White space separators are defined in the following syntax:

WhiteSpace ::= < Unicode blank characters (class Zs) > | LineContinuation

Comments

A single-quote character (') represents Visual Basic comments, or you can use the keyword **REM**. Comments can begin anywhere on a source line, and the end of the physical line ends the comment. I, like many others, had hoped for block comment ability in version 1 of Visual Basic .NET—something similar to the following:

```
/*
everything here is comments.
*/
```

Hopefully, it will arrive by the first service pack, because the lack of documentation-friendly features in Visual Basic .NET is one of the sore points (and there are several). Here is the current *limited* comment syntax:

Comment ::= *CommentMarker* [*Character+*]

CommentMarker ::= ' | **REM**

The compiler completely ignores the characters between the beginning of the comment and the comment line's terminator. The following code shows several comments:

```
'Hello program.
'This program writes "hello " to the console.

Module Hello

'Use hello when you mean goodbye
  Sub Main() 'This method must be named "Main".
    Console.WriteLine("hello ")
  End Sub
End Module 'goodbye
```

Identifiers

An identifier is the name you give an element so that the code providers (we, the developers), the code consumers (also we, the developers), and the compiler can identify it throughout the application. Visual Basic identifiers conform to Unicode 3.0 standard, Report 15, Annex 7. However, your identifiers may begin with an underscore (connector) character, although this is not recommended, as mentioned earlier in the "Naming and Notation" section. If you decide to write code like a C++ programmer and begin your identifiers with an underscore, be careful not to leave a white space between the underscore and at least one valid identifier character or the compiler will think you are signifying line continuation.

As mentioned earlier, you can escape the language's keywords with square brackets if you absolutely have to use one of the language's many keywords for an identifier. Escaped identifiers follow the same rules as regular identifiers except that they may match keywords and may not have type characters. The maximum identifier length an identifier can be is 16,383 characters. That's more than you need, because research has shown that identifiers and method names should not exceed 20 characters to preserve readability.

Here is some example code using the escaped keywords:

```
Class [class]
   Shared Sub [shared](ByVal [boolean] As Boolean)
     If [boolean] Then
       Console.WriteLine("true")
     Else
       Console.WriteLine("false")
     End If
   End Sub
End Class

Module Module1
   Sub Main()
    [class].[shared](True)
   End Sub
End Module
```

I think you'll agree the above example, while extreme, is very hard to follow. Identifiers are case insensitive, meaning case is ignored. So, if two identifiers differ only in case, they are considered to be the same identifier. (See also the discussion of **Option Compare** later in this chapter.) The following syntax applies to indentifiers.

Identifier ::=
NonEscapedIdentifier [TypeCharacter] |
EscapedIdentifier

NonEscapedIdentifier ::= < IdentifierName but not Keyword >

EscapedIdentifier ::= [IdentifierName]

IdentifierName ::= IdentifierStart [IdentifierCharacter+]

IdentifierStart ::=
AlphaCharacter |
UnderscoreCharacter IdentifierCharacter
IdentifierCharacter ::=
UnderscoreCharacter |
AlphaCharacter |
NumericCharacter |

CombiningCharacter |
FormattingCharacter

AlphaCharacter ::= < Unicode alphabetic character (classes Lu, Ll, Lt, Lm, Lo, Nl) >

NumericCharacter ::= < Unicode decimal digit character (class Nd) >

CombiningCharacter ::= < Unicode combining character (classes Mn, Mc) >

FormattingCharacter ::= < Unicode formatting character (class Cf) >

UnderscoreCharacter ::= < Unicode connection character (class Pc) >

IdentifierOrKeyword ::= *Identifier* | *Keyword*

Note   *When comparing identifiers, the Unicode standard one-to-one case mappings are used, and any locale-specific case mappings are ignored.*

Separators

The following ASCII characters are available as separators:

Separator ::= **(|) | ! | # | , | . | :**

Type Specifying Characters

A type character following a non-escaped identifier (with no white space between them) denotes the type of the identifier. You can use it in place of the "As *Type*" portion of declaration. For example, the following declaration:

```
Dim dubble#
```

is the same thing as

```
Dim dubble As Double
```

Type characters also detract from readability. If you use them be sure that if the declaration includes a type character, the character agrees with the type specified in the declaration itself; otherwise, a compile-time error occurs. If your declaration omits the type, the compiler will insert the type character implicitly substituted as the type of the declaration.

The following syntax lists the type characters available in Visual Basic .NET (there are no type characters for **Byte** or **Short**).

TypeCharacter ::=
IntegerTypeCharacter |

LongTypeCharacter |
DecimalTypeCharacter |
SingleTypeCharacter |
DoubleTypeCharacter |
StringTypeCharacter

IntegerTypeCharacter ::= %

LongTypeCharacter ::= &

DecimalTypeCharacter ::= @

SingleTypeCharacter ::= !

DoubleTypeCharacter ::= #

StringTypeCharacter ::= $

The compiler does not consider the type character to be part of the identifier. Also, white space between an identifier and its type character will choke the compiler. Here are some examples using type characters (as you can see, the code is prone to bugs):

Trying to append a type character to an identifier that does not have a type will generate errors.

For example, this declaration will not fly because a standard module cannot be typed:

```
Module Module1# 'try declare a module of type Double
End Module
```

The following code generates type compatibility problems because you cannot assign a value of type **String** to a value of type **Single:**

```
Public Sub TestTypeCharacter()
  Dim mySingle!
  Dim myString$
  mySingle = myString
  Debug.WriteLine(mySingle)
End Sub
```

However, the following fix makes it better:

```
Public Sub TestTypeCharacter()
  Dim mySingle!
  Dim myString$
```

```
    mySingle = Convert.ToInt16(myString)
    Debug.WriteLine(mySingle)
End Sub
```

because the **Convert** function converts the **String** value to a **Single** value.

Statements and Blocks

Statements are organized segments of code, which can be organized into blocks. Blocks are made up of labeled lines, and each labeled line begins with an optional label declaration, followed by zero or more statements, and then delimited by colons. For example:

```
Sub-Total:
```

Labels have their own declaration space and do not interfere with other identifiers. In the following example, the type characters for **bar** are used both as the parameter name and as a label name:

```
Function Foo(ByVal bar As Integer) As Integer
    If bar >= 0 Then
        GoTo bar
    End If
    bar = -bar
bar: Return bar
End Function
```

Note   *The treatment of labeled blocks is not covered in any meaningful way in this book as is the use of **GoTo** and **On Error** control-flow constructs. Such code is both controversial and outdated. See Chapter 6 for more information.*

The following syntax illustrates the use of labels and statements:

Block ::= [*LabeledLine+*]

LabeledLine ::= [*LabelName* **:**] [*Statements*] *LineTerminator*

LabelName ::= *Identifier* | *IntLiteral*

Statements ::=
[*Statement*] |
Statements [*Statement*]

Other types of blocks include conditional blocks such as **If**...**Then**...**Else**, **With** statements, the **SyncLock** statement, and so on. These constructs are covered in later chapters. Here is some example syntax:

WithStatement ::=
With *Expression StatementTerminator*
[*Block*]
End With *StatementTerminator*

SyncLockStatement ::=
SyncLock *Expression StatementTerminator*
[*Block*]
End SyncLock *StatementTerminator*

Nothing for Nothing or Something for Nothing

Nothing is a special literal that, as an operand assignee, represents the default value of the data type operand. **Nothing** is also not considered to have a type and, as such, is convertible to all types in the type system. When converted to a particular type, its value defaults to the default value of that type. If the type assigned to **Nothing** contains variable members, they are all set to their default values. Have a look at the following example:

```
Public Structure MyStruct
  Dim name As String
  Dim ort As Short
End Structure

Public Sub NothingForNothing()
 Dim Truct As MyStruct, intI As Integer, oolB As Boolean
 Truct = Nothing   'this line dereferences Truct
 intI = Nothing    'this line sets intI to 0.
 oolB = Nothing    'this line sets oolB to False.
End Sub
```

You will see in Chapters 8 and 9 that you can assign the reference variable of a reference type, an object, to **Nothing**. Doing this disassociates the variable from any object and makes the object a candidate for collection as garbage. For example:

```
Dim myObject As Object
myObject = Nothing   'No object is currently referred to.
```

However, setting a reference variable to **Nothing** does not itself bring about the termination of the instance. Only after the garbage collector has determined that no active references to the instance are remaining will it terminate the object and then release the memory and system resources associated with it. When you assign to **Nothing,** the reference variable no longer refers to any object instance, so it can be reassigned. The syntax is as follows:

Nothing ::= **Nothing**

See also the section "Null" later in this chapter.

Classes, Types, and Objects: What's the Difference?

The terms *type, class,* and *object* are often used interchangeably and by many (me included) without respect for what they truly refer to. In the loosest sense, however, classes are design-time constructs, like knitting patterns, architectural plans, of software. But classes are also groupings or collections of static runtime methods, and in this sense they are often referred to as operations classes. The members of so-called static classes can also be accessed at run time without the need for instantiation, just like ordinary dynamic link library (DLL) files.

Objects live in the run-time environment; they can only be accessed at run time and need to be instantiated before their members can be accessed. The term *types,* or *data types,* is more of a collective term, coined long before objects became the rage, and refers to both classes and objects, and what the common language runtime and type system relates to. In the world of object-oriented programming (OOP), the term *type* is often used to refer to the fundamental data types (or primitives), such as **Integer** or **Byte** (but you'll see in this chapter these types are also objects and are founded as classes; they are anything but primitive types).

There are six "species" of classes that derive from **Object** in the .NET Framework that you will use to build .NET applications. Let's examine them briefly:

■ **Class modules**   These are also known as standard *modules* in Visual Basic (modules are relevant only to Visual Basic). Modules are final and cannot be instantiated as objects (so they cannot refer to instances of themselves with the **Me** keyword). Their members are shared and they become self-contained applications. (Modules are discussed further in Chapter 9.) I don't understand why modules are even included in the language, because you can set any class to behave exactly as the module does with little effort (see Chapter 13 about the Singleton pattern). Modules do come with a number of limitations, however, and I suspect they were included in Visual Basic .NET partly to help with the migration from earlier versions.

■ **Standard classes**   The standard classes are used for all classes that form the building blocks of all .NET types and libraries. Standard classes are the basis of all reference types and are discussed in depth in Chapters 8 and 9, in which you will find out that you can only inherit implementation from one base class in the .NET Framework.

■ **Interfaces**   Interfaces are absolute abstract classes that are de-coupled from implementation. They must be implemented in classes that support or adapt the interface. Supporting an interface means providing its *implementation* (when implemented in standard classes). Adapting an interface means changing the interface so that other classes can reference the implementation that supports it. You are not allowed to include any implementation in an interface; their members (signatures) can only be defined—even if they are just simple events or the specifications for data fields. Interfaces are powerful application building blocks and are covered in detail in Chapters 10, 12, 13, and 14.

■ **Enumerations**   Enumerations, or "enums," are lightweight types that encapsulate constants of an ordinal value, such as **Integer**s, **Short**s, **Long**s and **Byte**s. Enum values are used in place of "magic" numbers that can make code hard to read. You can think of the enumeration class as a "container" type that provides a formal interface to a collection of enum values. Specific instructions on declaring and implementing enums are provided in Chapter 11.

■ **Structures**   Structures are value types and are also known as lightweight classes (because they are processed on the stack and not the heap like standard classes and objects). .NET's fundamental data types are value types, yet they still all derive from **Object** and are thus also objects. These classes or types are very lightweight and fast, and constitute a very powerful facility of the .NET Framework. You can build robust mission-critical applications using structures, enabling you to extend the language in a way never before imagined.

■ **Delegates**   The .NET Framework provides a construct for passing singleton method signatures as bound references to a consumer construct that has an interest in the execution of the method. The **Delegate** is a lot like a C++ function pointer, but it is type safe, secure, and object-oriented. **Delegates** are discussed in Chapter 14 in considerable detail, because they represent a major pillar of the .NET Framework, and a significant concept separating the .NET Framework from Java.

Classes: The View from Above

Classes come in two categories: [end] user classes (or custom classes), and Framework or API classes (also known as the base classes and the built-in types). The user classes are the ones you will build from scratch. As you will discover, you can derive your classes either implicitly—through automatic inheritance—from the root **Object**, or explicitly from one of the inheritable base classes or other custom classes.

User classes need to conform to the common language specification (CLS) or they will (at best) introduce bugs or (at worst) not compile (see Chapter 2). The Framework classes are the ones that ship with the .NET SDK. They also conform to the CLS (which ultimately supports the common language runtime—the CLR—discussed in the first two chapters).

All classes—as well as modules, enums, interfaces, structures, and delegates—are composed of a number of specific "spaces." A class typically is composed of a *directive space*, a *class declaration space*, and an *implementation space*. The compiler accesses the information in the spaces in a certain sequence of steps. These spaces are illustrated in Figure 4-1, and comprise the following:

- **Class declaration space**   The *declaration space* is where the class is declared and named. As we will discuss in the next section, the class declaration provides access information, the type of class it is (such as enumerator, module, and so on), whether the class is inheriting from a base class or implementing an interface (or both), class attributes, and so on.

- **Class directive space**   The *directive space* comprises data that directs compilation (**Option** statements), references external classes via their respective namespaces (**Imports**), scopes the class itself to a namespace, and so on. The directives are placed at the top of the class, which is also known as the *header space* in some languages, such as C and C++. The elements that go into the directive space are placed in an order of priority, which we will discuss in the next section because the order is important.

- **Class implementation space**   The implementation space is anywhere in the class between the class declaration and the class terminator symbol, which is the **End Class** statement (a closing outer curly brace in C#). The elements that go into the implementation space include methods, data fields, events, properties, and so on. We'll discuss these essential elements in more detail in this chapter and in other chapters.

The following sections discuss the preceding three spaces in the typical order in which you will work in them in the IDE: declarations, directives, and implementations.

The Class Declaration Space

You declare a class before doing anything else when you start coding in Visual Basic, which is why the declaration space is discussed first. The class declaration consists of several essential components in this space, starting with the class name and ending with the **End Class** terminator, as illustrated in Figure 4-1. The grammar notation provided by the .NET Framework SDK and Visual Basic language is as follows:

[*Attributes*] (Optional) *ClassModifier* ::= *AccessModifier* | **Shadows** | **MustInherit** | **NotInheritable** (Optional)

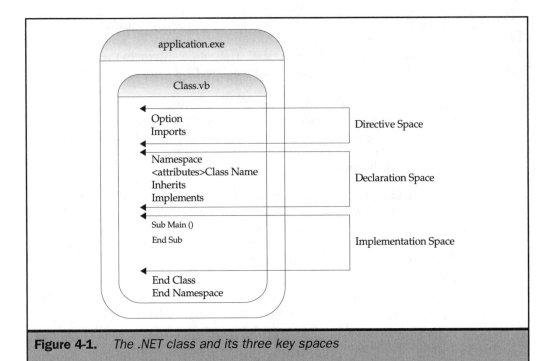

Figure 4-1. The .NET class and its three key spaces

ClassTypeName ::= **String**

ClassDeclaration ::=

    ClassBase ::= **Inherits** *TypeName LineTerminator* (Optional)

    InterfaceBase ::= **Inherits** *InterfaceBases LineTerminator* (Optional)

[*ClassMemberDeclaration+*] (Implementation)
End Class *LineTerminator*

The sections marked (Optional) are not essential elements for the development of simple classes. They may be left out, in which case the CLR assumes the default. For example, you can mark a class **Public**, but the CLR will assume **Public** if you leave out this modifier. However, the access modifiers modify the class to perform a specific role or to declare a certain level of visibility from the outside world. For example, if you need to explicitly seal a class (that is, prevent any of its implementation from being overridden or extended), then you need to modify the class as being **NotInheritable** (but we'll get back to the modifiers shortly).

Attributes

Attributes were introduced in Chapter 2, and are more a facility of the CLR and the CTS than of any individual .NET language. However, attributes can be used to decorate any specific language element in your source code by declaring **AttributeUsage** and **AttibuteTargets** modifiers in your code. The syntax is as follows:

Attribute Usage

Attributes ::= < AttributeList >

AttributeList ::=
Attribute |
AttributeList , Attribute

Attribute ::= [AttributeModifier :] TypeName [([AttributeArguments])]

AttributeModifier ::= **Assembly** | **Module**

Attribute Arguments

AttributeArguments ::=
AttributePositionalArgumentList |
AttributePositionalArgumentList, VariablePropertyInitializerList |
VariablePropertyInitializerList

AttributePositionalArgumentList ::=
ConstantExpression |
AttributePositionalArgumentList , ConstantExpression

VariablePropertyInitializerList ::=
VariablePropertyInitializer
VariablePropertyInitializerList , VariablePropertyInitializer

VariablePropertyInitializer ::= Identifier : = ConstantExpression

Attributes are discussed in further detail in *Visual Basic .NET Developer's Guide* (McGraw-Hill/Osborne, 2002) with the subject of reflection and runtime type information technology (RTTI). You will also learn how to create custom attributes and how to "decorate" classes and class members with attributes.

Table 4-11 lists the elements that can be decorated with attributes.

While creating custom attributes lets you "enhance" your classes, manipulate the compiler, and tame the CLR, you will mostly use built-in attributes provided by the .NET Framework.

The first element of the class declaration space—in front of the class access-modifiers and class name—is reserved for optional class attributes. The following line of code

Attribute Target	Example Applications
Assembly	Strong naming, information, identity
Module (as in DLL or EXE modules)	Information, identity (similar to assembly)
Class	Serialization, information, reflection
Struct (value types)	Layout of data fields in the class
Enum	Flags for bitwise combinations of values
Interface	How an interface is exposed to COM
Delegate	Reflecting on **Delegate**
Constructor	Tag names for Web control constructors
Method	Information for method reflection
Field	Information for field reflection
Event	Event reflection, security permissions
Parameter	Variable parameter lists
Return	Reflecting on the method return value
Property	Reflecting on properties

Table 4-11.   *Attributable Elements of Visual Basic .NET (and Any CLS-Compliant Language)*

illustrates how an attribute is applied to the target it is decorating the class as being serializable (serialization is discussed in Chapter 15):

```
<Serializable()> Public MustInherit Class Crew
```

The preceding attribute prepares the assembly and the compiler to serialize the object, which is the computer language equivalent of reducing pasta dough to dried spaghetti that can be later reconstituted into a magnificent bolognaise.

Class Access

The so-called *visibility* or *access* characteristics of a class from the outside world—its neighbors in the assembly, or classes and constructs in other assemblies or further away—govern how the class can be used and the level of encapsulation required.

The following syntax and code demonstrates the declaration of a publicly accessible class:

AccessModifier ::= **Public** | **Protected** | **Friend** | **Protected Friend** | **Private**

```
Public Class AforAway
  'Implementation Space
End Class 'Class AforAway
```

Class **AforAway** above is **Public**, while **BforBusy** defaults to **Friend** access:

```
Class BforBusy
  'Implementation Space
End Class 'Class BforBusy
```

There are five levels of access you can impose on a class: **Public**, **Friend**, **Protected**, **Protected Friend**, and **Private**. The levels and the rules for their usage are discussed in Chapter 9.

Note   *Only **Public** and **Friend** are valid modifiers for outermost classes. **Private**, **Protected**, and **Protected Friend** modifiers are only valid on composite classes. Furthermore, the default access (no modifier provided) is **Friend**, which is less risky as a default modifier than **Public**.*

Class Utility

The utility of a class is denoted by its so-called class modifier, which allows a class to be *shadowed, inherited,* or *sealed.* A shadowed class is a composite class that can redeclare and use the members of its outer class. A class that can be inherited is an abstract class that permits some or all of its members, if they so allow it, to be implemented in the deriving, or child, class. A sealed class cannot be inherited and thus its implementation is "final."

The Visual Basic .NET terms for shadow, inheritable, and sealed classes are **Shadows**, **MustInherit**, and **NotInheritable**, respectively. Each of these modifiers is discussed at length in Chapter 9.

Class Declaration

Class declaration comes immediately after your class is named and its access and utility are provided. Declaration starts with the optional declaration that the class either inherits from a single super class or implements one or more interfaces. The syntax for this declaration is as follows:

ClassDeclaration ::=

ClassBase ::= **Inherits** *TypeName LineTerminator* (Optional)

InterfaceBase ::= **Implements** *InterfaceBases LineTerminator* (Optional)

[*ClassMemberDeclaration+*] (Implementation)
End Class *LineTerminator*

If you need to extend a super or base class, such as the **Attribute** class or the **FileDialog** class, you need to do so with the **Inherits** keyword. And if you need to declare the implementation of one or more interfaces, you must declare this with the **Implements** keyword. The following example declares a public class called **NetHelpAttribute** that extends the **Attribute** class:

```
Public Class NetHelpAttribute
   Inherits Attribute
End Class
```

The Directive Space

The space above the class declaration space is where you provide specific directives for the compiler, references to namespaces and classes, and namespace declaration. The order of this information is important and must be as follows:

1. **Compiler options**   The first declarations—**Option Strict, Option Explicit,** and **Option Compare.**

2. **Namespace and Class References**   This section, which uses the **Imports** keyword, provides for the referencing of the types used in the class implementation.

3. **Namespace**   This section provides for the declaration of the namespace to which the class being declared and its inner types are scoped.

Compiler Option Directives

Visual Basic .NET provides many different compiler directives and we will investigate them in Chapter 17. Three of them are **Option** statements that, if used in your code, must be placed at the top of the class declaration before any other information. These directives to the compiler govern declarative and semantic elements of code construction, such as explicit declaration, late binding, typing and so on. The **Option** statements are as follows:

OptionDirective ::= *OptionExplicitDirective | OptionStrictDirective |
OptionCompareDirective*

■ **Option Compare**   This option directs the compiler to perform **String** value comparison using either a binary-processing algorithm or a text-processing algorithm. The binary option performs comparisons based on a sort order derived from the internal binary representations of the characters being compared, while the text option looks at the textual or **String** representations of the characters being compared, relative to locale. (See the "Comparison Operators" section in Chapter 5 for specific **String** comparison information and code. The syntax for the **Option** directives is as follows:

OptionCompareDirective ::= **Option Compare** *CompareOption LineTerminator*

CompareOption ::= **Binary** | **Text**

■ **Option Explicit**   This option forces you to explicitly declare all variables in your class. If you do not specify this option the compiler will assume the default setting, which is specified in the compiler configuration properties set in Visual Studio, at the project level (discussed later in this chapter). You can toggle the option using the statement **Option Explicit On | Off**. Specifically, **Option Explicit On** will prompt you to declare a variable before you can use it. The syntax is as follows:

OptionExplicitDirective ::= **Option Explicit** [*OnOff*] *LineTerminator*

OnOff ::= **On** | **Off**

■ **Option Strict**   This is a new option for the Visual Basic language that enforces strong type semantics, which thereby restricts implicit type conversions. The utility of this option is to prevent possible data loss through errant type conversions. The compiler environment stays one step behind you as you write your code and generally prevents narrowing conversions. The default setting for this option can also be set in Visual Studio at the project configuration properties level.

■ **Option Strict On** also reports an error on the following circumstances:

   ■ Late binding (`Dim myVar`); the variable must have an `"As"` clause (`Dim myVar As Integer`)

   ■ Undeclared variables, because **Option Strict On** implies **Option Explicit On**

The syntax is as follows:

OptionStrictDirective ::= **Option Strict** [*OnOff*] *LineTerminator*
OnOff ::= **On** | **Off**

The new **Option Strict** directive reflects the dilemma inherited by the Visual Basic .NET architects from the previous versions of Visual Basic and its inherent success as the world's most widely used software development tool. Visual Basic has traditionally been a very easy language to learn and thus to teach, so its semantic and declarative elements have traditionally been loosely enforced to aid learning, rather than to aid powerful application development now possible. While you can write strongly typed code with the earlier versions of Visual Basic they are a lot more lenient with typing, binding, and declaration.

Visual Basic .NET, however, is used in a variety of development environments for all manner of advanced and critical mainstream software construction. It thus makes sense to assume that gurus and experts are using the language, and that they have critical deadlines and a hefty responsibility to turn out quality products.

By setting **Option Strict** to **On**, you force the compiler to tighten the code construction process by checking for declaration errors, type conversion errors, and unintended late binding (see the section on "Method Binding" in Chapter 7).

For the most part, you should leave both **Option Explicit** and **Option Strict** set to **On** (make **On** the default in Visual Studio), because this aids code construction by tightening your code and reducing the number of possible bugs that may creep through. This also helps conserve resources that get used in exception handling, but it's not a reason to not use exception handlers in your code (see Chapter 11). In other words, it provides a filter for bugs that might otherwise have made it into the compiled code.

Setting **Option Strict On** does not imply that **Option Explicit On** becomes redundant. **Option Strict** will not catch unintended late binding.

Note	*When reviewing all code in this book, assume that both **Option Strict** and **Option Explicit** are toggled to the **On** position, because the two options will often be excluded from the code examples to conserve trees. If a specific reason exists for toggling the options to the **Off** position, then the statement will be included and noted.*

Another important consideration when setting the **Option** statements to **On** is that the directives set the compiler to continuous background checking. So, whenever you write a statement, Visual Studio waits for you to finish coding and then checks the code (and you need to work quickly or it will jump ahead of you). Sometimes, it takes a few seconds to finish its work and that can be an irritating distraction when you are working against time and are low on memory and processing power. If you are experienced enough to know how the compiler is going to react to "loose" code, you can code with these options set to **Off** and then come back and fix the errors later (or you can get a better computer). For more information, check out Chapter 11, which covers exception handling, and Chapter 17, which covers debugging and the command line compiler directives.

Importing Namespaces

The .NET Framework's class library is an excellent place to start to learn about the class namespaces, because it is a massive library of classes partitioned into many namespaces and packaged in a collection of assemblies. In many respects, it is the mother lode of classes, because it represents one of the largest collections of framework classes in programming history. Later in this chapter, I will give you some pointers to "mining" the treasure-trove of classes in the library. First, let's look at the syntax.

Imports Statement

ImportsDirective ::= **Imports** *ImportsClauses LineTerminator*

ImportsClauses ::=
ImportsClause |
ImportsClauses , ImportsClause

ImportsClause ::= ImportsAliasClause | RegularImportsClause

Import Aliases

ImportsAliasClause ::= Identifier = QualifiedIdentifier

Regular Imports

ImportsNamespaceClause ::= QualifiedIdentifier

But what is a namespace—in the software-engineering sense of the word? A namespace is a logical grouping of related classes (types) that ensures that the class names we concoct do not clash, and can thus be easily referenced. This is illustrated here.

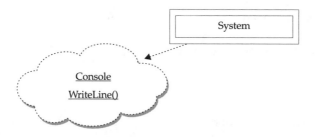

The discussion of structured programming and modules in Chapter 1 stated that, in OOP languages, the class is the unit of modularity. This means that it is possible for any programmer to create a class and give it the same name as one of your classes. And any class in the base class library or some other library could have the same name as one that you are creating.

Note   *Engineers who create classes for other engineers are principally referred to as* class providers *in this book. Engineers who use the provided classes (framework or custom) are principally referred to as* class consumers.

This means that it is entirely possible for class names to clash, because to ensure that every class ever created is given a unique name would be very limiting, well nigh impossible to implement, and not very practical. There are, however, other mechanisms for ensuring uniqueness, which are discussed in the next section.

The concept of a module namespace in programming was introduced in 1993 for the C++ language. The main purpose of a namespace specification was to prevent the clashing of classes and modules imported into the C++ application from different header files (.h extension), and to provide a reference or visibility (access) scope. This is achieved by making the class a member of a namespace. The combination of the namespace and the class ensures that class names do not clash and provides the developer with the freedom to name the classes without fear of name clashing.

Note   *A namespace is also a place to "park" your classes; thus, you can think of a "parking space" as more than a location to park your wheels.*

The fully qualified namespace (FQNS) name is the component that is kept unique within the programming environment. In other words, if you created a class called **Console** and tried to insert it into the **System** namespace (as demonstrated here), the IDE would politely warn you of your infringing ways, because a class of the same name already existed in the namespace. But you could comfortably create a namespace that starts with the root **Myreader** and put (your) **Console** class into it without any trouble. Referencing that class would be as follows:

```
Myreader.Console.ReadMylips("Do Something")
```

Or, better still, use the **Imports** keyword, as follows:

```
Imports Myreader
```

Or perhaps you could use the following:

```
Imports Myreader.Console
```

But you would still need to fully qualify the namespace for your **Console** class if there is a chance that your code references the **System** namespace, which also exposes a class named **Console**.

As demonstrated earlier, the **Imports** keyword references the namespace starting at the first word in the namespace and qualifying the references down to the class of interest. By just importing the namespace root, **Vb7cr**, we expose all the types in the **Vb7cr** assembly.

Tip   *While the root of a namespace and the assembly can have the same name, the two are unrelated. As discussed in Chapter 2, an assembly packages many namespaces. See Chapters 2 and 17 for information on naming assemblies.*

It does not make sense to expose the entire net worth of classes in a namespace, like the blast from a shotgun, if all you need is a reference to one or two classes. Thus, there is a lot to be said for referencing the entire namespace from the root to the last class in your code or on the **Imports** line, like a shot from a rifle, rather than just specifying the root on the **Imports** line.

On the other hand, if you do need to reference a lot of classes and repetitively reference the entire namespace for every class you reference, you are going to find yourself doing more typing than an Assembler programmer. Here's an example of the buckshot **Imports** vs. the rifle-shot **Imports**:

```
Imports Vb7cr 'buckshot, ok
Imports Vb7cr.MyClass 'rifle-shot, better
```

Declaring Namespaces

The last element to be included above the class declaration is the namespace declaration, and this needs to happens before you start constructing your class. The namespace declaration is the statement that *scopes* your class to its namespace. Here is the formal syntax:

NamespaceDeclaration ::=
Namespace QualifiedIdentifier LineTerminator
[NamespaceMemberDeclaration+]
NamespaceMemberDeclaration ::=
NamespaceDeclaration |
TypeDeclaration

TypeDeclaration ::=
ModuleDeclaration |
NonModuleDeclaration

NonModuleDeclaration ::=
EnumDeclaration |
StructureDeclaration |
InterfaceDeclaration |
ClassDeclaration |
DelegateDeclaration

End Namespace *LineTerminator*

A familiar example of a namespace is your Internet domain name—such as hq.sdamag.com. The unique part of this namespace is sdamag.com, which is being read from the top down on the Internet namespace. Normally you would read this as sdamag.com, but our class namespaces are read as com.sdamag.hq.

Registration of the unique parts of the namespace, with an Internet registrar, ensures that no other entity can create the identical domain namespace. The "hq" part of the namespace does not have to be unique, and it cannot. Thousands of companies have hq as a private subdomain on their respective namespaces, but the hqs of the world cannot clash because only one hq is allowed on the public Internet. Entities such as com and org are part of a *global* public namespace, and the same concept is extended into software engineering.

> **Note**   *Java, Delphi, and other languages provide similar strategies for module and class name clashing, such as packages.*

The dot notation will be the standard form used to illustrate namespaces throughout this book, both in various figures and in the text. Namespaces are not represented in UML (see Chapter 9).

> **Note**   *The C++ notation for a namespace reference is as follows:* **Myreader : : Myclass**. *Java also uses dot notation.*

The illustration demonstrates how it is possible that namespaces in the assemblies of various companies or class providers might clash. You and I could create the identical namespace and classes and they would work fine for us. But if we both happened to send our files to a third party, the namespaces would clash because we can't reference both namespaces in our code...even if they are in different assemblies.

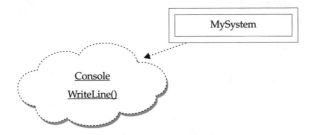

For this reason, it will pay you now to come up with a namespace that you will be able to rely on. A good suggestion borrowed from the Java world is to use your own Internet domain name (you have one right?) because you know it's unique. You can then provide a namespace as follows:

```
Com.Sdamag.Myclass
```

It is unlikely that such a company name exists, and we know that on the Internet (the real world for us hacks) the name is unique, thanks to DNS. Now you only have to worry about people in your own organization using this name. And, of course, you would think twice about a name such as Microsoft.VisualBasic.MyClass.

The minimum namespace name is the name on the extreme left (the first part of the name) of the first dot, and the class name on the extreme right (the last part of the name) of the last dot. While the root alone makes a namespace (root and class), it's best to provide a namespace root for all classes. As long as you have these two names and at least one dot, you have a clearly defined namespace. Referencing from the root to the class file means your are making a fully qualified reference to your class, no matter how many levels deep.

You are free to add whatever helps you to logically group the names in the middle. The following is a legal namespace, but it's not very helpful:

```
Vb7cr.NodeNotFoundException
```

The following example is better and typical of the namespace names that will be used in this book. Running two levels deep, they will help you relate the code to the book and the relevant chapter.

```
Vb7cr.Exceptions.NodeNotFoundException
```

 Microsoft suggests using your company name, as it does. I prefer the Internet domain name. It makes a lot more sense, and, unlike company names, there is not another one like it anywhere in the world.

Creating a namespace is simple and can be achieved in three ways. You can create the namespace for your class using the namespace declaration placed immediately above the class name in your class file. The syntax for declaring a namespace is as follows:

Namespace *QualifiedIdentifier LineTerminator*

[NamespaceMemberDeclaration+]

End Namespace *LineTerminator*

The following code demonstrates namespace declaration:

```
Namespace Vb7cr.Exceptions
  Class NodeNotFoundException
  'implementation space
  End Class
End Namespace
```

The other two ways to place a class into a namespace are via the command-line compiler option specifying the namespace, when compiling from the command line, or via the Visual Studio .NET interactive configuration options. The latter is accessible in the Property Pages dialog box for the project, in the General folder. These two options are explained in Chapter 17 in the "Visual Basic .NET Compiler" section.

| Tip | *When you specify a namespace do not include the name of the class as part of the root, or you'll end up with the class name repeated at the end of the namespace as shown in this example: Vb7cr.Exceptions.NodeNotFoundException.NodeNotFoundException.* |

That's all there is to a namespace. As you see, it is a logical naming system you use to organize and reference your classes. However, a namespace also implicitly encapsulates the scope of the type it harbors—its visibility outside its bounds. Types are by default **Public**, but they can also be exposed with the **Friend** modifier, which restricts visibility to the assembly, but we'll deal with that in Chapter 9.

| Note | *I was tempted to further expand the namespaces used in this book by adding a company name level, such as Com.Osborne, before identifying the title and the chapter in which the code is principally covered. However, namespace hierarchies are best kept to no more than three levels (four is already cumbersome and five would be the absolute limit). There is no technological limit to the number of levels, but you can overdo it and thus add unnecessary complexity and typing for your users. More than four levels and your consumers will begin to think your program is in the basement.* |

Remember, a namespace is a logical reference to a unique class name; it's not a physical file reference. The file reference is the *assembly*.

| Note | *You will see that you can declare multiple classes in a single Visual Basic source code file (*.vb, also known as the* class unit*), but you can only have one set of **Option** directives at the top of the file. Namespaces can, however, wrap each class in the file, thereby parking each class in its own namespace.* |

The Implementation Space

The implementation space is the entire class space between the declaration space and the **End Class** (and **End Module**) terminator. This section provides the declaration and functionality of the specific members of a class. Later in this chapter, we'll investigate the declaration spaces, contexts, and scopes of the class members.

Classes are composed of a number of constructs—called *class members*—the most fundamental of which are the fields that store data and methods. The list of these members is introduced here. The fundamental, built-in data types are further treated later in this chapter.

■ **Data fields** Classes can reference the values of composite *data types* such as what we understand as primitive values. The declaration of these types in a class directs the runtime to allocate a memory location where the data represented by the types is accessed. The locations for the data are known as the *fields*. The fields are accessible only to the runtime, on behalf of the class or object's members, which need access to the data. The data fields should (generally) be hidden (at the least behind property interfaces) and should not be accessed from the outside world (for a variety of reasons, discussed in Chapters 8 and 9).

■ **Variables** Fields hold variable information, hence the term *variables*. You can think of a variable as the fundamental storage unit used by your application. Variables are covered in more depth later in this chapter. Any value type or reference type can be associated with a variable.

■ **Constants** A class also has access to field data that is marked read-only or that cannot be changed. Such fields are called *constants* in the .NET Framework and in most languages, and are also known as *finals*. A constant is also a unit of storage, like variables, and is named and accessed in the same way as variables. (Constants are covered in more depth later in this chapter.) Any value type can be declared as a constant.

■ **Methods** Classes contain functions and procedures (collectively known as *methods* in OOP, which means nothing more than "a way of doing something"). These methods can modify data in their classes, interact with methods in the same class or with methods in other classes. Methods "talk" to each other through a process in OOP known as message passing. In the .NET Framework, the messages between objects and methods are known as *calls*, or method invocations. Function methods, like all functions, return data to the callers. Methods also perform specific services that change the state of the application. Methods are discussed exclusively in Chapter 7.

■ **Properties** The .NET Framework supports a construct that provides a structured and protected interface to the field data in classes. The constructs are known as *properties* and can be used to both access and change variable field data, under class control. Properties can be both static or instance members. The interface or access to a property is via its formal signature. Properties are principally discussed in Chapter 7.

■ **Events** Objects that need to notify other objects or any interested constructs that a certain action has been performed do so with events. Event notification is a key component of OOP, and, as such, OOP is often referred to as event-driven software development. By clicking a button, for example, the software fires an event that notifies *"subscriber"* or *"listener"* objects that the button has been clicked. You can then program "responses" to these events in specific event handling spaces, or *event handlers,* which delegate to another object in the application to do something in response to the event, such as opening a dialog box. A full discussion of event handling and the event-handling model, which is built on the **Delegate** architecture, can be found in Chapter 14.

■ **Indexers**   If your application creates a collection of like objects, you can index the collections as you would the elements of arrays or other collections. Indexers are instance members. See Chapter 12 for more information on collections.

■ **Operators**   You can't build software without operators, which are built-in functions that perform assignment, arithmetic operations, bit manipulation, type comparison, and so on. Chapter 5 is dedicated to the subject and demonstrates some operator services in action.

■ **Constructors**   To instantiate objects, you need to provide a constructor that will build the object for you and initialize its various data fields. Constructors run at object creation when you call **New**, and just after the object is instantiated. They cannot be directly called or invoked once the object is created. Constructors are not inherited, and the base class constructor can be called automatically by the CLR. However, you can overload constructors in the derived classes, and constructors can also be declared *shared* (static). Constructors are methods and are discussed in Chapters 7 and 9.

■ **Destructors and Finalizers**   These are constructs that facilitate the tearing down and cleaning up of an object. In unmanaged applications, the developer is responsible for explicit release of memory; however, managed environments like the .NET Framework depend on a garbage collector. See Chapters 2 and 7.

■ **Composite or Nested types**   Classes can be declared within the implementation space of another class. The "inner" or "nested" composite class can be a static class or instantiated. Composite types are discussed in Chapters 9 and 12 through 14.

Let's now investigate the fundamental value types and how these are declared and used as variables or constants. Keep in mind, however, that much of our discussion here is still from a very high level. The chapters that follow will, where appropriate, drill down into the subject in the context of the chapter and provide many examples. For example, how classes and object variables are referenced is discussed in depth in Chapters 8 and 9.

Elemental Value Types

The Visual Basic .NET language defines ten fundamental data types: **Boolean**, **Date**, **Byte**, **Char**, **Decimal**, **Double**, **Integer**, **Long**, **Short**, and **Single** (or 12 types if you count **Object** and **String**). These types are often referred to as primitive, or built-in, data types. All these terms refer to the same thing, but "primitive" is technically incorrect (even for **Boolean**), despite what the syntax says, because the .NET fundamental types are objects. I will refer to these types as the fundamental value types because they are first and foremost value types that descend from the root of the .NET object model, at the same time as being the elemental building blocks of all Visual Basic .NET applications. The syntax for these types is as follows:

PrimitiveTypeName ::= *NumericTypeName* | **Boolean** | **Date** | **Char**

NumericTypeName ::= *IntegralTypeName* | *FloatingPointTypeName* | **Decimal**

IntegralTypeName ::= **Byte** | **Short** | **Integer** | **Long**

FloatingPointTypeName ::= **Single** | **Double**

The **Date** is now considered a fundamental data type in .NET and I have included it in Table 4-12, which lists the storage size and values applicable to the elemental types that are available to Visual Basic .NET programs. The list is in alphabetical order. It also lists the framework's fully qualified type name, because all types derive from **Object** (see Chapters 7 and 10).

You will learn further in Chapter 8 that .NET types are separated into value types and reference types. All value types are stack-allocated; they may also be allocated inline in a structure. Reference types, on the other hand, are heap-allocated.

All .NET types derive from the root class **Object**, but the lightweight value types are able to behave and be treated like fundamental values and not as objects. When a value type needs to act like an object, such as when you call **myInteger.ToString**, a wrapper that makes the value type look like a reference object is allocated on the heap, and the value type's value is copied into it. The process is known as *boxing*.

The boxing is all done in Microsoft Intermediate Language (MSIL) and you don't need to provide any instruction to the compiler about boxing. The wrapper is marked in such a way that the system knows that it contains a value type. To return the object reference to the stack, the type is **unboxed**. The boxing technique allows any type to be treated as an object.

Computers classify and manage data according to the specifics of the declared type, the amount of memory allocated to each type, and where that memory is located. How the value types are referenced at their memory location by the runtime and your application is covered later in this chapter.

All computer languages provide facilities for converting from one type to another. Visual Basic .NET, however, is a *strongly typed language* under the **Option Strict** compiler directive. However, this language can also be weakly typed, and allows developers to provide custom type conversion handling scenarios and thus faster development (which of course leads to more bugs).

Type	.NET Framework	Size	Value
Boolean	System.Boolean	2 bytes (16-bit)	**True** or **False**
Byte	System.Byte	1 byte	0 to 255 unsigned
Char	System.Char	2 bytes	0 to 65,535 unsigned
Date	System.DateTime	8 bytes	January 1, 1 to December 31, 9999
Decimal	System.Decimal	12 bytes	+/-79,228,162,514,264,337,593,950,335 with no decimal point +/-7.9228162512264337593543950335 with 28 places to the right of the decimal point The smallest nonzero number would be a 1 in the 28th position to the right of the decimal point
Double	System.Double	8 bytes	-1.797693134862231E308 to -4.94065645841247 for negative values to 4.94065645841247 to 1.797693134862231E308 for positive values
Integer	System.Integer	4 bytes	-2,147,483,648 to 2,147,483,648
Long	System.Long	8 bytes	-9,223,372,036,854,775,808 to 9,223,372,036,854,775,807
Short	System.Short	2 bytes	-32,768 to 32,767
Single	System.Single	4 bytes	-3.402823E38 to -1.401298E-45 for negative values to 1.401298E-45 to 3.402823E38 for positive values

Table 4-12. *Visual Basic .NET Fundamentals Signed Value Types*

The ten fundamental value types can also be grouped as follows:

- **Ordinal numbers**   This group is represented by **Byte**, **Short**, **Integer**, and **Long**.

- **Floating and decimal-point numbers**   This group is represented by **Single**, **Double**, and **Decimal**.

- **Characters**   This group is represented by **Char** and **Date**.

- **Booleans**   This group has only one member, **Boolean**, which can represent either **True** or **False**.

Working with Numbers

When working with mathematical expressions, you have a choice of several classes of ordinal or integer types, the floating-point types, and the **Decimal** type, which is a number with a fixed decimal point. When working with the ordinal types, you should be aware that conversion from one type to another should not cause problems for your code. However, it is possible to encounter **OverflowException**s when converting from a type that can hold large values to a type that can only hold smaller values.

The integer types let you safely convert from a small integer type to a larger integer type without the possibility of **OverflowException**s and data loss. This is known as a *widening conversion*. When you try to convert from a larger value type to a smaller value type, say from **Long** to **Short**, data loss is inevitable if the number being held is large, and an **OverflowException** will occur that, if not handled, will shut down the application.

An analogy that, I believe, best describes the difference between widening and narrowing conversion and possible subsequent data loss is the cola bottle conversion problem. In one hand, you have a liter of cola and for whatever reason you want to transfer the cola to a smaller bottle. If the bottle is full and you try to move the cola to a 500ml bottle, the inevitable will happen—the smaller bottle will "overflow" and cola loss will result. You can, however, handle the "overflow exception" and drink half the cola first.

Integer Types

The most commonly used of the fundamental value types is the **Integer**, which is a type that represents a scalar, signed ordinal from -2,147,483,648 to 2,147,483,647. It is the most efficient and versatile type, which aliases **System.Int32**, because it is optimized for use on 32-bit processor systems, requiring 4 bytes of storage space, which at the time of this writing is the standard architecture of most of the world's servers and PCs.

While the **Integer** lets you work with a wide range of numbers, it sometime makes more sense to work with the value types that might need to be run on 16-bit or smaller computers. So the language includes the **Short**, a signed 16-bit ordinal type that only consumes 2 bytes, or 16 bits. The **Short** can thus represent numbers ranging from -32,768 to 32,767. The **Short** value type aliases **System.Int16**.

Even smaller than **Short**, however, is **Byte**, an 8-bit (1 byte), unsigned value type that is used to store binary data. **Byte**, which aliases **System.Byte**, has a range of values from 0 to 255. **Byte** value types are useful for handling raw binary data and working with streams and files (see Chapter 15).

If you need to work with very large numbers, more than can be represented by **Integer**, then **Long**, or **Systerm.Int64**, gives you the capability of working within a signed number range from -9,223,372,036,854,775,808 to 9,223,372,036,854,775,807. The **Long**, however, consumes 8 bytes for storage. It is a 64-bit ordinal and will become the standard type optimized for 64-bit processors.

When working with the integer or ordinal types, you should be aware that using the smaller types "because you can" does not necessarily mean that your applications will benefit from memory conservation. In fact, the **System.Int32** or **Integer** type performs better than the **Short** 16-bit type, because the so-called word—a fixed length of bits—of most modern computer systems is 32 bits, or 4 bytes, long.

Visual Basic 6 to Visual Basic .NET

Experts with Visual Basic 6 (and earlier) experience will very quickly pick up what's new in Visual Basic .NET by working with the language and going over the declaration examples and the code throughout this book. However, there are a few items to chew on at this early stage, especially if you have big upgrade plans.

 You can open a classic VB application in Visual Studio .NET. The IDE will create a new project for you and will make all the conversion changes that it can.

The ordinal data types you were used to in Visual Basic 6 have been widened in the .NET Framework. For example, the Visual Basic 6 **Integer** is 16 bits, but in the .NET Framework, it is a 32-bit-wide type. **Long** has been widened to 64 bits.

Point Types

This section discusses data types that can represent large number and decimal points, floating and fixed.

First we have *floating-point* numbers, also known as *floats* or *real* numbers, which are represented by two "float" value types—the **Single** and the **Double** (aliases of **System.Single** and **System.Double**, respectively). Floats are so named because they are represented in the computer as a sequence of digits and a "floating" decimal point, which changes position to represent various fractional values. For example, the number 110 can be represented as 1.10 or 0.110 by moving the position of the decimal point in the float value type.

The **Single**, which stands for single-precision floating point, is a value type that represents IEEE-754 (see the IEEE-754 sidebar in Chapter 5) floating-point number definitions that are 32-bit, 4-byte, values. The **Single** value can range from -3.402823E+38 to -1.401298E-45 for negative values and from 1.401298E-45 to 3.402823E+38 for positive values. The **Single** is safely converted to wider types of **Double** floats and the **Decimal** value type.

Double value types are allocated 64 bits to store their values and range in value from -1.79769313486231E+308 to -4.94065645841247E-324 for negative values and from 4.94065645841247E-324 to 1.79769313486231E+308 for positive values. **Double** values can be safely converted to values of the **Decimal** value type.

Single is sufficient for most operations. However, new computers are coming out with processors optimized for 64-bit floating-point operations and to support complex numeric algorithms.

The **Decimal** type stores a number in a wide 128-bit signed integer that ranges from a negative number of -79,228,162,514,264,337,593,543,950,335 to a positive number of 79,228,162,514,264,337,593,543,950,335, specifying no decimal places. While the **Decimal** represents a huge integral data type, it is included in this section because it can represent very large numbers that include a decimal point, albeit fixed. It can be used for algorithms that cannot afford precision loss caused by rounding. This type is fit for complex numeric processing, such as scientific calculations and financial applications.

You can declare a variable of **Decimal** as a signed, fixed-point value consisting of an integral part, or you can optionally include a fractional part. The integral and fractional parts consist of a series of digits that range from 0 to 9, separated by the decimal point symbol.

The binary representation of an instance of **Decimal** consists of a 1-bit sign, a 96-bit integer number, and a scaling factor used to divide the 96-bit integer and specify what portion of it is a decimal fraction. The scaling factor is implicitly the number 10, raised to an exponent ranging from 0 to 28 to specify the number of digits to place to the right of the point.

With a scale of 0—in other words, no decimal places—the largest possible value is 79,228,162,514,264,337,593,543,950,335, while at 28 decimal places the value is 7.9228162514264337593543950335. The smallest nonzero value is 0.0000000000000000000000000001 (+/-1E-28). Chapter 7 demonstrates method construction and provides specific examples of using the ordinal and point types in various arithmetic algorithms.

Characters

The .NET Framework's value type for storing characters is the **Char**. If you are a Visual Basic 6 programmer, then the **Char** will be a new type. But if you are from the world of C/C++, you might be tempted to think the .NET **Char** is the same as what you are used to—an 8-bit-wide integer data type. However, the .NET **Char** represents Unicode character values ranging from hexadecimal 0x0000 to 0xFFFF, or 0 through 65,356 (see Chapter 5).

The .NET **Char** is actually the same type as the Java **Char**, which also stores Unicode in 16 bits. The .NET hexadecimal values fit into the 16-bit field, which can give you the full range of 0 to 65,536 Unicode characters, a far cry from the ASCII range of 0 to 255.

Application of **Char** in algorithms and for international applications is covered in Chapter 17.

Booleans

The **Boolean** value type can only be one of two values, **True** or **False**; however, the underlying storage structure of the **Boolean** is 16 bits, or 2 bytes.

If you examine the underlying numerical value of the **Boolean**, you see that **False** is 0 and **True** is 1 for all .NET languages *except* Visual Basic. When you convert to or from these types to **Integers**, that's what you will get, for example, from a C# class.

For reasons that are not clearly known to me, Microsoft long ago decided that the value of **True** in Visual Basic 6 and earlier was equal to –1. The CLR, however, does not see it that way. To the CLR, **True** is 1 and **False** is 0 along with every other modern language in existence, and if you pass **True** to, say, C#, you'll see that **True** is passed through as 1.

During Beta 1 of Visual Basic .NET, Microsoft changed the value of **True** to be the same as all the other CLS-compliant languages—that is, "1." However, by Beta 2, it was changed back to –1 because half a million VB gurus threatened to burn down Redmond, WA (there's more legacy VB code than pollen in this world). You can, however, avoid a lot of confusion by just writing code with the reserved word **True** and avoid code that tests the numerical value—an old-fashioned idea that has, in any event, long outlived its usefulness in modern software development (see "Avoid Magic Numbers" later in this chapter and the section on Enumerations in Chapter 8).

Code examples for this value type can be found throughout the book; however, **Boolean** is the prime value type used in the logical operator expressions discussed in the next chapter on operators, and Chapter 6 with conditional statements such as **If** and **While**.

Literal Notation

A literal is a textual "decorator" that represents a particular value type and it forces the compiler to treat the object as that particular type. Literals perform a similar function to the Type Characters discussed earlier in this chapter. Literal decorators are available for **Boolean**, **Integer**, **Double**, **String**, **Char**, and **Date**. **Nothing** is a special literal (albeit it does not provide a decorator symbol); it is not considered to have a type and is convertible to all types in the type system. When converted to a particular type, it is the equivalent of the default value of that type. The following syntax describes literal usage:

Literal ::= BooleanLiteral | NumericLiteral | StringLiteral | CharacterLiteral | DateLiteral | Nothing

NumericLiteral ::= IntegerLiteral | FloatingPointLiteral

Boolean

BooleanLiteral ::= **True** | **False**

Integer

IntegerLiteral ::= IntegralLiteralValue [IntegralTypeCharacter]

IntegralLiteralValue ::= IntLiteral | HexLiteral | OctalLiteral

IntegralTypeCharacter ::=
ShortCharacter |
IntegerCharacter |
LongCharacter |
IntegerTypeCharacter |
LongTypeCharacter

ShortCharacter ::= **S**

IntegerCharacter ::= **I**

LongCharacter ::= **L**

IntLiteral ::= Digit+

HexLiteral ::= **& H** *HexDigit+*

OctalLiteral ::= **& O** *OctalDigit+*

Digit ::= 0 | 1 | 2 | 3 | 4 | 5 | 6 | 7 | 8 | 9

HexDigit ::= 0 | 1 | 2 | 3 | 4 | 5 | 6 | 7 | 8 | 9 | A | B | C | D | E | F

OctalDigit ::= 0 | 1 | 2 | 3 | 4 | 5 | 6 | 7

Floating-Point

FloatingPointLiteral ::=
FloatingPointLiteralValue [*FloatingPointTypeCharacter*] |
IntLiteral FloatingPointTypeCharacter

FloatingPointTypeCharacter ::=
SingleCharacter |
DoubleCharacter |
DecimalCharacter |
SingleTypeCharacter |
DoubleTypeCharacter |
DecimalTypeCharacter

SingleCharacter ::= **F**

DoubleCharacter ::= **R**

DecimalCharacter ::= **D**

FloatingPointLiteralValue ::=
IntLiteral . *IntLiteral* [*Exponent*] |
. *IntLiteral* [*Exponent*] |
IntLiteral Exponent

Exponent ::= **E** [*Sign*] *IntLiteral*

Sign ::= + | -

String Literals

StringLiteral ::= " [*StringCharacter*+] "

StringCharacter ::= < *Character* except for " > | ""

Character Literals

CharacterLiteral ::= " *StringCharacter* " **C**

Date Literals

DateLiteral ::= **#** [*Whitespace+*] [*DateValue*] [*Whitespace+*] [*TimeValue*]
[*Whitespace+*] **#**

DateValue ::= *MonthValue DateSeparator DayValue DateSeparator YearValue*

DateSeparator ::= **/** | **-**

TimeValue ::= *HourValue* [**:** *MinuteValue*] [**:** *SecondValue*] [*Whitespace+*] [*AMPM*]

MonthValue ::= *IntLiteral*

DayValue ::= *IntLiteral*

YearValue ::= *IntLiteral*

HourValue ::= *IntLiteral*

MinuteValue ::= *IntLiteral*

SecondValue ::= *IntLiteral*

AMPM ::= **AM** | **PM**

If you are writing code with **Option Strict** set to **Off** you do not need to declare the type of the literal value in your variable or constant declaration. The following code is an example of an implicit initialization of the variable's value to the literal value of 4 minus the declaration of the type:

```
Public myValue = 4
```

The problem with the preceding line of code, however, is that the compiler has no guidance to what "type" of value it is dealing with. In this case, it could be any of the ordinal or integer types, and the compiler will make it the default of **Integer**.

You can override the default with a literal type identifier that either encloses the value or is appended to it. For example, the default value type of **myValue** is **Integer** but we can override this by appending the literal notation character for the **Short** value type to the value as follows:

```
Public myValue = 4S
```

What you gain out of coding like this is speed, but you lose readability and a measure of self-documentation that comes with setting **Option Strict** to **On**.

Some experts who build classes their consumers are very unlikely to fiddle with believe that coding with literal values has its uses. For example, if you were to create a class that provides a large amount of constant values for a particular application, the following constant literal declaration would be acceptable:

```
Public Const BeginDate = #01/01/01# 'Date
Public Const EndDate = #12/31/99# 'Date
Public Const BeginTime = #11:59:59 AM# 'Time
Public Const FirstItem = 1% 'Integer
Public Const LastItem = 134443943789503723941D 'Decimal
```

The last item in the preceding code is worth a note. Even with **Option Strict** set to **On**, the value causes an overflow error because the compiler thinks the value is a **Long**. You will have to force the value to be taken as a **Decimal**, which can hold such a large number. The same applies with **Integer** division. Dividing by zero normally causes an **OverflowException** because the compiler defaults to **Integer** division. A **DivideByZeroException** would only arise if a **Decimal** were divided by zero (10D / 0).

Table 4-13 lists the value types that can take literal decorators, the respective literal type identifier, and the literal type character.

Some literals, however, require their targets to be quoted, such as the **Char** literal (C), as shown in Table 14-13. **Boolean** and **Byte** cannot take literal identifiers.

Data Type	Identifier or Enclosures	Literal and/or Usage
Char	"character"	C, "A"C
Date	#	#01/01/01#
Decimal	@	D, 234234324@
Double	#	R, 400.55#
Integer	%	I, 300I, 300%, or nothing
Long	&	L
Short	(none)	S, 4S
Single	!	F, 4.1S
String (Character)	""	"there you are"

Table 4-13.   *Value Type Literal Identifiers and their Respective Literal Type Character*

Type Conversion

Types can be converted from one type to another. This chapter, however, deals specifically with the conversion of one base value type to another. For example, you can convert from a **Short** to an **Integer**, from an **Integer** to a **Long**, and so on. The language provides several mechanisms for cast and conversion procedures.

When you convert from a smaller value type to a type that can represent more bytes of data, the old value is placed in a wider memory space (for example, 32 bits/4 bytes to 64 bits/8 bytes). This is called a *widening conversion*. The widening process does not generally cause data loss, as demonstrated in the earlier cola bottle analogy.

Converting from a larger value type to a type that has a smaller data structure is known as a *narrowing conversion*. The narrowing process might cause data loss and it might fail outright and result in an exception. After all, the cola bottle about which we spoke earlier might be half full.

Depending on the conversion, the code might automatically make the conversion for you without any trouble or requiring an explicit conversion function. This is known as an *implicit* conversion. A good example of such a conversion is declaring a **Decimal** that can easily fit the **Long** value type. If no decimal point is used with the number, the compiler will automatically convert to the **Long** because it uses fewer resources. The following code illustrates a common form of implicit or automatic conversion:

```
Dim myNumber As Integer = 10
Console.WriteLine(myNumber)
```

Here the variable **myNumber** of value type **Integer** is declared and represents the value 10. The **Console** class can write text to the command line using the **WriteLine** method and, in this case, implicitly converts the **Integer**'s declare value to a **String**. This implicit conversion takes place in the method, and you do not need to explicitly provide a cast function to perform the conversion to show the text. In other words, the following code is not necessary:

```
Dim myNumber As Integer = 10
Console.WriteLine(Convert.ToString(myNumber))
```

Another example:

```
Dim myNumber As Short   = 10
Dim ourNumber As Integer = myNumber
```

Here the declare is for a **Short** of value 10. The variable **ourNumber** is assigned to **myNumber** without any problems even though they are different types.

Setting **Option Strict** to **On**, however, will force you to use a cast function, even if a safe conversion can be made. This code, for example, will compile with **Option Strict Off:**

```
Dim myNumber As Integer = 10
Dim yourNumber As String = "34.54"
Dim ourNumber As Double = yourNumber / myNumber
```

But **Option Strict On** will raise an objection (refer to the section "Compiler Option Directives" earlier in this chapter) and will tell you that "Option Strict On disallows implicit conversions from 'String' to 'Double'." You will have to change the code to read as follows:

```
Dim yourNumber As Single = 34.54
```

or convert the value as follows:

```
Dim ourNumber As Single = Convert.ToSingle(yourNumber) / myNumber
```

Table 4-14 lists the safe conversions that can automatically or implicitly take place between the elemental value types, from smaller to larger (or narrow to wider), including point types and unsigned types. These are all widening conversions.

From	To[*]
Byte	Byte, Short, Integer, Long, Single, Double, Decimal, Object
Short	Short, Integer, Long, Single, Double, Decimal, Object
Char	Char, Object
Integer	Integer, Long, Single, Double, Decimal, Object
Long	Long, Single, Double, Decimal, Object
Single	Single, Double, Object
Double	Double, Decimal, Object
Decimal	Decimal, Object

*Unsigned and non-CLS-compliant value types apply.

Table 4-14. *Safe Conversion and Target Value Types*

Although automatic conversion can speed up your development, it is not always possible. Sometimes you will need to perform a narrowing conversion, or need to convert from an ordinal value type to a **Char**, **String**, or **Boolean**. To convert to and from various types, Visual Basic .NET provides you with a number of explicit cast functions, such as **CBool** and **CChar**.

Table 4-15 lists the cast functions that can be accessed from the Microsoft.VisualBasic namespace, which implements the classic VB conversion functions. The table also lists the modern framework conversion methods, which are accessed via the **Conversion** class. The syntax is as follows:

CastExpression ::=
CType (*Expression* , *TypeName* **)** |
CastTarget **(** *Expression* **)**

   CastTarget ::=
CBool | **CByte** | **CChar** | **CDate** | **CDec** | **CDbl** |
CInt | **CLng** | **CObj** | **CShort** | **CSng** | **CStr**

Classic Function	Conversion Class	Return Type
CBool	ToBoolean	Boolean
CByte	ToByte	Byte
CChar	ToChar	Char
CDate	ToDateTime	DateTime
CDbl	ToDouble	Double
CDec	ToDecimal	Decimal
CInt	ToInteger	Integer
CLng	ToLong	Long
CObj	ToObject	Object
CShort	ToShort	Short
CSng	ToSingle	Single
CStr	ToString	String
CType	ChangeType	Object

Table 4-15.   *Classic VB Conversion Functions and Framework Conversion Methods*

Here are more examples of code using the cast functions and the conversion methods:

```
Dim myNumber As Integer = 0
Dim booHoo As Boolean = CBool(myNumber)
Console.WriteLine(booHoo)
```

"False" is written to the console in the above example (by the way, the default value of **Integer** *is* 0).

Depending on your application's target platform, it might be safer to use the **Convert** class's methods instead of the classic Visual Basic cast functions (or any other cast functions wrapped for .NET usage). Your code will also be more palatable to other .NET languages, like C#. On the other hand, there might be a tradeoff in performance, because the call to one of **Convert**'s methods is not necessarily faster than the classic cast function.

In addition to the **Convert** class methods listed in Table 4-16 are a number of additional framework type-handling methods that are also accessible from the **Convert** class, such as **ChangeType** and **ISDBNull**.

Working with Variables and Constants

In the average life of an application, it is not uncommon, for example, to find a similar expression to the following in an application:

```
Private discount As Integer
Private total, amount As Double
'. . .
discount = 10
amount = 56.85

'Compute the discount percent
total = (amount * discount) / 100
```

This little "algorithm" computes two types of numbers—**Integer**s and **Double**s. As you know, an **Integer** is a data type that represents a whole number, an ordinal. A **Double**, on the other hand, represents fractions, a double-precision floating-point value, which in this example is holding the value 56.85. But **discount** and **total** have something in common. They are both *variables*.

The variable reserves a place in memory where its value is placed and where it can be accessed by the processor. In the preceding highly scientific example, the variable allocates 4 bytes of memory for the **Integer discount**, which may be any number between -2,147,483,648 and 2,147,483,648 and just happens to be 10. The variables

amount and **total** allocate 8 bytes each for a **Double**, which can be any number or fractional in a wide range of possibilities. The syntax for variable declaration is as follows:

VariableMemberDeclaration ::=
[*Attributes*] [*VariableModifier+*] [**Dim**] *VariableDeclarators LineTerminator*

VariableModifier ::= *AccessModifiers* | **Shadows** | **Shared** | **ReadOnly** | **WithEvents**

VariableDeclarators ::=
VariableDeclarator |
VariableDeclarators , VariableDeclarator

VariableDeclarator ::=
VariableIdentifiers [**As** *TypeName*] |
VariableIdentifier
[**As** [**New**] *TypeName* [**(** *ArgumentList* **)**]] [= *VariableInitializer*]

VariableIdentifiers ::=
VariableIdentifier |
VariableIdentifiers , VariableIdentifier

VariableIdentifier ::= *Identifier* [*ArrayNameModifier*]

Variable Initializers

VariableInitializer ::= *RegularInitializer* | *ArrayElementInitializer*

Regular Initializers

RegularInitializer ::= *Expression*

Without such a means of classifying, naming, and locating various types and their values, we would not be able to do much more with our computers besides $1 + 1 = 2$. Remember, computers store these values in Base 2, but in order for us to work with them, we have to dress them up in a variety of wrapping paper, with specific storage spaces and treatment instructions. Variable values can change at any time during execution, unless they are explicitly modified as read-only.

Constants are like variables and are declared in similar fashion. But, as the name implies, their values remain constant from the time they are initialized to the time they are removed from memory when the application or algorithm terminates. You do not have to declare constants read-only, which makes your code easier to read. The syntax for constant declaration is as follows:

ConstantMemberDeclaration ::=
[*Attributes*] [*ConstantModifier+*] **Const** *Identifier* [**As** *TypeName*] =
ConstantExpression LineTerminator

ConstantModifier ::= *AccessModifiers* | **Shadows**

Both variable and constant fields are private by default (see the section, "Keeping Data Private").

The following code demonstrates the declaration of a constant and the usage for such a declaration:

```
Const num As Integer = 100
Const lightSpeed As Long = 186355 'lightspeed is always constant
Dim feb As Integer = 28 'The number of days in February is not always 28
Const September As Integer = 30 'but there should always be 30 in September

Public Sub IncrNum()
  num = num + 1 'cannot happen because num is a constant
End Sub

Public Sub FlightTime()
  warpTime = warp * lightSpeed
End Sub
```

The first example may be a bad choice for a constant because the value of **num** needs to be changed. The call to the method **IncrNum** trashes the application. The second choice, **lightSpeed**, is an excellent choice for a constant because the speed of light is itself a constant that cannot change. Declaring **feb** as a variable is a good idea because the number of days in February changes from time to time. The number of days in September, on the other hand, is constantly 30. Constants are read-only values and can be used in place of literal values.

A variable is defined in your code with a name, the identifier, the data type it represents, and a value. Here's an example of the minimum declaration of a variable in Visual Basic .NET:

```
Dim myNumber = 1
```

The preceding line of code will compile and work fine as long as declaration and semantics checking are turned off, by setting both **Option Explicit** and **Option Strict** to **Off**. The reason it compiles is that the compiler can justify, by the initial value of 1, that the variable **myNumber** refers to an object "an **Integer**" with a value of 1. The compiler then keeps its fingers crossed and hopes for the best. In this simple case, nothing untoward happens and the code processes fine. However, this is not a very safe way of writing code, nor is it practical (see the "Compiler Option Directives" section earlier in this chapter, and the sections on late binding in Chapters 9 and 14). Switch both compiler options to **On** and you will notice the errors reported and that the compiler will continue only with the strongest of objections.

The code can be fixed with the following changes:

```
Dim myNumber As Integer = 1
```

This line of code adds a slew of characters to the declaration but it now represents a safe and fully declared variable called **myNumber**, which is declared "**As**" an **Integer**, the most widely used of the built-in data types. The formal syntax is as follows:

[*Attributes*] [*VariableModifier+*] [**Dim**] *VariableDeclarators LineTerminator*

Notice in the middle of the syntax the word **Dim**. **Dim** is the fundamental keyword for declaring a variable of a type, assigning it a value, and directing the compiler to allocate storage space for it. While **Dim** can be used almost everywhere in your code, you must further define the access level and thus "visibility" of the variable, or anything will be able to target the field data—an undesirable situation. **Dim**, however, is not used to declare constants, either within a method or anywhere else.

Also important to notice in the preceding declaration of **myNumber** is that the value is immediately assigned. This is known as *dynamic assignment*, which will be discussed further shortly. This immediate assignment or initialization, so to speak, is preferred over the longer syntax, which is as follows:

```
Dim myNumber As Integer
myNumber = 1
```

In addition, variable access varies according to its declaration space, where it is declared, and the context in which it is declared. In other words, declaring a variable at the class or module level is very different from declaring a variable inside a method block—within its declaration space. Also, the **Dim** keyword is automatically removed from class-level variables declared with the access modifiers. However, **Dim** is required for any declarations inside method blocks.

The following access modifiers can be applied to variables of the base data types:

- **Public** Variables declared as **Public** are visible from everywhere and thus become globally accessible even outside of the class in which they are declared. You cannot declare a **Public** variable inside the method declaration space and implementation.

- **Protected** Variables declared as **Protected** can only be accessed from within the class in which they are declared and from derived classes. You cannot declare a **Protected** variable inside the method declaration space and implementation.

- **Friend**   Variables declared as **Friend** can be accessed from the outside world but only from other classes of the assembly, which are classes that make up the application. You cannot declare a **Friend** variable inside the method declaration space and implementation.

- **Protected Friend**   Variables declared as **Protected Friend** are afforded the same protection as **Friend** access. The difference, however, is that you can also access these variables from derived classes. You cannot declare a **Protected Friend** variable inside the method declaration space and implementation.

- **Private**   Variables declared **Private** are only accessible within their declaration space. You cannot declare a **Private** variable inside the method declaration space and implementation because the variable is implicitly private.

- **Static**   Variables declared **Static** can be used in the implementation of methods and maintain their values even after the method has been processed. **Static** variables cannot be declared at the class level and cannot take **Shared** or **Shadows** as access modifiers.

- **Shared**   Variables modified with **Shared** are technically global variables and can thus be accessed from any class or file. You cannot declare a **Shared** variable inside the method declaration space and implementation.

- **Shadows**   Variables inherited from a base class can be identically redeclared in the derived class with the **Shadows** modifier, which does not affect the accessibility provided in the base declaration. In other words, if a base variable is declared **Private**, it remains **Private** in the shadowed declaration. You cannot declare a variable modified with **Shadows** inside the method declaration space and implementation.

- **ReadOnly**   Variables declared as **ReadOnly** cannot be changed by any local or derived process. The values these variables hold are thus constant. However, these variables can be declared with any access modifier, such as **Private**, and can be additionally modified with both the **Shared** and **Shadows** facility. You cannot declare a **ReadOnly** variable inside the method declaration space and implementation.

Note *See also Chapters 8 and 9 for additional specific variable declaration requirements.*

The scope of the preceding access and usage modifiers seems to be blurry at first glance, but they do have specific application.

Note *The use of the keyword **Static** is rather confusing for variables that survive the termination of the methods in which they are declared. For the most part, the term universally refers to shared global data and methods, the equivalent of which is **Shared** in Visual Basic. See the discussion of the C# **BitShifters** class in Chapter 5 for an example of so-called static methods. The words "static" and "shared" are frequently interchanged in general discussion throughout this book.*

Constants are similarly declared with access and implementation modifiers. The following code declares a public constant:

```
Public Const maxWarp As Integer = 9
```

Variable and Constant Declaration Shorthand

The declarations for both constants and variables can take the dynamic initialization shortcut, as demonstrated earlier for variables. Rather than declaring or initializing the variable or constants on the second line, like this:

```
Const hisNumber As Integer
hisNumber = 1
```

you can immediately assign the value as demonstrated in the following code:

```
Const hisNumber As Integer = 10
Const herNumber As Integer = 5
Const aCoupleAs Integer = hisNumber / herNumber
```

You can use any expression that will yield a legal value to be assigned to the variable or constant. In the preceding code, **aCouple** is assigned a value computed from the product of the two earlier constants. The following code, assigning the result of some fancy function, is also perfectly legal for a variable or constant declaration *and* assignment:

```
Const familyNumber As Integer = Complex(Sqrt(aCouple.AtWork))
```

Another form of declaration shorthand lets you declare—but not initialize—more than one variable (declarator) in the same expression. The following code declares three variables, and each variable is assigned the default of 0 by the CLR:

```
Dim hisNumber, herNumber, itsNumber As Integer
```

Both of the following lines of code, however, are not legal:

```
Dim hisNumber, herNumber, itsNumber As Integer = 1
Const hisNumber, herNumber, itsNumber As Integer
```

In the preceding incorrect examples, the first line fails because you are not allowed to assign values to multiple declarators in the same declaration; each variable declaration must be separately declared and initialized. The second example fails because you are not allowed to declare multiple constants in the same declaration expression. The correct style for each declaration example is as follows:

```
Dim hisNumber As Integer = 1, herNumber As Integer = 2, myNumber As . . .
Const hisNumber As Integer = 1, herNumber As Integer = 2, itsNumber As . . .
```

Default Initialization

The Visual Basic .NET compiler can also provide default values for the various value types. These values are listed in Table 4-16 and are assigned if the declarations omit any initial value assignment in the declaration of a variable or constant.

Null

The **Null** constant is no longer supported in Visual Basic .NET. If you need to represent a null value, such as a null database field, use the **System.DBNull** class and its **Value** field.

The following code generates a type mismatch error:

```
Public Shadows Sub ShadowMethod(ByVal myArg As Integer)
  myArg = System.DBNull.Value
End Sub
```

The compiler will tell you that you cannot convert an **Integer** value to **DBNull**.

Value Type	Default Value
Numbers (**Integers**, **Bytes**, **Longs**, **Decimals** and so on)	0
Boolean	**False**
Char	Character 0 or hex 0x0000
Date	#01/01/0001 12:00:00AM#
String *	Null

*String is included here because it is used a lot as a primitive type. However, it is not in the strictest sense a value type but rather an immutable reference type (see Chapter 15).

Table 4-16.   *Default Initialization Values for Value Types*

Many Visual Basic functions also no longer return **Null**, as was the case with **CurDir**, **LCase**, **LTrim**, **Left**, **Right**, and so on. In cases where it is possible to receive the **DBNull.Value** field, like null database records, you should test null with the **IsDBNull** function, as follows:

```
If (Microsoft.VisualBasic.IsDBNull(jField)) Then
'Do what's necessary
End If
```

Occasionally, it is legitimate to work with a field, such as a database field, that does not represent a known value. Many databases understand an empty field, nothing but white space, as a value. A good example is the second address line in a table, which is often left "blank."

The **DBNull** class differentiates between a null value (a null object) and an uninitialized value (represented by **DBNull** and its **Value** field, which is a shared public value). When a table contains records with uninitialized fields, these fields will be assigned the **DBNull** value. (This class is also used in COM-.NET interoperation to distinguish between a **VT_NULL** variant, which is associated with a null object, and a **VT_EMPTY** variant, which is associated with the **DBNull.Value** instance. See Chapter 14, which discusses COM adaptation.)

You cannot equate **DBNull** with anything. It is also a singleton class, which means only one instance of this class can exist at any given time in your application. That sole instance represents the **DBNull.Value**. Data-intensive applications accessing SQL databases must use the **System.Data.SqlTypes** classes, which have inherent support for null values.

If you need to reference a **Null** constant and **Nothing** is not useful to you, you can create your own **Null** object as described in the discussion of the Null pattern in Chapter 13.

Keeping Data Private

Variables and constants are declared at the class level or scope for two main reasons. The first and most frequently used reason is to allow the variable or constant fields to be accessed by all members of the class, and composite classes. Access to the field is either direct from the class methods or via class properties. The data is thus global to the class.

The second reason a field is scoped to the class level is to allow it to be accessed externally. To make it available or visible to the outside world, the field must be declared **Public**, **Friend**, or **Protected Friend** (**Protected Friend** makes the field visible to derived classes). An example of such a public field is the read-only **Value** field of the **System.DBNull** class. The value lives inside a singleton class and thus the "null" value is available to anyone that needs it.

You may have other reasons to make a class's field public, but you should stick to the practice of keeping fields, and thus the data, private. The reason for keeping data fields hidden, and thus off limits, is that it makes your code easier to maintain—making it more robust and less prone to errors (which also is a reason why variable lifetimes should be kept as short as possible).

Note *Research has shown that hidden data can improve code robustness by a factor of four. Other benefits of hidden data include security and reentrance.*

When data fields are kept hidden, only a small number of changes need to be made in the class when the field is changed. Changes to the fields will no doubt affect the methods of the class, but they should only affect the methods of the class that encapsulates them, not any consumers of the class (besides, the less you hard-code to global fields, the easier your software will be to maintain; see Chapter 7).

If you need to expose values of an object to the consumers of the object, you can do so via properties (see Chapters 7 and 9). The property acts as a "gateway" that conveys data to and from the field and the external environment of the class. Properties are methods, so the interface and implementation of the property allow later improvements without having to change the way a consumer accesses the data.

The principle of keeping fields private or hidden is one of the central tenets in both structured and object-oriented engineering. It extends the principle of black box functions in the structured design age. In object-oriented engineering, information hiding is known as *encapsulation*. Encapsulation refers to the containment and hiding of not only data fields, but all class members, so we will return to the subject again in later chapters, particularly Chapter 7 on methods and Chapter 9 on classes and objects.

Encapsulation makes the classes easy to version because a field and a referencing property cannot be changed to a property while maintaining binary compatibility. The following code example illustrates the correct use of private or hidden instance fields with **Get** and **Set** property accessors:

```
Public Structure Trajectory

   Private xCoord As Integer
   Private yCoord As Integer

   Public Sub New(ByVal xArg As Integer, ByVal yArg As Integer)
      Me.xCoord = xArg
      Me.yCoord = yArg
   End Sub

   Public Property PositionX() As Integer
      Get
```

```
      Return xCoord
    End Get
    Set(ByVal Value As Integer)
      xCoord = Value
    End Set
  End Property

  Public Property PositionY() As Integer
    Get
      Return yCoord
    End Get
    Set(ByVal Value As Integer)
      yCoord = Value
    End Set
  End Property
End Structure
```

And the above structure can be accessed as follows:

```
Dim spaceT As New Trajectory()
Public Sub Location(ByVal aArg As Integer, ByVal bArg As Integer)
  spaceT.PositionX = aArg
  spaceT.PositionY = bArg
End Sub
```

It is good practice to expose a field to a derived class by using a **Protected** property that returns the value of the field. This is illustrated in the following code example:

```
Public Class MyBaseControl
  Private visible As Boolean
  Protected ReadOnly Property IsVisible() As Boolean
    Get
      Return visible
    End Get
  End Property
End Class
```

Use public static read-only fields or constants for object instances that expose data for a predefined role. In most cases, however, you should use the facilities of structures or enumerations as discussed in Chapter 8. See also the discussion on using Pascal case in the "Visual Basic .NET Mini Style Guide" section earlier in this chapter.

Scope

Variables and constants can be written in any block in a class, the class itself, composite classes, or in any method. When a variable (and that means constants, as well, from here forward unless noted otherwise) is declared in the class body—not within a method body—it is typically accessible to all other class methods without qualification or additional reference. We call this unfettered access the "scope" within which a variable can be accessed. Viewed another way, we can say that generally a variable is not accessible outside the scope in which it is declared.

The scope of a variable can range from the deepest or narrowest level, in a block of code such as an **If…Then** block (see Chapter 6) to the widest level in the open declaration space of the outermost class (see Chapter 9).

Variables declared at the class level and modified as **Public** are "global" variables and this implies public access to the variable from outside the class, even a considerable distance away. "Class variable" is probably a better choice to describe a so-called "global" variable that is not public. However, a variable that is declared within the confines of a method or a block is known as a "local variable." For example, the following blocks of code encapsulate the variable in the narrowest scopes, methods, and blocks:

```
Sub CheckScope
Dim narrow As Integer = 2 'narrow
  If narrow <= 3 Then
    Dim moreNarrow As Integer = 1 'narrower
  End If
End Sub
```

So three key variable scopes exist in a .NET class: the scope that is defined by a class, the scope defined by a method, and the scope defined by a nested block of code within a method (such as the **If…Then** construct shown in the preceding example). Also, variables declared in composite or inner classes are not accessible from the outer or container classes.

Composite class methods can also access the variables but need to qualify the access—through inheritance or variable reference. This is demonstrated in the following code as in the following code two "out-of-scope" code segments:

```
'Example 1
Class Class1
  Dim myVar As Integer = 4
```

```
    Class Class4 : Inherits Class1
      Sub Sub4()
        Debug.WriteLine(myVar) 'myVar is an inherited member
      End Sub
    End Class
End Class


'Example 2
Class Class1
  Dim myVar As Integer = 4
  Class Class4
    Sub Sub4()
      Dim C1 As Class1
      Debug.WriteLine(C1.myVar) 'myVar is a member of reference C1
    End Sub
  End Class
End Class


'Example 3
Class Class1
  Shared myVar As Integer = 4
  Class Class4
    Sub Sub4()
      Debug.WriteLine(myVar) 'myVar sees the shared variable of Class1
    End Sub
  End Class
End Class


'Example 4
Class Class1
  Dim myVar As Integer = 4
  Class Class4
    Shadows myVar As Integer
    Sub Sub4()
      Debug.WriteLine(myVar) 'myVar sees the shadow variable of Class1
    End Sub
  End Class
End Class
```

In the first example, the inner class, nested several classes deep, "sees" the variable **myVar** because the variable is inherited from **Class1**. In Example 2, **myVar** is seen through the reference variable to **Class1**, which is **C1**. In Example 3, **myVar** is seen by virtue of the visibility **Shared** modifier. And in Example 4, **myVar** is redeclared using the **Shadows** keyword.

The hierarchy of access is from the inner classes to the outer classes. In other words, the innermost class members have the potential to "see" all the variables of each encapsulating class, but the outer classes cannot see the variables of the inner classes.

If you need to work with a variable from an outer class at the class level of a composite class, then you need to redeclare the variables in the composite class with the **Shadows** keyword.

Variable and Constant Lifetimes

The scope of variables and constants, previously discussed, also provides the "lifetime" that the variable has after its declaration. The variable is created when its scope is entered, and this can happen in several ways. When a class is referenced, its scope is entered and this serves to create the variable. For example, in this code, **Dim ClassOf69 As New MyClass** serves to begin the lifetime for the variables declared within the class, at the class level. The lifetime ends when the object is disposed of. The same lifetime policy applies to both static classes as well as instances of a class—an object's lifetime.

Variables local to methods begin their lives when the method is activated or called, and end their lives when the method code completes. Each time that the method or class is referenced, the variable is reassigned its default or initialization value.

Also, while a variable can be declared anywhere in the class or method, the code that uses the method must proceed the declaration. The compiler will pick up the following code as an error that cannot be tolerated:

```
Debug.WriteLine(myValue)
Dim myValue As Integer = 5
```

The first line cannot possibly write the value of **myValue** to the output window because the variable has not yet been declared. It's not difficult to remember this rule; just think of the classic chicken-and-egg or horse-and-cart clichés. In general, all variables and constants at the class level should be declared at the top of the class, and all variables and constants in methods should be declared at the top of the method, just after the signature. It is also important to remember that parameter declarations are scoped to the method and thus their scope is no different to variables or constants declared within the method body (see Chapter 7).

Span

The distance between a declare in a class or a method and the code that references the data is often referred to as *span*. In the following example, the space between the **lastName** declare and the line of code that accesses it is three lines. Thus, we can say that the *span* is three lines.

```
Dim lastName As String
Dim firstName As String
Dim birthDate As Date
GetName(lastName)
```

You can compute the average span in a class to test for its readability. But why should you be concerned about span? The short answer is that it makes it easier to construct code and to read the code you construct. Declares that are not used until much later in a method, or class, force you to keep referring back to areas higher up in the unit to refer to the data in the field.

Note   *You can declare variables without providing the initial value, because the compiler will always provide the default initialization value. For example, if you declare an **Integer** without an initial value, the compiler will automatically assign it 0.*

Keeping Lifetimes Short

Keeping lifetimes short also helps to make code less buggy and easier to maintain. Variables that are "live" from the moment a class is instantiated to its death introduce more opportunities for bugs. The live variables also make the code harder to maintain, even if the data is encapsulated in private fields. You are forced to consider all class members and code as possibly misusing a variable, as opposed to localizing the access to one line, a few lines away from where it first declared, or inside the methods that use them (see Chapter 7 for more on method parameter lists, passing arguments and so on).

This is, however, a somewhat controversial subject, because one school of thought says that declaring class variables and constants is better than having to pass the data though methods like a game of rollerball. I personally prefer to keep the class-level variables to a minimum, and instead pass arguments to method fields. The fields are more hidden, more secure, and easier to maintain, and the code is easier to read. In short, this keeps the problem of "hard coding" to a minimum.

Nevertheless, if data needs to be live for the duration the instance is live, then instance data is perfectly reasonable. However, a good rule is to use read-only fields instead of properties where the value is a global constant. This pattern is illustrated in the following code example:

```
Public Structure Int32
  Public Const MaxValue As Integer = 2147483647
  Public Const MinValue As Integer = -2147483648
End Structure
```

Avoid Magic Numbers

Magic numbers are the literal numbers that appear out of nowhere in the middle of your code. Here is an example:

```
Dim alarm() As Integer = {}
Dim intI As Integer
  For intI = 0 To 40
    alarm(alarmValue) = 190
  Next intI
```

The number 40 here is a magic number. Magic numbers should be avoided for several reasons:

- **Code is harder to read**   In the preceding example, it's not immediately apparent why 40 is the limit.

- **Changes are hard to make and can break code more easily**   In the preceding example, the array length (40) can't be changed without changing the **For...Next** loop. The value 190 is also a magic number that can cause errors.

- **Code is less reliable**   Magic numbers like this force you to make changes in every method that relies on the magic number. By using a named constant that all interested items can refer to, you only need to make the changes in one place. The preceding code eliminates the magic number syndrome by using the **UBound** function, as follows:

```
Dim alarm() As Integer = {}
For intI = 0 To UBound(alarm)
  alarm(alarmValue) = Alarms.HighAlert
Next intI
```

In this example, the expression **0 To UBound(alarm)** eliminates the magic number, because code depends on the **UBound** of the array (its upper boundary) rather than the magic number, which becomes useless if the array size changes. See the section "Enumerations" in Chapter 8.

Observations

We broke ground in this chapter and exposed the fundamental foundations of all Visual Basic applications. What do we know? We know that a Visual Basic application is a collection of classes that interact with each other. A Visual Basic application can be one class or a class module, or it can be made up of many classes.

We know that Visual Basic is a language with a rich and diverse syntax and that it has very peculiar and unique lexical and idiomatic elements that set it apart from all other languages. We also know that Visual Basic, while maintaining syntax and a number of grammatical similarities to its predecessor, has also been fundamentally changed—rewritten in fact from the ground up—to allow it to perform as a first class member of the .NET Framework.

We investigated the base or fundamental types in this chapter, often referred to as primitive types. We investigated where they derive from, and how they are declared, accessed, and used. And we also saw that there are some very important differences between the fundamental types of Visual Basic 6 and Visual Basic .NET.

The most important observation is perhaps that a Visual Basic class consists of three critical spaces. The first space is the class declaration space which names the class, declares how it can be accessed, and states whether it inherits from any other class. The second space is the **Options** space. Here we see that you can choose to write code either with loose semantics and syntax or with tight semantics and syntax by toggling the **Option Strict** and **Option Explicit** directives to the **On** or **Off** position. The **Options** space must precede all other declarations and code. The third space is the Namespace declaration space. Here we see how namespaces and classes are referenced such that they can be accessed from within the implementation space of the class.

The next three chapters deal more specifically with class implementation. Chapter 5 extensively covers the use of operators; Chapter 6 covers flow and control constructs as well as conditional constructs; and Chapter 7 provides the means of accessing the functionality through the construction and provision of the methods of our classes.

VB .NET FUNDAMENTALS

The Complete Reference

Visual Basic .NET

Chapter 5

Visual Basic .NET Operators

Operators are to computer programming what nails, staples, glue, and studs are to carpentry. Without these small elements, there would be no way to prevent the various parts of our creations from falling apart. This is true of standard operators: the many languages that exist within and outside of the .NET Framework use the same standard operators even though their symbol usage and data processing may differ.

Even if you know your operators, the information in this chapter will be worthwhile to assimilate because Visual Basic introduces fresh topics. This is also the first chapter that mixes in some C# code for some interesting language *interop* possibilities. We delve into bit shifting and see examples of how to use the C# shift operators in VB projects. This chapter lays the foundation for many of the algorithms we tackle in later chapters.

Note *The word* interop *stands for interoperation. In the context above it relates to the interoperation of C# code with Visual Basic code, or interop with a Visual Basic application. The term is also used to express the interoperation of .NET (managed) code with unmanaged code such as COM components.*

What an Operator Does

An *operator* performs an operation on one or two *operands*: a *unary operator* executes an operation on one operand, a *binary operator* does so on two.

Unary operators use prefix or postfix notation against their operands.

If the operator comes before the operand, it is a prefix unary operator, as is demonstrated here:

operator operand

or in code as

+ X

where **X** is the operand.

If it comes after the operand—which is an uncommon occurrence—it is a postfix unary operator. Here's an example:

operand operator

or in code as

X++

(The above ++ is the C# .NET unary operator for incrementing the operand by 1. The Visaul Basic .NET equivalent is **X += 1** or **X -= 1**, which are unary in "nature" but are considered binary because the operator increments or decrements the value on the left with the value on the right. In this chapter, we will elucidate the significant differences between Visual Basic .NET and C# .NET operators.)

A *binary operator* performs an operation on more than one operand and uses *infix* notation, because the operator is positioned between the operands as follows:

operand operator operand

or in code as

X < Y

The *ternary conditional operator* (?:), which is used in many languages such as C#, J#, and JScript, is "shorthand" for the **If...Else** conditional construct discussed in the next chapter (If = ? . . . Else = :). If you ever plan to use C# or JScript, it helps to know about this operator, which we will exemplify in C# sample code in this chapter.

Operators return the values based on their functions and on the type of operand. For instance, if you add two integers, the + operator returns the result of the integer addition. Operators thus *evaluate to their results*.

The operator returns the type of value (known as *operator resolution*) for which it has been defined. When dealing with operands of different types, you need to be sure that the operator is going to return the type you expect.

The default behavior of the operator is as follows: operands that are wider or narrower than the range for which the operator is defined will be *narrowed* to the type the operator will return. Conversely, operands that are narrower than the type for which the operator has been defined will be *widened* to the type the operator will return (see also Chapter 4).

Note   *An operand can be a single value or an entire expression, which should be enclosed in parenthesis for clarity and to minimize bugs.*

This chapter will also classify operators into their specific function groups as follows:

- **Arithmetic Operators**   Operators that perform arithmetic functions on the operands—such as +, - ,or *
- **Relational Operators**   Operators that perform relational evaluation of the operands—such as Is, Like, <, >
- **Assignment Operators**   Operators that return a value and then assign the value to the operand—such as = and +=
- **Concatenation Operators**   Operators that combine the data of their operands and then return the new combined value—such as + and &
- **Bitwise Operators**   Operators that perform *bitwise* (acting on the bits) operations on numbers and then return the bit result

Numbering Systems Reviewed

This section discusses the numbering systems that programmers of all languages use. Understanding them is key not only to coding useful algorithms and solving mathematical problems, but also to writing analysis software, working with arrays, and writing sophisticated game programs. These systems are also applicable to any software that communicates down to the so-called metal in the world, where only combinations of 1s and 0s are recognized currency. As you may know, .NET makes extensive use of large numbers for security uniqueness, complex mathematics, and numerical operations.

Here are the fundamental numbering systems used in computer programming:

- **Binary (Base 2)**   This is the language computers use internally to represent bits. Binary means 2 and the only digits used are 1 and 0. Digit 1 is known as the high-order bit (one less than the base of 2) and 0 is known as the low-order bit.

- **Octal (Base 8)**   This system encompasses digits 0 through 7 (one less than the base of 8).

- **Decimal (Base 10)**   This familiar numbering system is used for writing integers. These are the standard numbers which use digits 0, 1, 2, 3, 4, 5, 6, 7, 8, 9 (9 is one less than the base of 10).

- **Hexadecimal (Base 16)**   This system employs the 10 digits of the decimal system plus the letters A through F.

The octal and hexadecimal (hex) numbering systems are popular in computer programming because it's easier to work with their numbers versus binary numbers, which can become very large. Today's 32-bit systems are rapidly yielding to 64-bit computers and software (arriving in 2002/2003), which makes it imperative to fully understand the octal and hexadecimal systems, especially the latter one. The following table demonstrates the differences among the four systems.

Binary	Octal	Decimal	Hexadecimal
0	0	0	0
1	1	1	1
High = 1	2	2	2
Base 2	3	3	3
	4	4	4
	5	5	5
	6	6	6

Binary	Octal	Decimal	Hexadecimal
7	7	7	7
High = 7	8	8
Base 8	9	9
	High = 9	A (10)
	Base 10	B (11)
		C (12)
		D (13)
		E (14)
		F (15)
		High = F (15)
		Base 16

The hexadecimal number system is the most complex because it requires 16 digits, the last 6 of which are the letters A through F. It is thus possible to have a "hex" number comprising just numbers (345), numbers and letters (4C26D), or just letters (DEEE).

Positional Notation

Each numbering system employs a *positional notation*, which describes the *positional value* of the digit. In the decimal system, we describe the digit positions as *ones, tens, hundredths, thousandths* and so on. However, it's easier to refer to large numbers in terms of the power to which they are raised, such as 10 to the 5th power.

Base 2, or binary position lingo, describes the value of the bits from left to right. The number 5 in binary is 101, so we say that a high-order bit is in the right-most position, which is the *ones position,* the 0 is in the *twos position,* and the left-most bit of 1 is in the *fours position.* As the number increases, the notation grows from the right to the left by the power of the base—1, 2, 4, 8, 16—and so on. Increasing or decreasing the number is known as *shifting*. By shifting the bit 1 left in the *ones position* to the *twos position,* we are raising the number by the power of 2, the base. Shifting three positions is the same as raising the number to shift by the power of 4, such as 2 to the 4th power.

The positional values for the octal numbering system increase by its base of 8. So for a number like 350, we say that the 0 is in the *ones,* 5 in the *eights,* and 3 in the *sixty-fours* position.

Hexadecimal numbers work the same way, but the positional values rise by the power of the base, 16—*1s, 16s, 256th* positions, respectively.

The following tables list the positional values in each number system.

Binary Number System: Base 2 (. . . 128, 64, 32, 16, 8, 4, 2, 1)

Digit	1	0	1
Position	Fours	Twos	Ones
Power of base	2^2	2^1	2^0

Octal Number System: Base 8

Digit	3	4	8
Position	Sixty-Fours	Eights	Ones
Power of base	8^2	8^1	8^0

Decimal Number System: Base 10

Digit	5	6	5
Position	Hundredths	Tens	Ones
Power of base	10^2	10^1	10^0

Hexadecimal Number System: Base 16

Digit	D	0	E
Position	256ths	Sixteens	Ones
Power of base	16^2	16^1	16^0

Converting from One System to Another

Now that you understand the various conventions for positional notation within each numbering system, it will be easy to convert from one number in a system to another and to perform conversions in your code. Let's first see how we convert from the familiar decimal system to binary, octal, and hexadecimal. We'll begin by converting the number 42 from the decimal system.

Converting From Decimal to Binary, Octal, and Hexadecimal

In order to convert to binary, first decide which high-positional value shown in the binary positions and powers chart above is higher than the number 42. Then stop at the smaller positional value. In other words, 128 and 64 are bigger than 42, so we would need to stop at 32. Now how many times can 32 go into 42 and what's the remainder? Write down the results in the grid as follows:

Position	32	16	8	4	2	1
Division	42/32	10/16	10/8	2/4	2/2	0/1
Result	1	0	1	0	1	0
Remainder	10	10	2	2	0	1

The number 42 divides by 32 once and leaves a remainder of 10. So we write 1 in the result row and 10 in the remainder row. Then working from left to right, we divide 10 by the next positional value, (10 / 16). The result is 0, so we carry the 10 to the next position. There we find that 8 can go into 10 once, with 2 left over. Write down 1 for the result and 2 for the remainder under the 8s column. Then we try to put 4 into 2, which doesn't work; thus, 0 is the result and the remainder 2 moves to the right. Since 2 goes into 2 exactly once, we enter 1 in the 2s columns and 0 in the 1s column. Our binary number—10 1010—is now in the result row of the grid.

The same technique works for converting from decimal to octal, as seen here in the octal grid:

Position	512	64	8	1
Division	N/A	N/A	42/8	2/1
Result	N/A	N/A	5	2
Remainder	N/A	N/A	2	0

The result is that decimal 42 is octal 52.
Let's do the same thing now for hex:

Position	4096	256	16	1
Division	N/A	N/A	42/16	10/1
Result	N/A	N/A	2	10?
Remainder	N/A	N/A	10	10

The hexadecimal system makes sense for large numbers; however, with the number 42 there could be a slight confusion. The last column leaves us with 10, which is A in the hex system. Thus, the hex result is 2A.

Converting From Octal and Hexadecimal to Binary

Converting from these systems to binary is straightforward. You simply place octal and hex value positions up against the binary value positions in a grid. For example, octal to binary works by placing the octal right-most value up against the 3-digit binary equivalent like this:

Position	101	010
Octal	5	2

This yields the binary result of 101 010, or 10 1010. The hex to binary works similarly up against a 4-digit column:

Position	0010	1010
Hex	2	A

Converting From Binary, Octal, and Hexadecimal to Decimal

When you encounter one of the "alternate" numbers in your code, you'll need to convert the numbers to decimal to present them to users or do math that requires you to work with the decimal system. You can easily write software that multiplies 2A by 2A, but chances are very slim that 6E4 will mean anything to your user.

The formula for converting to decimal is very easy and can be derived manually or in a grid. With binary values, simply multiply the binary digit (starting left to right) with its positional value and sum the results. For example, to arrive back at 42 from 10 1010, perform the following math:

$$(1*32=32) + (0*16=0) + (1*8=8) + (0*4=0) + (1*2=2) + (0*1=0) \text{ Answer: } 42$$

Octal to decimal works along the same lines. Multiply the number value by its positional value:

$$(8*5=40) + (2*1=1) \text{ Answer: } 42$$

and hex:

$$(2*16=32) + (A*1=10) \text{ Answer: } 42$$

Operator Precedence

For simple operations, the left operand is always evaluated first at run time. We say that the operators are "left associative," which means that the operations on the expressions are performed left to right.

However, when expressions contain more than one operator, the precedence of the operator, not the order of appearance, controls the order in which the expressions are evaluated. For example, in the arithmetic group, if the multiplicative (*) operator comes after the additive (+) operator in the sequence, the two operands that straddle the multiplicative operator are multiplied, and the result is added to the operand on the left of the additive operator. The following example proves this:

```
Dim x As Integer = 5
Dim y As Integer = 1
Dim Z As Integer = 2
Dim Answer As Integer
Answer = x + y * Z
Debug.WriteLine(Answer)
```

The answer is 7 because y * z is the first procedure, which returns 2; the 2 is then added to the 5 to yield 7. If the additive had taken precedence over the multiplicative, the answer would have been 12.

Table 5-1 lists the precedence of operators when evaluating expressions.

Class of Operator	Precedence of the operators in the class
Primary *	(x), x.y, foo(x), foo[x], x++, x--
Exponentiation	^
Unary	+, -
Multiplicative	*, /, \, Mod, +, -
Concatenation	&, +
Comparison	=, <>, <, >, <=, >=, Like, Is, TypeOf...Is
Logical	Not, And, Or, Xor, AndAlso, OrElse
Bitwise	And, Or, Xor
Miscellaneous	Or, OrElse, New, TypeOf

Table 5-1. *Operator Precedence Table (*The ++ or -- Unary Operators are Not Accessible in VB .NET)*

Changing Precedence Order with Parenthesis

You can change the order of operations by enclosing the expression you want to process first between parentheses. In the preceding example, if we had bracketed the operands around the additive operator, we would have gotten 12 as the return value:

```
Dim x As Integer = 5
Dim y As Integer = 1
Dim Z As Integer = 2
Dim Answer As Integer
Answer = (x + y) * Z
Debug.WriteLine(Answer)
```

Now 12 is the output to the Debug window. Can you work out why? This complex example

```
Dim Value As Double
Value = 3 * 10 / 3 ^ 2 + 10 - 11
Debug.Writeline(Value)
```

writes 2.33333333333333 to the Debug window. But this one

```
Dim Value As Double
Value = 3 * 10 / 3 ^ (2 + 10 - 11)
Debug.Writeline(Value)
```

writes 10 to the output window. Let's process the operations as a stack, moving from the first operation to the last:

Example 1:

1. $3 \wedge 2 = 9$ (exponentiation is the highest operator in the expression)
2. $3 * 10 = 30$ (multiplicative comes second)
3. $30 / 9 = 3.33$ (regular divisional comes next)
4. $3.33 + 10 = 13.33$ (+ comes before -, but with regular math this is benign)
5. $13.33 - 11 = 2.33$

Example 2:

1. $(2 + 10) - 11 = 1$ (the parenthetical operation processes first)
2. $3 \wedge 1 = 3$ (exponentiation comes before multiplicative)
3. $3 * 10 = 30$ (multiplicative comes next)
4. $30 / 3 = 10$ (the regular divisional comes after multiplicative)

Here is a short list of additional rules to remember:

- The math or arithmetic operators evaluate first, followed by comparison operators, then by logical operators.
- The concatenation operator (**&**) precedes all of the comparison operators, but it follows the mathematical operators.
- The comparison operators have equal precedence.

Unary Operators

There are three unary operators supported by Visual Basic: **+, -,** and **Not** (**Unary Plus, Unary Minus,** and **Unary Logical Not,** respectively). They are defined as follows:

- **Unary Plus**   The value of the operand
- **Unary Minus**   The value of the operand subtracted from zero
- **Unary Logical Not**   Performs logical negation on its operand. (This operator also performs bitwise operations on **Byte, Short, Integer,** and **Long** [and all enumerated types], which we'll discuss later in this chapter.)

Unary Plus is also the additive operator. However, the operator is "overloaded" to perform a concatenation function if the operands are discovered to be of type *string*. For example, the following code

```
Dim S As String = "what is "
Debug.WriteLine(S + "this")
```

writes "what is this" to the Debug window.

 Use the & symbol for concatenation because it makes code easier to read.

Unary Minus converts a positive number into a negative one. For instance, this simple math

```
x = 3 + -1
Debug.WriteLine(x)
```

writes 2 to the Debug window. However, it's the same thing as 3 minus 1.

The **Unary Logical Not** is different altogether. It can change a **Boolean** result (**False** becomes **True** or **True** becomes **False**). As mentioned earlier, it can also perform a bitwise comparison on a numeric expression. Here are the rules for the **Unary Not Boolean** expressions:

■ If the *Expression* is **False,** then the *Result* is **True**

■ If the *Expression* is **True**, then the *Result* is **False**

Here's an example:

```
Dim x As Integer = 5
Dim y As Integer = 1
Dim z As Boolean = True
If Not (x > y = z) Then
  Debug.WriteLine("True")
Else
  Debug.WriteLine("False")
End If
```

Normally, the result would be "True" to the debug window, but in the above case truth is **Not** true. The **Boolean** condition inside the parentheses (this entire expression is the operand) is reversed—in this case **True** is made **False**. See Chapter 6 for examples of using the **Not** operator in conditional statements, especially **Null If** conditionals. You will also learn about Logical Operators and Bitwise Operators later in this chapter.

Arithmetic Operators

The full complement of arithmetic operators is available to Visual Basic .NET. **Unary Plus** and **Unary Minus** can also be considered arithmetic operators, as shown in Table 5-2.

Arithmetic operators are straightforward in their performance; however, there are several delicate situations. When number crunching, it is possible to cause a number of system exceptions, such as an **OverflowException**—when the sum of two operands is outside the range that the operator returns (see Table 5-3). For example, **Byte** is a data type that can have a value from 0 to 255. In the following code, the sum of the two operands raises the **OverflowException**, because the type cannot hold 258.

```
Public Sub TryItOut()
  Try
    Dim num1 As Byte = 253
    Dim num2 As Byte = 5
    Debug.WriteLine(num1 + num2)
  Catch Except As OverflowException
    Debug.WriteLine("Bad Byte Math:  " & "num1 + num---" & Except.Message)
  End Try
End Sub
```

Note   *Debug statements are stripped from release builds so the Debug statement inside the Catch handler will not be executed. For more information on using Debug, see Chapter 17.*

Operator	Description	Action/Usage
+	Addition	*Value = Expression + Expression*
-	Subtraction	*Value = Expression − Expression*
*	Multiplication	*Value = Expression * Expression*
/ and \	Division	*Value = Expression / \ Expression*
Mod	Modulus (division returns only the remainder; % in J#, C# C++, etc)	*Value = Expression **Mod** Expression*
^	Exponentiation	*Value = Expression ^ Expression*

Table 5-2.   *Visual Basic .NET Arithmetic Operators*

Exception : ArithmeticException	Purpose
DivideByZeroException	To handle an exception raised when an attempt is made to divide a number by zero.
OverflowException	To handle an exception raised when the result overflows the range of the type (usually the result of an invalid cast or conversion).

Table 5-3.   *Arithmetic Exceptions*

 Tip

Try...Catch are the constructs for structured exception handling (SEH). If you are new to SEH you can jump to Chapter 7 for a short treatise on SEH or tackle Chapter 11 which specializes in this subject, but I would not worry too much about the SEH stuff just now.

Assignment Operators

These operators assign values to variables, which are the left operands of an assignment expression. The assignment operators come in two forms, simple and compound, as listed in Table 5-4.

Operator	Description	Action/Usage
=	Assignment	*Value = Expression*
+=	Addition/Concatenation assignment	*Variable += Expression*
-=	Subtraction assignment	*Variable -= Expression*
*=	Multiplication assignment	*Variable *= Expression*
/= and \=	Division assignment	*FloatingPointVariable /= Expression* *IntegerVariable \= Expression*
^=	Exponentiation assignment	*Variable ^= Expression*
&=	Concatenation assignment	*Variable &= Expression*

Table 5-4.   *Assignment Operators*

The simple assignment uses the equal sign to assign the operand on the right side to the operand on the left side. For example, the following code

```
X = 5
```

assigns the number 5 to the operand x.

The compound version assigns the result of a numeric operation specified by the operator to the left operand. The most useful of these compounds is the += operator, which increments the left operand by the value of the right one and then assigns the result back to the left operand. For example

```
Dim x As Integer = 5
x += 1
```

increments the value of x by 1, so the new value of x is 6. This operator is the equivalent of the C# unary increment/decrement operators, ++ and -- respectively. However, you are not limited to incrementing or decrementing by 1. The following code is also valid.

```
Dim x As Integer = 5
x += 5
Debug.WriteLine(x)
```

This equation prints 10 to the debug window. The *= operator would yield 25, the -= would yield 0.

Tip   *When you declare variables, you can use a shortcut to make your code more concise and readable by assigning the value of the variable in the same line as its declaration: Dim X As Integer = 5 is the same as Dim X As Integer, X = 5.*

Notice how the compound operators function in an example of the addition/concatenation operator (+=):

```
Dim firstname As String = "Donald "
Dim lastname As String = "Duck"
firstname += lastname
Debug.WriteLine(firstname)
```

This writes "Donald Duck" to the Output window.

When using the assignment equals compound, remember that if the expression is numeric, the operation will be addition. However, if the expression is a string, it will be concatenation.

You can also use the compounds with array operations. In this example, an array value is incremented by 1 using the += operator.

```
Dim t(5) As Integer
t(1) = 1
t(1) += 1
Debug.WriteLine(t(1))
```

The answer is 2.

Comparison Operators

The comparison, or relational, operators evaluate an expression on the right side of the equal sign and return **True** or **False** (**Boolean**), depending on the comparison, as seen in Table 5-5.

When comparing types, the following behaviors must be noted:

- With **Byte**, **Short**, **Integer**, and **Long** we compare the numeric (literal) values of the operands.

- With **Single** or **Double** we compare the operands according to the IEEE 754 (see sidebar on the following page).

- With **Decimal**s we compare the numeric values of the two operands.

- With **Boolean** values (**True** and **False**) compared for equality, the equals operator (=) will return **True** if both operands are either **True** or **False**. The **Not Equals** (<>) is the reverse.

- With **Date**s we compare the complete date and time values of the two operands.

- With **Char**s we compare the Unicode values of the operands.

- With **String**s the operators perform either binary or text comparison. The two options can be set using the **Option Compare** (**Binary | Text**) directive (see Option Directives, Chapter 4). Binary mode compares the numeric Unicode value of each character in the operands. If each is the same, it returns **True**. Text mode makes the comparison on the current culture in use in the application environment (see Chapter 4).

Operator	Description	Action/Usage
<	Less Than	*Expr1 < Expr2*
<=	Less Than or Equal To	*Expr1 <= Expr2*
>	Greater Than	*Expr1 > Expr2*
>=	Greater Than or Equal To	*Expr1 >= Expr2*
<>	Not Equals	*Expr1 <> Expr2*
=	Equals	*Expr1 = Expr2*

Table 5-5.   *Comparison Operators Supported in Visual Basic .NET*

IEEE 754

IEEE 754 is the IEEE's (pronounced eye-triple-E, the acronym of the Institute of Electrical and Electronics Engineers) standard for computer specifications for floating-point operations—representing binary floating-point arithmetic.

It governs how number formats are represented, basic floating-point operations, conversions, and applicable exceptions. Another standard, IEEE 854, extends the scope of 754 to include decimal arithmetic. We anticipate IEEE will merge these standards that guide software language architects in accessing the floating-point facilities in modern computer hardware.

According the IEEE, the latest version of the standard proposes the following: "[754] provides a discipline for performing floating-point computation that yields results independent of whether the processing is done in hardware, software, or a combination of the two. For operations specified in this standard, numerical results and exceptions are uniquely determined by the values of the input data, sequence of operations, and destination formats, all under programmer control."

In particular, IEEE 754 specifies how software languages should provide support for precision, underflow, overflow, and extended precision. Software languages like Visual Basic and C# look to IEEE 754 for implementing square-root functions and the like.

Concatenation Operator

The concatenation operator, represented by the ampersand (**&**), combines two string operands and returns a single string expression. The usage is

Value = operand & operand

Here is an example:

```
Dim X As String = "1"
Dim Y As String = "23"
Debug.WriteLine(X & Y)
```

The result of the operation X & Y writes "123" to the debug window.

When this operator encounters integer operands, it will convert the integers to strings. The conversion is safe because the process results in a widening cast. The + operator is implicitly overloaded to perform concatenation when it encounters strings for operands. To avoid ambiguity, concatenate strings using the **&** operator.

Logical Operators

Logical operators take **Boolean** (logical) operands and return the **Boolean** result of their operations. Logical operators (see Table 5-6—logical **And**, **Or**, and **Xor**) can be confused with their bitwise counterparts because they have the same operator symbol. Classic VB documentation—as opposed to that of every other language—merged the two operator functions. Microsoft tried to introduce a more "logical" separation of these functions, but met with resistance from the VB community. Thus Visual Basic .NET remains "different" than the other .NET languages.

Bitwise operators return bits—they do not return **True** or **False**. It is important to understand and differentiate between the functions of logical and bitwise operators: both are critical in software development. Here we'll examine logical operators; we'll discuss bitwise ones in the next section.

> **Note**   *The operator is overloaded to return bits in Visual Basic .NET when it is required to operate on numbers.*

The key to understanding logical operations is to forget about numbers and bits. Think only in terms of **True** or **False**, which represent the types of operands and the

Logical Operators	Operation	C#, J#, or JScript
And (logical And)	Returns **True** if both operands are **True**—otherwise **False**	&&
Or (logical Or)	Returns **True** even if one of the operands is **True**—returns **False** only if both are **False**	|
Xor (logical Xor)	Returns **False** if both operands are either **True** or **False**—otherwise it returns **True**	!
AndAlso	Returns **True** if both operands are **True** returns **False** if only the first operand is **True** **but if the first operand is False**, the second operand is not evaluated and **True** is returned	**
OrElse	If the first operand is **True**, the second is not evaluated and the operator returns **True** Returns **False** if both are **False** and **True** if only the second operand is **True**	**

Table 5-6.   *Logical Operators and Their Functions, and C# and JScript Equivalents (** Not Applicable—All Logical Operators in JScript or C# Short-Circuit)*

return type of the operator. For example, in the following code, a logical **And** operation is performed on two **Boolean** operands:

```
Dim catlovesdog As Boolean = False
Dim doglovescat As Boolean = True
Dim weirdromance As Boolean
weirdromance = catlovesdog And doglovescat
Debug.WriteLine(weirdromance)
```

The operator **And** returns **False** here because the **Cat** operand is **False** (cats are unimpressed with dogs). If the **Cat** operand were initialized **True**, the operator would have returned **True**. Let's look at the different types of logical operators and their functions in Table 5-7, then we can examine how to use them.

Logical And, Or, and Xor

If cat loves dog	And dog loves cat	is love in the air?
True	True	True
True	False	False
False	True	False
False	False	False
If cat loves dog	**Or dog loves cat**	**is love in the air?**
True	True	True
True	False	True
False	True	True
False	False	False
If cat loves dog	**Xor dog loves cat**	**is love in the air?**
True	True	False
True	False	True
False	True	True
False	False	False
If cat loves dog	**AndAlso dog loves cat**	**is love in the air?**
True	True	True
True	False	False
False	Irrelevant	False
If cat loves dog	**OrElse dog loves cat**	**is love in the air?**
True	Irrelevant	True
False	True	True
False	False	False

Table 5-7.   *Conditions upon which Logical Operators Return True or False*

Short-Circuit Logical Operators

The **AndAlso** and **OrElse** are new short-circuit operators introduced to Visual Basic .NET. If you use **And**, the runtime will evaluate the entire expression, even if the first operand is **False**. Compare this to the **And** example in the preceding table—if the first operand is **False**, the operator returns **False**, even if the second one is **True**; thus you don't need to evaluate the second operand and the procedure "short circuits" the comparison. The best way to understand this is through code.

```
Module LogicTest
  Sub Main()
    Dim x As Integer = 1
    Dim y As Integer = 1
    If A(x) Or B(y) Then
      Debug.WriteLine("x= " & CStr(x) & ", y = " & CStr(y))
    End If

    If A(x) OrElse B(y) Then
      Debug.WriteLine("x= " & CStr(x) & ", y = " & CStr(y))
    End If
  End Sub

  Function A(ByVal v1 As Integer) As Boolean
    v1 = v1 + 1
    Return True
  End Function

  Function B(ByVal v1 As Integer) As Boolean
    v1 = v1 + 1
    Return True
  End Function
End Module
```

Copy and paste this code into Visual Studio or build and run the **LogicTest** console application in the Vb7cr solution (see the Introduction for instruction for downloading this demo). Insert a break point in the code at the following line:

```
If A(x) Or B(y) Then
```

When execution stops at the above breakpoint step into the code using the F11 key. You can now observe the short-circuit in action. The standard **Or** causes the compiler to invoke both methods **A** and **B**, but as you step into **OrElse** you will notice that method **B** does not get invoked.

Note   *See the project **LogicTest** in the Vb7cr solution.*

Originally, all Visual Basic .NET logical operators short-circuited, but in Beta 2 they reverted back to the way they operate in VB 6. We'd prefer to see "**Option Classic Off**" let "seventh generation" Visual Basic programmers choose the modern operators found in the other .NET languages.

Bitwise Operators

When your operands are numbers instead of **Boolean** values, **And**, **Or**, and **Xor** perform bitwise operations on the operands instead of logical ones. Instead of returning **True** or **False**, they return either a 1 or a 0 depending on the outcome. For example, in the following statement

expression1 **And** *expression2*

the operator returns 1 if both operands are 1; but it returns 0 if one of the operands is 0. However, the following statement

expression1 **Or** *expression2*

returns 1 even if only one of the operands is 1. It will return 0 only if both are 0. In the first example, nothing happens unless both operands are 1. This is fundamental electrical engineering: you have a gate and the circuit will be completed only if both the anode and the bnode are closed. In the second example above, only one operand *or* the other needs to be 0 to trigger the action.

You can use the bitwise **Not** operator with numerical expressions to negate the return value provided by the operator. The following rules apply to using **Not**:

- If the bit is 0, then **Not** makes the bit result 1.
- If the bit is 1, then **Not** makes the bit result 0.

Here's how to use this:

```
Dim x As Integer = 5
Dim y As Integer = 1
Dim z As Integer
z = (Not x)
Debug.WriteLine(z)
z = (Not y)
Debug.WriteLine(z)
```

The value returned is the negation of the bits that represent binary **x** and **y** (1s and 0s) ; thus, for x the value returned is –6 and for y it's –2. Looking at this in binary as demonstrated earlier, 5 is expressed as 00000101. Negating the bits turns the binary version of 5 into the following 11111010, which is –6 in decimal. This would be clearer seen in the following binary chart negating the bits representing 5 (Not 1 is 11111110, which is -2) :

| 5 = | 0 | 0 | 0 | 0 | 0 | 1 | 0 | 1 |
| -6 = | 1 | 1 | 1 | 1 | 1 | 0 | 1 | 0 |

Note   *See the **BitShifters** demo later in this chapter which can do the conversion for you.*

Table 5-8 shows the bitwise operators and the value they return.

Flag Sets

Bitwise operations are useful for manipulating flag sets (also known as bit sets, bit maps, bit tables, flag tables, or flag maps) for state management in a variety of applications and algorithms. You'll find many opportunities for employing flag sets, such as components, visual controls, state machines, schedulers, and database applications.

Bitwise Operators	Operation	C# or JScript
And (bit And)	Returns 1 if both operands are 1—otherwise 0. Valid types are **Byte**, **Short**, **Integer**, **Long**, or enumerated types.	&
Or (bit Or)	Returns 1 if either is 1—otherwise 0. Valid types are **Byte**, **Short**, **Integer**, **Long**, or enumerated types.	|
Xor (bit Xor)	Returns 1 if either operand is 1, 0 if both are 1, and 0 if both are 0. Valid types are **Byte**, **Short**, **Integer**, **Long**, or enumerated types.	^
Not (bit Not)	If the bit of an operand = 0, then bit in result = 1. If the bit of an operand = 1, then bit in result = 0.	~ (complement)

Table 5-8. *Bitwise Operators and the Values They Return; the C# and JScript Equivalents*

In computer telephony, PBX, or call-processing applications, flag sets are used to indicate the current state of a message (fax mail, email, or voice mail) or phone extensions (on-hook, busy, call waiting, signed off/on). A typical flag set for messages could be declared as follows:

- Accessed: No = 0, Yes = 1
- Archived: No = 0, Yes = 1
- Deleted: No = 0, Yes = 1

As soon as a mailbox receives a message, flags corresponding to its state are established in a database. All new messages would be enumerated so that the person accessing the mailbox would hear something like "you have 5 new messages." Then as soon as it is accessed, the system changes its accessed bit to 1 and the new value is saved to the database. The following grid represents the flag table for a message after it has first been retrieved—the accessed bit it set to 1.

Flag	Bit
Accessed	1
Archived	0
Deleted	0

The next prompt would be "you have 4 new messages and 1 accessed message." The user can do one of two things with it: archive it—its flag would be set to 1 and the value saved to the database—or delete it—its flag would be changed to 1. If the user deletes it, the dead-message collector would see that it's ready for trash, as illustrated here:

Flag	Bit
Accessed	1
Archived	0
Deleted	1

What would happen if the user decided to trash the message without first hearing it? How do you code the decision not to delete the message? You could use a conditional construct to check the flag value and then decide to delete or not. Or, you could perform various bitwise operations on the flags to test the message states rather than **Boolean** operations or **If** conditionals on the actual value.

The **GetMessages** application shown next loads the flag set for a message and then performs bitwise comparisons on the flags to control execution and flow. (See Chapters 13 and 14, which provide examples of state machines.) Besides exemplifying bitwise operators, this code uses **If Else** conditionals, **Select Case** construction, and nested exception handlers extensively. Chapter 6 covers the **If** conditional and **Select Case** and Chapters 7 and 11 cover exception handling.

```
Module GetMessages

  Dim menuChoice As String
  Dim inPut As String 'string to be blasted to bits
  Dim outPut As Integer
  Dim Completed As Boolean = False
  'Flags representing flag fields table for a message

  Dim messageFlag As Integer
  Dim isAccessed As Integer
  Dim isArchived As Integer
  Dim isDeleted As Integer
  Dim newMessage As Integer

  Sub Main()

    While Not Completed
      Console.WriteLine("                         ")
      Console.WriteLine("-----------MENU------------")
      Console.WriteLine("---------------------------")
      Console.WriteLine("Press 1 to hear message. ")
      Console.WriteLine("Press 2 to archive message.")
      Console.WriteLine("Press 3 to delete message.")
      Console.WriteLine("Press return to end.")
      Console.WriteLine("---------------------------")

      inPut = Console.ReadLine()
      If Not (inPut = "") Then
        Console.WriteLine("")
        Completed = ProcessMessage(Convert.ToInt32(inPut))
      Else
        Completed = True
      End If
    End While
  End Sub

  Public Function ProcessMessage(ByVal messageAction As Integer) As Boolean
    If (messageFlag And newMessage) = 1 Then
      Console.WriteLine("There are no more messages... ")
      Return False
    Else
      Select Case messageAction
        Case Is = 1 'Access the message
```

```
      AccessMessage()
    Case Is = 2 'Archive the message
      ArchiveMessage()
    Case Is = 3 'Delete the message
      DeleteMessage()
    Case Else
      Console.WriteLine("Not a valid input, try again... ")
      Return False
  End Select
End If
End Function

Sub AccessMessage()
  Console.WriteLine("Message accessed")
    messageFlag = 1
    isAccessed = 1
End Sub

Sub ArchiveMessage()
  If (messageFlag Xor isArchived) = 1 Then 'check if archived
    Console.WriteLine("The message is now archived")
    isArchived = 1
  Else
    Console.WriteLine _
    ("Cannot archive message until it has been heard.")
  End If
End Sub

Sub DeleteMessage()
  If (messageFlag And isAccessed) = 1 Then 'check if accessed
    If (messageFlag Xor isArchived) = 1 Then 'check if archived
      Console.WriteLine("The message was deleted")
      newMessage = 1
    Else
      Console.WriteLine _
      ("The message is archived and cannot be deleted")
    End If
  Else
   Console.WriteLine _
      ("Cannot delete message until it has been heard.")
  End If
End Sub

End Module
```

Note   *See the project **GetMessages** in the Vb7cr solution.*

Shifting Bits

Bit shifting is an important facility for enabling computer languages to handle sophisticated numeric programming and complex numbers. Visual Basic .NET does not have bit-shifting operators (or the ability to overload operators); its architects chose not to endow it with advanced numeric and number-crunching facilities (at least in the first version of Visual Basic .NET). However, C# has these features—language interop allows us to work with C# "muscle" by accessing C# classes and structure directly from Visual Basic.

Language interop makes it far less important that these features are missing in Visual Basic, because once you compile the entire application and reference C# class down to MSIL, the boundaries between the C# code and Visual Basic code vanish. C# becomes a natural extension of Visual Basic (and any other .NET language), something that has never been achieved before. The following code demonstrates both the language interop and C#'s bit-shifting operators. To keep this simple, I have created a console application that presents a menu similar to the **GetMessages** demo application discussed earlier. The menu lets you choose to return a decimal value in its binary form using the shift operators to populate a bit-mask. You can also choose to shift left or shift right a decimal value and simple return the decimal result.

You could have arithmetic exceptions in these operations so we have enclosed the calling methods between **Try . . . Catch** blocks.

```
Imports Vb7cr.BitShifters
Module SeeBits

   Private inPut, byShift As String
   Private outPut As Integer
   Private isCompleted As Boolean = False

   Dim E As BitShifters

   Sub Main()
      Private menuChoice As String
   \
      While Not isCompleted
        Console.WriteLine("                              ")
        Console.WriteLine("----------MENU-----------")
        Console.WriteLine("------------------------")
        Console.WriteLine("a: Decimal to Binary.")
        Console.WriteLine("b: Left Shift.")
        Console.WriteLine("c: Right Shift.")
        Console.WriteLine("d: Anything else to end.")
        Console.WriteLine("------------------------")

        Console.Write("Choose a process: ")
```

```
      menuChoice = Console.ReadLine()
      Select Case menuChoice
        Case Is = "a"
          DecToBinDemo()
        Case Is = "b"
          LeftShiftDemo()
        Case Is = "c"
          RightShiftDemo()
        Case Else
          isCompleted = True
      End Select
    End While

End Sub

Public Sub DecToBinDemo()
  Console.Write("Enter a number to convert from Dec to Bin: ")
    inPut = Console.ReadLine()
    If Not (inPut = "") Then
      Console.WriteLine("")
      isCompleted = ProcessInput(inPut)
    Else
      isCompleted = True
    End If
End Sub

Public Sub LeftShiftDemo()
  Console.Write("Enter a number to shift left: ")
  inPut = Console.ReadLine()
  Console.Write("How many shifts left?: ")
  byShift = Console.ReadLine()
  If Not (inPut = "") Then
    isCompleted = GoLeft(inPut, byShift)
  Else
    isCompleted = True
  End If
End Sub

Public Sub RightShiftDemo()
  Console.Write("Enter a number to shift right: ")
  inPut = Console.ReadLine()
  Console.Write("How many shifts right?: ")
  byShift = Console.ReadLine()
  If Not (inPut = "") Then
```

```vb
        isCompleted = GoRight(inPut, byShift)
    Else
     isCompleted = True
    End If
 End Sub

 Public Function ProcessInput(ByVal Num As String) As Boolean
   Try
      Dim a As String = getKibbles(CInt(Num))
      Console.WriteLine("Answer: " & a)
   Catch E As InvalidCastException
      Console.WriteLine("Not a number, try again...")
      Return False
   End Try
 End Function

 Public Function GoLeft(ByVal Num As String, ByVal Shift As String) _
   As Boolean
   Try
      Dim b As String = leftShift(CInt(Num), CInt(Shift))
      Console.WriteLine("Answer: " & b)
   Catch E As InvalidCastException
      Console.WriteLine("Not a number, try again...")
      Return False
   End Try
 End Function

 Public Function GoRight(ByVal Num As String, ByVal Shift As String) _
   As Boolean
      Try
        Dim c As String = RightShift(CInt(Num), CInt(Shift))
        Console.WriteLine("Answer: " & c)
      Catch E As InvalidCastException
        Console.WriteLine("Not a number, try again...")
        Return False
      End Try
 End Function

End Module
```

Note   *See the project **SeeBits** in the Vb7cr solution.*

The following C# source code is the class that contains the bit-shifting methods. The class is sealed and the methods are declared static (shared) so that the class does not need to be instantiated in order for you to use these bit-shifting methods.

```csharp
using System;
using System.Text;
namespace Vb7cr
{
  /// <summary>
  /// A C# utility class as a backend facility for
  /// shift operators which are not supported in VB .NET.
  /// Jeffrey R. Shapiro, Visual Basic .NET: The Complete Reference
  /// September 3, 2001
  /// </summary>
  public sealed class BitShifters {
  public BitShifters() {
    //
    // TODO: Add constructor logic here
    // Jeffrey Shapiro: "Nothing to do here."
  }
  public static String getKibbles(int value) {
     int kibbleMask = 1 << 31;
     StringBuilder sBuild = new StringBuilder(35);
       for (int s = 1; s <= 32; s++) {
         sBuild.Append( (value & kibbleMask) = = 0 ?  '0' : '1');
         value <<= 1;
         if (s % 8 == 0)
           sBuild.Append(' ');
       }return sBuild.ToString();

  }

  public static String leftShift(int value, int shiftBy) {
    value <<= shiftBy;
    return value.ToString();
  }

  public static String rightShift(int value, int shiftBy) {
    value >>= shiftBy;
    return value.ToString();
  }
 }
}
```

| **Note** | *See the project **BitsShifters** in the Vb7cr solution.*

Did you see anything you like? The interesting method is **getkibbles**, which we will examine in detail here. It's very simple and demonstrates both the shift and the bitwise **AND** in action:

```
public static String getKibbles(int value) {
   int kibbleMask = 1 << 31;
     StringBuilder sBuild = new StringBuilder(35);
       for (int s = 1; s <= 32; s++) {
         sBuild.Append( (value & kibbleMask) = = 0 ?  '0' : '1');
         value <<= 1;
         if (s % 8 == 0)
           sBuild.Append(' ');
       }return sBuild.ToString();
```

First, the bit-shifting operators of C# shift the left operand's bits to the left or right according to the number of positions specified by the right operand. So 16 shifted to the left by 4 returns decimal 256 as demonstrated in Table 5-9. If you compile and run the above code, you can try several numbers and shift them left or right by any number of positions.

In the **getKibbles** method, the first operation is to assign 1 shifted left by 31. The shift operator moves the 1 bit to the left 31 times and then drops it at position 32 (to give 32 bits). The positions to the right of this 1 bit are then filled in with zeros and we end up with a mask (**kibbleMask**) of 32 bits as follows 10000000 00000000 00000000 00000000.

Next we use a very useful class that you will learn about in Chapter 15, the **StringBuilder** class. This class allows us to build a string "buffer," which appends to and grows the string as we need (the standard **String** object is immutable and thus useless for something like this).

The next important piece of code is the for loop which for 32 loops does a bitwise **AND** of the value passed into the method against the mask. If the left-most bit **AND**ed yields 1, then 1 is appended into **sBuild**; otherwise 0 is. After each comparison, the loop left shifts the value variable by 1 (**value <<=1**).

```
for (int s = 1; s <= 32; s++) {
   sBuild.Append( (value & kibbleMask) = = 0 ?  '0' : '1');
```

Then at the end of the loop all we need to return is the string value in the **sBuild** object by calling its **ToString** method.

```
return sBuild.ToString();
```

Left shift	Yields Decimal	and Binary
1 << 1	2	10
2 << 1	4	100
4 << 1	8	1000
8 << 1	16	10000
16 << 4	256	1 00000000

Table 5-9.   *Resulting Decimal and Its Corresponding Binary Representation After Shifting Numbers by 1 or More*

The utility of both the bitwise operators and C#'s shift operators can be used in a single application. For example, you can design the algorithm around decimal numbers and then use the C# shift operators to move the decimals right or left as needed. You can then use the bitwise **And, Or,** and **Xor** to control program flow on the literal value of the numbers. Thus, if you shift "1" to the left by 1 you get 2, and if you shift "2" to the left by 1 you get 4, as seen in Table 5-9 above.

Specialized Operators

The .NET Framework defines a number of specialized operators. I have provided some light coverage in this chapter to introduce them. More examples are available in the chapters listed in Table 5-10.

Operator	Description	Action/Usage	See Also
Is	Compares objects	*Result = objectX **Is** objectY*	Ch. 8 and 9
Like	Compares string patterns	*Result = String **Like** Pattern*	Ch. 10
TypeOf...Is	Tests for the type of object	*If (TypeOf Object Is) Then*	Ch. 6, 8, 9, 10, 11, 15

Table 5-10.   *Specialized Operators*

Is

The **Is** operator takes objects as operands and compares them for equality. Using this operator can be tricky because it does not perform a comparison at the object level, rather at the reference-variable level (see Chapters 8 and 9). In other words, if two reference variables refer to the same object, you will receive **True** from the comparison. Here is a snippet of code that shows **Is** in action:

```
Dim ring1 As New String = "ring1" 'an object of type String
Dim ring2 As New String = "ring2" 'an object of type String
Dim isIt As Boolean
isIt = ecTor1 Is ecTor2 'Is returns False, which is assigned to isIt.
```

The **Boolean** result of the above operation is **False** because both **ring1** and **ring2** refer to different **String** objects. The following code, however, returns **True**:

```
Dim ring1 As New String = "ring1" 'an object of type String
Dim ring2 As New String = "ring2" 'an object of type String
ring1 = ring2
Dim isIt As Boolean
isIt = ecTor1 Is ecTor2 'Is returns True, which is assigned to isIt.
```

The **Boolean** result of the above operation is **True** because both **ring1** and **ring2** refer to the same **String** object by virtue of the expression "ring1 = ring2."

The use of **Is** will be clearer once you understand what a variable reference is. This is discussed in detail in Chapter 8. To compare the actual objects, you should implement the **Equals** method that is always inherited from the root **Object**. How to do this is discussed in Chapter 9. You may override and provide your own implementation to compare two objects and decide, for your purpose, what constitutes equality of the two objects.

Don't use the = (equals) operator to compare two objects. The = operator will feature heavily in Visual Basic's anticipated arrival of operator overloading.

Like

The **Like** operator is used as a pattern-matching utility for character, numeric, and wildcard-character operands. It returns a **Boolean** result. The operator returns **True** if the left operand matches the right. The **Like** operator, however, can take a mask character as a substitute to facilitate the pattern matching. Table 5-11 shows pattern making characters.

Character	Meaning
?	The wildcard for matching any single character
*	The wildcard for matching zero or more characters
#	The wildcard for matching any single digit (0-9)
[…]	The character list surrounded by the square brackets can match any character in the list you provide—example [VB .NET]
[!…]	The character list surrounded by brackets but prefixed by an exclamation point (bang) can match any single character not in the list
X – X	The characters separated by a hyphen can specify a range of Unicode characters

Table 5-11.   *Pattern Matching Mask Characters for Comparing Strings*

The following example demonstrates the **Like** operator and pattern matching in action:

```
Dim X As String
X = "boody"
If (X Like "b??dy") Then
  Debug.WriteLine("True")
End If
```

In the above code snippet the two wildcards ?? can be substituted for anything. For example, if expression **X = "buddy"** would also return **True**.

Operator Overloading

The .NET Framework permits its member languages to implement custom or "user-defined" operators. This is known as *operator overloading*.

Overloading an operator is simply the ability to redefine its operation for a specific type. The built in + operator is used as a unary operator, as the addition (infix) operator, and even as a concatenation operator. Clearly the very architecture of Visual Basic .NET supports operator overloading. Without overloading the + operator, or without the ampersand (&) concatenation operator, joining two or more strings would involve writing code like this:

```
Dim Str1 As String = "God"
Dim Str2 As String = " bless"
Dim Str3 As String
Str3 = Str1.Concat(Str2)
```

Instead, using the overloaded + operator, we have a much less complex alternative as follows:

```
Str3 = Str1 + Str2
```

or

```
Str3 = Str1 & Str2
```

You would also be surprised to find out how much the **Concat** method impacts performance (see Chapter 8).

In complex mathematics and numeric programming, the + and – operators can have very well-defined functionality. This means that in a C# class the + operator can be used to perform a complex operation between operands, something that might otherwise result in a lot of additional code.

Operator overloading provides notation in a customary style for mathematicians and statisticians. We would not be as advanced as we are today if the simple equation

```
E = MC²
```

had to be coded as

```
E = M.Multiply(C.Mulitply(C))
```

instead of

```
E = M *(Pow(C, 2))
```

or just

```
E = M * C * C
```

Operator overloading is especially important in endowing a language with high-end mathematical or numerical computing ability—floating-point operations. It is often the very high-end capabilities that elevate a language to critical acclaim. Java, for example, has struggled to penetrate the finance, statistics, and floating-point software markets precisely because it lacks operator overloading.

Not all .NET operators can or should be overloaded, however, because certain ambiguities may arise, which will only complicate rather than simplify development. For example, the compound assignment operators are split into two operators at the lower level, so there would be no way to change the definition of one or the other in the combination; besides, there would be no reason to. On the other hand, once operator overloading is made available to Visual Basic programmers, operators like Pascal's :=, might find their way into Visual Basic classes.

Visual Basic .NET currently does not provide the developer with the ability to overload any operators. We mention this for several reasons:

- C# does support it and that will make many Visual Basic programmers curious. Language interop is important in .NET and C# will often be used as an extension to Visual Basic and vice versa. Visual Basic programmers might switch to C# one day, specifically to develop a value type or some other class that overloads an operator (remember, even the floating-point "primitives" are objects).

- Controversy surrounding operator overloading has long preceded .NET and is worth investigating.

- Visual Basic programmers may be frustrated with Microsoft, as many Java programmers are with Sun Microsystems—for not allowing operator overloading in Java (see note).

- Microsoft has added some very powerful features to Visual Basic that without operator overloading may seem somewhat emasculated (see Value Types in Chapter 8 and Multidimensional Arrays in Chapter 12).

- Operator overloading will at some point be possible with Visual Basic .NET.

Note *A number of independent software vendors have been fighting for several years to get operator overloading into Java, as part of an effort to improve Java's ability to handle advanced numeric and precision algorithms.*

The debate over operator overloading centers on several issues. Its proponents claim that it is essential to doing complex numerical work in their language. Coding complex constructs can be very cumbersome without the ability to provide a custom operator. In many cases the standard notation and syntax elements are so complex and confusing that the best tack would be to use another language. A small percentage of Visual Basic programmers might think this way and then intermix C# classes in their code as I have in this chapter.

The opponents (in our case the Visual Basic .NET architects) believe (as Java's architects do) that operator overloading works against team projects and can make code harder to maintain. The following section makes the case for it facilitating complex numerics. (See Chapter 8.)

Exception Object	Purpose
DivideByZeroException	See the Arithmetic Operators section
InvalidCastException	To handle an exception raised when attempting to make an invalid type conversion
OverflowException	See the Arithmetic Operators section

Table 5-12.   *Referenced Exceptions*

Exceptions Referenced in this Chapter

Table 5-12 above lists important exceptions that you may encounter when working with operators. Arithmetic operators can cause divide-by-zero exceptions (**DivideBy Zeroexception**) when the right operand evaluates to zero. The **InvalidCastExamption** and the **OverFlowException** can be raised when implicit type conversion fails during assignment.

Observations

This chapter presented the first major encounter with C# mixins and language interop in a Visual Basic project. Many programmers will dislike this and wonder what C# code is doing in a Visual Basic book. Let's remember that it's not unusual to find HTML, JScript, and SQL in many books devoted to classic VB. More importantly, the common language runtime allows us to do something with other .NET languages that might not be that elegant, clean, or even possible with Visual Basic.

We believe that this "deficiency" will be short lived for Visual Basic and have therefore stopped short of elaborating upon operator-overloading code in C#. In fact, not long before the final release of the first version of Visual Basic .NET, Microsoft began laying the foundation for operator overloading in Visual Basic. When you consider that an expression like **A Mod B** is the equivalent of **A -Int(A / B)* B # CLng(Math.Sign(A))<> Math.Sign (B))***, then you will appreciate how important this is.

Finally, for further reading on floating-point arithmetic, a good starting point is the Internet, which links to many pages devoted to the IEEE 754 specification.

The Complete Reference

Visual Basic .NET

Chapter 6

Software Design, Conditional Structures, and Control Flow

The logical and typical flow of execution of a program is *top down*. Just as you read the words on this page starting at the top of the page and moving to the end, so too is it natural for execution to proceed in this sequential ordered manner. This is known as *sequential execution*. However, you can alter execution flow—to provide choices that execute one expression or a block over another—with statements that either *transfer control* to other locations of the method or otherwise *branch* or *jump* from the line that it is currently on to another area in the routine.

During the 1960s and 1970s, overuse of this transfer of control created programs that were hard to maintain and debug. A user could typically jump from one place to another with many lines of code in between. The problems programmers faced were often blamed on the infamous *goto* statement, which was cited as a reason advancements in software engineering were slow from the mid-1900s toward the end of the 20th century.

If you are new to programming, **goto** lets you transfer control to any number of labels in a method. The more labels you have the more incomprehensible the program becomes. In the early days of computing, most programs were reams of unstructured code that were to software what a mile of ticker tape is to modern communications.

You may remember programming like that in Dbase: trying to find a bug required printing miles of code on tractor-fed printer paper (laser printers cost about $8000 then). Those **goto** statements were like black holes in space—once you got sucked into one there was no way out.

The most important tenet of modern control-flow programming is to keep the line to be executed and the decision to execute that line as close together as possible. In other words, if you are going to execute a line based on a test that returns **True,** then that line should be the next line, not one that is 15 lines away.

Before the advent of structured programming, **goto** could transfer from line 15 to line 156443. Today, **goto** can only leapfrog short distances in the method, which is how it has been with classic Visual Basic. Now there is no reason for it to exist in object-based programming, or in the .NET languages. As a programmer, it's hard to see how **goto** is still with us for backward compatibility when so much legacy or classic code has to be rewritten.

Well-known engineers of the formative years of computer science, such as C.A.R. Hoare, Niklaus Wirth, Edsger Dijkstra, Corrado Bohm, and Guiseppe Jacopini, actively lobbied for the abolishment of **goto.** They held conferences and wrote many papers demonstrating the superfluousness of **goto.** Using flow diagrams similar to the ones in this chapter, they would demonstrate how alternative structured control/flow constructs, such as **Case** and **If**, could be used to control the sequence of execution and improve the readability and manageability of program code by an order of magnitude.

These constructs heralded the age of structured programming. Nevertheless, **goto** still made it into the BASIC language where it loiters to this day. Its inclusion in Visual Basic .NET is *not* auspicious to say the least, but we will discuss it again later in this chapter.

Before you embark on this chapter, keep this important rule in mind: The code in your methods should be organized as straight-line as possible. Avoid code that is anything but top-down. When you read this page you don't expect me to suddenly finish this sentence in the middle of the page, then jump to the sentence at the end and then return here. This can be avoided by keeping the related statements as close together as possible.

 See also Corrado Bohm and Guiseppe Jacopini, "Flow Diagrams, Turing Machines and Languages with Only Two Formation Rules." Communications of the ACM, Vol. 9 (May 1966), 366–371.

Control Structures

Although control and flow structures like **If** statements have been around for a while, old habits and poor education have carried structured software development into the world of object-based programming and object-oriented development. One example is how the code on Web sites suffers from this malaise, which is why Web sites cost so much to maintain. It's as if we are back where we started, four or five decades ago. ASP.NET goes further than any other technology to change that situation for Web developers (see Chapter 1).

The aforementioned Bohm and Jacopini showed us back in 1964 how programs (sans **goto**) could be expressed in terms of three core *control structures*—the *sequence structure,* the *selection* or *decision structure* and the *repetition structure.* These structures are further explained as follows:

- **The Sequence Structure**   The default of all .NET languages in which instructions are executed in sequence, as they are written.

- **The Decision Structure**   This structure uses the **If** statement to test the verity of a condition. Multiple choices for tests include the selection structures such as **Case.** These constructs interrupt the sequence and transfer control to another location in the program.

- **The Repetition Structure**   This structure—also known as the iteration structure—comprises actions that repeatedly execute lines of code until a condition changes, such as a number (until x = y) or when the end of a list or data structure is reached. They include the recurring **While**, **Do**, and **For** loops, and they are useful for iterating through lists, arrays, and other data structures. (Iteration is also achieved through recursive method calls, which are discussed in the next chapter.)

Control Flow

Algorithms will process one line of code after another if that's what we want them to do. We should always write code on the premise that the line of code after the one currently being executed may not always be the next logical choice of instruction or statement to process. Good program design and implementation should always be cognizant of the state of the program and its data, the environment, the machine, the user, the network, and thus of the entire system at any given time. Every line of code executed should be "fully considered." See the use of *assert* methods in Chapter 17.

Much of what we discuss in this chapter will also be applicable when enclosing code in the exception handling constructs (**Try . . . Catch . . . Finally**) discussed in Chapters 7 and 11, so pay attention. It's all very well saying "I will just send the command to the server and, if the connection is not open, an exception will be raised to take care of the error."

That's not good programming. Triggering or raising exceptions does not always happen immediately. So the program and the user sit waiting and wondering if the sky has fallen out of the universe before an error pops up saying "network not available" or "database is off-line." Exception objects are very useful and very important but they are objects that take up space in memory, processor cycles, and garbage collector "energy." Better to test the logic of making the call before shooting first and then "waiting" to see what happens (see Chapter 17).

Note	*If you are new to exception handling, see Chapters 7 and 11. Many lazy programmers— besotted on the wonders of SEH—rely too much on exception handling, which results in poor code.*

Every line of code you write that will alter the program's state should test a condition for every instruction you are going to give the computer. This is called *defensive* or *assertive* programming. You don't want to get carried away with this, though. It would be a waste of energy to perform a fancy logic check just to change the font of a label (see Chapter 17).

The introduction of and aggressive training in structured-programming techniques helped to accelerate the transformation of strictly top-down code execution to a more deterministic execution where, at any given time in a program, execution could substitute one course of action for another.

The scope of the jump in object-based programming has been narrowed to small and manageable methods. Inside our methods there may be lines of code that are never executed because the conditions are always favorable. If the flight deck is always kept clear when the jets land on the carrier, then there is no need to raise alarms.

A good example of code that programmers never expected to execute lay in the many thousands of lines of our Y2K software. Despite the billions spent to make sure such code remained unexecuted, there were still many annoying errors at the end of the century.

OOP and the intermessaging or call process between objects and between methods allow both concurrent execution and transfer of execution to take place in an organized fashion. The transfer or flow can be *intra-object*, which means one method calling another

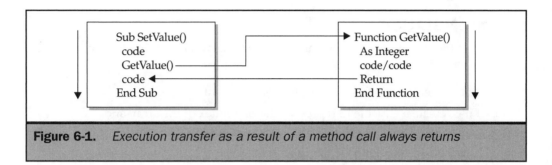

Figure 6-1. *Execution transfer as a result of a method call always returns*

method in a class (as illustrated in Figure 6-1), or *inter-object*, which means one method calling another method in another object, through message interchange, possibly even in another process, on another machine. Polymorphism between objects plays an important part in all this, as we will discuss in Chapters 10, 13, 14, and 15.

While the aforementioned calls transfer control out of a method, it is worth noting that they always return to the methods that made the calls. This return process is not only inherent in the .NET architecture, but in all modern object-oriented software development languages. While methods return you can write code that lets you continue with another process while the called method continues to work on its problem. This is known as an asynchronous method call (the target method makes a call back) and the techniques are discussed in Chapters 7 and 14.

Returns from method calls can bring back data in the form of references to objects and actual values. These are called *return values.* Standard subroutines return without data. Methods are discussed in greater depth in Chapter 7.

We call this continuous *execute-test data-transfer* model the control and flow, regardless of where it occurs in the program. Understanding the basics in this chapter will prepare you for the upcoming discussion of the construction and programming of objects.

Fully Sketched Code

In the software design process, it is imperative to design, model, and fully consider your algorithm before you code it. When you're constructing code, a number of formal "notations" allow you to "sketch" out a design. These include the following:

- Step-Form Notation
- Pseudocode
- Nassi-Schneiderman Charts
- Flowcharts

Step-Form Notation

This process helps you design algorithms by requiring you to list the steps of the code as illustrated here:

1. Determine if the array is longer than one element.
2. If it is, create a variable to represent the first index of the array and
3. Create a variable to represent the last index of the array.
4. Check if the value of the first index's element is less than or equal to that of the last one.
5. If the value is higher, swap the values.
6. While the first index variable is not at the end of the array and the last index variable is not at the beginning, increment the first index variable by one and decrement the last index variable by one.
7. Repeat step 6 until the index positions intersect in the middle of the array.

Designing algorithms in this manner, or with the notation discussed in the next sections, might seem tedious and unproductive. Yet, when you have a complex algorithm to code, you will discover that it's expeditious.

Pseudocode

Pseudocode is the "language" you use to "think" out your code before you convert it into Visual Basic code. There are no formal specifications, and it can intermix source code English, and other languages. However, you must keep the pseudocode consistent. We will use some pseudocode to explain concepts here and throughout the book.

The preceding step-by-step notation can be expressed as pseudocode like this:

1. *If array length is greater than 1, then*
2. *Create a variable for index 0 and then*
3. *Create a variable for the index at the length of the array.*

There appears to be little difference between these two forms of notation; however, the softer style of pseudocode lets you be more expressive, and thus more precise. Pseudocode is more popular for designing algorithms; in later chapters we'll sketch some algorithms and define the methods.

Nassi-Schneiderman Charts

Nassi-Schneiderman (NS) charts provide a more graphical means of expressing algorithms. These charts are represented using the symbols illustrated in Figure 6-2.

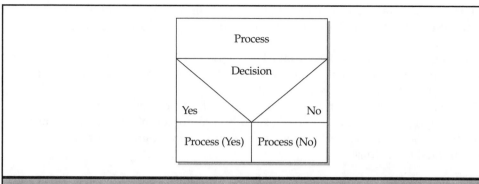

Figure 6-2.   *The Nassi-Schneiderman (NS) charts for graphically designing algorithms*

The NS chart in Figure 6-3 represents the formal design of our step-form and pseudocode notations described above (abridged).

NS charts are easy to use, yet difficult to maintain in larger programs; thus, few programmers use them currently. Most prefer to work with flowcharts, the de facto graphical notation for designing and expressing control flow and program states.

Flowcharts

Flowcharts formally express selection, decision making, and repetition using diagrams to depict the control and flow. These graphics use symbols that represent start and stop points. The decision diamond, the rectangle where processing (such as incrementing a number) occurs, is usually constructed with **True** taking the action path to the right and **False** taking the action path to the left.

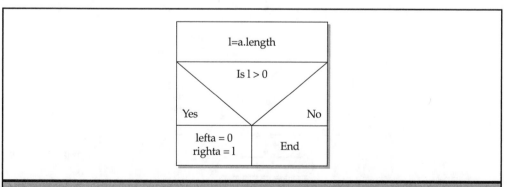

Figure 6-3.   *NS Chart for designing the process to step through the array*

Figure 6-4 illustrates the symbols used in simple flowcharts and, at the same time, represents the formal design of our step-form and pseudocode notation described earlier.

A number of advanced symbols have been added to the flowchart notation over the years. Refer to Visio 2002 for Enterprise Architect, for an extensive assortment of symbols and alternative flowchart structure.

Flowcharting is the best way to design software that requires a lot of switching, decision making, and selection. A good example is computer telephony programs in which you have a lot of selection constructs—press 1 for English, 2 for Xhosa, 3 for Zulu, and 4 for Yiddish.

Design Pitfalls

There's a point at which you must decide on a design and begin to write code. If you overdesign, either you never write or your customers get exactly what the model specifies, even if it's wrong. If you underdesign, your customers get everything *but* what they wanted. The latter is more common and often results in undocumented code. The only person who knows what's going on is the one who wrote it. Code should be written well enough that any programmer could quickly decipher the process and purpose at the code level.

The model provides the abstraction and identifies the scope, flow, and sequence of events. But the model is not the asset; the only true documentation for your code is the code itself—as long as it is well written. This is especially true of modern object-oriented

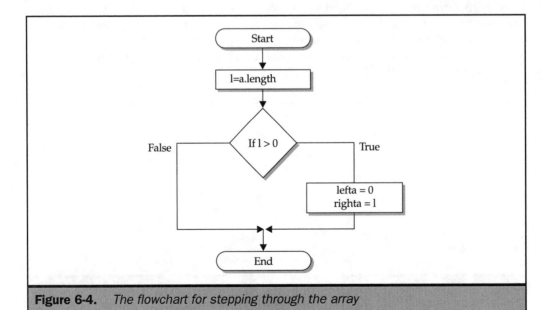

Figure 6-4.   *The flowchart for stepping through the array*

software development architectures. The various languages (including Java) are all so similar that if you can read one you can read them all.

Modeling languages like Unified Modeling Language (UML) are invaluable for high-level design. UML models could be used as the base for quality control, maintenance, and documentation if they could make the natural connection, or bridge, to the code more profound. In many projects, UML models turn out to be the sophisticated sketchpads—tools for abstraction—of the software architect's mind. But the programmers who write the code seldom get to work from the models.

Note	*Chapter 9 introduces basic UML constructs used in this book.*

Many code segments, however, need to be expressed in natural language before they can be converted to code. The mind that can think in code like this is rare. In many cases, designing complex data structure cannot be achieved without "playing" out the procedures in a flow diagram, pencil drawings, or in pseudocode.

You also need to fully understand what inheritance, aggregation, interfaces, and so on can do for your products. The biggest problem with object-oriented architectures is that few people are aware of all their features, know how to use them, or care to use them. Many programmers criticize features like inheritance and interfaces without really knowing why they have been provided.

Often code is repeated throughout an application, yet there is no formal design or architecture created via a pattern, interface definition, or diagram. It's no wonder that electrical engineers make such good software programmers. They often design software as they do circuit boards or CPU chips or light bulbs.

Conditional Statements

Conditional statements control the execution of other statements in our algorithms. To clarify this—the execution of certain statements is effected on the conditions that may be present in our code. These are determined by evaluating data that represents a condition, such as the following: a machine may be on; the temperature inside a fuel injector may be 10,000 degrees *Celsius*; our velocity may be increasing to a point that could cause system destruction.

The conditionals allow us to either execute the statement, or avert or circumvent its execution. They afford us the ability to fully consider taking important steps in our code, or redirecting the flow of execution to achieve certain objectives. Conditional statements have existed for decades in all programming languages and were first introduced by the doyens of our profession, such as C.A.R. Hoare (**Case**) and John McCarthy (**While**).

Visual Basic .NET supports several conditional and looping statements for control and flow in programs. We will also look at the **Error** conditional (**goto**'s partner) and cases shortly, but a much larger treatise of error handling and the new to Visual Basic structured-exception handling (SEH) constructs are covered in Chapters 7 and 11.

Table 6-1 lists the conditional statements that are supported by Visual Basic .NET. There are also a number of legacy conditional functions, such as **Else If**, that we will discuss later in this chapter.

If

The **If** statement is probably the most important conditional of all programming languages and is used in virtually every one. Conditionals derived from C often do not make use of **Then** in the statement, which is evident with C# and J#. The C-derivative languages use curly braces to delineate the block to be processed (see Chapter 4).

The condition can be one of two types. First and typical, it can evaluate if something is either true or false. This form of **If** is the classic usage. Second, it can test for the type of an object passed to a method using the **TypeOf** keyword or operator. The latter lets you code conditional routines depending on the type of object being referenced in a method.

The simplest form for this conditional is just plain **If . . . Then.** The entire **If** construct, however, must be terminated with the **End If** statement.

The **If** works as follows: If the test is found to be **True** (what you want to be so), the process continues into the block, and the code will be executed. If the test is found to be **False**, then the program jumps over the code directly after the test and exits the **If** block. Figure 6-5 shows how this works when your code is executed. We will use flow diagrams to explain these elements.

As we have seen, when a variable tests **True**, the statement after **Then** is executed. The syntax for the above flowchart is as follows:

If *condition* Then [Then *statements*]

And coding it is straightforward, as shown here:

```
If X = Y Then 'if condition is true then
   Debug.WriteLine("True") 'execute this statement
End If
```

Conditional Action	Statement
Decision Making and Switching	If. . .Then, Else, Else If, Select Case
Branching	GoTo, OnError

Table 6-1. *Conditional Statements*

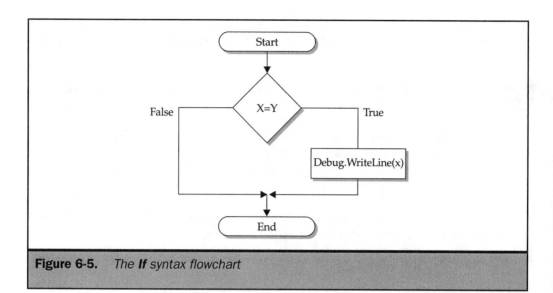

Figure 6-5. *The If syntax flowchart*

When the condition to test is complex, use brackets to make the code more readable. However, be sure the expression is being properly evaluated according to the operator rules of precedence. See Chapter 5, "Operators." Here is an example of such bracket usage:

```
If (i >= j > (j + z)) Then
   Swap(a(i), a(j))
End If
```

Stacking and Nesting If

You may often find yourself nesting or stacking **If** statements. The following example demonstrates the stacking of multiple **If** statements:

```
If (if a.Length > 0) Then
   pivotChar = leftSideIndex
End If
If leftSideIndex >= rightSideIndex Then
   swap(pivotChar, a(rightSideIndex))
End If
```

The above code is nothing more than independent **If** statements arranged one on top of the other. When you stack repeatedly like this, code becomes hard to read, is error prone, and might not perform as expected. When you need to test additional elements under the control of a single **If** construct, then use the **Else If** discussed later in this section.

Note   *Visual Basic .NET also supports a multiple-selection construct called **Select Case**, which we will investigate later in this chapter, so if you need to "stack" more than two If statements, your design may be better off with a **Select Case** statement. Also, there will be times when you need to construct a complex Boolean expression to test against and you may find that the functions contain superfluous variables. To build these correctly, you need to know how to articulate using high-level Boolean algebra, which you can accomplish using a Karnaugh map representation of a logic truth table.*

If the intention is to enact the second **If** statement on condition that the first **If** premise is true, then the preceding code must be nested as follows:

```
If (if a.Length > 0) Then
  pivotChar = leftSideIndex
    If leftSideIndex >= rightSideIndex Then
       swap(pivotChar, a(rightSideIndex))
    End If
End If
```

In this code, if the length of the array called **a** is greater than 0, the second **If** statement will be processed. If, however, **a.Length** is not greater than 0, the inner **If** statement will not be processed because it belongs to the executable code of the outer **If** statement.

Alternate Syntax for Simple If Statements

When the conditions are all placed on one line, the **If** statement can be executed using the new line marker ":" as follows:

```
If (i >= j > (j + z)) Then : j += 1 : Swap(a(i), a(j))
```

Notice that the **End If** terminator is not needed in the single-line construct.

Tips for If

You will find that the **Try . . . Catch** (SEH) construct discussed in Chapters 9 and 11 is a lot like the **If** conditional, and thus much of what we discuss here will be equally applicable for SEH.

Never put the code you are going to execute at the other end of the nested **If** blocks; put it right underneath the conditional test in order to execute it. Here's an example of what *not* to do.

```
If Inj1.IsOnline Then
   If cTemp <= 0 Then
     Inj1.oState = -1
   End If
     cTemp = Inj1.oTemp
End If
```

What's wrong with the above code? First we check if the **Injector** system (a space flight engine component) is online. We find that it is, so we test if the **cTemp** value is less than or equal to zero. The problem in the code, however, is that the line of code that obtains the current injector temperature, obtained from the object's **oTemp** property, is executed after the inner **If** block. This means that we are probably setting the **oState** on a stale value rather than a current one. This could result in an injector overload that could cause a major disaster. The right way to code this is as follows:

```
If Inj1.IsOnline Then
   cTemp = Inj1.oTemp
   If cTemp <= 0 Then
     Inj1.oState = -1
   End If
End If
```

Else

The **Else** statement is optional, but dependent on **If**, and it is executed only if the **If** statement tests false. The **Else** works as follows: If the test is found to be true (what you want to be so), the process will continue into the block, and the code will be executed. However, if the **If** test is found to be false, then the execution jumps over the code directly after the test and enters the **Else** block.

The syntax for the flowchart illustrated in Figure 6-6 is as follows:

```
If Condition Then
  (If Statements)
Else
  (Else Statements)
End If
```

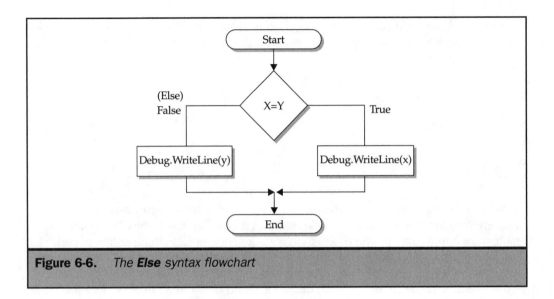

Figure 6-6.   *The **Else** syntax flowchart*

And coding it is straightforward, as shown here:

```
If Inj1.IsOnline Then
  cTemp = Inj1.oTemp
    If cTemp <= 0 Then
      Inj1.oState = -1
    End If
Else
  Inj1.oState = -1
End If
```

In the above code, the injector's state is set as –1 because it was found to be offline. Without the **Else**, the block would have terminated without the benefit of making a change based on the false result, or providing some other exchange.

Else If

We use **Else If** to advance the test to additional elements. It works as follows: If the first **If** test is found to be false, execution "jumps" over the code directly after the first test and enters the first **Else If** block. This next block then proceeds as *if* it were the original **If** test. In other words, this feature affords you additional chances to test a condition. Figure 6-7 shows how the conditional **Else If** works when your code is executed.

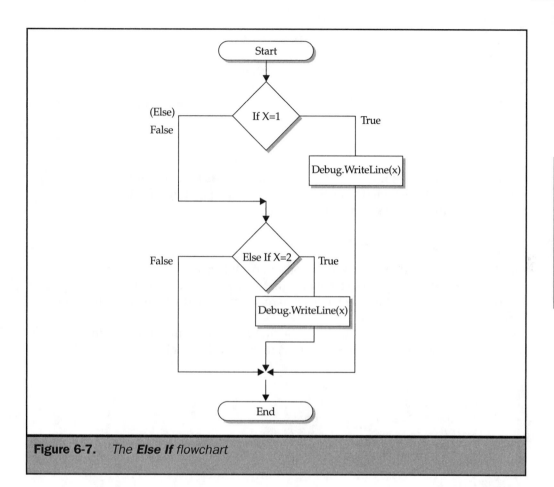

Figure 6-7.   *The **Else If** flowchart*

The syntax for the above flowchart is as follows:

If *Condition* Then
  (If Statements)
Else If *Condition-n* Then
  (Else If Statements)
Else
  (Else Statements)
End If

The **Else** statement is also optional and you can nest multiple **If** statements in the original block as well. The code for the above flowchart is as follows:

```
If numReceived = DialTone Then
  pTone = localDialtone
```

```
ElseIf numReceived = TieTone Then
  pTone = tieLineDialTone
ElseIf numReceived = OperatorTone Then
  TransferToOperator
Else
  pTone = fastBusy
End If
```

In the above code block, each **Else If** after the **If** tests for additional conditions. As soon as one variable is found to be true, the code inside that **Else If** block is executed and then the entire **If** construct is abandoned.

Tips for Else and Else If

Else If should be used to test multiple conditions. It is helpful in situations when you have two, or at the most three, statements that you want to test within the one logical **If** block. Your code will become too hard to read or debug if you are running more than three **Else If**s.

Using **Else If,** you can decide that if the first test is false, then possibly the next one might be true and if the second is also false, then the third might be true.

```
If level = desiredLevel Then
  ShutDown(ShuttleInjector)
ElseIf desiredLevel > 14 Then
  Alarms(Critical)
ElseIf desiredLevel < 24 Then
  Alarms(Warning)
  Exit Sub
End If
```

But if you need to evaluate only one variable, your code would be easier to read using the **Select Case** conditional.

Avoid a Null If

I have often seen code in which the programmer has chosen to do nothing when the condition tests true. This is known as a classic "null If" and looks like this:

```
If (intI >= intJ) Then
  '
Else
  intI += 1
End If
```

While this code compiles, it's pointless to include the **Else**. It is better to negate the predicate in the **If** statement and drop the **Else** option altogether. The code is better as follows:

```
If Not (intI >= intJ) Then
   intI += 1
End If
```

Badly Formed If Statements

A common mistake in nests is to interject the logical progression of the code with **Else** statements. At best, this makes the line hard to read and at worst, produces coding disasters. While the following code will compile, it not only makes it harder to read but prone to bugs.

```
If Inj1.IsOnline Then
   cTemp = Inj1.oTemp
Else
   Inj1.oState = -1
   If cTemp <= 0 Then
      Inj1.oState = -1
   End If
End If
```

What's wrong with this code? By interrupting the logical progression of the code with the **Else**, the code that should be executed is pushed to the end of the outer **If** block instead. The result is that values are changed in the wrong order.

This next example is better.

```
If Inj1.IsOnline Then
   cTemp = Inj1.oTemp
   If cTemp <= 0 Then
      Inj1.oState = -1
   End If
Else : Inj1.oState = -1
End If
```

The general idea, which also applies to the SEH **Try . . . Catch** blocks, is to fully code the outer **If** block before you mix in the nested blocks or alternative constructs. Once you have done this, make sure the line you need to execute on the first true condition is completed before you begin the next conditional (if the condition was true). When you have fully written the outer **If,** you can code the next **If** block and nest deeper.

If at the end of the construction the left side of the **If** block looks like a haphazard broken plank, then you have a problem. If on the other hand, through proper indentation, the code looks like an arrowhead and all the **Else If** and **Else** statements are neatly stacked under it, then you are on the right track. The entire collection of **If** statements should be on the upper part of the arrowhead.

Off-by-One Errors

You should also avoid off-by-one errors in **If** statements by fully considering when the less than or equal to operators (or the greater than or equal to operators) are more appropriate than the less than (or greater than) operators. In other words, the code:

```
If Inj1.Temp > CriticalTemp Then '40 degrees
```

is better written as

```
If Inj1.Temp >= CriticalTemp Then
```

if the temperature should absolutely not rise above 40 degrees. On the other hand, the following example produces the reverse of the desired results if you use the "less than or equal to" sign.

```
If Customer.Age <= legalAge then
  CanBuyBeer = False
Else
  CanBuyBeer = True
End if
```

While the age limit for buying beer is 21, this code forces the drinker to wait an extra year.

There will be times when the condition should be either less than or greater than; but the key is to not redirect or avert the process when in fact you should be executing. In the above example, if the critical temperature is 40 and above, then the operator should use >= to avoid the off-by-one error.

Select Case

What would a programming language be without its **Case** or **Switch** statements? The Visual Basic .NET **SelectCase** conditional structure is identical to the one in VB 6 and earlier versions.

The **Select Case** works as follows: An expression is passed to the **Select Case** function, which proceeds to test each "case" until it finds a **Case** *value* that matches the test expression. The procedure will then continue into the matching **Case** block, and its code will be executed. Afterward, the **Select Case** is abandoned. Figure 6-8 shows how the conditional works when your code is executed.

The syntax is as follows:

Select Case *expression_to_test*
Case Value1
Statements-for-value1
Case Value2
Statements-for-value2
Case Else
Case-Else-Statements
End Select

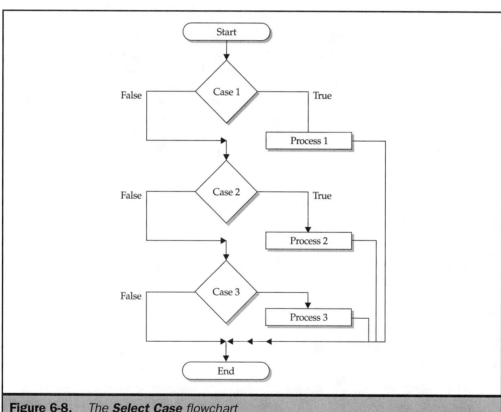

Figure 6-8.   *The **Select Case** flowchart*

Here is an example of **Select Case**:

```
Select Case Color
  Case Gray
    Grid.BackColor = Color.FromArgb(128, 128, 128)
  Case Red
    Grid.BackColor = Color.FromArgb(255, 0, 0)
  Case Black
    Grid.BackColor = Color.FromArgb(0, 0, 0)
  Case Else
    Grid.BackColor = Color.DefaultColor
End Select
```

In the above code segment, the method receives a variable representing the color chosen by a component user. For example, if the argument **Red** is passed to the **Color** parameter, the code in the second case (**Case Red**) is executed. The other lines are ignored. The optional **Case Else** is a safety net that triggers if the argument does not have a matching **Case** scenario in the **Select Case** construct. Normal execution resumes on any code that comes after the **End Select** statement.

Each **Select Case** expression can be complex and comprise elements such as function calls, multiple values, complex Boolean logic, and sundry comparison operators. When a **Case** expression is complex, the **Case** block that is executed will be the first one that matches the result of the complex call or computation. The following example demonstrates this:

```
Select Case Target.Position
Case TargetDown
'do something
Case TargetUp
'do something
Case TargetTurningIn
'do something
Case TargetTurningOut
'do something
Case TargetNoChange
'do something
```

You can use the new line symbol ":" to make the code easier to read for simple **Select Case** blocks as follows:

```
Select Case x
  Case 1 : x += 1
  Case 2 : x -= 1
End Select
```

The big difference between the **If. . . Else If** statements and the **Select Case** is that **If. . . Else If** can be used to test a number of alternative Boolean expressions in each block of the entire construct while **Select Case** examines only one and then uses the result to return the case paired with the **True** condition or run the code in that case.

GoTo

As mentioned earlier, **goto** (or **GoTo**) is still used in Visual Basic to help port code and assist with backward compatibility, though it is not essential to the .NET Framework. Since **GoTo** was one of the primary elements of classic BASIC and many other languages, programmers trained in these systems may find it difficult at first to write code without it.

It is surprising that C# supports **goto** because C# rarely needs to help port. This brings to mind only Java and J++ code, but Sun eliminated **goto** from Java so it wouldn't "pollute" the language.

Here's how it works. The **GoTo** keyword causes execution to jump from the current line to a label somewhere else in the block. The syntax is as follows:

GoTo *Label*

The following code illustrates the "disciplined" usage of **GoTo** branching. Anything more advanced would become too complex to understand and document.

```
Start:  str = Console.ReadLine()
        num = CInt(str)
        Goto Line0  'Check num and branch to its corresponding label.

Line0:  If num = 1 Then Goto Line1 Else Goto Line2
Line1:  Console.WriteLine("This is Line 1 and you typed 1")
        Goto Line3

Line2:  Console.WriteLine("This is Line 2 and you typed 2")
        Goto Line3

Line3:  If num > 2 Then Console.WriteLine() Else Goto Start
```

Notwithstanding its shortcomings, there are some rules that govern the use of **GoTo** in Visual Basic. They are as follows:

1. **GoTo** can be used to branch to regions of code only within the procedure blocks in which it is referenced. It cannot jump all around a unit of code as they did in the days of unstructured procedural programming.

2. **GoTo** can be used in the new **Try . . . Catch . . . Finally** blocks discussed in Chapter 11, but a **GoTo** in the **Try** block cannot direct execution to a label or line in the **Catch** or **Finally** blocks of the same SEH block.

3. A **GoTo** statement anywhere in the SEH block cannot direct execution to any line outside the entire handler.

OnError

The **OnError** statement will also be familiar to classic VB experts. The following **OnError** conditionals are supported:

- OnError GoTo *line*
- OnError Resume Next
- OnError GoTo 0
- OnError GoTo –1

The **OnError** statement is a conditional construct, which is why we have mentioned it here. It effects a jump to an error-handling code segment marked with a label that you need to specify. There is no inherent error-handling support built into the web and woof of the software language that is supported by the compiler, as there is with SEH. See Chapter 11 for examples of **OnError.**

Loops

Visual Basic supports the usual loop statements that let you execute one or more lines of code repetitively while a condition is a certain value, or until it becomes a certain value. The following loops are supported by Visual Basic .NET.

- Do . . . Loop
- For . . . Next
- For . . . Each . . . Next
- While

 *While is supported but it now terminates with **End While** and not **Wend,** as was the case with earlier versions of Visual Basic.*

Do...Loop

The **Do . . . Loop** command repeats the execution of a block of code for as long as a condition *remains* **True** or until it *becomes* **True**. The two variations use the key words **While** or **Until** to test the condition: the former uses **While,** the latter **Until.** The syntax for both tests is as follows:

```
Do [{While | Until} condition ]
    statements
Exit Do
    statements
Loop
```

Visual Basic .NET also supports the following variation:

```
Do
    statements
Exit Do
    statements
Loop [{While | Until} condition ]
```

Here is a simple example of the **Do . . . Loop**:

```
Do
  number = number + 1
  Debug.WriteLine("*")
Loop Until number = 50
```

Now we become more advanced with nesting and other techniques:

```
Dim incR As Integer
Dim conD As Boolean
  Do
    Do While incR < 500
      incR += 1
      Console.WriteLine("Now at: " + CStr(incR))
        If incR = 500 Then
        conD = True
          Console.WriteLine("Now at: " + CStr(incR) + " and Finished")
          Exit Do
        End If
    Loop
  Loop Until conD = True
```

There is no limit to the number of levels you can nest to, as demonstrated in the preceding code. But the more you nest, the more unreadable your code becomes. There is also not much difference between using **While** and **Until**. Use whatever makes your code more intelligible and suits the algorithm.

For. . . Next

The **For . . . Next** statement is a classic and has been preserved for this version of Visual Basic. The following example illustrates this loop:

```
sArray = s2.Split(seps)
  For intI = 0 To Ubound(sArray)
    Console.WriteLine(sArray(intI))
  Next intI
Console.WriteLine(s2.Join("*", sArray))
```

In this illustration, **I** is an **Integer** declared as a "counter" that increments every **Next I** of the loop ranging from 0 to the upper bound of the array (**0 To Ubound(sArray)**). You can run this loop for the duration of any range of ordinals, but you should avoid updating **Short** or **Long** counters because the **Integer** is a highly optimized type. Of course, the difference would impact your application only if you were performing thousands of operations, such as parsing a huge file or sorting a massive array. The following example would be slow if the counter **I** were declared a **Decimal**.

```
Dim foo As Long
For foo = 0 To Ubound(massiveArray)
 FillArray(sValue)
Next foo
```

If the number of elements in this array exceeded 32,767, you would have to declare **I** as **Long,** but it would run much slower than if **I** were an **Integer** because **Long** is much wider.

For Each . . . Next

For Each . . . Next is similar to **For . . . Next**, but it loops for each element or subscript of an array or collection instead of for a specified number of times. (See the chapters that cover arrays and collections and data structures, Chapters 12 and 13 respectively.) Here is the syntax for this loop:

For Each *(elementvariable)* In *collection*

'Statement block to be executed for each value of *elementvariable*.

Next [*elementvariable*]

For each iteration of the loop the variable *elementvariable* is set to one of the elements in the collection before the statement block is executed. When all the elements in the collection have been assigned to *elementvariable*, the **For Each** loop terminates and control passes to the statement following the **Next** statement.

You can choose to specify the element variable on the **Next** statement. Doing this will improve the readability of your program but you must specify the same variable that appears in the **For Each** statement.

The following method accepts a data structure and forces every object in the structure to erase its data fields:

```
Sub EraseAllNodes(ByRef OldTree As Tree)
   Dim OldNode As Node
   For Each OldNode In OldTree
```

```
    OldNode.Erase
  Next OldNode
End Sub
```

The elements of a *collection* can be of any data type; however, the type of *elementvariable* must be such that each element of the collection can be converted to it.

If you plan to loop through custom collections, the collection must be an object that exposes **GetEnumerator** method. **GetEnumerator** returns an enumerator object that exposes a **Current** property and a **MoveNext** method. (See Chapters 12 and 13 for information on the **IEnumerator** interface.) The Visual Basic uses these to traverse the collection. In addition, the elements returned by the **Current** property must be convertible to the data type of *elementvariable*.

Because arrays are implemented as collections, you can use a **For Each . . . Next** loop to iterate through them. This procedure presets all the elements of an array to 128:

```
Dim foo As Long
For Each foo In massiveArray
  FillArray(sValue)
Next foo
```

See the **FillArray** method in Chapter 12, which demonstrates advanced implementation of **For Each . . . Next.**

While

While executes a group of statements while a certain condition is **True.** The procedure is the same as it was in earlier versions of Visual Basic; however, this loop now needs to be terminated with **End While** and not **Wend.** The syntax for **While** is as follows:

```
While condition
  statements
End While
```

The *condition* parameter can evaluate to **True** or **False.** If the value is null, then it is considered **False.** As soon as the variable evaluates to false, the loop will end; as long as it evaluates to **True** the code in the *statements* section will be executed. The following is another way of executing the **Do . . . Loop** example provided earlier (**While** is actually more complex when taken to several nested levels):

```
Dim incR As Integer = 0
Dim conD As Boolean = True
  While conD = True
```

```
       incR += 1
       Console.WriteLine("Now at: " + CStr(incR))
       If incR = 500 Then
          conD = False
          Console.WriteLine("Now at: " + CStr(incR) + " and finished")
       Exit While
       End If
    End While
```

The **Exit While** keywords are redundant in this loop but are included for illustration. The loop will end at the next iteration of the outer loop because the Boolean value **Cond** will evaluate to **False** when the counter **Incr** reaches 500.

One or the Other Conditional Functions

The classic either/or selection functions (**Choose, IIF,** and **Switch**) have entered Visual Basic .NET via the **Microsoft.VisualBasic** namespace. We'll discuss them briefly in this section. The underlying architecture for all three functions is the same.

Choose

The **Choose** function is a conditional element that returns an index value based on a list of function arguments provided as choices. The first is index 1 (it is not a zero-based list), the second is index 2, and so on. The function looks like this:

```
Choose(index, choice-1[, choice-2, ... [, choice-n]])
```

and it works as follows:

```
Dim indx As Integer = 2
Console.Writeline(Choose(Indx, "Pears", "Apples", "Oranges", "Mangos"))
```

The list of four fruits in the example is indexed 1 through 4. The argument **indx** is an integer that is initialized to 2 in the example. Calling the function **Choose** and passing "2" as the index value for **indx**, results in selecting item 2 (Apples) from the list.

IIF

The **IIF** function returns one of two objects based on the Boolean result of an expression. Here's an example:

```
Function CanSwallowBeer(ByVal age As Integer) As String
  CanSwallowBeer = IIF(age = 21, "No swallowing", "OK to swallow")
End Function
```

The **IIF** function takes three arguments. If **age** is less than 21, the condition for the first argument to pass to the **IIF**'s first parameter will be **False** and the third argument will be returned. A **True** condition returns the second argument.

The syntax for this function is as follows:

```
Public Function IIf(ByVal Expression As Boolean, _
  ByVal TrueArg As Object, ByVal FalseArg As Object) As Object
```

All three arguments must be provided. The *Expression* is that which you want to test, the *TruePart* is a type that is returned if *Expression* evaluates to **True**; the *FalsePart* is a type that is returned if *Expression* evaluates to **False**.

You can pass method calls to this function as the first argument—in the first position, the call will return a Boolean result. **IIF** tests the function call passed as an argument, so expecting **IIF** to call a function based on the Boolean result of the first method call can be tricky, if not overly complex code.

This example uses the **IIf** function to evaluate the **level** parameter of the **CheckLevel** procedure and returns the word *Safe* if the amount is greater than 1000; otherwise, it returns the word *Critical*.

```
Function CheckLevel(ByVal level As Integer) As String
   CheckLevel = IIf(level = 500, "Safe", "Critical")
End Function
```

Switch

The **Switch** function evaluates a list of expressions provided in the form of a parameter array (see Chapter 7) and returns the type and data associated with the first expression in the list that is **True**.

The syntax for this function is as follows:

```
Public Function Switch(ByVal ParamArray VarExpr() As Object) As Object
```

The argument to send to the *VarExpr()* parameter must either be a single-dimension array containing an even number of elements or a list of object variables separated by commas (the function parses the list of subscripts, be it in list or array form).

The **Switch** function argument *VarExpr()* must comprise paired expressions and values because it analyzes them from lowest to highest subscript in the array or list and then returns the value associated with the first one that evaluates to **True**. For example, if *VarExpr(0)* is **True**, **Switch** returns *VarExpr(1)*, and if *VarExpr(0)* is **False** but *VarExpr(2)* is **True**, **Switch** returns *VarExpr(3)*, and so on. This code should elucidate the foregoing:

```
Function SwitchSuppressant (fire As String) As String
   Return Switch(fire = "Wood Fire ByVal", "Water", _
   fire = "Gas fire", "Sand", fire = "Chemical Fire", "Foam")
End Function
```

If you do not supply the *VarExpr* argument, **Switch** returns **Nothing**. If the number of elements in *VarExpr* is not divisible by two, an **ArgumentException** error occurs. As mentioned earlier, the foundation architecture on which these are built is the same, so be careful when including function calls in the list or parameter array.

Note	*Using these functions requires you to set **Option Strict** to **Off**, which permits the late binding. You need to also remember to Import the Microsoft.VisualBasic namespace or fully qualify the path to the method's class.*

Pausing, Resuming, and Exiting Iteration

Visual Basic provides the **Stop** and **Exit** keywords that can be used to suspend or break out of loops.

Stop can be used anywhere in methods to suspend execution, and it works like a breakpoint during debugging. **Stop** suspends processing; it does not close down the application, free resources, or close files and connections like the **End** keyword discussed in Chapter 4. However, the **Stop** statement works just like **End** if you leave it in a compiled, executable (.exe) file, so take care when removing it or comment it out in beta or release candidate code or when compiling in the so-called "retail" release mode (see Chapters 4 and 17).

This example demonstrates the **Stop** statement suspending executing for each iteration through the **For . . . Next** loop (see Chapter 17, "Getting Ready to Release").

```
Dim intI As Integer
For intI = 1 To maxChecks    'Starts the For...Next loop.
   ShuttleInjector.PostLevel(CheckLevel(CurrentCase))
   Stop 'Suspend execution during each iteration and wait for input
Next intI
```

Use the **Exit** statement to directly exit out if any conditional structure, loop, or method. Invoking **Exit** immediately transfers execution to the point in the code following the last control statement.

Exit is not used alone. You need to qualify the type of conditional or iterative construct you are exiting from so that Visual Basic can correctly intervene. The ensuing list enumerates the types of constructs in which you can call **Exit:**

- Exit Select
- Exit Try
- Exit Do
- Exit While
- Exit For

The same qualifying rule applies to exiting out of methods. You can exit directly from a **Function**, **Sub**, or **Property** procedure by specifying the type of method to qualify the Exit. The method qualifiers are as follows:

- Exit Sub
- Exit Function
- Exit Property

The method **Exit** statements can also be used inside the conditional and loop structures, for example inside **If . . . Then . . . Else** blocks. These are useful when you need to force a method to return at some point in your code.

Exit Idiosyncrasies

When **Exit** is encountered in nested control-flow or conditional structures, execution of code continues with the statement following the end of the innermost control statement of the kind specified in the **Exit** statement and execution returns to the previous level in the structure (**Exit** should not be confused with the **End** keyword). In the following example, **Exit For** is located in the inner **For** loop, so it passes control to the statement following that loop and continues with the outer **For** loop.

```
Public Sub InvertMyElements(ByRef myArray(,) As Double)
   Dim intI, intJ As Integer
   For intI = 0 To UBound(myArray, 0)
      For intJ = 0 To UBound(myArray, 1)
       If myArray(intI, intJ) = 0 Then
         Exit For
       Else
         myArray(intI, intJ) = 1 / myArray(intI, intJ)
       End If
       'this line is now processed when Exit For is executed.
```

```
        Next intJ
     Next intI
End Sub
```

You can also insert multiple **Exit** statements in conditional and control flow constructs. The following example shows this inside a **Do** loop:

```
Do Until level = desiredLevel
  If level <= desiredLevel Then Exit Do
    desiredLevel = CheckLevel(actualLevel)
Loop
```

The **Exit Do** statement works with all versions of **Do** loop syntax (with **While** or **Until**), and **Exit For** works with all versions of **For** loop syntax (with or without **Each**). Here is an example of **Exit** in all three places.

```
Sub CheckLevel(ByVal desiredLevel As Integer)
  Dim intI, level As Integer
  Do
    For intI = 1 To 5000
      level = CheckLevel(ActualLevel)
        If level = desiredLevel Then
          Exit For
        ElseIf level > 25 Then
          Exit Do
        ElseIf level < 0 Then
          Exit Sub
        End If
    Next intI
  Loop
End Sub
```

In the above code a **For. . . Next** loop of 1 to 5000 is set up inside a **Do . . . Loop**, which will end if not preempted before 5000 iterations. Inside the **For** loop we retrieve a value from a call into the **CheckLevel** method and test the result in the **If . . . ElseIf** construct. We can then decide on the finality of the **Exit** based on the result received from **CheckLevel.**

The **Exit For** statement lets you exit a **For Each . . . Next** loop before it has traversed the collection, which provides a nifty short-circuit feature. For example, you could decide to exit a loop upon detection of a condition that makes it unnecessary to continue iteration. A good example is acting on a user request to cancel a download or a file copy to a remote location. Also, if you catch an exception in a **Try . . . Catch . . . Finally**, you can use **Exit For** at the end of the **Finally** block.

Observations

We have devoted considerable time to the issues of control flow, iteration, and conditional structures because understanding these constructs will enable you to correctly apply these tools to creating your algorithms, no matter what the form, platform (Web or traditional applications), or problem may be.

Chapter 7 will take us to the next level—methods—and explore an important alternative iterative model to loops: recursion. It will further explore control flow in relation to recursion, method calls, and invoke-keywords. We will also apply the concepts studied in this chapter to method development and construction.

You will find more examples on iterating, traversing, and working with arrays in Chapter 12. Chapter 11 deals with structured exception handling. Traversing collections and data structures is further discussed in Chapters 12 and 13. For discussions on Boolean logic see Chapters 4, 7, and 16. See Chapter 4 for the scope and life times of variables that are declared inside conditional code blocks such as **If** and **Select Case**.

There is perhaps no better way to end this chapter than with a quote from one of the fathers of software development, Dr. Edsger W. Dijkstra: "We should do our utmost to shorten the conceptual gap between the static program and the dynamic process, to make the correspondence between the program (spread out in text space) and the process (spread out in time) as trivial as possible."

VB .NET FUNDAMENTALS

Visual
Basic
.NET

Chapter 7

Methods

We started the sojourn into the Visual Basic language by looking at the fundamentals, such as declaration, the built-in value types, and conversion. In Chapter 5, we explored operators and the operations they perform on types. Chapter 6 investigated the variety of control, iteration, and flow mechanisms used in Visual Basic algorithms. In this chapter, we bring together much of what we have covered in the past chapters to construct our algorithms, methods, and properties.

This chapter is about making methods. We will investigate what methods and properties are, what they constitute, their specific characteristics, and their application. This is a big chapter, divided into writing code to call framework methods and writing code to implement your own methods.

This chapter also introduces theory on method performance and the running time analysis of algorithms. The subject is not critical to building Visual Basic algorithms, but it is important if your focus will be on building iterative or recursive algorithms and time-, resource-, and computation-centric solutions (as opposed to data presentation). If you want to create the best possible solutions for your programming problems and challenges, the subject is invaluable (it will also help you understand the .NET Framework documentation, which makes more than casual references to algorithm performance).

In the pages to follow we will not only explore the implementation of methods but also the design and construction of methods. We will build on the foundations laid to create industrial strength algorithms and build sophisticated applications.

While this chapter is mostly about methods, it also discusses properties, which are sufficiently similar to methods in construction and purpose to warrant discussion in this chapter.

What Is a Method

A *method* is a unit of functionality, an operation, within a class or an object. Programs comprise multiple methods, organized in objects, and accordingly combined to solve a particular problem. As any dictionary will tell you, a method is simply a way of doing something. In OOP, methods are the way we do things with *procedures* and *functions*.

You can think of the term *routine* as a noun used to refer collectively to procedures and functions in structure-oriented languages like generic Pascal and BASIC, while *method* is the collective noun in OOP. Procedures are known as **Sub** methods in Visual Basic (short for subroutine) and do not return a value. To return a value, you use a **Function** method. Both method types, respectively, are demonstrated as follows:

```
'A Sub method
Sub MyMethod()
  'Make hay . . .
End Sub


'A Function method
```

```
Function MyMethod()As Integer
  'Make hay and return the amount made
  Return amount 'or
  Return MyMethod 'or
  MyMethod = Amount
End Sub
```

A *method* is the encapsulation of specific blocks of functionality and data within a class, no matter whether that method can be summoned or invoked statically (shared) or dynamically through object creation and the subsequent collaboration with that object (see Chapters 2, 8, and 9).

By encapsulating functionality, methods fulfill the tenet of structured programming, discussed in Chapter 1. Thus, methods provide the smallest unit or module of functionality in our Visual Basic applications. Methods avoid code repetition and promote reuse, because numerous consumers may execute the same code. The method thus has to be implemented only once in order to serve many.

Methods also provide additional levels—behind the object interface—of abstraction and encapsulation, the benefits of which are described in many places in this book. Specifically, hiding data and functionality behind methods reduces complexity, because once a method is defined, designed, and implemented, you can pretty much forget about it. Using the method's functionality becomes a simple matter of calling the method (or sending it a message as they say in Smalltalk circles). You no longer need to know or worry about how the method works…which means your method or class consumers don't either.

The illustration provides an abstract view of a method definition in a class.

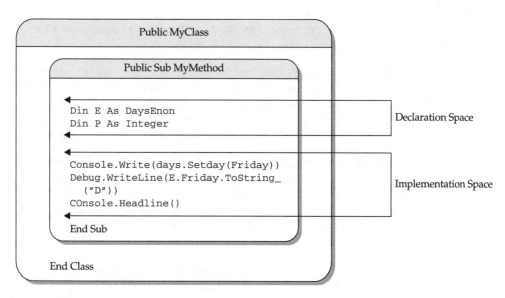

The following is the "formal" syntax for the declaration of Visual Basic methods. Do not worry if you do not understand the syntax at first (it's very cryptic); you'll pick it up as you check out the corresponding code.

MethodDeclaration ::= SubDeclaration | FunctionDeclaration
SubDeclaration ::=
[Attributes] [ProcedureModifier+] **Sub** *Identifier [([FormalParameterList])]*
[HandlesOrImplements] LineTerminator
  [Block] (implementation)
End Sub *LineTerminator*

FunctionDeclaration ::=
[Attributes] [ProcedureModifier+] **Function** *Identifier*
[([FormalParameterList])] [**As** *[Attributes] TypeName]*
[HandlesOrImplements] LineTerminator
  [Block] (implementation)
End Function *LineTerminator*

The method declaration consists of several essential components in this space, starting with the method name or identifier and ending with the **End Sub** or **End Function** method terminator.

The first elements in the declaration space of methods are the optional attributes, which were introduced in Chapters 2 and 4. Access and implementation modifiers, however, are required (although there are defaults).

Types of Methods

The generally accepted style for organizing methods in classes is to categorize them into two groups:

- **Accessor methods**   An accessor method (often called a "get method") is used to access information from another object or a local field in the current object and it does not manipulate the object or change its data in any way. An example of an accessor method is one that would allow us to query the current state of an object. Accessor methods are also often used to perform calculations and compute data.

- **Modification methods**   A modification method (often called a "set method") lets you manipulate an object and change its data. It can be designed to compute values, perform calculations, interact with external objects, and ultimately change the specific state of an object, values in variable fields, and so on. An object might have an "on" condition, for example, and you could use the modification method to set the condition to off.

Both accessor and modification methods can access the object's data fields (the instant variables and constants). The accessor methods access data and can even be activated or called by the other members of the class. The modification methods also use the data provided by the instance fields to perform computations and carry out the processing required by the algorithm. You don't have to organize your methods into the two groups, but doing so helps to logically organize a class.

Accessor methods are usually short and do little else other than access data and information. Accessor methods provide a return value (otherwise they would not work very well). They can (and should) also be used to let the consumer compute data or perform work without actually setting any variables in the object.

Note	*Properties, which we will discuss at the end of the chapter, can be substituted for accessor methods. I have my own rules for when to use a property and when to use an accessor method, which we will discuss later.*

You can also name these methods in such a way that consumers of the class can tell at a glance whether the method is an *accessor* method or a *modification* method. For example, accessor method names can be prefixed with *Get*, as in **GetSpeed** or **GetDriveState**. The modification methods, on the other hand, are given names that describe what they modify, change, or compute. For example, the modification method that changes the speed might be called **SetSpeed** and the modification method that changes the state of the drive might be called **SetDdriveState**.

Synchronous vs. Asynchronous Method Calls

Most of the method calls you make are *synchronous*, which means that your algorithm waits for the call to complete before you can carry on with the next line that follows the call. This is not something you can normally control. There is no keyword that amounts to saying "call the method and then wait for the result…give it five minutes and then give it the boot." If the method you are calling needs to perform a complex operation that could take many minutes to complete, your thread will be blocked waiting for the called method to complete. This is often felt when you try to open a connection to a database server that is having a hard time validating your security credentials, or when you try to log into a mailbox. There is nothing you can do but wait for your standard synchronous call to return.

On the other hand, there are occasions when you know in advance that the called method needs to go and do something else in order to serve your call. You can then make the call and attend to other tasks. This is known as an *asynchronous* method call. Such programming has specific and powerful support in the .NET Framework.

Another solution to the blocked calls from synchronous methods is to explicitly use another thread. Asynchronous calls and callbacks (when the asynchronous call returns to the caller with a result) is a subject beyond the scope of this book.

Threading is extensively covered in the aforementioned book in the chapter "Concurrent Programming." Threading is introduced in Chapter 17.

Method Data

Methods typically need to be provided with data (values or references to values) to process when they are called or contacted. They can get this data from four places:

- Class-level global data (see Chapter 4), or data the method can see elsewhere in the class
- Data from external classes and objects
- Method-level data (inside the method or within method blocks)
- Data passed to a method via its parameter list. Parameter fields expose data to the method.

Class-level data is data stored in the variable and constant fields, or within properties, which are scoped to the class. The following code shows a simple method accessing class-level data:

```
Public Class Calcs
  Const C As Integer = 186355 'mps
  Dim warp As Integer = 5 'not good to hard code like this

  Public Function FactorLightSpeed() As Integer
    Return C \ warp
  End Function

End Class
```

In the preceding code, the C is a class-level constant (global to the class) used by the method **FactorLightSpeed**. There are good things and bad things about class-level data fields used by methods. If you make it so your methods depend on class-level variables, then you are explicitly coupling methods that use the variable, one to the other, because a method that changes the data for itself changes it for all methods that used that variable. The methods in a sense become hard-coded, or hard-wired. In the preceding example, any method that changed **warp** affects the **FactorLightSpeed** method. Strive to maintain loosely coupled methods, as discussed later in this chapter.

Data from external objects or classes is data that is explicitly made available to calling methods. Such data is usually provided from properties, fields, or return values from methods that exist in an object with which the calling method is associated. In the following example, the calling method uses the data received from a specialist object to continue with its calculations:

```
Public Class Calcs
  Const C As Integer = 186355 'mps
```

```
Public Function FactorLightSpeed() As Integer
   Return C \ SpaceMath.CurrentFactor(warp)
End Function

End Class
```

Method-level data is data in variable or constant fields that is scoped local to the method or any block nested inside the method. Such data is the most encapsulated data in an object because only the method in which the variables or constants are declared has direct access to the data. The following example shows variables and constants declared inside the method:

```
Public Class Calcs
   Const C As Integer = 186355 'mps

   Public Function FactorLightSpeed() As Integer
      Const C As Integer = 186355 'mps
      Dim warp As Integer = 5
      Return C \ warp
   End Function

End Class
```

Visual Basic allows you to declare method-level static variables that have values that survive the termination of the method. In other words, the static variable is not disposed of with the destruction of the method call that comes after its completion. In the following example, a static method (the only place in Visual Basic you can use the **Static** keyword) retains its value after the execution steps exit the method:

```
Public Class Complex

   Public Function FactorLightSpeed() As Integer
      Const C As Integer = 186355 'mps
      Static warp As Long = 5
      Return C \ warp
   End Function

End Class
```

Note   *The use of **Dim** is optional with a static field.*

We will look at static variables again later in this chapter.

Data that is passed to a method's parameters comprises values or references required by the method to perform. This option is demonstrated in the following code:

```
Public Class Complex
   Const C As Integer = 186355 'mps

   Public Function FactorLightSpeed(ByVal warp As Integer)_
   As Integer
     Return C \ warp
   End Sub

End Class
```

The ability to pass data to a method in this fashion is the most powerful option you have for making data available to the method. It is also the most dynamic, soft-coded way. The caller or sender of the message maintains the utmost control over the data that is sent as an argument to the method's parameter. The method is also able to tightly control the data that it receives, because it can perform checks on the inbound references or values and take action accordingly. It can perform such checks in a number of ways, which includes specifying the type required, a built-in strong typing filter.

The level of method coupling varies in the previous four key options for providing data to the method. The highest level of coupling between methods results from the class level or global variables, while the lowest level of coupling is achieved when data is explicitly sent to the method via its formal parameter list. There will be more information on method data later in this chapter.

Method Data: Global vs. Local

Methods perform their work with local data or class data. When you need to modify variables for other methods in the class or for operations that interest the entire class, then use class variables. If no other method requires access to the variable or needs to use it, then declare it local to the method. In my opinion, you should not declare class variables if you don't need to, because the narrower the scope of access on a variable, the more secure it is and the less coupled your method will be to other methods in the class.

There is another school of thought, however, that says passing arguments to methods requires more resources from the run-time environment. I don't believe this is a valid argument (no pun intended) in the world of managed code and execution, because the common language runtime manages the call stacks with a very high degree of sophistication. Providing too many global variables eventually leads to problems.

Another criterion for declaring class variables or constants is when the values need to remain intact after the method has performed its work. Local variables are created and initialized either to the default values of their types or values you provide when the method is invoked or called. The data and references are subsequently destroyed when method execution ends. As mentioned earlier, you can use a static variable in a method if you require value persistence after execution, but static variables are more resource-intensive than class-level variables, because static variables are stored on the heap as boxed values (see Chapter 8).

Local variables are declared in either of two declaration spaces in a method: as a parameter in the formal parameter list space, or as a local variable in the method's local declaration space. The following illustrates the two declaration spaces we are talking about:

```
Public Sub Space(Parameter lists declaration space)
  local declaration space
End Sub
```

The method's local declaration space can also mean local to the block of code within the method implementation. This means that you can declare at any level as needed, because each nested block become its own declaration scope and context. This is demonstrated in the following code:

```
Public Sub BirdsNest ()
  Dim field1 As Integer = 1
  Const field2 As Integer = 2
  While field1 <= field2
    Dim field3 As Integer = 3
    Const field4 As Integer = 4
    While field3 <= field4
      field3 += 1
    End While
    field1 += 1
  End While
End Sub
```

Note the following rules for declaring variables and constants in method block and parameter lists:

- The variable declared in the parameter list cannot be redeclared in any method block.

- A variable declared in an outer or containing block cannot be redeclared in a nested block (or any other block for that matter). You cannot shadow method data, so consider the formal parameter list as the outermost declaration space before class data.

- Method declarations are scoped to the block in the method in which they are declared.

■ Method variables and constants are implicitly declared public, and you cannot modify the access characteristics with keywords like **Private** or **ReadOnly**.

■ The **Option Strict** and **Option Explicit** compiler directives (refer to Chapter 4) influence variable and constant declarations. You can implicitly declare (by simply just using the variable) and use loose syntax by setting both options to **Off** for the class. This practice is, however, greatly discouraged because it causes buggy and hard to maintain code. (Refer to Chapter 4 for more information on implicit and loose syntax declarations.) There is an exception to this rule, however. A local method variable may not be implicitly declared when it is the target of a function call, an indexing expression, or a member access expression. Also, implicitly declared locals are always scoped to the entire method body.

■ When you declare implicitly, the type of the variable defaults to **Object** if no type character was attached to the implicit declaration; otherwise, the type of the variable is the type of the type character. In the following example you can see how it is possible to set yourself up for problems with implicit declaration. The return value will continue to be wrong no matter what gets passed to the method until someone realizes the simple spelling mistake:

```
Public Function FactorLightSpeed(ByVal warp As Decimal)_
   As Decimal
   speed = 186355 \ waro
   Return speed
End Function
```

■ Variable initializers on method locals are equivalent to assignment statements placed at the textual location of the declaration. Thus, if execution branches over the local declaration, the variable initializer will not be executed. Also, if the method variable declaration is executed more than once, the variable initializer will be executed an equal number of times. It is important to note that locals are only initialized to their type's default value once, upon entry into the method (refer to "Local Declarations" in the next section).

Local Declarations

Local, or method, declarations can store both constant data using the **Const** keyword, which is no different from a class constant declaration, or variable data. Variables can be declared using the **Dim** keyword or the **Static** keyword. The following syntax represents local declaration:

LocalDeclarationStatement ::= *LocalModifier LocalDeclarator StatementTerminator*
LocalModifier ::= **Static** | **Dim** | **Const**

LocalDeclarator ::=
  LocalIdentifiers [**As** *TypeName*]
Identifier [*ArrayNameModifier*]
[**As** [**New**] *TypeName* [([*ArgumentList*])]] [= *VariableInitializer*]
LocalIdentifiers ::=
  Identifier [*ArrayNameModifier*] |
  LocalIdentifiers, Identifier [*ArrayNameModifier*]
LocalVariableName ::= *Identifier*

As the name suggests, constant data cannot be changed. It consists of read-only values, but the **ReadOnly** keyword is not valid in either of the method declaration spaces (see the "Properties" section later in this chapter).

Static Data

The **Static** keyword modifies a local variable declaration to static, which plays an important role in code reentrance, isolation, encapsulation, and recursion (see Chapters 4, 12, 13, and 14 and the later section "Recursive Design of Methods" in this chapter). When you declare static variables, their values are retained for future calls to the method.

It is critical to be aware that declaring a static local in a shared method means that the value of the static is retained for all references to the type. In other words, there is only one copy of the static local at all times. Dependence on the data held by the static must therefore be carefully reviewed. Remember that static methods (which are declared with the modifier **Shared** in Visual Basic and **static** in C#) are not instance methods. For all intents and purposes, the method and the static data are both global entities. (See the section "Improved Performance with Shared Classes and Modules" in Chapter 9.)

When you declare a static local in a nonshared method, which allows instantiation, then a separate copy of the static exists for each instance of the object, and the static's value is retained for the clients that have a reference on the object that encapsulates the static. The following code demonstrates declaring a static variable in a nonshared method (notice the use of Hungarian notation for clearly marking static variables):

```
Private Function ChurnOut(ByVal Param As Integer) As Integer
   Static stChurnval As Integer
   '...
End Function
```

Returning with Values

By default, all methods return to the caller or sender that called them. And as demonstrated in Chapter 6, you can use the **Return** keyword to terminate and exit out of a method at any point, even from a **Sub** method. In this regard **Return** works exactly like **Exit Sub**.

However, when you declare a function, you are advising the parties concerned that a value will come back from the method being called, so you must supply a return value and that value must be the same type as the value declared as the return value variable. This is demonstrated as follows:

```
Private Function ChurnIn(ByVal Param As Integer) As Integer
   '... do something with Param
   Return Param
End Function
```

The return value declared after the parameter list is a local variable declaration, just like the parameters and the variables declared in the body of the method. The function name is the name of the variable. For example, looking at the preceding method **ChurnIn**, you can see the variable declaration if you drop the parameter list as follows:

```
Function ChurnIn As Integer
```

To return **ChurnIn** as an **Integer**, you do not need to use **Return** unless there are several places in the function where return is possible (such as in a **Select Case** construct or a nested structure). However, if you do use **Return**, you must supply the value returned. Here are the additional variations to returning the value:

```
Private Function ChurnIn(ByVal Param As Integer) As Integer
   '... do something with Param and assign to ChurnIn
   'ChurnIn returned implicitly
   ChurnIn = Sqrt(Param)
End Function
```

or

```
Private Function ChurnIn(ByVal Param As Integer) As Integer
   '... do something with Param
   ChurnIn = Sqrt(Param)
   Return ChurnIn
End Function
```

or

```
Private Function ChurnIn(ByVal Param As Integer) As Integer
   '... do something with Param
   Dim valuable As Integer
```

```
    valuable = Sqrt(Param)
    Return valuable
End Function
```

Note *Chapter 12 investigates passing and receiving arrays from methods.*

Passing Arguments to Parameters

As discussed earlier in this chapter, the parameters of a method are declared by the method's formal parameter list. (The parameter list and method name, or identifier, are combined to form the method's signature.)

The parameter declarations of a method are the "placeholders" for the data sourced external to the method and the means by which the data can be "communicated" to the method for its use. For example, if a method needs to multiply two numbers represented by x and y, then you can communicate the value for x and the value for y by sending the respective values to the parameters.

The "sender" of the values refers to these values as the *arguments* for the parameters. Parameters are the "receivers"; you can think of them as pigeonholes or slots into which the arriving data is channeled. It's important to get the difference between *arguments* and *parameters* right. Many programmers confuse the terms to their own detriment (parameters receive; arguments send).

A method can receive a variety of types to its parameters: value types, reference types, and a collection (of types) that arrives as a comma-delimited list. The latter parameter is known as a parameter array. A fourth type of parameter is the "optional" parameter, which lets the sender choose not to send an argument. The method applies a default value to the optional parameter and then passes that into the method.

Method processing can be very tightly controlled by the optional parameter, as you will see later in this chapter and in later chapters.

The formal parameter keywords are listed in Table 7-1.

Parameter Type	Keyword
Value Types	**ByVal**
Reference Types	**ByRef**
Optional Parameter	**Optional**
Array Parameter	**ParamArray**

Table 7-1. *Parameter Types Excepted at Methods*

You can specify multiple parameters in the parameter list; however, each parameter declaration must be separated by a comma so that the compiler can discern the bounds of each parameter. You can use loose and implicit syntax in the declaration of parameters (if **Option Strict** and **Option Explicit** are set to **Off**), but if you use the **As** keyword for one parameter declaration, you need to use it for all. If you use implicit syntax and do not declare the type of parameter, then the type defaults to **Object**.

The syntax for declaring the parameter list is as follows:

FormalParameterList ::=
 FormalParameter |
 FormalParameterList, FormalParameter

FormalParameter ::=
  [*Attributes*] *ParameterModifier*+ *Identifier* [**As** *TypeName*]
 [= *ConstantExpression*]
 ParameterModifier ::= **ByVal** | **ByRef** | **Optional** | **ParamArray**

Pass by Value

Value parameters are passed by value and are explicitly declared with the **ByVal** modifier. If you omit the modifier in your code, the compiler automatically defaults the parameter acceptance mode to **ByVal**.

The **Value** variable is created when the method is called, and is destroyed when the method execution ends (returns). The scope of the parameter's variables is the entire method, including any nested blocks. Here's an example:

```
Public Sub ValueIn(ByVal Data As String)
   Console.WriteLine("Data received is: " &  Data)
End Sub
```

You are permitted to change the value received to the parameter (that is, the value that was sent to the method as the argument). Remember, once the value is passed to the parameter, changing the value in the method does not affect the source of the original data—the argument sent is a copy of the data, not a reference to it. As mentioned earlier, the parameter list is a declaration context, and the argument merely serves to initialize it with the value it carries to the method. This is demonstrated in the following example:

```
Public Function ValueIn(ByVal Number As Integer) As Integer
   Number += 5
   If (Number > 10)
     Return Number
   End If
```

```
    Return 0
End Function
```

Pass by Reference

When you pass by reference, the data and construct represented by reference are directly affected by the operations on the parameter. Passing by reference means you do not make a copy of the value and pass that to the method. No new storage location is created to hold any data. Think of the pass by reference as the baton in a relay race. There is only one baton being passed and if it gets dropped the passer gets disqualified.

You can pass both value types and reference types using the **ByRef** keyword. Passing by reference will become more clear in the next chapter and Chapter 9, which delve into the object reference models. When you pass a value by reference, you are essentially requesting the method to directly and immediately act on the original data. The following example demonstrates passing a value type by reference:

```
Public Sub ChangeUp(ByRef myVal As Integer)
   ChangeUp(myVal)
End Sub
```

Despite the declaration of a reference parameter, Visual Basic .NET may still use copy-in/copy-out semantics when a reference variable is passed to a **ByRef** parameter. This usually happens when there is either no storage location to pass a reference to, which is what happens when the argument references a property, or when the type of the storage location is not the same as the parameter type's. The latter situation happens, for example, when you pass an instance of a parent class to a **ByRef** derived class parameter—a technique called *upcasting*. Thus, a reference parameter may not necessarily contain a reference to the exact storage location of the object, and any changes to the reference parameter may not be reflected in the variable until the method exits.

Optional Parameters

Optional parameters can be passed to methods. An optional parameter is declared with the **Optional** modifier. Parameters that follow an optional parameter in the formal parameter list must be optional as well or you will choke the compiler. Thus, if you have numerous parameters in the parameter list, make sure all the optional ones are in their specific order and are placed after the other three parameter types. The following code provides an example:

```
Function DDB(ByVal rcost As Double, _
  ByVal rsalvage As Double, ByVal rlife As Integer, _
```

```
ByVal rperiod As Integer, _
Optional ByVal rfactor As Decimal = 2) As Double

  Dim book As Double = cost - salvage
  Dim deprec As Double
  Dim year As Integer = period
    While year > 1
      deprec = book * factor / life
      book = book - deprec
      year -= 1
    End While
  Return book

End Function
```

Optional parameters must specify constant expressions to be used as the default value if no argument is specified, as demonstrated in the bold type in the preceding code. This is the only situation in which an initializer on a parameter is valid. The initialization is always done as a part of the invocation expression, not within the method body itself. Also, optional parameters may not be specified in **Delegate** or **Event** declarations.

Passing a Parameter Array

A parameter array is a single dimension data structure that can be passed as an argument to a parameter. The differences between passing arguments to a parameter array and passing a regular array reference as the argument are as follows:

- The **ParamArray** parameter expects the argument as a value and not as a reference.

- You can only declare one **ParamArray** in the parameter list, while you can declare more than one parameter that expects a reference to a regular array or collection.

- The **ParamArray** parameter is useful for sending on-the-fly lists of data to the method, without the need to specially pass over a reference to any collection. It is ideal for varying the number of arguments needed by the method. This is demonstrated in the following code:

```
Module ParamArrayTest
  Sub Main()
    Dim arrayA As Double() = {1, 4, 2.5, 3.9}
    GetArrayVals(arrayA)
    GetArrayVals(10.6, 20, 30.0, 40.87, 987.3)
    GetArrayVals()
```

```
      Console.ReadLine()
    End Sub

    Sub GetArrayVals(ByVal ParamArray arrayargs As Double())
      Debug.Write(arrayargs.Length & " elements passed:")
      Dim intI As Integer
      For Each intI In arrayargs
        Debug.Write(" " & String.Format("{0:c}", intI))
      Next intI
    End Sub
  End Module
```

This example produces the following output:

```
4 elements passed: $1.00 $4.00 $2.00 $4.00
5 elements passed: $11.00 $20.00 $30.00 $41.00 $987.00
0 elements passed:
```

In the above code the first call simply passes a pre-packaged array to the parameter. The second call creates a five member comma-delimited list and passes the list. The third method call demonstrates that you can pass zero elements to the **ParamArray** parameter.

When you are passing a simple list to the **ParamArray** parameter it is often difficult to distinguish between the list of values and values in regular arguments because the argument list is not distinguishable from the list intended for the parameter array. While the compiler can make the distinction because it knows where the **ParamArray** starts in the receiving method, you may see the subtle "bug" when you make the call. For example, can you tell that the following call is actually sending two arguments?

```
GetVals(1, 10.6, 20, 30.0, 40.87, 987.3)
```

You can now if you examine the method signature as follows:

```
Sub GetVals(ByVal intI As Integer, _
ByVal ParamArray pArgs As Double())
```

You can avoid the problem by first avoiding hard-coding and doing away with magic numbers and arbitrary values in your code as shown in the following call:

```
GetVals(MyDayEnum.Sunday, MoneyToParamArray)
```

To send data to a parameter array your need to declare the parameter with the **ParamArray** modifier. And you cannot declare a parameter of type **ParamArray** without specifying the **ByVal** (**ByRef** is invalid). Like the optional parameter discussed earlier the paramarray parameter must be the last parameter in the formal parameter list. Unlike the optional parameter you do not have to provide default values. If the sender does not send an argument to the parameter array the array will default to an empty array.

Parameter array usage is as follows:

- The parameter array will perform a widening conversion on the argument if the argument is narrower than the parameter. However, if the argument is wider than the parameter array or incompatible an exception will be thrown.

- The sender can specify zero or more arguments for the parameter array as a comma-delimited list, where each argument is an option for a type that is implicitly convertible to the element type of the paramarray. An interesting activity takes place on the call. The caller creates an instance of the paramarray type with a length corresponding to the number of arguments, initializes the elements of the array instance with the given argument values, and uses the newly created array instance as the actual argument to give to the parameter.

- Paramarray parameters may not be specified in delegate or event declarations.

Parameter arrays are useful and you don't need to treat the parameter any different, from inside your method, as you do the regular array reference.

Calling Methods

Methods are called (or invoked) via an interface, which is accessed by referencing the class or object containing the method, followed by a reference to the method's *signature*—which is its name and (mostly) any arguments of the type and order, in the target method's parameter list. When you reference a method, you *invoke* it or *call* it. Some OOP experts also refer to the invocation of the method as "sending a message to the method." And thus the term *sender* is frequently used, especially in event models. Conversely, the method on the receiving end of the message or call is known as the *receiver*.

From time to time, we will refer to the construction of our code by the particular *method calls* that have to be made. Later in this chapter, we will see how Visual Basic methods can call themselves (recursion).

Call by Reference or Call by Value

As noted in Table 7-1, arguments can be passed to parameters by value or by reference. When you pass by value, you are passing the actual value to the method (some prefer to say "call by value"). When you pass by reference, you are passing only a reference to an object. Value types—such as the built-in **Integer**, **Short**, **Single**, and **Double**—are passed by value. Reference types—such as arrays, strings, and custom objects—are typically passed by reference.

VB .NET FUNDAMENTALS

Suppose the method you are calling needs to receive an array. You don't need to send the array to the method (although this was once the case some time ago) but rather a reference to the array. This means the object stays exactly where it is and the method can still go to work on the array. This will become clearer to you in Chapter 8, in the "Object Reference Model" section, which covers both how value types and reference types are references, and in the method design and construction sections later in this chapter.

The same procedure—passing the reference and not a copy of the value—applies when receiving the return value back from the function. If the function returns a value type, you'll receive a copy of the value; but if it returns a reference type, such as an array, you'll only get the reference to the array from the function.

Passing the actual value to the receiving method does not change any data that exists in the calling method or elsewhere, because a copy of the value is sent to the receiver. The value copy is then used and discarded. However, when you pass by reference, any changes made to the object by the receiving method affect the original object, because you don't send a copy of the object, you send a "message" telling the calling method where to find the object that needs to be worked on. The procedure is akin to sending someone the keys to a house, rather than the house itself. For example, when you send a reference to an array that needs to be sorted, all entities referencing the array will see the results of the sort. This is an important consideration to keep in mind when designing your software.

For the most part when you call a method, you do not need to worry about whether you are passing by reference or passing by value. Visual Basic enforces the calling procedure and knows whether it should pass by value or by reference (see Chapter 12 for information on passing and receiving arrays).

The following line of code is a typical method call found in many Visual Basic applications. Notice that this method does not pass any arguments.

```
Beep()
```

All this method does is make a call to the **Beep** function—which beeps the speaker—in the class maintained in the **Microsoft.VisualBasic** namespace. (The **Microsoft.VisualBasic** represents the classic VB runtime and its collection of types, libraries, and run-time constructs that provide the interface to the Win32 library for the classic Visual Basic languages. Any .NET language can now reference it thanks to the framework's interop layers and wrapper classes that adapt legacy code for access from the world of .NET.)

The fully qualified namespace for the method is as follows:

```
Microsoft.VisualBasic.Interaction.Beep
```

In other words, the **Beep** method can be found in the **Interaction** class contained in the **Microsoft.VisualBasic** namespace. Table 7-2 provides the entire list of legacy function calls you can access in this "wrapped" class.

Function	Purpose
AppActivate	Launches an executable (see also **Shell**)
Beep	Standard speaker beep
CallByName	Sets and gets properties and invokes methods at run time by providing arguments to the **CallByName** method
Choose	Selects and returns values from a parameter list
Command	Returns the argument portion of the command line used to launch VB apps
CreateObject	Creates a reference to a COM object
DeleteSetting	Deletes Registry settings
Environ	Returns the OS environment variables as a string
GetAllSettings	Returns all the settings related to an application's Registry settings
GetObject	Returns a reference to an object provided by a COM object
GetSetting	Returns a key setting from the Registry
Iif	Returns one of two objects passed as arguments and tested against a **Boolean** key
InputBox	Creates a dialog box for user input and then returns the input to the caller
MsgBox	Display a dialog box, presents options for the user, and then returns an Integer based on the choice of the user
Partition	Calculates a set of numeric ranges
SaveSetting	Saves an application's Registry setting
Shell	Runs an application and returns its process ID from the OS
Switch	Evaluates a list of expressions

Table 7-2.   *Legacy Functions in the **Microsoft.VisualBasic.Interaction** Class*

Function or Sub Methods

In all modern computer languages, methods can be constructed to return with or without a value to a caller. As mentioned at the start of this chapter, the methods that return a value are called *functions* and the methods that don't return a value are called *subroutines* or *subprocedures*. Visual Basic methods that return without values are declared with the **Sub** keyword.

Consider the **Beep** method we looked at previously. If you were to open up the **Interaction** class and search for the **Beep** method, you would find the following definition:

```
Public Sub Beep()
```

Public refers to the accessibility of this method (you can call it from anywhere). It is referred to as a **Sub** procedure because it does not return with a value.

Note *The .Net Framework documentation refers to the **Beep** procedure as a function, which is technically wrong. Technically, it is not a function because it does not return any value to the caller. But the VB runtime calls it a function, even though the .NET code defines it as a **Sub**. You will find many such inconsistencies in the documentation of various languages, .NET included. I even traded insults with another writer over the term method when first embarking on Visual Basic .NET.*

The following line of code is an example of a function call:

```
Public Function Choose(Index As Integer, ParamArray Choice() _
As Object) As Object
```

Choose is another classic VB function, and in this declaration, the method requires you to send an argument of type **Integer** for the **Index** parameter and the **Choice** array object for the **ParamArray** parameter. The returning type for this function is declared at the end of the method declaration; in this case, the return type is **Object**.

Choose is an interesting function. It returns with an object in the parameter array at the index position, 1 or higher, expressed in the **Index** parameter. In other words, if the argument to **Index** is "1" then the first item in the parameter array is returned to the caller.

You would invoke this method as follows:

```
Choose(num, "red", "white", "blue")
```

If **num** in the preceding call is 2, then "white" is returned to the caller. Digging around in the VB runtime (or what we used to call it before it got "inter-roped"), we find another useful function, the **Rnd** function:

```
Public Function Rnd() As Single
```

Rnd is also accessible to .NET, which returns a number (in this case, the number is of type **Single**) that we can use to generate a random number in a particular range. The VB runtime provides a **Randomize** procedure, which reads system internals, to produce guaranteed random selection.

Without going into the specific implementation "under the hood" of these randomizing functions, consider the following formula, which bubbles up from the VB runtime to the .NET Framework:

```
Int((3 * Rnd()) + 1)
```

This formula produces a random number in the range 1 to 3. Here we have another function called **Int**, which returns the number generated by the formula. With these constructs, we can program a game of chance using the **Choose** function. The following code demonstrates the preceding calls in action emulating a "loose" slot machine named "Pull":

```
Public Sub Pull()
  Dim key As Integer 'variable scoped to the method
  While (key <= 2)
    Randomize()
    num = Int((3 * Rnd()) + 1)
    Console.Write(Choose(num, "red", "white", "blue") & " | ")
  End While
  Console.WriteLine(" ")
End Sub
```

If you keep putting in the money, you'll eventually hit the jackpot, as demonstrated in the following output in line six:

```
red | white | white
white | red | red
blue | blue | red
blue | blue | white
red | red | red |
red | white | blue
```

Choose looks very much like a case routine, and can be very useful for quick conditional routines that return values for display. If you pass zero or a number greater than the total elements in the list, **Choose** throws an exception, which can be safely dealt with to provide a graceful resetting of the function. (See also Chapter 6 for information on **Choose** and similar control-flow constructs.)

When you call functions, you can access the return value by assigning a variable to the entire function call. However, it's the actual return value that is the predicate of the assignment. Look back at the **Pull** method. The following calls are assigned to variables (emphasized):

```
num = Int((3 * Rnd()) + 1)
Console.Write(Choose(num, "red", "white", "blue") & " | ")
```

The variable **num** is assigned to the return value of the **Int** function, while the entire argument in the method call to **Console.Write** is assigned to the return value of the call to **Choose**. In the latter case, part of the argument is itself a method call (under the hood, however, the return value from **Choose** represents the argument to the **Write** method). Table 7-3 lists the legacy functions available to us in the **Microsoft.VisualBasic .VbMath** class.

If it is not clear to you by now, programming against the .NET Framework consists of calling or invoking the thousands of methods that have been provided in the Framework classes. For the record you can also access additional classic VB "funcs" in the following classes:

- **Collection**   Collection Object utilities such as **Add** and **Count**
- **Conversion**   Simple conversion utilities such as **Int** and **Str**
- **DateAndTime**   Functions for working with date and time values
- **ErrObject**   Functions for programming against the legacy **Err** object
- **FileSystem**   File system utilities (see also the section "FSO" in Chapter 15)
- **Financial**   Functions for computing financial data
- **Globals**   Functions that return data related to the classic VB runtime
- **Information**   Useful utility functions (such as **UBound**, **LBound**, **IsDBNull**, and so on)
- **Interaction**   See Table 7-2 in this chapter for the full list
- **Strings**   String manipulation functions (see the full list in Chapter 15)
- **VbMath**   See Table 7-3 in this chapter for the full list

Function	Purpose
Randomize	Initializes the random number generator (**Rdm**). See also the **System.Random** class.
Rnd (Random)	Returns a random number of type **Single**.

Table 7-3.   *Legacy Functions in the* **Microsoft.VisualBasic.VbMath** *Class*

IF you have experience with these classic VB functions they can help you get up to speed with Visual Basic .NET very quickly. If you don't, the .NET Framework reference material will point you to the new .NET methods.

Method Access Characteristics

The characteristics listed in Table 7-4 describe the level of access (visibility) permitted on methods. The level of access to members and data and the implementation of members

Visual Basic	C#	Framework	Purpose
Public[*]	Public	Public	Provides unrestricted access from any class in any assembly (application)
Protected	Protected	Family	To restrict access to members of the class in which the method is declared, to composite or nested classes, aggregate objects, and derived classes
Friend	Internal	Assembly	To restrict access to members within the same assembly (program). **Friend** functions cannot be seen outside the assembly containing their class

Table 7-4.   *Access Modifiers and the Purpose for Each*

Visual Basic	C#	Framework	Purpose
Protected Friend	Protected Internal	Family and Assembly	The union of **Protected** and **Friend**—meaning one or the other
Private	Private	Private	To restrict access only to members of the class in which the method is declared, or a composite class

*Public methods are the only methods that can be accessed from a class in another assembly, program, or remote process.

Table 7-4. *Access Modifiers and the Purpose for Each* (continued)

can be controlled on several levels in the .NET Framework. For a conceptual discussion of information hiding and access control, see the section "Modularity" in Chapter 13. Also refer to the UML notation for "visibility" in Chapter 13.

Table 7-5 provides chart five visibility levels and the level of access sender methods have on receivers.

Caller to Sender	Public	Protected	Friend	Protected Friend	Private
Base to base	Yes	Yes	Yes	Yes	Yes
Base to nested	Yes	No	Yes	Yes	No
Base to derived	Yes	No	Yes	Yes	No
Assembly class to assembly class	Yes	No	Yes	Yes	No
Nested to base	Yes	Yes	Yes	Yes	Yes
Nested to instance*	Yes	Yes	Yes	Yes	Yes
External to assembly	Yes	No	No	No	No

*The above rules are valid for static methods only, which are declared with the **Shared** modifier (see next section). When you declare instance methods you only have access to the public methods of the instance class with which the caller is collaborating (unless you are making the call from a composite class and the method on the receiving end of the call belongs to the container).

Table 7-5. *Access Modifiers and How They Restrict Access*

Public is the most "permissive" level of access you can obtain on a method. **Public** methods can be called from anywhere. The access, however, stops at the method signature. You still do not gain access to any other information about a method, and there is no way of accessing the implementation or the internal data that is local to the method. The strictest level of access is **Private**; all other access levels are more permissive than **Private**.

The level of access (visibility or accessibility) to members and data and the implementation of members can be controlled on several levels in the .NET Framework.

Public Methods

A public method can be accessed from anywhere, and no restrictions are in place to prevent access to a public method. The following code declares a public method:

```
Public Sub StartInjector()
End Sub
```

It is critical to qualify or confirm the method that you specify as public, because it means that any function or procedure in an application can see and access the method. It is considered acceptable in some quarters, at the early stages of design and code, to declare methods as public—for the benefit of implementation teams and to make the development environment less rigid. Don't fall into this trap because you can't easily go back and hide your data and methods later without breaking code everywhere.

The use of **Public** is implicit in the following example:

```
Sub StartInjector()
End Sub
```

Public methods can thus be accessed from remote processes or method calls across process boundaries—through .NET "remoting" technology and the like—if the class so provides the required interface to access the method. Public access applies equally to static methods and instance methods. See Chapter 2 on application domains and security.

Protected Methods

Methods that are declared as **Protected** can be accessed only from other members of the class in which they are declared, and from composite, aggregated, and derived classes. However, a protected method can only be accessed from a derived class if the method is static (shared) or if the reference is to an instance method. If the method is not static both parent class containing the protected method and the child class must be collaborating as instances (a call to an object). Protected methods cannot be accessed from any other classes in the program. The following code declares a protected method:

```
Protected Sub StartInjector()
End Sub
```

As you can see, **Protected** modification affords a level of public access to classes that are directly related through composition and inheritance with the class in which the method is declared. No other classes in the application or outside of it can access a protected method.

Friend

The **Friend** modifier restricts access to the method to members of classes in the same assembly or application (DLL or EXE) in which the method is declared, nested classes, and derived classes. The members of a **Friend** class are not visible to classes outside the assembly in which it is contained. The following code declares a **Friend** method:

```
Friend Sub StartInjector()
End Sub
```

Friend essentially permits a level of public access to the members of classes that are essentially part of the same assembly (a .NET DLL or application).

Protected Friend

The **Protected Friend** modifier is the union of both **Protected** and **Friend** modifiers. In other words, it restricts access to the method to members of classes in the same application in which the method is declared, nested classes, and derived classes *and* applies the **Protected** access. The following code declares a **Protected Friend** method:

```
Protected Friend Sub StartInjector()
End Sub
```

Private Methods

The highest level of protection you can bestow on a method is achieved using the **Private** keyword. **Private**, as listed in Table 7-5, denotes that the method can only be accessed from within the class in which it is declared. However, **Private** methods can also be accessed from nested classes, because a nested class is part of the same declaration context or declaration scope of the **Private** method.

Composite or nested classes, which are discussed in Chapter 9, Chapter 13, and Chapter 14 are classes that are contained within classes—composition—and thus they also have access to the private members of a containing class. The reverse, however, is not true. Members declared **Private** in nested classes are not accessible to members of the containing class, because the scope or declaration context does not include the container class itself.

Private methods, for example, can be accessor methods that compute data, or modification methods that set internal class data that may be required elsewhere in the class, possibly to be accessed by the consumer of the class as a static method call.

The following code declares a **Private** method:

```
Private Sub StartInjector()
End Sub
```

The **Private** modifier is similar to the **Protected** modifier in that a composite class can see a **Private** method if the method is shared. If the method is not shared the composite must collaborate with the outer class via an object reference in order to see the **Private** method.

Controlling Polymorphism Characteristics of Methods

The implementation characteristics of methods define their polymorphic characteristics, because they are declared as nonvirtual by default. There is a good reason for this: Nonvirtual methods cannot be overridden, so the compiler does not need to look ahead and figure out all the variations of calls that may be invoked, which methods they apply to, and so on. Static methods stay nonvirtual, which means the compiler can bind to the call at compile time, a process known as a *method inline.* Polymorphism (which means many forms) is discussed in more detail in Chapters 9, 10, 13, and 14.

However, polymorphism is a central tenet of object-based programming (see Chapter 10), and the .NET Framework allows methods to be declared as virtual, which means they can be overloaded and overridden. Overriding, for example, achieves polymorphism by defining a different implementation of a method (and a property) with the same invocation procedure. Table 7-6 lists the polymorphism modifiers, followed by the alphabetical explanation of each modifier (note that C# modifiers are lowercase).

Final Methods (NotOverridable)

Final methods are methods that were virtual when they were first declared, which means they either were declared in classes using the virtual method modifiers or were simply overloaded or overridden in later implementations. However, prefixing the modifier **NotOverridable** to the method declaration specifies that the method is now final.

This modifier specifies that further implementation is stopped and the method is no longer virtual. In other words, it cannot be overridden or changed in a derived class. It is important to note that this has nothing to do with visibility or accessibility. A final method can be private or public, as demonstrated in the following code:

```
Protected NotOverridable Overrides Sub Finalize()
End Sub
```

Visual Basic	C#	Framework	Purpose
NotOverridable (used with overrides)	**sealed**	Final	You cannot override this member in a derived class; it is final
Overrides	**override**	A method that overrides	The method overrides the derived implementation from the base class
Overridable	**virtual** with implementation	A virtual method	The method can be overridden in the derived class
MustOverride with no implementation	**abstract** with no implementation	An abstract method	A method that is yet to be implemented in a subclass; the opposite of a final method
Overloads	No keyword necessary	Nonvirtual method that can be overloaded	Overloading allows you to implement methods of the same name but with different parameter lists
Shadows	Redeclared	Redeclared	Shadowing redeclares an inherited method in the derived class
Shared	**static**	Static method	The members retain their values no matter how referenced

Table 7-6.   *The Access and Implementation Characteristics of Class Members*

You will receive an error if you use this modifier on the first declaration or version of a virtual method in a base class, because you cannot seal the method when it is first declared. The method cannot be declared **NotOverridable** until it is actually implemented in a child class (see Chapter 9). You must first override the method in the child class and then prefix the **NotOverridable** modifier to the method.

Overriding Methods (Overrides)

Overriding is a means of allowing you to reimplement or implement from scratch— if the base method is abstract—a virtual method derived from a base or parent class. The overridden method must have the same signature (essentially the parameter list) as the method in the parent class (otherwise it becomes a method overload). You cannot override a final or static (nonvirtual) method.

> **Note** *The base method does not have to be abstract to be overridden. Overriding the method implies replacing the implementation, if any, in the parent or superclass.*

Overriding is an implementation characteristic and does not—and cannot—change the accessibility of the overridden member. In other words, when you override the member in the derived class, you must use the same access level modifiers for both base and derived classes.

Overriding in Visual Basic is specified using the **Overrides** keyword in both **Function** and **Sub** methods (and properties). In other words, where **Overrides** is used in a method statement, it means that you are overriding the method of the same signature in the parent class. The following code demonstrates the declaration of a method that overrides:

```
Protected Overrides Sub VirtualMethod(ByVal Param As Integer)
End Sub
```

Also, you cannot override a method in a base class that has not been explicitly declared "overridable" with the **Overridable** modifier. This is discussed in the next section.

Virtual Methods (Overridable)

As discussed in Chapter 9, a virtual member is not necessarily in its final form and it may be further implemented in derived classes, even overloaded and changed to a static state. A virtual member is declared virtual using the **Overridable** keyword.

> **Note** *According to the CLS, for every virtual method declared in or inherited by a class, there exists a "most derived implementation" of the method with respect to that class.*

The following code demonstrates the declaration of a virtual method that can be overridden:

```
Protected Overridable Sub VirtualMethod(ByVal Param As Integer)
End Sub
```

It does not make sense to modify an **Overridable** method with the **Private** keyword. See Chapter 8 which demonstrates overriding in more detail.

Abstract Methods (MustOverride)

Abstract methods—like abstract classes—are intended to be implemented in subclasses that derive from a base class, and the *abstract* modifier—**MustOverride**—is used to signal that no implementation in the method or provision of data exists. For all intents and purposes, the abstract members are nothing more than placeholders provided for conformance. The abstract method in a base class is merely declared and is devoid of any implementation; therefore, the method terminator (**End Sub** or **End Function**) is invalid. (See the sections covering abstract classes in Chapter 9.)

The following code declares an abstract method:

```
Protected MustOverride Sub VirtualMethod(ByVal arg As Integer)
```

A method or property that is declared as abstract is overridden in the subclass, because that is where the implementation of the method or property is handled. Abstract methods are thus implicitly *virtual*, because they can only be implemented in subclasses. Abstract members are thus the antithesis of final members.

 Declaration of abstract methods requires you to declare the base class with the MustInherit modifier. See Chapter 9.

Overloading Methods (Overloads)

Overloading is a feature of many OOP languages. .NET provides support for overloading of methods and properties. Overloading means that you can have multiple methods of the same name (identifier) but different signatures—the name, type, order, and number of parameters in the parameter list—and implementation.

Here's an example:

```
Function Traject(ByRef obj1 As Object,_
ByRef obj2 As Object) As Boolean
Function Traject(ByRef Obj As Object) As Boolean
```

From the point of view of the caller the method can be called and provided either one or two arguments.

Visual Studio automatically enumerates the overloaded methods of a class and makes them available to you when you code the calling routines (so the caller sees what amounts to a single method with the option to choose different parameter lists).

This is demonstrated in the illustration, which shows that a call to the **Console** class's **WriteLine** method has 18 overloaded variations. The following example shows you how to call an alternate variation of an overloaded method.

```
        End If
        Return 0
        Console.WriteLine(|
    End  ▲5 of 18▼  WriteLine (buffer() As Char, index As Integer, count As Integer)
         buffer: An array of Unicode characters.
```

The following call comes from the earlier example that calculates the area of a circle:

```
Console.WriteLine("The area in km is: {0:N3}", Area(inPut))
```

When you construct this method, you can choose which overloaded variation of **WriteLine** you need. Notice that some of the versions of **WriteLine** appear identical except for the value type of the argument you are to send. In many cases, you do not need to iterate through the list of methods looking for the exact method that corresponds to the value type being passed. Visual Basic will implicitly choose the correct overloaded method.

Shadow Methods (Shadows)

Shadowing is a blocking facility used in derived or child class implementations that allows you to prevent base class methods (and other elements for that matter) from subsequently conflicting with methods being implemented in the child class.

The problem is inevitable: You derive from a class that represents the bulk of what you need to implement in a certain case. However, the newly derived class is not complete, and thus you may need to both "override" and declare new methods in the child class. So, you implement a new method in the derived class and then discover later that the base class provider has created a new method of the same name that now conflicts with yours by virtue of your inheriting the provider's class.

This is something that is rather common when sucking down all kinds of classes from the Internet or from third-party providers. And it is also useful for working with nested classes. Shadowing is achieved in one of two ways: through overloading, as explained earlier, and by explicitly declaring a single version of a method as shadowed, using the **Shadows** modifier.

Shadowing will become clearer in the following chapters when we get down to inheritance. However, the following code demonstrates how to shadow a method (see also "Working with Variables and Constants" in Chapter 4):

```
Public Class Accessible
    Public Sub ShadowMethod(ByVal Arg As Integer)
        'base implementation
```

```
    End Sub
End Class

Public Class Additional : Inherits Accessible
    Public Shadows Sub ShadowMethod(ByVal Arg As String)
        'new implementation
    End Sub
End Class
```

Static Methods (Shared)

Methods declared **Shared** are *static* and are not associated with any instance. While you can declare static methods in a class that is instantiated or referenced as an object, or a structure, you will not be able to access the shared method. (See also "Working with Variables and Constants" in Chapter 4 and the section "Improved Performance with Shared Classes and Modules" in Chapter 9.)

Static methods are declared as follows:

```
Shared Sub Inject(ByVal Arg As Integer)
End Sub
```

However, they are called by referencing the fully qualified class name, as demonstrated in the following line of code:

```
InjectorClass.Inject(FuelGradeEnum.Refined)
```

Static methods are the antithesis of *dynamic* methods, which manifest when you create an object. Shared methods are considered thread safe, because multiple copies of them are not floating around an application (see Chapter 17 for an introduction on multithreading).

Mining the Framework's Methods

One of the secrets of object-oriented programming is to know which classes to reference and thus which methods to use in your applications. This knowledge is not something that you can gain overnight, nor can any book printed on paper impart information about every class and method. What you currently see in the .NET Framework is not the end of it, either. Over the years, the .NET Framework is bound to grow to thousands more classes, which will be compounded as well by myriad third-party classes that will be created, available for free or under a paid-for license. Worse for Visual Basic programmers is the fact that you also have methods you can access from the older run-time libraries, as demonstrated earlier. And, of course, there is all the COM stuff floating around out there.

Fortunately, an author *can* point programmers in the direction of various namespaces and their individual classes, and provide as many examples of the most important methods as possible—as has been done so far in this book. Some of the classes will be the focus of many articles, white papers, and so on. These include classes in **System.Data** (the ADO .NET technology), **System.Net** (TCP/IP stuff), and **System.Threading** (the multithreading namespace). These are the collateral libraries that expand your application-building horizons and save you the trouble and time of having to build the stuff yourself.

It is also important to know where and how to look for what you need. Throughout this book, I have made it a point to reference namespaces and classes pertinent to the subject at hand.

The Methods of System.Math

To kick off the discussion of how to work with methods belonging to the base class library (BCL) and the rest of the Framework—or simply to call methods you may or may not have written—let's investigate one of the most important classes in the **System** namespace: **Math**.

Every programmer for just about every task requiring some form of advanced calculation will likely use the **Math** class methods and the arithmetic operators discussed in Chapter 4. If you need the absolute value of a number, you'll find the function in **Math**. Need to work with PI? You can "call" on it here. Need the trigonometric tangent of *x*? **Math** is the place. Table 7-7 provides the complete list of public fields, and Table 7-8 provides the list of math methods that can be used in your applications.

Field	Description	Usage
E	The constant, e, specifies the natural logarithmic base.	Provides the field that holds the value 2.7182818284590452354.
Pi	Pi is a constant (3.17), represented by the symbol π, that specifies the ratio of the circumference of a circle to its diameter.	The value of this field is 3.14159265358979323846 $C = \pi * D$

Table 7-7. *Constants of* **System.Math**

Method	Description
Abs	Provides the absolute value of a number.
Acos	Provides the angle whose cosine is the specified number.
Asin	Provides the angle whose sine is the specified number.
Atan	Provides the angle whose tangent is the specified number.
Atan2	Provides the angle whose tangent is the quotient of two specified numbers.
Ceiling	Provides the smallest whole number greater than or equal to the specified number.
Cos	Provides the cosine of the specified angle.
Cosh	Provides the hyperbolic cosine of the specified angle.
Exp	Provides e raised to the specified power.
Floor	Provides the largest whole number less than or equal to the specified number.
IEEERemainder	Provides the remainder resulting from the division of a specified number by another specified number.
Log	Provides the logarithm of a specified number.
Log10	Provides the base 10 logarithm of a specified number.
Max	Provides the larger of two specified numbers.
Min	Provides the smaller of two specified numbers.
Pow	Provides a specified number raised to the specified power.
Round	Provides the number nearest the specified value.
Sign	Provides a value indicating the sign of a number.
Sin	Provides the sine of the specified angle.
Sinh	Provides the hyperbolic sine of the specified angle.
Sqrt	Provides the square root of a specified number.
Tan	Provides the tangent of the specified angle.
Tanh	Provides the hyperbolic tangent of the specified angle.

Table 7-8. *Methods (static) of **System.Math***

To investigate the constants and methods (and other members) of the **Math** class, open the Object Browser in Visual Studio. The easiest way to do this is to use the keyboard shortcut CTRL-ALT-J. The browser can also be accessed from the menus: Select View, Other Windows, Object Browser.

In the Object Browser, you need to drill down to the **System** namespace. As mentioned in Chapter 4, namespaces are preceded by the curly brace icon {}, while assemblies are represented by a small gray rectangle. Do not confuse the **System** namespace with the System assembly. **System**, the namespace, also lives in the mscorlib assembly, as illustrated in Figure 7-1.

Expand **System** and you can scroll down until you find **Math**. Expand the class and the complete list of members will be loaded in the right pane in the Object Browser. Every method is documented, as illustrated in Figure 7-2.

Programming with the Math Class

The following two examples, not by any means significant algorithms, demonstrate calling the methods in the **Math** class. Before you can use the methods and other members of the class, you need to first reference the class via its namespace. This can be done

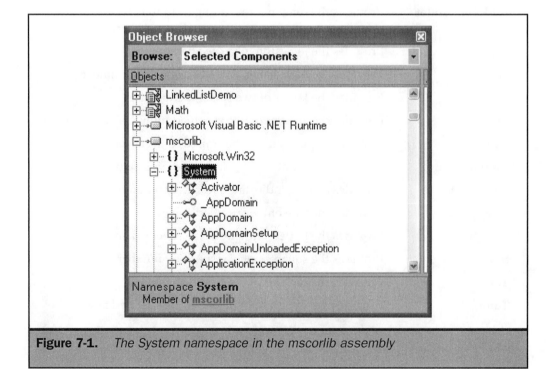

Figure 7-1. *The System namespace in the mscorlib assembly*

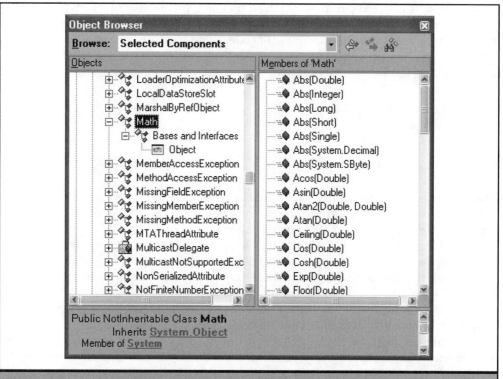

Figure 7-2.   *Browsing the members of the **Math** class*

using the **Imports** directive, as demonstrated in Chapter 4, the Project Imports folder that can be set in a project's Property Pages dialog box, or the following line of code:

```
X = System.Math.Sin(Y)
```

First let's have a look at the **Pow** method (power), which returns the number of the argument (of type **Double)** raised to a certain power. In this example, we call **Pow** twice to calculate the amount of energy that can be realized from a single gram of mass using the world's most famous equation, Einstein's $E = MC^2$:

```
Public Function E(ByVal M As Double) As Double
  Dim C As Double = 2.99792458 * (Pow(10, 8))
  E = M * (Pow(C, 2)) 'as joules
  'or E = M * C * C
End Function
```

By passing 1 to the M parameter in the E function, we are able to return the number 89,875,517,873,681,764 to the calling method. The return value of this method is implicitly returned in the following line of code:

```
E = M * (Pow(C, 2))
```

which is the equation in question as well as the name of the method we created. The output as a **Double** is

```
8.9875517873681E+16
```

which, if we harness this energy (other than by ramming molecules up against each other), would get us off the ground and on our way to the far reaches of our solar system. Rocket science, yes; difficult to calculate, no.

In the following example, let's build the support we need for determining the circumferences of the planets and their satellites in our solar system. Quite a few spheres exist out in space, so let's choose one of my favorite moons around Uranus, Ariel ("Air-ee-el").

Ariel was discovered by the British Astronomer William Lassell in 1851, and we know from later studies that the diameter of this rock is 1,158 kilometers.

The equation, using Pi, is $C = \pi*D$, where C is the unknown circumference and D is the diameter. Now we know that π is a constant of 3.14, so the circumference is 3.14 multiplied by 1,158. The circumference is therefore 3,636.12 kilometers (rounded to two decimal places). Let's write some code to express this:

```
Public Function Circumference(ByVal Diameter As Double) As Double
   Circumference = PI * Diameter
End Function
```

Simple enough, and we can glean more information about Ariel by also calculating its surface area. (These moons appear to have big chunks of ice, so if we ever run out of water on earth, we may need to put these planetary land surveying applications to work.)

The formula to calculate the area of a sphere such as Ariel is $A=4\pi r^2$ where A is the area of the planet.

This can be expressed with the following code:

```
Public Function Area(ByVal Diameter As Double) As Double
   Dim rad As Double = Diameter / 2
   Area = 4 * PI * Pow(rad, 2)
End Function
```

At approximately 1,053,191 kilometers, Ariel would be suitable for the next indoor Winter Olympics.

Here is the full listing of the **Math** demo:

```
Imports System.Math
Module Math
    Dim inPut As String
    Dim diameter As Double
    Dim Completed As Boolean

    Sub Main()

        While Not Completed
            Console.WriteLine("                            ")
            Console.WriteLine("-----------MENU------------")
            Console.WriteLine("--------------------------")
            Console.WriteLine("Please enter the diameter.")
            Console.WriteLine("or press return to end.")
            Console.WriteLine("--------------------------")

            inPut = Console.ReadLine()

            If Not (inPut = "") Then
                Console.WriteLine("                    ")
                Completed = ProcessMath(Convert.ToDouble(inPut))
            Else
                Completed = True
            End If
        End While
    End Sub


    'e=mc2 example
    Public Function E(ByVal M As Double) As Double
        Dim C As Double = 2.99792458 * (Pow(10, 8))
        E = M * (Pow(C, 2)) 'joules
        'same thing as E = M * C * C
    End Function

    Public Function ProcessMath(ByVal inPut As Double) As Boolean
      Console.WriteLine("The circumference in km is: {0:N3}", _
        Circumference(inPut))
      Console.WriteLine("The area in km is: {0:N3}", Area(inPut))
```

```
      Return False
    End Function

    Public Function Circumference(ByVal Diameter As Double) As Double
        Circumference = PI * Diameter
    End Function

    Public Function Area(ByVal Diameter As Double) As Double
        Dim rad As Double = Diameter / 2
        Area = PI * Pow(rad, 2)

        Area = 4 * PI * Pow(rad, 2)
    End Function

End Module
```

After entering 1158, the console displays the following:

```
The circumference in km is: 3,637.964
The area in km is: 4,212,762.651
```

The formatting is made possible with the {0:N3} specification in the **WriteLine** method (in **ProcessMath**). See Chapter 15 for information on formatting strings.

Math-Related Exceptions

Table 7-9 provides a list of the important exceptions that need to be handled when working with the **Math** class methods.

Exception	Purpose
ApplicationException	Thrown when a nonfatal application error occurs.
ArgumentException	Thrown when one of the arguments provided to a method is not valid.
ArgumentNullException	Thrown when a null reference (Nothing in Visual Basic) is passed to a method that does not accept it as a valid argument.

Table 7-9.   *Exceptions for **System.Math***

Exception	Purpose
ArithmeticException	Thrown for errors in an arithmetic, casting, or conversion operation.
FormatException	Thrown when the format of an argument does not meet the parameter specifications of the invoked method.
InvalidCastException	Thrown for invalid casting or explicit conversion.
NotFiniteNumberException	Thrown when a floating-point value is positive infinity, negative infinity, or Not-a-Number (NaN).
DivideByZeroException	Thrown when there is an attempt to divide an integral or decimal value by zero.
OutOfMemoryException	Thrown when there is not enough memory to continue the execution of a program.
OverflowException	Thrown when an arithmetic, casting, or conversion operation in a checked context results in an overflow.
StackOverflowException	Thrown when the execution stack overflows by having too many pending method calls.

Table 7-9. *Exceptions for **System.Math*** (continued)

VB .NET FUNDAMENTALS

Properties

A property is a construct that provides a well-defined interface for value retrieval. From the implementor's viewpoint the property works like an *accessor* method and a *modification* method combined into a well-structured package.

From the client or consumer's viewpoint, the property appears to be nothing more than a reference to a value. This is demonstrated in the following code changing the color of the cell background to yellow:

```
Cell.BackColor = Yellow
```

The name of the property is the name referenced by a client that accesses the property using similar semantics to retrieving a value from a standard public variable or constant. But the client is not referencing any storage. It is asking the property, **BackColor**, to set the color on its behalf. Behind the interface the property is free to implement whatever it needs to change the color. To the client the property appears to be a field or storage but any storage used by the property is completely off limits to the client. In fact the property may use several variable and constant fields, local or remote, in the algorithm it uses to return a value to the client, or set the value on behalf of the client.

Both *modification* and *accessor* properties, known as *setters* and *getters*, respectively, can and should be accessed via the public interface, which is the name of the object hosting the property followed by the dot and the actual property name. There are no white spaces in the property reference.

As class members, properties have the same standing as methods. So, they can be inherited (even as abstract declarations), overridden, sealed, and so on. Properties are listed in Visual Studio's declaration list for each class providing easy access. Properties are also parsed into the Properties window where they can be interactively accessed by the consumer (as opposed to programmatic access).

The property is exposed as a public property of the class or object, masquerading as a field (an intelligent one at that). They can also be hidden, which is, for security reasons, the default behavior if the property is inherited. The following is a simple usage for a property called **State** that does nothing but return the value held by the **oState** variable to the caller:

```
Dim oState As Integer
Public Property State() As Integer
  Get
    Return oState
  End Get
  Set(ByVal Value As Integer)
    oState = Value
  End Set
End Property
```

However, you have to be careful when you implement the property. Specifically, passing values to the property takes place via the setter's interface, which is the following statement in the property:

```
Set(ByVal myVal as Integer)
```

You implement a parameter list in the declaration statement of the property as shown here:

```
Public Property State(ByVal myVal as Integer) As Integer
```

Also, with **Option Explicit** set to **Off** the property will not complain if any variable it is trying to work with has not been declared, either in the global declaration space of the class, or in the local declaration space of the property itself (in the **Get** block). While you can declare in either the **Get** block or the **Set** block or both, anything declared in the **Set** block is not visible to the **Get** block.

If the property goes to work a variable that has not been declared or that it cannot see, it will cause a **StackOverflowException** to be raised.

You also need to provide the typing specifics for both the return value and the parameters of the property. This you do with the **As** syntax on the declaration line of the property as shown here:

```
Public Property State() As Integer
```

and in the parameter spaces as shown here:

```
Set(ByVal Value As Integer)
```

which only allows a single parameter. Also the return type and the set parameter type must be the same.

A property is declared and used as follows in Visual Basic .NET:

- If it does not carry the **ReadOnly** or **WriteOnly** modifiers, you must implement both **Set** and **Get** methods in the property.
- If the property is modified as **ReadOnly**, you must drop the **Set** method.
- If the property is modified as **WriteOnly**, you must drop the **Get** method.

The **ClearanceLevel** property can be written as follows, implementing only the **Get** method:

```
Public ReadOnly Property ClearanceLevel() As Integer
 Get
   Return cLevel
 End Get
End Property
```

The following code shows how a property is used internally in the class and still exposed to a client that may need to use the property value directly:

```
Public Class Clearance

  Private passWord As String
```

VB .NET FUNDAMENTALS

```
Private cLevel As Integer

Public Property ClearanceLevel() As Integer
  Get
    Return cLevel
  End Get
    Set(ByVal Value As Integer)
       cLevel = Value
    End Set
End Property

Public Function AuthUser(ByVal UID As String, ByVal PWD As String)_
As Boolean
  If PWD = passWord Then
    ClearanceLevel = ClearanceLevelEnum.AuthorizedGuest
    Return True
  End If
  ClearanceLevel = ClearanceLevelEnum.AuthorizedDenied
  Return False
  End Function
End Class
```

Properties vs. Fields

The property also provides a natural and elegant means of hiding instant fields. Information hiding is a subject I have a fair amount of passion for, and thus any construct that helps break the habit of publishing public globals gets my vote. Use properties as a rule to expose any value required by a client and keep all instance variables secret. Here are a few more examples of properties, as seen from the outside:

- **Cell.Length**   Sets or gets the length of a cell in a grid (for example, 10 to 40 pixels).

- **Sound.Volume**   Sets or gets the current volume setting (for example, 1 to 9).

- **Engine.State**   Sets or gets the current state of an engine (for example, on or off).

- **Background.Color**   Sets or gets the current color of the background (for example, blue, red, green).

On the other hand, if you are not looking to expose a property to the public, then a simple accessor method suffices. I don't really see much point to construct a property for the sake of access from the members of the same class in which a property is declared. It only tends to clutter the class, and introduces the possibility of bugs. A simple accessor method is, for all intents and purposes, simple. Using a private property to provide access only to private instance values is a lot like flying from D.C. to NYC via Moscow (unless you are a double-agent).

As long as the fields are private to the class, the private members do not need to access properties to work with that data; they can work with it directly and validate the data in their own implementation space or via a simple accessor. Besides, loosely coupled classes need to pass method data, and passing a property as an argument does not make any sense when a simple **Function** return or an instance field suffices. This is demonstrated in the following code:

```
Public Class Clearance
  Private passWord As String

  Sub Test()
    Console.WriteLine(AuthUser(Convert.ToString(PassCode)))
  End Sub

  Property PassCode() As Integer
    Get
      PassCode = 1233 + 1
      Return PassCode
    End Get
    Set(ByVal Value As Integer)
      passWord = Convert.ToString(Value)
    End Set
  End Property

  Public Function AuthUser(ByVal PWD As String) As Boolean
    If PWD = "1234" Then
      Return True
    End If
      Return False
  End Function

End Class
```

If you need to access private class fields, you can regulate the access and the modification with any method. For example, your method might check the value you are attempting to change the variable to and prevent the modification if it does not meet certain criteria. A private property can do the same thing, so in such a case, use the construct that makes sense or is easier to implement.

Properties vs. Methods

When would you use properties and when would you use methods? As you can see, there is a lot of overlap between the purpose of a property and the purpose of a method (especially an accessor method), and properties can contain just as powerful code as regular methods. In many cases, properties are easier and quicker to implement than simple methods. However, properties are called "properties" because they refer to a property characteristic of a class. Methods, on the other hand, are a way of doing something, as discussed at the beginning of this chapter. These respective definitions should thus guide your choices of the construct to use.

If you are looking to provide public access to a property characteristic of an object, such as **Palette.Color**, then use a property. In this respect, the property becomes a publicly accessible member that returns or sets a given characteristic in the object to an external party.

Properties are also value-oriented. You cannot pass-by-reference to the **Set** parameter of a property, nor would you want to.

The remainder of this chapter deals with the design and construction of methods and calling. We'll first deal with the easier concepts to grasp and then gradually make our way to some interesting and more complex topics.

Introduction to Exception Handling

We are starting to see in this chapter (as we will in subsequent chapters) code that is a lot more complex. So, the time has come to start looking at exception handling in our methods. The subject is extensive and an entire chapter (Chapter 11) has been devoted to the subject. This chapter, however, includes an introduction to exception handling because I really do not want to present code in the forthcoming chapters that does not include at least a hint that we are able to catch and deal with exceptions. Even if you are not new to exception handling, it is important to evaluate how we cater to error handling in all of our method definitions (where necessary) from now on.

In structured exception handling, a block of code is placed within a protected section, and each statement is provided guarded execution. The protection starts with the first line of code after the **Try** keyword, and ends at the last line of code before the first **Catch** keyword. An optional **Finally** section can be used that always gets processed after an exception is raised and handled. The **Try**...**Catch**...**Finally** block looks like this:

```
Public Sub ATrickyMethod()
  Try
    Protected or guarded code goes here...
Catch
    Exception handler code goes here...
  Finally
```

```
    End Try
End Sub
```

As soon as an error is detected within the protected section, between **Try** and **Catch**, execution is immediately halted and transferred to the catch area where the exception is handled. How, you might ask, is the exception handled? The best way to answer that question is to examine exactly what an exception is.

I'm sure you have lost your tempter on occasion. Remember that last bug that had you up until 4 A.M., that made you throw your monitor out the window? An exception is the same thing, only not as dangerous to passersby. It is essentially an object that can be "thrown" from one part of your method to another, or even to another class, when something goes wrong.

The brilliance of the throw exception, however, is that because an exception is a class that gets instantiated, it can implement a variety of methods and data structures to handle the error. For example, it might just report an error number, or it may translate the error number into something more meaningful.

The exception class, however, prevents the exception from doing any damage, and thus prevents the application from being terminated, or doing something dastardly that will get you into a lot of trouble.

The actual errors that cause your code to explode and throw fits occur for five reasons and they are listed as follows:

- **Syntax exceptions**   These exceptions are raised when something is declared incorrectly and the compiler does not realize it.

- **Run-time exceptions**   These exceptions occur when a program is executed. These errors can be produced by some of the simplest problems that arise during run time, but the errors do not normally mean the algorithm or application is flawed. An example of when such an error is produced is when someone tries to open a file that does not exist. If the file existed, normal execution would ensue; the code is technically correct, however. Other examples of when run-time errors are produced include when someone tries to connect to a database that does not exist, dial a telephone number with no modem attached, serialize an object to a full disk, process a lengthy sort with no memory, and so on. In all of these cases, if the resources existed, there would be no errors to talk about, and thus no exceptions to throw. Run-time exceptions usually come from the operating system, which detects the violations. These get passed through to the runtime, which passes them up to the application's exception handlers.

- **Logic exceptions**   These exceptions also occur at run time but they cannot be foreseen by any preprocessor or the compiler. A *divide-by-zero* error is a classic example. This is not an error until the program finds itself in a divide-by-zero situation. However, the fact that the logic of the algorithm led it to a divide-by-zero situation implies that the code is essentially flawed. Other examples of actions that produce logic errors include trying to access an element in an array that exceeds its upper boundary, reading beyond the end of a stream, trying to read from a file that has not yet been opened, or trying to reference an object that has long ago been dereferenced. Logic exceptions usually come from the operating system, which detects the violations. You may also provide custom exception classes to deal with your own logic errors.

■ **Conditional exceptions**   These exceptions are really there for custom exceptions you create, by extending the base exception class. You can raise exceptions on these "errors" if a certain precondition or postcondition exists in your code. For example, if a value is not 0 at the start of an algorithm, you could raise a custom, **ArgumentNotZeroException** exception to trap the condition. A postcondition exception would be raised if a condition you specify in the exception handler does not exist after the algorithm is processed. For example, if your code is supposed to leave the application in a certain condition before continuing, you could provide an exception right there and then—in a postcondition exception handler.

■ **Custom exceptions**   These are exceptions you can create to cater to anything you believe should be considered an error, such as something that requires an alternate course of execution, or requires the application to be shut down. You might find such an exception handler in your average treadmill software—if the device is not able to read a heart rate at regular intervals, it raises something like an **ExerciserIsDeadException** and shuts off. I guess that's its built-in fail-safe at work.

Why place exception handlers in Visual Basic .NET programs?

■ Applications need a facility to catch a method's inability to complete a task for some reason.

■ To process errors caused by a process accessing any functionality in methods where those elements are unable to directly handle any error that arises as a result of the access and the ensuing computation.

■ To deal with errors caused by the methods in components that are not able to handle any particular error in their own processing space.

■ To ensure that a large and complex program (actually any VB.NET program) can consistently and holistically provide a program-wide error-handling facility.

An exception handler is used to trap the error and handle the ensuing events. Handling the exception sustains the application and makes sure the data and the application are in a consistent state. Some handlers can simply roll back an error and continue silently, such as an array bounds exception, while others require you to advise the user what just happened (such as informing the user that the file he or she just tried to open no longer exists, and redirecting execution flow or resetting values.

Now that you know what an exception is, how does your code catch one after it is thrown, and what does it do with it once it's caught?

The Exception Handler

First you should know that if an exception is not handled, the standard course of action is to close down the application. This action is taken to prevent the application from risking damage to other applications and data. Allowing a half-dead application to continue trashing its environment has been shown to be troublesome. Closing down the application on any exception also forces developers to handle their less-than-perfect code. If an exception is ignored or not adequately dealt with, it may leave the application standing, but not in a very stable state.

The exception handler is your entire catch block, which contains a single exception "filter" that might apply to the error at hand. If the first catch block does not apply to the error, the code moves to the next one, if you provided it, and so on until the correct **Catch** block, or exception handler, is found. This is demonstrated in the following code, in which the so-called filters are represented in bold:

```
Try
  Protected code goes here...
Catch Except As EndOfStreamException
'handle this exception here
Catch Except As PasswordException When passWord = ""
'handle this exception here
Catch When passWord = ""
'handle this exception here
Catch Except As ArgumentException
'handle this exception here
End Try
```

The exception-handling filter mechanism is flexible. In the preceding code, **Except** is used repeatedly as an instantiation reference variable for the exception class. In other words, in the first catch block, **Except** is instantiated as an **EndOfStreamException** object if the code indeed blew up upon the unexpected encounter of the end of a stream.

It is also possible to catch an exception when something is **True**. Here's an example from the preceding code:

```
Catch Except As ArgumentException When passWord = ""
'handle this exception here
```

Here an exception is raised when something becomes **True**; in the preceding example, **the parameter expected a password and got nothing instead.**

The use of **When** in the catch block also allows you to test for an error number. This is demonstrated as follows:

```
Catch When ErrNum = Err_EndOfStreamException
'handle this exception here
```

If no handler is found for the exception, it is referred to the previous caller to look for the correct exception handler to deal with the exception. The exceptions will continue to be passed up the call stack until an exception class is found, or the generic exception code is used to process the exception. If no exception class is found, the program will terminate with an "unhandled exception" message.

Usually, the caller of a method handles the exception. It might also be necessary for the caller of the caller to handle the exception, and you might have to go quite far back on the call stack to handle an exception. You can also catch all exceptions in the method that caused them with a default handler called **Exception**. This is a useful technique; just remember to station it as the last exception handler in your list, because it will catch and dispose of the thrown exceptions before any intended handlers are reached.

Try ... Catch Blocks

If you're new to writing code inside **Try…Catch** blocks, it may take some time to get into the habit of doing so. While you can easily compile Visual Basic .NET code without a **Try…Catch** (and **Finally**) block, good code technique means writing **Try…Catch** blocks as if the language absolutely depended on them.

When you write code without a **Try…Catch** block, you are relying on the run-time system to serve up the default exception handler. But that's like flying on autopilot—eventually you have to take control to land the plane.

When you have been writing VB.NET code long enough, you begin to think in terms of **Try…Catch … Finally** in the same way you think in terms of objects and classes, or methods and their members—the inherent makeup of an object-oriented program. It just becomes natural to build blocks of functionality with the **Try** keyword, at least if there is the slightest chance that the algorithm might take *exception* to something you are trying to do in the code. See Chapter 11 for more information and advanced exception-handling techniques.

Design and Construction of Methods

Understanding data structures and studying both the basic and complex algorithms is a critical part of any programming or software development effort. This section thus deals with some of the key foundation concepts with respect to method design and construction. I will touch on some theory, but you will also get to cover some pretty sophisticated stuff that can actually be quite fun, in later chapters.

Data structures are especially important in graphics applications, games, financial and statistical analysis, expert systems, databases, simulation, and so on. Even Web-based applications rely on data structures.

Data structures are collections of data organized or arranged in a specific way. Algorithms are the recipes or step-by-step instructions used for solving problems; and methods are essentially the steps of those recipes. The algorithms you create or use employ data structures as utilities to complete the instructions. Algorithms can be single methods in an application, or the entire application, thus comprising many methods and other data elements. Before we look at data structures in Chapter 12, we first need to study methods.

A valuable—nay essential—technique for designing algorithms (no matter what the language) is to break down the problem into its constituent components. The components should be divided along task boundaries.

Think of your algorithm as a complete project that can be divided into separate tasks. The tasks should be compiled into a list, and the elements of the list should be arranged in order of priority and dependence. In other words, a task that is dependent on an earlier task or several tasks should be placed later in the list. (Decomposing the problem and task arranging is a design technique used also for *use case* creation and *class diagrams*.)

As soon as you have a list, you need to look at each task and determine if it can be further decomposed into tasks (task within tasks). This "atomization" is critical because you need to arrive at a level where the subtasks become easy to implement.

If a task can or should be broken down into subtasks, number them accordingly. For example, if Task 2 can be broken down further into two tasks, then list the subtasks of 2 as 2a and 2b.

Each small task should be simple enough to list as pseudocode. In fact, you can test whether the task has been sufficiently decomposed by determining whether you can write it as a single statement. If the task can be easily understood by a single line of code, then that will obviously suffice.

Consider the following list of tasks for an algorithm to calculate sales tax on a list of items:

1. Create a collection of *x* elements.

2. For each element in the collection, store a number.

3. Iterate through the elements and add 6 percent to each number.

4. Replace the value in the element with the new result.

Look at the task list and determine whether the collection of tasks can be implemented in a single method or would be better implemented as a collection of methods.

The pseudocode you write has another important role: documentation for your code, which is the critical element of any software project or effort.

When you list the tasks of your algorithms in the fashion described—and then determine whether the collection of tasks can be implemented in a single method or would be better implemented as a collection of methods—you are essentially self-documenting in the same step. The pseudocode forms the basis of the higher-level documentation, at the algorithm and method-implementation levels.

When a task is broken down into a subtask, it becomes much easier to document. In fact, all the documentation you have to do at such an atomic level for methods is to write one line of intelligent commentary. Here's an example:

```
'now adds the current tax
Public Sub AddSalesTax(ByVal Tax As Double)
'...
End Sub
```

For the most part, a method should perform the work required by a single task or subtask. When documenting your classes, you list the specification for each method by describing the task as a series of statements. This is known as functional or procedural abstraction. An abstract for the sales tax method might look like this:

- Method objective: To add sales tax to each value in an array element
- Task: Add a sales tax of 6 percent to the value
- Data type: **Double**
- Method signature: **Public Function ApplySalesTax(ByVal tax As Double) As Double**
- Expected (a preexisting condition): A value in the element
- Parameters: There is one parameter, **tax** as the percent of sales tax
- Exceptions: **BadTaxValueException**
- Returns with: The new value of the element with the applied sales tax

This form of task description *is* documentation. It is often referred to as a method abstraction or a method specification. Many programmers eschew such work. If you have key programmers on your team who feel this way, you need to employ a writer-cum-analyst to work on such specifications or come up with incentives to produce such documentation (like being grounded for the weekend).

Before you start writing a method, even a very simple one, you should write a method specification or abstraction. The following list recaps the sections you provide in the functional or procedural abstraction of a method:

- Preface/intro
- Expected/preconditions
- Exceptions
- Parameters
- Return values and postconditions

You can change the order of the section list if you prefer, but I prefer this order. The first section of the method "spec" is the Preface or Introduction. Using a few lines, simply describe the purpose of the method: why and how it came to be. (Remember, the method is the task or a subtask of your algorithm, so you should not need to write more than two or three lines. If you find yourself writing more, then the method needs to be analyzed for further decomposition.)

The next section of the abstract is the expected condition or precondition. The Expected section lists the preconditions that need to exist for the method to do its work. In the sales tax example, a precondition of the **ApplySalesTax** method is that the parameter variables are initialized.

Next you need to document the exceptions. Reference the exception you will throw on the wrong or bad precondition. Here you can simply describe what the code checks for and why the throw occurs. You could throw on the **Boolean** result returned from an **If** statement. Here's an example of a throw that checks for the correct precondition:

```
If (tax <= TaxScaleEnum.SecondLevel) Then
   Throw New IllegalValueException()
End If
```

Another possible exception to throw (depending on the method) is if the array even exists. If you discover that you have more than one exception to throw (more than one precondition), then take that as an indication that the method might be too complex and a candidate for further decomposition. In other words, strive to break the method down further so that you need to only check for one precondition (it does not cost you anything to add another method).

The Parameters section of the method spec lists the parameters and some information on how and why they are important to the method. In the **ApplySalesTax** method, the parameter **tax** is the percentage value to apply to the vector value. Without the parameter, the method is useless.

The final and essential section of the method spec is the documentation of the return values, conditions (also known as postconditions), return codes, and so on from the method. Future programmers (or concurrent members of the team) will be able to grasp the purpose of the method by reading the documentation you provide on the returns, results, and postconditions.

In the sales tax example, the method **AddSalesTax** goes beyond returning a single value or return code. It changes the values in every element of the array. What the method needs to do is check every iteration in the logic of the method for success and then return **True** if the entire iteration and update value process is successful—for every element in the array.

Class and Method Cohesion

While the constructors and instance variables bring an object to life, the methods make it useful. Methods allow you to organize a class logically. But poorly designed or written methods, or methods that do not clearly express either implementation or a management routine of a class (which is referred to as the "object policy"), can reduce the efficiency of your class and lead to poor design and the overcomplicating of the entire process.

A class should not try to do too many different things for the consumer. One school of thought believes that if you find your classes growing by more than 20 or 30 methods, then it may be time to break up your class. But I believe the number of methods in a class is not as important as strong method cohesion is.

What do we mean by *class cohesion*? Simply put, it means that the collection of methods comprises a cohesive collection. This means that the methods in the class all serve a common purpose. If the class contains ten methods that provide utilities for managing network operations, then adding another ten array utility methods to the same class is a bad idea. Rather, create a class for array utilities and another class for network operations. On the other hand, if a class has 500 methods that represent the best 500 array utilities this side of the galaxy, they may be better served by being separated into four highly cohesive classes.

Method cohesion, on the other hand, refers to the focus of the method. If a method tries to do more than one thing (be a Jack-of-all trades), we say it is weakly cohesive. If a method focuses on a single task, which usually means it does that task well, we say it is highly or strongly cohesive.

Highly cohesive methods are much more reliable than weakly cohesive ones. The more tasks you try to complete in a method, the more chances exist of things going wrong. The problem with methods that lack cohesion is that if one "subtask" of a method goes wrong, it has the potential of taking out the entire method. Sure, you can code a stack of **Try…Catch** blocks, but such code becomes hard to manage, document, and maintain.

The following list presents several levels of acceptable cohesion, from most acceptable to least acceptable (but still acceptable):

- **Functional cohesion**   The most desired form of method cohesion, in which a method does one thing and one thing only. The following code demonstrates a cohesive constructor whose sole purpose is to instantiate an object. It transfers control to another method that has its own tasks to perform.

```
Public Sub New()
  MyBase.New
  InitializeObject()
End Sub
```

- **Sequential cohesion**   Allows a single method to perform a series of steps in strict sequence in a single method. The steps must be performed in the order listed in the method, which together logically make up the entire process. A good example is a method that opens a file, writes to the file, and then closes the file. While you can easily transfer control to another method, it makes no sense to not complete the steps in a single method. On the other hand, if you were to insert a step that reads the data in the file and launches into some fancy operation with that data, perhaps then sending the data somewhere or sorting it, the method cohesion would break down. Rather, transfer control to another method to perform the next task, and then return to close the file.

■ **Communication cohesion** Allows several tasks to take place in a single method that all need to use the same facility. A good example is a method that opens a connection to a database for the purpose of writing some data to a table. It would therefore be acceptable to add a second operation that uses the same connection to read or write data to another table in the database. Because the steps do not need to happen in sequence, this level of cohesion can collapse when you start doing too many unrelated things at the same time. For example, the current method would not be the place to suddenly launch into a record count that updates a counter in the user interface, just because the door is open.

■ **Temporal cohesion** Allows a single method to perform a whole bunch of tasks that need to happen at the same time. The following code suggests temporal cohesion:

```
Shared Function DDBVal(ByVal choice As Integer, ByVal acq As
Double, _
   ByVal recovery As Double, _
   ByVal life As Integer, ByVal period As Integer, _
   Optional ByVal factor As Decimal = 0) As Double
   Dim book As Double = acq - recovery
   Dim deprec As Double
     If choice = 1 Then
       If factor <= 0 Then
         While period > 1
           deprec = book * 2 / life
           book = book - deprec
           period -= 1
         End While
       Else
         While period > 1
           deprec = book * factor / life
           book = book - deprec
           period -= 1
         End While
       End If
         Return book
     Else
       If factor <= 0 Then
```

```
            While period >= 1
               deprec = book * 2 / life
               book = book - deprec
               period -= 1
            End While
         Else
            While period >= 1
               deprec = book * factor / life
               book = book - deprec
               period -= 1
            End While
         End If
            Return deprec
         End If
      End Function
```

This example is on the borderline into the unacceptable group. Here you have two closely related tasks. But it is plain that the author is trying to use a single method to return either of two values, **book** or **deprec**. It would be best to use two methods instead, to channel each task to a pair of functionally cohesive methods. Also of particular concern is passing a variable to set up the choice between one or the other task, and the resulting clutter of unnecessary conditional elements.

Any methods that are less cohesive than the preceding example are considered unacceptable by many developers. A good example of weak cohesion that you often see in a program is a method that takes a control parameter that is used to decide which task in the method to perform. This is totally unacceptable method writing. Rather, break that method into submethods and use control flow in a single method that uses a **Select Case** conditional to determine which method to call.

Method Coupling

Methods in a class should also be loosely coupled, which means you should strive to make methods stand on their own and not be dependent on the operations of other methods. Coupling methods to methods in other classes is also a bad idea, because it is a form of tight coupling, hard coding, that increases complexity and leaves room for bugs to attack.

As mentioned earlier, when methods access or share global data, they become undesirably coupled to each other. If a method needs data to perform a certain task, use the facility of passing the data to the method's formal parameters.

In badly written applications, it is not unusual to find methods that have been delegated the task of writing to global variables for the benefit of other methods. This is a form of unacceptable data coupling. Rather, send the data to the method as an argument in the method call. The parameter list of a method is there for this reason, so use it.

The Length of a Method

How long should your methods be? This depends on the method. Again, I have learned not to impose such restraints on creativity. If a method has to be 100 lines, then that's what it has to be. Besides, there is ample research to show that long methods are no more troublesome to manage or debug than short methods.

On the other hand, like class and method cohesion, the method itself should not do too many things and should focus on a single purpose. In this regard, I am firmly of the school that says a method should be decomposed to a single task, returning a single value. This is known as the "divide-and-conquer" rule, which dictates that a problem should first be decomposed down to its constituent subproblems, at which point a number of methods can cater to the subproblems.

Recursive Design of Methods

At the method level, recursion solves a problem by invoking itself—either directly from within its own implementation or indirectly from some external implementation. At the algorithm level, recursion solves a problem by solving smaller instances of the same problem.

Recursive method calling is an important subject in computer programming, and the .NET Framework fully supports the concept of a method calling itself. Understanding recursion is vital for several reasons:

- Many problems you will be required to solve will be inherently recursive. In other words, the problem cannot be easily solved with the iteration constructs (loops) discussed in Chapter 6. The .NET Framework introduces a number of elements that beg to be expressed recursively. We will deal with some of them in this book. Toward the end of this section, I include a more specific checklist for using recursion.

- Even if you never have to program a recursive method yourself, you will no doubt encounter them everywhere, even in several places in this book. So, understanding what recursion is will make you a better programmer. It will certainly help you code tighter loops or consider alternative ways to code iterative constructs.

- Recursion often provides an elegant means of solving a problem, specifically because you have the ability to return with each recursive call and pass in fresh data that continues to erode the problem until it is solved or can no longer be eroded.

- Recursive method programming teaches you more about how to write great methods than any linearly structured methods. As you will see, recursion requires a sense of holistic awareness of software engineering.

- Recursion can be fun—depending on your outlook—because a good design that meets its objectives can be very rewarding. As the old saying goes: "The joy in tradition is in the repetition." Remember those words the next time your birthday comes around.

If an algorithm is a step-by-step "recipe" that arrives at the solution, then you could argue that recursion (and iteration) is the process that repeats the steps until the problem has been "diluted" to a point at which the final outcome can be put to some valuable use. Life has a similar process for solving its problems: History keeps repeating itself until life's problems are solved or mankind wakes up.

Looking at recursion as both a philosopher and an engineer or scientist, you might say that this ability to recursively erode a problem away is true only if everything in life is constant: that there are cases where continuous repeating of the steps does not distill the problem down to its logical conclusion; that there are bound to be times when the recursions ends before the desired result. In such cases, the problem might need to be solved by "brute force" or the definition of what the problem is needs to be changed. Of course, you could argue that brute force is the result of some other recursive design.

On the other hand, there are also possibilities that recursion could continue indefinitely until a stopping mechanism or a stopping condition is injected into the "loop" to bring an end to the giddy cycles. This also is a case of injecting "brute force" into the algorithm.

Here is a small example of recursion at work, but before we look at it in code or graphically, I must stress that these simple routines are not good choices for recursion. In fact, if you were to use recursion for such a problem at work, you would likely get fired. All languages have iterative constructs, as demonstrated in the previous chapter. The examples that follow may seem trivial, incurring unnecessary overhead, but they have been provided to assist you in grasping the concept, assuming you are new to it.

Let's look at some code to illustrate a small problem that can be solved easily by method recursion and iteration. The scenario is that we have a sequence of numbers in an array or list that is not in any particular order (like telephone extensions being saved on a caller ID). The sequence is as follows:

```
2189
2432
4391
3432
8932
```

The "problem" is that we need to turn the array upside down or swing it around. In other words, 2819 needs to be at the bottom and 8932 needs to be at the top. The pseudocode for the algorithm would be as follows:

```
'Interchange the values in the elements of the array.

If (first is less than last)
{Swap the value of first with the value of last
```

```
   Increment first by 1, decrement last by 1
   recall (recur) and repeat the process until
   first and last intersect or are of equal value.
}
```

Incidentally, while curly braces are a habit of mine from coding in C/C++, Java, and now C#, I also find them useful for delineating pseudocode segments. They will thus play a big part in my love affair with Visual Basic .NET. Now if you look at this method, you can imagine or sketch the processing that takes place (sketching works even for much more complex algorithms). Let's turn the array on its side for convenience:

```
round 1  [2189] [2432] [4391] [3432] [8932]
            f                           l
round 2  [8932] [2432] [4391] [3432] [2189]
                   f                l
round 3  [8932] [3432] [4391] [2432] [2189]
                         fl
```

In step one, the values of **f** and **l** are swapped and then the index values are incremented and decremented, respectively. The method can recur because **f** is still less than **l** and there are still elements left to swap. In the preceding case, we have five values, but the algorithm works even if we add another value to make it six, so that no value is left unswapped.

This brings us to two of the most important conditions of recursive methods or algorithms: base cases and stopping conditions.

The Base Case

A recursive method knows how to solve its simplest case. This is often referred to as the *base case*. The base case in the preceding array-reversal program is the reversal of at least two values. You would not need to recall the method on a single reversal, but throwing a huge array at the method means the method gets to work on one large problem and continues to erode it until it arrives at the base or simplest case. In other words, the problem keeps getting smaller until it no longer exists.

In more complex problems, the algorithm knows how to solve the problem, but because the problem is so big, the algorithm divides the problem into smaller problems and then calls itself to go to work on the smaller problems. (Refer to the discussion of "divide and conquer" in the previous section.) This is why you often see array sort methods using recursion, as you will in Chapter 12, because the method partitions the array into smaller arrays and then sorts each one recursively.

The Stopping Condition

Every recursive method must have a *stopping condition* or the recursion will continue until the computer runs out of memory. In the preceding example, the stopping condition is when first and last become equal or land on the same index. At that point, the method must return (using the **If...Then** construct) or the two values will intersect, reverse the procedure, and run off the bounds of the array, causing the method to explode.

In this example, the stopping condition is placed at the point where we decide we have achieved the desired result. Running out of memory because the recursion continues on indefinitely is a worst-case scenario you must protect against—just as you would with a **While** loop.

The method signature can thus be constructed as follows:

```
SwingArray(ByRef swinger() As Integer, ByVal first As Integer, _
  ByVal last  As Integer)
```

We pass the array reference, **first** (which is 0 or **swinger.GetLowerBound(0)**) and **last** (which is **swinger.Length-1** or **swinger.GetUpperBound(0)**). Inside the method implementation, we can swap the values as follows:

```
Module Module1
  Dim swinger() As Integer = {2189, 2432, 4391, 3432, 8932}
  Dim placeHolder As New Stack()
  Sub Main()
    SwingArray(swinger, swinger.GetLowerBound(0), swinger.GetUpperBound(0))
    PrintArray(swinger)
    Console.ReadLine()
  End Sub

  Public Sub SwingArray(ByRef swinger() As Integer, _
    ByVal first As Integer, ByVal last As Integer)
    If (first < last) Then
      placeHolder.Push(swinger(first))
      swinger(first) = swinger(last)
      swinger(last) = placeHolder.Pop
      SwingArray(swinger, first + 1, last - 1) '<-recursive call
    End If
  End Sub

  Public Sub PrintArray(ByVal swing() As Integer)
    Dim intI As Integer
```

```
    For intI = 0 To UBound(swing)
       Console.WriteLine(swing(intI))
    Next intI
  End Sub

End Module
```

The array is now reversed. Calling **PrintArray** provides the following output:

```
8932
3432
4391 <-f/l
2432
2189
```

Notice that we are using an **If** conditional because we don't need to loop inside the method. The recursive calls to the method—as marked—take care of the repeated runs through the code.

Of course, such recursion is really unnecessary, because a **While** loop (iteration) would handle the repeats. Here's the alternative using iteration:

```
Public Sub IterArray(ByRef swinger() As Integer, _
  ByVal first As Integer, ByVal last As Integer)
  While (first < last)
    placeHolder.Push(swinger(first))
    swinger(first) = swinger(last)
    swinger(last) = placeHolder.Pop
    first += 1
    last -= 1
  End While
End Sub
```

So, it should come as no surprise to you that you can write the recursive call with a **For** or a **While** loop. So why would you consider writing code that makes recursive calls? The first answer to this question usually comes in the form of a statement of surprise from many green programmers: "I did not even know there was any other way to do this—and I have loops that have completely lost their way."

But the first rule to consider is that if a problem can be solved effectively and quickly using loop constructs, then that should be your first choice. For most algorithms, loops are easier and quicker to write and are a natural component of your programming arsenal. Before you start thinking about moving a loop to a recursive call, explore tightening the loop by making it more efficient, choosing the correct operators, and so on.

Recursive method calls or algorithms, however, often offer us a natural and elegant way of dealing with a complex problem, and this is one of the reasons I brought the subject up in the first place. In Chapter 12 we are going to look at some data structures that can be elegantly manipulated with recursive algorithms; in some cases, recursion is the only way to deal with the problem.

The Impact of Recursion

You will find many algorithms that are inherently recursive and that may be better coded with recursion than loops. Keeping both the method and the size of the data structure being worked on small is very important, because recursive calls tend to impact the call stack, especially when the dataset explodes.

One of the worst reasons to use recursion would be to compute factorials or Fibonacci numbers. A good example (which I would never like to see in production code and thus will attempt to demonstrate) of such a case is processing the Fibonacci series:

```
"Start with 0 and 1 and then add the latest two numbers to get the next one
n: 0 1 2 3 4 5 6 7 8 9 10 11 12 13 14 15 16 ...
Fibonacci (n): 0 1 1 2 3 5 8 13 21 34 55 89 144 233 377 610 987 ...
```

Processing Fibonacci 20 results in 21,891 method calls, but processing Fibonacci 30 quickly racks up more than seven million calls. Why is this so dangerous? Clearly, it is very difficult to predict how seven million calls will impact the call stack. So unless you are certain what resources you will need or have for the recursive call, or what the worst case scenario of the recursion might be, you could be heading for a massive explosion (figuratively speaking) inside the computer.

Meanwhile, the following is a checklist to consider when choosing recursive methods:

- Make sure you have a stopping scenario. Every recursive algorithm must include an alternative nonrecursive path that is to be encountered in the path of execution. You thus have to code a routine that repeatedly tests for a certain condition and then returns the method and ends the recursion when that condition is encountered.

- Add a checking parameter to the parameter list. A checking variable can be passed in on every call and can be used to compute when it's time to bail.

- Watch that stack. Stack usage varies greatly depending on the algorithm. Test worst-case situations but build safety checks in the method to protect the target and the user. Get that debugger out and check the memory usage. Step the code through the paces and estimate how much of the stack the code chews up. While you should catch out-of-memory exceptions and the like, waiting for that to happen borders on lunacy.

■ Don't code recursion indirectly. This means that you should not reenter the method as a result of a call to another method. While I know some programmers have done that, I have not come up with a scenario in which such a situation is unavoidable, and I doubt I ever will.

■ Use recursion when the solution requires it. As you can see from the preceding tips, coding recursive routines is a lot of work. They are not exactly run-of-the-mill code. Using recursion for Fibonacci or to produce prime numbers is not the kind of software engineering you should be proud of. Keep your code simple.

■ Use recursion with divide-and-conquer logic. We've talked about this several times in the past. A recursive algorithm should not simply be a loop with an attitude, but rather a worthwhile step-by-step procedure to solving a problem recursively.

Understanding Method Performance

If a method is a task or a subtask of an algorithm, then the time analysis of an algorithm can be achieved by calculating the time it takes for each method to perform its operations. What do we mean by time analysis of a method? Think of an exercise you perform at the gym or health club. If you get onto a treadmill and program in parameters like weight and age and number of calories to burn, the program can determine how many steps you need to take to burn 500 calories. Similarly, it is possible to figure out how long it takes for a method to complete a task by counting the number of operations it takes to obtain the result and, more specifically, how long each operation takes.

Earlier we studied how to break down an algorithm into its constituent tasks and subtasks (methods), but you also need to break down a method to the number of operations it needs to perform to complete its task.

An array sort, or a tree-walking routine is essentially evaluated by the number of operations it takes to achieve the end result and for the operations of the method to end. If the operations continue ad-infinitum, then you have obviously "painted" yourself into a loop that cannot exit.

An *operation* is nothing more than a single statement in a method. These statements can be as complex as a multi-argument method call or as simple, yet critical, as the assignment of a variable or some calculation.

It should make sense, then, that a method that takes the longer list of input arguments is going to take longer to complete than a method that only has to deal with a short list. Going back to the treadmill example, the same logic applies: The exercise that results in the highest calorie burn will be the one in which you take the most steps and continue for the longest time.

In software engineering, we can formulate notation for computing time analysis by computing expressions where the number of steps is represented by the parameter n. In other words, you can write that to burn calories, you need to walk n steps at a constant rate. A time-analysis equation might look like this:

Time = timeN

or

Time = 60secs*500,
Time = 8hrs

Let's take the next step and look at the notation, using n as the base parameter, to do time analysis on a method. To repeat: A method operation can be simplistically defined as a statement in a method. A statement can be rather complex and involve other method calls. It can also be simple in scope, such as the assignment of a variable or simple math.

Notice again that I am talking methods here and not algorithms, although arguably a method is as much an algorithm as an application. It makes more sense, along our theme of decomposing algorithms and data structures, to be analyzing specific tasks of a program (methods) and not the program itself.

Software engineering experts have for decades pondered over the gauging of algorithm efficiency, and have provided us with several formulas for evaluating efficiency or performance, which you can use to determine how to handle a specific task. These apply equally to .NET languages, the Framework, and Visual Basic .NET as they do to unmanaged code, and you will find frequent reference to performance in the .NET Framework reference material.

Getting back on the treadmill, for example, you need to walk n steps to burn 500 calories, c, and it will take t time. If, for the 500-calorie burn, your body employs f function, you could just write the formula as $f(n) = c$, which is the function multiplied by the number of steps (n strides) to burn the calories (ignoring how long it will take).

In software development, the faster the process the better, so time analysis is the objective here. In other words, you rate the efficiency of your methods by how long it takes them to complete. For obvious reasons, you would not perform such exercises on simple programs that take a few seconds here or there to complete.

So let's review this by analyzing the operations of a simple Visual Basic .NET method. Consider an array-searching method simulating the use of a healthy body that can burn 500 calories by taking 6,000 strides in the treadmill's brisk walk program. The calorie-burning work is illustrated as the effort (function) to search the array until you reach the end. The last element in the array (plus 1 to be precise) must be equal to the exercise of 6,000 strides for the method to return **True**.

```
Public Function BriskWalk(ByRef strides() As Integer, _
   ByVal exercise As Integer) As Integer
   Dim aStride As Integer
   For aStride = 0 To strides.Length - 1
      strides(aStride) = exercise
      exercise += 1
   Next aStride
   Return aStride
End Function
```

Next we count the operations in this method. When the calorie-burning **For** loop starts, the first operation is the assignment of **aStride** to zero. The second operation is the **For** test to determine if **aStride**'s value is still less that the length of the **strides** array. The third operation is assignment inside the **For** loop (**strides(aStride) = exercise**) and the fourth operation is the increment that takes place after the assignment (**exercise += 1**).

The number of operations in the body of the **For** loop is expressed as f operations (the number of operations multiplied by the iterations of the loop). The number of operations is thus achieved by $f(n)$, as demonstrated earlier.

Finally, we have the **Return** statement after the loop is done, which, along with the first two operations, is also counted once. So, the formula for determining the total number of operations in this method is $f(n) + 3$.

Now clock the time to complete each operation, multiplying the operations that are repeated, to perform the time analysis of the method. To burn more calories, you would need to take more steps and increase the exercise. And the more steps you take, the longer it takes to complete the method.

Our big problem is that as the number of strides grows, the more time it takes to make each stride (for each iteration) because the healthy body begins to tire. The same thing happens with our methods and we begin to inject a new issue—*order of magnitude*—into the equations. Recursion is a good example, as discussed earlier. The longer the processing, the higher the impact on the stack and the less memory that is available. There are other variables that we have so far ignored, such as the strength of the compiler and the power of the processor, and we can think of those as the "friction" that keeps things from being anything but constant.

You can get bogged down pondering the math, and you should avoid that because this is about as far from Visual Basic .NET as we want to stray in this book. Instead, your sojourn into data structures and method performance requires you to understand that some algorithms work better than others (complete quicker) depending on the nature of the problem, the size of the input, and factors like growth rates and so on. Let's talk about that next.

Algorithms or the method techniques used in processing data structures can be classified for efficiency comparison using *asymptotic analysis.* Without getting into master's-level study, this mouthful permits us to accept that as we increase the size of the input data going into the algorithm, the efficiency of the algorithm is going be affected. In other words, an efficient algorithm for $10n$ may not be so efficient if the input size is increased to $100n$, depending on the algorithm.

This type of information can be expressed by a "yard stick" called *O*-notation (or to be precise, big-*O* notation). The *O* stands for order and the character used is a big *O*; hence the term big-*O* notation.

Big-*O* notation is useful because it lets us classify our methods or algorithms for efficiency comparison, but it does not prescribe how to write the algorithm. Rather, it classifies the algorithm, no matter what language it is written in, according to the time it takes, in theory, to complete the problem, and how the time increases or decreases as the algorithm works through the input data.

There are a number of such time analysis yardsticks, and if you stroll through the collection classes in the .NET Framework, you will find frequent references to the "*O*-ness" of a particular method used for sorting or searching data structures. Let's first talk about the three yardsticks you will encounter with everyday sort and search algorithms:

- **Linear time**   Your algorithm is said to be linear if by doubling the input size the number of operations can increase twofold. In other words, by doubling the input size, the time taken to complete the sort of a list of variables, such as an array, increases by approximately twofold. The notation for a linear algorithm is $O(n)$.

- **Quadratic time**   Your algorithm is said to be quadratic if by doubling the input size the number of operations increases by up to four times. In other words, if you double the list of variables in a sorting structure, the time taken to sort the list can take up to four times longer. The notation for a quadratic algorithm is $O(n2)$.

- **Logarithmic time**   Your algorithm is said to be logarithmic if by doubling the input size the number of operations only increases by a fixed number of operations. For example, depending on the input size, the number of operations may only increase by one or two operations. A logarithmic algorithm can thus work very efficiently on large sets of data, because the time taken to complete the computation of a larger input hardly increases. The notation for a logarithmic algorithm is $O(\log n)$. Several sort methods provided in the **System.Array** class use a logarithmic sort algorithm.

When you evaluate or design algorithms and methods for processing data structures, it is also important to understand the difference between worst-case results and expected results.

Expected results are hard to define when you do not have proven patterns or a scale on which to make comparisons. However, it can help you to make worst-case predictions based on the size of the data set and what you have to do with it, and fix your expectations from there.

In other words, when designing methods to search, sort, or otherwise process data structures, concentrate on the likely worst-case scenario. This is known as worst-case analysis. For example, let's say you have to sort a simple array of ten items. Instead of basing the performance of the array sort on 100 items, rather base it on the likelihood of the array being 10,000 items. (There may be a strong possibility that the input size will one day be as high as 10,000, and you need to decide how best to cater to that. Of course, you also have to balance this line of thinking against how the algorithm will work if the data set is small.)

I learned the hard way back in 1994 when I wrote an e-mail program that parsed e-mail addresses in a structure to extract malformed domain names and so on. The algorithm was sufficient when the size of the list was around 1,000 items, but became unusable at above 10,000 items because, unbeknownst to me, the number of operations had increased fourfold (a quadratic algorithm) and I was not sure why (memory constraints and ill-conceived code aside).

This was eventually fixed by changing the order of certain operations, tightening loops, making better use of bitwise operations, and so on. In 1999, I had to write a program that read data feed containing hundreds of thousand of check deposit records from about eight banks for one of the largest food distribution companies in the USA. The data needed to be streamed to the file, then sorted, and formatted into a common format before being transferred to the financial systems. So everything I learned about method performance over the years paid off here.

So, if you know that time in a sequential search will be linear, while in a binary search it will be logarithmic, why would you write a method that performs a sequential search of a large data set? Because it's easier.

The following additional key classes of efficiency are also described by big-O notation:

- $O(1)$ Constant time, typical of an Array index sort
- $O(n\log n)$ $n\log n$ time, typical of the quicksort algorithm (see "Quicksort" in Chapter 12)
- $O(n3)$ Cubic time, typical of matrix multiplication
- $O(2n)$ Exponential time, typical of set part partitioning

How do you know if the methods you are writing are up to standard? Do you just write a method and if it achieves what it sets out to achieve—it completes with the desired result—you are satisfied?

Being able to gauge the performance of a method is an important asset as a Visual Basic programmer (as any type of programmer, for that matter). Usually, you would not overly concern yourself with performance issues—that is, worry whether your application does X in Y milliseconds. But when you need to code real-time applications or create a process that requires optimum performance considerations, knowing how long it takes for a method to do its work is important. Remember, a method is a task or subtask of an algorithm, and all methods thus should be coded for optimum performance or one method may hold up the entire process.

To sum up this section: The time analysis of an entire algorithm can be achieved by calculating the time it takes for each method to perform its operations. You are obviously thinking that there are other factors to consider, and you are right. But for the most part, you should not try to inject factors like kernels, processor bandwidth, hard disks, and so forth into the equations, because these factors hardly remain constant and most of the time you have no control over them. The quality of your code does remain constant, and it matters how you code a method to ensure that it completes in the quickest time. The quality of your code and how you code a method is something you have very fine control over.

You have studied how to break down an algorithm into its constituent tasks and subtasks (methods), but you also need to break down a method to the number of operations it needs to perform to complete its task. In the study of data structures, it becomes clear that there are many ways to achieve a result. But only one way completes in the fastest time. We will return to sorting and searching in Chapter 12.

Observations

There is a lot to methods besides the implementation aspects. We have to worry about access to methods, the polymorphic behavior of methods, method attributes, class cohesion and method coupling, and so much more. As important as methods are to an OO application, becoming too fanatical about them doesn't help either, because that has the potential of distracting you from the bigger picture of OO design and architecture. We will focus on methods again in Chapter 12, with respect to sorting and searching.

The
Complete
Reference

Part III

Classes and Objects

The Complete Reference

Visual Basic .NET

Chapter 8

Types, Structures, and Enumerations

In Chapter 2 we looked at the .NET Type System and learned a little about the hierarchy that descends from the root type, which is called **Object** (see Figure 2-1). We also investigated the two branches of the type model: *value types* and *reference types*. This chapter will expound upon these two strands.

By now it's clear that the type system underpinning .NET is one hundred percent object-oriented. This means that even the fundamental, simple types like **Integer** and **Boolean** are first class objects. This is not the case with Java whose primitive type architecture is modeled on C.

Value types derive from the root object and include built-in fundamental-data types as well as user-defined types cradled in structure and enumeration "garb." The built-in value types are the so-called *primitive* or *elementary* types that derive from classes like **System.Int16**, **System.Int32**, **System.Int64**, and **System.Double**. From a purist's viewpoint, *primitive* is a misleading descriptor for .NET's built-in value types, because primitive types herald from the procedural age of software engineering and are not objects—value types *are* objects. (See the comments comparing Java primitives to .NET value types at the end of this chapter.)

Most types you program with or against are processed on the heap, the allocation of random access memory (RAM) on your computer. We call heap objects *reference types* because of the semantics used to reference them. What value types do have in common with reference types is inheritance. They derive from their base type **ValueType**, which itself derives from the root metatype, **Object**. Thus, you can create your own "custom" value types, known as *structures*. From our perspective, this is where the similarity between value types and reference types ends.

There are a number of differences between value types and reference types. The most important difference is that value types are "value oriented"—representing a single value or collections of values. They also live in the CLR-managed stack, a highly efficient memory for such lightweight classes. The CLR stack is not garbage-collected. Reference types, on the other hand, are more function- and algorithm-oriented (rather than being value-oriented) and define methods that operate on or work with the values of value types.

Semantics for the two types are also dissimilar. Furthermore, the compilers and the CLR treat the two very differently, especially in regard to keeping value types lightweight and efficient while allowing them to be referenced as objects when the need arises. The division of the object model into two type models keeps the .NET Framework purely object-oriented, while still allowing values to be processed efficiently.

Note   *See the discussion of fundamental types in Chapter 4.*

We'll now begin our investigation into these two models: starting at the beginning will help us better understand the differences between them—a critical requirement for avoiding subtle and unnecessary bugs and performance hogs in your code.

The Value-Type Model

Custom value types are efficient constructs and perform similarly to the built-in, simple data types. However, the term "built-in" indicates that the base-class library already provides the simple types; thus, compilers "know" about them and can manage them more efficiently than your custom types.

You can even build your own version of **Integer** and override some of the base methods that value types inherit from both the **ValueType** and root-**Object** classes. Yet, the value-type class is not meant to replace the built-in fundamental types. That would be redundant for a type like **Integer**. **Double** might be a different story, as we'll see later. The base **ValueType** class allows you to create specialized, efficient value types that can provide utility that exceeds the utility of the built-in ones.

The **ValueType** class, for example, lets you develop complex numeric types for use in scientific, numerical, and statistical problems. You can create value types that represent collections of the fundamental types (like enumeration constants) and present them in forms and with values resulting from mathematical operations—even functions for linear algebra and statistical operations requiring double-precision operations.

| Note |

Since Visual Basic .NET has the support for custom value types, which provide the necessary foundation for the advancement of numerical computing on the Windows platform, I expect the next version to include support for operator overloading. It may possibly even come in a service pack.

Some important facts about values types:

■ They have value semantics. When you assign an existing value type, the operator performs a *deep copy* of the object bit-for-bit and doesn't work on the pointer to some other "place," as described later for reference types. A *deep comparison* also examines the objects bit-for-bit and doesn't evaluate whether the left and right sides of the **Is** operator refer to the same object on the heap.

■ Their variables always have a value. If none is assigned at declaration, the value type's field defaults to zero, or you can specify a value in the default constructor (which must have parameters). Those that store strings default to an empty **String**. Value types are always final, which lets the compiler perform important type processing economics at compile time.

■ A value type does not incur dispatch overhead or require a dispatch pointer, because the class is always final (in other words the compiler knows what it is and what it does at compile time). Subsequently, only one version exists in the stack and you don't need the **New** keyword to create it (although it is not a sin if you use **New**).

- They do not require finalization. When the variable's life ends, the CLR—not the garbage collector—immediately removes it from stack memory. When the value type goes out of scope, such as an **Integer** declared in a method, it's done, there and then.

- Value types can implement interfaces. This is considered a big bonus from Microsoft, because it can't hurt the specification of a custom value type, and it provides a powerful facility. To some, however, this feature detracts from its lightweight virtue. To use the famous words of Muhammed Ali, a value type should "float like a butterfly, sting like a bee."

- Value types cannot have virtual methods, nor can they or their members be abstract.

- They are implicitly sealed; thus, they cannot be used as a base for deriving new types. You cannot, for example, inherit from **System.Int32**. Value types are implicitly declared **NotInheritable**.

- Value types are shared, which means there is only one copy of the type's value in the system. For this reason they default to private access.

Note   *See also the Flyweight pattern (Erich Gamma, Richard Helm, Ralph Johnson, and John Vlissides.* Design Patterns: Elements of Reusable Object-Oriented Software. *Addison-Wesley, 1995).*

Referencing value types is done implicitly via their identifiers, their names. If you name an **Integer** "voila," then voila it is, and the following code is perfectly legitimate.

```
voila = voila + voila
```

However, this name is not carried down to IL; the compiler assigns it a less elegant one.

How Value Types Work

Value types are small, lightweight, and efficient. Some people call the simple built-in types "the hard currency" with which all software is created. I would then add that the value type model itself is the means that the .NET architects give you to add more currency to the type system—to extend it so you can build any software for any problem.

The best way to understand the value type is to declare one and then compare it to the other base types and standard classes in order to see how it lives in the computer. Before we do that, we need to understand what a value type is and why its model and architecture in .NET are so significant.

When you work with a simple type, such as the **Double** (which represents double floating-point precision), you will notice the abundance of methods, properties, and other members "attached" to this object. In case you have not investigated what lies "beneath" a value type like **System.Double**, try the following experiment: Declare a variable of type **Double**. Reference the variable in a method and insert a dot after the variable as follows.

```
Public Sub TestDouble()
  Dim dbl As Double = 5.5
  dbl.
End Sub
```

When you hit the period key, you discover a whole world of methods and things you never thought existed. If you don't have the IDE open in front of you, the illustration demonstrates this (there's even a field for **Epsilon**).

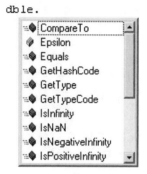

There are three ways to declare a variable of a value type:

```
Dim dbl1 As Double = 5.5
Dim dbl2 As New Double()
Dim dbl3 As New System.Double(5.5) Initialization produces a compiler error
```

The first is the short cut used by the compiler to deal with the type in value type semantics. It knows to create the object without the **New** keyword because, as you will learn in the next chapter, **New** creates a reference to a heap-based object. The second uses the **New** keyword, which is also valid but, for value types, this style does nothing different from the first style. In the third example, using the **New** keyword and trying to initialize the variable will not work because **Double** cannot be initialized in this fashion. Value types do not have a default constructor. The syntax you choose is not important here, because the compiler will produce the same IL code.

To investigate how value types behave let's look at some simple value assigning. The following code first writes the value of **dbl1** (first with defaults) to the Output, Debug window (Step 1). Then it writes the value (still 0) of **dbl2** to the output window (Step 2). Next it initializes **dbl1** to the value of 5.5 and displays the values of both variables again

CLASSES AND OBJECTS

(Steps 3 and 4). At this point, only **dbl1** is 5.5. Next it copies the value of **dbl1** to **dbl2** and then displays both values (Steps 5 and 6). At this juncture, both values are identical because the copy is "deep." The code then finally raises the value of **dbl2** to the power of itself. The final output to the output window confirms that **dbl1** is not affected by the process that changes the value of **dbl2** (Steps 7 and 8).

```
Dim dbl1 As Double
Dim dbl2 As Double
  Sub Main()
     Debug.WriteLine("Step 1: " & dbl1)
     Debug.WriteLine("Step 2: " & dbl2)
     dbl1 = 5.5
     Debug.WriteLine("Step 3: " & dbl1)
     Debug.WriteLine("Step 4: " & dbl2)
     dbl2 = dbl1
     Debug.WriteLine("Step 5: " & dbl1)
     Debug.WriteLine("Step 6: " & dbl2)
     dbl2 = System.Math.Pow(dbl2, dbl2)
     Debug.WriteLine("Step 7: " & dbl1)
     Debug.WriteLine("Step 8: " & dbl2)

     Console.WriteLine("Normal exit: Press 'q' to quit the sample.")
     While Chr(Console.Read()) <> "q"c
     End While
  End Sub
```

The output to the Debug window is as follows:

```
Step 1: 0
Step 2: 0
Step 3: 5.5
Step 4: 0
Step 5: 5.5
Step 6: 5.5
Step 7: 5.5
Step 8: 11803.0648208644
```

As you can see, the two value types are referencing their own values. If they both referenced an object on the heap then both **dbl1** and **dbl2** would return the value in Step 8. But what would happen if we were to *box* one of the types? The next section will explain this concept in case you are unfamiliar with it. This is not essential knowledge for most applications; however, your algorithms will benefit from your understanding the boxing/unboxing process, especially if they are complex or scientific.

Boxing

A quick summary is in order before we proceed. We know that the value type lives in stack memory where it can be efficiently accessed. We also know that the value types are themselves objects, part of the type system's "family tree," of which **Object** is the root type (see Chapter 2).

We also see that each variable of a type has its own underlying methods, fields, and properties that act on the variable. So what happens to **dbl1**, for example, when we ask it to tell us more than its value—like giving up its **Epsilon** value—or if we ask it to compare itself to another value? What happens to the type when we need to talk to it more as an object and less as a value?

In order to work with the value type using object semantics, it first has to be boxed. This technique creates a new object in heap memory, where reference objects live, and copies the value of the value type to that location. The new version of the value type moves into the object spotlight as the old version on the stack recedes. Have a look at the following two methods; only one of them results in a box operation:

```
Module TestBox1
  'to box or not to box
  Sub Main()
    Dim dbl1, dbl2 As Double
    dbl1 = 5.5
    dbl2 = 5.6
    Console.WriteLine(dbl1.CompareTo(dbl2))
  End Sub
End Module

Module TestBox2
  'to box or not to box
  Sub Main()
    Dim dbl1, dbl2 As Double
    dbl1 = 5.5
    dbl2 = 5.6
    Console.WriteLine(dbl1.ToString.CompareTo(dbl2.ToString))
  End Sub
End Module
```

The methods are nearly identical and return identical results. There is one tiny difference. The first method, **TestBox1**, requires a boxing operation to compare **dbl1** to **dbl2** with the **CompareTo** method because **CompareTo** takes an object as an argument. The boxing operation extracts the value of both variables to make the comparison. The second method **TestBox2** does not require a boxing of the types because we extract the values in the type's **ToString** fields beforehand and compare the values returned from the **ToString** calls.

We can confirm this using the .NET Framework IL Disassembler (ILDASM) tool described in Chapter 2 to inspect the MSIL code. The first example is from **TestBox1** and indicates a box operation (in bold). The second method is the code from **TestBox2** and does not indicate a box. Have a look:

```
.method public static void  Main() cil managed
{
  .entrypoint
  .custom instance void [mscorlib]System.STAThreadAttribute::.ctor() = ( 01 00 00 00 )
  // Code size       52 (0x34)
  .maxstack  2
  .locals init ([0] float64 dbl1,
           [1] float64 dbl2,
           [2] float64 dbl3)
  IL_0000:  nop
  IL_0001:  ldc.r8      5.5
  IL_000a:  stloc.0
  IL_000b:  ldc.r8      5.5999999999999996
  IL_0014:  stloc.1
  IL_0015:  ldc.r8      5.7000000000000002
  IL_001e:  stloc.2
  IL_001f:  ldloca.s    dbl3
  IL_0021:  ldloc.1
  IL_0022:  box         [mscorlib]System.Double
  IL_0027:  call        instance int32 [mscorlib]System.Double::CompareTo(object)
  IL_002c:  call        void [mscorlib]System.Console::WriteLine(int32)
  IL_0031:  nop
  IL_0032:  nop
  IL_0033:  ret
} // end of method TestComplex::Main
```

TestBox2 does not indicate a box operation.

```
.method public static void  Main() cil managed
{
  .entrypoint
  .custom instance void [mscorlib]System.STAThreadAttribute::.ctor() = ( 01 00 00 00 )
  // Code size       58 (0x3a)
  .maxstack  2
  .locals init ([0] float64 dbl1,
           [1] float64 dbl2,
           [2] float64 dbl3)
  IL_0000:  nop
  IL_0001:  ldc.r8      5.5
  IL_000a:  stloc.0
  IL_000b:  ldc.r8      5.5999999999999996
```

```
    IL_0014:   stloc.1
    IL_0015:   ldc.r8      5.7000000000000002
    IL_001e:   stloc.2
    IL_001f:   ldloca.s    dbl3
    IL_0021:   call        instance string [mscorlib]System.Double::ToString()
    IL_0026:   ldloca.s    dbl2
    IL_0028:   call        instance string [mscorlib]System.Double::ToString()
    IL_002d:   callvirt    instance int32 [mscorlib]System.String::CompareTo(string)
    IL_0032:   call        void [mscorlib]System.Console::WriteLine(int32)
    IL_0037:   nop
    IL_0038:   nop
    IL_0039:   ret
} // end of method TestComplex::Main
```

You may be wondering why this is relevant since the CLR manages the code. Consider this in response: Boxing is a resource-intensive process that slows down your code. This may seem negligible when you're working with a small segment of code, as in the above example. However, for a complex algorithm, writing code that boxes heavily will negatively impact performance.

It's not difficult to inspect your code and evaluate it for boxing overhead. Using the ILDASM tool referred to previously, open the assembly and double-click the method you want to inspect. Instructions to box value types are embedded in the MSIL code. Using the ILDASM tool in this way, you can quickly evaluate the assembly for boxing bottleneck.

Why are Value Types Objects?

This is an important question that can be asked in another meaningful way: why aren't value types primitive? The most crucial of many reasons we'll examine concerns mixing object semantics and primitive semantics within an object-oriented language; this causes problems at the source level for the architects of a software language and for its intended audience. Primitive or native types are fundamentally incompatible with objects. There will be problems if they coexist in the same type system, especially within a framework that boasts strongly typed and secure software.

To understand the architecture, let's look at the roots of the issue. Objects are reference types that live in heap memory. When you create an object with the **New** keyword, it is placed in a heap-based memory location and you are given a reference to work with, rather than the object itself. This reference is a variable that holds a memory address where the bits of the object can be looked up.

Hence, the statement **obvar1 = obvar2** denotes that you are making **obvar1** and **obvar2** point to the same object. It does not means **obvar1** and **obvar2** are equal. We'll discuss the object-reference model later in this chapter.

Many software gurus, including Java's architects, believe object management is too cumbersome for essential software types, such as the elemental-data types. When you declare an **int** in Java, you are creating a variable that holds the data assigned to it and is stored on the stack, where it is processed more efficiently than your average object is. Java's primitives are not objects, and you cannot "talk" to them in reference type semantics.

Java's native types are powerful, slender, and fit—always there when you need them. Reference types are fat and lazy living on the heap, waiting for the garbage truck to collect them. But the .NET reference type object model is far from inefficient. Although heap memory is not as fast as the stack, which has a direct connection to the CPU, many object-oriented purists believe that Java's inventors erred greatly in NOT making the native types objects.

For starters, mixing primitive types with objects quashes polymorphism, because you can't place a primitive type in a field asking for an object. You first have to convert it into an object.

Also, primitive types cannot be easily deployed in an object model that provides runtime type information (RTTI) or reflection ability (see Chapter 2). In order to work with pure objects, we would have to first wrap the values manually in cumbersome wrapper classes, creating problems and setbacks in performance gains.

Currently, Java programmers must explicitly wrap an **int** every time it is needed in an object realm. A powerful contingent within Java is lobbying its creators to implement lightweight classes and convert primitives into objects—thus rendering Java 100 percent object-oriented.

The .NET architects benefited from this debate and adopted the lightweight class architecture—although they are not divulging exactly why the CLR works so well. Was it possible to have it any other way? After all, the Common Language Specification (CLS) makes .NET the framework for all languages—except of course for C++, which, with its primitive type model and hybrid semantics, is far from being a pure object-oriented language.

This value-type model seems to provide the best of both worlds. It allows us to work with true objects on the stack and copy them to the heap when needed. We have the freedom to create new value types, which is a major benefit compared to the Java model, which even struggles with enumerations. The downside is the overhead of boxing, and only time will tell if the .NET inventors upped the ante on Java.

Structs and Enums Ahoy: Creating New Value Types

Let's now create our own value types, which are categorized in two groups deriving from the **ValueType** class specified by the Common Type System. They are called structures (or structs) and enumerations (which actually issue from **System.Enum**). The illustration shows the **ValueType** hierarchy and its two derivatives, which we'll discuss in this chapter.

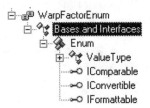

> **Note** *While Structures (and Enums) ultimately derive from **System.ValueType**, you cannot explicitly inherit from either base class (using the **Inherits** keyword). Instead, special classes called **Structure** and **Enum** implicitly derive the value type and all its respective members for you.*

Structures

Structures, or "structs" as they are called in C# (a name inherited from C), are used to build simple or efficient types in which their variables directly represent their data, rather than pointing to locations on the heap. Thus, the variables of structure types include both the reference—in this case the variable's name—and the value or data of the type. When you reference structures in an application, you are working on the actual data, not a reference to the data.

> **Note** *The Visual Basic 6 **Type . . . End Type** statement is not supported in Visual Basic .NET.*

The syntax for the structure is as follows:

[*<attrlist>*] [{ **Public** | **Protected** | **Friend** | **Protected Friend** | **Private** }] [
Shadows]
Structure *name*
  [*Implements interfacenames*]
  variabledeclarations
  [*proceduredeclarations*]
End Structure

It would be redundant to try to create a structure that replaces one of the built-in simple types. But there is one fundamental type that lends itself to some creative adaptation—the **Double**.

When you referenced a variable of the **Double** object previously, the first thing you noticed was a plethora of methods that can operate on the value. If you look at the members of the **Integer** class, you'll see that **Integer** pales in comparison, because **Double** is used for complex math.

For example, you can compare the **Double** to another **Double,** or you can check if it evaluates to negative infinity, positive infinity, and other fancy conditions for complex numerical values as provided by the IEEE 754 specifications (see Chapters 4 and 5). But to do any sophisticated numerical computing we would need a new value type that can compute and return complex values to a client.

The following **Structure** class provides such a data type. It defines the structure as the object **Complex** and takes two **Double**s, one for the *real* part of the complex number and one for the *imaginary* (*unreal*) part of the complex number. It defines several functions and properties for computing the complex numbers, such as multiply and divide. I also included standard **Double** math operations in the same class. Complex math functions typically run into the hundreds, so you can imagine you would need several value types to represent or encapsulate these operations, and then make the types available to scientific applications, like digital signal processing (DSP), encryption, and plotting.

```vb
Public Structure Complex
'floats for real and imaginary parts of complex numbers
'or use both for simple float math
  Public real, unreal As Double
  Public Sub New(ByVal re As Double, ByVal unre As Double)
    real = re
    unreal = unre
  End Sub

  Public ReadOnly Property BasicProduct()
    Get
      BasicProduct = real * unreal
    End Get
End Property

  Public ReadOnly Property BasicDivide()
    Get
      BasicDivide = real / unreal
    End Get
End Property

  Public ReadOnly Property Reciprocal() As Complex
    Get
      If real = 0.0 And unreal = 0.0 Then
        Throw New DivideByZeroException()
    End If
     Dim div As Double = real * real + unreal * unreal
     Return New Complex(real / div, -unreal / div)
    End Get
End Property

  Public Shared Function ComplexToDouble(ByVal aReal As Complex) _
    As Double
    Return aReal.real
  End Function

  Public Shared Function RealToComplex(ByVal dble As Double) _
    As Complex
```

```
      Return New Complex(dble, 0.0)
   End Function

   Public Shared Function ToPositive(ByVal aReal As Complex) _
      As Complex
      Return aReal
   End Function

   Public Shared Function ComplexToNegative(ByVal areal As Complex) _
      As Complex
      Return New Complex(-areal.real, -areal.unreal)
   End Function

   Public Shared Function AddComplex(ByVal areal As Complex, _
      ByVal breal As Complex) As Complex
      Return New Complex(areal.real + breal.real, areal.unreal + _
      breal.unreal)
   End Function

   Public Shared Function SubtractComplex(ByVal areal As Complex, _
      ByVal breal As Complex) As Complex
      Return New Complex(areal.real - breal.real, areal.unreal - _
      breal.unreal)
   End Function

   Public Shared Function MultiplyComplex(ByVal areal As Complex, _
      ByVal breal As Complex) As Complex
      Return New Complex(areal.real * breal.real - areal.unreal * _
      breal.unreal, real.real * breal.unreal + areal.unreal * breal.real)
   End Function

   Public Shared Function DivideComplex(ByVal areal As Complex, _
      ByVal breal As Complex) As Complex
      Return MultiplyComplex(areal, breal.Reciprocal)
   End Function

   Public Overrides Function ToString() As String
      Return String.Format("({0}+{1}i)", real, unreal)
   End Function

End Structure
```

The following console-based code tests the **Complex** value type:

```
Public Class TestComplexed

  Public Shared Sub Main()
    Dim acomplex As New Complex(2.7, 1.5)
    Dim bcomplex As New Complex(7.5, -2)      Console.WriteLine("")
    Console.WriteLine("The acomplex is " & acomplex.ToString)
    Console.WriteLine("The bcomplex is " & bcomplex.ToString)
    Console.WriteLine("Here's the idea...")
    Console.WriteLine("Multiply two doubles = " & acomplex.BasicProduct)
    Console.WriteLine("Divide two doubles = " & acomplex.BasicDivide)
    Console.WriteLine("ConvertToDouble = " & _
      Complex.ComplexToDouble(acomplex).ToString)
    Console.WriteLine("ConvertToComplex = " & _
      Complex.RealToComplex(5.5).ToString)
    Console.WriteLine("Here's the complex idea...")
    Console.WriteLine("acomplex + bcomplex = " & _
      Complex.AddComplex(acomplex, bcomplex).ToString)
    Console.WriteLine("acomplex - bcomplex = " & _
      Complex.SubtractComplex(acomplex, bcomplex).ToString)
    Console.WriteLine("acomplex * bcomplex = " & _
      Complex.MultiplyComplex(acomplex, bcomplex).ToString)
    Console.WriteLine("acomplex / bcomplex = " & _
      Complex.DivideComplex(acomplex, bcomplex).ToString)
  End Sub
End Class
```

The above code prints the following to the console:

```
The acomplex is (2.7+1.5i)
The bcomplex is (7.5+-2i)
Here's the idea...
Multiply two doubles = 4.05
Divide two doubles = 1.8
ConvertToDouble = 2.7
ConvertToComplex = (5.5+0i)
Here's the complex idea...
acomplex + bcomplex = (10.2+-0.5i)
```

```
acomplex - bcomplex = (-4.8+3.5i)
acomplex * bcomplex = (23.25+5.85i)
acomplex / bcomplex = (0.286307053941909+0.276348547717842i)
```

Note *The code for the above **Complex** structure is the ComplexTypes project in the Vb7cr solution.*

Here's another illustration of a financial structure encapsulating a financial function found in numerous function libraries, like those in Microsoft Excel®. The following structure implements methods for computing financial information. I have just shown an attempt at the straight-line Double-Declining Balance formula (*book-value * 2/useful life*), which computes depreciation on an asset for a number of years.

The **DDB** function is computed iteratively. In the following code the book value starts out at a value minus the current salvage value (what the item can be sold for on Ebay today). The methods respectively return the amount the book value decreased in the specified period in its useful life and the amount of depreciation to report.

```
Imports System
Public Structure Accounting
  Dim cost, salvage As Double
  Dim life, period As Integer
  Dim factor As Decimal

  Public Sub New(ByVal rcost As Double, ByVal rsalvage As Double, _
    ByVal rlife As Integer, ByVal rperiod As Integer, _
    Optional ByVal rfactor As Decimal = 2)
    cost = rcost
    salvage = rsalvage
    life = rlife
    period = rperiod
    factor = rfactor
  End Sub

  ReadOnly Property DDBValue()
    Get
      Dim book As Double = cost - salvage
      Dim deprec As Double
      Dim year As Integer = period
      While year > 1
        deprec = book * factor / life
        book = book - deprec
```

```
              year -= 1
          End While
          Return book
      End Get
  End Property


  ReadOnly Property DDBDepreciation()
      Get
          Dim book As Double = cost - salvage
          Dim deprec As Double
          Dim year As Integer = period
          While year >= 1
              deprec = book * factor / life
              book = book - deprec
              year -= 1
          End While
          Return deprec
      End Get
  End Property
End Structure
```

The **Accounting** value type can be used as demonstrated here. The following code:

```
Public Sub PrintDepByYear(ByVal intI As Integer, ByVal life As Integer)
  For intI = 0 To DepreciationPeriodEnum.SeventhYear
      Dim deprec As New Financial(53000, 3000, 10, life, )
      Console.WriteLine("Year " & life & ": " & String.Format("{0:c}", _
          deprec.DDBValue) & ", " & String.Format("{0:c}", _
          deprec.DDBDepreciation))
      life += 1
  Next intI
  Console.ReadLine()
End Sub
```

produces this output

```
Year 0: $50,000.00, $0.00
Year 1: $50,000.00, $10,000.00
Year 2: $40,000.00, $8,000.00
Year 3: $32,000.00, $6,400.00
Year 4: $25,600.00, $5,120.00
Year 5: $20,480.00, $4,096.00
Year 6: $16,384.00, $3,276.80
```

Note | *The code for the **Financial** structure is the FinancialStructure project in the Vb7cr solution.*

Structures serve other purposes beyond number crunching or simple value use. The following example shows a structure encapsulating a collection of color properties for a given component. The properties call the **Color.FromArgb** method found in the **System.Drawing** class, which takes three arguments representing parameters for Red, Green, and Blue (RGB) color combinations. The structure allows the user to choose custom RGB colors (which can be used as a palette you provide in an application). In the **GridColors** structure the colors are returned as objects of **System.Drawing.Color,** which lets you use the colors anywhere a parameter requires you to pass a **System.Drawing.Color** object:

```
Imports System.Drawing
Public Structure GridColors
  Private colorDefault As Color

  Public Sub New(ByVal red As Integer, ByVal green As Integer, _
    ByVal blue As Integer) As Color
    colorDefault = Color.FromArgb(red, green, blue)
  End Sub

  ReadOnly Property grWhite() As Color
    Get
      grWhite = Color.FromArgb(255, 255, 255)
    End Get
  End Property

  ReadOnly Property grLightGray() As Color
    Get
      grLightGray = Color.FromArgb(192, 192, 192)
    End Get
  End Property

  ReadOnly Property grGray() As Color
    Get
      grGray = Color.FromArgb(128, 128, 128)
    End Get
  End Property

  ReadOnly Property grDarkGray() As Color
    Get
      grDarkGray = Color.FromArgb(64, 64, 64)
    End Get
```

```
End Property

ReadOnly Property grBlack() As Color
  Get
    grBlack = Color.FromArgb(0, 0, 0)
  End Get
End Property

ReadOnly Property grRed() As Color
  Get
    grRed = Color.FromArgb(255, 0, 0)
  End Get
End Property

ReadOnly Property grPink() As Color
  Get
    grPink = Color.FromArgb(255, 175, 175)
  End Get
End Property

ReadOnly Property grOrange() As Color
  Get
    grOrange = Color.FromArgb(255, 200, 0)
  End Get
End Property

ReadOnly Property grYellow() As Color
  Get
    grYellow = Color.FromArgb(255, 255, 0)
  End Get
End Property

ReadOnly Property grGreen() As Color
  Get
    grGreen = Color.FromArgb(0, 255, 0)
  End Get
End Property

ReadOnly Property grMagenta() As Color
  Get
    grMagenta = Color.FromArgb(255, 0, 255)
  End Get
End Property
```

```
   ReadOnly Property grCyan()As Color
     Get
       grCyan = Color.FromArgb(0, 255, 255)
     End Get
   End Property

   ReadOnly Property grBlue() As Color
     Get
       grBlue = Color.FromArgb(0, 0, 255)
     End Get
   End Property

   Public ReadOnly Property UserDefined() As Color
     Get
       Return colorDefault
     End Get
   End Property

   Public WriteOnly Property SetUserDefined(ByVal red As Integer, _
     ByVal green As Integer, ByVal blue As Integer) As Color
       Set(ByVal Value As Color)
         Value = Color.FromArgb(red, green, blue)
       End Set
   End Property
End Structure
```

You could then use the **Color** structure as follows:

```
Dim Col As New GridColors()
CommCon.BackColor = Col.UserDefined()
```

or

```
Dim Col As New GridColors(200,255,30)
CommCon.BackColor = Col.UserDefined()
```

or

```
Dim Col As New GridColors()
CommCon.BackColor = Col.grLightGray
```

CLASSES AND OBJECTS

As shown in the above code, structures are useful for returning related pieces of information about a data type. Instead of declaring a new variable for each color in the example, we simple declare a structure and change the color it represents by changing one of its member properties. Once you declare the structure it becomes a standard value type that can be referenced like any of the built-in data types.

The code for the **GridColors** structure is the Palette project in the Vb7cr solution.

Structure Behavior

The structure is an extremely efficient and flexible construct. The following behaviors of structures provide the flexibility to use them in a variety of applications and algorithms.

Nested Structures

In nested structures, you can declare and implement one or more structures inside another one as shown in the following code:

```
Public Structure GridColors '
   Private colorDefault As Color
   '. . .

   Private Structure Hue
   Dim defaultHue As Integer
      '...
   End Structure
End Structure
```

You can also reference other structures—any one of the fundamental value types, for starters—in yours. Let's examine how the method **ClRed** in the following code:

```
Private colorDefault As Color
Public Sub ClRed()
   colorDefault = System.Drawing.Color.Red
End Sub
```

sets the default color to **System.Drawing.Color.Red**, which is itself a structure provided by the **System.Drawing** namespaces.

Passing Structures to and from Methods

You can pass structures as arguments to method parameters **ByValue** and **ByReference**, just as you can with any value type. This is critical, especially for returning arguments from methods. While you can pass several arguments to the formal parameter list of a method, you cannot return more than one value type or built-in data type.

There are many situations in which you can return a value type that sends more than a single value *as a single value*—notwithstanding the oft-cited rule and condition that you can and should only return a single value from a method.

Structures Can Reference Objects

Structures can reference objects, even collection objects like arrays. The upcoming example includes objects and other structures:

```
Public Structure Target

  Private targetColor As TGridColors 'target colors
  Private targetPosition As TGridCoordinates 'x,y positions on the grid
  Private targetSpeed As TSpol 'significant percentage of lightspeed
  Private targetType As TCraft 'the type of craft
  Private targetDistance As TDistance  'distance from our ship
  Private targetVector As TVector 'is the target going or coming
  Private targetHistory As History

End Structure
```

Structure Constructors

You cannot initialize a structure's members in the declaration, but you can initialize its variables in the constructor. The following code, from the earlier **GridColor** example, initializes the **colorDefault** variable of **System.Drawing.Color** structure in the **New** constructor.

```
Private colorDefault As Color
Public Sub New(ByVal red As Integer, ByVal green As Integer, _
  ByVal blue As Integer)
  colorDefault = Color.FromArgb(red, green, blue)
End Sub
```

You are not required to provide a constructor for a struct, as you would be to create an object instance. Even if you provide the **New** method, you do not need to call **New** in the declaration. Please note: if you neither provide nor call a constructor, zero will be the default for the struct's fields. This also explains why you cannot provide a parameterless constructor.

Note *It is also worth noting that structures cannot take destructors, because they are not collected by the garbage collector. When they are no longer needed the CLR knows to get rid of them.*

CLASSES AND OBJECTS

Enumerations

In Chapter 4 we talked a little about *magic numbers*, the constant ordinals that represent array bounds, character positions, coordinates, subscripts, indexes, flags, and other literal number values in your algorithms. Whenever you need to refer to these values in your software, you must name the magic numbers before you use them; otherwise, your code becomes extremely hard to read and maintain—especially when these numbers appear suddenly and without explanations.

As a rule, any number other than 0 or 1 will likely be magical and should be given an identifier, its name. All modern software-development languages support named constants and global variables, so there is no excuse for leaving magic numbers in your code.

When you need to work with a list of constants that represent magic numbers, organize them in a group for uniform reference and ease of management. Standard classes and structures would be the first "containers" that come to mind for encapsulating named constants. Classes, however, are too cumbersome and would always place your collection of constants in heap space. Accessing the members of the class requires object-reference semantics, which is clumsy for something so basic. Access and visibility are also considerations for constants encapsulated at the standard-class level.

A structure would be a better container because it's efficient, although it's not ideal. Fortunately, the .NET Framework is equipped with an enumeration or enumerated type—the **Enum**—that provides that facility for you.

Note   *Do not confuse the term* enumeration *with the term* enumerator, *which is an object that iterates over a collection, or counts a collection of values (see Chapter 12).*

The **Enum** is a value type, like a structure; however, it does not have a structure's facilities for methods and properties, which represent baggage in this context. It's only a place for naming your constants, a place for hiding magic numbers. **Enum** types are thus ideal to represent collections of symbols that correspond to ordinal values.

Within these enumerations, you can manage the symbols in familiar terms as your named constants. And you don't need to explicitly initialize them with values. In addition to having a formal type for symbolic names, enumerations provide a strong type utility. In other words, you cannot pass the value **TemparatureEnum.Hot** to a method that requires an argument of type **BouquetEnum.Roses**. It is also more helpful in debugging and documentation to be shown meaningful symbols rather than meaningless numbers. You can easily see what enumerations cater to in the following code:

```
'good
If TemparatureEnum.Hot Then
   Cooler.Start
```

```
End If
'bad
If temp > 120 Then
  Cooler.Start
End If
```

The user-defined **Enum** inherits from **System.Enum**, which in turn inherits from **System.ValueType**. It is processed in stack memory.

In addition to being an efficiently managed type, the **Enum** offers exceptional reference semantics. It is an elegantly implemented type, infused with a very useful collection of methods that render the **Enum** one of the most pleasurable constructs to work with in the .NET Framework. Enumerated types, like interfaces, are part of the fabric that makes up the web and woof of the framework.

Here's an example of using the enumeration: Let's say we need to set up a grid on a monitor for rendering—plotting the flight path of a space ship across a sector in space, which the grid must refer to and represent. The grid would function as a "window" to the sector in space.

We need some frame of reference for the grid and a collection of methods that manage it in relation to the inbound data it's rendering. For starters, the grid would be referenced on its left bound at pixel 0 and on the right bound at pixel 480 (for argument's sake). These values might represent the length of a monitor's viewing areas, but they could also represent the grid within a user interface (probably surrounded by instrumentation).

As the space ship travels, the grid represents its path, but remains unchanged. The monitor would have to pan in order to track the object as it approaches the edge of the grid's field of view. A method for this would regularly test the ship's location; if it were near or on one of the edges, the grid would move to keep it in view. The grid could remain fixed until the object approached the bounds, or it could fix the space ship onto coordinates and continuously pan as the ship moves, and stop as the ship rests.

Using magic numbers to compute the trajectory of the object would make the code hard to read. For example, with a magic number the code would read as follows:

```
If (ObjectPosition >= 75) Then
'. . . do something
End If
```

Better to use a named constant as follows:

```
If (ObjectPosition >= GridVectorsEnum.MaxRight) Then
'. . . do something
End If
```

If the numeric value of **MaxRight** changes from 75 to 65, we need to change the constant in only one place in our software. Using the magic number, we would be forced to change the value from 75 to 65 wherever it was referenced. Manually replacing the unnamed constants would be laborious and impractical. The resulting code would be both hard to read and prone to bugs, especially in a large program.

If we needed to maintain a large set of coordinates for our grid, we could list a collection of them in an enumeration and assign them the constants of their respective grid values. The following example uses the **Enum** to represent such a collection of grid constants:

```
Public Enum GridVectorsEnum
  MaxRight = 480
  MaxLeft = 0
  MaxHeight = 300
  MinHeight = 40
  PixelDistance = 12 'the number of pixels to move left
                     'for right for each Kilometer traveled
End Enum
```

To work with the **GridVectorsEnum** enumeration in our code, reference it with the **Imports** statement or directly in the class and declare the type as follows:

```
Dim Grid As New GridVectorsEnum
```

Using it in the code couldn't be easier:

```
If (ObjectPosition >= Grid.MaxRight) Then
'. . . do something
End If
```

Working with System.Enum

While enumerated types are familiar to many programmers of languages like Delphi and C++, they are much more useful in the .NET Framework. They are typically processed in the stack area, but can also be boxed onto the heap as objects.

Every **Enum** must have an underlying type that represents one of the ordinal built-in types: **Byte**, **Integer**, **Long**, and **Short**. If you do not initialize the enumeration constants with values, they default to **Integer**. The following example specifies constants of the default **Integer** type:

```
Public Enum DaysEnum As Integer
   Sunday
   Monday
   Tuesday
```

```
      Wednesday
      Thursday
      Friday
      Saturday
      Noday
   End Enum
```

When you create and reference enumerated types, they are essentially compiled to constant fields. So the following **Enum** called **EnumDays**,

```
Public Enum DaysEnum
   Sunday = 1
   Monday = 2
   Tuesday = 3
   Wednesday = 4
   Thursday = 5
   Friday = 6
   Saturday = 7
   Noday = -1
End Enum
```

is handled by the compiler as if you had written this:

```
Class MyDays
   Public Const Sunday = 1
   Public Const Monday = 2
   Public Const Tuesday = 3
   Public Const Wednesday = 4
   Public Const Thursday = 5
   Public Const Friday = 6
   Public Const Saturday = 7
   Public Const Noday = -1
End Class
```

The same goes for the **DepreciationPeriodEnum** enumeration we used earlier with **Accounting** structure, as shown here:

```
Public Enum DepreciationPeriodEnum
   FirstYear = 0
   SecondYear = 1
   ThirdYear = 2
```

```
    FourthYear = 3
    FifthYear = 4
    SixthYear = 5
    SeventhYear = 6
    EighthYear = 7
    NinthYear = 8
    TenthYear = 0
End Enum
```

If you look under the covers of these constant fields, you will not find much. However, with **Enum** it's another story. Apart from the inherited members, you also have the marvelous collection of mostly static utility methods, listed in Table 8-1, at your disposal.

Enum Members (abridged list)	Utility
CompareTo (i)	Compares this object to the object passed by value to a single parameter. The function returns an indication of their relative values.
Format	Converts the specified value of an enumerated type to its equivalent **String** representation according to the specified format.
GetName	Returns the name of the constant passed with the specified enumeration.
GetNames	Returns an array of the names in the enumeration passed to the method.
GetTypeCode	Returns the **TypeCode** for the object.
GetUnderlyingType	Returns the underlying type for the enumeration.
GetValues	Returns an array of the values of the enumeration.
IsDefined	Returns a **Boolean** whether a specified constant exists in the enumeration.
Parse	Converts the string representation of the name or value of an enumerated constant to an equivalent enumerated object.

Table 8-1.   *Member of System.Enum*

To return the underlying type of an enumerated type, you can use the **GetUnderlyingType** method as follows:

```
Public Sub EnumUncovered()
  Debug.WriteLine(E.GetUnderlyingType(E.Saturday))
End Sub
```

We can also easily declare the enumerated type in this way:

```
Dim dayoweek As DayEnum.Saturday
Debug.WriteLine(dayoweek.ToString)
```

This will print "Saturday" to the output window. **Enum**'s **ToString** internally calls the **Format** method for various output options, as described in Table 8-1. To return the ordinal value of **DayEnum.Saturday**, you can specify the "D" format argument, which returns a **Decimal** value for Saturday. This is shown here:

```
Debug.WriteLine(dayoweek.ToString("D"))
```

You can also work directly with the **Format** method, which obviates the need to create an instance of the type. Here's an example:

```
Console.WriteLine(DaysEnum.Friday.Format(E, 4, "G")
```

Table 8-2 provides an abridged explanation of the **Format** method's parameter-value options.

Format option	Utility (abridged)
"G" or "g"	If *value,* passed to the second argument, is equal to a named enumerated constant, then the name of that constant is returned; otherwise, the decimal equivalent of *value* is returned. (See also the discussion on flags later in this section.)
"D" or "d"	The value is returned as a decimal value.
"X" or "x"	The value is returned as a hexadecimal, sans the 0x notation.
"F" or "f"	The value is treated as a bit field.

Table 8-2. *Options for the Format Method's Parameter Value*

CLASSES AND OBJECTS

If you need to look at the **Enum**'s collection of constants, you can retrieve an array of values using the **GetValues** method. **GetNames** also returns an array, but instead of values you get the collection of names. This code exemplifies both of the aforementioned methods:

```
Console.WriteLine(DaysEnum.GetNames.Format(GetValues(E)))
```

If you just need to pass a value and recover its name, the **GetName** method will do the trick. Interestingly, Microsoft did not implement an equivalent single value of the **GetValues** method. As you realize, returning an array doesn't help much when you simply need to recover a single value for the symbol passed to the method. An array also consumes more memory than a single value, especially if your type is an enumeration of more than a handful of values.

I thought about implementing a method to capture the single value, but realized I could not derive from **System.Enum**, so there is no way to override one of the above "Get" methods. However, we can make use of the **Parse** method to solve our dilemma.

Parse lets us convert a symbol in an instance of **Enum**. We can then retrieve the value from the process that represents the enumeration. This is shown in the following code:

```
Dim periodVal As Integer
periodVal = [Enum].Parse(GetType(DepreciationPeriodEnum), "FifthYear")
```

and thus **periodVal** is initialized to 4. And in the following code

```
Console.WriteLine([Enum].Parse(GetType(DepreciationPeriodEnum), "7"))
```

the output to the console is **EighthYear**.

> **Note**   *Parse is a very useful method for converting the **String** representation of a numeric type into a numeric type.*

The last method to look at is one you will use frequently—**IsDefined**. As mentioned in Table 8-1, this method verifies that the argument specified as a particular constant actually exists in the enumeration. You get **True** or **False** depending on whether the type is defined or not. Here is an example:

```
Public Sub GetDay(ByVal day As DaysEnum)
  If Not (Enum.IsDefined (Friday)) Then
    Return Enum.NoDay
  End If
End Sub
```

The following code declares an enumeration for warp speeds (so there can be no errors when choosing):

```
Public Enum WarpFactorEnum
   Impulse = 0
   ImpulsePlusOne = 1
   ImpulsePlusTwo = 2
   ImpulsePlusThree = 3
   ImpulsePlusFour = 4
   ImpulsePlusFive = 5
   ImpulsePlusSix = 6
   ImpulsePlusSeven = 7
   ImpulsePlusEight = 8
   ImpulsePlusInfinity = 9
End Enum
```

We can then test if the helmsperson has entered the right values, as shown here, so that we do not rocket away to infinity:

```
If [Enum].IsDefined(GetType(WarpFactorEnum), _
 "ImpulsePlusTen") Then
    Throw New ArgumentOutOfRangeException()
End If
```

Flags

We typically use enumerations for lists of named constants, such as days of the week, spectrum of colors, and stars in a solar system; on the other hand, we generally rely on bit fields to combine qualities or quantities of these constants. Here's an example in code:

```
If (isAccessed AND isArchived)
'. . . do something
End If
```

In Chapter 5 we discussed bit flags and bit maps in the context of operators, and now we'll examine them in the context of enumerations. The framework employs the **Enum** type for various purposes, and one of them is to represent collections of bit flags. You'll see a lot of these in the **System.Forms** namespace, as discussed in Chapter 16.

Using the WinCV tool, you can browse for many enumerations that encapsulate collections of bit states. These include enumerations for visual states, appearances, the state of controls, forms, tables, databases, file attributes, and button shapes. Figure 8-1 illustrates the framework's enumeration for database table columns (they are all in C#).

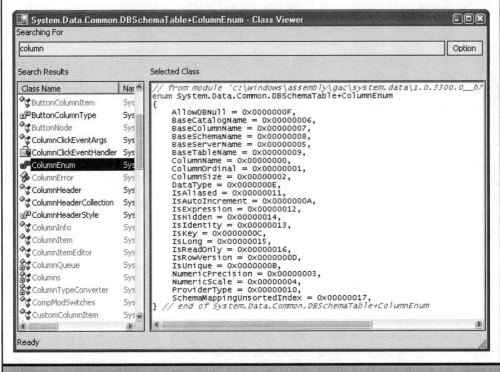

Figure 8-1. *Using WinCV to look at the built-in enumerations*

Using the **Enum** type, we can similarly represent a collection of bit flags for any application. Looking at the enumeration shown in Figure 8-1, one can conclude the following: an expression that checks for **IsUnique** and **IsKey** seems perfectly feasible, as does one that verifies whether a file **IsCompressed | IsEncrypted** or **IsHidden AND IsReadOnly** with the **FileAttributes** enumeration.

We can do the same for the message flag constants demonstrated in the **GetMessages** example listed in Chapter 5. Remember the following collection of flags:

```
Dim messageFlag As Integer = 2
Dim isAccessed As Integer = 4
Dim isArchived As Integer = 8
Dim isDeleted As Integer = 16
Dim newMessage As Integer = 32
```

This collection would be better represented inside an enumeration. We can call the enumeration **MessageFlagEnum**, as depicted in this code:

```
Public Enum MessageFlagEnum
  MessageFlag = 0x0001
  IsAccessed = 0x0002
  IsArchived = 0x0004
  IsDeleted = 0x0008
  NewMessage = 0x0016
End Enum
```

We don't have to initialize the symbols with hex values, although it doesn't hurt, and the symbol values can still be easily stored in the database. We also don't necessarily need to represent the bit flags in any special sequencing—here I have raised each bit flag to the power of two.

However, as you have seen, the **Enum** semantics don't typically lend themselves to bit-flag semantics, in which it's normal to write an expression evaluating the combined state of more than one symbol. So, when you execute the following code,

```
Dim MsgState As MessageFlagEnum.IsAccessed | MessageFlagEnum.IsArchived
Debug.WriteLine(MsgState.ToString())
```

you are going to get the value 0x0006 to the console instead of the combination of the two symbols. Thus, if the intention is to write "**IsAccessed, IsArchived**" to the Debug window, it will not happen. To force the enumeration to return the latter, you can pass the "F" argument listed in Table 8-2 to the **Format** method or to the **ToString** method as shown in the forthcoming code:

```
Dim MsgState As MessageFlagEnum.IsAccessed | MessageFlagEnum.IsArchived
Debug.WriteLine(MsgState.ToString("F"))
```

This is a little cumbersome; however, Microsoft has developed a cleaner approach to making the enumeration think it's a collection of bit flags. We can use the **Flags** attribute to denote bit-field or bit-flag semantics. While the runtime itself does not distinguish between traditional enumerations and bit fields, you can make this distinction in your code via the **Flags** attribute, allowing you to use bitwise operators transparently on all bit fields. At runtime, therefore, you get what you ask for. This amended **Enum** portrays the use of the flags attribute seen here decorating **MessageFlagEnum**:

```
<Flags>
Public Enum MessageFlagEnum
```

```
    MessageFlag = 0x0001
    IsAccessed = 0x0002
    IsArchived = 0x0004
    IsDeleted = 0x0008
    NewMessage = 0x0016
End Enum
```

Final Words on Enums

Here are some final considerations before you implement the **Enum** type in your applications:

- Enumerations can represent any of the ordinal built-in data types (except **Char**). Remember, the "magic words" are "magic numbers," not "magic **Boolean**s" or "magic characters."

- You can assign a value of the underlying type to an enumeration and vice versa (no cast is required by the runtime).

- You can create an instance of an enumeration and call the methods of **System.Enum**, as well as any methods defined on the enumeration's underlying type. However, some languages might not allow you to pass an enumeration as a parameter when an instance of the underlying type is required (or vice versa).

- **Enum**s cannot define their own methods.

- **Enum**s cannot implement interfaces.

- **Enum**s cannot define properties and events.

- Reduce operations with **Enum**s that create a lot of boxing/unboxing code as demonstrated earlier in this chapter. Since some of the methods entail casting symbol values to objects, moving values to the heap may detract from performance requirements. Try re-writing your code to use minimal boxing overhead.

- Finally, if only one class or object is using the **Enum**, don't nest or encapsulate it in the class. It won't be long before other classes in the application will need the **Enum**, and you'll be forced to define it at the level of those classes as well. This may not seem problematic for a small **Enum**, but imagine the difficulties if dozens of methods were depending on that **Enum**. Nesting also detracts from the elegant **Enum** semantics you have at your disposal, because **Friend** classes still have to access the encapsulating object's interface before they can reference the **Enum**. As you have seen, all **Enum**s defined for the framework are identified at the same level as all standard classes.

Other than noting the few items in the above list, the enumeration is an especially powerful and fun construct to work with.

Note   *The code for the above enumerations is the Enumerations project in the Vb7cr solution.*

The Object-Reference Model

It is important that you obtain an unshakable understanding of the object-reference model and how it differs from the value-type reference model before you progress to programming with classes and objects in the chapters to follow.

The *object-reference model* specifically ensures that objects are accessed only via a reference variable that points to a location in memory where the object is stored. To best illustrate how this model works, let's evaluate an example that shows various ways of accessing and working with objects.

Imagine that we are asked to design an object representing the fuel injector of a space ship. The injector's main purpose is to increase the sub-warp (significant percentage of light speed) velocity of the space ship. We can design a class to represent an **Injector** object containing a number of methods that manipulate the injector and interact with the many other space ship components and services. Assume we already have this class—its methods control the velocity of a space ship—since designing and implementing it is not the subject of this section.

The **Injector** class we are discussing follows a pattern written expressly for your creating multiple instances of **Injector** objects that are completely reentrant. This means you can use them in your application and be sure that the data fields in each object remain completely isolated and protected from any calls to methods in other **Injector** objects. The data in each **Injector** object is also completely isolated from the data in other objects that have been created in the same application space.

Once you create an **Injector** object, you access it by referencing its name, as we see in this code:

```
Dim Sim1 As New Injector
Sim1.StartInjector()
```

The first part of the expression, **Dim Sim1**, declares a new variable called **Sim1**. The second part, **New Injector**, creates a new **Injector** object by calling the type's instance constructor—the **New** method. We create the new **Injector** object and initialize **Sim1** to reference it on the heap. **Sim1** is thus a variable reference *and* a reference variable to an instance of the **Injector** class.

CLASSES AND OBJECTS

In the early days of OO software development, the object-reference variable and the object were one and the same, like value types; the reference did not function as a "pointer" to the object's data in memory. When you declare the reference variable, you do not necessarily have to create the object and connect the dots. The following code is an example of late binding (see the illustration):

```
Dim Sim1
```

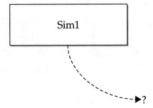

 Note *Switching **Option Strict** to **On** forces you to declare the variable with the As clause and to thus assign a type at the same time. See Chapter 4, which explains the Option directives, and Chapters 7 and 9, which talk about late binding.*

To create the reference variable and associate it with just the root object, you can use the following code:

```
Dim Sim1 As New Object
```

Here we are referring to nothing more than an instance of **Object**, which for this purpose is inconsequential. Nevertheless, we have created an object with the specific use of the **As** keyword and **New** (albeit **New** is what breaths life into the object *As* a **Type**). The reference variable is tied to the object and can perform certain actions on it. For example, we can create an instance of the **Injector** class with the following code:

```
Dim Sim1 As New Injector()
```

Now you have an **Injector** object loaded in memory and you can access it through the name **Sim1** as illustrated here.

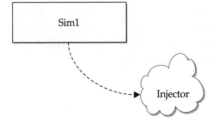

The **Injector** object is loaded in memory and you can access it through **Sim1** using this procedure:

1. Start with **Sim1**, which is the reference used to manipulate and access data in the object. The reference is then followed by a period thus:

```
Sim1.
```

2. Visual Studio now automatically gives you a drop-down list of the public members that are available to you. Choose a method you want to call, such as the accessor method or property **IsWarpdriveOn**, which is shown here:

```
Dim checkIsOn As Boolean
checkIsOn = Sim1.IsWarpdriveOn()
```

3. If the method call requires you to supply arguments, they will go between the braces and each will be separated by commas. This corresponds to the method's parameter list, as you saw in Chapter 7. In the above case, we are calling a method that will return a **Boolean** value, telling us if the warp drive is on or off. If the return value is **True**, the drive is on; if it's **False** . . . . We can also use the method call as follows:

```
If Not Sim1.IsWarpdriveOn() Then
'. . .
End If
```

The above code takes the flow-of-execution into the **If. . . Then** structure and processes the code inside. The call to **IsWarpDriveOn** returned **False** (the default at start up), so you first need to turn the drive on. This is achieved with the following modification method call:

```
Sim1.StartInjector()
```

The method **StartInjector** is a **Sub** procedure and does not return a value. Also it does not need an argument, because you would want to start warp engines and remain at warp 0. Nevertheless, the call modifies the object because the method changes the data and the state of the object.

The next step would be to set the warp speed for the simulation. The method call to do that is **Sim1.SetWarpSpeed**. This requires an argument—the constant for the **newWarpSpeed** parameter, from the **WarpSpeedEnum**. The method takes an **Integer** and can be written as follows:

```
Sim1.SetWarpSpeed(WarpFactorEnum.Impulse)
```

The above call passes the enumeration symbol to the parameter, which sets the warp speed to **WarpFactorEnum.Impulse**. But this example is "hard-coded." The following example lets you enter the value at the command line. Using the console class' method to read input from the command line, you can send various arguments for warp speed to the **Injector** object as follows:

```
Sim1.SetWarpSpeed(CInt(Console.ReadLine()))
```

To get feedback from the object, you can access the **warpSpeed** field (remember this is one of the instance variables that gets initialized in the instance constructor). But these variables are privately encapsulated in the class and are thus off limits to the consumer. So when you type **Sim1** in the IDE, **warpSpeed** will not be among the publicly accessible members. To access the warp, use the accessor method **GetWarpSpeed** as shown here:

```
Sim1.GetWarpSpeed()
```

The final example of calling the custom methods in **Injector** is the call to the accessor method **GetMPS**. This method multiplies the warp factor passed to the parameter by the speed of light in miles-per-second (MPS) and then returns the value to you. Write it as follows:

```
Sim1.GetMPS(WarpFactorEnum.Impulse)
```

You do not want to hard code the parameter, so pass the return value of the method call to **Sim1.GetWarpSpeed** as follows:

```
Sim1.GetMPS(Sim1.GetWarpSpeed())
```

You can then write the return value to the console using the console object's **WriteLine** method as shown:

```
Console.WriteLine("Light speed is  " _
+ CStr(Sim1.GetMPS(sim1.GetWarpSpeed())) & " miles-per-second.")
```

What happens if you specify a parameter for warp that is greater than **WarpFactorEnum.ImpulsePlusSeven**? The class' method **SetWarpSpeed** evaluates the value as it passes into the method with an **If . . . Then** statement as follows:

```
If WarpSpeed > WarpFactorEnum.Infinity Then
  Throw IllegalWarpParamException
End If
```

The exception handler "throws" the execution flow into the catch section of the **Try ... Catch** structure, which turns off the injector as seen here:

```
warpDrive = False
```

This works because the variable or field named **warpDrive** is visible to the members of the class. With **warpDrive** set to **False**, your code can take the natural course of action to immediately stop the injector.

The entire implementation of the console-based simulation is presented in this module:

```
Module WarpSim
  Sub Main()
    Dim Sim1 As New Injector()
    Console.WriteLine("Testing injector simulation...")
    Try
      If Not Sim1.IsWarpdriveOn() Then
        Console.WriteLine("The injector is off. _
        Enter to start or any key plus enter to abort test.")
        If Console.ReadLine() = "" Then
          Try
            Console.WriteLine("Starting injector...")
            Sim1.StartInjector()
            Console.WriteLine("The injector is on... _
            ready to engage warp drive....")
            While Sim1.IsWarpdriveOn
              Console.WriteLine("Enter warp speed....")
              Sim1.SetWarpSpeed(CInt(Console.ReadLine()))
              Console.WriteLine("Warp speed is set to: " & _
              CStr(Sim1.GetWarpSpeed()))
              Console.WriteLine("Light speed is " & _
              CStr(Sim1.GetMPS(Sim1.GetWarpSpeed())) & _
              " miles-per-second.")
              If Sim1.GetWarpSpeed() = 0 Then
                Sim1.StopInjector()
```

```
            End If
          End While
        Catch
          Console.WriteLine(oState.ToString)
        End Try
      End If
    End If
  Catch
    Console.WriteLine(oState.ToString)
  End Try
 End Sub
End Module
```

As you can see, the object's reference variable is a versatile feature. In the unmanaged world, we would also have used it to destroy the object or remove it from the memory it occupies on the heap (such as **Sim1.Free** or **Sim1.Destroy**). But in the managed world of .NET, the garbage collector takes care of that (see Chapter 2 for an introduction to the garbage collector).

When we are finished with an object, we can cut the connection between it and the reference variable—like cutting a lifeline between a soul and its body. This prompts the garbage collector to clean up.

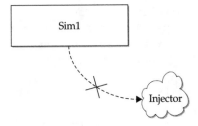

You are essentially placing the object out of scope, which can be noted thus:

```
Sim1 = Nothing
```

Another means of cutting the "lifeline" is to assign the variable reference to another object. You'll need to create this object if you don't have it. Look at how we achieve this:

```
Dim Sim1 As New Injector
Dim Sim2 As Object
```

We now have two object variables called **Sim1** and **Sim2**; they refer to different objects. **Sim2** refers to **Object**, which will do nothing for it, while **Sim1** refers to an instance of **Injector**. The objects and their reference variables are demonstrated here.

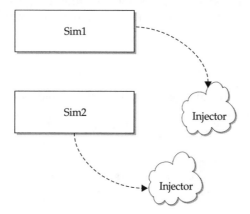

To render **Sim2** more useful, we can make it refer to the same object as **Sim1** as demonstrated:

```
Sim2 = Sim1
```

In the illustration, Sim1 and Sim2 now refer to the same Injector object, at the same location in memory.

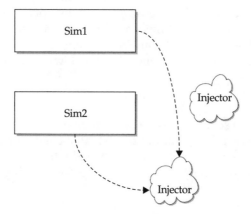

Declaring and using more than one object of the same type is not uncommon. If the class allows this, you can add as many **Injector** objects as you need to the application. You will often be working with patterns that require you to create more than one instance of the same object.

You can program a class to allow only one instance of itself to be created. This is called a singleton class; its pattern is demonstrated in Chapter 13.

Creating more than one object of the same type requires only another call to the **Injector** class' constructor. All you need is a new name, as shown here:

```
Dim Sim1 As New Injector()
Dim Sim2 As New Injector()
```

You can now reference each object through the variables **Sim1** and **Sim2** independently, as illustrated.

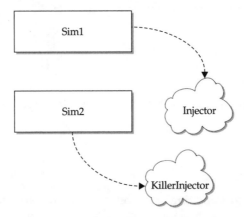

The data in each object is encapsulated in its own field, so modifying data through **Sim1.SetWarpSpeed** does not affect the **warpSpeed** field of **Sim2**. Remember, you have created two distinct variables: **Sim1** and **Sim2**. But you have also explicitly created two **Injector** objects, and each variable references its own object.

For **Sim1** and **Sim2** to refer to the same object, you will need the following code:

```
Sim1 = Sim2
```

In other words, if you set the warp speed by calling **Sim1.SetWarpSpeed(WarpFactorEnum.ImpulsePlusSeven)** and then call **Sim2.GetWarpSpeed**, the return value will be **WarpFactorEnum.ImpulsePlusSeven** because **Sim1** and **Sim2** now refer to the same object (see the discussion on enumerated types). As a further example:

```
Sim1.GetMPS(Sim2.GetWarpSpeed())
```

This call returns the value for MPS even though you never explicitly made the call to **Sim2.StartInjector()**. The difference between standard types and reference types should now be crystallizing (isn't OO wonderful?).

Null Reference

We can explicitly cut the reference variable's lifeline to an object by telling it to reference "nada." Using the so-called **Null** reference (represented by the keyword **Nothing** in Visual Basic) makes the variable assign to nothing, as show here:

```
Sim2 = Nothing
```

This does not necessarily hasten the work of the garbage collector; nonetheless, it is a good idea to set the reference to **Nothing** when the object becomes orphaned.

Does this mean you can still use the reference variable **Sim2**? Yes it does. It was declared, so re-setting **Sim2 = Sim1** is valid because all you are doing is telling **Sim2** to get a life, like **Sim1**. But setting **Sim1 = Sim2** will cause catastrophic failure. Why? **Sim1** cannot refer to the **Null** reference, and the code will throw off the **NullReferenceException**. Make a note somewhere about this **Null** reference error, because it is easy to cause this bug in your code (see Chapter 11, which covers exception handling).

Also, make a note that setting a reference variable to **Null** does not nullify the actual object, only the reference to it. If there is only one reference to the object, it is orphaned and earmarked for collection. But if more than one variable references the object and just one variable is set to **Null**, then only that reference is unaffected.

Note *See Finalization in Chapter 9 and Chapter 17.*

What the Reference Refers To

Experts as well as programmers new to Object-Oriented software development often refer to the reference variable—such as **Sim1**—as the actual object. This is incorrect. **Sim1** and **Sim2** are not themselves the objects of class **Injector**; they are just the reference variables. Thus, it is fallacious to say "the injector **Sim1** has been set to… " It is accurate to say "the injector that **Sim1** refers to has been set to. . .".

Naturally when you are sitting around a table talking code with one of your buddies, it's fine to say things like "**Sim1** just blew up the space ship; it must be the code in your class." But when you need to prepare formal documentation, use the longer expression. It will help keep your documentation clear and easier to understand.

The Object-Reference Model and Equality, Comparison, and Assignment

You may also encounter confusion when you test equality and make assignments or comparisons between and among objects. Are you performing these functions with regard to the references or their objects? Actually, you can do both. The **Equals** method compares objects for assignment or reference data. **Equals** is inherited from **System.Object**.

To test if one reference compares to another you can use the **Is** operator. The **Is** operator is not the same thing as the = operator (see Chapter 5, "Visual Basic .NET Operators" and Chapter 9, "Classes"). This code tests whether **Sim1** equals **Sim2**:

```
If (Sim1 Is Sim2) Then
  . . .
End If
```

If **Sim1** and **Sim2** reference the same object, then the **Is** comparison returns **True** . . . and **False** if they do not. For example:

```
Dim Sim1 As New Injector()
Dim Sim2 As New Injector()
Sim1 = Sim2
If (Sim1 Is Sim2) Then
   Debug.WriteLine("Sim1 is Sim2")
End If
```

This might be more easily understood through an illustration. The illustration shows **Sim1** and **Sim2** referencing the same object; therefore, **Is** returns **True**.

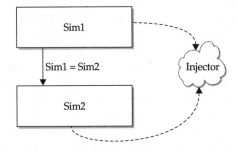

Let's see what happens when we introduce a third **Injector**:

```
...
Dim Sim3 As New Injector()
```

```
Sim2 = Sim3
If (Sim1 Is Sim2) Then
   Debug.WriteLine("Sim1 is Sim2")
End If
```

Is does not return **True** anymore, because **Sim1** and **Sim2** no longer reference the same object. However, **Sim2 Is Sim3** returns **True**. There is a quirk: as long as two or more variable references refer to the same object, they are considered equal. Also, **Null** references (**Sim1 = Nothing**) also return **True** when compared with the **Is** operator.

To compare the objects, you should implement the **CompareTo** method defined by the **IComparable** interface or bridge to a *comparator* (see Chapter 12). You will be able to write code here that compares the bits of objects rather than the reference variables. Chapter 10 provides an in-depth discussion of this subject.

What *Me* Refers To

When you have a class that can be instantiated multiple times, you'll find that the **Me** keyword—an internal reference variable—conveniently references the object from within its own instance space. From this viewpoint, everything is visible, yet still protected from the outside world. Here we model the **Injector** object calling its own **GetType** method:

```
Public Function WhatAmI() As String
   Return Me.GetType().ToString
End Function
```

| Note | *Me is the same as the keyword **This** in C#. It is also not legal to use it in a class module.* |

As you will learn in the next chapter, there are limits to using **Me**. For instance, it is not valid in shared classes that cannot be instantiated.

Observations

Microsoft is not alone in implementing primitives as first-class lightweight objects—several other languages have taken the same approach, including ADA and Smalltalk.

I scrutinized Java's primitives earlier in this chapter and concluded that they are primitive, or native, types and not first-class objects like .NET's value types. You can place Java primitives on the heap using wrapper classes that ship with the Java SDK. In this process, manual boxing/unboxing, you have to couch your primitives in object semantics, adapt them. So in these respects the type models are very similar. In one case the boxing is manual (Java) and in the other case it is done automatically (.NET).

CLASSES AND OBJECTS

I am not privy to enough information to criticize the makers of Java—nor do I want to detract from the subject of .NET Value Types—for adopting an approach that makes Java not really as pure an object-oriented language as is believed. They have claimed a number of acceptable reasons. Yet, others have criticized Sun for this. Their detractors include both object-oriented technology purists and a small percentage of engineers with highly sophisticated programming needs.

Some of you may say, "who cares, this is not a book about Java." But I think it is worth your while to fully grasp how the automatic boxing process in .NET affects your code's performance. You'll also develop better code by knowing what Microsoft is doing under the covers. This knowledge will endow you with critical mastery of the workings of NET types.

There is talk at Microsoft about possibly including generic types in the next major release of the .NET Framework. Whether they make it into the CLS, or are just made available to C# and not to Visual Basic .NET and other languages remains to be seen.

Chapter 9

Classes

I firmly believe that you cannot be a good .NET programmer without continuously *thinking* about your applications in terms of classes and objects. Thinking in terms of classes and objects (in other words, thinking in terms of object-oriented programming) means thinking about the bigger picture and not only about code. This is not an easy thing to do and takes many years of experience. It means thinking about how you *can* organize your objects as a cohesive system—in much the same way as your body is organized as a cohesive system.

Thinking in terms of OOP need not detract from cohesion at the method level, nor how brilliant you might be at writing method code. Being able to design and implement good OO design and still write tight methods is what makes a brilliant programmer. In fact, I have an obsession with objects, and yet that does not stop me from doing my best to optimize methods to as few lines of code as possible. After more than a decade in this business, I still struggle to come up with clean, stable OO design. You'll find that as you master smaller systems, the bigger ones take you back to square one.

Why do I feel so strongly about this? Why the detail presented in this chapter, in a book that is clearly a reference to core Visual Basic .NET, and not one about OOP? The main reason is that Visual Basic is a pure object-oriented language. It's not a hybrid per se language in the sense that it has to be absolutely backward-compatible with VB 6 and earlier code. From start to finish, Visual Basic .NET is about designing and implementing classes and objects.

> **Note**   *When Microsoft embarked on the making of Visual Basic .NET, it decided that the only way forward was to provide a pure object-oriented language and forgo backward compatibility with classic VB code. While you can migrate some VB 6 code to "VB 7," it is not the same migration level you had moving VB 5 code to VB 6.*

If you don't have an unshakable understanding of object-oriented programming (OOP), you will never be an effective or efficient .NET programmer. Everything you do in .NET is OOP, no matter the language—and requires an understanding of the workings of classes, class relationships, objects and their roles, polymorphism, encapsulation, abstraction, delegation, interfaces and so on, the subject of the next couple of chapters. Sure, there are a lot of buzzwords, but it eventually all "clicks" into place.

I would go as far as to say that unless your understanding of OO development is as solid as concrete, your abilities will be severely limited. If you have already experimented with Visual Studio .NET and created a form, then you will soon discover that what you have done is *inherited* a new **Form** class from one of the framework's base classes. Thinking in terms of objects also liberates your creativity and widens the field of opportunity for your code because objects have "legs" and can travel, beyond proprietary platforms and technologies. By writing Common Language Specification (CLS)-compliant classes, other programmers will be able to use your classes with any other CLS-compliant language. That's how Java has become as successful as it has. It caters to the consumer "plug-in" paradigm perfectly. Java programmers all around the world share classes. Some classes are freely contributed, for the greater good of the language; others can be purchased from programmers who make a living selling their code. Such opportunities have not been readily available to VB 6 programmers. After this chapter and the others to follow there will be an added bonus to being good at OO; besides Visual Basic you'll also be able to easily tackle any design—for any language including J#, C#, Java, or otherwise.

> **Note** *If you are an experienced OO programmer, you can skim over this chapter, focusing just on the stuff you need to understand .NET classes, the Visual Basic .NET idioms, and how Visual Basic .NET differs from what you might know using classic Visual Basic, Java, Delphi, or whatever. But don't skim too lightly, because this chapter covers important concepts, and aspects of .NET class construction, not covered elsewhere in this book. Also, if you are new to object-oriented technology and have no idea what a class is, I recommend reading one of the best books on the market, Grady Booch's* Object-Oriented Design with Applications *(The Benjamin/Cummings Publishing Company, Inc., 1991).*

Forms-oriented programming has been around for more than a decade. The forms-based model of programming is what made Visual Basic the most popular language in the world, because Visual Basic got so much of the world's so-called "old economy" applications done far quicker than anything else did. But now, especially with highly distributed, concurrent, asynchronous applications, you need to kick the habit, thinking primarily about "forms" when you think about writing applications and think classes and "objects" instead.

It also seems tough to ask many Visual Basic programmers to think in terms of programming classes and objects rather than programming forms, and that is one of the challenges of this book. A key objective of this chapter is to understand that the bases for forms are also classes. But so much programming today is distributed, which is important. Invoking methods on remote servers, for example, has nothing to do with forms.

This chapter thus begins a mammoth expedition into the world of classes and objects, object-based programming, and object-oriented software development using Visual Basic .NET. If by the end of Part III you have started to think in terms of objects, then I will have succeeded in my objective.

Getting the Semantics Correct

Before we get cracking, you should be clear on the difference between *classes* and *objects* and *types*, because we all have the habit of using the terms loosely to mean the same thing. Both classes and objects may be thought of as types, which is correct; however, classes and objects have very different roles in your application design and construction. We touched a little on this in the last chapter.

A class is a blueprint, a template, a specification, a pattern, or any other founding definition of an object. Objects absolutely depend on classes; without classes, you don't have objects. This should be clear from Figure 9-1, which shows that a class must exist before you have an object, just as the egg must come before you can have a chicken.

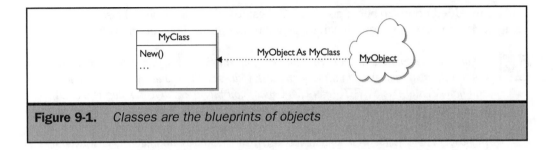

Figure 9-1.   *Classes are the blueprints of objects*

In this regard, most of this chapter is about classes rather than objects. Later in the chapter, however, we'll investigate what it takes to "lay" an object. Classes are almost always a design-time construct, whereas objects can only exist at run time. A process called *instantiation,* as indicated in Figure 9-1, manifests objects. In other words, when you need an object during the course of a running application, you must create an *instance* of the class, which is an object.

You can typically create many instances of a class, but you can also program a class in such a way that only one instance of it can be created. This class is called a *singleton.* The singleton class is discussed in more depth in Chapter 13.

Calling class constructors creates objects. The ultimate constructor of a class is the **New** method, as you will discover later when constructors are discussed in some depth in the pages to follow.

While objects are a run-time phenomenon, you can also design and implement classes that can be accessed for functionality only at run time. Just like calling a function in a typical function library in a procedure-oriented language like C, these classes never need to be instantiated. They are not given constructors because you do not need to instantiate them. The members of these classes are shared and we typically refer to them as operations classes. The **File** class is one good example of an operations class. When you need file system objects you can instantiate **FileInfo**, which provides identical instance methods to **File.**

Of Classes and Types

Type and *class* mean the same thing to many people, and in many respects, I use these terms interchangeably in this book—not a problem. However, if you really want to excel at this, it will pay dividends to realize the subtle difference between the word "class" and the word "type."

I am always on the lookout for a good explanation of the difference. Perhaps the best one can be found in the following quote from Grady Booch's book *Object Oriented Design with Applications*: "Typing is the enforcement of the class of an object, such that the objects of different types may not be interchanged, or at the most, they may be interchanged only in very restricted ways."

Most modern languages in use today are strongly typed. This means that there are specific rules and safeguards that protect against unfettered type conversion and casting. Visual Basic and all the .NET languages have specific rules that govern how types are converted from one type to another. This was discussed at length in Chapter 4, which demonstrated how Visual Studio is configured to enforce strongly typed semantics.

Semantics and Notation

Before we can design classes (or types), it is vital that we all talk the same language. Trying to describe classes and objects in code is not impossible but it is as cumbersome as taking a dip in a tide pool with a windbreaker and gumboots.

Many modeling languages and notations have thus been introduced down the ages of OO engineering. The most popular ones are Booch notation, Object Model Technique (OMT), and Unified Modeling Language (UML).

UML has emerged as the principal class design and object modeling language in use today; much of its constructs and elements really derive from several earlier modeling languages and notation that have survived the past few decades.

You don't need to be fluent in UML, but you do need to know UML notation to define and model classes and applications. This is what we are going to tackle in the next section. A full-blown discussion of UML and, for that matter, object-oriented analysis and design using UML is beyond the scope of this "little" book.

Modeling

What is a model? This may seem like a dumb question in the middle of a book, but millions of developers have absolutely no clue how to answer it. A model is essentially a representation or an abstraction of some "thing" before it is actually built—no more, and no less.

Step outside of our profession for a few minutes. Architects build models, in the form of miniature constructions of the actual buildings, houses, or complexes they are going to construct. Landscapers build models, in the form of miniature gardens that represent, almost identically, the land they intend to sculpt. Boat builders build miniature boats, complete with engines, tiny plastic crew members, bunk beds, and so on.

A model can be an almost identical representation of the actual thing to be built. A model omits all the nonessential details, although some model builders can get carried away. Some architects will build models of shopping centers and malls, and add real miniature lakes and waterfalls.

It is a natural human behavior to model. Modeling permits us to deal with complexity. It permits us to test and evaluate before building something. Mankind has been modeling for thousands of years, not long after Adam started wearing a fig leaf. One of the world's most famous model builders was Leonardo da Vinci. His pencil sketches of aircraft and other mechanical contraptions far exceeded what was possible for him to actually build. He built models of contraptions that were hundreds of years ahead of their time.

Modeling is a fundamental requirement for any hardware and software system. Before building a complex application, the software engineer must model the system—abstract different views of the system. If you don't model, the odds are very much in favor of disaster—only the smallest systems can escape the modeling stage. However, once a system begins to grow, the risk of leaving out or wrongly implementing key components is very great. You don't hear of architects leaving out the parking garages, or the lobby, or elevators, or the sprinkler systems of their office buildings.

A software engineer should use precise notation and the appropriate illustration to confirm that the software satisfies the requirements of the system. After the modeling is complete and indeed does satisfy the proposed uses or requirements, the engineer can begin to transform the model into actual code and, finally, implementation.

Software Modeling

There are several good reasons to model software applications (and no excuse not to). Consider the following benefits of a model.

Testing

No engineer worth his or her pizza and can of Jolt cola would consider building something in its entirety before testing it. Engineers place models of airplanes and cars in wind tunnels to test their aerodynamics. Bridge builders build miniature bridges to test the arches and to confirm stability.

Computer simulations allow us to test almost any software-rendered model. You just input the data variables and constants into the systems, and the software will calculate the precise dynamics and the result expected in the real world.

In the movie "Hollow Man," there is an excellent example of genetic modeling being performed by scientists, simulating how gene manipulation might make someone become invisible and then visible again. All cartoons start as storyboards, and their characters start life as sketches, or computer-rendered wire-frame drawings.

Visualization and Communication

A model allows you to visualize the end result. With a model, you can envisage how your ideas will look after they are built, and how they flow and interoperate. A software model lets you demonstrate the critical components of a system, to communicate what it will be to developers, project managers, and ultimately users and customers.

Reduction of Complexity

Reduction of complexity is probably the most important benefit of modeling. Software engineering is an extremely complex science. It is also an art form at the same time. All systems are far too complex to understand directly. No matter how well you can read code, the human brain is not advanced enough to "see" what is being envisaged or achieved as quickly as possible. An application of even 10,000 lines of code may take several days to understand, possibly longer if no documentation exists.

Even the smallest applications, if not properly modeled, can explode beyond the original specifications and become completely unmanageable. Software models allow you to divide and then conquer the software development process. Software development is far less complex and risky if you take the time to model your application.

The software modeling process begins at a very high level of abstraction above your code. I call this the "mile-high" view of your application. The mile-high view allows you to suppress the aspects of the software that are unimportant during the design phase, so that you can easily isolate your design and functional and developmental requirements.

Viewpoints

A good model is one that captures the critical aspects of the application—the essential elements that identify the goals and objectives of the application. Even the seemingly simple Web site or e-commerce application needs to be properly modeled. But how do you model? And exactly how "high" is your mile-high view of your application. We will answer the "how to model" issues in a bit. First, let's investigate the viewpoints of a software model.

To capture all the important requirements and functional aspects of an object-oriented system, you can work within the bounds of three fundamental and distinct models of the software that represent the viewpoints of the model. These viewpoints are really your means of looking into the future to see something as close to the final product as possible. The three models are defined in the Object Modeling Technique (OMT) as follows:

- The object model
- The dynamic model
- The functional model

These three core models, illustrated here, are not mutually exclusive and, in fact, are interdependent upon each other to provide a complete model of a system.

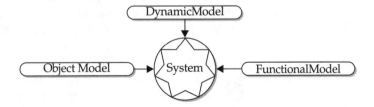

However, each model can be separated from the trio and examined exclusively. The best model builders create interconnections between the three models but avoid designing them in such a way that they become inseparable to the extent that the objectives of the models in the first instance are lost. A good model is one that incorporates the three views into the system yet still isolates the different aspects of the system while limiting the associations between them.

Before embarking on the modeling process, it is important to accept that the three models will evolve during the development cycle. The modeling process should not be one that limits or prevents flexibility in the design of a system. Actually, the fundamental reason to model is to allow the software development process to provide input to the models during the development of the system, to provide the necessary assurances for all parties that have high expectations.We should also enforce the idea that the three stages of software construction—analysis, design, and implementation—respectively sit adjacent to the three models (object, dynamic, and functional). The three stages and their collaboration with the models makes up the software development life-cycle.

The Object Model

The *object model* is the most abstract of the models because it describes the structure of the objects in your software. An object model (and you could call the entire .NET Framework one huge object model) identifies the objects and the relationships between them. It also defines their attributes and what they do. The object model is very much the focus of this chapter. Even though we will be talking about classes, the net result is a system of objects.

When we talk about an object model framework, we mean the framework into which both the dynamic and functional models can be placed. Life can be considered one huge object model. As discussed earlier in this chapter, the natural object models in nature, in us, comprise the cohesive objects that make up our existence—from the highest level going all the way down to the molecules and subatomic matter.

Object models are the most abstract of the three models. Object models provide that so-called mile-high view of the system. No matter the problems we are trying to solve or the applications we are trying to build, the object model should be easy to understand and its concepts should be easy to grasp. If you are modeling a business problem, your models should reflect concepts that business people can understand. The terms and visuals of the business-problem model should be familiar to business people. The same strategy applies to engineering problems, scientific problems, and so on.

Object models for software systems are built using graphical notation languages that render object diagrams that will ultimately represent class libraries and their elements. Later in this chapter, we will explore class and object diagrams in more depth.

The Dynamic Model

The *dynamic model* represents the aspects of a software system that represent time, sequencing, and changes in state. A dynamic model will also represent control. It will not necessarily describe actual operations, but rather the operations that take place in the system, what they operate on, and how they are implemented.

A dynamic model is represented with state and sequence diagrams. It shows the state and event sequences that are permitted in the system for a particular class of objects. Another way to look at the dynamic model with its sequence diagrams is that the state diagrams represent or correspond to functions in the function model (to be discussed next) and also represent operations on objects in the object model.

The Functional Model

The *functional model* captures what a system does, not necessarily how it does it, when it does it, or with what it does it. Another way to understand the functional model is that it represents the aspects of a software system's control over the transformation of values.

Functional models are represented with data-flow diagrams that show the dependencies between values that are computed, as output values, from input values. A functional model does not necessarily represent how the values are computed. It is not concerned with the inner workings of classes and methods or how the methods are executed.

Model Relationships

While each model alone describes various aspects of a software system, the combination of all of them, with references to each other, fully describe the software system. For example, the operations in the object model relate to events in the dynamic model and the functionality in the functional model. The dynamic model, on the other hand, describes the control structures of the objects in the object model. And the functional model represents the functionality that is achieved by the operations in the object model and the actions in the dynamic model.

It is important to understand that the models you create can never be exact representations of the actual software system. There is an accepted deficiency level because no model or abstraction can capture everything about the actual system or thing being modeled. Remember that the goal is to simplify the construction process and not burden it with overly detailed models.

Unified Modeling Language

Strange as it may seem, if you stop John or Jane developer in the lunchroom and ask him or her what modeling language they use, chances are they will think you are nuts, because modeling is still not something a programmer considers important. This is especially the case with Visual Basic programmers, because classic Visual Basic as a language has never really lent itself to requiring such discipline in engineering. This is beginning to change in a hurry, because Visual Basic programmers now have full membership to the object-oriented club and are expected to have the correct disciplines. This is one of the reasons I decided to introduce this chapter with a backgrounder on modeling and modeling languages.

The visual modeling techniques we just covered are supported by an underlying modeling language—supported by standards—that a number of modeling tools support. When modeling software systems, if you cannot convey the model to interested parties the model will not mean much or be very useful. A visual model of a software project is not like a wooden model of a boat that is easily interpreted by physical look and feel.

So, the software-engineering world came up with several notations over the past few decades, the most popular being the Unified Modeling Language (UML).

Visual modeling tools like Visio and Rational Rose support the three aforementioned notational or modeling languages. UML, however, is now by far the standard that has become the most popular. It is supported by austere governing boards such as ANSI and by the Object Management Group (OMG).

Over the years, object-oriented analysis, design, and modeling have relied on the collaborative efforts of a gang of wizards from several technology havens, especially Rational Software Corporation. The wizards include Grady Booch (Chief Scientist at Rational), Dr. James Rumbaugh, Ivar Jacobson, Rebecca Wirfs-Brock, Peter Yourdon, and several others. In particular, Booch, Rumbaugh, and Jacobson, the so-called "three amigos" that work at Rational, can be considered the caretakers of UML, and continue to work on the refinement of the language.

UML comprises a system of symbols that you use to build your software models. The symbols are similar to the Booch and OMT notations. UML has borrowed the notation elements from other notation languages, as well.

UML has thus been in the works for more than a decade; however, it officially became known as UML in 1996. The first version, UML 1.0, was handed over to the Object Technology Group in 1997. On November 14, 1997, OMG released UML 1.1 as the official industry-standard release.

Many software companies now adopt UML, including Microsoft. In fact, Microsoft has more than standardized its technology on UML; it has fully implemented it. The Enterprise Architect's edition of Visual Studio .NET is tightly connected with Visio for Enterprise Architects. It allows models to export Visual Basic or C# source code, and you can use Visual Studio to reverse-engineer IL code or source code to UML models. Rational Software Corporation's Rational Rose—the premier modeling suite to support UML—is also now tightly coupled to the .NET Framework. UML modeling is also taught in the Microsoft certified Solutions Developer courses.

UML allows you to develop a number of different diagrams. These diagrams are combined to represent the object, dynamic, and functional aspects and requirements of your system as originally specified by the Object Modeling Technique (the object, dynamic, and functional models discussed earlier).

The visual elements of the UML models enable you to encapsulate relationships between entities, and concepts such as inheritance, aggregation, association, and so on. So powerful is UML that many technology companies now require all engineers to be fully disciplined in the use of UML tools. It has become a prerequisite for many new hires.

UML Diagrams

UML defines a host of diagram types that can represent the object model, the functional model, the dynamic model, and so forth, of your application. When designing a Visual Basic .NET application, or an application in any language for that matter, it behooves you to properly design your applications using model diagrams like the ones offered in UML.

UML lets you design with various graphical elements to represent real-world scenarios interacting and interfacing with your software. UML enables you to design with several different types of visual diagrams that represent the various views of a software application or system. A Web application, for example, allows you to design the baseline requirements of a system and represent it with several types of diagrams that you can create in UML. These include process diagrams, use-case diagrams, and sequence diagrams.

Process diagrams are developed to identify high-level system functionality within the application owner's business domain. The use-case diagrams are developed to describe each process within the process diagrams, in terms of detailed functional steps required to accomplish the high-level system functionality desired by the business owners. The domain model is developed to illustrate the functionality described in the use-case diagrams in terms of business entities specific to the business domain.

Most UML tools support the development of these models using the following notations and diagrams:

- Use-case diagrams
- Sequence diagrams
- State charts
- Collaboration diagrams
- Class diagrams
- State-transition diagrams
- Component diagrams
- Deployment diagrams

The diagrams you will become familiar with in this book mainly include class diagrams.

 While the class diagrams show you the interactions between classes in a system, to fully benefit from the modeling objects, take the time to become conversant with UML. There are many books available that specialize in the subject, and you should invest in a good tool like Visio or Rational Rose.

UML Notation for Class Diagrams

A class diagram is a diagram that comprises classes, class interfaces, and the relationships between the classes. The classes themselves are quadrangles that you divide into several compartments. A typical class component in UML contains three specific compartments, as illustrated in Figure 9-2.

CLASSES AND OBJECTS

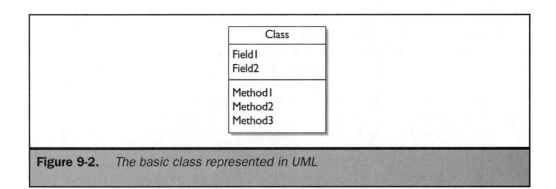

Figure 9-2. *The basic class represented in UML*

The top compartment represents the class name. The middle compartment represents the class attributes or variables—the data of the class. The bottom compartment represents the class methods. Figure 9-3 illustrates a simple class that will shut down the application.

Notice that you can assign an initial value to your variables. In the preceding example, we have provided a **Boolean** named **Down** and have assigned it an initial value of **False**. Now let's look at the variables or attributes a little closer. Find the difference between the class represented in Figure 9-4 and the earlier ones. (Tip: We are looking for three key differences.)

If you only spotted the new data item **Counter**, you have found only one of the key differences. If you noticed that the instance variable, **Counter**, is also underscored, you have scored two out of three.

Before we discuss the third difference, let's talk about the underscored part. If a variable in a UML class object is underscored, it means that the variable is static. Methods, which can also be static (shared) are similarly underlined.

 Rational Rose provides a purer form of UML in its modeling tools than Visio 2002 provides.

UML Notation for Class Relationships

Classes in an object-oriented system are not completely isolated from each other. While some classes are more independent than others, all classes relate to each other in a

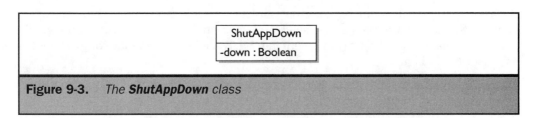

Figure 9-3. *The **ShutAppDown** class*

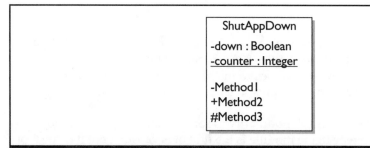

Figure 9-4.   *The **ShutAppDown** class with additional variables*

formal way. Over the years, OO technology has identified five key relationships that classes can have with each other. These relationships are inheritance, implementation, association or collaboration, nonexclusive aggregation, and composition.

Figure 9-5 illustrates the UML graphical notations used to denote the five key relationships among classes and interfaces. We will employ this notation in various places in this book.

Now that we have a basis for modeling applications and representing classes, we can embark on an exciting journey of designing classes for our applications. We have a lot of ground to cover between this point and the end of the chapter, because we are going to look at *all* of the various roles and responsibilities our classes can play, as well as the patterns that dictate their construction.

However, before we can look at OO specifics, we need to discuss a critical concept that actually has its roots in structured design—modularity.

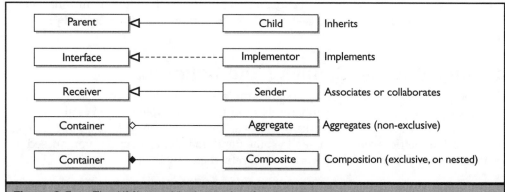

Figure 9-5.   *The UML graphical notation for expressing the relationships among classes and interfaces*

Modularity

Many software development experts jump at the chance to point out that modularity is a critical component of structure design and was inherited by the OO rage. They are one hundred percent correct. However, while modularity is not per se a founding OO principal, it is critical to understand modularity in terms of the object-oriented software development.

What is *modularity?* We discussed modularity to some extent in Chapter 1, but let's dig a little deeper here. To repeat, the module is the unit of encapsulation. It is the tool we use to divide up a system or an application into a collection of individual components or compartments. Modularity follows the principal of divide and conquer; it allows us to reduce complexity and size to a degree that the individual modules can become manageable by the programmer or a team of programmers.

OO programs are not organized as collections of modules, however; they are organized as collections of classes. Classes, nevertheless, serve a similar function as modules. The difference between modularization in structured- or procedure-oriented technology and *classification* in object-oriented technology is that modules are concerned with the meaningful grouping of routines and procedures that forms a cohesive collection. Classes, on the other hand, are concerned with how objects and their contents are grouped and connected to form the structure of the application.

> **Note**   *Interestingly, Visual Basic .NET implements the concept of a class module, which is not found in any other .NET language. At the IL code level, class modules are simply static classes that contain static methods and static fields, which means that all the members are shared. Modules cannot be instantiated (so there is only one copy of each field) and all data is global.*

Programming for modularity in OOP is, however, just as important as it is in the procedure-oriented world. Encapsulation, one the founding principals of OOP, depends on modularity. In OOP, however, encapsulation is concerned with both information-hiding—the maintenance of secrets—as well as the hiding of methods behind public interfaces.

Modularity Metrics: Coupling and Cohesion

So, if programming for modularity is so desirable, even for OO software design, how do we know that our classes are inherently modular? It's simple really. We just have to follow the two most important metrics of modularity—*coupling* and *cohesion.* The coupling and cohesion metrics were discussed in some depth in Chapter 1, and if you missed the boat back then, you may want to return for a refresher.

Coupling

It is worthwhile repeating here that strong coupling detracts from the benefits of OO design because it makes the overall system harder to understand and maintain. When classes depend on each other for data and functionality, they become tightly coupled—and this should be avoided. This is especially important when designing a system of objects, because tightly coupled objects detract from concurrency, reentrance, persistence of objects, and other such desirable traits (and benefits) of object-oriented systems. It becomes harder to maintain and understand classes the more dependent they become on other classes.

You should know that the coupling metric has a vital contraindication in OOP—inheritance. The concept of inheritance denotes a hierarchy of classes, where children depend on parents for their inheritances, data, and implementation.

Inheritance classes are thus tightly coupled; however, the loose coupling metric is elevated to the class hierarchy or the family. We will talk more about this in the "Inheritance" section later in this chapter.

Cohesion

The cohesion metric also came to life in structured design and is a critical principal of procedure-oriented software development. While coupling covers the relationship between classes, cohesion covers the degree of connectivity between the members of classes and their data.

Cohesion, discussed in Chapter 7, applies equally to all members of classes as well as the collection of methods within them. Strong cohesion among the elements of classes is what we strive to achieve.

The best-constructed classes are the ones that avoid coincidental cohesion, in which you just toss unrelated elements into a class. As discussed in Chapter 7, our aim is to construct classes that are strongly cohesive (functional cohesion), in which methods and data are exactly all the class needs to fulfill its role and duties and no more.

The Classes Are the System

When you think about your application as a system and not as a huge collection of "function points," it become possible to see the bigger picture and not be mired down in the minute details that can be so debilitating. For example, I have been working on a spacecraft simulator and can vouch for how quickly you can get buried in the specifics of designing classes, such as deciding which classes play what roles, what their duties and responsibilities are, and how they interrelate. Nevertheless, imagine looking at a spacecraft from the deck of a space station. The image you see in your mind is a magnificent machine, an abstraction for your imagination provided by the likes of movie series such as "Star Trek," "Star Wars," and "Babylon 5."

Behind the hull, however, it's a different story—one that you seldom see. Thousands of highly complex systems make up the spacecraft. The models for a spacecraft's systems are many and massive, so they need to be decomposed to comprehensible and—at the same time—logical units. You have systems for weapons, systems for environmental control, systems for flight, systems for navigation and trajectory, systems for life support, and so on. The list is endless. You would have to design many models on various levels, perhaps starting with a small collection of the most abstract parts that partition the architecture of the entire craft.

If we see ourselves as engineers focusing on getting a spacecraft moving through space, we do not need to care about life support (at least not in the early stages or for the building of the software systems that cater to space flight). So, it makes sense for us to work on a model that caters to all the systems the spacecraft depends on for movement and velocity.

The illustration depicts a model that indicates, at the conceptual model level, the collection of systems that make up our "engineering systems." We have systems for controlling temperature, systems for controlling velocity, systems for controlling the environment around the "coils," systems for controlling the matter-antimatter collision process, systems that generate electricity, systems that monitor, systems that diagnose, and so on. At this point, we do not need to see the other systems of the ship in our model, because until we get moving, we aren't going to need them.

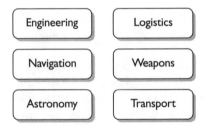

Even just focusing on engineering is still daunting, and in an actual project like this, many large teams work on the various systems within these systems. By decomposing the model further (in the same fashion we decomposed methods in Chapter 7), we can arrive at a system that a specialized and cohesive collection of engineers can work on—the antimatter (fuel) injector. This is illustrated here. (It would in fact detract from the objectives to make the team working on the fuel injector systems work on, say, the environment control systems. The job of the project manager is to determine when it is time to move an "injector" engineer to help the environment control team.)

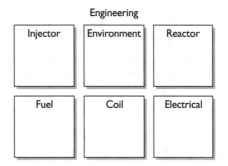

Each system, algorithm, or application thus comprises a collection of classes that relate to each other for the benefit of the greater system. The following list identifies these key relationships and roles and the chapters in which we will primarily explore that relationship:

- **Abstract classes**   The roots of our class hierarchies. (Abstract classes are covered next.)

- **Inheriting classes**   Extending classes and building class hierarchies. (Inheritance is covered in this chapter.)

- **Composite classes**   Reuse of code and association through exclusive composition or containment of one class in another (composition is covered in this chapter, and in Chapters 12 through 14).

- **Aggregate classes**   A form of non-exclusive composition whereby the classes are embedded in the container class but not defined (aggregate classes are discussed later in this chapter and are also discussed in Chapters 13 through 16).

- **Associate classes**   These are classes that associate or collaborate directly with other classes. They typically gain access to implementation in other classes by instantiating and then collaborating with the object (associate classes and collaboration are discussed in all chapters).

- **Delegate classes**   Classes that act as intermediaries between a sender or client class and a receiver or server class. This is a form of association or collaboration, but through indirect method calls where the call is made via a delegate or proxy object. (Formal **Delegate**s, which encapsulate a pointer to a method in a receiver class, are covered extensively in Chapter 14.)

- **Final classes**   Classes that are sealed, which finalizes the inheritance hierarchy (final classes is discussed in this chapter).

- **Singleton classes**   Classes for which only one object can exist (the Singleton pattern is discussed in Chapter 13).

- **Shared classes**   Static or operations classes that are not instantiated (shared classes are discussed in this chapter and throughout the book).

- **Bridge classes**   Classes that allow two or more separate classes to collaborate (the Bridge and Strategy patterns are discussed in Chapter 13).

- **Interfaces**   A class that provides a formal definition of an interface that concrete classes can implement (interfaces are discussed in Chapter 10).

- **Wrappers and adapter classes**   These are classes that adapt the interface of other classes, thereby providing an interface for clients that would not normally be able to use the original interface. (Wrappers and adapter classes are discussed in Chapter 14.)

Figure 9-6 shows a system of classes, and the UML notation indicates the relationships between them.

Class Characteristics

While this book is dedicated to Visual Basic, the .NET Framework provides both a design-time and run-time environment that is common to many compliant languages. The remainder of this chapter thus applies equally to Visual Basic B .NET, C# .NET, JScript .NET, and all the other languages that have been "retrofitted" or "resurrected" to work on the .NET Framework (such as Pascal, COBOL, and Smalltalk). However, every language has its own compiler, and each compiler supports different things in different ways, but the differences are very small and are mainly along idiomatic lines.

What you can do with the language of your choice is dependent on its compiler, and how it works with the BCL and your custom classes. For example, the C# compiler understands how to deal with overloaded operators, but this is not *yet* available to the

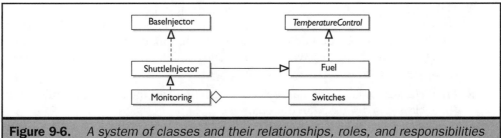

Figure 9-6.   *A system of classes and their relationships, roles, and responsibilities*

Visual Basic programmer, even though operator overloading is well within the realm of possibilities of the Visual Basic compiler.

You should not see this as a limitation at all, because these "differences" are actually there for a reason, and some of them make Visual Basic .NET even more powerful than any other software development tool available on this planet. Take Java, for example. Based on C++, its architects started building it only after deciding to ditch everything that gives programmers such a hard time—multiple inheritance, pointers, operator overloading, and so on.

Classes come in two flavors, user classes (or custom classes) and the Framework or API classes (aka the base classes). The user classes are the ones you will build from scratch. Actually, as you have seen, you first derive them—inheritance—from the base classes (at the least you will derive from **Object**) and other custom classes.

User or custom classes need to conform to CLS; otherwise, at best, they will introduce bugs, and, at worst, they will not compile. The framework classes are the ones that ship with the .NET SDK. They also conform to the CLS (which ultimately supports the Common Language Runtime, or CLR, discussed in the first two chapters).

Table 9-1 provides a list of CLS-documented class characteristics, which apply to both API classes and any user classes you create.

CLS Characteristic	Purpose	VB .NET Usage
Sealed (final)	This class does not permit subclasses.	**NotInheritable**
Implements (interfaces)	This class provides implementation access required or specified by one or more interfaces.	**Implements**
Abstract (virtual)	You cannot instantiate this class. If you want to use it, you must create a child class and provide an instantiation constructor for the child class.	**MustInherit**
Inherits	This means that a child class inherits from a parent class, which is either a base class or a parent in a class hierarchy.	**Inherits**

Table 9-1.   *The Characteristics of .NET Classes*

CLS Characteristic	Purpose	VB .NET Usage
Public	The class itself is visible to all other classes.	**Public** (optional; if omitted, it is public by default)
Exported/Not Exported	This class cannot be exposed or accessed from outside its assembly.	**Friend**

Table 9-1.   *The Characteristics of .NET Classes* (continued)

In the Beginning ... Abstract Classes

I have often drawn a parallel between classes and cells, in which respect I am not being original at all. Many OOP experts have shown how OO systems are modeled on nature, and I am merely drawing on a logically sound concept. In fact, the earliest object-oriented thought processes were directly modeled on cellular biology. And since then it has become a controversial topic—especially in light of the late 2001 announcements about the success of stem cell and human embryo cloning.

Organisms comprise many different types of cells, and each type is a cohesive object in its own right. But all cells start out as stem cells, which are the ultimate cells from which all elements in the organism derive. Many scientists consider stem cells "life-less." What they say is that before DNA is added to a cell, all stem cells are considered identical and completely abstract. Only after a "child" cell, which derives from a stem cell, is given meaningful or life-indicating attributes can it be considered a life form.

The controversy that currently rages in our time is whether or not the stem cell itself is considered a living thing. What's more perplexing is the process or phenomenon that decides what a stem cell will become—its purpose in life, and thus when life itself happens.

The illustration shows a new type of cell deriving from a stem cell. All living things generate stems cells. In humans, a single cell is created at the moment a sperm fertilizes an egg. The cell is known as a *totipotent* cell, which means that it has total potential to divide and continue a process that will result in the development of a human being. When placed into a woman's uterus, these cells have the potential to develop into a fetus.

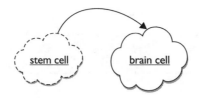

When two such cells make it into the uterus and develop as separate entities, the process gives rise to twins. More time passes and the original cells begin to divide into new cells that give rise to the process that will lead to the creation of organs, tissue, and skin.

For example, blood stem cells give rise to various types of blood cells, while skin stem cells give rise to various types of skin cells. All cells have a particular function. They are highly cohesive entities that know exactly what they have to do to perpetuate life. Blood stem cells, for example, live in the bone marrow of every person. Their function is to continually replenish the organism's blood system.

The analog of stem cells in OO software is the *abstract* class. The root class, **Object**, in the .NET Framework is the ultimate abstract class. It is the single "totipotent" class that has the potential to create additional "stem classes" from which we will produce our class hierarchies and give our applications life.

An *abstract* class is simply a class that cannot be instantiated because, on its own, it is not complete and cannot serve the function of an accessible object. It requires further implementation in deriving classes (called concrete classes). In other words, an abstract class is simply a class that is intended to be derived from, and either all or part of the class implementation has been postponed for construction in the child class.

Factoring Out Commonality

It would be clumsy to pack all the functionality of an injector into one class and then seal it. We would certainly want other developers to take the class, derive base and generic services from it, and use it as they see fit, or extend it or adopt (and adapt) it for use in other spacecraft. After all, all spacecraft require fuel injection systems, no matter whether they are full-blown battleships or little shuttles that zip down to planets and back.

The injector engineers thus work on the base specifications for fuel injector software programs that are required by all spacecraft. This is then the point at which we would create our ultimate abstract class as the base class from which further classes are derived, classes that would be concrete or that might extend the class hierarchy even further (perhaps to go where no developer has gone before). But we have to start somewhere.

The base injector class, **BaseInjector**, thus provides the abstract members that all injector classes will have, the most important ones being **StartInjector** and **StopInjector**. These members also include methods that signal to other systems that increase or reduction in velocity is required, information that the injector is on or off, and properties that provide other critical information back to the injector, such as the state of the coils, core temperatures, and fuel levels.

In addition to overriding or overloading the base functionality, we would also want class consumers to improve the classes with their own methods—using our abstract class, or at least the next generation of it, as a starting point. We are thus creating a "blueprint" or a template, so to speak. All injector objects derived from this base class will have common characteristics when they are born—just like humans at the embryo stage. The illustration demonstrates the **BaseInjector** object with its initial abstract methods.

```
BaseInjector

StartInjector
StopInjector
SetWarpSpeed
GetSpeed
MPS
DriveState
InjectorState
```

*Remember, the **BaseInjector** class also implicitly inherits from **Object**, so there are additional members in this abstract class that are not shown. You will not normally see the inherited members in your class. However, the process of reflection (which provides type information) lets you look at a class and see the inherited members. See "Reflecting Classes" in Chapter 13.*

All software systems have to start somewhere. It's not imperative that you start with an abstract class. Some of you might start with a form (so that you can see results early) and make that the "center" of your application. Some of you will start with a single abstract class, which becomes the root class for the entire system. This class might be an abstract class that serves a particular function or purpose expressed during the design of a system. You might also create several abstract classes and create a system that's not unlike the human body described earlier, which produces stem cells as the basis for all of its elements.

I design applications using the latter approach, starting with the design of a single abstract class and extrapolating the entire system from it. Even forms, which are complex hierarchies of many classes, ultimately derive from **Object**, the .NET stem cell. Many years ago (in the days of Borland's Object Vision language and then moving on to Delphi), I would start with a form, and everything would herald from there. But as analysis and design tools (especially UML) matured, it became less important to get cracking on the user interface and easier to identify the place or places in your model as starting points. Your models point out where to start with an application; a team of developers can often start in a number of places at the same time, independent of each other. If you can delegate like this, then you are on the right track.

You declare an abstract class in Visual Basic .NET as follows:

```
Public MustInherit Class BaseInjector
   'on its own it cannot be instantiated
End Class
```

Caution   *Be sure not to forget the **Public** access modifier or the class will default to **Friend** which cannot be exported, and you will not be able to inherit from it as the base class.*

There are two ways to generate the source for our abstract class. The first and most convenient way is to export the class to Visual Studio from Visio or another tool you have used to create the UML diagrams. The second approach is to simply construct the class manually. The code for the entire abstract **BaseInjector** class is as follows:

```
Public MustInherit Class BaseInjector
   Public MustOverride Sub StartInjector()
   'must be overridden in child class
   Public MustOverride Sub StopInjector()
   Public MustOverride Sub SetWarpSpeed(ByVal newWarpSpeed As Integer)
   Public MustOverride ReadOnly Property MPS() As Integer
   Public MustOverride ReadOnly Property GetSpeed() As Integer
   Public MustOverride ReadOnly Property DriveState() As Boolean
   Public MustOverride Property InjectorState() As String
End Class
```

The Members of Abstract Classes

Abstract methods are intended to be implemented in subclasses that derive from a base class, and the *abstract* modifier, **MustOverride**, specifies that the child class is required to implement the methods. For all intents and purposes, the abstract members are nothing more than a definition of the member signatures the implementor must adhere to. The abstract method in a base class is thus merely a definition and is devoid of any implementation.

A method or property that is declared as abstract is overridden in the subclass, because that is where the implementation of the method or property is handled. Abstract members are thus implicitly *virtual*, because they can be implemented in subclasses. Abstract members are thus the opposite of final members.

An abstract class cannot be sealed, which would in any event defeat its purpose. Sealing a class prevents it from being further extended.

The members of an abstract class do not necessarily themselves need to be abstract. In other words, you can derive complete functionality from an abstract class (which you cannot do with an interface). In this regard, you can declare variable and constant fields in the abstract class. This allows the fields to be inherited by the descendant classes (this is not possible with an interface; see Chapter 10).

Since you cannot instantiate an abstract class, using the **New** operator as an attempt to create a new instance of the object would result in an exception. The code for the abstract class, **BaseInjector**, previously shown, does not define a constructor. However, there is nothing stopping you from defining collateral constructors. The **New** constructor merely passes through to the child from the parent of **BaseInjector** (in this case **Object**) on which it depends for the constructor implementation. Classes that derive from **BaseInjector** can thus call **New** for instantiation.

When you derive an abstract class, you must override all abstract methods in your implementation, even if you just declare the methods and leave out the meat. Let's now get down to inheriting from the base class.

Inheritance

Inheritance is pervasive across the .NET Framework and in all of your custom classes. First, you implicitly inherit from **Object** every time you create a class. Second, when you are ready to create a new class, your first consideration is to decide whether it is appropriate to extend a base class—create a subtype. But first we must ask, what exactly is inheritance?

Inheritance, as described in the previous section on abstract classes, is nothing more than a mechanism in which the data, attributes, properties, and behavior of classes propagate from parents to children. Again, inheritance in software is modeled on inheritance in nature. Mother Nature uses inheritance as a mechanism for perpetuating her species, and to maintain collections of species that share common specialized attributes.

Like our ability to inherit brown eyes or acting ability, which may be debatable, from our parents, the inheritance relationship between two classes implies that code implemented in the parent class is derived to the child class where it can be used. Figure 9-7 shows the inheritance of the definitions and any implementation from **BaseInjector** to **ShuttleInjector**.

In this figure, **ShuttleInjector** inherits several methods from **BaseInjector** including the implementation of the **GetHashCode** method that was originally derived from the ultimate base class, **Object**. We will return to the implementation of **ShuttleInjector** shortly.

It is vital to understand that one major difference exists between inheritance in nature and inheritance in OO software technology. In nature, organisms inherit the traits, attributes, and behavior of their parents, which manifest in them. You just have to look at your children (or your parents) to see this at work. But after birth, there is no longer a connection (at least a physical one). Looking at it another way, just because

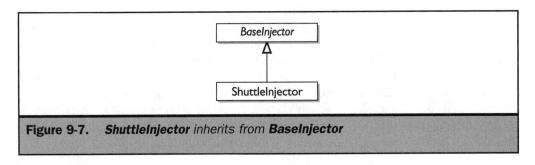

Figure 9-7. *ShuttleInjector* inherits from *BaseInjector*

your dad decides to eat 100 pancakes today does not mean you will wake up tomorrow weighing 20 pounds more.

Classes that inherit are always tied to their parents, or superclasses. An inherited method is not replicated in the child or extended class; the implementation remains at the parent, while the functionality can be accessed from the child as if it were its own method. This is what we refer to as *code reuse*. It does not mean that we select code in class **A** and paste it to class **B**. This type of inheritance also means that any changes to a method in a parent class will affect the child. To avoid such behavior, you need to implement a mechanism to block the inheritance, such as overriding or shadowing in the child class, or sealing the member in the parent class.

How do you know when you should create a class that inherits from a parent. Determining whether or not inheritance should occur is easy if you follow the cardinal rule of inheritance. If a new class **B** *is-a* class **A**, then **B** should inherit from **A**, or at least there is good reason for **B** to inherit from **A**. In other words if **A** is a cat and **B** is also intended to be a cat then the determination is that **B** *is-a* **A** or **B** is a cat. The *is-a* rule is simple to follow. To demonstrate the rule in action, let's now move to another part of the spacecraft, to the **Crew** manifest. Classes that represent a hierarchy of crew members may be easier to visualize in an inheritance structure than **Injector** objects.

> **Note** *I introduced this example, the **Crew** class, in my book,* Visual Basic .NET Developer's Headstart *(McGraw-Hill/Osborne, 2001) and felt that repeating it here in more detail was worthwhile.*

On every spacecraft is a crew. The crew may be human, or it may be a multitude of species, like the crew of the Enterprise or Voyager on "Star Trek." The crew may also contain a compliment of primates, highly trained chimpanzees that work with their human associates.

So, our spacecraft's systems require a hierarchy of classes representing crew. The first job of the designers is to create a base abstract class, called **Crew**, and encapsulate in it all the attributes and behaviors that will be common to all crewmembers. Factoring out the commonalties is not a difficult problem. Create a class in UML and add to it all the elements common to crewmembers.

You should not need to think about this too hard. All crewmembers have names. So, the first fields you might add to the **Crew** class would be **firstName**, **middleInitial**, **lastName**. Next on the list of common fields would be **age**, **sex**, and **religion**. Besides the commonalties of all people, there are also commonalties specific to crewmembers, such as **crewID**, **rank**, and **clearanceLevel**. With these elements in hand, the base **Crew** class should look like the one in Figure 9-8.

Creating subclasses, or child classes, of **Crew** is simply a matter of inheriting from it using the **Inherits** keyword. Suppose you need to create classes that represent engineers and security staff. Both types of crewmembers will now have different attributes and

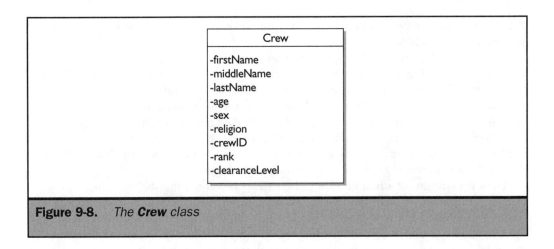

Figure 9-8. *The Crew class*

other elements. Engineers, for example, may require specialized classification of certain skills, whereas security staff will be assigned side-arms that need to be checked out of the armory at the start of every shift and checked in at the end of every shift.

> **Note** *The inheritance rule states that inheritance is represented by is-a relationships between classes. If **ClassB** is-a (kind of) **ClassA**, then **ClassB** should inherit from **ClassA**.*

Thus, when an application or solution requires the creation of an **Engineer** class you simply derive from the base **Crew** class—in other words you extend **Crew**—when **you declare the new class. On the other hand, even the Engineer** class may be too general for a spacecraft that employs about six different types of engineer. It may in fact make sense to deepen the hierarchy and derive **InjectorEngineer** from the **Engineer** class. Injector engineers represented by the **InjectorEngineer** class may need to check in for a medical every 48 hours to ensure that working too close to an antimatter environment has not affected their molecules.

The deeper the hierarchy, the more specialized are the *most derived* classes. The classes closer to the base or abstract class are more generalized. **InjectorEngineer**s have certain members that differ from **Gunner**s, **Cook**s, **Medic**s, and **Captain**s. But a class at the end of a class hierarchy also inherits from all the previous classes.

InjectorEngineer is now considered a subclass or a subtype of **Engineer**, and both are subtypes of **Crew** (which is a subtype of **Object**). This hierarchy is presented for purposes of illustration, but you can see that inheritance can also be overdone when you create hierarchies that run to double-digit levels. You should have very strong and valid reasons to create a subtype. We can also override certain methods in our derived classes and thus change the functionality to suite the subtype. It is better to override a bunch of methods than to unnecessarily deepen the hierarchy. In other words, further extending a type just to create a new class is getting carried away.

Inheritance and Polymorphism

Looking back at the discussion of polymorphism in Chapter 1, you can see how perfectly inheritance supports this key foundation tenet of OO software development. Extended or derived types not only inherit the interface from parent classes, but the implementation as well.

Where is the polymorphism? It manifests in every inherited class. It is no matter that the class is used as is or the method is overridden; you can send the same message to all the classes in the hierarchy, and the correct method behind the interface will respond and be processed.

However, it is also possible to override this functionality, and in the case of abstract classes, the methods, properties, and events are often defined with the **MustOverride** modifier, which means that you must override and implement the methods in the subclasses. So, again, the message is sent, and the interface and the method signature are the same. The only difference is the class and the implementation.

So, polymorphism is served and the type system extended because a single interface (which is defined in a base or an abstract class) can be implemented repeatedly in many forms. We will investigate method overriding in this context later in this chapter (refer also to Chapter 7).

Inheritance and Coupling

A child class is tightly coupled to its parent, because it depends on functionality and data created in the parent class. This means that you can't simply take your child class and go and reimplement it at will or make it into something it is not intended to be— explicitly overriding methods that should not be overridden or otherwise violating the *is-a* rule. Although nothing stops you from creating a class **FlightEngineer** that derives from **BaseInjector**, that would not make sense.

Although class hierarchies represent tightly coupled classes, the tight coupling does not work against the application or the algorithm in the same way that global data couples classes to each other. Coupling that results from inheritance is coupling by design. In this respect, you should think of a hierarchy of classes as a logical unit, not as a collection of tightly coupled classes, the one depending on the other like two conjoined individuals. As long as you stick to the information-hiding/encapsulation recommendations and practices described later in this chapter, you will never see a detrimental result created from the inheritance mechanism.

Inheritance can actually detract from the encapsulation you have taken care to implement in your class. As an example, imagine that you decide to extend a class and use a method or some data as is from the base class. Now the class provider—a neat freak who just keeps improving his or her classes—goes and makes a change and reissues the assembly you are referencing (of course, that neat freak could be you), and now you have a problem. Because of the direct inheritance, the change ripples down the class hierarchy like a long line of dominoes. At the end of the line is your application, which gets knocked over.

Sounds like a big problem, but it's not really if you know what you are doing. In properly and carefully designed applications, you use the ability to override base functionality wisely. If you extend a class and absolutely need to depend on a new implementation in the child class, overriding effectively stops the domino ripple in its tracks. We will see how this works later in this chapter.

You can't override inherited variables and constants derived from on high. But any class designer worth more than a pound of salt is not simply going to change an **Integer** you are using to a **Double** or a **Decimal**. Chapters 2 and 4 illustrated just how type safe the .NET Framework can be. With the correct configuration, it is very difficult to make changes without Visual Studio stopping you dead in your tracks. Despite that, you should shadow data fields that have the same name in parent classes, or declare new variables and constants in the child classes.

The coupling effect of inheritance no doubt has to be considered. It is also possible to change implementation or add override functionality along a deep hierarchy, which can result in some nasty conflicts. A cohesive development team implementing a framework will be able to manage the process with common sense. In other words, you still have to be careful.

If you don't intend your derived classes to be further derived or you are getting ready to implement your derived classes for the greater good of the application, then methods and other implementation can be sealed or made final, thereby preventing other users of the class from further overriding your methods. We will delve into this in more detail later in this chapter, after we have reviewed all the various ways of constructing classes, the roles of classes, and the relationships among classes.

Multiple Inheritance

Mother Nature is much more intelligent than any guru writing software is. She can easily fashion new life from the genes of more than one parent. For example, Laila Ali might punch like her famous daddy, Mohammed Ali, but the world knows that she also has her mother's looks.

Multiple inheritance (MI) allows a design and implementation concept known as a *mixin* in OO parlance. A mixin would allow us to inherit from more than one class and thus inherit the definition and implementation from the mixin. This is illustrated in Figure 9-9, where the new subtype of two or more parents contains the inherited elements of all the mixed-in classes.

MI in software, some believe, is too problematic for us rank-and-file software geeks, so we can't do mixins. The .NET type system thus only supports inheritance from a single parent. But it turns out there is good reason. MI adds to the complexity factor, which goes against what we are trying to achieve with inheritance in the first place.

One of the most common problems encountered with MI deals with identical method signatures that derive from more than one class. The problem you have to face when you derive from two or more parents with identical methods is determining which method to implement?

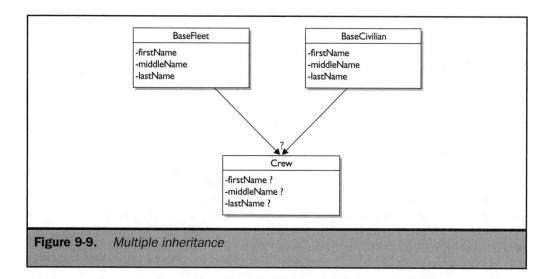

Figure 9-9.   *Multiple inheritance*

The purest form of MI lets a subclass inherit fields and implementation from different parents at the same time, and many class providers feel that the added flexibility and power is worth the extra care required during implementation. C++ changed to MI long after the language was introduced. Eiffel was built from the ground up using MI. Languages like Java and Delphi have opted for single inheritance only. This is the case with the .NET languages. (If you try to add a second **Inherits** statement to your class, the compiler will politely tell you to get lost.)

But single inheritance does not necessarily mean you only have one super or parent class. It means that inheritance can only be implemented through a single object hierarchy. While a language like C++ has multiple object hierarchies, the .NET languages only inherit from one hierarchy. The root **Object**'s members always manifest in every new class. So, a child class derives not only from your new custom base class, but also from **Object**. You can by all means derive from your custom class, and thus you would have a new child class that contains elements of three superclasses. This is acceptable (if not overdone) as long as there is only one logical hierarchy.

Order and Control with Inheritance

Classification provides order and control in software development projects, which so often becomes a chaotic situation. I have been involved in many extensive software development projects over the years, from classic applications such as highly efficient state machines/schedulers for telephony systems and telephone switches, to business applications such as accounting systems and CRM applications, to multimillion dollar e-commerce sites. In all of these projects, I have seen how quickly a team of developers can lose control over their code.

CLASSES AND OBJECTS

Classification of classes into hierarchies provides a means of order and control. It is a good idea to assign the responsibility of base class creation to a single developer or a group of developers—class providers—and enforce the inheritance and extension of subclasses at the class consumer level, with the developers who need to use the classes.

Figure 9-10 shows how a chain of command is established for the class. Consumers know what they need to do to use the class in the application, and the providers know what they need to do to maintain the base classes. When consumers and the architects require new common class members to be added to the base classes, that responsibility falls back to the developers maintaining the classes.

As the figure indicates, I propose providing class hierarchies for all classes in a project. The class hierarchies should thus evolve to become a framework, in the same context and for the same purpose as the .NET Framework. Some class hierarchies will be deep and lightly extended. Others might be shallow and heavily extended.

The creation of frameworks using inheritance thus implies a separation of objectives in the software development process. On the one hand, you are using inheritance to create new classes, polymorphism, and interfaces to feed the development, and provide new classes. On the other hand, developers use the framework to build their applications. I stumbled across an excellent analogy in a pottery shop at about the time I wrote this chapter. In this particular shop, you could buy the vase in its raw state, already shaped and baked, and simply paint it. So, the pottery shop provides the base and you provide the finishing touches without having to get your hands fouled up with sticky clay.

Reduction of Complexity

Developing class hierarchies and frameworks substantially reduces complexity. First, the class hierarchy is properly factored, as discussed earlier. So, documentation, adherence to models and specifications, interface usage and exposure, guidelines for deployment, and so on all become available to the team. Developing applications within a framework of classes that is well thought out and well documented is much easier than developing them within a hodgepodge of code that is just stuffed into classes like leftovers stuffed into Tupperware boxes.

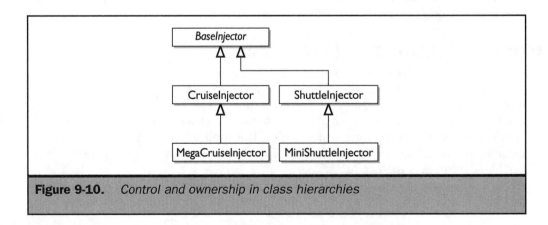

Figure 9-10.   *Control and ownership in class hierarchies*

At the same time, creating the framework provides a benefit that is obtained implicitly and without huge effort on the part of the project manager. No single person becomes the indispensable keeper of his or her "code" either through some desire to protect some interest or because a class is created on-the-fly and on-the-quiet. Often, classes are written as an afterthought, or for some other reason known only to the creator, without inclusion in the model or the specification, or without any forethought or inclusion or agreement from any other team members and the project manager.

It thus becomes much more difficult to lose control over documentation and source code when code is classified and admitted to a framework of class hierarchies. Well-written source code does not have to be fully documented to the extent that the developer writing the code explains in plain English (or any other lingo) exactly for what reason every variable, constant, method, or property exists. This is especially true with OO code. The code is to a very large extent self-documenting, and if you can read Visual Basic .NET source code, you can comprehend what is going on in the class. (Contrast this to the classic BASIC code, described in Chapter 1.)

However, the bigger problem is at the higher level of abstraction, at the class level. When you have a class that does not exist in a model and the framework, or it is difficult to discern how the objects interoperate with each other, how they relate, or how they depend or don't depend on one another, you have the ingredients necessary for disaster. This has been a big problem with many Web sites and e-commerce systems targeting the likes of Microsoft's old Active Server Page technology. The mixing in of Visual Basic script, Java, JavaScript (or JScript), HTML, XML, and various other language constructs in a collection of flat, seemingly boundless modules (ending up with what many call "spaghetti code") has led to many wasted nights trying to find errors and bugs.

Not having the models and the proper design documents and diagrams (such as use cases, sequence diagrams, and state charts) has seen many millions of dollars go down the drain in e-commerce systems that become impossible to decipher once the original developers fade into the twilight. This is very different with ASP.NET, in which an entire e-commerce application can be assembled from a collection of highly cohesive classes.

Maintenance

Class hierarchies are easily maintained. The class providers control the base classes and the core functionality and data required by all subclasses in the hierarchy. Consumers that have extended the classes down the line become responsible for the maintenance of their own classes. But when commonality among the classes in a collection is identified, the common constructs can be added to the base class, and all derivatives benefit.

The same process works for maintenance of the common members in the base classes. A developer maintaining a base class can return to a method and rewrite it or update it. Perhaps the method requires an optional parameter, perhaps it needs to be souped up, or perhaps it just needs to be reimplemented from scratch. Definitions can be changed in the abstract classes, and the changes trickle down to the subclasses.

Code Reuse

Code reuse is another concept that does not really have its roots in OO. The idea of code reuse came a lot earlier—in fact, OOP only helped popularize the concept. However, code reuse is now synonymous with inheritance and is often cited as the most important benefit of inheritance. As you have now seen, by directly inheriting a method from a base class, you do not need to reimplement the method. This makes sense; why would you want to rewrite extensive, well-tested code when it already exists?

The skeptics of inheritance—oldies who can't get the hang of OOP—will tell you that you don't need inheritance to reuse code. They suggest you are better off just copying and pasting code from one module to another. But the problem with that approach is so obvious that it's ridiculous. When implementing an extensive algorithm or application, we discover many situations that require identical code. Getting back to the **Crew** class, you can see several possibilities for code reuse. For example, suppose the **Crew** class implements a database lookup, or encrypts a stream. By cutting and pasting code for each new type of crewmember, you end up with additional code in additional classes all over the place. Every constructor, **Equals** method, **GetType**, **GetHashCode**, and more will have to be rewritten with this very sophisticated and advanced feature called *cut and paste*.

A bigger problem with the cutting-and-pasting scenario arises when you need to improve or change the original method that does the encryption or the database lookup. You now have to go to every place the code was pasted to and paste in the new code. This not only wastes a lot of time, but the potential for introducing bugs is enormous. That's not code reuse; that's code misuse.

You might also stumble across recommendations to avoid inheritance completely and use aggregation and containment techniques. This is not sound advice either. Nothing in life is a perfect fit; there are no constants. In some scenarios, inheritance points the way; in others, aggregation or another pattern points the way. The problem is not that one technique is bad and another is good. The problem arises when you use the techniques for the wrong reason.

It is true that inheritance has been overhyped in many quarters; and as a result, rather than learning when to correctly use inheritance, novice programmers start using it everywhere. The problem is that when they finally grow up, they can't shake the bitter experience of having to redesign applications and learn new tricks, so they slam inheritance and tell you not to use it. That's a difficult pill to swallow when you work with a framework, like .NET, in which inheritance underpins the entire infrastructure.

Implementing a Space Ship's Fuel Injector Software

We've come a long way with the theory in this chapter, but now for some code that shows inheritance in action. We are now ready to implement the **ShuttleInjector** class, which will comprise the following elements:

- **Instance Fields**   These are the variable and constant data fields—of course, they represent objects—of our class. For every instance of the class, there will be a separate and totally private copy of the object's fields that can only be accessed from within the instance they are part of.

- **Instance Constructors**   In this class, we only need one essential constructor, the **New** method.

- **Properties**   Properties are implemented to obtain status information related to the injector's on/off state and current velocity, and so on.

- **Methods**   A number of methods will be implemented from the base class.

The **Inherits** keyword in a class specifies a class to be derived from. In other words, the class intends to inherit the interfaces, methods, and fields of the base or superclass.

The following code demonstrates the new class for an object (a simulator) that can control an injector, about to inherit from the class **BaseInjector**. Visual Studio will report to you that you need to implement a lot more than just **New**, specifically as directed by the base class through the facility of the **Inherits** keyword:

```
Public Class ShuttleInjector
   Inherits BaseInjector

   Public Sub New()
     MyBase.New()
   End Sub

'there are methods to implement

End Class
```

In the preceding declaration, the **Inherits** keyword specifies that the derived class, **ShuttleInjector**, inherits the properties, methods, and any initialization data from the parent class, **BaseInjector**. However, understand that the use of the **Inherits** keyword does not circumvent any non-inheritable or non-overridable members in the base class. These remain sealed if that is what you intended. The inheritance will become clearer in the next section.

Note   *The .NET Framework suggests using PascalCase notation when naming members, such as methods and class names, and using camelCase for variables and fields. For a detailed discussion on notation recommendation for .NET code, refer to Chapter 4.*

Instance Fields

The first thing we do after creating an empty class is provide (declare) a number of instance (or member) variables, which will reference the data fields of the object. Remember, these data fields are nothing more than objects of the fundamental types contained in both the **BaseInjector** and **ShuttleInjector** classes. So, let's jot down the following variables and constants in our **ShuttleInjector** class specification:

- First variable, **warpSpeed**   This represents an integer to store the warp speed of 0 through 9, which represents light speed plus a significant percentage thereof.

- Second variable, **warpDrive**   This is a **Boolean** value used to store the on/off state of the warp drive.

- Third variable, **injectorStatus**   This is a **String** for storing information about the status of the injector.

- First constant, **C**   This constant represents the speed of light, which is 186,355 miles per second. The term "warp" or "warpspeed" for this simulation shall thus mean light speed plus a certain level above it. (It is, however, believed that traveling at or beyond the speed of light slows the aging process, and that would inject new considerations in our algorithm, which of course we will just have to ignore for this trial.)

The variables and constants are declared as follows in the class:

```
Private warpSpeed As Integer
Private warpDrive As Boolean
Private injectorStatus As String = "Injector is Offline"
Const C As Integer = 186355
```

All Visual Basic variables are initialized to their default values when the class is created or instantiated, and *do* require access or visibility modifiers regardless. Declaring with **Dim** alone modifies the fields to **Private** access. This is required by CLS; however, not all .NET languages use the same default values. In Visual Basic, integers default to 0 when initialized, but C# integers required explicit initialization.

 *The use of **Dim** is not required for instance variables that are modified. If you try to use **Dim** with **Private**, **Public**, **Shared**, and so on in the declaration of the instance variable, Visual Studio will, cheekily, remove it. Check out Chapter 4 and Chapter 7 for a refresher of the variable and constant declaration basics.*

When the first variable is initialized to zero, it means that the warp drive is online but that no antimatter is present in the annihilation chamber of the warp drive (annihilation is similar to the combustion technology of the average motor vehicle used as transport during the Information Age).

The second variable gets initialized to *off*, which you represent as **False** by using the **Boolean** type. If **warpDrive** is set to *off*, it means the spaceship may be stationary or traveling under "impulse" drive. If the **warpDrive** is set to *on*, it means the spaceship has engaged warp drive by starting up its warp engines.

Do you need to declare instance variables for every class you create? No. You can create a class that does not require instance variables or fields at all. Or you can create a class that declares variables or constants and leaves them initialized to their default values.

Place your instance or class fields directly after the declaration of the class. While the scope or visibility of the variable is global to the class, the instance variables are declared private, which thus hides them from being accessed by the outside world. This is the essence of encapsulation—the hiding of information (discussed in Chapter 1). If you really think about it, nothing else, other than the members of the class, needs access to these variables, and no matter what or where your code resides in the class, you always have access to the class variables. The visibility and scope of variables is discussed at length in Chapter 4, and in Chapter 13, which tackles the subject of encapsulation.

The code in your IDE window should thus now look like the following showing the methods and properties that are yet to be implemented:

```
Public Class ShuttleInjector
   Inherits BaseInjector

   Private warpSpeed As Integer
   Private warpDrive As Boolean
   Private injectorStatus As String = "Injector is Offline"
   Const C As Integer = 186355

   Public Overrides ReadOnly Property GetSpeed() As Integer
     Get
     End Get
   End Property

   Public Overrides ReadOnly Property MPS() As Integer
     Get
     End Get
   End Property

   Public Overrides ReadOnly Property DriveState() As Boolean
     Get
     End Get
   End Property

   Public Overrides Property InjectorState() As String
```

```
      Get
      End Get
      Set(ByVal Value)
      End Set
   End Property

   'Gentlemen start your warp engines
    Public Overrides Sub StartInjector()
    End Sub

    'Stop the warp engines
    Public Overrides Sub StopInjector()
    End Sub

    'Set warp speed
    Public Overrides Sub SetWarpSpeed(ByVal newWarpSpeed As Integer)
    End Sub
End Class
```

Visual Studio will stop complaining about implementing the abstract methods as soon as you have overriden all inherited definitions.

Instance Constructors

The next member to define and code is the instance constructor, which requires the **New** keyword. The **Injector** class is one that is going to be activated or instantiated as an object, so we need a constructor to "bootstrap" the object when we send it the message to construct itself as a *new* object.

The instance constructor is nothing more than a method that can initialize the object's data fields and other initial tasks in a class, at its creation as an object. Its purpose is to provide control over the state of the object at its creation. The code in the **New** method is processed before any other code in the class.

The preceding code includes the call **MyBase.New**, which is required at the beginning of the instance constructor. If you omit this line, the CLR makes the call for you, but if you need to either lock the class (prevent its instantiation) or do more with the **New** method, you will have to implement it. In the preceding example, using the base class's constructor will work.

As mentioned earlier, your constructors do not need to initialize the class instance variables. And you can thus call such constructors *no arguments* or *parameterless* constructors. If the class can be created without constructor code, you can leave the constructor block empty, or you can leave it out altogether because the CLR invokes the parent's constructor, derived from **Object**, which you will learn about in a few minutes.

Using the *specification notation* you learned about in Chapter 7, you can now go ahead and write up the specification for the injector's instance constructor as follows:

■ **Constructor definition**   The constructor **New** creates an instance of injector and initializes the object's data.

```
Public Sub New()
```

■ **Preconditions**   The **warpSpeed** = 0 and the **warpDrive** variable is **False**; that is, **warpDrive** = off.

■ **Postconditions**   After the activation of the object, the warp drive is off and warp has not been engaged.

■ **Parameters**   None

■ **Exceptions**   None

So, let's code the constructor as follows:

```
Public Sub New()
  MyBase.New()
  injectorStatus = "Injector is offline"
End Sub
```

In the case of our **ShuttleInjector** class, however, we have only one instance variable that needs to be initialized with a value no matter the default variable assigned by the consumer language of your class. In this case it's the injector's **injectorStatus** variable, which needs information pertaining to the state of the injector when the object is first created.

The **warpDrive** naturally defaults to **False**. You want to know that when a **ShuttleInjector** object is created, it will be in a useful or "kosher" state to protect the consumer from something unexpected. When you start a car, it does not suddenly jump into a drive gear; it first idles in neutral. We want the same behavior when consumers use our injector software.

Here are the CLS rules for instance constructors:

■ The name of the instance constructor must be **New**, which ensures that the code in this method is the first processed before any other code in the class.

■ The instance variables are only assigned or initialized after the activation of the base class constructor—even if you explicitly provided the call to the parent constructor (with **MyBase.New)**, which must always be the first line of code in the constructor.

■ The constructor looks and behaves like a method; however, it is activated when the object is itself created using the **New** keyword. You cannot explicitly or directly call the class constructor after the object is activated, and the constructor cannot call or invoke itself (the compiler will not let that code through either).

■ The constructor does not return any values to its activation mechanism; thus, using the keyword **Return** in the constructor does nothing but waste white space.

You can have more than one constructor in a class along with the instance constructor. Constructor code is processed when the program is executed or when an object is created, but only one constructor method, **New**, is automatically invoked by the CLR. Additional constructors must therefore be called by code provided to **New** for them to fire when the object is created. The other custom constructors can also set various instance variables and perform post-creation checks to ensure algorithm or object integrity.

As mentioned earlier, you do not need to explicitly include **MyBase.New** at the beginning of your instance's constructor block, because the default behavior of the CLR is to call the base class constructor regardless (in the example shown earlier, the **New** constructor explicitly calls the constructor of the root **Object** class).

Also, as mentioned earlier, if you declare **New** as **Private**, consumers of your class will not be able to derive from the class or instantiate it. This behavior can be useful and further protects a class that has been explicitly sealed for inheritance.

Properties

While you might provide a property method to return the warp speed (using the **WarpFactorEnum** enumeration constants set up in the last chapter), you might also find it useful to provide a property that can be used to determine the actual velocity in terms the average human would understand.

 Properties were introduced in Chapter 7.

Let's write a specification for a simple "get" property to get the actual warp speed settings of the injector (the property must return a value, so the property behaves like a function and returns a value).

■ **Property signature: GetSpeed.** This read-only property is used to access the current warp speed as the warp factor (0-9). It takes no arguments. The full declaration of the property is as follows:

```
Public ReadOnly Property GetSpeed() As Integer
```

■ **Return value:** This property gets the current warp speed and returns it to the caller as an **Integer** value.

The code can be written as follows:

```
Public Overrides ReadOnly Property GetSpeed() As Integer
  Get
    Return warpSpeed
  End Get
End Property
```

When the simulator is executed, the default warp speed will be reported as 0. Notice that this accessor does not have a parameter, and you will not need to test for any precondition. The data required by the accessor property is provided by the instance variables and is available to the members of the class. The **warpSpeed** data is private but not exactly hidden either. Notice that the property is public and thus can be called by any class (see the section "Class Characteristics" earlier in this chapter). Placing the variable behind another layer in the class, a property, can further hide the direct access to the already private **warpSpeed** field.

Remember, warp speed is (in our case) light speed plus a significant percentage of light speed. If warp factor, represented by the constant value C, is equal to one light year, you can easily calculate the miles per second (MPS) of, say, warp 5 (**WarpFactorEnum .ImpulsePlusFive**). So, you could write a property called **MPS** that computes and returns the value as MPS. Let's now do the specification and code for the method to convert the warp speed to MPS:

- **Property definition: MPS.** This read-only property gets the current speed in MPS.

  ```
  Public Property MPS()
  ```

- **Returns:** The property gets the current warp speed from the **warpSpeed** field that is global to the instance and converts the speed to MPS.

The code should be as follows:

```
'Get the MPS speed of the warp factor
Public Overrides ReadOnly Property MPS() As Integer
  Get
   MPS = warpSpeed * C
  End Get
End Property
```

Now we need to implement **DriveState**, which returns a value **True** or **False** for the current state of the warp drive (on or off) as set in the **warpDrive** field. The specification is as follows:

- **Property definition: DriveState**. This property gets the current state of the warp drive. If the drive is on, then the return value as a **Boolean** type will be **True**; if the drive is off, then the return value will be **False**.

  ```
  Public Overrides ReadOnly Property DriveState() As Boolean
  ```

- **Returns:** The property returns **True** if the drive is on and **False** if the drive is off.

The code should be as follows:

```
'Check the state of the warp drive
Public Overrides ReadOnly Property DriveState() As Boolean
  Get
    Return warpDrive
  End Get
End Property
```

The last property to implement is **InjectorState**, which returns the current **String** value held by the **injectorStatus** field. The property may also be used to supply new data to the **injectorStatus** field. The specification is as follows:

- **Property definition: InjectorState**. This property gets the current state of the injector held in the field's **String**.

  ```
  Public Overrides Property InjectorState() As String
  ```

- **Returns:** The property returns the **String** value from the **injectorStatus** field.

The code should be as follows:

```
'Check the state of the warp drive
Public Overrides Property InjectorState() As String
  Get
    Return injectorStatus
  End Get
  Set(ByVal Value As String)
    injectorStatus = Value
  End Set
End Property
```

Methods

The next members will be implemented as methods. You will need to increase warp speed, so you will need to pass an argument to a parameter that represents the level of warp speed that you want to set. However, we may also need to throw exceptions in this method and perform other tests and calculations that could be complex. This is the point at which I prefer to forgo properties for standard modification methods.

To kick off the simulation of warp speed, we need to implement at least two modification methods for the **ShuttleInjector** class. We will need a method to start the injector coils and a method to shut down the injector coils. We also need a method to set the warp speed, which is more involved. All three methods manipulate and change the object and can still be implemented as properties, rather than methods. Now, let's look at the specification for the first method:

- **Method definition: StartInjector.** The method starts the injector and sets the state of the warp drive to on (no preconditions or parameters are required).

  ```
  Public Sub StartInjector()
  ```

- **Postcondition:** The state of the warp drive is set to on.

The code should be as follows:

```
'Gentlemen start your warp engines
Public Overrides Sub StartInjector()
  warpDrive = True
  injectorStatus = "Injector is Online"
End Sub
```

Notice that **StartInjector** is a simple **Sub** method, because it does not need to return anything to the caller. The method also does not take any arguments, because it does little else, in the current version, other than to change an instance variable. Later, as you get into writing more complex methods, you will probably always be passing reference or value arguments to parameters.

You also do not need to provide any preconditions at this stage. Later, you can code in certain requirements to increase the validity of the simulation. For example, you might need to test for injector temperature, subspace anomalies, and so on. I have also not provided any special exception handlers here. You don't really need them at this stage. But you would need to add exception handlers if you were testing for temperature and other preconditions before starting up the injector.

Note   *Exception handling is discussed in depth in Chapter 11.*

Now, if you are going to start the warp engines, you will need to stop them as well, so write another simple modification method to do this and call it **StopInjector**. The code for this method is identical to the code for the **StartInjector** method, only it performs the opposite. The specification and code for the **StopInjector** method is as follows:

■ **Method definition: StopInjector**. The method stops the injector and sets the state of the warp drive to off (no preconditions or parameters are required).

```
Public Sub StopInjector()
```

■ **Postcondition:** The state of the warp drive is set to off.

The code should be as follows:

```
'Stop the warp engines
Public Overrides Sub StopInjector()
  warpDrive = False
    injectorStatus = "Injector is Offline"
  End Sub
Public Sub
```

Before you execute code that actually increases warp speed, you need to check if the warp drive is set to on. The following is the specification for the **SetWarpSpeed** method:

■ **Method definition: SetWarpSpeed (ByVal newWarpSpeed As Integer)**. The method sets the warp speed (no preconditions are required).

```
Public Sub SetWarpSpeed(ByVal newWarpSpeed As Integer)
```

■ **Parameters:** The parameter **newWarpSpeed** is provided in the range of 0 – 8 (warp 9 has not been tested yet).

■ **Precondition:** The method must first test if the warp drive is on (or the warp core could breach, because there would be no place to transfer the energy). It must then test if the **newWarpSpeed** parameter is legal (less than warp 9).

■ **Postcondition:** The state of the warp drive is set to on.

■ **Exceptions:** This method throws exceptions.

By throwing exceptions, you will test the precondition (instead of using flow control statements). **DriveNotOnException** is thrown if the warp drive is not set to on (**warpDrive = True**) and **IllegalWarpParamException** is thrown if the engineer (or any accidental activation of the method, for that matter) tries to set the warp speed above 8 with the **WarpFactorEnum.ImpulsePlusInfinity** value (lest you'll take the ship to infinity—ne'er to be heard from again).

When working with exception handlers, code is placed between **Try** . . . **Catch** blocks. This was introduced in Chapter 7 and is fully discussed in Chapter 11. While

Visual Basic still supports the classic **On Error** mechanisms of the past (mainly to help porting), you will not find many examples of it in this book.

The following code represents the first version of the **SetWarpSpeed** method:

```
    'Set warp speed
Public Overrides Sub SetWarpSpeed(ByVal newWarpSpeed As Integer)
  Try
    If Not warpDrive Then
      Throw New DriveNotOnException()
    End If
    Try
      If newWarpSpeed > warpSettings.ImpulsePlusEight Or
        newWarpSpeed < warpSettings.Impulse Then
        Throw New IllegalWarpParamException()
      End If
      warpSpeed = newWarpSpeed
    Catch F As IllegalWarpParamException
      'shut down warp drive to prevent warp core breach
      warpSpeed = warpSettings.Impulse
      StopInjector()
      injectorStatus = "Stopping on invalid warp setting. "
    End Try
  Catch E As DriveNotOnException
    'update object status field
    injectorStatus = "warp drive was not started"
    Return
  End Try
End Sub
```

That's the entire implementation of the **ShuttleInjector** class (verion 1.0). You can access in the Vb7cr solution, in the Shuttles project. The **BaseInjector** assembly also includes the enumeration for warp factor constants and the two exception classes you see in the **SetWarpSpeed** method. I know you are anxious to test this code, so let's dive into publishing and using the **ShuttleInjector** class.

Publishing the ShuttleInjector Class

Publishing your class, or making it available to consumers of your application, is very simple on the .NET platform. There are two ways to use the **ShuttleInjector** class. You can directly import the source class file into your application, or you can compile the class and lock it up in an assembly. If you have no issue distributing the source, or your user has permission to use the source, then compiling it is the extra step you might not need.

To simply compile your class and place it into an assembly and use it in your application, go to the Build menu in Visual Studio and choose Build (the shortcut is CTRL-SHIFT-B). To use the class directly or reference the assembly, follow the steps described in the next section. If you are not yet familiar with the Visual Studio compiler, I suggest you read Chapter 7 and Chapter 17.

Typically, you would want to build the class and make it an assembly, or include it with other files in your collection. The main reasons you do that are to prevent consumers from changing the class and for version control. If you publish a class and secure it to a central location on your developer network, then the consumers of the class can all use the class, and will be able to trust that no other consumer has altered it, or changed its original specification.

The ingeniousness of a class is that it can be used in many different ways. In the following example you will see how you can use the object behind a simple user interface, an interactive testing form, to test each property and method. (Console-based applications are useful for testing classes and observing how your methods will be used in other applications, because you do not have to waste a lot of time inheriting forms and coding events under button clicks, and so on. However, as soon you need a little interaction from a user, console-based applications are no longer useful. As a rule, consoles should be used as a simple facility for displaying information and taking simple command-line arguments.)

Activating the ShuttleInjector Class

To use the **ShuttleInjector** source code in your new project, follow these steps:

1. Go to the Project menu in Visual Studio .NET and choose Add Existing Items. You can also do this on the Project menu in Solution Explorer.

2. Locate the file and click OK. (You can also right-click the Project node in Solution Explorer and choose Add, then choose Add Existing Items.) The source file now appears in Solution Explorer, under your project node.

3. Before you can use the class to instantiate **ShuttleInjector** objects, you must include the **Imports** statement immediately after the options directives (which always come first), as follows:

```
Imports VB7cr.Shuttles
Public Class YourClass

. . .
```

If you want to use the assembly containing the **ShuttleInjector** class, then follow these steps:

1. Go to the Project menu in Visual Studio .NET and choose Add Reference.

2. Locate the assembly and add it as a reference, and then click OK. The source assembly now appears in Solution Explorer, under your project's References

node. (You can also expand the Project node in Solution Explorer, right-click the References node, and choose Add Reference.)

3. Before you can use the assembly to instantiate **ShuttleInjector** objects include the **Imports** statement immediately after the options directives, as shown in the earlier code.

Now we are ready to start using the referenced classes in our application.

To test the **ShuttleInjector** class, we need to activate a single **ShuttleInjector** object and let it send status information to a simple user interface. We can also use the user interface to get input from the engineer, such as starting and stopping the injector, setting the warp speed, and so on. To reference an object of type **ShuttleInjector** from the user interface we need to provide the necessary code to instantiate it. This is achieved as follows (after first importing the assembly that contains the **ShuttleInjector** class):

```
Dim shuttleInj As New ShuttleInjector()
```

We do not need many components on the initial form to begin interacting with and testing the **shuttleInj** object. Starting and stopping the injector requires user input so we'll need a start and a stop button to let the user start and stop the injector. We can wire up the properties and methods to the button, as demonstrated in the following code:

```
'start button
Private Sub Button1_Click(ByVal sender As System.Object, _
  ByVal e As System.EventArgs) Handles Button1.Click
  shuttleInj.StartInjector()
End Sub

'stop button
Private Sub Button2_Click(ByVal sender As System.Object, _
  ByVal e As System.EventArgs) Handles Button2.Click
  shuttleInj.StopInjector()
End Sub
```

We also need the user to select the warp factor. This can be best provided using a **ComboBox** control, and the standard one that ships in the Visual Studio toolbox is sufficient. The following line of code submits the warp factor value to the **SetWarpSpeed** method in the **shuttleInj** object.

```
'choose the warp speed
Private Sub ComboBox1_SelectedIndexChanged(ByVal sender As Object, _
```

```
    ByVal e As System.EventArgs) Handles
CommandBox1.SelectedIndexChanged
    If shuttleInj.DriveState Then
        shuttleInj.SetWarpSpeed(ComboBox1.SelectedIndex)
    End If
End Sub
```

Notice in the above code that we first test the **DriveState** value so that we don't cause the injector to blow a fuse. Lastly, a timer component would be useful to update the information being displayed on the form. This is achieved easily in a timer's **Tick** event handler:

```
Private Sub Timer1_Tick(ByVal sender As System.Object, _
    ByVal e As System.EventArgs) Handles Timer1.Tick
    ListBox1.Items.Clear()
    ListBox1.Items.Insert(0, "Drive State: " & shuttleInj.DriveState)
    ListBox1.Items.Insert(1, "Injector State: " & shuttleInj.InjectorState)
    ListBox1.Items.Insert(2, "MPS: " & shuttleInj.MPS)
    ListBox1.Items.Insert(3, "Current Warp: " & shuttleInj.GetSpeed)
End Sub
```

Firing up the injector is simply a matter of executing the form and clicking the start button (of course, the **ShuttleInjector** is just a simulator that still needs to be wired to I/O ports and interfaced to a warp coil injector before it can be any more useful than it currently is).

The running application is shown here.

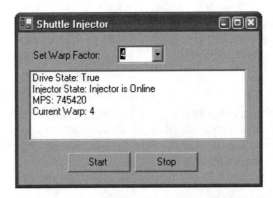

You can test its tolerance for exceptions by selecting an invalid warp value in the **ComboBox** control. The object simply "absorbs" the exception behind the scenes as it tests the incoming values in the **SetWarpSpeed** method and sends a message to the user interface, as shown.

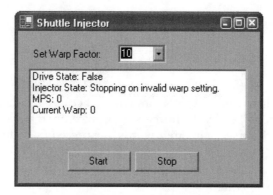

For more information on event-driven programming and forms, see Chapters 14 and 16, respectively.

The Inherited Members of Object

As mentioned earlier in this chapter, there is more to the class you created than meets the eye. This is true because the root object of all types in the .NET Framework is **Object**. No matter what class you create, it will inherit the members of **Object** the framework requires to be inherited. The **Object** hierarchy is introduced in Chapter 2. Chapter 3 demonstrates using Visual Studio .NET's Object Browser.

Note *While modules are attached to the **Object** hierarchy, they do not inherit, nor can they be part of any inheritance hierarchy.*

If you inspect the **ShuttleInjector** object in the Object Browser, you will notice the members it inherited from **Object**. Another place to observe the inherited elements is with the WinCV application. Chances are you already observed this when writing the class, as demonstrated earlier. These methods are exposed to you for a good reason. For example, the **New** and **Finalize** methods are the constructor and destructor definitions, respectively—and you cannot create objects without them, even though they often do nothing until implementation is called for. So, let's look at these inherited methods and what they give you.

Testing for Reference Equality with Equals

In the last chapter, we talked about the difference between comparing objects and comparing the reference variables to them (what they refer to). Now, let's look at how you can use the **Equals** method on objects.

The **Equals** method is a function that has only one argument, an object **Obj** (or **Object**). When you execute the following code,

```
If Sim1.Equals(Sim2) Then
'  . . .
End If
```

would you expect the method call to return **True** and cause the code to step into the **If...Then** structure? If you said yes, you are wrong, because the default behavior of the **Equals** method as prescribed by the framework is to compare the variable references and not the value of the objects. In other words, the preceding code is no different than the following:

```
If (Sim1 Is Sim2) Then
'  . . .
End If
```

But, if you wish to compare the objects (that is, check whether the values of the two objects are value for value, bit for bit, the same), you need to both overload the method (replace its parameters) and reimplement (override) it in the derived class. (Overloading and overriding are similar concepts and are discussed in Chapter 7.)

This reimplementation of the **Equals** method is a powerful feature because you, the class implementor, get to decide what constitutes equality of the values of objects derived from the same type. Have a look at the following method you enhance in the injector class:

```
Public Overloads Overrides Function Equals(ByVal Obj As Object)_
   As Boolean
If (Obj.GetType() Is Me.GetType()) Then
    Return True
End If
```

Has it sunk in yet? Here's what's going on: The method in the base class **Object** only compares the references, and we learned earlier that if the references reference the same object, the return value will be **True**. So, by reimplementing the method in **ShuttleInjector**, you can customize what gets evaluated, how it gets evaluated, and what gets returned. The specification and implementation of your **Equals** method is left entirely up to you.

In the preceding example, we have decided to compare the objects by simply calling the inherited **GetType** method (discussed shortly), and if the **GetType** methods of both objects return the same values, the comparison will be **True**.

Now, check out the code used by the consumer of the **Injector** class:

```
If Sim1.Equals(Sim2)Then
. . .
End If
```

Gee. It's the same code used earlier, only this time it returns **True**, because we are no longer comparing references; we are comparing payload. Reason: We are calling the new **Equals** method and not the version in the base class. The only problem with the implementation shown here is that **GetType** is not appropriate for comparing objects value for value. **GetType** only returns the exact run-time type of the instance. You need to compare the members and the data of each object as well.

Yet the flexibility you have can also be a loaded shotgun. The consumer of your classes might make decisions on a return value of **True** while some critical values remain different. So, you obviously need to document the API and the method calls very carefully and be sure of your design. You can also implement the **Equals** method in such a way as to be sure that each object being compared actually compares, from one end of the object to the other. A few tricks are available to help, discussed later in this chapter and in the forthcoming chapters.

ToString

What the heck is **ToString**? This is a question I hear from many new programmers, in the Java world as well. This is another *overridable* method that, in many implementations, simply returns a string representing the fully qualified object name (FQON). But it is most often used to provide the **String** representation of a type's value. So, the following code,

```
If Sim1.Equals(Sim2) Then
  Console.WriteLine(Sim1.ToString())
  Console.WriteLine(Sim2.ToString())
End If
```

will output to the console as follows:

```
ConsoleApplication.Injector
ConsoleApplication.Injector
```

Notice that it returns the name of the instance, not the name given the reference variable.

However, *overridable* is the key here and, thus, like **Equals**, you can implement the derived method to suit your application. For example, take a peek at the following code:

```
Dim Str As String = "Foo Bar"
Console.WriteLine(Str.ToString())
```

This **ToString** call does not return the FQON. Instead, it returns the actual string assigned the object. So the console output is **Foo Bar**.

You can have a lot of fun with this method, and it can be very handy with other stuff you will learn in later chapters (and you also saw it in action with the **Structure** and **Enum** classes in the last chapter). For now, let's override the method because the default return value not only is boring, it also is not very useful to consumers of the class. Here's a new version of the **ToString** method you can add to your injector class:

```
Public Overrides Function ToString() As String
   Return "Injector Class, Version 2.0. June 2001."
End Function
```

Cloning

You will find a number of frequently used patterns in OO software development where it is convenient for you to make additional, identical instances of an object. This is known as *cloning*. A clone is an identical copy of an object, but it remains a completely separate entity from the master copy—just like Dolly the sheep. When you clone an object, you end up with a new object and a new reference variable to that object.

The CLS supports two types of clone procedures: *shallow clones* and *deep clones*. A shallow clone lets you make an identical copy of an object, as illustrated in the next chapter. A deep clone lets you make a copy of the object and any references to other objects being maintained by the object.

To make a simple shallow clone, the root **Object** gives you a method called **MemberWiseClone**. This is illustrated in the following example:

```
Public Sub Carbonize()
   Dim Sim1 = New Injector()
   Dim Sim2 = New Injector()
   Sim1.SetWarpSpeed(4)
   Sim2 = Sim1.MemberwiseClone();
End Sub
```

The **MemberWiseClone** method is protected, which means you cannot override its functionality and reimplement it (that, of course, does not stop you from creating a custom **Clone** method that clones an object according to a new pattern you wish to implement). But to use the base method, it will only be available to derived classes or **Me**, the current instant of the class. You will deal with cloning, deep cloning, and the **ICloneable** interface in Chapter 10. (By the way, the Java architects also spelled their **Cloneable** interface with an *e* in the middle—which is not exactly correct. Interesting coincidence, or is it that all software architects can't spell?)

GetHashCode

A discussion of genetic cloning will almost certainly lead to discussions about DNA. When talking about the cloning of objects, the discussion will usually include the hash code subject. A simple definition of a hash code is that it is an integer key, created on the contents of an object, which can be used as a means of searching and sorting objects.

The **GetHashCode** method is used to implement hash tables, which are used for doing fast lookups by key. A hash table makes use of the key to increase the efficiency of searching and sorting objects, and there are various tried patterns for its use.

Every object in .NET produces a hash code, and the **GetHashCode** method implements a very simple hashing function that produces a simple key. In fact, everything you do generates hash codes, because everything in .NET is an object. The elements in a list of URLs in a browser have associated hash codes, a collection of IP addresses have associated hash codes, and the elements in an array have associated hash codes. Every .NET programmer should have an unshakeable understanding of hash codes and hash tables.

In Chapter 12, you will look into what's involved in using hash tables, but for now, check out what the **GetHashCode** method retrieves. Adding the following line to your code,

```
Console.WriteLine(Sim2.GetHashCode())
```

writes integer "3" to the console (your compiler will probably return some similar number). How amazingly scientific is *that* result for one of the cornerstones of computer science?

You are probably thinking, "That doesn't look very unique either." It isn't. **GetHashCode** is another important method that is left up to the class implementors to override. The base class version simply returns an index value representing the class instance (the CLR chooses it, and not long after I tested it, it returned 3 for an **Object** that had already been disposed of), so it is very possible that it will not be unique. In fact, only the strongest hashing functions will produce a (relatively) unique hash code for you.

Making **GetHashCode** overridable is correct behavior, similar to the reason **Equals** is overridable. This mandates that you reimplement it using the hashing algorithm of your choice. This is the case with all OO languages. Stay tuned for more on this subject in Chapter 12.

GetType

You had a look at the **GetType** method earlier, in the discussion of the **Equals** method, so you know that it returns the exact run-time type of the argument. So, the statement

```
Console.WriteLine(Sim2.GetType)
```

just returns the FQON.

ReferenceEquals

The **ReferenceEquals** method lets you compare the variable references of two objects, to determine if they refer to the same object. It works like the default implementation of the **Equals** method, but you do not have to override the implementation (the method is *not* overridable).

You might be tempted to ask why the architects provided this method, if it has the esteemed **Equals** to do that work? If you do decide to reimplement the **Equals** method as shown earlier, then when you need a simple conditional element to check if two variables reference the same object, **ReferenceEquals** comes to the rescue. Here's an example:

```
Sim1 = Sim2
If Object.ReferenceEquals(Sim2, Sim1) Then
  Debug.WriteLine(Sim1.GetHashCode())
  Debug.WriteLine(Sim2.GetHashCode())
End If
```

In this piece of brilliant code, **Object.ReferenceEquals** returns **True** because the variable references were assigned one to the other (**Sim1 = Sim2**). And as an added bonus, the **GetHashCode** statements display "3" to the console on both lines—because both variables refer to the same object.

Finalize

The architects of CLS decided to give us a **Finalize** method. What is it good for? In its original state—absolutely nothing. And that's because a garbage collector (or GC, as discussed in Chapter 2) does the housekeeping for you, making sure that discarded objects are purged from the CLR, an so on.

When an object is discarded, or when an application or process terminates, the GC automatically cleans up for you. But there might be a specific pattern or algorithm that requires you to override this "placeholder" method. Just making it a habit of good design is reason enough to call **Finalize** in its simplest form: a method that overrides **Finalize** to provide a mechanism to call the base **Finalize** method to do some customer housekeeping and "mark" the current object for collection by the GC. The following code is one example:

```
Protected Overrides Sub Finalize()
  MyBase.Finalize()
End Sub
```

Class implementers and component writers might require such control, and interoperability with legacy objects. In the COM world for example, objects will require explicit finalization. For the most part, you can work without worrying about this method.

Aggregation and Composition: Reuse by Containment

As you work with classes, you'll begin to discover certain repetitive patterns emerging that dictate how classes relate to each other. You'll find that the initial design of the framework and implementation of the class diagrams are effectively achieved with inheritance, but as you get into the details of how that application actually works, continuous extension of classes neither applies nor works.

As stated earlier, inheritance has its place in the foundations of your class hierarchies, but implementation (putting it together) requires alternative thought and design. Think like a farmer: First you till the soil, then you sow the seeds, then you harvest. You can't sow the seeds or harvest until you have tilled the land, but all the steps are required before you can start thinking about going to market.

We have sown the seeds with inheritance and implementing base classes, but now we need alternative techniques to reap what we have sown. Aggregation and composition are two techniques in OOP that allow us to reuse existing code and collaborate with other implementations.

Some OOP experts make a distinction between *composition* and *aggregation;* others will tell you they both mean the same thing. At the conceptual level, expressing an alternative to the *is-a* relationship, that may be true. But at the implementation level there are important differences, as you will shortly see.

While inheritance represents the *is-a* relationship between classes, aggregation and composition represent the *has-a* relationship between classes. A bus, for example, *has* seats for its passengers, but a bus *is not a* seat. The seats are embedded in the bus as member objects. Seats have their own class hierarchy, as do busses. The hierarchies of both classes remain separate and distinct because a bus cannot be a seat and visa versa. This is shown in Figure 9-11.

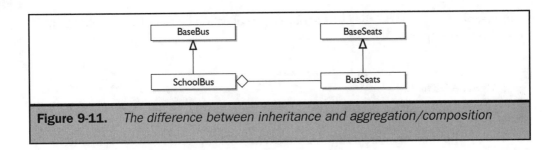

Figure 9-11. *The difference between inheritance and aggregation/composition*

Aggregation is exactly how your form classes come to life with all manner of functionality. You embed components and controls onto the form, like buttons and text boxes. Forms, buttons, and text boxes, however, are distinctly separate objects. A form is not a text box and a text box is not a button (although there may be traces of a common ancestor far back up the chain in the base classes for components and controls).

The aggregation rule states that aggregation is represented by has-a *relationships between classes. If* **ClassA** *has-a* **ClassB**, *then* **ClassB** *should be aggregated or composed in* **ClassA**.

Where *aggregation* differs from *composition* is that aggregate objects or *aggregates* are sub-types that are *embedded* in the container class and composite classes or *composites* are classes that are *composed* in the container class. Aggregates are not exclusive to their container and may be embedded in other containers. Aggregates can be any exposed types in any assembly that can be declared and instantiated in the container class. Composites on the other hand are exclusive to their container. They are formally declared and implemented in a container class as a composite or *nested* class.

Additionally you always have direct access to the implementation, or source code, in a composite class. Aggregate objects are not exposed in this manner; you have no access to their implementation and source (their non-exclusivity is represented in UML by the open diamond shape shown in Figure 9-6). The remainder of this section explores aggregation in more detail while composition is pervasive in the patterns described in Chapters 12 through 14.

To understand when we need to aggregate let's tackle another space-age project. Imagine that on our spacecraft, the captain decides that the food replicator should be extended to cater to fast food. One of the first recipes she or he wants coded into the system is a good old-fashioned burger from the 20th century and you have the job of upgrading the replicator software. So, you set out to first design a class for your burger patty. Burger patties are usually round, and we'll want to specify certain sizes for our patty, including the circumference, area, and so on. Thus, initially, it makes sense to extend the class **Circle** as the base for the **Patty** class.

But the **Circle** class is missing a method to specify the height of the patty. So, do we now add a height method and field to our **Circle** class, or do we look for a class that already implements a height method? Turns out the more-specialized class **Cylinder** is available with the exact functionality we need. So, our **Patty** class can safely extend **Cylinder**, which extends **Circle**.

As Figure 9-12 illustrates, we now have a class hierarchy as the basis for generating patties out of thin air.

When we are ready to broil our burger patties, we will need to construct a method that creates the patty. We will thus be able to send a message to the inherited methods that set the size of the patty, a method for patty diameter, and a method for patty height (and other ingredients, the discussion of which is beyond the scope of this book). This inheritance chain is demonstrated in the following code:

```
Public Class Circle
  Function CreateCircle(ByVal diameter As Integer) As Circle
  'to be implemented
  End Function
End Class

Public Class Cylinder : Inherits Circle
  Function CreateCylinder(ByVal height As Integer) As Cylinder
    'To be implemented
  End Function
End Class

Public Class Patty : Inherits Cylinder
  'declare patty ingredients here
  Sub Createpatty(ByVal height As Double, ByVal diameter As Double)
    'To be implemented in the year 2345
  End Sub
End Class
```

At this particular point, you can see that **Patty** qualifies to inherit from the aforementioned class hierarchy, because a patty *is-a* **Circle** and (also) *is-a* **Cylinder**. But is this where the inheritance line ends?

As you can see, we can create the dimensions for a patty by using the functions inherited from **Circle** and **Cylinder**. But now we need to add more ingredients to our burger. Tomatoes are a requirement of burgers, and we can easily add a **CreateTomato** method to the **Patty** class. This would really be a silly idea, though, because surely a method

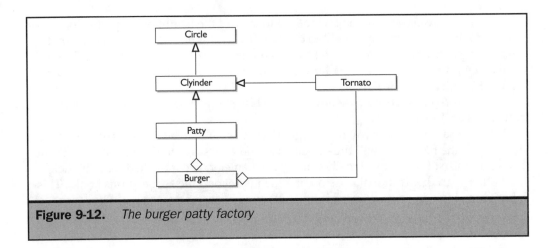

Figure 9-12.   *The burger patty factory*

for replicating tomatoes exists in the replicator software already. Guess what? It does. A stand-alone **Tomato** class that also ultimately inherits **Circle** and **Cylinder** exists.

How do we reuse the methods in **Tomato**? For starters, we could simply make it that **Patty** extends **Tomato**. Okay, hold it, time out; we have just made the classic inheritance mistake. (The skeptics are now saying "See, told you so!") How can **Patty** extend **Tomato**? We have just insulted every vegetarian in the universe. Besides, while there is nothing stopping us from doing this, we will really muck up our clean code, good and proper. What happens when we just want to replicate a burger patty and not add tomatoes? **Tomato** has a right to exist as a separate class because tomatoes are used in many recipes.

The multiple inheritance (MI) would also muck up our code, even if it were possible in .NET. The first problem would be the clash of method signatures, because we would have two hierarchies deriving from **Circle** and **Cylinder**. So, think about the burger for a moment and not the code or the class. Tomatoes are placed inside burgers, between the patty and the bun. Why not just add the **Tomato** and the **Patty** class to a **Burger** class, just as you would in the kitchen?

This pattern (which is a technique) is called *aggregation*. As mentioned earlier, the application of the rule to determine when composition is valid is similar to the application of the inheritance rule. Instead of asking if a thing *is-a* thing, you ask if the thing *has-a* thing. In our case, the rule fits. A burger has a tomato or more, and has a patty or two; tomatoes do not have burgers, nor patties. And for that matter, our inheritance architecture is also sound because we know that a circle *is-not-a* burger. Remember, the rule states that aggregation (and composition) is represented by *has-a* relationships between classes. If **ClassX** *has-a* **ClassR**, then **ClassR** should be contained in **ClassX**.

You'll probably be surprised to learn that we have been using aggregation from the very beginning, even before we inherited one line of code. As discussed in the previous chapter and in Chapter 4, the fundamental types are also objects. So, we are really using the technique when we declare an **Integer** or a **String** object to reference the variable or constant data in our class. We are simply embedding these objects in our new class. Back to patty making.

We can now begin constructing our patty by referencing both **Patty** and **Tomato** classes in the **Burger** class. Once we have done this, adding the other classes, like **Pickle**, **Ketchup**, and **Onion**, should be a no-brainer. Adding methods for controlling calories and fat is a different matter, however.

The code for our **Burger** class can now be basically implemented as follows:

```
Public Class Burger
  Friend Patty1 As Patty()
  Friend Tomato1 As Tomato

  Private Sub GoBurger()
    Me.Patty1.Createpatty(2, 10)
    Me.Patty1.Location = New BunPosition(60, 140)
    Me.Tomato1.CreateTomato(1, 8)
    Me.Tomato1.Location = New BunPosition(60, 140)
  End Sub

End Class
```

If you now look at the code, you'll notice something truly incredible with OOP. Through both inheritance *and* aggregation, we are able to reuse all the previously implemented code for the benefit of the **Burger** implementation. We are reusing not only the code previously written only for the independent **Tomato** class, but also the code for any other "ingredients" of **Burger**. We will not implement the **Burger** class further because I am sure you now have the idea, and besides, replicator technology has not yet been invented (and when that day comes we will be ready).

It is also important to mention that classes that make wise use of composition patterns—using sealed classes as often as possible—will provide much potential for the improvement in performance of your applications. See the section "Ending Inheritance with Sealed Classes," later in this chapter.

More Aggregation at Work: A Form for Testing

Another good example of how inheritance and aggregation come together to create extensible composite objects is the **Form** class. As mentioned earlier in this chapter, forms derive from a long line of ancestors. If you examine the **Form** hierarchy in the .NET Framework documentation, you see a line of "in-laws" long enough to make your hair stand up. Imagine, without inheritance, we would have to re-create all of that each time we needed a form, or at least make an untold number of copies of it. It was once like that, mind you, when it would take a week just to draw a dialog box.

If you have created a Windows application project and looked at the code behind the main form, the first thing you probably noticed is that it inherits from **System .Windows.Forms.Form**. But there is not much else for something as complex as a form; there must be more to it than what meets the eye. There is; just examine the **Form** class in WinCV and you'll quiver at the long list of members hiding in the hierarchy. This is very different from how forms were given to us in VB 6 and earlier, in which the forms just seemed to come from nowhere.

Creating a Windows application is easy. You just go to the New Project dialog box in Visual Studio, as described in Chapter 3, and select the Windows Application icon. Visual Studio automatically generates a single form and provides all the necessary innards to render the form in the designer. The Toolbox, which is chock-full of visual controls, is also activated when you are in Design mode—that is, when you are looking at the form and not the code behind it.

So, let's create a Windows application. But instead of taking the shortcut and having Visual Studio set up the whole project, let's do the job of creating the form manually. By the end of the exercise, it will be clear to you how we create a composite object, such as a form for interaction, from inheritance and containment.

Instead of creating a Windows application, just create a project and add it to a single class. Name this class **Formlet** and then take the following steps:

1. Add a reference to the assemblies System.Drawing and System.Windows .Forms. These assemblies contain the classes that you'll need for drawing the forms and the components, like buttons.

2. Add an **Imports** statement to the class and reference the class **System.Windows .Forms.Form**. You can also reference the namespace in the Imports list in your project's Property Pages dialog box (this is described in Chapter 3). As soon as you reference the **Form** class, Visual Studio picks this up and shows the default form to you in the designer.

3. Go back to the Property Pages dialog box. Under the Common Properties folder, select General and then choose Windows Application for the Output Type. This will allow the compiler to run the **Formlet** application for you as a stand-alone application for testing purposes. (You can also invoke the form from any other class, as we intend to do in a bit.)

4. Provide a **New** constructor as follows. You now have the makings of a form. The code for the **Formlet** class should now look like the following:

```
Imports System.Windows.Forms
Public Class Formlet
   Inherits System.Windows.Forms.Form
   Public Sub New()
     MyBase.New()
```

```
   InitializeComponent()
End Sub


Protected Overloads Overrides Sub Dispose(ByVal disposing_
   As Boolean)
   If disposing Then
     If Not (components Is Nothing) Then
      components.Dispose()
     End If
   End If
   MyBase.Dispose(disposing)
End Sub


End Class
```

This code now activates the functionality in the hierarchy to produce a blank form. You can view the form in all its glory by selecting the little form icon in Solution Explorer under the project you created. Right-click the form and select View Designer.

5. The next option is to add some useful controls to the form. Again, you can drag and drop the controls you need from the Toolbox's Windows Forms tab to the form. But by doing it the easy way, you miss observing composition and containment in action. Rather, change the code view by right-clicking the form again under your project in Solution Explorer and selecting View Code. You will now be back at the code behind the form. Now, we need to add a textbox to the form for output, a couple of edit fields for input, and a button to make something happen. Do we do this by inheriting from the classes of these components? Not on your life (remember the burger example; a button is not a form and a form is not a textbox). The way we add components is by nesting each class in the form class. The form class thus becomes the container, the outer class, for the inner component classes. In fact, the form class can now become the container for a lot of inner classes that would be awkward to reference by association, as you will soon see. We can embed the components as demonstrated in the following code:

```
Private components As System.ComponentModel.IContainer
Friend WithEvents Button1 As System.Windows.Forms.Button
Friend WithEvents Button2 As System.Windows.Forms.Button
Friend WithEvents ListBox1 As System.Windows.Forms.ListBox
Friend WithEvents ComboBox1 As System.Windows.Forms.ComboBox
Friend WithEvents Label1 As System.Windows.Forms.Label
Friend WithEvents Timer1 As System.Windows.Forms.Timer
```

This code simply declares reference variables that will instantiate the contained visual components aggregated to the **Formlet** class. The aggregate objects can thus directly collaborate with the container form class. (Refer to Chapter 4's section for information about the visibility provided by the **Friend** modifier. The modifier **WithEvents** is discussed in Chapter 14 and Chapter 16.)

6. The following code now sets up and positions the visual components on the form:

```
Private Sub InitializeComponent()
    Me.components = New System.ComponentModel.Container()
    Me.Button1 = New System.Windows.Forms.Button()
    Me.Button2 = New System.Windows.Forms.Button()
    Me.ListBox1 = New System.Windows.Forms.ListBox()
    Me.ComboBox1 = New System.Windows.Forms.ComboBox()
    Me.Label1 = New System.Windows.Forms.Label()
    Me.Timer1 = New System.Windows.Forms.Timer(Me.components)
    Me.SuspendLayout()

    Me.Button1.Location = New System.Drawing.Point(60, 140)
    Me.Button1.Name = "Button1"
    Me.Button1.TabIndex = 0
    Me.Button1.Text = "Start"

    Me.Button2.Location = New System.Drawing.Point(140, 140)
    Me.Button2.Name = "Button2"
    Me.Button2.TabIndex = 1
    Me.Button2.Text = "Stop"

    Me.ListBox1.Location = New System.Drawing.Point(13, 44)
    Me.ListBox1.Name = "ListBox1"
    Me.ListBox1.Size = New System.Drawing.Size(260, 82)
    Me.ListBox1.TabIndex = 2

    Me.ComboBox1.Items.AddRange(New Object() {"0", "1", "2", "3"})
    Me.ComboBox1.Location = New System.Drawing.Point(120, 16)
    Me.ComboBox1.Name = "ComboBox1"
    Me.ComboBox1.Size = New System.Drawing.Size(56, 21)
    Me.ComboBox1.TabIndex = 3
    Me.ComboBox1.Text = "0"

    Me.Label1.Location = New System.Drawing.Point(16, 20)
    Me.Label1.Name = "Label1"
    Me.Label1.Size = New System.Drawing.Size(96, 16)
    Me.Label1.TabIndex = 4
    Me.Label1.Text = "Set Warp Factor:"
```

```
    Me.Timer1.Enabled = True
    Me.Timer1.Interval = 10
    Me.AutoScaleBaseSize = New System.Drawing.Size(5, 13)
    Me.ClientSize = New System.Drawing.Size(288, 177)
    Me.Controls.AddRange(New System.Windows.Forms.Control() _
      {Me.Label1, Me.ComboBox1, Me.ListBox1, Me.Button2, Me.Button1})
    Me.Name = "Form1"
    Me.Text = "Formlet"
    Me.ResumeLayout(False)
  End Sub
```

That's all there is to creating a form we can now use instead of a console application to interact with the user. While there is no small amount of code on this form and "above" it in the framework, using it for some of the more complex things we want to do in later chapters will be much easier than using the **Console** class, as you saw with our little Shuttle Injector application shown earlier.

With that ultimate and highly elegant demonstration of combining inheritance and aggregation or composition, we move on to two important options for classes where inheritance and aggregation do not play a part—sealed classes and shared classes.

Ending Inheritance with Sealed Classes

Sealed classes are also known as *final* classes in object-oriented parlance. In other words, a sealed class cannot be derived from and thus cannot beget child classes or become a superclass or a base class. This sealing off of the class applies to its members as well. The methods of a sealed class can be called, but they too are final—locked down in a sealed object. An attempt to derive from a sealed class will not go down well with the compiler.

The following code creates a sealed class:

```
NotInheritable Class FinalInjector
   Inherits RocketInjector
End Class
```

Why would you seal a class? Two reasons: First, you may not feel it appropriate to allow other classes to derive from this class (at least not until you are ready to release it). Second, a sealed class can increase run-time performance because the compiler can inline any implied virtual (inheritable) function member invocations into nonvirtual function member invocations. In other words, the compiler does not need to provide for an alternate implementation at a later time, and thus the memory addresses of the members and the method implementation are set at compile time.

Unless you intend a class to be extended, you should seal it. Whenever the compiler encounters inheritance potential, it has to provide for this potential with various binding and referencing techniques, all of which cater to polymorphism, binding, and so on. This is not the case with sealed classes that can be used in composition design, which thus would improve performance.

Improved Performance with Shared Classes and Modules

Shared classes are classes that are explicitly declared not inheritable (so they are final) and can be made so they cannot be instantiated, which means there will always be only one copy of the class and its members. Shared classes (also known as static classes) are useful for collections of like utility methods that do not need the overhead of instantiation into objects.

A good example of such a utility method is a method that opens a file. There is no need to have more than one copy of this method in your application, because once the method has serviced a thread, it is ready to service another thread. The data passed to the method's parameters is discarded and a new argument arrives to provide new data (a new file and path name) of a file to be opened. The **File** class is a good example of a .NET Framework shared or final class. The following code is an example of a sealed class that is also shared and thus cannot be instantiated:

```
NotInheritable Class TheEnd

   Shared ata As Integer
   Shared ing As String
   Shared ouble As Double
   Shared cimal As Decimal

   Private Sub New()
      'this sub aint going anywhere
   End Sub

   Shared Sub StaticSub()
   End Sub

End Class
```

How do you make a class static? Simply declare it **NotInheritable**, as demonstrated in the preceding code. This is, however, not enough to prevent instantiation, so you need to provide a **New** constructor and lock it down with the **Private** modifier. This will prevent a consumer or user of the method from attempting to invoke **New**. They will just get a compiler error.

Declaring a class as **NotInheritable** does not implicitly make all the class members static or shared. To make each class member (including fields and properties) static, modify them to static with the **Shared** keyword.

Visual Basic, however, provides an additional shared class over the other .NET languages: the module (the equivalent of the C# *sealed* class). Modules do not have any instantiation potential whatsoever, and using them is akin to creating modules in structure-oriented languages. All the members in a class are implicitly shared, which is very convenient. When you automatically create a console application, for example, via the New Project dialog box, Visual Studio automatically puts all the contents of the console application in a single module.

Refer to the chapter on methods, Chapter 7, for more information on shared methods. Also check out the .NET implementation of the famous **Singleton** pattern in Chapter 13.

Observations

There were many things to learn in this chapter, but the most important concepts we studied were inheritance and composition with .NET classes and the major differences between them. As you have seen, inheritance provides an elegant facility for code reuse and maintenance. It also supports what is fundamental to all software development, iterative and incremental development.

Inheritance provides a facility for isolating bugs in new code because the new bugs will mostly manifest in the classes that derive from the tested and debugged base classes. You can be sure that when a bug arrives in your class, the problem is in the extended class. Of course, this means too that we are putting a lot of faith in the base class library. It seems highly unlikely that in a collection of several thousand classes, there are no bugs in .NET.

We also looked at composition and containment as a means of reusing implementation and associating objects one with the other. It is thus important to point out inheritance is not a facility to get hooked on and start using everywhere and anywhere. Most of the time, your application's classes will come to life by interacting with each other through association, aggregation, composition, delegation, substitution, and various other roles and responsibilities.

A final word before we embark on a lot more code in the coming chapters. While applications need to move bits around the computer, you don't get very far in OOP by constantly dwelling in the basement where the functionality is. Instead, you should be thinking in terms of classes and objects and learn how to transform the logical and dynamic view of your models into meaningful technology that caters to the problem domain expressed by your client.

The Complete Reference

Visual
Basic
.NET

Chapter 10

Interfaces

In software development, the interface is the faculty of abstraction, coupling (loose or tight), and polymorphism. It's easy to see how interfaces facilitate polymorphism because only one version of an interface exists in a system or a framework, yet many people can implement it or program against it in *many forms* and in many places. The emphasis is on *many forms*, which is what polymorphism is.

Interfaces are deemed so important for software construction that they are one of the key Fundamental Design Patterns published in the groundbreaking work *Design Patterns* (Gamma et al.). The formal interface design pattern referred to by the object-oriented community is the *Abstract Factory* pattern. Its intent is to create families of related or dependent objects by specifying interfaces without having to specify or provide *concrete* classes (refer to Chapter 9).

> **Note**   *See* Design Patterns: Elements of Reusable Object-Oriented Software *by Erich Gamma, Richard Helm, Ralph Johnson, and John Vlissides. (Addison-Wesley, 1995.)*

But patterns are also found in many other formal patterns, such as the key Structural Iterator pattern (described in Chapter 13). In this chapter, we examine the forces behind the emergence of interface patterns and investigate the various ways in which interfaces play a role in software development. The chapters that follow will take interfaces to more advanced levels.

First we will look into abstraction: how it facilitates developing software by abstracting and hiding the complexity of the implementation behind the interface. We will also explore the implicit interfaces that exist in all .NET classes and objects, and the explicit interface you can create by using the special interface class.

We will also examine how interfaces are declared and referenced, and the various styles used to bridge interfaces to implementation classes in order to collaborate with the data and functionality behind the interface. Finally, we will examine both how to define an explicit interface and how to implement custom interfaces and the .NET interfaces that ship with the framework. In particular, we will look at the implementation of the **IClonable**, **IComparable**, and **IEnumerable** interfaces.

The formal interface class provides an important facility for polymorphism in .NET, which will be the principal concept discussed in this chapter. This chapter will also present the pros and cons of using abstract classes versus interfaces.

> **Note**   *See also "Abstract Classes" in Chapter 9.*

Abstraction and Interfaces in Object-Oriented Software Design

We take eyesight and our eyes so much for granted that we rarely think what it would be like to suddenly lose them. The act of seeing, however, is a vastly simpler act than the actual processing of the images behind the scene.

Stop and think about your eyesight for a minute. While reading this page, you likely are unaware of the intricate "implementation" of image processing that is going on behind your lenses, such as how light passes through the retina, gets inverted by the lenses, and is interpreted by the nerves at the back of your eye sockets before being processed by the brain.

Unless you are an eye surgeon, you don't think about this—you just see. Can you even imagine that the image you are currently looking at is really upside down? If you try and imagine it, you'll soon begin to notice some lightheadedness. That's the essence (and benefit) of abstraction—a process that enables us to cope with the many incredible complexities around us.

You are able to ignore the details and focus on what's relevant. If you had to stop and think about how you see every time you see, you would simply not be able to see. Abstraction is the same for software engineering. If you had to constantly focus on the minute details over every function, and even into the molecular level of the operators, you would find it impossible to write code.

In procedure-oriented design, procedural programming, the unit of abstraction is the procedure or the function. In object-oriented design, the unit of abstraction is the class, and ultimately the object of that class—a much higher level of abstraction. By encapsulating methods, properties, and data in classes, it becomes much simpler to tackle complex problems and make some headway in programming the large systems that exist today.

Another example: When a racing car driver gets into a car, he or she focuses on the drive, the road, navigation, and the competition. If the racing car driver had to focus on the engine, the gas, and the combustion forces going on inside the pistons, he or she would not be able to drive a centimeter.

Grady Booch's marvelous book *Object-Oriented Design with Applications* (The Benjamin/Cummings Publishing Company, Inc., 1991) has been an arm's reach away from my keyboard for more than a decade. In it is the following definition for abstraction in software engineering: "An abstraction denotes the essential characteristics of an object that distinguish it from all other kinds of objects and thus provide crisply defined conceptual boundaries, relative to the perspective of the viewer."

A good designer/programmer can provide a clear and concise design in the arrangement and interrelationship of objects. That same programmer or another can then write a clearly defined interface for the objects represented in the design. And that same programmer or another can write a good implementation behind that interface.

However, it is vitally important to keep each level of abstraction in the hierarchy of problem or abstraction domains separate in practice—from highest-level design to the very lines of code in the method implementations. You need to keep the various levels of abstraction in their own domains. This border between the domains, which hides the implementation and thus provides the abstraction, is called the interface.

Note | *See Chapter 7 for information on the decomposition of methods and the inner interfaces between methods in a class; see Chapter 9 for information on modeling, and Chapter 13 for more information on class secrets and information hiding.*

CLASSES AND OBJECTS

This is the reason why it is important to separate the implementation from the interface in object-oriented design and know why you are doing it. It matters not that the separation is split between two Visual Basic source code units or that the separation is within a single source code unit, with one class declaring the interface and the other declaring the implementation. It matters more that the separation actually exists and that it's part of the design. Figure 10-1 shows the "interface" in graphical terms.

Getting Passionate (or Radical) about Interfaces

Interfaces are so elegantly integrated into the .NET Framework that I cannot help being passionate about the subject. Let's explore the reason for explicit interfaces further.

To fully understand object-oriented software development "philosophy" and its many concepts, you need to understand the concept of both abstraction and interfaces and why they are so important to .NET. Not only that, explicit interface design and implementation is a key requirement for "professional grade" .NET software development—both for standard applications and algorithms and for component development. Please don't think you can program without them.

Formal interface design and implementation is not new to software development, but it is one of its most misunderstood concepts. And, as mentioned in Chapter 2, interface implementation has often been blamed for DLL hell and versioning problems. The common language runtime's versioning features and side-by-side execution environment provide a haven for numerous versions of an interface—even if they are identical—thus freeing the programmer of the burden of maintaining versions of interfaces in a registry.

A large number of interfaces actually ship with the .NET Framework base class library. They carry no implementation, which is left to the programmer who can either implement directly or bridge the interface to an implementation that may already exist.

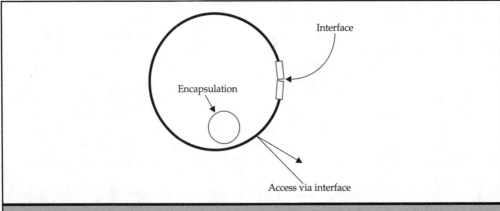

Figure 10-1.   *To access an object, you reference its interface*

Implementing an interface is a lot like implementing a Mini or some other car that everyone loves but that no one might be making any more.

Imagine walking into a store and buying just the Mini's chassis and the body and then being told by the salesperson that you now have to take home the shell and build your own internals, engine, seats, drive shaft, dashboard, and so on. You would probably be very confused at the prospect—if you don't have a nervous breakdown at the idea. Why buy a car that *you* have to implement to drive?

Here's your dilemma: As a driver of past Minis, you've never really paid much attention to the implementation. It has always been abstracted away from you. You have had only to interact and communicate through the interface: the steering wheel, shift or gear stick, accelerator, and breaks. When something went wrong with the car, you took it to the shop, which knew the ins and outs of the "implementation." Now you are faced with all the messy details of the implementation…the idea of getting your hands all greasy is the last thing you were thinking about when you bought the "interface."

Looking at the interfaces in the base class library (and there are many of them), you, the programmer, might be excused for thinking the same thing. You design and implement a really cool application that the IT department is going to love you for, and a day before your are ready to deploy, the head of the financial applications department tells you she must have encryption support. No problem! The last time you checked in the huge collection of namespaces, there were encryption classes out the wazoo.

You rush to plug one of those encryption classes into the application, and all you find are empty shells, the signatures of methods, properties, and events that are yet to be implemented. "Shucks, Microsoft was so late in delivering .NET it forgot to finish up these classes," you think. You might chuckle here, but I have actually heard exasperated calls for help along the lines of, "Okay, I plugged in **IPluggable**, but where's the beef?" I too was as befuddled years ago, when I found myself staring at empty interface classes with just the interface declares present, and searching the rest of the file proclaiming, "What's up with this? Invisible code?"

Understanding interfaces is a little easier if you understand modern engineering practice. Let's go back to the store selling Mini shells. You decide to go along with the Mini "interface." You ask the salesperson how you implement the Mini, and she refers you to a list of companies that specialize in Mini implementation. Each one of these companies implements the Mini differently, but on the outside, the Minis all look the same, only some Minis go faster than others, one implements a turbo drive, and another implements a rocket engine. There's even a company that specializes in do-it-yourself Mini implementation. For pocket change, you can read the company's manual on how to build your own Mini internals and implement them. After a while, you can become so proficient at Mini implementations that you might even go into business implementing Minis for other Mini lovers.

What do you see emerging here? You can have a whole collection of Minis that all look the same and all drive pretty much the same, except one can travel at a significant percentage of the speed of sound. No matter which Mini you climb into, the gears, steering wheel, brakes, clutch, and so on are all in exactly the same place. But you have multiple implementations of the same Mini interface…the Mini implementation is in "many forms." You are staring at "Mini-morphism" in all its glory.

The expert or practiced search routine software writers can all implement the same encryption interfaces. The interface members must be implemented, but they can all be implemented differently. For example, a search method behind an interface might implement a conditional routine to test the value of **Integer** types, but another implementation might use bitwise operations instead. The implementations are different, in many forms, but the interfaces remain the same. They have to.

Interfaces and Inheritance

One of the main factors contributing to the confusion about interfaces in object-oriented languages is the proclamation that they are a substitute for multiple inheritance and the "limitations" of even single-parent implementation inheritance. I have read this sorry confused excuse for interfaces in Java, .NET, and the official documentation of other languages: "X doesn't support multiple inheritance…but that's okay, because it supports interfaces." This is technically correct, but I have a problem with this blasé and simplistic explanation for interfaces. I believe you are just not getting it if you are going with this line.

Interfaces are not a formal substitute for inheritance, which, as discussed extensively in the last chapter, is a facility for creating families of closely related, and thus tightly coupled, classes. Thus, when a class inherits from a base class, the child or derived class is coupled to its parent—and one of the key benefits, aside from classification, is code reuse.

Interfaces do not promote the classification of objects. It is simply not why interface classes are uncoupled from the concrete classes that contain their implementation. Read the definition of the Abstract Factory pattern in *Design Patterns…* (Gamma et al.), and you will see that interfaces promote loose coupling, by allowing separate classes to interoperate.

Inheritance relationships are born of the close relationship of one class to another, a child to its parent. For example, consider employees at a company or (one of my favorite examples) the crew on a spaceship. All "staffers" are first crew or employees before they are captains, engineers, cooks, pilots, gunners, medics, and so on. In other words—as demonstrated in the UML diagrams for inheritance in Chapter 9—the communications officer on a spaceship *is-a* member of the crew. The parent class is thus **Crew**, and the subordinate, child, extended, or derived class is the **ComEngineer**.

The **Crew** class bestows all that is common about crewmembers to the descendent classes. **ComEngineer**, for example, will inherit the base members and either override, overload, or shadow the parent members.

Interfaces, on the other hand, do not allow inheritance of data and implementation, because (as we have discussed at some length) they have none.

It should thus be clear that inheritance promotes a tighter coupling of classes, while interfaces, by separating implementation from the interface, are able to promote loosely coupled and completely disconnected classes and the ability to access the implementation of unconnected objects. Most important, however, is that the interfaces drive polymorphism in the system of classes and objects that makes up your applications.

Despite the confusion about interfaces being a substitute for multiple inheritance, it is clear where the misunderstanding originates. Suppose you need to provide a new object to represent a new type of crewmember on the spaceship—the logistics crew. So, you create the class **Logistics** and derive from **Crew** to inherit all the common attributes and properties of **Crew**, such as **CrewName**, **CrewRank**, and **CrewID** fields, and methods used in authentication, sign-on, time on duty, and so on.

In the derived class, you extend the base class with members and implementation that applies to the **Logistics** class, even though the **Logistics** engineers are derivatives of **Crew**. Now you want to add support for comparing **Logistics** objects that compares fields unique to the **Logistics** objects.

The **Comparer** methods do not exist in **Crew**, so you'll have to implement the **IComparer** interface in **Logistics** instead or bridge in an implementation that already exists, to get the desired functionality available to the class. But is this a substitute for multiple or even single inheritance? No. How can the **Logistics** class, which we have said *is-a* crewmember, also be a child of the **Comparer** class? **Logistics** does not share an *is-a* relationship with the **Comparer** class—in the same way that a *raptor* is not a member of the *canine* family, or a bicycle *is-a* train when it feels like going choo, choo, choo.

In other words, *inheritance* is used in object-oriented engineering only for two purposes (as repeatedly stated in Chapters 1 and 9): to represent the *is-a* relationship (and all of its benefits) among classes, and to express a tight coupling between the classes, for code reuse.

We also touched on multiple inheritance in Chapter 9. But multiple inheritance detracts from class structure. Even if you could inherit from multiple parents, the benefit of maintaining that focused class hierarchy would be very quickly lost.

Interface implementation and class inheritance, multiple or single, do share one thing in common, however: they both contribute to polymorphism between objects and methods. But interfaces *do not* make up for the lack of multiple inheritance in object-oriented languages, because they serve distinct and very different roles.

Thus, while the *architecture* for "inheriting" the definition of an interface is technically the same for standard class inheritance, proclaiming interface inheritance a substitute for multiple inheritance without understanding the difference is completely misguided and counterproductive.

Realizing the Benefits of Interfaces

The driving force behind modern object-oriented frameworks like .NET is to be able to engineer software that can be easily extended and changed. Engineers are taught to design software with this idea in mind; computer science grads, sadly, often are not.

The engineer will design software for the problem at hand, but provide the facilities in his or her software to change the implementation as the problem changes. The implementations, for example, might require calls to different operating systems, different hardware platforms, and new indirect method calls.

In other words, we as software engineers must provide interfaces that are as general or as abstract as possible. The implementation, however, need not be as general. And, in many cases, it cannot be. But the interface has achieved the polymorphism objective of delivering method implementation in many forms, which means you are given the flexibility to implement in a variety of ways.

Implicit Interfaces

All standard class declarations and member declarations implicitly expose interfaces so that their objects can be referenced and instantiated, and their functionality and data accessed in predefined and regulated ways. This implicit, but always present, interface comprises the standard object's identifier and the encapsulated method signatures (as well as other class members, such as constants, variables, and properties).

Without the implicit interface, you would never be able to reference a class or instantiate an object and access its methods and data. In other words, the interface in the standard class is said to be automatically defined. The implicit interface is evident in a standard class declaration, as follows:

```
'The MyDay implicit interface declaration
Public Class MyDays
  'The method definition or signature declared is the interface
  Dim Days As New DaysEnum
  Function SetDay(ByVal Day As Integer) As String
    Return 'something
  End Function
End Class
```

and sending a message to this interface—or calling the method—is done by the client as follows:

```
Public Function GetDay(ByVal day As Integer) As String
  GetDay = MyDays.SetDay(Days.Saturday)
End Sub
```

where **Days.Saturday** is a variable of type **Integer** (as a constant of the **DaysEnum** enumeration) that is passed to the **SetDay** method. In the preceding code, this method is implicitly implemented in the **MyDays** class. In other words, **MyDays** implicitly implements the interface **MyDays.SetDay**. The class or code-level representation of the implicit interface is demonstrated in Figure 10-2.

Visual Basic and all .NET languages implicitly provide the interface for the implementation in standard classes. You might not be thinking about the interface when you create a class and begin coding a method, but you are actually providing an interface on-the-fly. Object Pascal or Delphi source files make you more aware of the interface in every unit. For every class, you must first declare the interface as follows:

```
{interface}
type
  TMyDays = Class
  public
    function SetDay(Day: Integer) : string;
{}
    {implementation}
    function TMyDays.SetDay(Day: Integer) : string;
    begin
      SetDay := Day;
    end;
end;
```

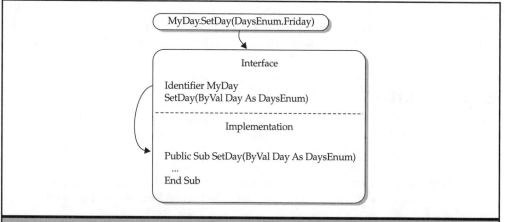

Figure 10-2. *The implicit interface and the implementation behind it*

The Visual Basic equivalent is as follows:

```
Class MyDays
  Function SetDay(ByVal Day As Integer) As String
    SetDay = Day
  End Sub
End Class
```

The only difference between the two languages is that, in the Visual Basic example, the class name and the method signature (in bold) *are* the (implicit) interface (and there's about 30 percent less code apparent in the Visual Basic version).

Visual Basic can also be very flexible when it comes to deciding where to place the interface and where to place the implementation—and how to tie the two together. For example, the standard base class (**MustInherit**) can also be *abstract,* which implements the interface (well sort of) but provides no code in the implemented methods—a job left to the deriving class. The abstract class must be inherited so that the method can be implemented or used in the deriving class. The abstract class would be declared like this:

```
'example of abstract class that implements interfaces
Public MustInherit Class MyDays
  Dim Days As New DaysEnum
  Function SetDay(ByVal day As Integer) As String
  MustOverride
End Class
```

As you learned in the last chapter, this class cannot be referenced or instantiated because it cannot provide any service. And its true abstract methods are modified with the *abstract* modifier, **MustOverride**. Only the deriving class that inherits the interface and its abstract methods and implements them can be referenced and instantiated.

Explicit Interfaces

.NET provides a form of reference type that allows you to explicitly declare an interface and keep it completely separate from any implementation. In other words, the interface class and the class that implements the interface represent the most loosely coupled arrangement of classes you can achieve in the .NET Framework.

Interface classes are a fundamental construct used in many places in the .NET Framework. They have been provided to ensure that when implementing certain algorithms, such as cloning, comparing, encrypting, iterating, and so on, consumer classes are guaranteed to implement the supported operations specified by the interface.

By implementing the interface according to its definition, polymorphism is ensured. What do we mean by *ensured?* As you know, polymorphism means *many forms*. Thus, an interface that defines a method forces all implementors of that method to conform to the method definition. For example, if an interface method **CompareTo** has two parameters expecting objects, and you reimplement it with three parameters, or change the identifier to **CompareObjects**, the polymorphism would be broken. Interfaces do not allow that.

How polymorphism permeates around the .NET application is evident in the ability to pass a reference to an object's implemented interface as an argument to a method parameter. This allows two totally uncoupled classes to exchange functionality as shown in the following example:

```
Public Sub CompareTo(ByRef val1 As IComparable)
```

You can now pass any object that implements the **IComparable** interface as the argument for the **val1** parameter, even though the implementations of the various **IComparable** objects may be very different from each other.

In this regard, the interface acts as a filter and forces an implementor to support the definition of the interface regardless of how it is implemented. The interface is thus a contract that must be honored by the implementor. You can think of the interface as defining a contract for conduct by the implementor. It forces the implementor to work with the required parameter types and to return the required return types (when the method is a function). It also enforces usage of the correct data as well as properties and events.

Another objective of the interface is that the .NET architects help you implement standard and supported operations that are not viable candidates for implementation in formal classes. This is why many interfaces only have a single method for you to implement (such as **Clone**).

You will design and implement interfaces for a variety of reasons. Here are several of the most important ones, in addition to the abstraction facility and polymorphism provided:

- Interfaces can and should be used for types that are not part of any identifiable class hierarchy, or that on their own form the basis for types that *are not* any particular "animal," typical of utility classes. As you will see later in this chapter, several interfaces can be coupled together to provide a single utility class.

- Interfaces can and should be used for developing classes in situations where inheritance of implementation from base or parent classes is not required. Class hierarchies, *is-a* relationships, and interface declaration and implementation serve very different design requirements.

- Interfaces can and should be used in situations that call for interface implementation. A good example is the **Structure (Value Type**s) that cannot inherit implementation via standard class inheritance (see Chapter 9).

- Interfaces should not be used as a substitute for the lack of multiple inheritance. That's not the premise for their inclusion in the .NET Framework, or any other object-oriented framework. Multiple inheritance does not have its place in the .NET Framework; interfaces do and have nothing to do with multiple inheritance. This is further discussed in this chapter. Also see "Inheritance and Multiple Inheritance" in Chapter 9.

- Interfaces are great for structure and formality in a class—great tools for class providers to force conformance by class consumers. If your classes seem like badly packed, jumbled up, holiday suitcases (the whole family's togs tossed into one bag), then it's in need of the structuring that interfaces provide.

- Finally, and most importantly, interfaces allow you to delegate. This is probably their most advanced and useful purpose. By being able to collaborate with an interface that is a bridge to an autonomous class that implements the interface, the client to the interface has a way of targeting the implementation. By being totally decoupled from the class that references the interface and the class that implements it, the client class can use an interface to delegate functionality to classes specially designed to play certain roles for them. In other words, rather than working under *is-a* relationships, classes collaborate on the basis of being able to play the role of something else. And the interface, a form of delegate or agent, is the middle person in the relationship. This concept is discussed in detail in the next few chapters and is the basis for .NET event handling. So don't worry now if you did not understand a word of what I have just said.

Abstract Class or Explicit Interface

When do you use an interface and when do you use an abstract class? Understanding the difference between the two is important and can be confusing because both declare abstract members and they cannot be instantiated.

To recap from the last chapter: An *abstract class* is a class that cannot be instantiated, but must be inherited from. In this regard, all abstract classes are declared with the **MustInherit** modifier. The main difference in terms of implementation is that an abstract class may be fully or partially implemented in its declaration space, while the formal interface class cannot be implemented in its declaration space in any way, shape, or form. Abstract classes form the basis for inheritance hierarchies and, as such, they are usually partially implemented. The abstract class thus serves as the basis for encapsulating common functionality for inherited classes. **Object** is the ultimate abstract class.

Classes can inherit from only one base class, and while you can provide polymorphism by deriving from the base class, all classes that need access to that polymorphism must inherit, directly or indirectly, from your abstract class. This can be a limiting factor in the design and layout of your application.

A positive aspect of abstract classes is that, through inheritance and the implementation of the members, all deriving classes gain access to the same functionality. Interfaces cannot provide this facility, and the consumer of the interface must manually provide the access to the implementing or referencing objects.

While I strongly believe that interface implementation and class inheritance capabilities have distinct roles—and I intend to expose the differences later in this chapter—here are some recommendations for choosing between the two constructs (assuming polymorphism rather than classification is the objective):

- Abstract classes provide a simple and easy way to version all deriving classes. By updating the base class, all the inheriting classes get automatically updated. This is not possible with interfaces, as you will see in this chapter.

- If you need to create functionality that will be used by a wide range of unrelated objects, then the interface is your choice. As discussed in Chapter 9 (and often repeated in this chapter), abstract classes provide the base class for classes of objects that are closely related. Interfaces are best suited for providing common functionality to unrelated classes and are not a substitute for the lack of multiple inheritance. If you fully understand inheritance, as discussed in the previous chapter, then this distinction will be clear to you.

- As mentioned earlier, interfaces are great for targeting functionality that resides in other classes and that can be used in a wide variety of places, even in abstract classes in which the implementation can be inherited, and the polymorphism thus propagated.

Note *Chapter 9 provides extensive coverage of abstract classes, for further reference.*

An Introduction to Interface Design and Implementation

The interface can be explicitly declared with the **Interface** class as demonstrated in the following code. (Don't worry about copying any of this code; just follow along and try to understand what is taking place. Later in this chapter, we'll go through creating and implementing an interface step by step.)

```
'The IMyDays Interface declaration
Public Interface IMyDays
  'The method definition or signature declared in the interface
  Function SetDay(ByVal day As Integer) As String
End Interface
```

CLASSES AND OBJECTS

Note   *As shown earlier the implementation of **IMyDays** interface makes use of the **DaysEnum** enumeration that we constructed in Chapter 8. Great code reuse, huh!*

No implementation is allowed in the preceding class. As you can see, you are not allowed to provide the terminating **End** keyword for the method, such as **End Function**. The interface is then implicitly implemented in another class (often called the *concrete class*) in the following fashion:

```
Class MyDayManipulator
  Implements ImyDay

  Sub New()
  End Sub

  Function SetDay(ByVal Day As Integer) As String Implements
IMyDays.SetDay
     Select Case Day
       Case 1
      Return "Monday"
        Case 2
      Return "Tuesday"
        Case 3
      Return "Wednesday"
        Case 4
      Return "Thursday"
        Case 5
      Return "Friday"
        Case 6
      Return "Saturday"
        Case 7
        Return "Sunday"
      Case Else
        Return "No such day matches the number"
      End Select
    End Function
End Class
```

What you are seeing here is a loose coupling of classes, which can be better visualized with the graphic in Figure 10-3 (which, as you can see, is very similar to Figure 10-2).

Note   *Members of an interface are public by design, and access modifiers are invalid in the interface class.*

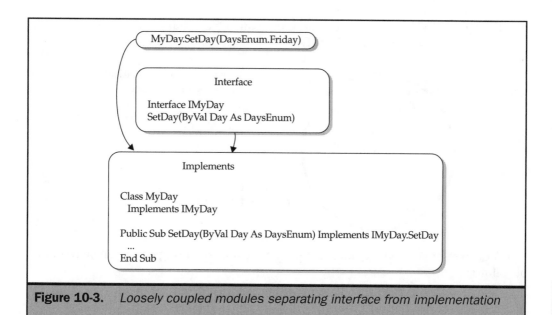

Figure 10-3. *Loosely coupled modules separating interface from implementation*

You can now access the implemented method by simply sending a message to the **MyDayManipulator** object, as follows:

```
Class MyDay
  Dim mydayman As New MyDayManipulator
  Function GetDay(ByVal Day as Integer) As String
    GetDay = mydayman.SetDay(Days.Tuesday)
    'GetDay is now given the string value of day 3 and you _
    'can now do something with it
  End Sub
End Class
```

Many classes in the .NET Framework implement classes in this fashion. Examples include implementation of the **IClonable** interface, implemented in many classes, **IComparer**, and **IEnumerator**.

Depending on your design requirements, the preceding style of referencing the interface can be a little inelegant and rigid because you are referencing, from a logical point of view, the object rather than the interface. However, you can first create a reference variable of the actual interface and then "plug" it onto any object that implements the interface. .NET lets you do that, and thus you can reference the interface anywhere in your code and reuse any object that provides the implementation, where appropriate. The illustration demonstrates this idea.

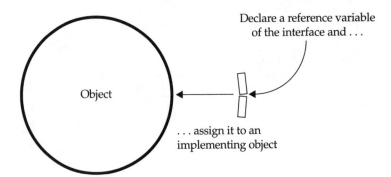

Declare a reference variable
of the interface and . . .

Object

. . . assign it to an
implementing object

Code to reference the interface rather than the implementing object can be written as follows:

```
Imports Vb7cr.Interfaces
Public Class InterfaceTester

    Shared Sub Main()
        'instantiate the object that implements the interface
        Dim daymanipulator As New MyDayManipulator()
        'create the reference variable of the interface
        Dim Day As IMyDay = daymanipulator
        'reference the interface rather than the object
        Console.WriteLine(Day.SetDay(Days.Friday))
        Console.ReadLine()
    End Sub
End Class
```

The **InterfaceTester** code writes **Friday** to the console.

Many classes in the .NET Framework implement interfaces. You can then use the implementing classes by referencing variables of the interface as just described. This is known as interface indirection and it is discussed further later in this chapter and in the chapters ahead.

Accessing and Using the Implementation

How do you thus use the explicit interface? There are several implementation access styles that point the way in terms of fundamental design. We looked at these styles earlier, but they are worth repeating.

The first style to discuss, because it is the most often used, directs that the class that needs access to the implementation of an interface explicitly implement the interface (in other words, the class that implements the interface is also the class that requires direct access to the implementation). A good example of this is the implementation of the **IClonable** interface in many classes, even in the base class of a hierarchy.

While abstraction and polymorphism are still served here, because the interface exists separately from the implementation, this style may clutter the container class, especially if the class implements more than one interface, which it can.

For example, if your class **Trajectory** inherits from class **Astro** and then implements **IWormHoleTransform**, **IEngageWarp**, **IHyperJump**, **IBendSpace**, and so on, life in the class can become very crowded. This interface crowding is illustrated in Figure 10-4.

Interface crowding can also produce problems of method signature clashing. In other words, ambiguities arise because you might attempt to implement two interfaces that declare the same method signature. So, one of the methods cannot be implemented. You can't simply expect to overload all method signatures either, because some interfaces might forbid it.

The second style suggests you implement the interface in a separate class file and provide access to the implementation via an interface bridge. This is also known as *interface indirection*. This is demonstrated in Figure 10-5.

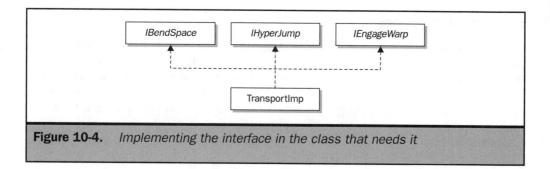

Figure 10-4.   *Implementing the interface in the class that needs it*

CLASSES AND OBJECTS

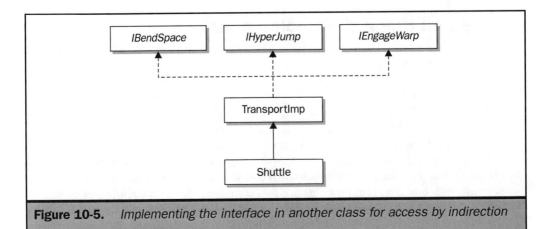

Figure 10-5. *Implementing the interface in another class for access by indirection*

Granted, you might still get ambiguities because you could easily reference more than one class that declares the identical method, but the signature clashing is more easily overcome through fully qualifying the method through the class's namespace (see Chapters 4 and 9). To access the implementation, simply create a reference to the interface and assign it to an implementing object. This is an elegant means of accessing implementation that I like a lot.

You can also pass interfaces as arguments to method parameters. An example of this style is presented later in this chapter, in the section "Implementing IComparable."

Compound Interfaces

Using interface inheritance, multiple interfaces can be merged to form a single compound interface class. In other words, you can create a base interface class and then create a child interface that derives from it. A third-generation interface can also inherit from the second generation and thus inherit the interfaces from both its parent and grandparent, forming what is called a compound interface or an interface hierarchy. The resulting interface can then be implemented in either of the two kinds of implementation styles discussed earlier. Here is an example of the compound interface:

```
Public Interface ICompare
   Function Compare(ByRef ObjA As Object,_
   ByRef ObjB As Object) As Boolean
End Interface

Public Interface IEncrypt :
```

```
Inherits ICompare
  Function Encrypt(ByVal Value As String) As Object
End Interface

Public Interface IIterator : Inherits IEncrypt
  Function GetNext() As Object
End Interface
```

The interface **IIterator** in the preceding example has inherited the definitions of both **ICompare** and **IEncrypt**.

Interfaces thus support multiple inheritance, meaning one interface can inherit multiple interfaces to form one compound interface. Have a look at the following example, which does the same thing as the previous code—it's just a cleaner approach to coupling the interfaces:

```
Public Interface IIterator : Inherits IEncrypt, ICompare
  Function GetNext() As Object
End Interface
```

With such flexibility, it is unavoidable to end up inheriting an interface more than once. In the preceding code, **IIterator** actually inherits the **ICompare** interface twice, once through **IEncrypt**, which originally inherited **ICompare**, and a second time by implicitly inheriting **ICompare**. However, the compiler lets this go because it only sees one **ICompare** in the hierarchy, no matter how many references there are to it. The illustration shows how Visual Studio automatically enumerates and merges the inherited interface members, but it does not duplicate the definitions inherited twice.

If you implement an interface, you also have your side of the deal to fulfill. The contract requires you or your client to implement the entire interface, and every aspect of the interface as it is defined. So, compounding the interfaces or inheriting multiple interfaces also has its downside, as demonstrated in the following code, which requires you to implement the methods of all interfaces inherited by the interface you are implementing:

```
Public Class Iterator : Implements IIterator

  Private Function Compare(ByRef ObjA As Object, ByRef ObjB As Object) _
    As Boolean Implements IIterator.Compare
```

```
    End Function

    Function Encrypt(ByVal Value As String) As Object _
        Implements IIterator.Encrypt
    End Function

    Function GetNext(ByRef ObjA As Object, _ ByRef ObjB As Object) As Boolean _
        Implements IIterator.GetNext
    End Function

End Class
```

What is clear in this code is that if you implement the compound interface, you must implement the entire compound interface, even if you only need to implement one method specified. If you do not need the whole shebang, rather implement a single interface that contains only the definitions you need.

Another technique is to use an adapter class—a proxy interface that adapts another interface for access—which is discussed in Chapter 14. Or, you can place all the interfaces—compound, inheriting, or otherwise—into an abstract class, and then inherit that abstract class. The abstract class lets you implement only what you need to, although you lose the only implementation inheritance "lifeline" you have in the process, which would be a waste and considered bad design.

Designing and Defining Interfaces

Designing an interface is known as *interface factoring*. This factoring is the process of deciding what properties, events, and methods are to be included in a certain interface. When you design or at least construct an interface, it is important to know what the interface is intended to hide and the abstraction behind that interface. You should thus make sure that each interface abstracts a single tightly focused implementation. When you start cluttering up the interface with unrelated methods and properties, you obscure the abstraction domains and place unnecessary burden on the implementor.

Thus, if you are going to design an interface for a collection of encryption methods, it makes no sense to "toss" the definition for comparing objects, or disposing of objects, into the same interface just because you don't feel like creating another interface project.

While you should take care to assemble definitions of a common purpose in one interface and not confuse the interface, at the same time, you should not split up an interface into too many related components. For example, splitting a collection of ten financial methods for an accounting interface into two interfaces, one for debits and one for credits, would be silly. They are better packed into one clean interface.

It is best to start small and get the interfaces up and running quickly. The interface can then evolve, because you can add more definitions and interfaces as needed.

*Convention calls for giving the interface an initial capped letter I. This is not necessary but it helps you and your consumers to distinguish interfaces from the classes that implement them. The initial-capped I is the convention used by Microsoft for interfaces published in the .NET Framework (for example, **ICloneable**, **IComparer**, and so on).*

Interfaces, Once Published, Must Not Change

As you know from the previous code examples demonstrated, for interfaces to succeed, they cannot change. In other words, the abstract definition encapsulated by the interface class must always remain the same. If the definition of a method, property, or event must change, you must create a new interface definition or member, leaving the old one in place for backward compatibility—for consumers that depend on it and that have implemented it, directly or indirectly.

Once your interface has been published, there is no telling who has implemented it and where. Changing the interface while other classes have already implemented it breaks software. Implementation thus depends on the interface to remain constant. It is thus often said that an interface must obey an unseen "contract" it has with the consumer or implementor, a contract that must be maintained because the consumer has implemented the interface on the trust that it *will not* change. This is known as *interface invariance*.

You can't simply add more methods to an existing interface and hope your interface consumers will not notice. Remember, the consumer or contractee must implement the entire interface. If you add a method, the consumer will be forced to implement that method the next time he or she compiles.

Interface Invariance

Interface invariance protects existing software that has been written to use the interface. So, when you clearly need to add new definitions or alter an existing definition, a new interface should be created instead. The best way of publishing the interface is to give it the same name and add a version number onto the end of the name (and then properly document the changes and additions). So, the **IEncrypt** interface mentioned earlier might be published as **IEncrypt2** or something similar that clearly identifies it as a new version of an interface that already exists.

CLASSES AND OBJECTS

Constructing the Interface

You declare or define the interface within the **Interface** and **End Interface** keywords as demonstrated with the following formal syntax:

InterfaceDeclaration ::=
[*Attributes*] [*InterfaceModifier*+] **Interface** *Identifier LineTerminator*
[*InterfaceBases*+]
[*InterfaceMemberDeclaration*+]
End Interface *LineTerminator*

InterfaceModifier ::= *AccessModifier* | **Shadows**

A simple code equivalent is written like this:

```
Public Interface IFace
End Interface
```

You can also add the optional **Inherits** statement after the interface identifier to list one or more inherited interfaces, as demonstrated earlier in this chapter. The **Inherits** keyword can be on a new line after the interface identifier, or you can place it directly after the identifier in front of the new-line colon symbol, as follows:

```
Public Interface IFace
   Inherits IGullible
' . . .
End Interface
```

or

```
Public Interface IFace : Inherits IGullible
' . . .
End Interface
```

The **Inherits** statements must precede all other elements in the declaration except comments. All remaining declaration statements in the interface definition keywords can then be **Event**, **Sub**, **Function**, and **Property**. Remember, you cannot add **End Sub**, **End Function**, or **End Property** terminating statements to the interface.

Interface statements are public by default and you cannot declare them as being anything else (it would be illogical to hide the interface). However, you can modify the implementation of the interfaces by using any valid member modifier, such as **Private**, **Friend**, or **Protected Friend** (see Chapters 4, 7, 8, and 9), which can carry out any secret design or information hiding needed in the class. There is only one exception: The keyword **Shared** defines a static class method and is therefore illegal on an interface method. You can also overload the methods and properties on an interface with the **Overloads** modifier, but using any of the polymorphism **Overrides**, **MustOverride**, or **Overridable** modifiers is illegal. Table 10-1 provides a list of the legal and illegal modifiers for implemented interface members.

Access and Polymorphism Modifiers	Legal/Illegal
Public	Illegal in the interfaces itself
Protected, Friend, Protected Friend	Legal only for implementations
Shared	Illegal in interfaces and on implemented members
Overrides, MustOverride, Overridable	Illegal in interfaces, legal on implemented members
Overloads	Legal in interfaces and on implemented members

Table 10-1.   *Legal and Illegal Access and Polymorphism Modifiers in Interfaces and on the Implemented Members*

Getting Started with the Interface Definition

The steps to take to create an interface are straightforward, but there are a few angles to tackle this task. First, you could create the interface definition in the same way you create the abstract class, by just providing the abstract methods and not going into any implementation at all for now. This approach would also allow you to first model the interface in UML with tools like Visio or Rational Rose, which would allow you to write the definitions out to Visual Studio code units.

Another approach would be to implement and provide the methods of a standard class and then later decide if it makes sense to extract an interface using the formal **Interface** class.

The latter approach is often how interfaces come into existent, but that does not mean you need to forgo the benefits of modeling the classes in UML first. You will likely first model a standard class and then fully implement it. Then you will decide whether or not the class would benefit from the creation of a formal interface to it (or the provision of adapter interfaces).

This is, in fact, how the **IIterator** interface introduced earlier in this chapter came into existence. I first fully implemented it in the linked list class (discussed in Chapter 13). But it is better served as an interface that can be implemented apart from the list class. I thus made it available for many other forms of collections, data structures such as lists, and so on.

It is also worth noting that **IIterator** is a formal behavioral design pattern documented in the book *Design Patterns*, mentioned at the beginning of this chapter. The book describes the intent of the pattern as a means to "...provide a way to access the elements of an aggregate object sequentially without exposing its underlying representation."

My motivation for implementing **IIterator** external to a **LinkedList** class was to prevent the class from becoming bloated with the various traversal and list traversal functionality that was going into the **IIterator**. I noticed that my simple **LinkedList** class was in fact becoming bogged down with iterator-specific methods that were detracting from the clean implementation of the **LinkedList** and its data elements encapsulated within (see Chapter 13).

The **IIterator** interface thus allowed me to extract the construct from the **LinkedList** class and allow it to be used with objects that have other traversal and iteration needs. (By the way, this is also the motivation behind Java's iterator interface—a very clean adaptation of the formal **IIterator** pattern.)

Basically, our objective is this: Define an interface for accessing a collection of objects in a linked list. The iterator has the job of accessing the collection, iterating from one object to the next, forward (in the case of singly linked lists) and backward (in the case of doubly linked lists), and so on. The following list represents the formal requirements of the **IIterator** object:

- The **IIterator** object must be able to gain access to the list to iterate over.

- The **IIterator** object must be able to obtain a reference to the first item (node) in the list.

- The **IIterator** object must be able to keep track of, or record, the current element.

- The **IIterator** object must be able to keep track of previous elements iterated over.

- The **IIterator** object must know when it has reached the end of the list, the last object.

- The **IIterator** object must be able to communicate to the list object information the list object requires to do its work, such as adding, inserting, removing, and changing data.

Figure 10-6 illustrates the relationships between the **LinkedList** object, the **IIterator** interface, and an **IIterator** implementation (any **IIterator** implementation).

An important objective of creating the **IIterator** interface is to allow list objects to work with their own **IIterator** objects. A **LinkedList** object will therefore reference an **IIterator** interface and work with a suitable implementation, or create its own **IIterator** object by implementing the **IIterator** interface.

The following code is an example of the **IIterator** interface:

```
Public Interface IIterator : Inherits IComparable
   Function GetNext(ByRef ObjA As Object,
_ByRef ObjB As Object) As Boolean
   Function HasNext() As Boolean_
'is there a node after the current position
   Property Current() As Object
   Sub AddClone()
   Sub Add(ByRef Obj As Object)
   Sub Remove()
End Interface
```

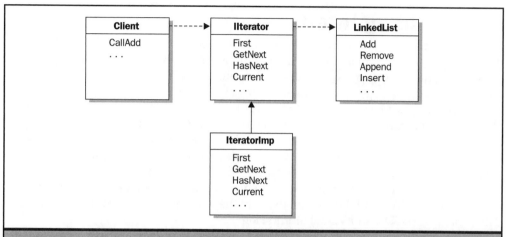

Figure 10-6. *The class that instantiates a **LinkedList** object also instantiates a reference to an **IIterator** interface in order to access the functionality of the **IIterator** for the list in question*

The next two examples show the two ways a class can reference the interface and instantiate an **IIterator** object for its use:

```
Imports Vb7cr.Iterator
Public Class TreeWalker
  Dim iterImp As Iterator
  Public Sub GetObject(ByRef Obj As Object)
    MyTree.Node = Iter.GetNext(Obj)
  End Sub
End Class
```

Or better yet:

```
Public Class TreeWalker
  Dim Iter As IIterator = New Iterator
  Public Sub GetObject(ByRef Obj As Object)
    MyTree.Node = Iter.GetNext(Obj)
  End Sub
End Class
```

Chapter 13 provides the complete implementation of the **IIterator** interface in the class **IIterator**, and demonstrates its employment with the **LinkedList** class. The chapter also examines the .NET Frameworks **IEnumerator** interface, which is also an iterator for collections and how **IIterator** can inherit **IEnumerator** in order to support .NET **ICollection** objects.

Implementing Interfaces

The .NET Framework's collection of interfaces is extensive and there are literally dozens of interfaces for many different operations. There are interfaces for graphics, networking, data structures, databases, and so on. All .NET interfaces are prefixed with an uppercase *I* for easy identification as an interface.

You can use the Object Browser to browse the collection of interfaces in the various namespaces. If a particular collection of classes provides interfaces, you find them by expanding the class tree down to the Bases and Interfaces node in the Object Browser tree. Selecting the interface in the browser brings up a summary of the interface in the Details pane of the browser. Interfaces are also listed higher up the namespaces.

You can also explore the interfaces that ship with the Framework with the Class Viewer tool, WinCV. And they are all listed in the documentation that ships with the .NET Framework SDK and Visual Studio Help.

With so many interfaces, it would be meaningless to list them all and explain them here. However, let's look at the implementation of two of the few well-known interfaces, **IClonable** and **IComparable**, which will give you an idea of what's required to support and implement an interface. Later chapters will implement some of the other built-in interfaces, as well as custom interfaces. First, let's go over some of the interface semantics to put us on the right track.

Interface Implementation Semantics

You use the **Implements** keyword as demonstrated earlier to signify that a class implements a specific interface. You can implement multiple interfaces in a single class as long as you list the classes being implemented. This is achieved by providing a comma-separated list behind the **Implements** keyword, as follows:

```
Public Class SeaFood
    Implements IShrimps, IScallops, IOysters, ICrabs
```

In addition to the **Implements** keyword that comes after the class declaration, you must also provide the **Implements** keyword after the name of the interface member (method, property, or event) being implemented. This is demonstrated in the following code:

```
Function Select(ByVal Food As String) As Boolean Implements IShrimps.Select
End Function
```

Interestingly enough, you do not need to use the same identifier for the implemented member name and the interface member name, which was a required convention (**InterfaceName_MethodName**) used in the classic versions of Visual Basic. For example, the following code shows the implementation of a method (in bold) given a different name in the interface (also in bold):

```
Sub FindNext(ByVal aNext As Integer) _
Implements IIterator.GetNext
```

The method signature, however (including any return type), must not change; otherwise, the interface will complain. Still, the most common way to implement an element of an interface is with a member that has the same name as the interface member, as shown in the previous examples, and it's best to stick to what's easiest and not overly complicate matters unless you are avoiding name collisions.

| Note | *When a private member implements a member of an interface, that member becomes available by way of the interface even though it is not available directly on object variables for the class. This is a very important facility for event handling and delegation, as described in Chapter 14.* |

Implementing ICloneable

The ability to clone (a fancy synonym for "copy") an object is a fundamental operation in object-oriented systems. You have object "a" and for some reason you need to create object "b" as an exact copy of "a." Looking at the class members, the first method you'll notice is **MemberwiseClone**, which we discussed in the previous chapter.

This method performs a shallow copy of the object and is implemented throughout the framework, providing standard shallow copy functionality. But what if the shallow copy is not appropriate? What if you have a special object that requires a deep clone (copy the object and any objects it refers to) and need to implement the cloning in a special way? A good example of such a deep copy is making a copy of a linked list object. The list itself references a collection of objects, which are its data elements or nodes, so by a deep copy, you would want to copy all the objects maintained by the list and not just the references to the original nodes.

First you might ask: "Why would the base class not implement a deep clone method that I can use in any class I create?" The basis for this thinking is that the cloning methods would be used in all objects, and thus it would make sense to implement a **Clone** method in **Object** so that everyone inherits these methods. But this is only part of the reason deep cloning is not supported in the base **Object** class.

Implementing alternatives to the **MemberwiseClone**, such as a deep clone, is not appropriate in all objects, and because of the variety of ways of cloning, if you want to implement a deep copy, then you need to implement it yourself. The way of doing this would be via the **ICloneable** interface.

ICloneable is a simple interface and provides only one member definition, the method **Clone**. In the following example, **ICloneable** is implemented in a simple class representing an object that stores a reference to another object:

```
Public Class Node
  Implements ICloneable

  Public Data As Object

  Public Sub New()
    MyBase.New()
  End Sub

  Public Function Clone() As Object Implements ICloneable.Clone
    Dim baseNode As Node
    baseNode = Me.MemberwiseClone()
    baseNode.Data = Me.Data
    Clone = baseNode
  End Function

End Class
```

The **Node** object is now endowed with the ability to return an exact copy of itself, first by cloning its members and then by cloning the objects that are encapsulated within its structure.

Implementing IComparable

The next interface we will investigate lets you provide support for comparing the current object to another object. Again, the interface only specifies one method, **CompareTo**. In the following method, the object of type **Node** must be passed to the **CompareTo** method, which makes a value comparison to the current object (**Me**):

```
Public Function CompareTo(ByVal tnode As Object) As Integer _
  Implements IComparable.CompareTo
  If (Not (TypeOf (tnode) Is Node)) Then
    Throw New ArgumentException("Argument must be of type Node")
  End If
  If (Me.Data Is tnode.Data) Then
    Return 1
  ElseIf Not (Me.Data Is tnode.Data) Then
    Return 0
  End If
End Function
```

As you can see in the preceding code, we are given the liberty of defining the implementation rules for our method—the freedom to determine how to implement a method that compares one object to another. Thus, we can determine what constitutes a comparison (and returns 1 or 0) and what does not (and returns 0 or -1).

To compare two objects (for example in a binary tree, as demonstrated in Chapter 13), we would construct a method called **CompareTo** as follows:

```
Public Function CompareTo(ByVal tnode As Object) As Integer _
   Implements IComparable.CompareTo
   If (Not (TypeOf (tnode) Is Node)) Then
     Throw New ArgumentException("Argument must be of type Node")
   End If
   If (Me.Data Is tnode.Data) Then
     Return 1
   Else
     Return 0
   End If
End Function
```

The preceding code is straightforward except for one thing that might throw you. While you are passing in object arguments to the method's parameters, the parameters are asking for **IComparable** objects, hence the parameter declares are **As IComparable** and not **As Object**. As such, the method is laying the ground rules for you to submit only objects that implement **IComparable**, and if you try to submit an object that does not implement the interface, you write the necessary code to raise an exception. This is demonstrated in the following code:

```
Public Function Max(ByVal val1 As IComparable, ByVal val2 As IComparable) _
   As IComparable
   If (val1.CompareTo(val2) > 0) Then
     Return 1 'val1 > val2
   End If
   If (val1.CompareTo(val2) <= 0) Then
     Return 0 'val1 <= val2
   End If
End Function
```

Both of the preceding methods are useful in implementations of linked lists. The latter method will be revisited in the example of binary trees in Chapter 14.

Some last thoughts about interfaces: Interfaces can have static members, nested types, abstract or virtual members, properties, and events, but any class implementing an interface must supply the full definitions for the abstract members declared in the interface. Without the full definition, the compiler will complain bitterly.

An interface can require that any implementing class must also implement one or more other interfaces as a precondition.

The following restrictions apply to interfaces:

- An interface can be declared with any accessibility, but interface members cannot be anything other than public.

- Security permissions cannot be attached to interface members or to the interface itself.

- You can define a "discreet" constructor in an interface, calling it anything you want, but you naturally cannot define the **New** constructor.

Exceptions Covered in this Chapter

The following three exceptions are used in interface implementation and are principally discussed in Chapter 7:

- **ArgumentException**
- **ArgumentNullException**
- **ArgumentOutOfRangeException**

The exception object that is most important in the use of interfaces is **ArgumentException**. This exception is commonly raised when passing to method parameters. The exception is raised by the receiving method upon testing the argument for its support for a particular interface. See "Implementing IComparable," earlier in this chapter.

Observations

The subject of interfaces is extremely interesting and complex at the same time. However, it is important, nay vital, to understand that interfaces are a fact of .NET programming—and all OOP environments for that matter. There are going to be very few scenarios that will not require any significant implementation of an interface, and possibly a definition of a new interface.

To recap the important facts about interfaces in .NET: It should be clear to you that interfaces provide a key facility for polymorphism. This is true for both implicitly defined interfaces that are automatically defined in standard classes and explicitly defined interfaces defined in the formal **Interface** class.

Interfaces provide a facility for implementing small, loosely coupled objects or instances of functionality that are not part of any formal class hierarchy. In this regard, they should not be considered a substitution for multiple inheritance but rather as a facility to provide functionality to classes external to and without consideration for any class hierarchy. In other words, interfaces can usually be implemented or accessed anywhere and can be considered neutral constructs.

The .NET Framework provides interfaces to help you support a number of important operations. These interfaces are so defined to ensure that you stick to supported operations and standards.

One final and important observation for your consideration: If you are planning to provide interfaces to consumers (customers or fellow programmers), it makes sense to provide good example code and documentation to help your consumers implement the interface. It's all very well to provide the definition for an extensive interface, such as a drawing interface or a text interface, but if you don't help your customers understand how to implement them, you are not going to be highly regarded. This should not be a difficult thing to do, because you should not release a formal or explicit interface unless *you* have fully tested the definition of the interface, which is done by fully implementing it.

The Complete Reference

Visual Basic .NET

Chapter 11

Exceptions: Handling and Classes

S *tructured Exception Handling* (SEH) is new to the Visual Basic language. Although it prevents further execution of troublesome code in a manner similar to the familiar **On Error Goto** construct, it is a very different construct to **On Error Goto**. When a program encounters an error in classic VB, all further processing of statements after the violating line is suspended, and the execution is transferred to a region in the current routine where the programmer can deal with the error. That's where the similarity ends.

The classic Visual Basic error handling, while still supported in Visual Basic .NET, is a form of unstructured error handling that did not serve VB programmers well. Visual Basic unstructured error handling is not a holistic approach to guarding code and properly dealing with an error. Visual Basic 6 and earlier code often suffers from lack of error handling specifically because **On Error Goto** statements are left sterile, and don't provide much error management at all. A good example of this is the following VB 6 code, providing so-called inline error-handling:

```
On Error Resume Next
```

which sometimes serves no purpose other than to defer the handling of the error and leave holes everywhere in the code.

SEH is a critical component of programming against the common language runtime (CLR). You cannot write reliable software without it, for a number of reasons. The CLR terminates any application that does not catch an exception; so even the slightest error that otherwise would allow your software to continue without much risk of application failure will result in your application being terminated. The approach forces the programmer to deal with the inherent problems in his code.

 Note   *SEH in Visual Basic .NET works like SEH in Visual C++, Object Pascal, and Java.*

It has been one of my observations, as both a programmer and a project manager, that developers often treat error handling like loathsome documentation. They try to ignore it until all functionality is written. They believe writing error-handling code is tedious and often insist they can program functionality correctly the first pass. This malady is also prevalent in so-called death-march development projects. The deadline is so tight that the code to handle the exceptions and errors is skimped on.

The exception-handling code is thus left until the last minute before a product is passed to beta or, worse, shipped to customers. The problem is that the bigger and more complex the application, the higher the chances are that areas that require explicit error handling will be overlooked or forgotten about come release time. There is often a last-minute rush to go through all the methods and write the exception-handling code. Like documentation, exception handling should be considered along with the method specification (as demonstrated throughout this book, most notably in Chapter 7 and Chapters 12 through 17), not after the product has been released to manufacturing.

Chapter 7 provided a brief introduction to exception-handling code, so you may feel that you have already covered some of the material presented in this chapter. But this chapter also covers advanced subjects, such as custom exception classes and exception filters.

The older, unstructured error-handling practices are not covered in this chapter, for the reasons previously mentioned, with one exception (no pun intended): a description is provided of how to tap into the Visual Basic **Error** object that is supported in Visual Basic .NET.

In any event, the **On Error** syntax cannot be used in a method that exploits SEH constructs. I have never felt comfortable about **On Error** and its **Goto** construct, and I believe that the sooner you port your code to SEH and fully adopt it, the better. Unstructured error handling is simply unstructured and comparing VB 6 error handling code to SEH is like comparing break dancing to ballet.

If you don't handle exceptions as they are raised, your application dies. The CLR closes down your application, and there's nothing you can do to recover or save data. The CLR is a safe execution environment. As mentioned in Chapter 2, its priority is to protect the execution environment. SEH should not be left out of your methods unless the construct or what you have written does not require an exception handler, or if any exceptions can be handled somewhere else on the stack, in other methods, or even in other classes and objects.

Why Do We Need Exception Handling?

We inject exception-handling code into our programs to trap errors and "handle" them "gracefully" and to prevent a program from terminating unexpectedly. Some errors don't result in an application crashing. But if we were to allow a program to continue mortally wounded it would present undesirable results to the user or risk trashing data. Instead SEH anticipates the impending disaster and presents a viable rescue plan.

Visual Basic .NET provides us with the facility to catch all types of exceptions. We can code specific handlers to catch only certain types of exceptions, or exceptions generated by related types, or classes. We can also force an exception, and even use the exception as a flow mechanism that leads to alternate functionality provided by a method (but this is discouraged, because there are formal constructs for flow control that are much less resource-intensive than the instantiation of exception objects).

To summarize, we need exception handling for the following reasons:

- Applications need a facility to catch a method's inability to complete a task.

- To process exceptions caused by a process accessing any functionality in methods, libraries, or classes where those elements are unable to directly handle any exception that arises as a result of the access and the ensuing computation.

- To process exceptions caused by components that are not able to handle any particular exception in their own processing space.

- To ensure that large and complex programs (actually, any Visual Basic program) can consistently and holistically provide program-wide exception handling.

Exception- and error-handling routines need to be part of the code that defines any method. Get into the habit of making sure that for every method you write, you include code in the method that jumps in if the method does not complete as excepted or produces results contrary to what is expected. (A trained SEH writer will look to assert, test conditions and states, and fully consider code and only bring on the exception handler as a last resort or failsafe. Such patterns and techniques are explored in more depth in Chapter 17.)

Structured Exception Handling 101

The concept of SEH is straightforward. Code is optionally enclosed in a block that sets up a guarded perimeter around the code to be executed. This guarded code is everything that falls between the **Try** and **Catch** keywords. Here is an example. The statement in bold is in the guarded or protected section, in the code from line 14 to line 16:

```
13 Try
14    GetTrim = Call(SetFalloff) <- begin protected code
15
16 <-end protected code
17 Catch
18 End Try
```

As soon as an exception is raised, all further execution of the method's code is halted and transferred to a catchment area. The catchment area is the **Catch** block between **Try** and **End Try**.

You need to think ahead of the possible exceptions that may be raised by your code. For example, consider if it's possible to get stumped on a memory exception or an arithmetic exception. If so, then you need to provide an exception handler for that exception. You can also provide a default exception handler that will catch the exception, if nothing earlier catches it and if you are not sure what exception class to activate. We will discuss the default handler later in this chapter.

When the CLR begins to process the code in the **Catch** section, it looks for an exception handler, the exception instantiation code, in the local catch sector that matches the exception anticipated. When a match is found, an exception object to cater to the exception is created to deal with the exception.

If the CLR finds no match for the exception in the local method's **Catch** block, the CLR rolls back up the call stack—to methods that were previously called—looking for a handler in one of the earlier methods. (It will not go to the call stack if you do not first attempt to catch an exception.) And if no exception handler is found on the stack, the application will be terminated with an unhandled exception violation.

Note *You can also rethrow an exception to another method, and even to another class, and avoid walking up the stack. These concepts are further explored later in this chapter.*

Exception objects are no different from standard instances. They derive from the root **Exception** class and contain the necessary methods and data to deal with the information generated by the CLR. As you will later see, exception objects trap error information, trace the stack, and so forth. Customer handlers you write can even provide fancy methods to deal with the error in your own special way. For example, you can easily write the error to the Windows error-logging facilities, a technique we'll explore later in this chapter.

Exception objects also have access to local and class data (variables), which lets them correct errors that resulted in the exceptions in the first place. Once you have caught and "handled" the exception, the exception object is dereferenced, marked for destruction, and immediately collected by the CLR.

The processing scenario just described will be illustrated in the following code. **Main** starts a "roll" through three methods of which the last causes an overflow exception. However, only the first method can handle that exception an thus the exception handlers will pop off the stack until the first method's default **Exception** handler handles the exception:

```vb
Module FindExcept
  Dim var1 As Integer 'default is 0
  Dim var2 As Integer = 10

  Sub Main
    'first will call second and second will call third which
    'causes an overflow exception
      FirstMethod()
    Console.WriteLine("Press 'q' to quit the sample.")
    While Chr(Console.Read()) <> "q"c
    End While
  End Sub
  'FirstMethod has a default catch that can process the exception
  'later on in the flow
```

CLASSES AND OBJECTS

```
Public Sub FirstMethod()
  Try
    SecondMethod()
  Catch Except As Exception
    Console.WriteLine("First: " & Except.Message)
    If var1 <= 0 Then
      var1 = 5
    End If
  End Try
End Sub

'This method will not handle the exception
Public Sub SecondMethod()
  Try
    ThirdMethod()
  Catch Except As DivideByZeroException
    Console.WriteLine("Second: " & Except.Message)
  End Try
End Sub

'nor will this method
Public Sub ThirdMethod()
  Try
    var2 = var2 / var1
  Catch Except As DivideByZeroException
    Console.WriteLine("Third: " & Except.Message)
  End Try
End Sub
End Module
```

Which mechanism manages the entire process? Every method in your executable code, regardless of whether or not it declares a **Try…Catch** block, is apportioned space in an internal exception information table that is managed by the CLR. This table is automatically created when you run your application. The table is maintained by the CLR throughout the life of the executable. You don't have to know anything about this table, nor do you need programmatic access to it.

A region of the exception information table is provided to every method. If your method does not provide SEH, its portion of the table will be empty. If a method does provide SEH, the information in the table is used to describe the block under protection and any exception handlers associated with it.

The exception information table represents four types of exception handlers for protected blocks:

- The default exception handler that must process an exception.
- The exception object–filtered handler, which handles an exception object of a specified class or any of its derived classes.
- A user-filtered handler, which runs user-specified code to determine whether the exception should be handled by the associated handler or should be passed to the next protected block.
- A **Finally** handler, which executes whenever code exits either of the **Try**...**Catch** handlers, regardless of whether or not an exception occurred. If a **Finally** block is not provided, this section of the table is also left empty.

When an exception is raised by a method, two things happen. First, the CLR searches the table for the exception handlers associated with the errant method. Since the table stores information about every protected method, the CLR can very quickly link the exception to the method that caused it, and then access the handler provided to deal with the exception.

Second, the CLR creates the exception object to wrap all associated data generated over the exception. It will then execute any statements you provide in the catch handler. Your catch handler code can directly access the exception object and its properties, methods, and other members. See the section **"System.Exception"** later in the chapter for more details.

Exception objects are processed and collected almost immediately after the CLR or the application no longer needs them (which is usually as soon as the method that raised an exception returns normally). As such, memory consumed by exception objects is released back to the environment far quicker than memory consumed by objects in both managed and unmanaged code. This makes exception handling by the CLR far less resource-intensive than what is possible in an unmanaged environment, such as standard C++ unmanaged exception-handling code.

Exception-Handling Models

Two exception-handling models are used in modern object-oriented programming:

- The resumption model
- The termination model

The CLR is based on the termination model, which means that the block in the method that caused the exception in the first place is terminated. If the exception is not handled, application termination ensues.

The Resumption Model

The resumption model dictates that after code blows up, you need to return things to normal; but in this model, the execution returns to the "raise point" in the code where things got hairy in the first place—after the exception is handled.

Handling this scenario takes some skill because you need to resume normal execution without reraising the exception. You are thus forced in the handler to change flow, logic, and data to be sure the exception is not reraised. A forced "rerun" of the code (with new input) may sound like the right thing to do, but it also makes programming a lot harder and, in fact, more prone to disaster. Programming against possible exceptions is not good OO programming practice either.

The Termination Model

The termination model dictates that you cannot (normally) return to the point in the code where the exception was first raised. This is how Visual Basic has always worked, even with the old **On Error** construct. The exception kicks you out of the block of code that erupted, nixes the block on you, and forces you to deal with the mess or make a hasty exit.

If you do handle the exception, control returns to the line immediately after the **Try…Catch** code, as demonstrated in the following method. In the following **FireEvent** method **mdArray(CurrentCode)** in bold causes an exception. After the exception is handled, however, the code after the **End Try** in bold executes

```
Public Sub FireEvent()(I ByVal CurrentCode as Integer)
Dim code As Integer = -1
  Try
    code = mdArray(CurrentCode)
  Catch Except As IndexOutOfRangeException
    Console.WriteLine(Except.Message)
  End Try
Dim EDA As New EventDataArgs(True, code)
OnEvent(EDA)
End Sub
```

The preceding method raises an **IndexOutOfRangeException** exception when it tries to access an element that is out of the upper bound of the **mdArray**. After the exception is handled, the execution continues after the **End Try** statement and the **OnEvent** call continues with –1 as the value for the code argument. In other words, **code** did not get changed.

What if you need to execute the code in the **Try** block that blew up? Handling the exception "gracefully" and then "leaving it at that" is not always enough. That's where the termination model used by .NET shines. You can always recall the method in the code after the **End Try**. Rerunning the code block can also be made possible from a **Finally** block that comes after the catch. Later we'll see how to use the **Finally** block.

It important to understand the two models, with the objective of writing code that is less buggy and easier to document and follow. Your error handling does not need to end in the **Catch** blocks of the method that caused you grief. The neat aspect of the underlying exception-handling architecture is that you can direct control through any **Catch** handlers until a handler that is specifically defined to handle the exact infringement is found—no matter how deeply nested the source of the problem. As you'll see later, you can delegate the exception handling to another object entirely.

The exception handling process is analogous to a baseball game: After the pitch (the entry into the method), the errant ball is caught in the catcher's mitt and then thrown to second base to catch the runner trying to steal second. No luck at second base, so the defensive on second flings the ball to third base. Third is not tagged in time and the ball is thrown to home plate to catch the runner coming down from third.

While you do not need to "throw" an exception from one side of your application to another, you can use it to specifically rethrow or reraise the exception, even transfer it out of the original **Try**…**Catch**…**Finally** block to another method. You can also do whatever you need to do to fix the problem that caused the original hiccup and then return to the original method to try again (passing the ball back to the pitcher to have another shot). The exception-handling code and the code you can place in a **Finally** block can be used to roll back and clean up. It is key to remember that whatever happens in the exception-handling code, execution will resume with the code that comes after the **End Try** statement.

Recovering from Exceptions

There are exceptions from which you cannot easily recover. You can recover from your application or custom exceptions, but you cannot easily recover from most run-time exceptions without changing conditions in the system and hardware underpinning the application. What's the difference between exceptions raised from run time errors (in the CLR and even beyond its borders) and the custom exceptions?

Exceptions can be raised for the following reasons:

- **Syntax errors**   These errors can occur if something is declared incorrectly and the compiler does not realize it. Syntax errors slip by unnoticed when syntax checking is turned off, by setting **Option Strict** to the **Off** position. A good example of a syntax error is an element or member of an object being accessed when the object has not been created.

- **Run-time errors**   These errors occur during execution of your code, but may have absolutely nothing to do with your code. They can be produced by some of the simplest problems that may arise during run time, but the errors do not normally mean the algorithm or application is flawed. An example of such an error is an attempt to open a file or database that does not exist because the administrator moved the server. Your duty, however, is to write code that anticipates that a time may come when an idiot decides to delete a production database and bring the whole company, and your application, down.

Other examples of actions that cause run-time errors include trying to dial a telephone number with no modem attached, serializing an object to a full disk, and processing a lengthy sort with no memory. In all of these cases, if the resources existed, no errors would result and no exceptions would be thrown. Run-time errors usually come from the operating system, which detects the violations in its part of the world, beyond the borders of the CLR where operating system services live.

■ **Logic errors** These errors are similar to syntax errors because they go unnoticed by a preprocessor or the compiler. A *divide-by-zero* error is a classic example. This is not seen as an error until the program finds itself in a divide-by-zero situation—the logic of the algorithm leads the program to code that is essentially, but not inherently, flawed. Other examples include trying to access an element in an array that exceeds its upper boundary, reading beyond the end of a stream, trying to close a file that has not yet been opened, or trying to reference an object that has been terminated. Logic exceptions usually come from the operating system, which detects the violations. You may also provide custom exception classes to deal with your own logic errors.

■ **Conditional errors** These are exceptions, usually custom-built by deriving from a base exception class, and are explicitly raised. You would raise exceptions only if a certain precondition or post-condition exists or does not exist in your code. For example, if a node of a custom linked-list class is not found at the start of an algorithm or block of code, you could raise a custom **NoSuchElementFoundException** exception to trap the condition. A post-condition exception would be raised if a condition you specify in the exception handler does not exist after the algorithm is processed. For example, if your code is supposed to leave the application in a certain condition before continuing and does not, you could provide an exception right there—in a post-condition exception handler.

You can create custom exceptions to cater to anything you believe should be considered an error and that is not provided by the default exception classes provided in the base class library.

Note *Using the directive **Option Explicit On** at the top of your class files forces the Visual Basic compiler to forward-check your syntax before it is compiled. It lets you be sure that all code is free of syntax errors before run time.*

An exception is an object that is derived from the superclass **Exception**. When you add an exception handler to a method, you are essentially providing a means of returning control to the application and resuming execution as normally as possible. What would life be like if humans were provided with error or exception handlers like this? Just as you are about to make a gargantuan mistake, an error handler would catch the "error" and put you back on track. Humans learn from mistakes; unfortunately it takes a lot of effort to write heuristic software.

You can make it so that the caller of a method handles the exception raised in the target method. It might also be necessary for the caller of the caller to handle the exception, and you might have to go quite far back on the call stack to handle an exception.

When a method that bombs on an error is unable to deal with it, we say it has *thrown an exception.* This term comes from C++ and has caused many developers to balk at the idea of a class having a fit any time something goes wrong in a program. You might think of handling the "throw" as being similar to catching a ball at a baseball game. Drop the ball and miss the catch and you let the team down. Such exception handling is not a new idea. For example, structured exception handling has been part and parcel of the Object Pascal language and Delphi since its inception.

Exception Statements

To catch exceptions in Visual Basic, you need to enclose your code in a **Try**…**Catch** block. The guarded code to execute is placed in the **Try** section of the block, and any errors are handled in one or more **Catch** blocks. After the last **Catch** block, you can provide the optional **Finally** block that will always execute regardless of whether or not an exception occurred. The **Finally** block is mandatory if no **Catch** block is used. Later, I will show you how you can use the **Finally** block to reset resources and provide some housekeeping.

Try

Back in the early '90s when I was a "newbie" Delphi programmer, I made an effort to code 99.9 percent of my stuff in **try**… **except/try**… **finally** blocks. In other words, no matter what routine I was writing, as soon as I arrived at the point in the method where the algorithm starts, the first line of my code was **try**. I am not ashamed to admit that I often did stuff like this:

```
      Try
   Y/0;
except
   on EZeroDivide do HandleZeroDivide;
end;
```

I did this (Object Pascal code) at a time when exception handling had just been introduced to the new object-oriented programming languages that were emerging. Clearly, more than a decade ago, many of us wrapped code in these exception-handling blocks just to "play it safe." You may laugh, but at least it was better than adding the line **On Error Resume Next** at the top of every routine regardless of what that routine did.

This habit carried over into my Java programming by 1995 and I always believed this until I decided to investigate exception handling in much more detail than I needed to. Before you get carried away, consider the following advice:

- Not all code produces exceptions. There's no point enclosing the call to **BackGround.SetColor** between a **Try…Catch** block. First, you do not really have the ability to handle the exception properly, and second, it's unlikely that a property like this will be coded in such a way that it can risk exceptions. And even if a property were prone to exceptions, the exception handling should not be handled by a method that calls faulty code. Imagine asking a restaurant patron to "handle" his or her own "fly-in-the-soup" exception.

- Exceptions not handled by the method that raised them may, and often should, get handled by methods that came before it. In other words, the methods are popped off the call stack one by one until a suitable handler is found. So not handling the exception at the point it was raised does not mean your application is going to go to hell on the A-train. The **FindExcept** class presented later shows how this "delegation" works.

- Variables and constants declared inside the **Try…Catch** blocks are only visible inside the block in which they were declared. In other words, their visibility does not extend beyond the scope of the guarded block of code. You will also not be able to see the variables from the **Catch** or **Finally** sections of the handler.

These points suggest that you should not willy-nilly enclose everything in **Try…Catch** blocks but rather should think through your code properly—according to the design patterns, models, and well-scripted method specifications discussed in Chapter 7. If you do this, you'll easily be able to figure out exactly where you need to put a handler and the purpose it will serve.

Catch

The code that handles your exception begins at the **Catch** statement as follows:

```
Catch Except As Exception
```

or

```
Catch E As Exception
```

The preceding statements serve to instantiate the exception object that can handle the type of exception. Each exception object is a reference type, and in the preceding code, **Except** and **E** are the reference variables. The variable reference model at work here is the same object reference model described in the previous chapter, and you can work with or on any exception object as you would with any other instance.

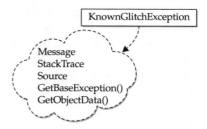

What the illustration shows is this: At the point an error is detected, the next line of code processed is the **Catch** line, which instantiates an exception object to deal with the exception. The exception object is accessed by way of its reference variable. As soon as you have instantiated the object, you can get to work on handling the error. "Handling" can range from doing practically nothing to doing a whole lot. The first job might be to consider the user who might be inconvenienced, and report information to that user. So, we could display a message to the user, as demonstrated in the following code, which produces the message box seen in the illustration below.

```
Public Sub CheckForModem()
  Try
    If Not ModemExists Then
      Throw New Exception()
    End If
  Catch E As Exception
    MsgBox("Can't find the modem.", MsgBoxStyle.Exclamation, _
      "The Complete Reference")
  Finally
    isCompleted = False
  End Try
End Sub
```

CLASSES AND OBJECTS

Only provide the user with information he or she has the power to change or can use. It makes no sense to tell a user that a *"**DivideByZeroException** just occurred."*

Naturally, you would want to use common sense here and communicate with the user in a manner he or she will be able to relate to. If the exception is a matter of concern for the program and its creator, then there's no need to report the exception and the contents of the exception object's message field to the user. Simply handle the exception and move on if possible.

Table 11-1 lists the members of the framework's base class library exception objects (r signifies read-only and r/w signifies read and write). Let's go through these members and see how they can be used to handle exceptions.

GetBaseException

This method returns the root cause of an exception. In a chain of exceptions, there will always be a link back to the root exception via the **InnerException** property. You can gain access to the root exception, read any information from it, and pinpoint exactly in your code where the trouble started in the first place. The **ToString** method of the root exception will provide you with the type of current exception and will identify the line that raised the exception. Have a look at the following code:

```
Public Sub GetToStringOfException()
  Dim ex As Object
  'set up the exception for out of range error
  Dim mdArray(5) As Integer
  Try
    mdArray(6) = 10 'oops
  Catch Except As IndexOutOfRangeException
    ex = Except.GetBaseException
    Console.WriteLine("Info: " & ex.ToString)
  Finally
    isCompleted = False
  End Try
End Sub
```

The output to the console window is as follows:

```
Info: System.IndexOutOfRangeException: Index was outside the bounds
of the array.   at Vb7cr.ExceptionTests.GetToStringOfException() in
C:\Vb7cr\Exceptions\ExceptionTests.vb:line 157
```

See also the discussions on **InnerException** in "Creating Your Own Exception Classes" later in this chapter.

Exception Member	Usage
GetBaseException	Returns the root cause of the exception
GetObjectData	Serializes out the exception object's data
GetType	Gets the type of the current object
HelpLink (r/w)	Sets a link to a help file associated with the exception
InnerException (r)	Returns information about the exception caused by the previous exception object
Message (r)	Returns any error message that describes the exception
Source (r/w)	Gets or sets the name of the application that caused the exception
StackTrace (r)	Takes a snapshot of the call stack and places the information in a string you can access
TargetSite (r)	Returns the name of the method that threw the exception
ToString	Returns a string representation of the current exception (maybe the same data as the message)

Table 11-1.   *Methods and Properties of an Exception Object*

GetObjectData
This method serializes out the exception object's data.

HelpLink
This is a property you hard code as a constant to the class and set it whenever your class is raised. The link can be provided to the user in a variety of ways. The consumer of the class may display it to a message box and from there let the user visit a Web page with further information or as a means to collect debug data. See "Creating Your Own Exception Classes" later in this chapter.

InnerException
This property stores the reference to an exception object that may have preceded the current exception. There are two ways that another exception can arise as the result of an exception. The first way is that the code in the current exception handler itself

causes another exception. After all, the **Catch** block itself has as much power to process code as the **Try** block. I don't believe you should add 101 lines to the **Catch** block. That's not good programming. But even one line of code can be a problem.

The second way is if you explicitly raise another exception with an explicit **Throw** from the **Catch** block. The latter way is a more likely scenario, because you may have something else to test in the **Catch** block and decide to raise another exception. The second exception raised can be used to take the flow of execution to the handler provided in the method that originally called the method that started the exceptions.

Later, in the section "Creating Your Own Exception Classes," we'll look at some code that specifically accesses the **InnerException** property.

Source

This property stores the name of the class or instance in which an exception was raised. Combine the **Source** property with the **Message** property and other data to create a detailed report on an exception. The entire string can then be stored and shipped off to a log, saved to a file, or made available to an administrator that can have access to a window that has access to the information.

In the example that follows, I concatenated **Source** with the **Message** property and pushed it onto a stack object storing my exception information for the class:

```
Public Sub LookAtSource()
  Dim mdArray(5) As Integer
  Dim myErrorStack As New Stack() 'remember stacks need New for activation
  Dim myErrorSource As String
  Try
    'this next line raises another IndexOutOfRangeException
    mdArray(6) = 10
  Catch Except As IndexOutOfRangeException
    myErrorSource = Except.Source & ": " & Except.Message
    myErrorStack.Push(myErrorSource)
    Console.WriteLine(myErrorStack.Pop)
  Finally
    isCompleted = False
  End Try
End Sub
```

The StackTrace Property

This property is similar to **Source** but the information is a lot more detailed. You get the exact call from the main call stack for the application. The call returned is the method call and the line number in the class where the exception occurred. This property is very useful for debugging, as the following example shows:

```
Public Sub LookAtStackTrace()
  Dim mdArray(5) As Integer
```

```
   Try
      mdArray(6) = 10
   Catch Except As IndexOutOfRangeException
      Console.WriteLine(Except.StackTrace)
   Finally
      isCompleted = False
   End Try
End Sub
```

This code writes the following line to the console window:

```
at Vb7cr.ExceptionTests.LookAtStackTrace() in
C:\Vb7cr\Exceptions\ExceptionTests.vb:line 190
```

See also the discussion on **InnerException** in "Creating Your Own Exception Classes" later in this chapter.

 *The stack trace begins at the throw-point, the statement that causes the exception, and ends at the **Catch** statement that catches the exception, so be aware of this fact when deciding where to place a **Throw** statement.*

Message

We examined the **Message** property earlier. It provides a message created by the author of the exception object, and hopefully provides details about the cause of an exception. Often it's just information about the type of exception raised, such as "Index was outside the bounds of the array."

The message string may be in the language specified by the **Thread.CurrentUICulture** property of the thread that throws the exception.

TargetSite

This property returns the method that raises your exception. You can combine it with some of the other properties, like **Source**, to supply your own information concerning the classes and method in which exceptions originate.

Finally

When an exception occurs, execution stops and control is given to the closest exception handler. This often means that lines of code you expect to always be called are not executed. There are times when resource cleanup, such as closing a file, must always be executed even if an exception is thrown. To accomplish this, you can use a **Finally** block. A **Finally** block is always executed, regardless of whether an exception is thrown and regardless of whether you used a **Catch** block to handle the exception.

The following code example uses a **Try...Catch** block to catch the
IndexOutOfRangeExceptions we have been looking at for the past couple of examples. In
the following listing the **Finally** block executes regardless of the outcome of the action
and sets the **isCompleted Boolean** variable to **False** in order to return to the menu
rather than close down the application.

```vbnet
Public Sub Main()

  Dim menuChoice As Char
  While Not isCompleted
    Console.WriteLine("                        ")
    Console.WriteLine("----------MENU-----------")
    Console.WriteLine("------------------------")
    Console.WriteLine("a: Test the NodeNotFoundException.")
    Console.WriteLine("b: Test exception parser.")
    '...
    Console.WriteLine("i: Get a LookAtStackTrace.")
    Console.WriteLine("Q: Q or nothing to quit application.")
    Console.WriteLine("------------------------")
    Console.Write("Choose a process:  ")

    menuChoice = Console.ReadLine()
    Select Case menuChoice
      Case Is = "a"c
        GetNodeNext()
      Case Is = "b"c
        TestParser()
      '...
      Case Is = "h"c
        LookAtSource()
      Case Is = "i"c
        LookAtStackTrace()
      Case Else
        isCompleted = True
    End Select
  End While
End Sub

'lots of methods in between

Public Sub GetNodeNext()
  Try
```

```
    Throw New NodeNotFoundException()
  Catch NExcept As NodeNotFoundException
    Console.WriteLine(NExcept.Message)
  Finally
      'we need this line to keep the menu in the console alive
      isCompleted = False
  End Try
End Sub
```

The **Finally** section in the preceding method returns the user to the **Console** and provides for a normal exit from the application, no matter what the exception.

The preceding technique is useful, but in most applications and services, the **Finally** block is used to clean up after the code in the blocks that preceded it, no matter whether an exception was raised or not. Because the **Finally** block is always called, you never want to recall the method, either directly or indirectly, from the **Finally** block because you'll end up putting the method on a carousel.

The **Finally** block will also be processed after an **Exit Sub** or an **Exit Try** statement aimed at knocking the execution out of the entire method. It will also process after a **Return** anywhere in preceding blocks. And the **Finally** block is also executed after an exception is passed up the call stack to a method that was pushed down onto the stack earlier and even within inner and nested exceptions.

The **Finally** block is also not restricted, so it's quite possible for it to raise another exception. Should that be the case, the exception will be passed up the call stack to a method that has a suitable **Catch** handler that can be delegated the task. Keep code in the **Finally** block simple and as exception-proof as possible, because it makes no sense to be raising exceptions after a lengthy cleanup.

When an exception is handled by a method further into the call stack, or not by a handler in the method that caused the exception, the code that comes after the exception (after the **End Try** *statement) is not processed. This is normal behavior regardless of whether* **Finally** *is used or not.*

When Filters

The **When** keyword in a **Catch** handler is a new concept that lets you "filter" exceptions according to criteria you specify. Interestingly, only Visual Basic and C++ support this concept of user-filtered exceptions. Since exception handling has been around for many years without such a concept, I wondered in what situations such an idea would be useful. Turns out that it helps reduce the amount of exception-handling code by letting you decide when you want to handle an exception in the local handler or let the exception through to be handled further into the call stack.

CLASSES AND OBJECTS

It is also useful when a particular exception object corresponds to several errors. For example, several areas in your **Try** code can raise *argument, null reference,* and similar exceptions. The syntax for using the **When** condition is as follows:

```
Catch Except As Exception When Something is True
```

In the following simplistic example, which works like an **If...Then** statement, we set up two **Stack** objects that will render exceptions of type **DivideByZeroException** (a **Decimal** divided by the default values of **denom** and **demon2**) rather than the overflow exception. Calling the method with **denom** as zero causes the first exception to be picked up be **E1**. However, when we fix **denom** with the value 10 the **When** keyword takes the code over **E1** to be caught by **E2**. Check it out:

```
Public Sub CatchWhen()
  Dim myStack As New Stack()
  Dim yourStack As New Stack()
  Dim value As Decimal = 10
  Dim denom As Integer
  Dim denom2 As Integer
  Try
    myStack.Push(value / denom)
    yourStack.Push(value / denom2)
  Catch E1 As DivideByZeroException When denom = 0
    Console.WriteLine(E1.Message & " at myStack")
  Catch E2 As DivideByZeroException When denom2 = 0
    Console.WriteLine(E2.Message & " at yourStack")
  Finally
    isCompleted = False
  End Try
End Sub
```

In the preceding example, the custom **MyDivideByZeroException** will be instantiated only when the **denom** variable is zero; otherwise, all other **DivideByZeroException**s will be handled by the second handler.

When Filters and the Error Object

Visual Basic maintains a global and system-wide error object that you can tap into by using the **When** exception filter as follows:

```
Try
   mdArray(6) = 10
Catch Except As IndexOutOfRangeException When Err.Number = 9
   '...
End Try
```

In the preceding example, you can access the **Error** object (**Err**), which typically has a property that contains the specific error code associated with the error. You can use the error code property in the expression to select only the particular error you want to handle in that **Catch** clause.

The following Visual Basic example illustrates the **Catch**...**When** statement:

```
Try
   '...
Catch When Err = VBErr_ClassLoadException
   '...
End Try
```

or

```
Try
   '...
Catch When Err.Number = 9
   '...
End Try
```

While using **When** with the error object appears useful, it doesn't offer anything more powerful than standard SEH **Catch** handlers. The following example does not present you with a reference variable:

```
Try
   mdArray1(6) = 10
Catch When Err.Number = 9
   MsgBox(Err.Description)
End Try
```

However, you can use the **Err** object to create an exception because the SEH architecture and the **Err** object basically get their error grist from the same mill. Still, it's better to work with exception objects and work the **Err** object out of your future.

Nesting Try Blocks

If you're new to writing code inside **Try**…**Catch** blocks, it can take some time to get into the habit of doing so. While you can easily compile Visual Basic code without a **Try**…**Catch** block, good Visual Basic design guards code whenever necessary.

I often have thought that the compiler and the run-time environment should require, in most cases, that the **Try**…**Catch** blocks be mandatory for certain syntax. When you write delicate code without a **Try**…**Catch** block, you are relying on the run-time system to serve up the default exception handler. But that's like flying on autopilot—eventually you have to take control to land the plane.

When you have been writing Visual Basic code long enough, you begin to think in terms of **Try**…**Catch**…**Finally** in the same way you think in terms of objects and classes, or methods and their members—the inherent makeup of an object-oriented program. It just becomes natural to build blocks of functionality with the **Try** keyword.

It should come as no surprise, therefore, that a single **Try** block does not always cater to complex methods. Many circumstances will require you to create additional **Try**…**Catch** blocks inside of your outer ones. In other words, as a matter of course, you'll be nesting the blocks for complex and perhaps very long methods. Sometimes you might find reason to nest these blocks to several levels.

When the code being executed enters an outer **Try** block, the so-called context of that exception is pushed onto the stack. When something goes wrong and the current exception does not have the correct handler, the code reverses back up the stack and the next **Catch** statement is scanned for a handler. The code continues to back out of the stack until a handler is found or the run-time system is forced to handle the exception. You saw this at work at the beginning of the chapter, but have a look at the following example:

```
Public Shared Sub TestNest(ByVal value As Integer, ByVal value2 As Integer)
   Dim result As Integer
   Dim array(5) As Integer
   Try
     result = value / value2
       Try
         array(6) = 10
       Catch Except As IndexOutOfRangeException
         Console.WriteLine(Except.Message)
       Finally
         Console.WriteLine("Inner Finally")
       End Try
   Catch Except As OverflowException
     Console.WriteLine(Except.Message)
   Finally
     Console.WriteLine("Outer Finally")
   End Try
End Sub
```

What's happening here? This code nests one **Try**...**Catch** block within another. At first a potential divide-by-zero exception is set up so as to deal with it on the outer **Try**...**Catch** block. The code does drill into the **Try** nest as you would expect, so it never encounters the **IndexOutOfRangeException**. The reason is simple: as noted earlier, the code in the entire outer **Try** block is ignored, and that goes for any nested **Try** statements inside of it.

If the outer **Try** code checked out, then the inner **Try** would still be live code and the processing would go on to encounter the **IndexOutOfRangeException**. However, if no suitable exception were found, the outer **Catch** block would be tried for a suitable handler. In the preceding example, the handler might be found at the level of the calling method, which has a default handler for any **Exception** object.

Nesting **Try** statements is not easy, and you can often waste a lot of time with misplaced closing **End Try** statements and out-of-position **Catch** statements, which result in a compiler error reporting that the **Try** is catchless. Here's a tip: First create and complete the outer **Try** statement, complete with its **Catch** and especially a **Finally** block, if you need one. Then go into the inner **Try** block and code the new inner **Try**...**Catch**...**Finally** from start to finish. Do not leave out *all* the **Catch** blocks until after the **Try** blocks are done. You'll tear your hair out trying to properly place the **Catch** and **Finally** blocks with the correct **Try** blocks. Follow similar design logic to the steps suggested back in Chapter 6 for nested conditional statements.

While you can practically nest to as many levels as you need to, your code will become very hard to follow and maintain, and that's not good design. When you code methods that have the potential of generating many exceptions, stack the **Catch** handlers rather than nest them. This has the same effect as a deeply nested collection of **Try**...**Catch** blocks, but it's far easier to follow, as the following code demonstrates:

```
Public Shared Sub TestStack(ByVal value As Integer, ByVal value2 As Integer)
Dim result As Integer
  Dim array(5) As Integer
  Try
    result = value / value2
    array(6) = 10
  Catch Except As OverflowException
    Console.WriteLine(E.Message)
  Catch Except As IndexOutOfRangeException
    Console.WriteLine(Ex.Message)
  Finally
    Console.WriteLine("Only one Finally")
  End Try
End Sub
```

While you gain clarity in your code, stacking the handlers rather than nesting the **Try**...**Catch** blocks has a significant downside: You are limited to one **Finally** block when you stack handlers. Nested **Try** blocks give you a **Finally** block for every exception handler. In other words, if you nest to five levels, you get five **Finally** blocks. This may be an important consideration, depending on the objectives of the method. However, there is yet another technique that is discussed later, in the section "Delegating to an Exception Handling Class."

While stacking and nesting ability is powerful, too much of either suggests that your method needs to be decomposed as discussed in Chapter 7. A method can be hundreds of lines long if it has to be but you will write better code, which will be easier to read and maintain, if methods are functionally cohesive units.

Throw

The exceptions that are raised or instantiated in the code examples that we have seen so far in this chapter are automatically raised by Visual Basic. You don't have to raise an **ArithmeticException** because Visual Basic implicitly does that for you if your code fouls up. There are also occasions when you can explicitly raise an exception, when you deem it necessary or need to meet specific objectives. You do this by using the **Throw** keyword, followed by **New** constructor to create the object.

Using the **Throw** keyword is simple. At the so-called "throw point," simply raise the exception as follows:

```
Throw New SomeKindOfException
```

Notice that we use the **New** keyword because we are essentially instantiating an object, a derivative or specialization of **System.Exception** or its children.

There are several uses for the **Throw** keyword. We have seen the first use several times already in this chapter. We decide to raise or reraise one of the standard exceptions that come included with the base class library and that the CLR knows about. Usually, we use **Throw New** because of some condition in our code that requires it. We might decide to throw the exception based on a certain precondition not existing in a method or a post condition also not existing (or existing).

Another important use is to raise a custom exception that the CLR might not know about. You can create your own exception class for certain custom conditions, and you'll need to raise the custom exception with **Throw New** because only you can determine, at design time, why and when to raise it. We can also use **Throw** to delegate exception handling to another exception class, but I will get into that idea a little later in this chapter.

So how do you handle exceptions that the CLR is not prepared for? You can write code that is able to distinguish between violations that are always caught by the CLR and violations that are not caught by the CLR (it does not know about them), and you need to provide the facility in your method to catch these exceptions.

To check and raise exceptions that your code might create, and thus protect callers of the method, you can add a **Throw** statement to the method as shown in the following method.

```
Public Sub Factor()
  Try
    If myStack.Pop <= 0 Then
      Throw New DivideByZeroException
    End If
  Catch Except As DivideByZeroException
    Console.WriteLine(E.Message)
  Finally
    isCompleted = False
  End Try
End Sub
```

If you declare the exception with the **Throw New** statement, you are essentially forcing prior callers to handle the exception. Using this technique is good programming practice because, as your code evolves and increases in complexity, you know you have the reinforcement bar in place should your concrete come under unexpected pressure.

Two interesting items to note here:

- Visual Basic gives you the ability to create a new exception object, thus enabling you to set up a new exception-handling scenario. This is useful if you need to create specialized exception-handling code that does a better job for your situation than the default exception-handling classes.

- Visual Basic lets you pass text and **InnerException** data to the new exception object's constructor. In the declaration and instantiation object, the **Message** property, normally read-only, is overloaded, and two of the alternative methods are read/write.

You can pass data to the parameters of the new object's constructor as follows:

```
Catch Except As DivideByZeroException
  Throw New DivideByZeroException("I come from ExceptTests.FirstMethod")
Finally
'...
```

Note *The ability to pass data on **Throw New Exception** is not immediately apparent from the Visual Basic documentation.*

The Double Play: Rethrowing an Existing Exception

Imagine, as we did earlier, that the exception is a baseball runner trying hard to ruin your game. The defensive players covering the bases are the exception handlers, "trying" hard to "catch" the runner. After the first throw from the pitcher, an exception handler (the catcher) picks up the ball and "throws" it to first base. This is, in fact, the second chance the team gets to handle an exception.

Visual Basic lets us set up a similar scenario. An exception can be caught once and then rethrown to another handler using code similar to the following:

```
Catch Except As OverflowException
  Except.Source = Me.ThrowPoint
  Throw Except 'double-play
Finally
'...
```

Where would you use the double, or even triple, throw? Sometimes you may have a need to catch an exception, add information and data to its read/write properties, and then rethrow the exception. This example rethrows the exception but not before first adding information to the **Source** property, which for some exceptions is left empty. You can also add a URL link to a page on a Web site somewhere or to a local help file by populating the **HelpLink** property and then rethrowing the exception. Here is a more concrete example:

```
Public Module ExceptionTests
  Shared Sub Main()
    Try
      TestThrow(10D, 0)
    Catch Except As Exception
      Console.WriteLine(Except.Message & " " & Except.HelpLink)
    Finally
      Console.WriteLine("Normal exit: Press 'q' to quit the sample.")
      While Chr(Console.Read()) <> "q"c
      End While
    End Try
  End Sub

  Public Sub TestThrow (ByVal value As Decimal, ByVal value2 _
    As Integer)
    Dim result As Decimal
    Try
      result = value / value2
    Catch Except As OverflowException
      Except.HelpLink = "http://www.codetimes.com/adfwe54353fef.htm"
      Throw Except
    Finally
```

```
        Console.WriteLine("Outer Finally")
    End Try
  End Sub
End Module
```

This may be a little hard to follow, so let me explain. The method that caused an exception is called **TestThrow** (adapted from **TestNest**, shown earlier), which comprises a **Try…Catch…Finally** block. This method is called by **Main**, which causes an **OverflowException** object caused by passing in **Decimal** 10 to be divided by **Integer** 0 to **TestNest** parameters. An inner handler takes care of the exception and tacks on the URL to the **HelpLink** property.

The next line is **Throw Except**, which rethrows the exception, this time complete with the data in the **HelpLink** property. The second throw point does not create a new exception; it just rethrows the exception. The exception is caught by the handler in the method that called **TestThrow**—in this case **Main**.

> **Note** *When you rethrow an exception or throw a new exception as demonstrated in the preceding example, the CLR passes the rethrown exception object to a handler in the previous method, because the current **Try** and **Catch** blocks are out of scope. Only the **Finally** lives on, and the flow of execution dictates that the **Finally** from the current method is processed before the newly thrown exception is handled by the method the flow of execution returns to.*

Using Throw to Delegate to an Exception-Handling Object

Another technique used in other object-oriented environments that have SEH is the delegation of exception handling to an exception-handling object or operations class.

When a complex method has the potential to raise several different types of exceptions, or when you have many methods in a class that all have exception-raising potential, you may have to nest **Try…Catch** blocks to many levels or stack the **Catch** handlers to several "stories." This can make the method hard to read, maintain, and manage as I mentioned earlier. You can instead catch any exception caused by the method in a single default catch handler and then pass the reference to another method that can better handle the exception object. To use the baseball analogy again, it's like throwing the ball to the catcher at home plate and then letting the catcher decide where to throw next.

The pattern is simple as shown in the UML diagram here.

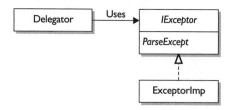

Create a static class or instance with methods that receive the reference variable to the exception's object instantiated elsewhere in your application. Then, in the method that raises the exception, catch the object using the default exception handler. With the exception object "in your mitt," pass it by reference to the exception-handling method in the exceptions class or object delegated to handle the exception.

Once the reference has been received by the method in the exception-handling class, it can be rethrown to an assortment of exception handlers. The following code shows how I implemented this idea. The class contains a method that does not do much except throw an exception to simulate the real thing.

```
Imports Vb7cr.Exceptions
Imports System
Public Class ExceptionTests

Private Ex As IExceptor = New ExceptorImp()
Public Sub TestParser()
  Try
    Throw New Exception()
  Catch Except As Exception
    Console.WriteLine("came back with: " & Ex.ParseExcept(Except))
  Finally
   isCompleted = False
  End Try
End Sub
```

The method **TestParser** can call the **ParseExcept** method of the **IExceptor** interface and pass it a reference to the object. The following interface and implementation code is on the receiving end of the call:

```
Interface IExceptor
  Function ParseExcept(ByRef Except As Exception) As String
End Interface

Class ExceptorImp
  Implements IExceptor

  Public Function ParseExcept(ByRef Except As Exception) _
    As String Implements IExceptor.ParseExcept
    Try
      Throw Except
    Catch E As DivideByZeroException
      Return E.Message
```

```
      Catch E As DivideByZeroException When E.Source = _
        "ExceptionTests.ThreeInOne"
        Return "Right place pal " & E.Message
      Catch E As IndexOutOfRangeException
        E.Source = ""
        Return E.Message
      Catch E As NodeNotFoundException
        Return E.Message
      Catch E As Exception
        Return "Two mules for sister Sarah " & E.Message
      End Try
   End Function
End Class
```

The method **ParseExcept** in the above code implements a number of options depending on the type of exception. It gets the reference to the exception object and simply rethrows it to its own **Catch** blocks. The stack of **Catch** blocks can filter the exception until the correct exception object is found. It can then be dealt with, as you deem necessary. The **ParseExcept** method returns normally to the method that called it, so any additional lines of code, or a **Finally** block, are still executed by the **caller**.

| Note | *The above code was taken from an e-mail server I wrote a couple of years back. Any network programming you do, particularly sockets, has the potential to create many scenarios you'll want to throw exceptions on (and many that will give you no choice). These include losing connections, receiving bad data, receiving invalid responses from hosts, getting malformed URLs from the sockets, parsing malformed domain names and e-mail addresses, and so on.* |

You can be as creative as you need to in the **ExceptorImp** class. The code in **ExceptorImp** also implements an exception filter with the **When** keyword, as shown earlier in this chapter, so you can tighten the connection between the class that caused the exception and the **ParseExcept** method. The following code demonstrates two exception handlers for different **DivideByZeroException** objects filtered according to source:

```
Catch E1 As DivideByZeroException When E.Source = "Delivery.GetPercenatages"
   Return E1.Message
Catch E2 As DivideByZeroException When E.Source = "Receiving.GetPercenatages"
   Return E2.Message
```

One thing I should point out as a matter of interest: The class that parses the exception is implemented here as an interface and implementation. You could just as easily couple interface and implementation in a standard class. However, de-coupling the interface from the implementation like this is useful for varying the implementation and reusing the interface for a number of situations. This is made possible with the following declaration used eariler:

```
Private Ex As IExceptor = New ExceptorImp()
```

This code couples the interface **IExceptor** (as **Ex**) to an implementation of it (in this case **ExceptorImp**. The pattern is known as Strategy and is covered in more detail in Chapters 13 and 14.

Exception-Handling Tips

Structured exception handling is very important, but you should not overuse it. Here are some important tips to make sure you do not:

- Avoid using Visual Basic exception handling for anything other than handling errors. Often, developers will find that **Try…Catch…Finally** blocks make for interesting flow-control structures, but using them for this purpose only serves to damage the structural integrity of the program and consume resources.

- Creating custom exception classes for every error you might encounter doesn't make sense. Creating equivalents of the run-time exception classes only wastes time and resources.

- Notwithstanding the usefulness of the **Throw** feature, you should handle exceptions, as far as possible, in the method in which they were raised. This, too, conserves resources and makes your code easier to follow.

- When using nested **Try** blocks or multiple **Catch** blocks, you need to remember to place the default **Catch E As Exception** as the last **Catch** block, because placing it earlier will prevent any later exception classes (both custom or built-in) from ever getting executed.

- Handle all exceptions; do not simply catch exceptions and then do nothing with them. Providing "sterile" exception-handling code does not mean you do not have to deal with the exceptions, and they should not merely be "swept under the carpet."

- As mentioned in Chapters 5, 6, and 7, you should carefully evaluate if you need to throw an exception or if the implicit throw can be avoided. Program defensively. Use flow control and iterative routines to check for conditions that would cause an exception, and then program around those conditions. Here is an example that causes an exception, and you now have to deal with it:

```
Try
    conn.Close()
```

```
Catch ex As InvalidOperationException
   'now you have to deal with it.
End Try
```

- In the following example, the exception is avoided because you have tested the code for exception "potential":

```
If conn.State <> ConnectionState.Closed Then 'avoid the exception
   conn.Close()
End If
```

Note *See the State pattern in Chapter 13 and the discussion of state machines in the same chapter.*

- Here is another example that can potentially raise exception hell but avoids it through other mechanisms:

```
Class FileRead
   Sub Open()
     Dim stream As FileStream = File.Open("myfile.txt",
FileMode.Open)
     Dim b As Byte
     'Method ReadByte returns -1 at EOF (the end of the file).
     While b = stream.ReadByte() <> True
       'Do something.
     End While
   End Sub
End Class
```

- On the other hand, if the test or conditional routines require you to write more code or more resources, or both, than the exception, you should rather raise or throw the exception and then provide the means to deal with it.

- When you need to create custom or user-defined exceptions that will be used in remoting or transapplication domain scenarios, you must ensure that the assemblies that contain the metadata for the exceptions are available to the code executing remotely, or across the application domains. For example, if an application in an application domain throws an exception that is contained in an assembly not under its application base, the CLR will throw a **FileNotFoundException**. To avoid this situation, put the assembly into a common application base shared by both application domains, or if the domains do not share a common application base, sign the assembly containing the exception information with a strong name and deploy the assembly into the global assembly cache (refer to Chapters 2 and 19 for more-specific information).

- Prefer exceptions to returning error codes or **HRESULT**.

- Provide a message that informs; watch the language and grammar. Users and consumers appreciate grammatically correct and informative messages. An obnoxious **E.Message** that reads something like "user is a loser" will not help your reputation.

Creating Your Own Exception Classes

We've covered working with the Visual Basic built-in, or class library, exception handlers. But solid exception-handling code often requires custom exception handlers.

Creating your own exception classes is not a difficult task. These exceptions need to be derived from class **Exception**, or the derivatives of **Exception**. Classes that derive from **Exception** inherit the base methods and properties of this class. While you can still derive from **Exception**, you might be better off inheriting from the children, the specialized classes, of **Exception** (not necessarily the ones that come installed with the .NET Framework) and gain access to specific functionality you need, not typically implemented in the root exception class. To create your own exception class, you can override the methods of the parent as needed. Before we proceed to create our own exception class, let's investigate the .NET exception class hierarchy.

The .NET Exception Hierarchy

We know that two main types of exceptions can be thrown or raised by an executing program: application exceptions and exceptions generated by the CLR. However, some exception classes can be thrown by either an application or the CLR.

The **Exception** class is the base class for exceptions in the .NET Framework. Several built-in exception classes inherit directly from **Exception**. These include **ApplicationException** and **SystemException**. These two classes form the basis for almost all run-time exceptions.

Most exceptions that derive directly from **Exception** add no functionality to the **Exception** class, so it's uncertain for the first version of the Framework why the architects chose to split the hierarchy into two descendant paths: **ApplicationException** and **SystemException**. For example, the **NullReferenceException** class hierarchy is illustrated here.

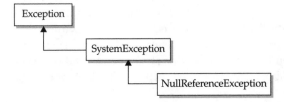

When the CLR detects errors that result from failed run-time checks (such as array out-of-bounds errors that can occur during the execution of any method), it throws the appropriate derived class of **SystemException**. On the other hand, **ApplicationException** is preferred as the base class to derive from for exceptions thrown by a user program.

The Framework architects suggest that if you are designing an application that creates new exceptions, you should rather derive custom or application specific exceptions from the **ApplicationException** class. According to the SDK documentation, the Framework architects do not recommended that you catch objects derived from **SystemException**, and they believe it is not "…good programming practice to throw **SystemException** in your application."

Without knowing what specifically lies under the exception class "hood," I can't really explain why this is suggested, because **ApplicationException** does not appear very different from the root of the exception hierarchy, **Exception**. My guess is that later versions of the .NET Framework may enhance **ApplicationException**. Whatever the reason, it does no harm to inherit from **ApplicationException**.

> **Note**   *The most severe exceptions that can be caught are those thrown by the CLR, and include ExecutionEngineException, StackOverflowException, and OutOfMemoryException.*

Choosing a Base Class from which to Inherit

Whether you decide to derive from **Exception**, **SystemException**, **ApplicationException**, or one of the specific child exceptions, such as **NullReferenceException**, all exceptions ultimately inherit from **System.Exception**. Thus, you can throw any object that derives from the **Object** class as an exception. Microsoft recommends you throw and catch only **Exception** objects, or exceptions that derive from it, because not all .NET languages will be able to throw non-**Exception** exceptions.

Table 11-2 provides a concise reference to .NET Framework exception classes. It lists the runtime exception hierarchy.

The CLR has a base set of exceptions deriving from **SystemException** that it throws when executing individual instructions. You should look up the standard exceptions provided by the CLR and determine the conditions under which you should create a derived class. For example, interoperation exceptions derive from **SystemException** and are further extended by **ExternalException**. For example, **COMException** is the exception thrown during COM interoperability operations and derives from **ExternalException**. **Win32Exception** and **SEHException** also derive from **ExternalException**. There is no need to specifically declare the new exception class as long as it is linked into your namespace (refer to Chapters 2 and 4). You must reference the custom exception with both the **Throw** and the **New** keywords.

As a class or toolkit provider, you may want your consumers to be able to programmatically distinguish between various error conditions your product needs to cater to. The best way to do this is with your own user-defined exceptions. Each of the Framework's specific exception classes defines a specific exception, so in many cases, you only have to catch that exception, or derive from it. On the whole, however, you can simply derive from the **ApplicationException** class and be sure you are following supported practice.

Exception Class	Parent	Description
Exception	None	The base or parent class for all exceptions. This class is not used as an exception object itself.
SystemException	Exception	The base class for all runtime-generated errors. Use a derived class of this exception for custom system exceptions.
IndexOutOfRangeException	SystemException	Thrown by the runtime when an array is indexed improperly or when referencing an indexing outside its valid range.
NullReferenceException	SystemException	Thrown by the runtime only when a null object is referenced.
InvalidOperationException	SystemException	Thrown when something invalid is done.
ArgumentException	SystemException	Base class for argument exceptions.
ArgumentNullException	ArgumentException	Thrown when an argument is not allowed to be null.
ArgumentOutOfRangeException	ArgumentException	Thrown when an argument is not in a given range.

Table 11-2.   *The .NET Framework Runtime Exception Hierarchy*

Exception Class	Parent	Description
ExternalException	SystemException	Base class for exceptions that are external to the CLR.
ComException	ExternalException	Exceptions that encapsulate the COM **HRESULT** information.
SEHException	ExternalException	Exceptions that encapsulate Win32 structured exception handling information.

Table 11-2.   *The .NET Framework Runtime Exception Hierarchy* (continued)

CLASSES AND OBJECTS

Tip   *Whichever way you choose, it is always a good idea to end the class name of your custom exception class with the word* Exception.

All exceptions inherit the overloaded **New** constructors from the base class. The first constructor is parameterless and thus takes no arguments when you invoke it. Simply make the call as follows:

```
Throw New OutOfCandyException()
```

The second version of the **New** constructor contains a single parameter that sets the message field in the exception, which is accessible via the **Message** property after you raise the exception object. To provide a message to this exception, you can invoke the constructor as follows:

```
Throw New OutOfCandyException("Sorry, Halloween's over")
```

The third version of the **New** constructor provides for the inner exception property as well as the message information. That call is as follows:

```
Throw New OutOfCandyException(message, inner)
```

It is also good practice to implement the three recommended common constructors, as shown in the following example. You can call secondary constructors if you need to and add custom private methods in the new class that provides the message and inner exception information internally as soon as the object is instantiated.

In situations where you are using remoting, you must ensure that the metadata for any user-defined exceptions is available at the server (callee) and to the client (the proxy object or caller). For example, code calling a method in a separate application domain must be able to find the assembly containing an exception thrown by a remote call. For more information, see "Exception-Handling Tips."

In the following example, a new exception class, **NodeNotFoundException**, is derived from **System.NullReferenceException**. Three constructors are typically defined in the class, each taking different parameters. The parameters are: no message for the **Message** property that is accessible to the constructor, the inclusion of a message, or the inclusion of a message and data for the **InnerException** property.

```
Imports System
Imports System.Runtime.Serialization

<Serializable()> Public Class NodeNotFoundException
  Inherits NullReferenceException

  'Constructors
  Public Sub New()
    MyBase.New("No such node found.")
  End Sub

  Public Sub New(ByVal message As String)
    MyBase.New(message)
  End Sub

  Public Sub New(ByVal message As String, ByVal inner As Exception)
    MyBase.New(message, inner)
  End Sub
End Class
```

This is the extent of the newly derived class. There is no need to expose the members of the parent to our class, or override any base method, because the functionality we derived works just fine. If there is something specific you want to add to the new class, declare a new method or property.

Note *Do not forget to make the derived class serializable with the **<Serializable()>** attribute (see Chapter 15 for more information on serialization).*

The new exception class is tested with the following method:

```
Public Shared Sub TestNodeNext()
  Try
    myList.NodeNext
    If (NodeNext = Nothing) Then
      Throw New NodeNotFoundException()
    End If
  Catch Except As NodeNotFoundException
    Console.WriteLine(Exceptions.ParseExcept(Except))
  Finally
      'stay on current node
  End Try
End Sub
```

Observations

This chapter provided a thorough overview of exception handling in Visual Basic .NET because the subject is extremely important. It also served to supplement the introduction to exception handling in Chapter 7, which provided information on writing code with exception handlers as early as possible in this book. Exception handling is a vital facility in the design and construction of high-quality algorithms and robust methods.

An observation that I feel is imperative to point out in this chapter is that the pure inheritance in .NET comes into maximum use for creating your own user-defined, specialized, or custom exceptions. It makes perfect sense to derive from the base exceptions, as demonstrated earlier, because exceptions are all one of a kind. They all do the same thing and are tightly focused on handling exceptions raised in your code. Exceptions are thus tightly coupled and form a natural class hierarchy that is accessed by all parts of an application. It would make no sense, waste a lot of time, and cause a lot of anguish to your users and class consumers if you were to reinvent the wheel and develop your own hierarchy of exception classes.

The Complete Reference

Visual Basic .NET

Chapter 12

Collections, Arrays, and Other Data Structures

The .NET Framework provides exhaustive support for the implementation and deployment of many classic data structures. Easily accessible to Visual Basic .NET, these structures can be used for all manner of local and distributed algorithms, for visual and nonvisual applications, with Web services, ASP.NET, XML, and SOAP applications.

The data structure namespaces are underpinned by a powerful assortment of classes that can be used to search and sort data and to store and manage like and unlike collections of objects. The following is a list of common data structures you will encounter in this book:

- **Arrays** The most popular data structure—or "collection object" in object-oriented parlance—is an array. An array is an ideal means of storing and manipulating data (as you will later see), and for all the power that it packs, like the ability to reference its items through an index, it is surprisingly easy to work with. While the first data structure that always seems to come to mind is an array, a number of other data structures are more suited or more convenient to managing collections of data. Nevertheless, this chapter provides extensive coverage on arrays.

- **Lists** A list is also a very common data structure. The basic list, known as a "singly linked list," maintains a collection of objects that hold the data for each logical item, and a pointer to the next object in the list. The head of the list is a pointer to the first item; the last item points to null. Like arrays, lists typically process data at $O(n)$ time (refer to Chapter 7). Linked lists are ideal for storing unsorted data where the iteration and searching are more important than having sorted data and ad-hoc access via the indexed element. You could use a list to store recently loaded Web pages, data feed from serial ports, shopping carts, and any serialized streams of data. In a singly linked list, you use an *iterator* or *cursor* (or an *enumerator*, in .NET terminology) to "walk" or traverse the linkage of nodes. In a doubly linked list, the iterator can traverse the list in both directions. You can easily move the list data to an array. The .NET Framework, however, provides a highly optimized "cross-breed" between an array and a list, called the **ArrayList**, which provides similar utility to a linked list.

- **Trees** A tree is a hierarchical data structure comprising list-like structures in which nodes point to each other, like branches on a tree. However, a tree is a nonlinear structure. In other words, the elements of a tree do not point one element to the next, as they do in lists. Each parent element points to a left child and a right child. Trees are highly efficient search structures that typically process data at $O(\log n)$ time. A tree is useful, for example, for representing a file system or a directory structure. Trees are implemented and discussed in depth in *Visual Basic .NET Developer's Guide* (McGraw-Hill/Osborne, 2002).

- **Hash tables**   Hash tables are one of the cornerstones of computer science and one of the most widely used structures for sorting and accessing objects. A hash table stores the elements of lists in array-like structures and provides a very convenient means of accessing objects through a key (the hash code) based on data of the object. Hash tables are highly efficient and flexible, and we will spend some time reviewing them later in this chapter.

- **Stacks**   A stack is a very simple data structure to work with. It is a structure or container of elements that are rigidly ordered by pushing elements into the collection at one end, and then removing them again from the same end, like a stack of plates in a cafeteria or dining room. Items in a stack are typically referenced according to their position from the top of the stack. Items are "pushed" and "popped" from a stack on a last-in, first-out (LIFO) order. Another name for the LIFO stack is a *push-down* stack. The call stack of an operating system or the common language runtime is a similar structure, in which calls that are pushed down into the structure are suspended until the calls pushed on top of them are processed.

- **Queues**   Queues work in a manner opposite to stacks. In other words, the elements of queues are accessed according to a first-in, fist-out (FIFO) order. The elements in queues are like people standing in line at the theater. The elements that arrived in the queue first get serviced first.

A stack is a much simpler structure than an array and does not carry the overhead of an array. A queue is also technically much simpler than an array. But arrays have a lot more features, as we will see, and are thus used in many algorithms.

NET's Array and Collections Namespace

The .NET Framework organizes its data structure classes and interfaces into two principal namespaces: **System.Array** and **System.Collections**. The former namespace contains only the **Array** class, while the latter contains a variety of collection-oriented classes and interfaces. You cannot explicitly inherit from **Array**; only Visual Basic can do that for you. To create and use an array, you use Visual Basic's special constructs, which instantiate the **Array** for you.

The data structures in the **Collections** namespace that are similar to arrays maintain a collection of types that can be referenced to and managed as logical units. The most important difference between collections and arrays, however, is that the members of an **Array** object must all be of the same type, because an array is intended to be a strongly typed collection. In other words, the declaration syntax of the **Array** class instantiates the array to contain objects of only a certain type. Many of the collections we will be looking at do not require explicit typing at instantiation.

The **System.Collections** namespace contains a variety of interfaces, classes, and utilities that define various collections of objects, such as lists, queues, bit arrays, hash tables, stacks, and dictionaries. These members are listed in the tables that follow in this section. We do not have sufficient time and space to review all of them here, but once you understand the workings of the most important classes and interfaces, the others are just trivia.

Table 12-1 lists the various interfaces in the **Collections** namespace. Many of the collection classes—including the **Array** object—implement one or more of these interfaces. The **Array** class, for example, implements **System.Collections.IList**, which defines methods for accessing objects in a collection via an index. **Array** thus qualifies to be categorized as a collection.

Table 12-2, which lists and describes the collection classes, also indicates the various interfaces implemented by collections. These include interfaces such as **IEnumerable** and **ICloneable**, introduced in Chapter 10.

Interface	Description
ICollection	Defines a method for obtaining the amount of objects in a collection, synchronization methods, and a method for copying data from collections to an array
IComparer	Exposes a method that compares two objects
IDictionary	Represents a collection of key-and-value pairs
IDictionaryEnumerator	Enumerator support for the the elements of a dictionary
IEnumerable	Exposes a method used to bridge to a collection for simple iteration (see Chapter 13)
IEnumerator	Supports a simple iteration over a collection
IHashCodeProvider	Supplies a hash code for an object, using a custom hash function
IList	Represents a collection of objects that can be individually accessed by index

Table 12-1. *Interface Members of the **System.Collections** Namespace*

Classes	Purpose	Implements
ArrayList	An efficient array-like structure whose size is dynamically increased as required; it implements the **IList** interface.	IList, ICollection, IEnumerable, ICloneable
BitArray	A compact array of bit values, which are represented as **Boolean** values, where **True** indicates that the bit is on (1) and **False** indicates that the bit is off (0)	ICollection, IEnumerable, ICloneable
CaseInsensitive Comparer	A utility that compares two objects for equivalence, ignoring the case of strings	IComparer
CaseInsensitive HashCode-Provider	Supplies a hash code for an object, using a hashing algorithm that ignores the case of strings	IHashCodeProvider
CollectionBase	The abstract base class for a strongly typed collection	IList, ICollection, IEnumerable
Comparer	A utility that compares two objects for equivalence, where string comparisons are case-sensitive	IComparer
DictionaryBase	The abstract base class for a strongly typed collection of key-and-value pairs	IDictionary, ICollection, IEnumerable
DictionaryEntry (structure)	Defines a structure for a dictionary key-and-value pair that can be set or retrieved	N/A
Hashtable	A collection of key-and-value pairs that are organized based on the hash code of the key	IDictionary, ICollection, IEnumerable, ISerializable, IDeserializationCallback, ICloneable

Table 12-2. *Collection Classes (**Array** is not a member of **System.Collections**)*

Classes	Purpose	Implements
Queue	A standard FIFO collection of objects	ICollection, IEnumerable, ICloneable
ReadOnly CollectionBase	The abstract base class for a strongly typed read-only collection	ICollection, IEnumerable
SortedList	A collection of key-and-value pairs that are sorted by the keys and are accessible by key and by index	IDictionary, ICollection, IEnumerable, ICloneable
Stack	A standard LIFO collection of objects	ICollection, IEnumerable, ICloneable

Table 12-2.   Collection Classes (**Array** is not a member of **System.Collections**) (continued)

Specialized Collections

In addition to the standard collections, the .NET Framework also provides advanced or specialized collections, which are grouped in the extended **System.Collections.Specialized** namespace. These are listed in Table 12-3.

Class/Structure	Description	Implements
BitVector32 (structure)	Provides a simple structure that stores **Boolean** values and small **Integer** values in 32 bits of memory	N/A
BitVector32.Section (structure)	Represents a section of the vector that can contain a integer number	N/A
CollectionsUtil	Creates collections that ignore the case in **Strings**	N/A
HybridDictionary	Implements **IDictionary** by using a **ListDictionary** while the collection is small, and then switching to a **Hashtable** when the collection gets large	IDictionary, ICollection, IEnumerable

Table 12-3.   Classes in **System.Collections.Specialized**

Class/Structure	Description	Implements
ListDictionary	Implements **IDictionary** using a singly linked list. Recommended for collections that typically contain ten items or less	IDictionary, ICollection, IEnumerable
NameObject CollectionBase	Provides the abstract base class for a sorted collection of associated **String** keys and **Object** values that can be accessed either with the key or with the index	N/A
KeysCollection	Represents a collection of the **String** keys of a collection	ICollection, IEnumerable
NameValue Collection	Represents a sorted collection of associated **String** keys and **String** values that can be accessed either with the key or with the index	N/A
StringCollection	Represents a collection of **Strings**	N/A
StringDictionary	Implements a hash table with the key strongly typed to be a **String** rather than an object	IEnumerable
StringEnumerator	Supports a simple iteration over a **StringCollection**	N/A

Table 12-3.   *Classes in **System.Collections.Specialized*** (continued)

Before we get down to working with the actual data structures, let's first investigate four important interfaces that underpin collections and arrays: **ICollection**, **IList**, **IEnumerator**, and **IEnumerable**. While we will discuss these interfaces and what they define in this chapter, we are only doing so to understand what's at work "under the hood" of the already implemented classes discussed in this chapter, such as **Array**, **HashTable**, and **Queue**. Implementation of these interfaces in custom classes is left for Chapter 13, which also covers the subject of aggregation in more detail.

ICollection

- The **ICollection** interface is the base interface that most collections implement. It not only provides definitions for the most important utilities of collections and arrays, it also provides the definitions used in all classes that represent containers of objects, such as **ListBox**, **ComboBox**, **ListView**, **CookieCollection**, **DataView**, and **MenuItem**.

ICollection defines the **Count** property and **CopyTo** methods, which are the more commonly implemented members. While the definitions for synchronization are supplied, this does not indicate that collections are guaranteed to be thread-safe. On the contrary, you need to exercise special care when multiple threads in an application access the same collections. **ICollection** is implemented in Chapter 13 (the synchronization methods have been merely declared without implementation).

IEnumerator and IEnumerable

The **IEnumerator** and **IEnumerable** interfaces support iteration through a collection of objects. You must also implement them if you want to use the **For Each…Next** loop construct with your collections, because **For Each …Next** knows how to delegate to an enumerator to loop up the collection's elements. See Chapter 13 for an example of this.

IEnumerator's implementation provides all the functionality needed for an *iterator*— a device that moves from one object to the next in a collection. **IEnumerable** is a proxy interface given the task—through exposing of a single member, a method—of returning an iterator (enumerator) for the target collection (see Chapter 10 for a discussion on interfaces).

> **Note** *IEnumerator was a bad choice of name for this interface, because until you know that it implements an iterator, your first impression is that it defines counting (it does not even define the **Count** method). However, it is similar enough to the formal iterator pattern to have been named **IIterator**. You'll notice that when referring to the actual object, I use the word "IEnumerator" or "enumerator"; but I use "iterator" when referring to the concept of iteration from one element to the next. It's also easy to think the IEnumerator interface has something to do with enumerations (enum value types) which is does not.*

IList

The **IList** interface defines various properties and methods that, when implemented, provide the necessary functionality for constructing and maintaining a collection. **IList** also inherits **ICollection** and **IEnumerable**, which thus provides the necessary interfaces for iteration, counting, and working with the collection.

- As a descendant of **ICollection**, **IList** is given the honor of base interface for all lists and the **Array** class. It defines methods such as **Add**, **IndexOf**, **Insert**, **Contains** and so on. See Chapter 13, "Linked Lists and Trees."

Fixed-size lists, indicated by the **IsFixedSize** property, do not allow the addition or removal of objects after the initial creation of the list. Read-only lists, indicated by **IsReadOnly**, cannot be modified.

Stacks

Stacks have been around for millions of years—well, at least the noncomputer kinds. Ever since we learned how to store and horde, we have been stacking objects. We stack plates, money, books, tortillas, cards, and so on. In OOP, we use a stack to store objects, one on top of the other. Figure 12-1 provides a simple graphical analogue of a software-implemented stack.

A stack is also known as a *push-down store,* and the implementation of a stack on a silicon wafer works the same way as stacking waffles on a plate in the kitchen. We take off from the stack the last item we placed onto it; hence, the term "push-down." If you need a waffle or a plate from a stack, you would not pull one out from under the stack—the stack would probably topple.

Simply defined, a *stack* is a data structure comprising a stack of ordered objects, where the objects are added to the top and can only be removed from the top. We say the stack is "ordered" because we can only add and remove at one end. We can also say the stack is a LIFO construct.

When objects are placed onto a stack, we say the objects are "pushed," and when the objects are removed from the stack, we say they are "popped." Picture the stack of plates in your local buffet-style restaurant. These stacks are usually supported on a spring, so the hungry patrons can easily "pop" off plates as they file past the food wagons.

Programming an object-based stack with the .NET Framework is easy. And, yes, the language does have a prebuilt stack class that has already implemented the interfaces we discussed earlier. You can locate the stack at **System.Collections.Stack**.

CLASSES AND OBJECTS

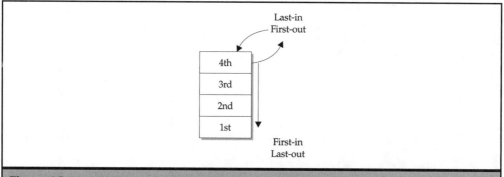

Figure 12-1.   *Objects on a stack can only be accessed last-in, first-out from the end of the stack*

The methods of the **Stack** class are as follows:

- **New** The **Stack** constructor is overloaded to allow you to specify a source collection or an initial capacity
- **Push** Pushes an element onto the top of the stack
- **Pop** Pops an element off the top of the stack
- **Peek** Looks at the topmost element of the stack without removing it
- **Clear** Flushes all elements from the stack
- **Contains** Looks for a certain element in the stack
- **CopyTo** Copies the contents of the stack to an existing one-dimensional array, starting at the specified array index
- **ToArray** Copies the contents of the stack to a new array
- **GetEnumerator** Gets an enumerator object for the stack (see the earlier discussion of **IEnumerable**)

Stack implements **ICollection**, **IList**, and **IEnumerable**, so the **Count**, **IsSynchronized**, and **SyncRoot** properties are included.

The code for declaring and using a stack is as follows:

```
Dim myStack As New Stack()
```

Tip *Remember to use the **New** keyword or you'll end up with a **NullReferenceException**.*

The following application demonstrates the important methods of the **Stack** class:

```
Imports System.Collections
Module Stacker

  Private inPut As String
  Private outPut As Integer
  Private isCompleted As Boolean

  Dim myStack As New System.Collections.Stack()

  Sub Main()
    Dim menuChoice As String
    While Not isCompleted
      Console.WriteLine("                              ")
      Console.WriteLine("----------MENU-----------")
```

```
Console.WriteLine("-------------------------")
Console.WriteLine("a: Push.")
Console.WriteLine("b: Pop.")
Console.WriteLine("c: Peek.")
Console.WriteLine("d: Print.")
Console.WriteLine("e: Find.")
Console.WriteLine("f: Clear.")
Console.WriteLine("g: Anything else to end.")
Console.WriteLine("-------------------------")
Console.Write("Choose a process: ")

menuChoice = Console.ReadLine()
Select Case menuChoice
  Case Is = "a"
    PushDemo()
  Case Is = "b"
    PopDemo()
  Case Is = "c"
    PeekDemo()
  Case Is = "d"
    PrintDemo()
  Case Is = "e"
    FindDemo()
  Case Is = "f"
    ClearDemo()
  Case Else
    isCompleted = True
End Select
    End While
End Sub


Public Sub PushDemo()
Console.WriteLine("Type something to push")
inPut = Console.ReadLine()
  If Not (inPut = "") Then
    Console.WriteLine("")
    isCompleted = PushIt(inPut)
  Else
    isCompleted = True
  End If
End Sub
```

```vbnet
Public Sub FindDemo()
Console.WriteLine("Type the string to find")
inPut = Console.ReadLine()
  If Not (inPut = "") Then
    Console.WriteLine("")
    isCompleted = FindIt(CType(inPut, Object))
    Console.WriteLine(Convert.ToString(isCompleted))
    isCompleted = False
  Else
    isCompleted = False
  End If
End Sub


Function PushIt(ByRef instuff As String) As Boolean
  Try
    myStack.Push(instuff)
  Catch E As InvalidOperationException
    Console.WriteLine("An error occurred: {0}", E.Message)
    Return False
  End Try
End Function


Public Function PopDemo() As Boolean
  Console.WriteLine("Enter to pop")
    Try
      Console.WriteLine(myStack.Pop())
    Catch E As InvalidOperationException
      Console.WriteLine("An error occurred: {0}", E.Message)
      Return False
    End Try
End Function


Public Function PeekDemo() As Boolean
  Try
    Console.WriteLine(myStack.Peek())
  Catch E As InvalidOperationException
    Console.WriteLine("An error occurred: {0}", E.Message)
    Return False
  End Try
End Function


Public Function PrintDemo() As Boolean
```

```
      Try
        Dim myIterator As System.Collections.IEnumerator = _
        myStack.GetEnumerator()
        While myIterator.MoveNext()
          Console.Write("Current: {0}", myIterator.Current)
        End While
        Console.WriteLine()
      Catch E As InvalidOperationException
        Console.WriteLine("An error occurred: {0}", E.Message)
        Return False
      End Try
    End Function

    Public Function FindIt(ByRef obj As Object) As Boolean
      Try
        FindIt = myStack.Contains(obj)
        If FindIt Then
          Return True
        Else
          Return False
        End If
      Catch E As InvalidOperationException
        Console.WriteLine("An error occurred: {0}", E.Message)
        Return False
      End Try
    End Function

    Public Function ClearDemo() As Boolean
      Try
        myStack.Clear()
      Catch E As InvalidOperationException
        Console.WriteLine("An error occurred: {0}", E.Message)
        Return False
      End Try
    End Function
  End Module
```

How to Program Against a Stack

If there is one thing that is apparent about stacks, it's that you really need little effort to program against them. As long as you remember that you are pushing and popping objects at the top of the stack and not at the bottom, you'll have no problems. In fact, stacks are so incredibly easy to work with, you may wonder whether they really have any utility. After all, the first thing most of us grab at is an array, even for the simplest of algorithms that don't require all the overhead of an array. But stacks do have many uses, and they are very efficient.

For starters, the CLR uses a stack to keep track of method calls and parse syntax. I find stacks very useful as a place simply to store items that I need to refer to at a later time (like a couple of seconds later) in a particular method or algorithm (as demonstrated later in this chapter). Stacks are very fast, tiny, and efficient and provide a central location to reference data. If you need to juggle data and only have two hands, then a stack is what you need. Also, it often makes more sense to push a variable onto a stack than to store it in a temporary field. Of course, you need to keep track of the items you push into the stack.

You have to remember that the stack is a LIFO structure, so what goes in last comes out first. Here's an example:

```
Dim myStack As New System.Collections.Stack()
Public Sub MakeDuck()
  myStack.Push("L")
  myStack.Push("O")
  myStack.Push("V")
  myStack.Push("E")
End Sub
```

You are pushing the characters that make up the word "LOVE" onto the stack. But when you pop them, what do you get? Check this out:

```
Public Function PopAll() As Boolean
  Try
    While Not (myStack.Count <= 0)
      Console.Write(myStack.Pop)
    End While
  Catch E As InvalidOperationException
      Console.WriteLine("An error occurred: {0}", E.Message)
      Return False
  End Try
End Function
```

Answer: EVOL is written to the console. This probably is not what you expected, but this is perfect for many operations that require you to store a chronologically acquired order of string objects. Here's an example that can be developed to keep track of the path a user takes through the Web site:

```
Public Sub MakeList()
  myStack.Push("http://www.sdamag.com/vb7cr/;$sessionid$QHDT1")
  myStack.Push("http://www.sdamag.com/ vb7cr /;$sessionid$AQBT5")
  myStack.Push("http://www.sdamag.com/ vb7cr /;$sessionid$AQBT6")
End Sub
```

The last item to go onto the stack is the last link the surfer came from. The preceding implementation is pretty straightforward. Often you get the most utility from a stack when you reference it from within nested, iterative, and recursive structures. The following code shows the pushing and popping from within the fabric of a recursive construct:

```
Public Sub Transpose (ByRef array() As Integer, _
  ByVal first As Integer, ByVal last As Integer)
  If (first < last) Then
    placeHolder.Push(array(first))
    array(first) = array(last)
    array(last) = placeHolder.Pop
    Transpose(array, first + 1, last - 1)
  End If
End Sub
```

Now, stand in line for a peek at queues.

> **Note** *RemoveAt is not implemented in the **Stack** class, which would defeat the LIFO utility of a stack. Remember, you can't pull a plate from the bottom or middle of a stack, or else you end up with a lot of broken china. However, you can pull a plate from the bottom or middle of a list. A **RemoveAt** implementation is covered in Chapter 13 in the Linked Lists and Trees section.*

Queues

What's a queue? Or rather, what's in a queue? A queue is a FIFO software construct used practically everywhere to process items in an ordered fashion. A queue is the opposite of the stack, on which the elements ahead in the stack are pushed down. Figure 12-2 provides a simple graphical representation of a queue.

The specification for a queue is one of the easiest specs you'll ever need to prepare. Why? Look around you. From the moment you wake up to the moment you go to bed, you are standing in queues. For example, we have two showers between a three-member family, yet I still have to stand in line every morning just to get five minutes under spray. As soon as the object (me) hits the bathroom, it encounters a queue.

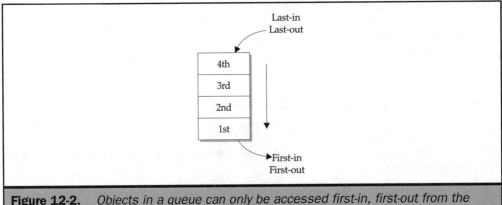

Figure 12-2.   Objects in a queue can only be accessed first-in, first-out from the front of the queue

The software queue works the same way. To get into the queue, we need a method to stand "in" line. But we also need a method that services the object in the front of the line—an "out" method. We also need a method to check if anything is currently in the line. That could be handled by the **Count** property defined by the **ICollection** interface, which would return an **Integer** value to us. Fortunately, the .NET Framework provides such a utility, and then some.

A good example of a queue in an application is the caller-on-hold structure of an automatic call distributor (ACD). Calls come in, but operators are busy, so the callers get placed into a queue. As soon as an operator frees up, the caller at the front of the queue is taken from the front of the "line" and processed.

The queue data structure represents a collection of ordered items; objects are inserted at the back of the queue and serviced from the front. The **Queue** class implements the same interfaces as the **Stack** class, so the **Stacker** example shown earlier for **myStack** will work the same if you just declare a **Queue** instead (**myQueue** instead of **myStack**). Like **Stack**, the **Queue** class also implements the **Count**, **IsSynchronized**, and **SyncRoot** properties.

Besides putting people on hold, what else are queues good for? Queues have a lot of applications. In multitier applications, they are used to schedule objects waiting for processor time. In fact, any algorithm that has chronological limitations will need to process a queue. Take for example the keyboard I am using to write this section. I might be typing at 75 words per minute, but each keypress is a serial process. My computer thus maintains a keystroke buffer, a queue, that deals with each character in chronological order; the last character in is the last one to the screen.

Despite the similarity to the **Stack** class, I provided a demo called **Queuer**, for the **Vb7cr** solution that accompanies this book. The members of **System.Collections.Queue** are listed as follows:

- **New**   The **Queue** constructor is overloaded to allow you to specify a source collection or an initial capacity

- **Enqueue**   Places an element into the queue
- **Dequeue**   Services an element from the front of the queue
- **Peek**   Looks at the element at the front of the queue without removing it
- **Clear**   Flushes all elements from the queue
- **Contains**   Looks for a certain element in the queue
- **CopyTo**   Copies the contents of the queue to an existing one-dimensional array, starting at the specified array index
- **ToArray**   Copies the contents of the queue to a new array
- **GetEnumerator**   Gets an iterator for the stack (see the earlier discussion of **IEnumerable**)
- **TrimToSize**   Trims the capacity of the queue to the actual number of elements

The following example shows how to program against the queue data structure:

```
Dim myQueue As New System.Collections.Queue(10)
Public Sub EnqueueDemo()
  Console.WriteLine("Type something to Queue")
  inPut = Console.ReadLine()
  If Not (inPut = "") Then
    Console.WriteLine("")
    isCompleted = EnqueueIt(inPut)
  Else
    isCompleted = True
  End If
End Sub


Function EnqueueIt(ByRef qStuff As String) As Boolean
  Try
    myQueue.Enqueue(qStuff)
  Catch E As InvalidOperationException
    Console.WriteLine("An error occurred: {0}", E.Message)
    Return False
  End Try
End Function
```

Unlike the stack, a queue, as discussed, processes the elements at the front of the structure. Thus, the preceding example "love" is not printed out as "evol" in the following example:

```
Public Function DequeueAll() As Boolean
  Try
```

```
      While Not (myQueue.Count <= 0)
        Console.Write(myQueue.Dequeue)
      End While
    Catch E As InvalidOperationException
      Console.WriteLine("An error occurred: {0}", E.Message)
      Return False
    End Try
End Function
```

LOVE is written to the console instead of EVOL as demonstrated in the earlier stack example.

How to Program Against a Queue

Despite the many applications for queues, so few programmers I talk to think of coding one just to deal with "work flow" in their apps. The structure is very easy to define and code. The following collection of methods places filenames into a queue for processing. The filenames are taken from the front of the queue for processing; processing will continue as long as more files are added to the queue before it finishes.

```
Public Function WorkQueue() As Boolean
   Dim fileQueue As New System.Collections.Queue(10)
   fileQueue.Enqueue("file one")
   fileQueue.Enqueue("file two")
   fileQueue.Enqueue("file three")
   Try
     While Not isCompleted
       isCompleted = ProcessWork(fileQueue.Dequeue)
     End While
   Catch E As InvalidOperationException
     Console.WriteLine("An error occurred in the work process: " _
     & E.Message)
     Return False
   End Try
End Function

Public Function ProcessWork(ByRef filename As Object) As Boolean
   Try
     Console.WriteLine("Processing: " & filename.ToString)
     ProcessWork = True
   Catch E As InvalidOperationException
     Console.WriteLine("An error occurred in the process: {0}", E.Message)
     ProcessWork = False
   Catch E As Exception
```

```
      Console.WriteLine("An error occurred in the process: {0}", E.Message)
       ProcessWork = False
   End Try
    Console.WriteLine("Processing is finished...")
     ProcessWork = False
End Function
```

ProcessWork writes the following to the console window:

```
Processing: file one
Processing: file two
Processing: file three
An error occurred in the work process: Queue empty.
```

Two useful methods implemented by both **Stack** and **Queue** are the **ToArray** and **CopyTo** methods, which copy the contents of the structures to new or existing arrays, respectively. The **ToArray** method is shown in the following example (do not worry if you are unfamiliar with array declaration syntax; that's coming in the next section):

```
Public Function CopyToArray() As Boolean
  Dim myArray() As Object
  Dim intI As Integer
  Dim result As String
  Try
    myArray = myQueue.ToArray()
    For intI = 0 To UBound(myArray)
      Console.WriteLine("Item " & intI & ": " & CStr(myArray(intI)))
    Next intI
  Catch E As InvalidOperationException
    Console.WriteLine("An error occurred: {0}", E.Message)
    Return False
  Catch E As IndexOutOfRangeException
    Console.WriteLine("An error occurred: {0}", E.Message)
    Return False
  Catch E As InvalidCastException
    Console.WriteLine("An error occurred: {0}", E.Message)
    Return False
  Catch E As Exception
    Console.WriteLine("An error occurred: {0}", E.Message)
    Return False
    Finally
    'dereference the object for this demo
```

```
        myArray = Nothing
    End Try
End Function
```

Arrays

Few programming topics are as important, and as deserving of discussion, in a core reference book as *arrays*. Every programmer, no matter the project, will use an array—a data structure for managing collections of identical data types, such as integers, characters, strings, and even custom reference types. The array is to the programmer what the chisel is to the carpenter or the scalpel is to the surgeon.

Arrays find themselves in all algorithms—even ASP.NET applications, Web services code, and various components along the data supply, storage, and retrieval route. This section thus presents not only an introduction to arrays, but also advanced topics, such as how to use arrays, insert values into them, sort them, search them, and put them to work. We will also build on Chapter 7's discussion of how arrays can be passed to methods and how methods can return arrays. This will not be the only chapter in which arrays and array usage will crop up. Later chapters present some sophisticated techniques and algorithms that require array implementation and access.

An *array* is a collection of objects of the same type, conveniently packaged in an indexed, sortable, and searchable construct. The structure itself, which derives from **System.Array**, is a collection of objects (as mentioned earlier, it implements **ICollection**) that are referenced via the container's name and an index location.

One of the main attractions of arrays is that their elements, the values they hold, can be randomly accessed. As you saw, this was not possible with the **Stack** and **Queue** classes, which also do not allow you to insert at a certain location or remove at a certain location.

Figure 12-3 provides a representation of an array. It has a "bottom" and a "top." The array can grow and shrink. You can copy the array, reference any element in the array, sort the array, search the array, reverse the elements of the array, and much more.

The array is referenced with a reference variable (see Chapter 9 for more details on referencing objects), and you use it to store and retrieve variables of a like type, the *elements* of the array. The values are stored, retrieved, and manipulated by referencing the index—or *subscript*—of the array element (the slot or pigeon hole in which array objects are "logically" stored). The first element in the array is indexed at number 0, which means it is a zero-based structure. The zero element is also known as the array's *zeroth element*, or *lower bound element*(or *LBound*) element. An array cannot have zero length; there is always at least one element, which is the *zeroth* index, as illustrated in Figure 12-3.

Not all variables referenced in the array are referenced in the same way. **String** objects, for example, are referenced by references to the string data (in other words, the array's string elements are just references to the string objects), while numeric data is stored directly in the array (see the "Boxing" section in Chapter 8).

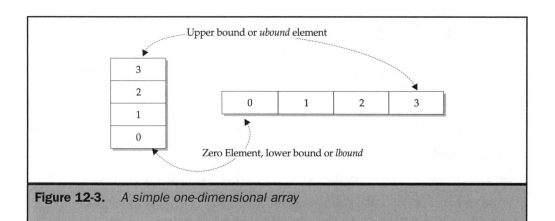

Figure 12-3. *A simple one-dimensional array*

The elements of an array and its contents can be accessed or referenced through the index (see Figure 12-4), which would be like punching a hole in the stack or queue to access an element's value in the body of the structure instead of at one of the ends.

You refer to the element of the array as the *element type*. The element type is created when you create the array, and destroyed when the array is destroyed. Naturally, the only type that cannot be the element of the array is the array itself.

Note *As demonstrated in the earlier queue example, **CopyToArray**, an array can be declared as type **Object** and then upcast to another type later.*

Arrays can also comprise more than one dimension, and the elements in the dimensions can be referenced separately from the elements of the surrounding dimensions, as we will see later in this chapter.

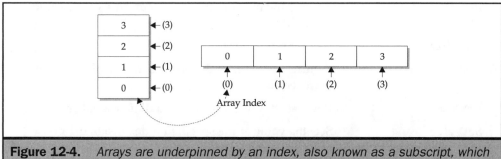

Figure 12-4. *Arrays are underpinned by an index, also known as a subscript, which gives you direct and random access to any element in the array*

The Array Class

All arrays derive from the base class **System.Array**. This includes the **Length** property. The class contains a number of useful methods and properties, which are listed alphabetically in Table 12-4.

Class Member	Purpose
BinarySearch	Searches a one-dimensional array for a value
Clear	Sets a range of elements to zero, null, or **False** in a one-dimensional array. (See also "The **Erase** Statement," later in this chapter.)
Copy	Copies the entire array or a range of elements in a one-dimensional array to another array
CopyTo	Specifies the starting element to copy to in the target array
CreateInstance	Represents alternative array creation syntax for late binding
GetEnumerator	Returns an instance of the **IEnumerator** implementation
GetLength	Returns the length of a dimension
GetLowerBound	Returns the lower bound element of a dimension
GetUpperBound	Returns the upper bound element of a dimension
GetValue	Returns the value at a specified index in any dimension
IndexOf	Returns the index at the first occurrence of the value searched for
Initialize	Not yet implemented
LastIndexOf	Returns the index at the last occurrence of the value searched for
Reverse	Reverses the elements in a one-dimensional array
SetValue	Sets the value at the specified index in a one- or multidimensional array

Table 12-4. *The Members of **System.Array** (Excludes Members Inherited from **Object**)*

Class Member	Purpose
Sort	Provides built-in sort operations
IsFixedSize	Returns **True** or **False** if the array size is fixed
IsReadOnly	Returns **True** or **False** if the array is read-only
IsSynchronized	Returns **True** or **False** if the array is synchronized (thread-safe)
Length	Returns the length of a one-dimensional array
Rank	Returns an ordinal representing the number of dimensions in the array
SyncRoot	Returns an object used to synchronize access to the array

Table 12-4.   *The Members of **System.Array** (Excludes Members Inherited from **Object**) (continued)*

Note   *Table 12-4 does not include the members inherited by **System.Array**, such as **GetType** and **ToString**.*

Declaring and Initializing Arrays

When you create an array, you need to declare a length for each of its dimensions. The length of the array is the number of elements that you need to store. As you now know, .NET array elements (no matter the language) are referenced through a zero-based index, which, as mentioned earlier, means the first element of the array is given the index value 0. So, to specify the length of the array, you defer to the range of indices counting from and including 0.

Arrays are declared in the same manner as you declare any variable. Visual Basic array grammar includes parentheses or brackets after the data type (as opposed to square brackets used by other languages). In the following example, an array reference variable called **sAlarms** is declared, the intention of which is to reference an array of ordinal values:

```
Dim injectorAlarms(10) As Integer
```

If you need to declare an array reference variable that will reference **Double** value types, you could declare the array reference as follows:

```
Dim latinumPercentages(10) As Double
```

How many values can either of the preceding arrays hold? Tip: While they are declared as arrays of ten elements (0 to n-1), you'll be surprised to discover that you won't get ten. The Visual Basic architects did something here that confuses a lot of programmers. Using the **For**...**Next** iteration structure (discussed in the previous chapter), let's find out what gives:

```
Public Sub OffByTwoArrays()
  Dim injectorAlarms(10) As Integer
  Dim intI As Integer
    For intI = 0 to injectorAlarms.Length
    Next intI
  Dubug.WriteLine(intI)
  Debug.WriteLine(injectorAlarms.Length)
End Sub
```

Holy mackerel! The **injectorAlarms** array has 11 values (0 to n-2). Talk about getting what you didn't ask for. (What's worse is that **intI** after the **For** loop ends up at 12 (because it started at 0).) Why did the VB architects do this? To make it easier to convert from the 1-based arrays supported in the classic versions of Visual Basic (version 6 and earlier), under the covers, the Visual Basic implementation of the .NET arrays tacks on the zero element and thus adds one more element to the declaration of, in this case, 10.

When you convert a Visual Basic 6 or earlier array, you get the extra element over and above (or would that be "under and below"?) the original array length—in the zeroth position. The problem is that C# and other .NET languages do not work that way. The same declaration in C# produces a ten-element array (0-9). To thus declare arrays to the exact length you specify in the declaration, you can use the following kluge code:

```
Dim latinumPercentages(10 - 1) As Double
```

It's not elegant but it will do until Visual Basic's array declaration works like C# or J# declarations, or we get a new array class that's not as confusing (or you take the bold step of creating a new array class from scratch).

The preceding lines of code thus declare the array reference variable named **injectorAlarms** with the "potential" to hold 11 **Integer** or **Double** values. In other words, the preceding code does not yet lead to the creation of the actual object. The object gets constructed implicitly at the attempt to assign variables to the declared elements and when you call **New** in the declaration. This means that we can create the array reference variable but delay initialization and activation of the array object, a tactic you can get away with when you set **Option Explicit** to **Off** to allow implicit typing declaration.

The constant between the parentheses does not have to be a number. Any legal means of obtaining the constant will do; even a value in a queue will work, as demonstrated here:

```
Dim latinumPercentages(ArrayQueue.Dequeue) As Double
```

The array reference variable should not be confused with the array element values, which are also variables (of types). The array variable is really nothing more than a reference to an array object, as you will learn about in the following chapter.

To initialize the array object in the declaration of the reference variable, you need to call the **New** constructor. The following example creates the array object **Alarms** to hold four **Integer** variables (in elements 0 through 3):

```
Dim Alarms() As Integer = New Integer(4) {}
```

What does this code do? As you are aware, an array in .NET is an object that derives from **System.Array**. The **New** operator thus accesses the constructor of the array class and passes the argument to create the array of five elements. The array can thus be illustrated as in Figure 12-5.

In addition to the creation or activation of the array object with **New**, the array object must be initialized with the trailing curly braces (the same idea is used in C# and Java). You cannot leave out the curly braces, because that will generate an error, but you can leave the pair of braces empty, as illustrated in the preceding code, or use the curly braces to provide the initial variables for the array elements, as demonstrated in the next section.

Note *In case you were wondering, the Visual Basic 6 syntax of specifying lower bound to upper bound elements, such as* `Dim Days(1 to 20) As Integer` *is no longer supported in Visual Basic .NET.*

If an array is an object, then assigning the object to another reference variable shouldn't be a problem. This can be done if you leave off the parentheses with an assignment statement, as follows:

```
oAlarms = sAlarms
```

Both reference variables reference the same object, as illustrated in Figure 12-6.

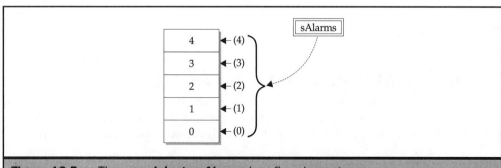

Figure 12-5. *The array injectorsAlarms is a five-element array*

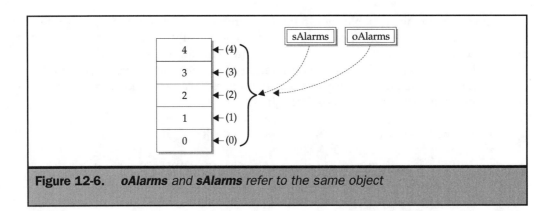

Figure 12-6. *oAlarms* and *sAlarms* refer to the same object

Note *The Object Reference Model is discussed in Chapters 8 and 9.*

To initialize the array object with data, use a comma-separated list between the curly braces, as follows:

```
Dim sAlarms() As Integer = New Integer () {1, 2, 3, 4, 5}
```

To recap, first declare the array, add an equal sign, and then follow the equal sign with the list. (You can also leave out the **New** keyword, and the compiler will implicitly make the call. If you make the call to **New**, however, you must include the pair of curly braces on the end of the statement, even if the pair is empty.)

The number of elements in the array can be accessed by the **Length** property of the array. You can test these array declarations using the **Length** property. Here's an example:

```
Debug.WriteLine("There are {0} elements in sAlarms", sAlarms.Length)
```

Behold, **sAlarms** is truly one element larger than you declared:

```
There are 11 elements in sAlarms
```

Declaring Multidimensional Arrays

You can use a multidimensional array to reference elements in more than one dimension. The construct is well suited for simple referencing of two-dimensional data, much like a spreadsheet. To declare an array of more than one dimension, use the following syntax:

```
Dim sAlarms(4,4) As String
```

This is a rectangular array that has two dimensions. You can think of the array as a table with columns—each column represents the dimension, as illustrated in Figure 12-7.

The number of dimensions declared in an array determines the *rank* of the array. An array of one dimension has a rank of 1; an array of three dimensions has a rank of 3, and so on. You can't go nuts with dimensions, either, because arrays are limited to 32 dimensions. The following syntax for declaring multidimensional arrays is acceptable to the .NET runtime:

```
Dim mdArray(,) As Integer
Dim mdArray1() As Integer = {New Integer(), New Integer(), New Integer()}
Dim mdArray2(,,) As Integer = New Integer(5, 5, 5) {}
Dim mdArray3(,) As Integer = {{1, 1}, {2, 2}, {3, 3}, {4, 4}, {5, 5}}
```

The first **mdArray** declaration creates a two-dimensional array that is not initialized with values. The second **mdArray1** declaration creates an array of three dimensions.

Note *When calling the **Ubound** function on a multidimensional array, omitting the dimension returns the upper bound of the first dimension.*

Knowing the rank of an array is not important until you need to work with more than one array and need to convert from one array to another. See the discussion of **ArrayTypeMismatchException** in the "Array Exceptions" section later in this chapter.

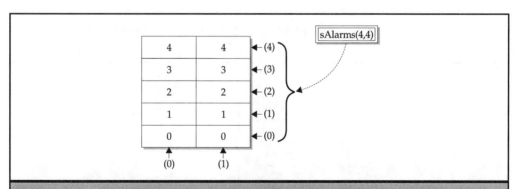

Figure 12-7. *A multidimensional array of two dimensions*

Jagged Arrays

A *jagged* array is an array of more than one array, or an array of arrays. It is useful for working with two-dimensional data where the structure is not rectangular, as in a multidimensional array. Imagine declaring two arrays, sticking them together, and then referencing them through a single reference variable. Each array can be a different length and have multiple dimensions. The shape of such an array is jagged rather than rectangular or square. The jagged array is illustrated in Figure 12-8.

Declaring, initializing, and working with the jagged array can be tricky. The array illustrated in Figure 12-8 comprises two arrays, which can be declared as follows:

```
Dim sAlarms(2)() As Integer
Dim sAlarms()() As Integer = {New Integer() {5, 6, 7}, _
  New Integer() {10, 24, 63, 82}}
```

After the jagged array is initialized, you can access the elements in either member array using code, demonstrated as follows:

```
Dim sAlarms()() As Integer = {New Integer() {5, 6, 7}, _
  New Integer() {10, 24, 63, 82}}
Dim intI As Integer
For intI = 0 To UBound(sAlarms(1))
  Console.WriteLine(sAlarms(1)(intI))
Next intI
```

Jagged arrays are not as universal or powerful in utility as single arrays. Many .NET constructs do not (yet) know how to access a jagged (and even multidimensional) array. Two good and familiar examples are the **CopyTo** and **ToArray** methods,

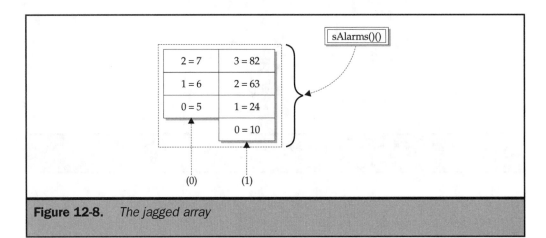

Figure 12-8. *The jagged array*

discussed earlier. You typically need a lot of funky code to get a good system going against the collection of arrays, and you might be better off just creating an array of objects, as discussed later in this chapter.

Programming Against Arrays

This section deals with the peculiarities of Visual Basic arrays and demonstrates usage of several important methods of **System.Array** and a number of stand-alone keywords and statements, native to the Visual Basic language, created to make working with arrays easier. The legacy array-handling keywords can be accessed via the **Microsoft.VisualBasic.Information** namespace.

First, we need to get data into the arrays before they can be of much use. You can populate the array elements by referencing the index value that represents the position in the array. This is done as follows:

```
sAlarms(0)  =  14320
sAlarms(1)  =  12390
sAlarms(2)  =  14870
sAlarms(3)  =  14975
```

Arrays are simple to work with, although they do have their nuances, as we will see shortly. The initial value of an array is **Nothing**. In other words, in the **sAlarms** declaration shown earlier, each element of the five-element array is **Nothing**. Referencing the **Nothing** literal is not impossible, as the following code shows:

```
Public Sub CheckOnNull()
Dim incR As Integer
Dim conD As Boolean = True
Dim AlistIndex(10) As String
  For incR = 0 To UBound(AlistIndex)
    Console.WriteLine("Element {0} = {1}", incR, AlistIndex(incR))
  Next
End Sub
```

This chunk of code reports the value of each element in the array. Since nothing in the code is assigning values to the elements then you get nothing. The same routine correctly displays **Nothing** for **Integer** elements as zeros. The output to the console is as follows:

```
Element 0 =
Element 1 =
```

```
Element 2 =
Element 3 =
. . .
Element 10 =
```

Let's now declare an Integer array and check the results:

```
Public Sub CheckOnNotNull()
Dim incR As Integer
Dim conD As Boolean = True
Dim AlistIndex(10) As Integer
  For incR = 0 To UBound(AlistIndex)
    Console.WriteLine("Element {0} = {1}", incR, AlistIndex(incR))
  Next
End Sub
```

The output to the console now shows values:

```
Element 0 = 0
Element 1 = 1
Element 2 = 2
Element 3 = 3
. . .
Element 10 = 10
```

Notice that we need to test on the value of **UBound** to end the **Next** loop without throwing an exception. This demonstrates that the array is zero-based (0 to 10). You need to watch this or the method will throw an out-of-range exception (**IndexOutOfRangeException**) when it tries to access the nonexistent eleventh element (see "The UBound Statement" next and the "Array Exceptions" section later in this chapter).

The UBound Statement

To find the upper bound, or size, of an array, we use the **UBound** statement, a keyword that can be accessed via the **Microsoft.VisualBasic.Information** namespace. The syntax is as follows:

UBound(*arrayname*[, *dimension*])

The *arrayname* parameter is the required name of the array, while *dimension* is an optional parameter, of the **Long** data type, representing the dimension of which array you wish to retrieve the upper bound. Use 1 for the first dimension, 2 for the second dimension, and so on. In the following example, we use **UBound** to get the array's upper bound to terminate the loop without the chance of throwing an exception:

```
For incR = 0 To UBound(AlistIndex)
   Console.WriteLine(CStr(AlistIndex(incR)))
Next
```

By using **UBound** effectively, we will never get an exception that states we passed the boundary limit of an array, so our code is less troublesome. An alternative to the **UBound** keyword is the **Length** property, which is a member of **System.Array** and not a Visual Basic information keyword like **UBound**.

> **Note** *While the **Microsoft.VisualBasic.Information** namespace also provides access to the **LBound** keyword, which was used to declare VB 6 arrays, its utility is really redundant in .NET because the **LBound** of an array is now 0.*

Use the **Length** property (and don't forget to add –1) as you do the **UBound** keyword. The following code demonstrates this usage:

```
For intX = 0 To sArray.Length - 1
   Console.WriteLine(CStr(sArray(intx)))
Next
```

Using either **Length** or **UBound** in your code instead of hard-coding the number of elements makes for code that is easier to maintain. Arrays tend to change, and the following code is a time bomb (the emphasized value) waiting to destroy your software:

```
For intX = 0 To 10
   Console.WriteLine(CStr(sArray(intx)))
Next
```

If you must use a value less than the **Length – 1** or **UBound** of the array rather use an enumeration constant, an **Enum** value, instead of a magic number, as discussed in Chapter 8. For example:

```
For intX = 0 To BlockEnum.SecondLimit
   Console.WriteLine(CStr(sArray(intx)))
Next
```

When or why would you use **Length - 1** over **UBound**? When **UBound** is no longer supported. Because it still sits in the classic VB runtime it stands a chance of being discontinued. Until that happens, if it in fact does, you stand more of a chance of causing off-by-one hell in your code because it's not difficult to forget to add the – 1 after the **Length** property.

Redeclaring Arrays

Visual Basic .NET supports explicit redeclaration of arrays using a **ReDim** statement, and thus the ability to keep expanding the array as needed. The cool aspect of this behavior is that you can preserve the data of the original array. Essentially, the array can keep growing ad infinitum, as you will see shortly. The **ReDim** syntax is as follows:

RedimStatement ::= ReDim [Preserve] *RedimClauses+ StatementTerminator*

RedimClauses ::=

  RedimClauses |

  RedimClause, RedimClauses

RedimClause ::= *VariableExpression ArrayInitializationModifier*

The syntax takes the following arguments:

- **Preserve** An optional keyword that you use if you wish to keep (preserve) existing array data when expanding the upper limit of the array dimension.
- **Varname** Required name of the variable name of the array.
- **Size** Required size of the new array dimension.
- **Type** Optional variable data type.

The array must be initialized before the upper bound can be changed. This means that you must first declare the array, after which subsequent calls to resize the array can be used with the **ReDim** statement. The type of data that the array contains cannot be changed. If the array is declared as **String**, then you cannot change the data type of the array to **Integer**. If you use the **ReDim** statement to make the array smaller, the elements in the upper bounds of the array that you eliminate will obviously be gone forever, so be careful when using the **ReDim** statement.

In the following example, we have taken the code demonstrated before and increased the array size by one:

```
Public Sub TestPreserve()
Dim incR As Integer
Dim conD As Boolean = True
Dim AlistIndex(10) As String
   For incR = 0 To UBound(AlistIndex)
```

```
      AlistIndex(incR) = Convert.ToString(incR)
      Console.WriteLine("Element {0} = {1}", incR, AlistIndex(incR))
   Next
   ReDim Preserve AlistIndex(UBound(AlistIndex) + 5)
   incR = 0
   For incR = 0 To UBound(AlistIndex)
      Console.WriteLine("Element {0} = {1}", incR, AlistIndex(incR))
   Next
End Sub
```

The new output to the console is as follows:

```
Element 0 = 0
Element 1 = 1
Element 2 = 2
Element 3 = 3
. . .
Element 10 = 10
Element 11 =
Element 12 =
Element 13 =
Element 14 =
Element 15 =
```

The following are some rules to follow when resizing arrays:

- You cannot change the number of dimensions in the array (refer to the earlier section "Declaring Multidimensional Arrays").
- **ReDim** does not allow you to change an array from one data type to another.
- When working with multidimensional arrays, **ReDim** only lets you extend the **UBound** of the last dimension.
- If you shrink the array, you will lose the data stored in the eliminated elements.
- **ReDim** is only valid in the implementation space of a method.

The Erase Statement

The **Erase** statement releases the instance of an array, essentially "erasing" the array values. If you wish to zap more than one array, you can pass a comma-delimited list of array names to the **Erase** statement. The syntax is as follows:

Erase *arraylist*

Consider the following example:

```
Dim animals(5) As String
animals(0) = "Dog"
animals(1) = "Cat"
Erase animals 'Now the array is kaput
```

The **Erase** statement is destructive and hardly recoverable. If all you need to do is ditch the values in the array and still keep the object intact for additional use, use the **Clear** method of **System.Array** (defined in **IList**). Simply call the **Array.Clear** method and pass it the array (sans index brackets), the starting index of the element to clear from, and the ending index of the element to clear. The following code purges the entire array, setting the values to 0 because the array is of type **Integer**:

```
Array.Clear(sAlarms, 0, sAlarms.Length)
```

In other words, the clearing starts at the **LBound** and erases every element for the length of the array. The following example does the same thing:

```
Array.Clear(sAlarms, 0, UBound(sAlarms))
```

The IsArray Function

The **IsArray** function returns a **Boolean** value indicating whether a variable *is* an array. The syntax to use the function is as follows:

IsArray(*variablename*)

The following is an example:

```
Dim AlistIndex(10) As String
Dim incR As Integer
Debug.WriteLine(IsArray(AlistIndex))    'writes "True"
Debug.WriteLine(IsArray(incR))          'writes "False"
```

Array Exceptions

There are not too many ways you can screw up code when working with arrays. Table 12-5 lists the exceptions that can be raised when good arrays turn bad.

ArrayTypeMismatchException raises exceptions when the element's data type in the source array cannot be implicitly converted to the data type in the elements of the target array. (Array covariance provides for the implicit conversion from one array to another when the arrays are declared to be of the same rank and type.)

Exception Object	Purpose
ArrayTypeMismatchException	Raised if you attempt to interchange data between arrays that are not of the same rank and type
IndexOutOfRangeException	Raised if you attempt to access an element index value outside the lower or upper bounds of the array (refer to the discussion of **UBound** in the section "The UBound Statement" in this chapter)
NullReferenceException	Raised if you try to reference elements that don't exist or that have not yet been declared
SafeArrayRankMismatchException (Interop exception)	Raised when the rank of an unmanaged **SAFEARRAY** does not match the rank specified in the managed signature
SafeArrayTypeMismatchException (Interop exception)	Raised when the type of an unmanaged **SAFEARRAY** does not match the type of the array specified in the managed signature

Table 12-5. *Array* Exceptions

Suppose you have an **Integer** array and a **String** array. You cannot copy data from an element of one array to the other because the array data types are different. The following example raises this exception:

```
Dim sAlarms1() As Object = New String(10) {}
Dim sAlarms2() As Double = New Double(3) {1, 2, 3, 4}
sAlarms1(0) = sAlarms2(3)
```

The exception message is as follows:

```
A first chance exception of type 'System.ArrayTypeMismatchException'
occurred in arraystest.exe Additional information: Attempted to
store an element of the incorrect type into the array.
```

In this code, we are trying to copy a string from a **String** array to a **Double** array. It does not work and the exception is raised, which, if not handled, will result in the termination of your application.

The message field for the preceding exception reports the following: "Attempted to store an element of the incorrect type into the array." The "bad" code escapes detection if **Option Strict** is set to **Off**.

The next array stumbling block arises when you try to access the elements of an array that do not exist. In other words, you access the array "out of its bounds." This throws the **IndexOutOfRangeException**.

Looking again at our array **sAlarms**, consider the following code that generates some bitterness for the Visual Basic compiler:

```
Dim sAlarms() As Integer = New Integer() {1, 2, 3, 4, 5}
sAlarms(-1) = 40
sAlarms(5) = 10
```

The first line that throws an exception makes use of an index that is lower than the base of 0 (–1). This is not a common error, because it is obvious that the array's lower bound is not an index value less than 0. But the second error is more common, because it is not difficult to inadvertently reference an element beyond the upper bound of the array, especially when you use magic numbers in your code. The array **sAlarms** has only five elements (0 to 4), but the index is zero-based, so the upper bound is actually 4 and element 5 does not exist.

The **NullReferenceException** is raised when you try to work with an array object that has been declared without elements. The following code, which escapes detection if **Option Explicit** is set to **Off**, will thus not work unless it is properly constructed and initialized:

```
Alarms()
```

To fix it, you need to declare the array with elements (remember, the name and the braces are just a reference variable to the array object itself. If you need to declare the array now and then provide the length (number of elements) later, declare the array with one "zero" element and then **ReDim** the array later to expand it:

```
ReDim Preserve Alarms(numElements)
```

Here, **numElements** represents a variable that sets the new length of the array.

The two **SafeArray** exceptions are raised when the rank or data types of unmanaged so-called safe arrays differ from what's expected (the target signatures) in the managed world.

Passing Arrays to Methods

We can easily pass an array as an argument to a method. To accomplish this, you just have to leave the brackets off the end of the array name when you do the passing. Have a look at the following statement:

```
SortArray(sAlarms)
```

This code passes the array **sAlarms** to the method **SortArray**. Why do we not need the brackets and the element **Length** information? The arrays do not need to schlep such extra baggage when they get passed around because the array object is "aware" of its own size, and the actual array object remains put. The **Length** property holds the size. So, when we pass the array, we implicitly pass the length data as part of the object's data, because only the reference variable to the array is passed.

Obviously, you cannot simply pass an array to any method that has not defined the array parameter. The method that is to expect the array needs to make room for the arriving reference. The receiving method's definition should thus make arrangements for the array in its parameter list, like this:

```
Sub SortArray(ByRef sAlarms() As Integer)
'do something with the array
End Sub
```

This code specifies that the **SortArray** method is to expect an array of type **Integer** as the parameter. Bear in mind that arrays, like all objects, get passed by reference (or call by reference), so you are not actually sending the entire object to the method, just the reference to it. By passing by reference and not by value, we can "pass" a huge array to the method without issue (refer to Chapter 7 for a discussion on pass by value and pass by reference).

The latter part of this chapter shows how to pass array references to methods, return array references, and use the various methods and built-in functions to work with arrays. In fact, without the ability to pass arrays to methods and return them, we would not be able to do much with our arrays.

Receiving Arrays from Methods

You can receive an array of values from a method call (or the array reference variable). Typically, you pass the array to some utility method, which sorts or populates the array or does something exciting with the values in the array. Then the array is returned to your calling method. The following example calls the **GetArray** method, which delivers a reference to an array of bytes:

```
Public Sub PrintByteArray()
  Dim bite As Byte = CByte(54)
  Dim intI As Integer
  Dim ReturnArray() As Byte
  ReturnArray = FixArray (bite)
  For intI = 0 To ReturnArray.GetUpperBound(0)
    Debug.WriteLine("Byte {0}: {1}" intI, ReturnArray(intI))
  Next intI
End Sub
```

The following function performs the operation and returns the byte array:

```
Public Function FixArray(ByVal bite As Byte) As Byte()
  Dim newByteArray(2) As Byte
  newByteArray(0) = bite
  newByteArray (1) = bite + bite
  newByteArray (2) = bite + CByte(50)
  Return newByteArray
End Function
```

You'll find much more information on passing and receiving arrays in the following sections on searching and sorting.

Searching and Sorting Arrays

The simplest array search algorithm is typically known as a sequential search, because you iterate through each element in the array, one element at a time in sequence, to find the element that matches what you are looking for. The following code does exactly that, using a **For** loop to "iterate" through the array. The example looks for a specific value in the array and then returns the index value holding the matching variable.

```
Sub WhatIndex(ByRef array() As Integer, ByVal ArrayVal As Integer)
  Dim intI As Integer
  For intI = 0 To UBound(array)
    If ArrayVal = array(intI) Then
      Console.WriteLine("Found the value {0} at index {1}", _
      ArrayVal, intI)
    End If
  Next intI
End Sub
```

This method receives the reference of the array to iterate through. It uses the **For...Next** loop to iterate through the array until the variable passed to the **ArrayVal** parameter matches the value of the element in the array. Here's how you call it:

```
Console.WriteLine(WhatIndex(Alarms, 87))
```

As an alternative, you can instantiate an iterator over your array and loop through it with a **MoveNext** method. An iterator that implements **IEnumerator** is ideal for this job, and since **System.Array** implements **IEnumerable**, we can make an iterator with the **GetEnumerator** method in the same fashion as we did with the **Stack** and **Queue** classes.

The following code demonstrates the instantiation of an iterator over an array:

```
Sub WhatIndex(ByRef array() As Integer, ByVal ArrayVal As Integer)
  Try
    Dim index As Integer
    Dim myIterator As System.Collections.IEnumerator = _
    array.GetEnumerator()
    While myIterator.MoveNext()
      index += 1
      If CType(myIterator.Current, Integer) = ArrayVal Then
        Console.WriteLine("Found the value {0} at index {1}", _
        ArrayVal, intI)
      End If
    End While
    Catch E As InvalidOperationException
      Console.WriteLine("An error occurred: {0}", E.Message)
    End Try
End Sub
```

But you do not really need such elaborate code. The **Array** class provides a similar "ready made" method that can return the indexes of both the first and last encounters of the value (plus several variations in between). Check out the following code:

```
Public Sub FindIndex()
  Dim IndexFinder() As Integer
  With IndexFinder
    Console.WriteLine(.IndexOf(Alarms, 87))
  End With
End Sub
```

Can you tell what's cooking here? First, we need a reference variable to the array class. Then, we use the reference to invoke the **IndexOf** method.

As for the iterator, you learned earlier that it runs at *O(1)* so for large arrays it might be a lot more efficient than the **IndexOf** method. You should also be aware that **IndexOf** is defined in **IList** so varying implementations of it exist, both custom implementations and framework implementations. Also, as you'll see exactly in the section "The IndexOf Method" in the next chapter, **IndexOf** itself may implement an **IEnumerator** object to iterate over a collection.

The BinarySearch Method

The **BinarySearch** method is simple to use. It essentially looks for the first occurrence of the element value you specify and returns an **Integer** representing the index value of the element holding the first occurrence of the value. If the method is unsuccessful, it will return –1 to the caller.

The following code declares an array of type **Double** and then searches for the occurrence of 4.0:

```
Dim sAlarms() As Double = New Double(3) {1.3, 2.5, 3.0, 4.0}
Console.WriteLine("Found at index: {0}", _
sAlarms2.BinarySearch(sAlarms2, 4.0)
```

The method returns 3 to the caller, which just so happens to be the **UBound** element of this **sAlarms** array. The **BinarySearch** algorithm can be used for a variation of array search criteria, but you must remember to sort the array first for the best performance. Here's why: When you perform a binary search, the algorithm bisects the array it searches and then checks the last value in the first part of the array. If the value found is less than the search value we are looking for, the algorithm will only search the second part. If it turns out that the value is more than the search value, then the value we are looking for might be in the first part of the array—in which case the second part of the array is ignored. This is why the algorithm is called *binary search*; it has nothing to with the binary representation of the value.

The method makes the assumptions just described because it knows that the data in the array is sorted and that if an item is not in one part of the array, it must be in the other. Thus, only part of the array is searched, which is why binary search is so fast.

The method is overloaded as follows:

```
BinarySearch(Array, Object) As Integer
BinarySearch(Array, Object, IComparer) As Integer
BinarySearch(Array, Integer, Integer, Object) As Integer
BinarySearch(Array, Integer, Integer, Object, IComparer) As Integer
```

While the **Array.BinarySearch** method is documented to require you to first sort the array, it does not specify the behavior of the method if it encounters an unsorted array. The following example seeds an array with values and then sets **BinarySearch** on it before and after sorting. The results are not surprising. The first example,

```
Sub FindMyValue()
  Dim sArray() As Integer = {12, 82, 23, 44, 25, 65, 27}
  Debug.WriteLine(Array.BinarySearch(sArray, 27))
End Sub
```

writes –2 to the Output window. However, what happens if we first sort the array?

```
Sub FindMyValue()
  Dim sArray() As Integer = {12, 82, 23, 44, 25, 65, 27}
  Array.Sort(sArray)
  Debug.WriteLine(Array.BinarySearch(sArray, 27))
End Sub
```

We now get 3 written to the Output window, which is correct.

Results are not only produced faster by an order of magnitude if the array is first sorted, they can also be relied on. Thus, let's now talk about the important job of sorting arrays. We will return to binary search in the section "Working with Trees" in Chapter 14.

The Basics of Sorting Arrays

Most algorithms that use arrays will require the array to be searched for one reason or another. The problem with the code in the preceding section is that the array we were searching was at first not sorted—and you saw the result. If the value we are looking for turns up at the end of the array, we will have iterated through the entire array before hitting the match, which means we take longer to get results because the binary search cannot perform the $n/2$ operation. If the array is huge, searching it unsorted might give us more than unpredictable results.

Sequential searching like this will suffice when the size of the data set is small. In other words, the amount of work a sequential search does is directly proportional to the amount of data to be searched. If you double the list of items to search, you typically double the amount of time it takes to search the list. To speed up searching of larger data sets, it becomes more efficient to use a binary search algorithm—or an $O(logn)$ algorithm. But to do a binary search, we must first sort the array.

Search efficiency is greatly increased when the data set we need to search or exploit is sorted. If you have access to a set of data, it can be sorted independently of the application implementing the searching algorithm. If not, the data needs to be sorted at run time.

The reason array sorts are so common is that sorting a list of data into ascending or descending order not only is one of the most often performed tasks in everyday life, it is also one of the most frequently required operations on computers (and few other data structures can sort and search data as easy as an array).

The **Array** class provides a simple sorting method, **Sort**, that you can use to satisfactorily sort an array. The **Sort** method is static, so you can use it without having to instantiate an array. The following code demonstrates calling the **Sort** method statically and as an instance:

```
'with the instance method
With sAlarm
  .Sort(sAlarm)
End With
'or with the static method
Array.Sort(sAlarm)
```

The sorting method comes from the **Array** collection of methods. Simply write **Array.Sort** and pass the array reference variable to the **Sort** method as an argument. The **Sort** method is overloaded, so have a look at the enumeration of methods in the class to find what you need.

The following code sorts an array (emphasized) before returning the index of **Integer** value 87, as demonstrated earlier:

```
Public Function GetIndexOfValue(ByRef myArray() As Integer, ByVal _
  ArrayVal As Integer) As Integer
  Array.Sort(myArray)
Return .IndexOf(myArray, ArrayVal)
  End With
End Function
```

While the **System.Array** class provides a number of **Sort** methods, the following sections demonstrate typical implementations for the various array-sorting algorithms, such as *Bubble Sort* and *Quicksort*. These have been around a lot longer than .NET and translate very easily to Visual Basic code. Porting these sorts to Visual Basic provides a terrific opportunity to show off what's possible with .NET, the **Array** methods, and built-in functions.

As discussed, **Array** comes preloaded with a version of *quicksort*, but having access to your own sort code will be invaluable for many occasions.

Bubble Sort

The *bubble sort* is widely used to sort small arrays and is very easy to work with. It gets its name from the idea that the smaller values "bubble" to the top, while the heavier ones sink (which is why it's also known as "sinking sort"). And if you watch the values move around in your debugger's Locals windows you see why it's called bubble sort (see the "Debugging With Visual Studio .NET" section in Chapter 17).

What you should see this code produce is as follows: The array **sAlarms** is initialized to capture the alarm IDs and descriptions that are pulled from a database or direct feed (I just initialize the array here).

The **PrintArray** method is called twice to show the array both unsorted and sorted. The bubble sort is called before the second call to **PrintArray** to display the sorted list out to the console:

```
Public Module BubbleTest
Dim Alarms() As Integer = New Integer() {134, 3, 1, 23, 87, 342, 2, 9}

Sub Main()
  PrintArray(Alarms)
  BubbleSort(Alarms)
  PrintArray(Alarms)
  Console.ReadLine()
End Sub

  Public Overloads Sub PrintArray(ByRef Array() As Integer)
  Dim result As String
  Dim intI As Integer
    For intI = 0 To UBound(Array)
      result = CStr(Array(intI))
      Console.WriteLine(result)
    Next intI
  Console.WriteLine("—-")
  End Sub

  Public Sub BubbleSort(ByRef Array() As Integer)
  Dim outer, inner As Integer
    For outer = 0 To Array.Length - 1
      For innerI = 0 To Array.Length - 2
        If (Array(innerI) > Array(innerI + 1)) Then
          Transpose(Array, innerI, innerI + 1)
        End If
      Next innerI
    Next pass
  End Sub

  Public Overloads Sub Transpose(ByRef Array() As Integer, ByVal first _
  As Integer, ByVal second As Integer)
    Dim keep As Integer
```

```
      keep = Array(first)
      Array(first) = Array(second)
      Array(second) = keep
   End Sub
End Module
```

The output to the console shows the list of elements of the array unsorted, and then sorted after the array reference variable is passed through the **BubbleSort** method. The output is as follows:

```
134
3
1
23
87
342
2
9
---
1
2
3
9
23
87
134
342
```

In the initializer for the console, I created the array and initialized it with a collection of numbers (the list of alarms coming out of a queue, popped off a stack or off the back of a serial port). The code used to do this is as follows:

```
Dim sAlarms() As Integer = New Integer() {134, 3, 1, 23, 87, 342, 2, 9}
```

Then the array is passed to the **PrintArray** method, which prints the values of each element to the console. The **PrintArray** method is useful and will save you from having to write the **For** loop every time you want to print out the array, or stream the values out to some place like a screen or a file or a remote location. I have overloaded the method to provide some useful implementations, especially to use an **IEnumerator** instead of the **For...Next**:

```
Public Overloads Sub PrintArray(ByRef Array() As Integer)
  Dim result As String
  Dim intI As Integer
    For intI = 0 To UBound(sArray)
      result = CStr(sArray(intI))
      Console.WriteLine(result)
    Next I
  Console.WriteLine("—-")
End Sub
```

In the preceding code, we use the **For** loop to write the random numbers with which the array has been initialized to the console. This demonstrates that the array is currently unsorted. After generating the array, we then called the **BubbleSort** method and passed it the reference of the array to sort. This is achieved using the following method:

```
Public Sub BubbleSort(ByRef Array() As Integer)
  Dim outer, inner As Integer
  For outer = 1 To Array.Length - 1
    For inner = 0 To Array.Length – 2
      If (Array(inner) > Array(inner + 1)) Then
        Transpose(Array, inner, inner + 1)
      End If
    Next inner
  Next outer
End Sub
```

How does this bubble sort work? Notice that there are two loops, an outer loop and an inner loop. (By the way, this is pretty standard stuff, and many people use this sort for a small array, or small collections. I adapted it directly from the C version and several Java versions. I have not seen a C# one yet, but it would probably be identical to the latter variation just mentioned.) The outer loop controls the number of iterations or passes through the array. An **Integer** named **outer** is declared, and thus the outer **For** loop is as follows:

```
For outer = 0 To Array.Length - 1
  'inner For loop in here
Next pass
```

Upon the first iteration, **outer** is set to start at 0. Then the loop repeats for the length of the array, determined by incrementing **outer** (**Next outer**) with each pass of the array until **outer** is equal to the array's **Length –1** property (it does not need the final iteration).

For each loop of the outer array, we run the inner loop as follows:

```
For inner = 0 To Array.Length - 2
Next inner
```

The variable **inner** is first initialized to 0. Then, with each iteration of the loop, as long as **inner** is less than the length of the array minus 2, we do a comparison of each element against the one above it, as shown in the pseudocode here:

```
If Array(inner) is greater than Array(inner + 1) then swap them
```

For example, if **Array(inner)** is 3 and **Array (inner+1)** is 2, then we swap them so that 2 comes before 3 in the array. Often, it pays to actually sketch what's happening with the code, as demonstrated in Figure 12-9, a technique used by many gurus who believe that the mind is the *model* of invention.

The method that does the swapping is **Transpose**, which looks like this:

```
Public Overloads Sub Transpose(ByRef Array() As Integer, ByVal first _
As Integer, ByVal second As Integer)
  Dim keep As Integer
  keep = Array(first)
  Array(first) = Array(second)
  Array(second) = keep
End Sub
```

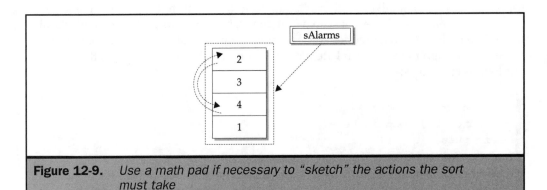

Figure 12-9. *Use a math pad if necessary to "sketch" the actions the sort must take*

The **Transpose** method shown here gets a reference to the array we are sorting. We also pass into **Transpose** the element positions we are going to swap around. It helps to see this without the placeholders in pseudocode, as follows:

```
Transpose(The Alarms array, the first element, the second element)
```

First, we create an **Integer** variable called **keep** to hold the value of the first element passed in:

```
keep = Array(first)
```

Then, we can assign the second element to the first one, as follows:

```
Array(first) = Array(second)
```

Now we give element 2 the value of element 1, as follows:

```
Array(second) = keep
```

When the **Transform** method completes, it returns us to the inner loop, and the new value in the higher element of the two previous elements is compared to the one above it.

Notice that the **Transpose** method is separated from the **BubbleSort** method. Why did we do that when we could have just as easily included the swapping routines in the **BubbleSort** method? Two reasons. First, we are following the rule discussed in Chapter 7 covering the construction of methods: It's better to decompose the algorithm into separate problem-solving methods. While this is a border line case—because the method is small enough to be included in the one method—expanding the **BubbleSort** method later becomes more difficult if the **Transpose** algorithm is left in (as you will see shortly). Also, the code is more readable and more maintainable like this. Another thing to consider is that the **Transpose** method can be useful outside of the **BubbleSort** method and can be defined in a sort interface or a utility class containing sorting methods (loose coupling and high cohesion). There may just be other opportunities to use the method, as the forthcoming code will demonstrate.

In the following code, a "slick" alternative uses the **Xor** operator discussed in Chapter 5 to evaluate ordinal values (**Short**, **Byte**, **Integer**, and **Long**). This method is an overloaded version of **Transpose**.

```
Public Overloads Sub Transpose(ByRef Array() As Integer, ByVal first _
As Integer, ByVal second As Integer)
  Dim keep As Integer
```

```
    Array(first) = Array(first) Xor Array(second)
    Array(second) = Array(first) Xor Array(second)
    Array(first) = Array(first) Xor Array(second)
End Sub
```

A third variation of **Transpose** pushes the **keep** variable onto a stack. I mentioned this technique earlier in the chapter:

```
Public Overloads Sub Transpose(ByRef Array() As Integer, ByVal first _
As Integer, ByVal second As Integer)
  Dim keep As Stack
  keep.Push(Array(first))
  Array(first) = Array(second)
  Array(second) = keep.Pop
End Sub
```

I have never found that using a stack in this way has any adverse effect over the running time of the sort. Later, the technique is again used in this book's version of the quicksort algorithm.

The **BubbleSort** method looks very efficient from a distance, but when you strip it down line by line and operation by operation, you can see that for a large array, its running time will explode. For small arrays (like 25 elements), it's great and it's fast because we do not have to do any fancy partitioning with the array object. But we'll need something more efficient for larger data structures, which tend to beg for dissection. Let's see what happens when the array gets much bigger, as discussed in the following section. The next section maintains the simplicity of the bubble sort but attempts to keep the size of the arrays to sort as small as possible.

Partition and Merge

The divide-and-conquer philosophy discussed in Chapter 7 can be applied to large data structures like a large array. Instead of running **BubbleSort** for one large array and then running out of "bath water," we can divvy up the array into smaller arrays, or portions, and then sort the portions separately. After that, we need to merge the portions back into one large array. Remember, **BubbleSort** walks through every element in the array, so **BubbleSort** on one large array is not efficient. But what if we were to chop the large array into two smaller ones? The result is an *n/2* sort, and if the array is small enough, the running time will still be linear. In essence, we can now use **BubbleSort** on two small arrays instead of one large one.

There are two parts to this algorithm. The first part divides a large array into two smaller arrays and then sorts the subarrays or portions. The second part merges the two sorted subarrays back into one large array.

So how would you divide the array? Since we have access to its **Length** property that's actually the easy chore. The following code can be used for the division:

```
bound = Array.Length \ 2 'bound represents the upper bound of the first part
'or bound is the other part's upper bound
bound = Array.Length - 2
```

What have we here? Firstly, the array is only logically split into two arrays; we still have one array. But when we make the calls to the **BubbleSort** method, we first sort up the middle of the array, then we start over again and sort the second part of the array. Once you run the arrays through the **BubbleSort** method, you end up with the two portions of the same array, both sorted in the same call. We can kick off this idea as demonstrated in the following example:

```
Public Sub BubbleSort(ByRef array() As Integer)
   Dim outer, inner As Integer
   For outer = outerStart To array.Length \ 2
     For inner = innerStart To array.Length \ 2
       If (array(inner) > array(inner + 1)) Then
         Transpose(array, inner, inner + 1)
       End If
     Next inner
   Next outer

   Dim outerStart As Integer = outer
   Dim innerStart As Integer = inner

   For outer = outerStart To array.Length - 2
     For inner = innerStart To array.Length - 2
       If (array(inner) > array(inner + 1)) Then
         Transpose2(array, inner, inner + 1)
       End If
     Next inner
   Next outer
End Sub
```

What's cooking here? The **BubbleSort** now does two sorts in one method. It first sorts the first part of the array and then it sorts the second part. But before we look at the innards of the method do you notice that the stack of sorts seems a bit of kludge. The stack of sorts seems inelegant. It is. But trying to combine the two iterative routines into one iterative routine that still sorts the two parts separately is extremely cumbersome. If you look at the two separate sorts you will see how the method now lends itself to recursion. As we discussed on the section on recursion in Chapter 7, there are times when recursion is the best solution (and sometime the only one) when you need to use divide and conquer techniques to solve a problem.

However, designing recursion can be hairsplitting as well. You need to decide what gets passed to the method for the first sort and what gets passed for the second sort. Have a look at the following code. You'll notice we now have to pass variables to the method instead of fixed values. These variables cater to the start and end points at which to logically partition the array.

```
Public Overloads Sub BubbleSort(ByRef array() As Integer, _
   ByVal outerStart As Integer, _
   ByVal innerStart As Integer, _
   ByVal bound As Integer)
```

(**BubbleSort** must now be overloaded to cater to the multiple versions of this method we can come up with (we still preserve the original for simple sorts on small arrays).) The **outerStart** and **innerStart** parameters expect the starting position on the array for both **For** loops in the method. The **outerStart For** loops for each element in the array and the **innerStart For** loops for the number of comparisons that must be made for each element. The **bound** parameter expects the upper bound of the array part to sort to. The recursive method to sort the two parts can be implemented as follows:

```
Public Overloads BubbleSort(ByRef array() As Integer, _
   ByVal outerStart As Integer, _
   ByVal innerStart As Integer, _
   ByVal bound As Integer)
   If outerStart >= bound Then
     Exit Function
   End If
   Dim outer, inner As Integer
   For outer = outerStart To bound
     For inner = innerStart To bound
       If (array(inner) > array(inner + 1)) Then
         Transpose(array, inner, inner + 1)
       End If
     Next inner
   Next outer
   BubbleSort(array, outer, inner, array.Length - 2)
End Sub
```

The recursive call is highlighted in bold. Before we continue, take note of the stopping condition (also in bold).

```
If outerStart >= bound Then
  Exit Function
End If
```

If we forget to include a stopping condition the method will explode. We can now call this method as follows:

```
Dim sArray() As Integer = {102, 82, 23, 44, 25, 65, 27, _
45, 7, 234, 54, 5, 22, 4, 343, 0, 56}
BubbleSort(sArray, 0, 0, sArray.Length \ 2)
```

After the first part on the array is sorted the recursive call goes to work on the second part.

As demonstrated in the preceding code, we divided the array into two parts and sorted the elements in the two parts recursively. Now we have both halves of the array sorted by the **BubbleSort** method, but we still need to merge the two sorted halves back into one whole, sorted array. That's the harder part of the algorithm. What do we know about the results of the recursive partition bubble sort so far? Figure 12-10 illustrated the current sorted state of the array.

To merge the two sorted parts, we have to allocate a new temporary array called **Temp** and copy the sorted elements into **Temp**. We can merge into **Temp** by comparing the value in the first element of **part1** with the first value in the first element of **part2**. Now the algorithm requires that we keep track of how many times we copy a value to **Temp** (call it **copytemp**), and how many times we copy from **part1** and **part2**, respectively. Suppose we compare **part1**(*index*) and **part2**(*index*) and find that **part2**(*index*) is less than **part1**(*index*). We must then copy the value of **part2**(*index*) to the back of the temporary array and increment **copytemp** by 1 and **part2** by 1.

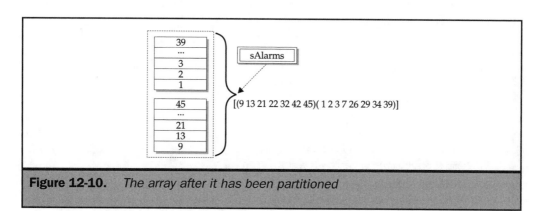

Figure 12-10.   *The array after it has been partitioned*

CLASSES AND OBJECTS

The pseudocode for the algorithm can thus far be written as follows:

```
Allocate array temp, Integers copytemp = 0, part1 = 0,
part2 = array.Length \ 2 + 1
While there are uncompared elements in both halves
  if the next element of part1 is less than or equal to
  the next element of part2 then copy the next element
  of part1 to temp, increment copytemp and part1 by 1
  Else Copy the next element of part2 to temp and
  increment copytemp and part2 by 1
End While
```

The code for the merging process can be implemented as follows:

```
Public Sub Merge(ByRef array() As Integer)
Dim part1, copytemp As Integer
'get the start of the second part
Dim part2 As Integer = array.Length \ 2 + 1
'a temp array the length of Array-1
Dim Temp(array.Length - 1) As Integer
  While (part2 <= array.Length - 2) And (part1 <= array.Length \ 2)
    If (array(part1) <= array(part2)) Then
      Temp(copytemp) = array(part1)
      copytemp += 1
      part1 += 1
    Else
      Temp(copytemp) = array(part2)
      copytemp += 1
      part2 += 1
    End If
  End While
  While (part1 <= array.Length \ 2)
    Temp(copytemp) = array(part1)
    copytemp += 1
    part1 += 1
  End While
  While (part2 <= array.Length - 1)
    Temp(copytemp) = array(part2)
    copytemp += 1
    part2 += 1
  End While
  array = Temp
End Sub
```

The **While** loop will continue to process until there are no two items to compare. The best way to refine the pseudocode and finally translate it into source code is by sketching the arrays and graphically representing each iteration, comparison process, and copy process element by element. That way, you'll be able to decide how to code out the math you need to do the job in an algorithm.

The **Merge** can be called independently or from within the stopping conditional in the **BubbleSort** method as follows:

```
Merge(Alarms)
PrintArray(Alarms)
```

The results are printed as follows:

```
0
4
5
7
22
23
25
27
44
45
54
56
65
82
102
234
343
500
--
```

Yes, there is a lot going on behind the scenes, but to sort the array, we simply pass it by reference to the **Merge** method. What this algorithm costs is debatable. One of my objectives is to show you more ways of handling array sorting. The **Merge** method is very fast because the parts of the array are already sorted so there is much less iteration.

The speed, however, does not result from the apparent concurrency. Recall the discussion in Chapter 7 on running time analysis of an algorithm and big-O notation. Running time is not constant and ranges from linear to quadratic time (and worse) the larger the data set. The effect of the partition ensures the sorts are kept at $O(1)$ and thus not at $O(4)$. In other words, sorting one large array takes much longer than dividing the array into smaller bits and then sorting each division, one after the other.

The sort goes faster because we are sorting two smaller arrays instead of one large one. Incidentally, the **Array** class is thread-safe, which means that it's not out of the question to put recursive sorts into their own threads, or solicit the help of a free processor.

While the merge process is very effective, it is also a little resource-intensive and wasteful on massive arrays that just get partitioned into two large arrays. Surely, there is a better way of sorting an array than creating a temporary array that you use to hold the elements of the original array. After all, creating the temporary array means extra computing steps; and then having to put all the values back into the original array seems a little odd. The bigger the data input, the harder it is to process. Nevertheless, it is a useful method.

One of the reasons to take you through the previous exercise was to show you that one of the basic tenets of sorting in particular, and computing in general, is to divide larger work units into smaller work units so as to keep the running time curve from arcing upwards.

As mentioned at the beginning of this section, sorting arrays is a precursor to searching them. Searching is practically impossible on large arrays if data is unsorted. This is true for searching not only arrays, but also all types of linear data structures. Try to search an unsorted list of values in a spreadsheet or a database table and see how hard it is in comparison to searching these structures if they are sorted in ascending or descending order.

To take the next step in sorting our data structures, we should strive to maintain the good ideas, such as the divide-and-conquer rule, and toss out the parts that result in extra computing, such as creating unnecessary extra data structures, which requires more code and more resources.

A good example of such a sorting algorithm is the famous *quicksort*, discussed next.

Quicksort

The well-known scientist C. A. R. Hoare invented the quicksort algorithm more than 40 years ago (and it's still running in various forms to this day). The premise of the algorithm is to partition an array into smaller partitions and then recursively sort the partitions, in a similar fashion to what we have just covered. It is similar in concept to the partition and merge bubble sort, but the partitioning is a lot more slick because instead of having to merge two partitions into one at the end of the sort, with quicksort, the end result is a fully sorted array, and no merging is required. We also do not need to create a temporary array.

The specification of this algorithm is as follows:

1. Choose an element in the array, which is often called the "pivot."

2. Partition the array at the pivot into two groups.

3. Send the values that are less than the pivot to the one side.

4. Send the values that are greater than the pivot to the other side.

5. Sort each side recursively.

The pivot element is exactly that—pivotal. This sort is fast because once a value is known to be less than the pivot, it does not have to be compared to the values on the other side of the pivot.

This sort is faster than the sorts we coded earlier because we do not have to compare one value against all the other values in the array. We only have to compare them against n/2 values in the entire array—divide and conquer.

Exactly how fast is the quicksort? Taking its best case, we can say that the first pass partitions the array of n elements into two groups, n/2 each. But it is possible to partition further into three groups, n/3 and so on. The best case is where the pivot point chosen is a value that should be as close to the middle of the array as possible, but we'll get back to that after we have coded the algorithm.

Quicksort has been rewritten for nearly every language, and it has been implemented using a variety of techniques. The .NET Framework architects have also implemented it in C#, and it's a static method you can call from the **Array** class. But let's code the algorithm ourselves. Later, you can check out which implementation of quicksort works faster, the Visual Basic .NET one or the C# one.

To recap, the element that sits at the intersection of the partition is called the pivot element. Once the pivot is identified, all values in the array less than or equal to the pivot are sent to one side of it, and all values greater are sent to the other. The partitions are then sorted recursively, and when complete, the entire array is sorted.

The recursive sorting of the partitions is not the difficult part; it's finding the pivot element that is a little more complex. There are several things we don't know going into this algorithm:

- We don't know anything about the array elements and their values. When an array is passed to you for sorting, you don't get any advanced sorting information, such as the best element to use as the pivot.

- We don't know where the pivot element may finally end up in the array. It could be in the middle, which is good, or it could end up close to—or at—either end, which actually slows down the sort (and, of course, that's bad).

So, to begin somewhere and without any information, we might as well just pick the first element in the array and hope that it's possible to move it to an index position that intersects the array as close to its final resting place as possible. But we still don't know where that might be (incidentally, you can also use the last element as the pivot). Let's look at another array to sort, represented here by its declaration and "on paper" in Figure 12-11 (it's easier now to represent the array horizontally):

```
Dim sAlarms() As Integer = {43,3,38,35,83,37,3,6,79,71,5, _
78,46,22,9,1,65,23,60}
```

This array is unsorted and yields the number 43 in the first element. So, we now need a method that will take all the numbers in the array less than or equal to 43 and

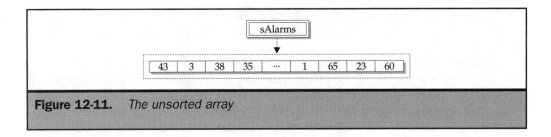

Figure 12-11.   *The unsorted array*

move them to the beginning of the array. However, because we have chosen the first element as the pivot, we still don't know how far we need to move the less than or equal to elements to the one end of the array or how far we need to move the greater than elements to the other end.

The way this problem has been solved over the years is like this: Start at each end of the array—from the element after the pivot (0) to the other end of the array—comparing the value of each element with the value of the pivot element until we find an element value that is less than or equal to the pivot value and one that is greater than the pivot value. So, we start at the beginning, skipping the first value because it is the pivot, and stop at the element holding 83.

Now we need to go to the other end of the array and test each element value until we find an element value that is less than or equal to the pivot value. In our case, we stop at the element holding 23. The two elements are emphasized in the array example in Figure 12-12.

We need to create two variables to hold the indexes of the two elements, because the next step is to exchange the two element values. The value 23 is moved to the index of the 83 element, and 83 goes to the index of the 23 element. In other words, the elements swap their values at their index positions in the array. The result is shown in Figure 12-13.

We have to continue with the process, starting from the left and stopping at the element holding 79. On the right, we keep marching to the left, stopping at 9. We repeat the process, and we note the index positions and exchange the two element values. We can perform the interchange because we know the index of each element.

We keep doing this until the march from the left crosses over the march from the right. This point then becomes known as the array partition intersection, the point at which the array is partitioned for us. The array ends up as shown in Figure 12-14.

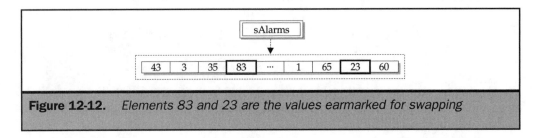

Figure 12-12.   *Elements 83 and 23 are the values earmarked for swapping*

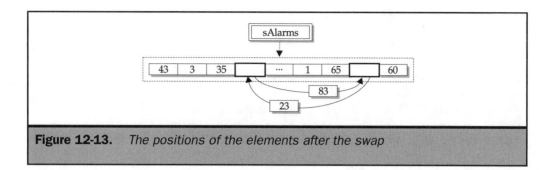

Figure 12-13.   *The positions of the elements after the swap*

If we examine the array, we see that on the left side of the intersection, we have elements less than or equal to the pivot, and on the right of the intersection, we have all the elements greater than the pivot. At this point, the array is partitioned and the star (*) represents the position for the pivot element. However, we still have not positioned the pivot at the intersection of the partitions (its final resting place). So, the last piece of the pivot puzzle is to interchange the last element value of the lesser or equal to values with the pivot. The pivot is now at the intersection of both partitions, as shown in Figure 12-15.

Next, we need to write the code to programmatically achieve what we did here, after which we can write the code to recursively sort each partition. So, the algorithm uses the chosen pivot value to partition the array by looping through each array index position from the left and from the right, and comparing each index value to the pivot value.

If the values meet the "change sides" condition, they are swapped; otherwise, they are left alone and the loop advances the left-side index to the right and the right-side index to the left. It will keep going until both operations intersect the array and overlap.

As the algorithm loops from left to right and from right to left, the point of the intersection is then used as the partition point and the location to where we move the pivot's value. The algorithm swaps the value that is less than or equal to it with the value of the pivot, the value in the first element. Let's begin designing this algorithm.

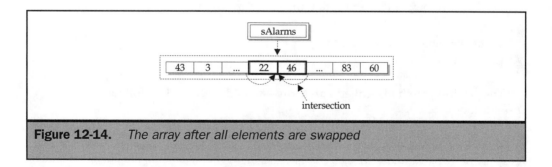

Figure 12-14.   *The array after all elements are swapped*

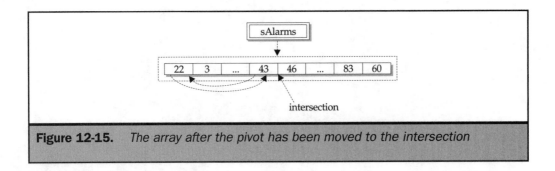

Figure 12-15. *The array after the pivot has been moved to the intersection*

Note *The array example here provides a best-case scenario, because 43 invariably ends up in the middle of the array or very close to the middle. A worst-case scenario would be to find the first element to be sitting at a low index, like 1, or somewhere up near or at the end of the array, which would result in the pivot not partitioning the array in any useful way for the recursive sort. So, the worst case is an n1 sort.*

We can prep the algorithm as follows:

- Integer **n** is the length of **sAlarms**.
- Integer **pivotChosen** is the zero index of **sAlarms**.
- Integer **leftSideIndex** is the index of **sAlarms** from the left.
- Integer **rightSideIndex** is the index of **sAlarms** from the right.
- Integer **reCall** is a holding "cell" for an index value used for swapping.

With this information, you can create pseudocode and then write the method. The pivot element would be obtained as follows:

```
pivotChosen = Alarms(0) 'or Alarms.Length - 1
```

which, remember, is the arbitrarily chosen pivot.

The lesser or bigger elements are represented as follows:

```
leftSideIndex = myArray(1)
rightSideIndex = n - 1
```

The partition method—called **PartArray**—would then work as follows (pseudocode):

```
While the leftSideIndex is less than the rightSideIndex, and
   While leftSideIndex is not at the end of Array and
   Array(leftSideIndex) is less than or equal to the pivot
```

CLASSES AND OBJECTS

```
    value then increment leftSideIndex.
And
  While the rightSideIndex is greater than or equal to the leftSideIndex,
   and While Array(rightSideIndex) is greater than or equal to the pivot
    value then decrement rightSideIndex.
But
  If (Array(leftSideIndex) > (Arrray(rightSideIndex))
  swap the values of both index positions.
```

When the preceding code is done swapping, the partition can be made as follows:

```
1) remember the value at rightSideIndex
2) remember the value at pivotChosen
3) swap the values
```

This can now be implemented. First we create the array and then pass it to the **QuickSort** method as follows:

```
Dim sAlarms() As Integer = {43,3,38,35,83,37,6,79,71,5,78,46,22,9,1,65,23,60}
QuickSort(sAlarms,0,0,0)
```

This code passes the array and the initial starting positions for the partitioning process. Have a look at the method's signature:

```
Public Overloads Sub QuickSort(ByRef Array() As Integer, _
  ByVal outerStart As Integer, _
  ByVal innerStart As Integer, _
  ByVal bound As Integer)
    Dim outer, inner As Integer
  'get the middle of the array from the pivot returned from QuickPart
  If Not (outerStart >= Array.Length - 1) Then
    If (bound <= 0) Then
      bound = QuickPart(Array)
    End If
  'sort to follow...
End Sub
```

This method is also recursive and checks to see that the **outerStart** parameter is not positioned at the end of the array, which would indicate the array sort is finished (the first bold emphasized line). Then a conditional is introduced to determine if the array has already been partitioned (the second bold line). The partition function, **QuickPart**, also returns to us the starting position of the second sub-array to sort. **QuickPart** is implemented in the following example:

```
Private Function QuickPart(ByRef myArray() As Integer) As Integer
Dim n As Integer = myArray.Length
'just choose the first element
Dim pivotChosen As Integer = myArray(0)
Dim leftSideIndex As Integer = 1
Dim rightSideIndex As Integer = n - 1
'checks for intersection
  While (leftSideIndex < rightSideIndex)
    While ((leftSideIndex < rightSideIndex) And _
      (myArray(leftSideIndex) <= pivotChosen)) 'keep going until false
      leftSideIndex += 1 'increment the left side's index position
    End While
    While (myArray(rightSideIndex) > pivotChosen)
      rightSideIndex -= 1 'decrement the left side's index position
    End While
    If (leftSideIndex < rightSideIndex) Then 'swap sides
      Transpose2(myArray, rightSideIndex, leftSideIndex)
    End If
  End While
  'move pivot to the intersection
  Transpose(myArray, 0, rightSideIndex)
  Return rightSideIndex
End Function
```

Now let's add the recursive sorting part of the method, which will call itself one more time to sort the second part of the array:

```
Public Overloads Sub QuickSort(ByRef Array() As Integer, _
  ByVal outerStart As Integer, _
  ByVal innerStart As Integer, _
  ByVal bound As Integer)
    Dim outer, inner As Integer
  'get the middle of the array from the pivot returned from QuickPart
  If Not (outerStart >= Array.Length - 1) Then
    If (bound <= 0) Then
      bound = QuickPart(Array)
    End If
    For outer = outerStart To bound
      For inner = innerStart To bound
```

```
      If (Array(inner).CompareTo(Array(inner + 1))) > 0 Then
        Transpose(Array, inner, inner + 1)
      End If
    Next inner
  Next outer
  QuickSort(Array, outer, inner, Array.Length - 2)
  End If
End Sub
```

Naturally, if you were going to package these utilities in a single class you would provide a simple interface for the client to call **QuickSort** and not have to specify the various parameters other than the reference variable of the array to sort.

Notice that in the preceding code the method makes use of the **CompareTo** method to determine if a value in the array is greater than, less than, or equal to the value to the right of it. **CompareTo** returns a value greater than 0 if the left-hand value is greater than the right-hand value. It returns 0 if the values are equal, and –1 if the left-hand value is less than the right-hand value.

The **QuickPart** method works well with a pivot that is chosen from the value sitting in the zeroth index of the array. But what if that value at the zeroth index turned out to be one of the lowest or one of the highest values in the array? As mentioned earlier, this would result in little or no improvement in the running time for the sort. In fact the effort to try and partition an array that cannot be partitioned is added to the increase in time to sort one large array and the running time might be worse that anticipated.

We will return to sorting again in Chapter 14, demonstrating how we can use the method pointing facility of the **Delegate** to replace the recursive call. The code for these sorting examples can be access in the Vb7cr.ArrayUtils project.

Sorting Strings and Other Objects

The sort methods we have studied so far only sort ordinals, but we all know that, more often than not, we need to sort through a collection of objects, especially **String** objects. The sort methods can thus be overloaded as needed to take different arguments and thus provide different implementations of the sorts.

Like the static **Sort** method in **System.Array** your typically overloaded method signatures might accept objects that implement **IComparable** interface (you already saw some use of the **CompareTo** method in the **QuickSort** method). These are typically referred to as **IComparer** objects—**String** is one. We typically refer to such arguments as **IComparable** arguments. See Chapter 15 in the section on "Strings" for more information comparing **String** values.

CLASSES AND OBJECTS

Populating Arrays

Inserting values into array elements one value at a time, as demonstrated earlier, can be a bit of a bind. You can use the optional curly braces to pass a comma-delimited list of values to the array constructor, but that only works if you know the values at design time, which means they are hard-coded. The following code demonstrates an alternative that is more elaborate:

```
Sub ArrayPopulate()
Dim arrayVal(50) As Integer
Dim intI As Integer
  For intI = 0 to UBound(arrayVal)
    arrayVal(intI) = 10
  Next Int
End Sub
```

However, the preceding method only populates the array with identical values. We can still get a little more creative, however, by changing the values for every new iteration of the **For** loop:

```
Sub ArrayPopulate()
Dim arrayVal(50) As Integer
Dim intI As Integer
  For intI = 0 to UBound(arrayVal)
    arrayVal(intI) = intI * 2
  Next intI
End Sub
```

The preceding code now changes the value (see the highlighted line), so instead of an array filled with the number 10, the array is now filled as 0, 2, 4, 6, 8, 10 , and so on. It's an improvement, yes—but not much of an improvement. Often, we need to fill an array with a predetermined range of values, objects, different items, and so on. So, if we focus on the emphasized line in the preceding code, we should be able to devise the necessary algorithms to return a list of values, and place each different value into a separate slot in the array.

We can use stacks and queues to copy values to the array, but we are still stuck with the problem of getting the values to the other data structures in the first place. The source of true random and external data for array and data-structure, however, comes from files and streams. For example, we can read (line by line) from a file (such as an e-mail document or a word-processing file) and then load that data into an array or a linked list.

In Chapter 15, we will look at several classes, such as **File**, **Directory**, and **Stream**, that you can use to open a text document, parse through each line in the file, and extract the values using various regular expressions. After scrubbing the data you have in hand, you can then bridge to an array or another type of collection object and copy the values to it.

Arrays for Objects

Often, you will find a need to work with data in a tabulated format or grid-like structure, like a database table or a spreadsheet. Of course, you can always access the ADO and ADO.NET libraries and work with data in recordsets and datasets, but that's not always convenient or even always possible.

In a normalized collection of tables, data you need to pull and analyze could be in many tables, even in different databases. While you can assemble a killer SQL statement with the mother of all joins, and pull the exact data you need, operating on the data is not always convenient or practical with a standard record or data set. If you have had some hands-on process control or operations management work, or got your hands greasy programming OLAP (online analytical processing) cubes, then you know what I mean.

Also, not all data is stored to or retrieved from a database table. A spreadsheet is a good example; the last time I used Excel, I don't remember saving my spreadsheet to Access or SQL Server. Logs are another good example of tabulated data that does not always need to be stored in a database. A flat file often suffices and is a lot cheaper to use as storage.

There are several ways to collect related data in such a way that you can perform complex analyses and calculations on it. You just need to look at the data structures in this chapter and the next and you see several alternatives to arrays for collecting objects.

But arrays are a powerful data structures because they provide the most functionality for accessing data in any random order and for sorting and searching in very powerful ways. First, let's think about a particular need. If you were an injector engineer and operations manager, you typically would need to collect and analyze data in myriad ways. For example, you may need to calculate the life of an injector, how long it takes to repair an injector, how many shifts and assistant engineers you need, and what might be the useful life of an injector before it begins to burn more fuel than considered normal.

In our **Injector** object we started building in Chapter 9, we could extract and tabulate five sets of data:

- **Date**   The date this injector was placed into service
- **Time**   The time this injector was placed into service
- **Temp**   The average temperature of the injector since startup
- **Burnrate**   The average amount of fuel burned since startup
- **Velocity**   The average velocity we have been traveling at since startup

This data can be computed and reported on in various ways, but we are studying the data structure to hold the data, and not operations management. So, don't concern yourself with what we are trying to calculate.

The first solution you might think of to hold this data and have the facility to perform any manner of complex computation on the data, and still extract it for reports or archiving, is to use five separate arrays for each variable. The declaration for the collection of arrays would look something like this:

```
Dim lDate(1000) As Date
Dim lTime(1000) As DateTime
Dim lTemp(1000) As Integer
Dim lRate(1000) As Integer
Dim lFuel(1000) As Integer
Dim logVelocity(1000) As Integer
```

To reference the data, or load the five "columns" into your report or user interface, you would need to reference the subscripts of all five arrays at the same time in your method. If you try to iterate through the array, the method must also be able to work with all six arrays at the same time. Your collection of arrays would look like the concoction illustrated in Figure 12-16.

The method you might create would be a real grizzly. Such a method can get very hairy and impractical when the length and number of arrays grow. This structure sometimes is called the "parallel array structure," but you don't need to name it, because such code is not what makes software fun, and you should forget this approach.

Could a better solution be to declare an array of six dimensions, as demonstrated in the following declaration? (Careful, this is a trick question.)

```
Dim InjectorStats As Integer = {New Date(), New DateTime(), _
New Integer(), New Integer(), New Integer(), New Integer()}
```

You are not going to get very far with the preceding **InjectorStats** array because of one fundamental limitation. Arrays are strongly typed, so the other dimensions must also be **Integer**s. Even if you could create a multidimensional-multitype array, this code is also exactly the definition of "inelegant." Really, it's not practical either.

This is where you need to put your object-thinking cap on. What if you did not store any of the actual values in the array and only stored references to objects? After all, that's how arrays of **String** work. By storing objects in the array, we only have to

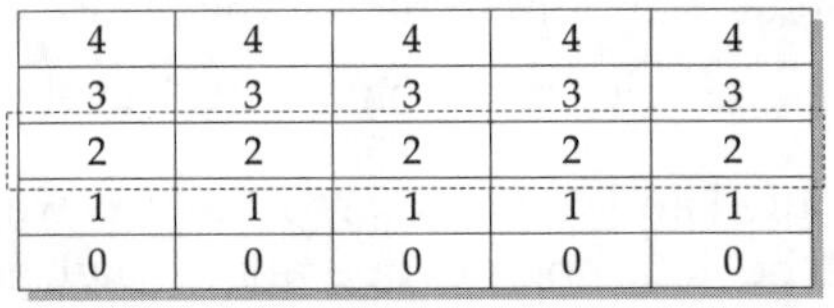

4	4	4	4	4
3	3	3	3	3
2	2	2	2	2
1	1	1	1	1
0	0	0	0	0

Figure 12-16. *Accessing five arrays at the same subscript at the same time*

collect the reference variables. No injector data is stored in the array. Instead, we create an object that will contain the five data fields we require. Every reference variable stored in the array thus becomes a reference to the six data fields.

What do we achieve with this approach? First, we only need a simple one-dimensional array. No parallel arrays and no multidimensional arrays are needed. Second, the array can hold any object, as long as the objects are all of the same type. So, we don't have a type mismatch issue with the array, which can continue to behave in its strongly typed way. Third, the data contained by the actual objects can now be processed and managed in any sophisticated way you may conceive. Fourth, your algorithm can be easily changed and adapted. The array of your custom type never needs to change, while the object itself can be extended and adapted as needs dictate.

The data can also be printed, sent to Crystal Reports and persisted through serialization (see Chapter 15), or stored in a database or a data mart. When we are finished with the objects, we can leave the garbage collector to clean up the bits left lying around. Not only is this all possible, but it's one of the most elegant ways to meet this type of data processing requirement.

First, we need an object that represents a record (like a tuple or row in a database table). We can call this object **Row**. While we can declare the container array wherever we need to work with **Row**s we need to create a class for the **Row** object so that **Row**s can be instantiated as needed (the number of **Row**s would be limited to the available memory). The class must have a constructor so that it can be instantiated with the following syntax:

```
Dim InjectorRows As New Row
```

Using object semantics, you can encapsulate six objects as fields of the container object. The first cut of our class might look like this:

```
Public Class Row

Private ldate As Date
Private ltime As DateTime
Private ltemp As Integer
Private lburn As Integer
Private lfuel As Integer
Private lvelocity As Integer

End Class
```

You can then access the data in the fields via accessor methods and modify the data via modification methods. But properties are ideally suited to the public visibility required by the **Row** object. It's always better to expose such values via property interfaces. The

Row values can remain hidden and secret, yet they can easily be used via the property interfaces.

The class can then be extended with properties as follows:

```
Public Class Row

  ' . . .

  Property LogDate() As Date
    Get
      Return ldate
    End Get
    Set(ByVal Value As Date)
      ldate = Value
    End Set
  End Property

  Property LogTime() As DateTime
    Get
      Return ltime
    End Get
    Set(ByVal Value As DateTime)
      ltime = Value
    End Set
  End Property

  Property Temparature() As Decimal
    Get
      Return ltemp
    End Get
    Set(ByVal Value As Decimal)
      ltemp = Value
    End Set
  End Property

  Property BurnRate() As Integer
    Get
      Return BurnRate
    End Get
    Set(ByVal Value As Integer)
      lburn = Value
    End Set
```

```
      End Property

      Property Fuel() As Integer
        Get
          Return lfuel
        End Get
        Set(ByVal Value As Integer)
          lfuel = Value
        End Set
      End Property

      Property Velocity() As Integer
        Get
          Return lvelocity
        End Get
        Set(ByVal Value As Integer)
          lvelocity = Value
        End Set
      End Property
    End Class
```

With properties we can easily access any other method in the **Row** class—even to perform a behind-the-scenes computation. Now all we need to do is to come up with the methods to create the array, create and insert **Row** objects into the array, and manage the array. Accessing the **Row** objects and the **Row** properties is easy, as you will see. But first we need to create the structure. In the following class, we create the **InjectorStats** array and add **Row**s to the array. The method caters to capturing data for installment into the "columns" of each row object:

```
Class RowArray
  Dim InjectorStats(1000) As Row
  Public Sub AddRows(ByVal rownumber As Integer, _
    ByVal ldate As Date, _
    ByVal ltime As DateTime, _
    ByVal ltemp As Integer, _
    ByVal lburn As Integer, _
    ByVal lfuel As Integer, _
    ByVal lvelocity As Integer)

    InjectorStats(rownumber).LogDate = ldate
    InjectorStats(rownumber).LogTime = ltime
```

```
      InjectorStats(rownumber).Temparature = ltemp
      InjectorStats(rownumber).BurnRate = lburn
      InjectorStats(rownumber).Fuel = lfuel
      InjectorStats(rownumber).Velocity = lvelocity
  End Sub
'...
End Class
```

Notice that the array is declared as type **Row**. In this declaration, the array is initialized to hold 1000 **Row**s. However, just because the array is declared to be of type **Row** does not mean rows get magically added. You still need to instantiate the row objects and add them to the array. This can be arranged rather simply with code resembling the following in the constructor for the **RowArray** class:

```
Dim InjectorStats(1000) As Row
Dim newRow As New Row()
Dim count As Integer
Public Sub New()
  MyBase.New()
  While count <= 1000
    InjectorStats(count) = newRow
    count += 1
  End While
End Sub
```

While the size of the array is hard-coded in the above example you can just as easily extend the class with a handful of methods that allow for variable sizes and even extending the array size as needed. Or once the array fills up you can overwrite the data in the row, just like your standard Windows event logs.

The following code demonstrates how we can access a **Row** and change or manipulate the **Row** data via the **Row** object's properties:

```
Public Sub AddToLog()
  InjectorLogs.AddRows(GetRowNumber, GetDate, _
  GetTime, GetTemp, GetBurn, GetFuel, GetVelocity)
End Sub
```

With our injector engineer thinking caps on, what else might we need to do with the **Row** data? Printing the rows would be helpful, especially to a console opened up over the live injector for real-time monitoring. A single print method, **PreparePrint**, can be constructed to perform the assemblage of the data from the **Row** object, while another method, **PrintData**, can be constructed to print the data to a console. Displaying the data to the console from a row in the **InjectorStats** is simply a matter of accessing the properties of each **Row** as follows:

```
Public Sub PrintRow(ByVal rownumber As Integer)
  Console.WriteLine(InjectorStats(rownumber).LogDate)
  Console.WriteLine(InjectorStats(rownumber).LogTime)
  Console.WriteLine(InjectorStats(rownumber).Temparature)
  Console.WriteLine(InjectorStats(rownumber).BurnRate)
  Console.WriteLine(InjectorStats(rownumber).Fuel)
  Console.WriteLine(InjectorStats(rownumber).Velocity)
End Sub
```

which outputs the raw data as shown here:

```
3/3/2002
3:39:05 PM
1459723
75645
1523688980
888348
```

Of course you can redirect this data to a hard-copy printer method (which does a nice job of formatting it), to a report engine, or to other methods to handle whatever form of persistence or presentation is required.

Sorting the data and searching would not be that difficult to do. You would simply sort on a particular property in a particular **Row** you make the key field, much like a database table column. In fact you could override the **Row** object's **ToString** field to hold the key value to sort on, which in any event is unused space.

What you now know is that the architecture can easily underpin a graphical cell-like component for manipulating data, possibly even a construct that can be packaged as a control that can be dropped onto a form.

Any time you need to work with related data in two or more arrays, you should determine whether a single array that stores objects might be a better solution. An array of objects also makes for very adaptable and easily maintainable code, which is precisely what OOP is all about.

Hash Tables

A hash table is a data structure that stores a related pair of items—a key and its partner value. Hash tables work like arrays and lists (in fact, they are a combination of arrays and lists), and implement sophisticated mathematics—hashing algorithms—to create a highly efficient data structure for storing and retrieving data.

The difference between a hash table and an array, however, is that an array maintains an ordered collection in which a value is paired with an index number that corresponds to the element in the array that stores the data. The hash table has no such index value and it is not ordered. You simply send the data you want to retrieve to the hash table and remember a key that you will use later to get the data back. The following real-world analogy illustrates the utility of hash tables.

There you are at the TechEd 2004 about to go in to a huge hall to listen to Bill G. talk about Version 8 of Visual Basic .NET. You have your overcoat with you and you don't feel like schlepping it into the hall. So you make your way over to the overcoat "keep" and hand it to the person behind the counter. He or she hangs it along with the other 15,000 overcoats belonging to the other eager developers who came to listen (or get free breakfast). The person returns with a tag and writes 13,987 on the tag for you.

After you are done getting all fired-up by Bill, you return to the coat keep and hand in your (key) tag. If you lose the tag you will need to sort through 15,000 overcoats, and that will make you very late for your first session.

Hash tables are to software engineering what a telescope is to an astronomer, and the implementation of the **Hashtable** class in the .NET Framework saves us a lot of time because we do not have to construct our own hash tables from scratch. The whole reason we have a framework like .NET is to reuse its no-doubt expertly architectured classes, like the **Hashtable**.

Investigating every aspect of the construction of a hash table and studying its underpinning science is beyond the scope of this book. If you are interested in the subject, possibly to provide your own hash table to the Framework, one of the best places to start is Robert Sedgewick's seminal work, *Algorithms in C, Parts 1-4* (Addison-Wesley, 1999). However, a cursory investigation of the hash table is essential to understanding the practical uses of this simple yet highly practical data structure. Later, we'll also look at implementing custom hashing algorithms to replace the standard **GetHashCode** method inherited from **Object**.

A hash table can be used for any need that you have to associate some data—which is often a "pointer" to something more complex stored somewhere else—with a key that can quickly be looked up. The crux of a hash table is that the key value is "hashed" to generate a highly efficient search condition (such as an index value) that can be efficiently accessed in the hash table.This is especially valuable when you have values that are themselves hard to index, such as the nine-digit U.S. social security number or complex stocking or cataloging numbers (like the International Standard Book Number—ISBN), or when you require indexable values to be extracted from a combination of values, such as the X and Y coordinates on a grid, or the coordinates that might represent an object suspended in a multidimensional space. In OOP, hashing is important because it allows us to represent searchable objects as hashed values.

A value is passed to a hashing algorithm, an implementation of a hash code function in a hash table class, which returns the hash code to the table. The resulting hash code is then used as an "index" in the hash table where the associated information is stored. This is demonstrated in Figure 12-17.

An analogy of the internal operations of the hash table in the physical world is a modestly sized collection of mailboxes that typically stands in front of a corporate office park or office complex. To efficiently deliver all the mail, the post office employee needs only associate a company name with a mailbox number on a lookup chart. So, for example, all mail for Jacaranda Communications would be placed in mailbox 1, all mail for Osborne in mailbox 2, and all mail for McGraw-Hill in mailbox 3.

If all the mailboxes were identified by company name instead of by number, and there were 50 companies in the office park, delivering the mail would take much longer. A post person finds it easier to mentally translate the company name to a mailbox number when sorting. In other words, when sorting the mail, all letters for Jacaranda go into one pile, which can be inserted in mailbox 1. This analogy is illustrated in Figure 12-18.

You might say that the name Jacaranda was "hashed" to mailbox "1" to make it easier to find the mailbox. If the company names were not hashed and instead placed on each mailbox, then looking for the mailbox would take more time, because numbers are easier to find in a collection than complex strings of characters.

You might also argue that after a long time, the mail person would know the location for a particular mailbox, and thus it would not matter whether or not the mailbox had identification. But if that person were to call in sick, the replacement would not be able to deliver anything. He or she would have to read all the names in order to find the correct mailbox, which is much slower than looking up a number "hashed" out of a company name.

This hash table is used so often in software applications that it is probably implemented more than most algorithms. For starters, compiler and run-time environments like the CLR use hash tables all the time to store data such as method and variable identifiers and so on.

An easily translatable analogy to the world of computers is the generation of a hash value (or hash code) from a URL key, which is more often than not a string that relates to the complex Web address of a particular page of information. The URL is associated

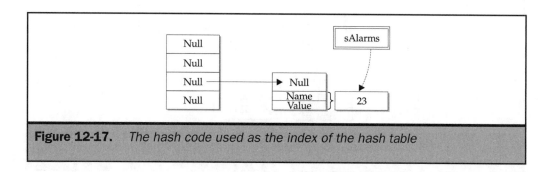

Figure 12-17.   *The hash code used as the index of the hash table*

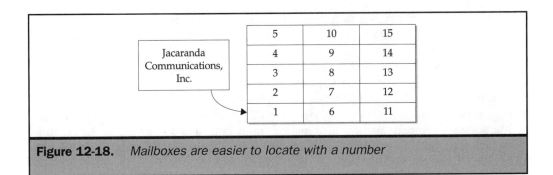

Figure 12-18.   *Mailboxes are easier to locate with a number*

with an easily identifiable name, like the name of the Web page and the actual URL, as illustrated in Figure 12-19.

But instead of searching on a string, no matter how simple, the name is hashed to an efficient **Integer** value, which becomes the key the hash table uses to look up the URL in the hash table. This is illustrated in Figure 12-19, which shows the associated **String** identifier of the URL hashed to its new key value.

Hash tables are considerably faster to search than standard binary searches, which require data in an array to be sorted (otherwise, the binary search will be meaningless). The underlying structure of a hash table has been implemented over the years in a number of different algorithms. Some implementations are better than others for certain types of information.

The hashing—so-called because the value extracted from the process is a "hash-up" or "scrambling" of numbers that represent a string—produces key values that are used to identify the location, or the subscript, of the hash table.

To avoid the collision of hash values that hash to the same location in the hash table, key values are organized in so-called *buckets* that associate the hash value with a list of items that share the key. A technique called *chaining* keeps the list of associated values together. The buckets and chains are shown in Figure 12-20.

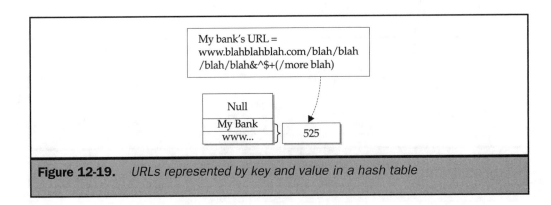

Figure 12-19.   *URLs represented by key and value in a hash table*

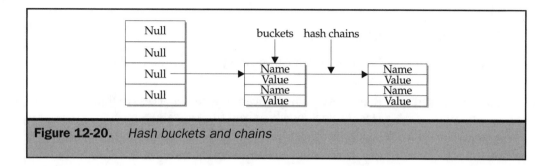

Figure 12-20.   *Hash buckets and chains*

Why is a hash table, which typically operates at *O(1)*, so much faster to search than a vanilla array? As we saw earlier in this chapter, in the section "The BinarySearch Method," we literally have to go through every element of the array to find what we are looking for. The only way to speed up the search is to partition arrays, sort the partitions, and scrounge for shortcuts, such as eliminating values that do not fall within the search range.

A hash table, however, is organized in such a way that when you pass it a key to retrieve, it knows exactly which bucket to look into. In the same way, we do this when we fetch the mail. We don't sift through a pile of envelopes from 50 companies; we just know to go look in the first mailbox.

In other words, the hash table only has to look through a subset of all the elements, which, for a binary search, is like not having to first sort and then partition the array, a process that would cut the time to find the element by an order of magnitude. By and large, you can think of the hash table as having knowledge of a shortcut to the data, whereas an array only knows the official route.

The **Hashtable** class is referenced in the **System.Collections.Hashtable** namespace and implements the following interfaces: **IDictionary**, **ICollection**, **IEnumerable**, **ISerializable**, **IDeserializationCallback**, **ICloneable**, **IList**, and **ICollection**. Thus, many of the methods (such as **GetEnumerator**) have been discussed before and don't need to be reviewed.

Hashtable's members are listed in Table 12-6.

Class Member	Description
Count (p)	Retrieves the number of key-and-value pairs contained in the **Hashtable**
IsFixedSize (p)	Retrieves a value indicating whether the **Hashtable** has a fixed size

Table 12-6.   *The members of **Hashtable**. The class implements **ICollection**, **IEnumerable**, and **IList***

Class Member	Description
IsReadOnly (p)	Retrieves a value indicating whether the **Hashtable** is read-only
IsSynchronized (p)	Retrieves a value indicating whether access to the **Hashtable** is synchronized (thread-safe)
Item (p)	Retrieves or sets the value associated with the specified key. In C#, this property is the indexer for the **Hashtable** class
Keys (p)	Retrieves an **ICollection** containing the keys in the **Hashtable**
SyncRoot (p)	Retrieves an object that can be used to synchronize access to the **Hashtable**
Values (p)	Retrieves an **ICollection** containing the values in the **Hashtable**
Add	Adds an element with the specified key and value into the **Hashtable**
Clear	Removes all elements from the **Hashtable**
Contains	Determines whether the **Hashtable** contains a specific key
ContainsKey	Determines whether the **Hashtable** contains a specific key
ContainsValue	Determines whether the **Hashtable** contains a specific value
CopyTo	Copies the **Hashtable** elements to a one-dimensional array instance at the specified index
GetEnumerator	Returns an **IDictionaryEnumerator** that can iterate through the **Hashtable**
GetHashCode	Inherited from **Object**, it serves as a hash function for a particular type, suitable for use in hashing algorithms and data structures like a hash table
GetObjectData	Implements the **ISerializable** interface and returns the data needed to serialize the **Hashtable**
OnDeserialization	Implements the **ISerializable** interface and raises the deserialization event when the deserialization is complete

Table 12-6.   *The members of **Hashtable**. The class implements **ICollection**, **IEnumerable**, and **IList*** (continued)

Class Member	Description
Remove	Removes the element with the specified key from the **Hashtable**
Synchronized	Returns a synchronized (thread-safe) wrapper for the **Hashtable**
Comparer (protected property)	Retrieves or sets the comparer to use for the **Hashtable**
hcp (protected property)	Retrieves or sets the object that can dispense hash codes
GetHash	Returns the hash code for the specified key
KeyEquals	Compares a specific object with a specific key in the **Hashtable**
GetEnumerator	Returns an **IEnumerator** that can iterate through the **Hashtable**

Table 12-6.   *The members of **Hashtable**. The class implements **ICollection**, **IEnumerable**, and **IList*** (continued)

The following code demonstrates how to instantiate and add elements (car name and accompanying registration) to a hash table:

```
Public Module Hasher
  Dim Tablet As Hashtable = New Hashtable()
  Sub Main()
    AddToTable()
    FindItem("Galant")
    FindKey("BOND007")
    Console.ReadLine()
  End Sub

  Public Sub AddToTable()
    Tablet.Add("GYX 523", "Corrola")
    Tablet.Add("FX1 82A", "Galant")
    Tablet.Add("BOND007", "I386")
  End Sub
```

```
Public Sub FindItem(ByVal item As String)
  If Tablet.ContainsValue(item) Then
    Console.WriteLine("Found {0} in the hashtable.", item)
  End If
End Sub

Public Sub FindKey(ByVal key As String)
  If Tablet.ContainsKey(key) Then
    Console.WriteLine("Found {0} in the list.", key)
  End If
End Sub

End Module
```

This is pretty straightforward code, and because you are probably an expert on collections you can imagine how the other methods, such as **Remove**, work. **Hashtable** allows you to search and retrieve key-value pairs on search-by-value and search-by-key. But search-by-value is very slow and thus defeats the reason for placing the data into the hash tables in the first place. The fast search capability of the hash table is only available, like retrieving your coat in the earlier example at the beginning of this section, when searching by keys (so don't lose them).

It's also important to understand that a hash table is only as good as its hashing algorithm. As mentioned in Chapter 9, the implementation of the **GetHashCode** method in **Object** is pretty weak, and if you want to ensure you receive strong hashes on instances of the same type, you may need to get into the bits of each object and implement a better hashing algorithm. This is exactly one of the reasons why the **Hashtable** class can be inherited, which then allows you to override the **GetHashCode** and **GetHash** methods. The other methods you need to implement in the extended class can be conveniently overloaded or overridden, which is clearly what the .NET authors of the class intended.

Observations

This has been a long and especially important chapter because it deals with many of the fundamental processes of computer science, the processing of data. Despite the effort to pound the concepts of object-oriented software development home, and to highlight its benefits, this chapter also makes clear that underneath that "O-ness" of the class still lies the raw implementation of our code. It should thus be clear that the OO model is not just about classes and how they relate to each other, but how methods in classes are implemented and how that functionality is made available to other objects through interfaces.

We also learned that sequential searching works well when the size of the data set is small. In other words, the amount of work a sequential search requires is directly proportional to the amount of data to be searched. If you double the list of items to search, you double and even quadruple the amount of time it takes to search or sort the list. It is thus important to learn how to divide large sets of data into smaller sets, to keep the running time of algorithms as linear as possible.

You also learned that search efficiency is increased when the data set you need to search or exploit is sorted—and you cannot do a binary search on data unless the data set is sorted. If you have access to a set of data, it can be sorted independently of the application implementing the searching algorithm. If not, the data needs to be sorted at run time or you need to implement a binary search method that invokes a sort or returns an error on an unsorted list.

We have discussed a number of important data structures or collections in this chapter, and we could carry on for another few hundred pages just talking about how to program against them. However, much of what we have covered in this chapter is applicable to all data structures, and thus you should have no trouble transferring the concepts and comprehending the implementation of the interfaces that all of these classes implement.

The material presented here, while critical, is pretty straightforward. Later, we are going to look at some advanced concepts that also involve arrays and array sorting. For starters, the recursive nature of the sorting algorithms we looked at in this chapter can be achieved using delegates, the very involved subject of Chapter 14. In that chapter, we will briefly look at alternatives to the recursive calls for implementing both the bubble sort and the quicksort.

In the next chapter, we will stick with the data structures, to discuss linked lists and trees. In Chapter 14 we will also investigate iterative and more advanced search methods. However, the theme of the next chapter is the implementation of patterns such as Bridge, Strategy, State, Composition, and so on.

The
Complete
Reference

Visual
Basic
.NET

Chapter 13

**Advanced Design
Concepts: Patterns,
Roles, and Relationships**

In Chapters 8, 9, and 10, we covered the core foundation or structural patterns of object-oriented software, such as interfaces, abstract classes, inheritance, aggregation and composition, and association. In this chapter, we will look at some advanced concepts in class design and implementation, as we keep these patterns, class relationships, and class roles in mind.

Our sojourn into these advanced class concepts will be allied with continued treatment of data structures and algorithms started in the previous chapter. Often class or object theory can become boring because we are discussing concepts that are at a higher level than code and data. Admittedly the theory is great, but there is nothing as rewarding as implementing the grand design, getting down to the code that returns results.

Designs on Classes

In Chapter 9, we looked at the key differences between inheritance, association, aggregation, and composition; here we will investigate some advanced patterns that give us the collateral needed for richer analysis, design, and depth. I have handpicked the following class design patterns because they have become the formative patterns in OO and are applicable in the .NET Framework. I discuss other patterns in subsequent chapters.

- **Singleton Pattern** The creational pattern that describes how to ensure that only one instance of a class can be activated. All objects that use the singleton instance use the same one.

- **Bridge Pattern** The structural pattern that prescribes the de-coupling of the implementation of a class from its interface so that the two can evolve independently of each other.

- **Strategy Pattern** The structural pattern that prescribes the de-coupling of the implementation of a class from its interface so that algorithms, or any operation or process, can be interchanged. Algorithm implementation can thus vary independently from the client or consumer objects that need it. Strategy is very similar to Bridge; however, Strategy is used to interchange implementation at runtime.

- **State Pattern** The behavioral pattern that provides a framework for using an object hierarchy as a state machine—as an OO alternative to constant or variable state data, complex conditional statements, enumeration constants, and map tables.

- **Composite Pattern** The structural pattern that prescribes how classes can be composed (and aggregated) into tree-like hierarchies.

- **Iterator Pattern** The behavioral pattern for a class that provides a way to access the aggregated or composite elements of objects of a collection (as mentioned in Chapter 12, Microsoft's name for its iterator-like object is the "enumerator"). This chapter will implement an iterator as an implementation of The **IEnumerator** interface as described in the previous chapter (see the "IEnumerator and IEnumerable" section).

■ **Adapter Pattern**   The structural pattern that prescribes the conversion of an interface to a class into another interface a client object can use transparently. Adapter, affectionately known as Wrapper, is discussed at length in Chapter 14.

■ **Null Pattern**   A behavioral pattern providing an alternative to **Nothing** in Visual Basic .NET (see Chapter 14, "Iterating over a Tree").

■ **Delegate Pattern**   The Delegate pattern prescribes how to wrap a singleton method signature in a special class, which is then used as a "pointer" to a method in another class or object. (Chapter 14 is dedicated to the Delegate pattern).

Singleton

Often in applications you need to instantiate an object (as opposed to a static class) but limit the application to only one instance of the class. This single instance follows what is commonly referred to in OO circles as the Singleton pattern. Here are some reasons for implemening a single instance of a class.

■ **Provision of Concurrency, Reentrance, and Safety**   You can improve the safety of applications by ensuring that access to an object and its data can only occur through a single controlled interface. The **Singleton** class, once instantiated, encapsulates the sole instance of its data and methods so it can have strict control over who and what access it.

■ **Eradication of Global Variables**   The Singleton pattern may be a better solution than static or shared variables that tend to pollute an application and make it much harder to maintain and debug. The Singleton thus provides an alternative to a shared operations class with the benefit of instance methods.

■ **Object-Oriented Alternative of the Class Module**   The Visual Basic .NET class module is probably the only construct in Visual Basic .NET that is not object-oriented. You cannot derive from modules, you cannot inherit with them; all their members are implicitly shared and they offer no encapsulation or polymorphism (no interface implementation is allowed). You don't need it for console applications, because a console application can be constructed easily in a standard class. The module may thus be useful for implementing an operations class, which contains only a pile of static functions and procedures. But such an operations class can be easily implemented in a standard class, which is better maintained and managed by explicitly declaring static members, such as **System.Math.** The **Singleton** class provides the value of a global interface channeled to a single instance of a class and the benefits of dynamic methods and data—such as being able to use the **Me** keyword that allows the object to reference itself, which cannot be done with a module. You can also easily prevent a **Singleton** class from instantiation, as described in the "Improved Performance with Shared Classes and Modules" section in Chapter 9.

- **Replacement of Static Classes** **Singleton** classes provide more flexibility than static classes, which only offer traditional VB or C++ style class operations to the application (this was described in Chapter 9 and in the preceding section).

- **Flexibility in Design and Implementation** This pattern is very flexible. You can easily change the Singleton to a "Doubleton" or a "Tripleton" if you need to. The pattern can be preserved as a base or abstract class providing the ability to extend or subclass the Singleton through inheritance.

Session managers, such as in remoting applications, or managers that pool and manage connections to a database, should not be instantiated more than once or session conflicts will arise. This is also true of objects that perform specific tasks, such as opening and closing folders to check the contents. In all cases, having more than one object perform the work can cause object processes to clash with one another. Figure 13-1, illustrated with the UML class diagram, shows how to design in such a way that only one instance of an object can be created.

To create a class that qualifies as a **Singleton** we must intercept the constructor and prevent its returning the new instance, while ascertaining that at least one instance of the class is afloat; we then return that instance to the thread that needs access to the object.

A perfect place to implement this pattern is in our spacecraft's software (see Chapter 9), in which we would consider the Singleton when we are ready to put our **Injector** object onto the actual fuel injector system. We would not want to create two **Injector** objects and risk having the application access one that starts the injector and another one that inadvertently closes it down. In any event, why would we want more than one **Injector** object when there is only one injector system in the spacecraft?

The simplest way to implement the singleton **Injector** object is to make its constructor private. Thus, it cannot be invoked through any public interface. Instead, we create a shared method that tests if the object has already been instantiated, and if not, it calls

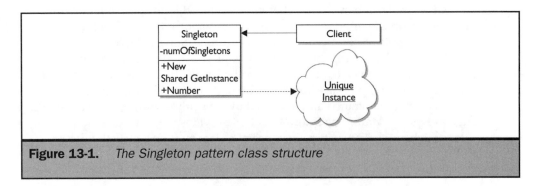

Figure 13-1.   *The Singleton pattern class structure*

the private constructor to create at least one of the objects. The following code demonstrates this (I have included the base class in this example for clarification):

```
Public MustInherit Class BaseSingleton
  Dim numOfSingletons As Integer
  Property Number()
    Get
      Return numOfSingletons
    End Get
    Set(ByVal Value)
      numOfSingletons = Value
    End Set
  End Property
End Class


Public NotInheritable Class Singleton
  Inherits BaseSingleton
  Private Shared Singleton As Singleton
  Shared Function GetInstance() As Singleton
    If (Singleton Is Nothing) Then
      Singleton = New Singleton()
      Singleton.Number += 1
      Return Singleton
    End If
  End Function

  Private Sub New()
    MyBase.New()
  End Sub
End Class


Module TestSingleton
  Dim Zingleton As Singleton
  Sub Main()
    Zingleton = Singleton.GetInstance()
    'this outputs "1", the value of numOfSingletons.
    Debug.WriteLine(Zingleton.Number)
  End Sub
End Module
```

Instead of directly invoking the **New** method, this code lets us call a custom constructor, **GetInstance**. This is a static method that lets us call a non-instance method. Also, by declaring it static with the shared modifier, there will be only one version of it in your application space, and it thus becomes the global interface to which all calls to activate the **Singleton** object will arrive.

The **GetInstance** method goes on to do a few things. First it checks to see if an instance of the object already exists. It achieves this by testing if the reference variable is connected to an actual object. If not, we can instantiate it by employing the standard **If ...Then** conditional.

Next we increment the **Number** property to 1 in order to test the number of times the **New** constructor is called. Let's create a **Singleton** object and test if indeed there is only one instance of it. The following code creates an instance of the **Singleton** class and tests the value assigned to **Number**. If **Number** is higher than 1, then "Houston, we have a problem."

The pattern we have implemented here also lets us declare a reference variable to the **Singleton** object without having to use it initially. Actual activation can occur at a later stage in the scheme of things. The following code accomplishes this:

```
Public Shared Zingleton As Singleton
```

This line of code creates the reference variable without having to access the **New** method, which graphs the object into memory. Well, as you will recall you can't summon **New** directly because it is declared **Private**. So after the reference variable declaration, we can call the **GetInstance** method to activate the object as follows:

```
Zingleton.GetInstance
```

As long as you maintain at least one reference to the instance you will not have any trouble. Once the object goes out of scope it will be garbage collected, and you'll then be able to create a new instance of the object.

Another benefit of the Singleton pattern, as mentioned earlier, is that you can change your implementation to allow more instances later. You can use the singleton's constructor code to create more instances of the object if need be. You control this by inserting into the **GetInstance** method a conditional that increments numbers to a certain level and then blocks calls to the **New** constructor when the desired number of instances has been activated. The forthcoming code shows how to do this:

```
Public NotInheritable Class Singleton
  Inherits BaseSingleton
  Private Shared Singleton As Singleton
  Shared Function GetInstance() As Singleton
    Singleton = New Singleton()
    Singleton.Number += 1
    If (Singleton.Number >= 2) Then
      Throw New NotSupportedException()
    End If
      Return Singleton
```

```
      End If
   End Function

   Private Sub New()
      MyBase.New()
   End Sub
End Class
```

In essence, the **GetInstance** constructor defines the policy for activation of the object. By encapsulating the policy, you can change it as determined by your needs—possibly providing many variations of the conditions for instantiation.

A problem you will stumble upon with respect to the number of instances is decrementing the **numOfSingletons** value when an object is de-referenced. One solution is to implement **Finalize** before putting the object out of its misery, as shown here:

```
Protected Overrides Sub Finalize()
   Number -= 1
End Sub
```

You would also need to watch the global shared data if you planned on instantiating pairs or trios of singleton objects. If you start finding yourself needing more and more instances of the singleton you might just be better off going with standard object activation.

Child Singletons

Unlike modules and static classes, singleton classes can belong to a hierarchy. You can create the base or abstract class for a singleton and then extend subclasses to accommodate your application's design. However, you have to be careful.

The crux of the Singleton pattern is providing a unique interface for client or associate objects to access and ensuring that only a single instance of the class can be created. As you have seen, this requires you to "privatize" **New** and call it via a proxy or secondary constructor (**GetInstance**) that controls the instance creation. The problem is that declaring **New** and modifying **Private** in the base class will essentially seal the class and prevent it from being extended as a subclass. The subclass cannot be instantiated because it has no way back to the parent's constructor, which is blocked by virtue of the **Private** keyword.

Another issue you have to consider is the shared quasi-constructor, **GetInstance**. If you implement it in the base class, you will not be able to override it (although you can shadow it), because it will have been declared static in the base class. So what's a Singleton-architect to do? Simply implement the Singleton's constructors in the final class, which you will seal with the final keyword **NotInheritable**. The final lock-down comes from using the optional keyword **MustInherit** in the base class, which kicks out any **New** methods in the base class and prevents the class from being instantiated in any event.

CLASSES AND OBJECTS

The **Singleton**'s heritage was depicted at the beginning of this section showing first the abstract or base class declared **MustInherit** and then the child class declared **NotInheritable**. See the section covering the State pattern later in this chapter for more examples of the Singleton pattern in use.

*Be sure to declare the **New** constructor in the final class, because if you don't, a default constructor will be automatically provided and Visual Basic will make it publicly accessible.*

Bridge

The Bridge pattern is an advanced structural pattern that can be used to alleviate the awkwardness that often results from the tight coupling of interfaces and implementation in object hierarchies. In Chapter 9 we learned that although inheritance is a critical component of frameworks, it also promotes tight coupling between classes in the hierarchy and between the interface and the implementation. Simply inheriting and then fulfilling the definitions in the base class permanently binds the implementation to that interface. That's not always nice.

To show inheritance at work, we discussed (in Chapter 9) how to configure a root **Injector** class (**BaseInjector**) and derive classes that can be used in the injection systems of different types of spacecraft, such as shuttles, cruisers, warships, and strike-craft.

To recap, the abstract class defines the interface the client objects use (because it is inherited in the child class), while the concrete or child classes implement the abstraction in varying ways as they deem fit. This is illustrated in Figure 13-2.

The binding or coupling of abstract-class interface and concrete-class implementation is unalterable, which means you cannot easily provide varying independent implementation without creating clusters of specialized classes. This is not a desirable trait for an object hierarchy—such as an injector hierarchy, in which all spacecraft use identical fuel-injector systems. But what if they did not? Suppose we needed to provide injector software for different systems—one for a Lockheed Martin Mark V shuttle, one for a Boeing Interplanetary cruiser, and one for an "Earth Alliance" Xion Class battle-craft.

While each specialized class uses the same definitions for its members, they may have to differ in the actual operations (that is, at the implementation level), and data used. For example, a cruiser may need to respond to certain levels of sub-light speed differently than a shuttle does. Each injector may require different ratings to calibrate each respective drive differently at startup. How would you handle the differences?

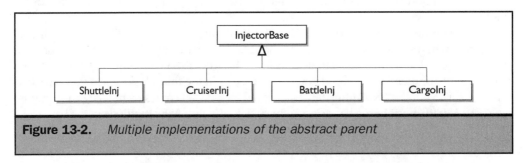

Figure 13-2. *Multiple implementations of the abstract parent*

One solution is to create new specialization subclasses to provide new implementation and calibration. We would want to keep the method definitions, the signatures, the same. Otherwise, the classes would be harder to reuse, and the specialization classes would be more cumbersome for clients. If we continued extending the classes the clients would in fact have to be changed out and recompiled whenever we needed to change or extend the injector objects. Dynamically switching to different objects at runtime would be impossible because the client would find itself using an object that might contain methods it has no clue how to call. This awkwardness— known as "nested generalizations" in the industry— is shown in Figure 13-3.

Here we see that each subclass implements **BaseInjector**, so any differences among injector systems need to be defined and configured in the subclasses. We would need to create separate hierarchies in order to keep them separate from each other. This is not a practical or elegant way of creating a framework of specialized classes, because for each new specialization or extension of the abstract class, we couple another subclass to hierarchy. And as each class needed specialized code and data so would each class become less generic. How would you then provide the specialization and still keep the classes generic and small in number?

Rather than "clustering" the classes in this fashion, it would be better to de-couple the specialized code in the child class with the use of a technique called a "bridge." Instead of a single hierarchy that fans out into an elaborate pyramid of classes that inherit from a common base, you can create separate classes of implementations and then "bridge" the implementations back to the concrete classes with interfaces. Any client can access the specialized code using the interface as the so-called bridge. This bridge is shown in Figure 13-4.

The base class here is still the root of all immediate specialization classes. However, the specialization classes don't implement any of the fancier code themselves. Instead they "bridge to" the code in any decoupled implementation class they need—via the services of the interface—and clients needn't be the wiser about what implementation is being accessed.

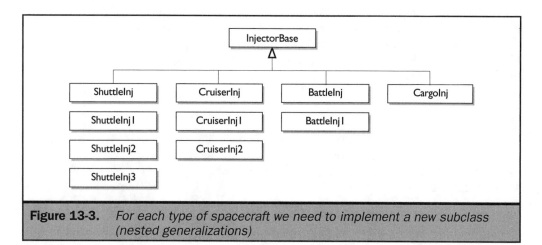

Figure 13-3. *For each type of spacecraft we need to implement a new subclass (nested generalizations)*

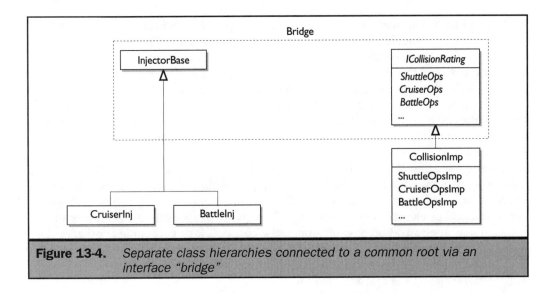

Figure 13-4. *Separate class hierarchies connected to a common root via an interface "bridge"*

The ensuing code demonstrates how to de-couple the implementation from the subclasses. Instead of adding antimatter collision monitoring code into each sub-class, we can provide a separate concrete class that specializes in the calculations required. This target class can implement a host of algorithms for each type of space ship in the fleet, and it can continue to be refined and upgraded without ever having to affect the injector classes that need access to the algorithms. To allow any other class to use the implementation, we simple de-couple the interface as demonstrated:

```
Public Class LockheedCruiserRaterImp

  Implements ICollisionRating
  Function RateCollision(ByVal shipType As Integer, _
    ByVal coilSize As Integer) As Integer Implements _
    ICollisionRating.RateCollision
      'rate the collision and returns the rating
  End Function

End Class

Public Interface ICollisionRating
    Function RateCollision(ByVal shipType As Integer, _
      ByVal coilSize As Integer) As Integer
End Interface
```

A client needs to only instantiate the original specialized sub-class of **BaseInjector**. It knows nothing about the classes, as shown above, that will be bridged to for the implementation. When the specialized injector class is ready to bridge to the specialized "rating" code it can make the bridge as follows:

```
Public Class CruiserInjector
  Inherits BaseInjector
  Dim ColliderRatesBridge As LockheedCruiserRaterImp
  Dim ColliderRates As ICollisionRating = ColliderRatesBridge
  Dim rating As Integer
  Public Overrides Sub StartInjector()
    rating = ColliderRates.RateCollision(ShipTypeEnum.Cruiser, _
      CoilSizeEnum.CruiserClass)
    warpDrive.Calibrate(rating)
    warpDrive = True
    injectorStatus = "Injector is Online"
  End Sub
End Class
```

As you can see, the object providing services to the client simply instantiates the implementation, gets a reference to the interface to access the implementation and fires away (no pun intended). We can extend this by providing a simple conditional structure that allows the client to switch to different implementations at runtime.

A word of warning: be careful not to transpose the implementation and the interface when you attempt to bridge, otherwise you just end up instantiating the implementation. This may result in an error if the implementation's constructor cannot be invoked. The following code makes the error of switching the interface identifier (bold) with the implementation identifier:

```
Dim ColliderRatesBridge As ICollisionRating
Dim ColliderRates As LockheedCruiserRaterImp = ColliderRatesBridge
```

To prevent consumers from making this mistake have them invoke a method to make the bridge instead. The "bridge" method is a function (which may be shared) that returns the implementation as shown in the following code:

```
Public Shared Function GetBridge() As LockheedCruiserRaterImp
  Dim CruiserImp As New LockheedCruiserRaterImp()
  Return CruiserImp
End Function
```

You can now bridge to the implementation using the following declaration:

```
Dim ColliderRates As ICollisionRating = _
LockheedCruiserRaterImp.GetBridge()
```

This Bridge pattern is useful in the following circumstances:

- You find that the collection of subclasses in a hierarchy is becoming bloated and the hierarchy is beginning to look like a wide-based pyramid with specialized classes fanning out from left to right. This nested generalization occurs because you need to provide alternate implementations for the operations defined in the abstractions.

- You need to switch or select implementation at runtime without the client or consumer objects being affected (see the Strategy pattern in the next section).

- Client code at design time should not have to be changed and in many cases cannot be changed. Changing the implementation must not impact the clients in any way. This is especially important if you are shipping product to clients you have no control over.

- Implementation should be extensible and alterable when you subclass and specialize. By unhinging the interfaces, more than one implementation can vary independently.

- Implementation needs to be shared among many objects.

De-coupling the implementation from a standard-class hierarchy that does not demand access to varying implementations of specialized code may seem like overkill. However, it can be useful in certain circumstances—for example, if you want to provide an implementation that can change in the future and allow the clients to continue using the class they originally instantiated.

You will also gain control and flexibility in design by being able to delegate when and what implementation to use in the algorithm. Such a scenario will be introduced to us in the latter part of this chapter, where we will use the **GetEnumerator** method to return an implementation of the **IEnumerator** interface. The example is much more concrete and a lot less fanciful than the "rating" example shown here for expediency.

The Bridge pattern also fulfills the promise of multiple inheritance—inheriting implementation from two parent classes to form a composite specialized implementation—but without the drawbacks that have hounded multiple inheritance out of OO frameworks like .NET and Java. In Chapters 9 and 10, we alluded to the fact that using interfaces to bridge to the implementation is one of several examples of how interfaces obviate the need for multiple inheritance (but be sure you understand interfaces are not a substitute for multiple inheritance).

Also, .NET provides a far more flexible and elegant solution to the dynamic switching of implementation than C++ does, specifically because the C++ core language does not offer native support for providing interfaces—and for that matter, neither does classic VB. The next pattern takes the use of interfaces to an even more advanced level.

Strategy

While the Bridge pattern defines a model for interchanging implementations at design time, the Strategy pattern defines a similar model—de-coupling interface from implementation using interface classes—for interchanging algorithms and operations at runtime. After implementing and experimenting with Strategy and Bridge, you'll never think about multiple inheritance again.

Going back to our spacecraft example, suppose that for each increase in the significant percentage of light speed a craft travels at, different dynamics come into play that require varying treatment from the injector algorithms for the type or version of warp drive and other factors. At a speed that is more that 50 percent of light speed, we may need to make certain computations to compensate for the possible effects received from the disruption of the time-space continuum.

Should the injector instruments and measuring devices pick up certain conditions, we might need to switch to an alternate algorithm that takes the new dynamics into account. For example, we might change to different communication protocol, because one may be better suited than another to deal with the new conditions.

The Strategy pattern allows us to configure an application that both accommodates the range of behaviors that arise at runtime and interchanges algorithms to facilitate the different behaviors. This pattern also obviates the need for implementing long and complex code in conditional structures and switch statements that vary the implementation. This is illustrated in Figure 13-5.

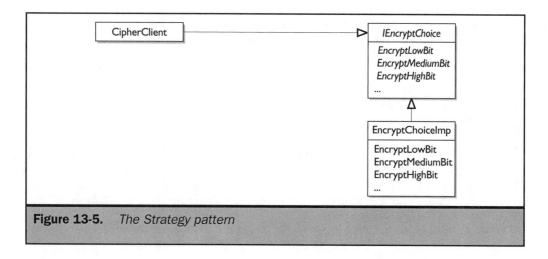

Figure 13-5.   *The Strategy pattern*

CLASSES AND OBJECTS

The following code illustrates how the injector software chooses alternate implementation by accessing a different interface for each case in a **Select Case** statement. You can say that each case provides a different strategy to invoke, depending on the conditions, at runtime.

```
Public Class CruiserInjector
  Inherits BaseInjector

  Dim ColliderRates As ICollisionRating = _
  LockheedCruiserRaterImp.GetBridge()
  Dim compensationLevel As Integer

  'Bridge to speed algorithms
  'handle impulse
  Dim Impulse As IImpulseHandler = _
    LockheedCruiserImpulseHandlerImp.GetBridge
  'handle level one light speed
  Dim PlusOne As ILightPlusOneHandler = _
    LockheedCruiserPlusOneImp.GetBridge
  'handle level two light speed
  Dim PlusTwo As ILightPlusTwoHandler = _
    LockheedCruiserPlusTwoImp.GetBridge

  Public Overrides Sub StartInjector()
    rating = ColliderRates.RateCollision(ShipTypeEnum.Cruiser, _
      CoilSizeEnum.CruiserClass)
    warpDrive.Calibrate(rating)
    warpDrive = True
    warpSpeed = WarpFactorEnum.LightPlusOne
    compensationLevel = Compensate(warpSpeed)
    injectorStatus = "Injector is Online"
  End Sub

  Public Function Compensate(ByVal warpspeed As Integer) As Integer
    Select Case warpspeed
      Case 0
        Compensate = Impulse.Compensation(InjectorVerEnum.Class3, _
          ShipTypeEnum.Cruiser)
      Case 1
        Compensate = PlusOne.Compensation(InjectorVerEnum.Class3, _
          ShipTypeEnum.Cruiser)
      Case 2
```

```
        Compensate = PlusTwo.Compensation((InjectorVerEnum.Class3, _
          ShipTypeEnum.Cruiser)
        Case 3
          '. . .
      End Select
  End Function
End Class
```

If the above code is a little too "spaced-out" for you then here is an example you might more easily identify with. Suppose you need to encrypt an object with one of several possible encryption algorithms. As you know, the more secure the encryption, the more powerful the algorithm must be. The algorithms that provide less security typically process quicker than those that provide better security (a weak algorithm may only work with 16-bit encryption while a very strong one would use 128-bit numbers and higher). You can thus present a user with the opportunity to decide to encrypt data as quickly as possible or as securely as possible. The first choice prevents a blockage that may arise in the application, and cause other side effects. The second choice would use stronger algorithms to produce more secure results, but it would take longer to process. Here's an example that bridges to a single implementation that contains facilities for all three levels of encryption (the interface definition is included for clarity):

```
Public Interface IEncryptionLevel
  Function EncryptLowBit(ByVal obj As Object) As Object
  Function EncryptMediumBit(ByVal obj As Object) As Object
  Function EncryptHighBit(ByVal obj As Object) As Object
End Interface

Public Class Obfuscate
  Dim Cipher As IEncryptionLevel = EncryptionLevelImp.GetBridge
  Public Function Encrypt(ByVal level As Integer, ByVal obj As Object) As Object
    Select Case level
      Case 0
        Encrypt = Cipher.EncryptLowBit(obj)
      Case 1
        Encrypt = Cipher.EncryptMediumBit(obj)
      Case 2
        Encrypt = Cipher.EncryptHighBit(obj)
    End Select
  End Function
End Class
```

Is it not evident that your specialized class need not implement this code at all, and still have access to an implementation it remains completely disconnected from? Such is the wonder of interfaces . . . and polymorphism. This technique, or pattern, provides many benefits and is useful in a number of situations. You should consider using the Strategy pattern in the following circumstances:

- You are constructing an application in which a client may need to use one of many algorithms or implementations behind a single interface at runtime. In other words, your application can call for numerous variants of the implementation that may be needed by the client.

- Clients do not need to know about the data and code used in the implementation. By moving the implementation out to discrete classes in a separate class hierarchy, users are completely isolated from this data and code. This pattern not only allows clients to function unchanged despite the interchanging of implementations—which makes them easier to manage and maintain—but it also hides the implementation from clients that do not need this information.

- You need to get rid of client-dependent conditional structures and the related code, thereby encapsulating the functionality in separate **Strategy** classes.

Inheritance offers the ability to specialize subclasses, yet it also hardwires implementation to the interface, which results in the same awkwardness described in the earlier Bridge pattern.

Your clients, however, need to be aware of the different strategies available to them, as demonstrated in the encryption application earlier in this section. So this pattern actually becomes applicable when clients understand the reasons for the interchanges and can make informed choices. In other words, the variation in algorithms must be relevant to the client.

One drawback is that Strategy creates more classes than would have been created if the clients had implemented the different behaviors or algorithms themselves. As a tradeoff, with respect to the latter course, the client is never independent of the implementation; thus, all clients have to be changed whenever the algorithms change. The other drawback to not using Strategy is that the clients, which may be implemented by remote customers in other companies, get access to more implementation knowledge than they need. The Strategy pattern and **Delegate** construct share the same objective (see Chapter 14).

State

Regardless of your programming background, you have most likely encountered the need to manage various states in your application. State affects everything and is relevant everywhere—not only in your application. Here are some program-related examples.

A form or dialog box presents a state so that you can select the correct event or action to match the current state of the application. For example, data may be in a volatile state; therefore, the user interface should prompt you to save to a database. It may even block you from doing anything else until the data is saved.

Connections have to be managed according to the state they are in at any given time. A database or network connection may be open, closed, established, listening, receiving, or disconnecting.

Telecommunications and telephony applications are huge state machines that schedule operations according to the state of many different variables. Such applications are often called state machines. They are used so often in software solutions that they are part of the first year curriculum of every computer science course.

A PBX tests state and doles out operations accordingly. Lines and stations may be in busy state, off-hook state, on-hook state, ready state, out-of-service state, or logged-out state. These conditions are usually represented by enumeration constants.

In procedural programming worlds, state machines are typically managed in long and complex conditional elements such as **If...Then** and **Else If** constructs and **Case** and **Switch** blocks. But long conditional statements that test flags and values are undesirable in both procedure-oriented programming and Object-Oriented programming, because they make programs hard to read and maintain.

Mapping state transitions in a map table is an outmoded practice, although it is still used—even in OO circles. If you recall, we reviewed something similar in the **GetMessages** example in Chapter 5—and we used a map table in order to not preempt the discussion of classes and objects that began in Chapter 8.

Often programmers set up state machines without thinking ahead to how the application may change in the future. Thus, they must alter the machine frequently, and as they apply new conditions and operations, the entire design begins to unravel.

The State pattern lets us drop such conditionals and "lookup" constructs completely. This pattern permits us to create instances of state objects, or stateful objects, that derive from a hierarchy in which the concrete-state classes represent the states in the application. This hierarchy is illustrated in Figure 13-6.

The client object that needs to maintain the state machine does so by maintaining references to the state objects. Figure 13-7 shows how our **ShuttleInjector** object references objects of type **BaseDriveStateMachine** to determine the applicability of certain operations dependent on the state of the injector at any given time.

For example, an injector cannot be placed into warp-ready state unless it has been started, and you would not want to try and start the warp drive if it has already

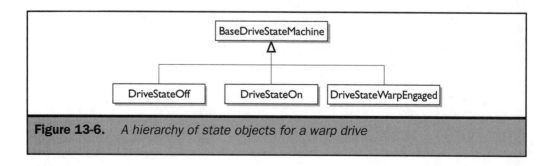

Figure 13-6.   *A hierarchy of state objects for a warp drive*

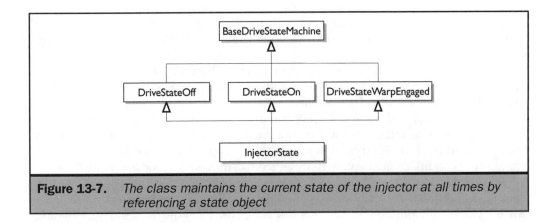

Figure 13-7. *The class maintains the current state of the injector at all times by referencing a state object*

been started. So the first state the injector would reference on the warp drive would be **DriveStateOff**. Our **BaseInjector** code can thus define the state-aware methods for all subclasses. For example, before the **Start** method of a **ShuttleInjector** object is called, our code should reference the **State** object and return the current instance. If the instance returned is the **DriveStateOff** object, the object itself can respond to events needed by the client before startup, such as the initialization of certain data and conditions. Upon returning the **DriveStateOff** instance, the client can then invoke the **Start** method. On successful completion of the **Start** method, the client can reference **DriveStateOn** object and make it the current state.

The following code shows the implementation of the **InjectorState** hierarchy illustrated in Figure 13-7.

```
Public MustInherit Class BaseDriveStateMachine
  Dim objectNumber As Integer
  Public MustOverride Sub StateHandler()
End Class

Public Class DriveStateOff
  Inherits BaseDriveStateMachine
  Private Shared DriveStateOff As DriveStateOff
  Shared Function GetInstance() As DriveStateOff
    If (DriveStateOff Is Nothing) Then
      DriveStateOff = New DriveStateOff()
      Return DriveStateOff
    End If
  End Function

  Private Sub New()
    MyBase.New()
```

```
      End Sub

      Public Overrides Sub StateHandler()
        'add fancy state handling code here
      End Sub
End Class

Public Class DriveStateOn
   Inherits BaseDriveStateMachine
   Private Shared DriveStateOn As DriveStateOn
   Shared Function GetInstance() As DriveStateOn
     If (DriveStateOn Is Nothing) Then
       DriveStateOn = New DriveStateOn()
       Return DriveStateOn
     End If
   End Function

   Private Sub New()
     MyBase.New()
   End Sub

   Public Overrides Sub StateHandler()
     'add fancy state handling code here
   End Sub
End Class

Public Class DriveStateWarpEngaged
   Inherits BaseDriveStateMachine
   Private Shared DriveStateWarpEngaged As DriveStateWarpEngaged
   Shared Function GetInstance() As DriveStateWarpEngaged
     If (DriveStateWarpEngaged Is Nothing) Then
       DriveStateWarpEngaged = New DriveStateWarpEngaged()
       Return DriveStateWarpEngaged
     End If
   End Function

   Private Sub New()
     MyBase.New()
   End Sub

   Public Overrides Sub StateHandler()
     'add fancy state handling code here
   End Sub
End Class
```

Notice that the **BaseDriveStateMachine** defines an abstract method called **StateHandler** that will be overridden and implemented in each subclass. In other words, when the client changes the state to **DriveStateOff**, the **DriveStateOff**'s **StateHandler** method will be activated to perform any necessary computation, communication, or events.

Pay special attention to the Singleton logic here. Unless you have special reason to create multiple instances of the state objects, they should be instantiated once and implemented as Singletons. The following code shows the client **ShuttleInjector** object using its references to the state machine to make decisions and process various operations accordingly.

Make note of the **ShuttleInjector**'s **StartInjector** method. **StartInjector** starts the state machine and assigns the **State** reference variable to the **DriveStateOn** object. **State** can then invoke the **DriveStateOn** object's **StateHandler** method. The following code shows the implementation of the **StartInjector** method.

```
Imports Vb7cr.Injectors
Imports Vb7cr.ShuttleExceptions
Imports Vb7cr.InjectorStates
Public Class ShuttleInjector
  Inherits BaseInjector
  Dim State As BaseDriveStateMachine
  Private warpSpeed As Integer
  Private warpDrive As Boolean
  Private injectorStatus As String = "Injector is Offline"
  Const C As Integer = 186355
  Dim warpSettings As New WarpFactorEnum()

  Public Overrides Sub StartInjector()
    warpDrive = True
    State = DriveStateOn.GetInstance()
    State.StateHandler()
    injectorStatus = "Injector is Online"
  End Sub
  '. . .
End Class 'ShuttleInjector
```

This technique, or pattern, provides a number of benefits and is useful in a variety of circumstances:

- State-specific behavior can be encapsulated in dedicated objects. As demonstrated with the earlier patterns, this allows you to vary implementation and state-specific code by merely replacing or enhancing the **State** object. New variations can be easily created by extending the **BaseState** class and constructing subclasses.

- The transition to a new state is more explicit, specifically because each **State** object encapsulates its own functionality and data. This is a much better idea than working with enumerator values or constants and large blocks of conditional constructs that are difficult to maintain.

- The state transitions are also atomic, which means state changes occur by explicitly de-referencing only one state for another.

- **State** objects can be shared, as singletons, especially if they do not need to maintain instance data.

- Table value or flag lookup is not nearly as efficient as the **State** object alternative, in which transition is effected by a simple method call. Map tables also provide no facility for additional logic, event processing, or the ability to easily change the representation of the state in the dynamic way the **State** object does. Essentially, the table-driven approach defines state, while the State pattern models a framework for state-specific behavior.

The remainder of this chapter will be devoted to a study of the Composite pattern, implementing a base class for linked lists and trees (collections of nodes), and applied against the .NET Framework's support for collections.

Linked Lists and Trees

Linked lists and trees are an important alternative data-structure to many of the collections we talked about in the previous chapter. Most of us hit the array for virtually all data-management constructs needed in a class—without considering (or without knowing) other structures that may be more suitable. Linked lists are as easy to use as arrays and are very efficient structures for storing and accessing collections of data. Insertion and removal of a list's elements are very fast. Trees are a little more difficult; nevertheless, they are extremely useful for many types of algorithms.

Linked lists and trees are inherited into OO frameworks (no pun intended) from procedural languages like C and Pascal. The formulation of these data structures in the OO world is facilitated by the key structural pattern known as the Composite. This is the first reason for discussing linked lists and trees in this chapter.

Linked lists and trees provide ideal candidates for demonstrating composition of classes and aggregation of objects. They make an ideal platform for discussing the Composite pattern. The linked lists and trees we are going to implement contain objects—called *nodes*—that demonstrate this capacity. The **Node** classes are composed in a container class at design time, and then aggregated to the container object at runtime. The nodes can hold all types of data; you can easily maintain a list that has some nodes containing **Double** data, others with **Strings**, and some with **Longs**, as you will see. Strongly typing a linked list or tree is not a difficult exercise either.

A second reason for examining them here is that we can easily build the classes and instantiate the objects in an object-oriented framework, such as .NET. Linked lists and trees are perfect constructs for demonstrating class and object creation and management principles. The third reason for going into linked lists and trees is that the .NET Framework's base-class library does not include a native linked list or tree class that we can use or extend (although linked-list implementation is directly employed in some of the classes in the base class library, such as the structure behind a **Delegate** that maintains a collection of subscribers to an event). So we have to do it ourselves. Fortunately, it's very easy.

> **Note** *As you saw in Chapter 12, the **System.Collections** namespace provides classes that can handle some of the duties of linked lists and trees. However, there are many applications in which a custom linked list or tree would be the better way to go. In this chapter linked lists also provide a great OOP learning tool.*

Finally, we are going to implement the Iterator pattern (or at least a pattern that closely resembles it) in this chapter. We will build an iterator to traverse the lists we create by first implementing the **IEnumerator** interface provided in the **System.Collection** namespace. It is worthwhile to investigate incorporating the "comparer" interfaces into our data structures to facilitate recursive searching and applying the Delegate pattern for iterating across trees.

Where would we use a linked list or a tree, especially a binary tree? It's easy to find uses for these data structures. Any part of an application or algorithm that needs to maintain a collection of data would benefit from them. For example, a Web browser might need to maintain a list of Web sites you have visited during a surfing session.

Also, an accounting system might use a list to manage a roster of items moved from one account to another. The list would make it easy to reverse debit/credit activity, because every action would be recorded (periodically persisted) in chronological order.

A shopping cart application presents another opportunity. Every time you place an item into the cart, a node representing that item can be added to the list and removed when needed. When you see components that present data sequentially, a linked list is probably being employed behind the scenes. In Chapter 15, I use a linked list to maintain a collection of noise words and characters to filter out of Index Server searches because they are a lot lighter than arrays. The linked list also provides a much faster data structure than an array for a Web-based application.

Is there a place for a linked list or a tree in our spaceship's computer systems? Definitely. The spaceship's "trajectory console" is one such component. Trajectory software assists us in plotting a course from one point to another. We also want to collect data on these points in relation to celestial bodies like stars, where we have already been. A tree is an ideal structure that keeps spreading out. It can be easily traversed and searched.

We could gather data to determine how long it took us to get from one point to the next, and what took place within the ship at certain times, given certain coordinates. Once we ascertain this, we can project with some certainty how long the overall journey or individual segments will take (at light speed, of course). Implementing trees is a much more advanced subject so the remainder of this chapter focuses on the linked list.

Understanding the Linked List

The basic linked list represents a collection of items in a list-like format where one item is linked to the next with a linker or a pointer. The links are nested, which provides the backbone for the list. The data and the link itself are encapsulated in an object that forms the single element or item of the container, otherwise known as the node.

The list resembles a stack, where nodes enter at one end and pile on top of each other on a last-in, first-out basis. The difference is that we can add and delete nodes anywhere in the list structure, and we can traverse the list from one end to the other.

The first node on the list—the first we create—does not link to anything, because it represents the deepest node in the collection and there is nothing ahead of it. It is often called the *tail node*, and it is usually the last one removed if the nodes are peeled off from the top down. It is customary, though not always necessary, to maintain a reference to the tail node. Any node added below or in front of the tail node takes its place at the end.

The second node we create is linked to the first via a linker to the previously inserted node. This pointer is a reference variable in one node that refers to the next link in the list. For example, when you add a third node to the collection, it maintains a link to the second item. The illustration provides a graphical representation of such a linked list.

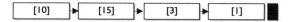

In the illustration, the first node in the list, the tail, contains the **Integer** value 1. It represents the first item in the list. The last node, currently the *head node*, contains the **Integer** 10 and links to a node containing 15. Every linked list is built in this fashion. When we create the first node at the beginning (if no node precedes it), we mark the end with an end-of-list symbol. The letter "E" suffices, but in the actual code the link points to *null* (**Nothing**).

Visual Basic, or any other language for that matter, knows nothing about linkers and nodes in lists and trees. We represent these "concepts" programmatically using classes, objects, and data.

As mentioned earlier, linked lists operate like the standard stack or queue (see Chapter 12). The only difference is that you can insert new nodes—the data—anywhere in the structure of the linked list by maintaining references to *next* and *previous* nodes. How a node is referenced (last, first, current, previous, next, top, and so on) depends on the operation you need to perform relative to the current reference, the current position. From the perspective of the "current node" the node that was created after it is the next node and the node that was created before it is the previous node. This may be clearer in the illustration.

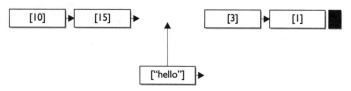

When you insert, only the neighboring nodes need to change. Inserting is similar to people jostling for positions in a lunch line. The illustration on the previous page shows this "pushing in" activity.

Removing a node follows the same pattern. You affect only the neighboring links and need to manage the references on both sides so that you can "plug" the hole that results upon the removal of a node.

Perhaps you are wondering why this is significant, since you can do this with arrays. Furthermore, arrays let you access an element or subscript value anywhere in the structure by virtue of the index. The specialty of the linked list, however, is that insertion, removal, and iteration are much faster and less resource-intensive than array insertion and removal, which indexes the elements for random accessing, sorting, and searching. Linked lists don't have the overhead associated with managing indexes. You gain speed but lose the benefit of random access. If you index the linked list, you are only steps away from concocting a custom array.

You cannot simply access any node in a list as you can an indexed element of an array. To remove or insert a node at a certain position in the list, you need to iterate through the entire sequence, one node at a time. This scrolling activity is very fast and used mostly to display or print the list—and feed data to an array or other data structure or a stream (see Chapter 15).

Note	*If you are going to implement linked lists (and trees for that matter), and you expect them to grow big, don't formally index the structure. Linked lists are typically used for algorithms that don't need random access to elements. You typically process the roster as a unit. If you need a structure that gives you random access via an indexed element, use an array (see Chapter 12).*

Looking at our examples of lists and trees, we realize that we don't need to sort the items. Furthermore, sorting would violate the integrity of the list. The list of Web sites recently visited, for example, would be worthless if you decided to sort it. On the other hand, the nodes of a list are easily accessed, so sorting them would not be very difficult. It is also quite easy to transfer the data to an array (as we will discover later in this chapter) and back again to a list.

Designing a Base-Container Class for Lists (and Trees)

Looking at Figures 13-8 and 13-9, we need to develop the base class from which we can create and maintain the structures represented in the above figures. To facilitate the class design, we will investigate the Composite pattern.

The Composite pattern has been tried and tested over many years and provides us with a model from which to implement our link-oriented structures. This pattern also specifies how all the **Node** objects in the list or tree can or should be consistently manipulated.

*An interesting observation to make here is that while the **Node** class in a tree or list container is a composite class (nested), its instantiation results in the object being easily aggregated to the container class.*

Two key forces drive this pattern. First, we have a container object that becomes a collection of identical objects (**Nodes**) that need to be organized in a logical hierarchy (and that hierarchy needs to facilitate iteration, possibly recursively). Second, it is desirable to limit the number of different child node objects that make up the composite nodes of the tree. While we should be able to encapsulate any type of data in the composite nodes, the **Node** objects should be of the same type—**Node**. In other words, the list or tree should be strongly typed.

Strong typing is more than possible because the aggregate **Node** objects can only be of type **Node**, so every composite object created for the type of collection contains identical members and fields. At the same time, the nodes themselves should have the ability to encapsulate data and functionality of different data types, which is what makes lists and trees so powerful and useful. Should the implementor require strong typing of data within the actual node (remember a field in .NET is nothing more than another object, a value type, or a reference type), then that too is entirely possible. Let's continue creating the collection container and return to the definition and implementation of the composite node later.

The first task in implementing the Composite pattern is to provide the parent or base container class. The class should be abstract and inheritable; however, a number of properties and methods can be implemented in the base class with the potential to be overridden in any child class. This class is the ancestral super-class of all list and tree structures. There is so little difference between linked list and tree classes, that it makes sense to "grow" a container framework that specializes in the collection of nodes.

Figure 13-8 illustrates the hierarchy for the container class for linked lists and trees. We shall call this base class **BaseNodeCollection**.

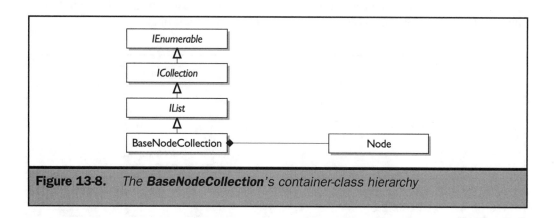

Figure 13-8.   *The **BaseNodeCollection**'s container-class hierarchy*

The following code illustrates the simple construction of the **BaseNodeCollection** class:

```
Imports System
Imports Vb7cr.Exceptions
Public Class BaseNodeCollection
  'IList inherits ICollection and IEnumerable
  Implements IList
  '. . .
End Class
```

<blockquote>

Note
*This above code example shows only that it implements **IList**. **IList** inherits both **ICollection** and **IEnumerable** so you must implement all three at the same time.*

</blockquote>

Now that we have the container base class let's get to work constructing the composite **Node** class.

Implementing the Node

The best way to represent a node in a linked list or tree is to create an object to represent it and aggregate it to the root container or collection object—in this case, the **Node** object is encapsulated in the base **BaseNodeCollection** class.

An object is more than an ideal facility for a linked list or tree node. Each **Node** object can contain data fields, methods, and properties and can be easily referenced from within the confines of the collection container. You can even create nodes that contain other objects, making the node a multifaceted container. The **Node** object maintains its own aggregated objects—the data represented by the node—and the linking objects, which point to other nodes as illustrated in Figure 13-9.

Our implementation of the nodes and the container itself will not be sealed, which gives us the ability to extend the classes and thus improve on the foundation we have created in version 1.0. Extending the base class so it can be used for a multi-node tree is the next logical step in the evolution of the **BaseNodeCollection** class.

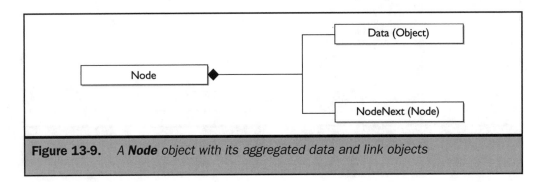

Figure 13-9. *A **Node** object with its aggregated data and link objects*

The **BaseNodeCollection** class provides a perfect scenario for the implementation of nested or inner classes, aggregation, and composition, as discussed in Chapter 9. You can think of the node as a leaf, the linkers as branches, and the container class as the trunk. The UML diagram representing this arrangement is illustrated in Figure 13-10.

The **Node** class used to represent a node in the collection can be defined as follows (the outer **BaseNodeCollection** class is shown here to provide the composite context):

```
Public Class BaseNodeCollection
   'carries in ICollection and IEnumerable as part of the hierarchy
   Implements IList
   '. . .
      Public Class Node
        Public Data As Object
        Public NodeNext As Node

        Public Sub New()
          MyBase.New()
        End Sub

        Public Overrides Function ToString() As String
          Return String.Format("Node({0})", Data)
        End Function
    End Class
End Class
```

This is the beginning of our **Node** object—notice how class **Node**, the *composite*, is nested inside **BaseNodeCollection**, which is also known as the *outer* class. But **Node**

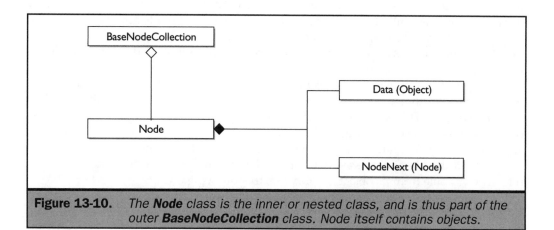

Figure 13-10.   *The **Node** class is the inner or nested class, and is thus part of the outer **BaseNodeCollection** class. Node itself contains objects.*

itself is also a container. We need to provide a facility for a linker object and an object to hold the data of the node. While we could easily use the inherited **Node.ToString** facility (overridden in the **Node** class) for **Node**'s data, doing that will limit us to a single data field, and you'll see later when you extend **Node** for tree support that one field for data is not enough.

The composite classes to nest in **Node** are thus **Data** and **NodeNext**, the data field and the target **Node** to link to respectively. (The **Node** can hold characters, fractions, and other forms of data, but for now we'll work with simple numbers and strings to facilitate your understanding the concepts.)

Note that **NodeNext** is itself an object of type **Node**. The **Node** object, as **NodeNext**, becomes the "linker" object that connects each **Node** to the next. This is what holds a list or tree together. The first node references the second one, which references the third, and so on. The references form a chain that results in the list or tree. The UML class diagram for the **Node** object and its composites can be thus represented by the illustration.

Node
Data : Object NodeNext : Node

The **Node** class declares the following aggregate objects:

- **Data** An object (required) of type **Object** that represents the data field of **Node**.
- **NodeNext** An object of Type **Node** (required) that represents the next **Node** in the chain.

We have now seen how it is possible to create objects that represent nodes of a linked list or tree, which can be instantiated from the outer container class. The Composite pattern or technique lets us keep the node-object data private inside the outer class, but the members and data of the inner class can be freely accessed via instances of **Node** by the various list-manipulation methods of the outer class. The **Node** object is aggregated to the **BaseNodeCollection**, in the same fashion that a **ListBox** component is aggregated to a form. And we thus have the same access to **Node** from **BaseNodeCollection** as **Form** has to **ListBox** or **Label**.

The first node that was created in the collection, which usually becomes the last node removed from it, can't link or point to any object ahead of it. So its linker must point to **Nothing**. This can be achieved simply by specifying **Nothing** for either the previous node of the object or the next node of the object. This will become more apparent as we instantiate **Node** and begin to work with it from the outer class.

The **Nothing** literal discussed in Chapters 4 and 8 suffices to de-reference the reference variable from its object graph. Thus the following code:

```
NodeNext = Nothing
```

serves to cut the link to the next node. **NodeNext** gets collected, and the current node becomes either the first node of the list or the leaf node in a tree (the leaf at the end of the branch).

(Using the Null pattern is useful if you have specific business rules for keeping an object alive at the head or end of a list or tree. A **Null** object is referenced by **NodeNext**, but the object does nothing and can simply be a sterile copy of **Object**. This technique offers the advantage of being able to upcast the so-called **Null** object as soon as you are ready to add a node to the beginning or end of the data structure. You can then add a **Null** object to the next node or create a new **Null** object after you have upcast the existing one.

But how do we reference the various nodes from the parent container? By aggregating the **Node** class to **BaseNodeCollection**. Remember back in Chapter 9 we saw the same technique used to aggregate controls to a **Form** class, before they are instantiated and used. Aggregating **Node** to **BaseNodeCollection** is done as follows:

```
Private CurrentNode As Node
Private NodePrevious As Node
Private LastNode As Node
Private NextNode As Node
```

The four **Node** declarations here represent the following roles the nodes play in the list. In other words, each node can be any referenced as any one of the four positions.

- **CurrentNode**   A node that represents the current (cursor) position in a list.

- **NodePrevious**   A node that represents the node before the **CurrentNode**. In other words, **NodePrevious** links to **CurrentNode**. **NodePrevious** is thus closer to the tail of the list than **CurrentNode**.

- **NextNode**   A node that comes after **CurrentNode**. **NextNode** is thus the node that is closer to the head than **CurrentNode**.

- **LastNode**   The node at the head or end of the list. This node points to **Nothing** above it (it has no reference to a **NextNode**). The second-to-last node in the list is this node's **NodePrevious** (which is the earlier created **Node** object's **NodeNext** reference).

We now have enough in the **BaseNodeCollection** to begin implementing its methods and properties.

Implementing the Container

The root **BaseNodeCollection** class defines the various members of the container class for managing the collection as a unit. The Composite pattern provides the model for defining the members as shown in the class diagram in Figure 13-11.

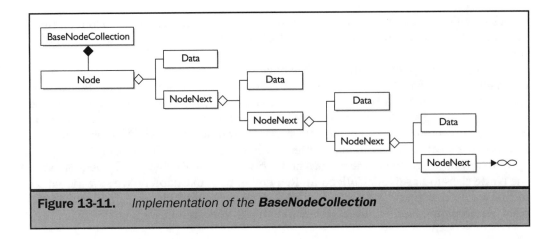

Figure 13-11. *Implementation of the **BaseNodeCollection***

The following list includes methods and properties defined in **IList, ICollection,** and **IEnumerable**. The interfaces are listed in Chapter 12 because they are implemented in various other collections, such as **Array** and **Stack**.

- **New**   A constructor for the **BaseNodeCollection** object
- **Add**   A method that adds a node to the top of the list
- **Clear**   A method that clears the list
- **Contains**   A method that determines if a node contains the specified data
- **CopyTo**   A method that copies all the data in a linked list to an array
- **Count**   A property that maintains the number of nodes in the collection
- **CurrentPosition**   A property that maintains a reference to the node in focus in a collection
- **FindItem**   A method that applies the **CurrentPosition** to the node containing the last instance holding the specified data
- **GetEnumerator**   A method that gets an **IEnumerator** object on the specified list
- **IndexOf**   A method that provides a facility to find the first index or location of a particular item or value in the list
- **Insert**   A method that inserts a node at a specified location in the list
- **Item**   A property that retrieves or sets the current value of the referenced node
- **Last**   A property that retrieves a reference to the node added last to the list, the head node
- **PreviousNode**   A property that retrieves a reference to the node that comes before the current node
- **Remove**   A method that removes the specified node from the list
- **RemoveAt**   A method that removes the node at the specified location in the list

If you understand interfaces (Chapters 10), you know that the **System.Collection** namespace includes three interfaces that suddenly become relevant in implementing the Composite pattern. Since **BaseNodeCollection** is an abstract class, we can elegantly implement **IList, ICollection**, and **IEnumerable** in it and convert our Composite-adherent container into a fully-fledged .NET Framework-aware **Collection** class. This provides many advantages, such as accommodating the **For Each . . . Next** conditional statement (see Chapter 6 for an introduction to this conditional). (Chapter 12 describes the definitions that the **IList, ICollection**, and **IEnumerable** bring to our abstract class.) We can implement the **ICollection** as well. By implementing **IEnumerable** we are setting ourselves up to implement **IEnumerator** in our iterator object.

We should start with the essential method of the container class, which is the one that builds our list. We can thus begin our effort by implementing **IList.Add**.

The Add Method

The **IList.Add** method adds nodes to the top of a list. This requires the node pushed down to alter its link reference to point to the new node as shown in Figure 13-12.

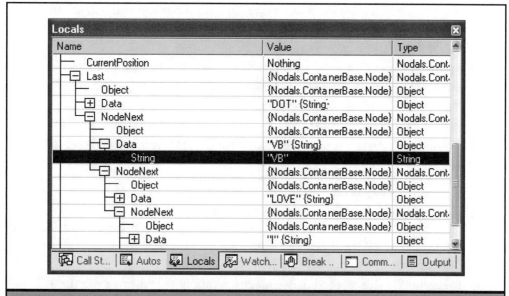

Figure 13-12.   *Inspecting the objects in the Locals windows during debugging (see Chapter 17) shows the linked list in action, the head of the list, the tail, and the body*

Recapping, linked lists (and trees) work like push-down stacks (although you can be deep in the structure and insert at the current node referenced). Nodes are typically added at the beginning and pushed down (or into) the structure. So, as soon as a new node is added to the head of the list, the first one created becomes the node farther away from the head. (Later we'll discuss how to insert nodes at the current location in the list using the **Insert** method.)

Before we create the definitions for the other methods, let's develop the **Add** method. There's a good reason for this: once we have the main method that can effectively add nodes to a **BaseNodeCollection** object, the other methods will fall into place to manipulate the structure taking shape.

Don't be afraid to get out a pencil and paper and draw the data construct and the algorithms. The "drawing" shown in the earlier figures help us visualize the container and determine how to work in it and on the list. From it we can see that once you have a **BaseNodeCollection** containing more than two nodes, only the first and last nodes are easily accessible.

You'll find that once you can add a node to a list, you naturally have a reference to it, and because it's easy to find the first one, it's just as easy to delete it or add a new one. As you look back at the illustrations and the class diagrams shown earlier (which make convenient abstractions and models of the actual classes) you will see the **BaseNodeCollection** beginning to make sense. The definition for the **Add** method is as follows:

- **Method Name: Add**   The method adds a node to a **BaseNodeCollection** object
- **Method Signature**   The method takes an argument of type **Object**, which represents the data encapsulated in the node

  ```
  Public Function Add(ByVal obj As Object) As Integer Implements IList.Add
  ```

- **Parameters**   The parameter **obj** is an instance of **Object**, which is yet to be cast to a particular type, or left as is. The **obj** parameter will be used to represent the data type encapsulated by the node. It is not the node itself. The return type is an Integer, which is not used here.

- **Precondition**   The method should first test if a node already exists on the list. It does this by checking if **LastNode** references an object that may have already been created or it references **Nothing**.

- **Postcondition**   No postcondition

- **Exceptions**   This method may engage operations that throw exceptions. The example code forgoes exception handling for simplicity at this stage.

An implementation of the **Add** method is as shown in the following code:

```
Public Function Add(ByVal obj As Object) _
  Dim TopNode As New Node()
  With TopNode
    .Data = obj
```

```
      .NodeNext = CType(LastNode, Node)
      If (LastNode Is Nothing) Then
        LastNode = TopNode
      Else
        NextNode = LastNode
        LastNode = TopNode
      End If
    End With
End Function
```

Let's step through this code. The first statement in the method creates the new **Node** object called **TopNode**, which does not play a role at the class level (which is why it was not mentioned earlier). It immediately places the data represented in the **obj** object into the node (in **TopNode.Data**). If you look back at the **Node** class you'll see where **Data** comes from. It is one of two composite objects in **Node**. (Without the **Data** object there would be no point to this whole exercise.)

The next line of code converts the composite **NodeNext** to an object of type **Node**. **NodeNext** then gets ready to play the role of **LastNode** (the head of the list) as shown here:

```
.NodeNext = CType(LastNode, Node)
```

At this point in the method, the data structure looks like the example in the illustration.

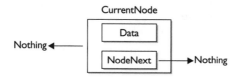

Next, a conditional checks to see if a **LastNode** might already exist, which means that a list may have already been started. If indeed there is no prior node then **LastNode** is added as the first node and the list is born. This it does by making **LastNode** the **TopNode,** which is now scoped to the container where everyone can now see it.

If the conditional test fails the method jumps over the assignment of **TopNode** and simply adds a new node. This is done in the following code:

```
Else
  NextNode = LastNode
  LastNode = TopNode
End If
```

(The process of adding and removing nodes in the middle of the **BaseNodeCollection's** structure—and how you navigate it—must still be puzzling. Traversal and iteration will factor into this conversation, which we will pursue later in this chapter. But first let's implement the other key methods and properties in the base class.)

Before we move on there has to be an important addition to the **Add** method. We need a facility for keeping count of how many nodes are manifesting in the container—how many nodes are currently in the list. This is achieved by providing an **Integer** field to **BaseNodeCollection** as follows:

```
Private num As Integer
```

Now every time we add a node to the list we need to increment the number. We can place the code that achieves this at the end of the method, the last line of code executed upon the successful addition of a node. This line is shown in the updated **Add** method in bold:

```
Public Function Add(ByVal obj As Object) _
Dim TopNode As New Node()
  With TopNode
    .Data = obj
    .NodeNext = CType(LastNode, Node)
    If (LastNode Is Nothing) Then
      LastNode = TopNode
    Else
      NextNode = LastNode
      LastNode = TopNode
    End If
    num += 1
    Return num
End With
End Function
```

The **num** variable plays an important role in the **Count** property, which is used in several places to report on the number of nodes in the list. **Count** is implemented shortly and the role of **num** will become more apparent.

The following code shows how to use **Add**:

```
Dim CopyList As New BaseNodeCollection()
Dim BigNode As BaseNodeCollection.Node
For Each BigNode In List
  CopyList.Add(BigNode)
Next BigNode
```

The Clear Method

The **IList.Clear** method clears all nodes from the list. This is a very easy method to implement. We simply de-reference the last node and the entire list collapses like a stack of cards. The garbage collector will conclude that there is no longer an interest in the entire chain and will collect all the objects accordingly.

The definition for the **Clear** method is as follows:

- **Method Name: Clear**   The method clears the reference to a list in **BaseNodeCollection**

- **Method Signature**   The method takes no arguments

  ```
  Public Sub Clear() Implements IList.Clear
  ```

- **Parameters**   None

- **Precondition**   None; simply assigning **LastNode** to **Nothing** severs the connection to the list

- **Postcondition**   None

- **Exceptions**   None; this method will not throw an exception, even if the list does not exist

An implementation of the **Clear** method is as shown in the following code:

```
Public Sub Clear() Implements IList.Clear
  LastNode = Nothing
End Sub
```

The **Clear** method can be called as follows.

```
List.Clear()
```

The Contains Method

The **IList.Contains** checks to see if the specified value is contained in the **Data** object of the **Node**.

The definition for the **Contains** method is as follows:

- **Method Name: Contains**   The method checks for the first existence of the specified value and returns **True** or **False** representing success or failure respectively. This method uses the **IndexOf** method shown later to make the determination.

- **Method Signature**   The method takes no arguments.

  ```
  Public Function Contains(ByVal obj As Object) _
  As Boolean Implements IList.Contains
  ```

CLASSES AND OBJECTS

- **Parameters**   Expects an argument (**obj**) of type **Object**
- **Precondition**   None
- **Postcondition**   None
- **Exceptions**   None

An implementation of the **Contains** method is as shown in the following code:

```
Public Function Contains(ByVal obj As Object) _
  As Boolean Implements IList.Contains
  If IndexOf(obj) < 0 Then
    Return False
  Else
    Return True
  End If
End Function
```

The **Contains** method can be used as follows:

```
If Not (List.Contains("buyer")) Then
  SendEmail("The web site is broke")
End If
```

The CopyTo Method

The **ICollection.CopyTo** copies the values held in the nodes' **Data** object to an array. The definition for the **CopyTo** method is as follows:

- **Method Name: CopyTo**   The method copies the entire list's values to an array.
- **Method Signature**   The method takes two parameters

  ```
  Public Sub CopyTo(ByVal array As Array, ByVal index As Integer) _
  Implements ICollection.CopyTo
  ```

- **Parameters**   This method expects a **System.Array** argument and an **Integer** to specify the index in the array to copy to
- **Precondition**   The method engages an iterator of type **IEnumerator** to traverse the list
- **Postcondition**   None; the list is left as **CopyTo** found it
- **Exceptions**   This method throws an exception of type **ArgumentOutOfRangeException** when the index specified does not exist in the array (it is thus outside the bounds of the array). By throwing exceptions you will test the precondition (instead of using flow-control statements) and allow the user to handle the exception. The **Catch** handler also writes the exception's message to the **exceptInfo** field which is scoped to **BaseNodeCollection**.

An implementation of the **CopyTo** method is as shown in the following code:

```
Public Sub CopyTo(ByVal array As Array, _
  ByVal index As Integer) Implements ICollection.CopyTo
  Try
    Dim myIterator As System.Collections.IEnumerator =_
      Me.GetEnumerator()
    While myIterator.MoveNext()
      CurrentNode = myIterator.Current()
      array(index) = CurrentNode.Data
      index += 1
    End While
  Catch Except As ArgumentOutOfRangeException
    exceptinfo = Except.Message
  End Try
End Sub
```

The **CopyTo** method can be used as follows:

```
Dim ProcessArray(2000) As Object
List.CopyTo(ProcessArray, 0)
```

The Count Property

Being able to keep track of the number of items in a collection is very useful. **Count** is a simple read-only property that returns the number of nodes in the linked list. The definition for **Count** comes from the **ICollection** interface. The easiest way to implement **Count** is to have it simply report the current value of the **num** variable, which is scoped to the container as discussed earlier. The **Add**, **Insert**, and **Remove** methods increment and decrement a counter and **Count** just reports the current value.

Here is its definition:

- **Property Name: Count**   The property counts the number of nodes in the collection.

- **Property Signature**

  ```
  Public Overridable Overloads ReadOnly Property Count() _
  As Integer Implements ICollection.Count
  ```

- **Parameters**   The property returns an **Integer**

- **Precondition**   None

- **Postcondition**   None

- **Exceptions**   None

Count can be implemented as follows:

```
Public Overridable Overloads ReadOnly Property Count() _
   As Integer Implements ICollection.Count
   Get
      Return num
   End Get
End Property
```

You can use **Count** with the other methods as follows:

```
Public Sub InsertNode()
   List.Insert(Count - 1, 100.54)
End Sub
```

This method inserts the value at the end of the list.

Let's review the stage we are at now. We have the model and code for the container called **BaseNodeCollection.** We have also implemented the following **BaseNodeCollection** members: **Add, Clear, Contains, CopyTo,** and **Count.** While we can certainly cook up a list we can't do much with it yet. The next forthcoming group of members to implement will begin to make things a lot more interesting.

The CurrentPosition Property

The **CurrentPosition** property returns a node that is currently in focus, the so-called **CurrentNode.** While **CurrentNode** is referenced internally the purpose of this property is to allow a node to be referenced from the public interface to **BaseNodeCollection.** Later you will see that the iterator uses this property to traverse the list because it is implemented externally and works with an external reference the **BaseNodeCollection.** **CurrentPosition** and similar public properties allow the iterator to find its way to the list.

The definition for the **CurrentPosition** Property is as follows:

- **Property Name: CurrentPosition**   The property specifies the **CurrentPosition**

- **Property Signatures**   The property takes no arguments to its **Get** method and an object of type **Node** to its **Set** method. It returns the **CurrentNode** object

  ```
  Property CurrentPosition() As Node
  Set(ByVal Value As Node)
  ```

- **Parameters**   The **Set** method expects an argument of type **Node**

- **Precondition**   None

- **Postcondition**   None

- **Exceptions**   None

An implementation of the **CurrentPosition** property is as shown in the following code:

```
Property CurrentPosition() As Node
  Get
    Return CurrentNode
  End Get
  Set(ByVal Value As Node)
    CurrentNode = Value
  End Set
End Property
```

This property is used by the iterator, or any external object, to specify the node considered to be at the current position during traversal.

The Find Item Method

The **FindItem** method is a custom method that makes the node at the specified location in the list the **CurrentNode**. The **CurrentNode** can then be referenced by any other methods and properties as needed. The definition for this method is as follows:

- **Method Name: FindItem**   The method makes the node at the specified location the **CurrentNode** object, returned by the **CurrentPosition** property

- **Method Signature**   The method takes a single argument of type **Integer** as an index value representing the node number in the list

  ```
  Private Sub FindItem(ByVal nodeIndex As Integer)
  ```

- **Parameters**   Expects an argument of type **Integer**

- **Precondition**   Checks first to see if the provided argument is outside the bounds of the list

- **Postcondition**   None

- **Exceptions**   This method throws an exception of type **ArgumentOutOfRangeException** when the index specified does not exist in the list (it is thus outside the bounds of the structure—that is, below zero and higher than **Count**). The **Catch** handler also writes the exception's message to the **exceptInfo** field which is scoped to **BaseNodeCollection**.

An implementation of the **FindItem** method is as shown in the following code:

```
Private Sub FindItem(ByVal nodeIndex As Integer)
  Try
    If (nodeIndex < 0 Or nodeIndex > Count) Then
      Throw New ArgumentOutOfRangeException()
```

CLASSES AND OBJECTS

```
      End If
        Dim myIterator As System.Collections.IEnumerator = _
          Me.GetEnumerator()
        Dim intI As Integer = -1
        While intI < nodeIndex
          myIterator.MoveNext()
          CurrentNode = myIterator.Current()
          intI += 1
        End While
    Catch Except As ArgumentOutOfRangeException
      exceptinfo = Except.Message
    End Try
End Sub
```

This method requires a little more explanation. If the **nodeIndex** parameter is valid the first step required is to bridge an iterator object to the list. This is achieved in the following lines of code:

```
Dim myIterator As System.Collections.IEnumerator = _
  Me.GetEnumerator()
```

The nifty thing about this code is that it uses the **Me** "handle" to send a message to the current **BaseNodeCollection** object's **GetEnumerator** method. **GetEnumerator** is implemented to support instantiating the **IEnumerator** object. (The discussion of the **GetEnumerator** is coming up next.)

The next job of the method is easy. Once we have the iterator (of type **IEnumerator**) we can simply enter the list at the head, and iterate over the list until we arrive at the *n*th node specified by the **nodeIndex** parameter.

The iterator itself has a handle on the node it lands on via the **IEnumerator**'s current method (you will see how this works when we tackle the implementation of the iterator object with **IEnumerator** later in this chapter).

The GetEnumerator Method

As mentioned, we will implement an iterator that supports the .NET **IEnumerator** interface towards the end of this chapter, so this discussion of the **IEnumerable.GetEnumerator** method may seem a little premature. However, **GetEnumerator** is required by all methods that seek a handle to the list in order to traverse it (and do other things to it). We use an iterator extensively from within **BaseNodeCollection** (allowing the container to work on its own list) but we also need to implement it to support the likes of external constructs, such as **For Each ... Next,** which will not work without a **GetEnumerator** implemented in the target object. **For Each ... Next**, as discussed in Chapter 6, essentially uses our custom iterator to loop up the list, but it needs **GetEnumerator** to bridge to the iterator. Later on in this chapter you will see how this all comes together like peas in a pod.

Here is the definition of **GetEnumerator**:

- **Method Name: GetEnumerator**   The method returns an instance of an iterator that implements **IEnumerator**

- **Method Signature**

  ```
  Public Function GetEnumerator() As IEnumerator Implements _
     Enumerable.GetEnumerator
  ```

- **Parameters**   The method returns an instance of an **IEnumerator**

- **Precondition**   The method must first instantiate an **IEnumerator** (our iterator)

- **Postcondition**   None

- **Exceptions**   None

GetEnumerator can be implemented as follows:

```
Public Function GetEnumerator() As IEnumerator Implements _
   Enumerable.GetEnumerator
   Dim iterator As New Iterator(Me)
   Return iterator
End Function
```

This is not a difficult method but it requires one critical item to make it work. It needs to pass a reference to *this* object (**Me**) to the iterator's constructor. The iterator will then use the reference to bridge to the current **BaseNodeCollection** object to be "iterated." It may help to see this from inside the iterator. The following codes show the receiving end of the instantiation call to the **Iterator**'s **New** method.

```
Public Sub New(ByRef list As BaseNodeCollection)
   MyBase.New()
   workList = list
End Sub
```

An object of type **BaseNodeCollection** is passed to the constructor, which assigns it to its **workList** variable. The iterator can then get to work on the **workList**, which is connected by reference to the target **BaseNodeCollection** object.

The IndexOf Method

The **IList.IndexOf** method is implemented to provide a facility to find the first index or location of a particular item or value in the list. This method requires some **String** comparison work because we have to iterate through the list and compare that data in each **Data** object to the object passed as an argument specifying the value to search for. Here is the definition of **IndexOf**:

- **Method Name: IndexOf** The method provides a facility to find the first index or location of a particular item

- **Method Signature**

  ```
  Private Function IndexOf(ByVal obj As Object) _
  As Integer Implements IList.IndexOf
  ```

- **Parameters** The method takes an object representing the value or item to find in the list. It returns the index of the first node that has data matching the value specified

- **Precondition** None

- **Postcondition** None

- **Exceptions** This method throws an exception of type **NodeNotFoundException** which is raised when the method compares every node in the list and comes up empty handed. The **Catch** handler also writes the exception's message to the **exceptInfo** field, which is scoped to **BaseNodeCollection**.

IndexOf can be implemented as follows:

```
Private Function IndexOf(ByVal obj As Object) _
  As Integer Implements IList.IndexOf
  Dim intI As Integer = -1
  Dim Nodal As New Node()
  Nodal.Data = obj
  Dim myIterator As System.Collections.IEnumerator _
    = Me.GetEnumerator()
  While myIterator.MoveNext()
    CurrentNode = myIterator.Current()
    intI += 1
    Try
      If (String.Compare(CurrentNode.Data, Nodal.Data) = 0) Then
        Return intI
      End If
    Catch E As NodeNotFoundException
      Return -1
    End Try
  End While
  Return -1
End Function
```

This method uses the **String.Compare** method to compare the value of the **obj** parameter with **CurrentNode.Data.** The **obj** parameter is, however, first assigned to the **Data** object in a node, so that we don't run into type mismatch incompatibility problems during the comparison.

The Insert Method

The **IList.Insert** method is one of the more challenging methods to implement because it requires jostling around nodes in the middle of a list. The interface specifies that you must pass in an **Integer** that represents a position on the list somewhere and the data to insert into the list. The application of the data to the list is pretty straightforward because once you are fixed on a position in the list and have successfully inserted a new **Node** object into the list, you can simply copy the data to the node's **Data** composite.

Here is the definition of **Insert**:

- **Method Name: Insert**   The method inserts a new node in the list or collection and copies the specified data to the new node

- **Method Signature**

```
Public Sub Insert(ByVal index As Integer, _
  ByVal obj As Object) Implements IList.Insert
```

- **Parameters**   The method takes an **Integer** representing the position in the list to insert the new node, and an object encapsulating the data for the new node

- **Precondition**   Checks first to see if the provided **index** argument is not outside the bounds of the list

- **Postcondition**   None

- **Exceptions**   This method throws an exception of type **ArgumentOutOfRange Exception** when the index specified does not exist in the list (it is thus outside the bounds of the structure—that is, less than zero and higher than **Count**). The **Catch** handler also writes the exception's message to the **exceptInfo** field, which is scoped to **BaseNodeCollection**.

Insert can be implemented as follows:

```
Public Sub Insert(ByVal index As Integer, _
  ByVal obj As Object) Implements IList.Insert
  Try
    If (index < 0 Or index >= Count) Then
      Throw New ArgumentOutOfRangeException()
    End If
    Dim myIterator As System.Collections.IEnumerator _
    = Me.GetEnumerator()
```

```
      Dim intI As Integer
      While intI < index
        myIterator.MoveNext()
        intI += 1
      End While
      Dim NewNode As New Node()
      Dim JostleNode As New Node()
      NewNode.Data = obj
      JostleNode = CurrentNode.NodeNext
      CurrentNode.NodeNext = NewNode
      NewNode.NodeNext = JostleNode
      num += 1
    Catch Except As ArgumentOutOfRangeException
      exceptinfo = Except.Message
    End Try
  End Sub
```

Once **Insert** has checked that the location to insert to is kosher it can call on the services of the iterator and run over to the desired location. The location can be anywhere in the list, including the node after the tail node, the first node position, and anywhere in between head and tail. The important part of this method is the code required for jostling the nodes around to accommodate the insert. It is represented in the following section:

```
Dim NewNode As New Node()
Dim JostleNode As New Node()
NewNode.Data = obj
JostleNode = CurrentNode.NodeNext
CurrentNode.NodeNext = NewNode
NewNode.NodeNext = JostleNode
num += 1
```

This code creates two new nodes; one is called the **NewNode** and one is called **JostleNode**. The data passed to the method is first copied to the **NewNode**'s **Data** object, so once that part is done the data-transfer part is out of our way.

The next job of the method is to make the node that bears the honor of the **CurrentNode** link point to the **JostleNode**. This is achieved by assigning **JostleNode** to **CurrentNode.NodeNext**. Then we point **CurrentNode.NodeNext** to the **NewNode**, which brings the new data into the list. Finally, **NewNode.NodeNext** is assigned to **JostleNode**, so that we don't lose the rest of the list. This may be clearer if represented graphically as shown in Figure 13-13.

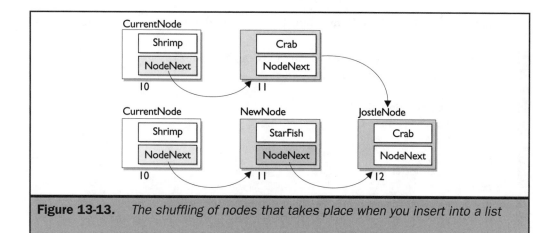

Figure 13-13.   *The shuffling of nodes that takes place when you insert into a list*

The **Insert** method can be used as follows:

```
Public Sub InsertNode()
  List.Insert(0, "Start")
End Sub
```

The Item Property
The **IList.Item** property retrieves or sets the value in the referenced node. This is an easy property to implement because it merely references the **CurrentNode** object and retrieves or changes the data in **CurrentNode.Data**.

The definition for the **Item** property is as follows:

- **Property Name: Item**   The property sets or returns the data in **CurrentNode.Data**

- **Property Signatures**   The property takes arguments to both **Set** and **Get** methods

  ```
  Public Property Item(ByVal nodeIndex As Integer) _
    As Object Implements IList.Item
  Set(ByVal Value As Object)
  ```

- **Parameters**   The **Get** method expects an **Integer** representing the position in the list to iterate to. The **Set** method expects an object representing the data to install in the target's **Data** object

- **Precondition**   None

- **Postcondition**   None

- **Exceptions**   None

An implementation of the **Item** property is as shown in the following code:

```
Public Property Item(ByVal nodeIndex As Integer) _
  As Object Implements IList.Item
  Get
    FindItem(nodeIndex)
    Return CurrentNode
  End Get
  Set(ByVal Value As Object)
    CurrentNode.Data = Value
  End Set
End Property
```

The Composite pattern also defines a method that returns the data of a node. The pattern calls it **GetChild. GetChild** and **IList.Item** do the same thing. From within **BaseNodeCollection**, we can vary operations that return one of several items, such as the data in **Data**, information about the current state, or any other information you care to program into the **Node** object.

If you are a stickler for formality you can change the name of **Item** to **GetChild** because interface implementation allows you to change the name of the identifier.

The **Item** method can be used as follows:

```
List.Item(3).Data = "oh no"
```

The Last Property

The **Last** property is a custom property that returns the node currently assigned to **LastNode**. The **LastNode** is essentially the head of the list.

The definition for the **Last** property is as follows:

- **Property Name: Last**   The property returns the **LastNode** object.
- **Property Signatures**

  ```
  ReadOnly Property Last() As Node
  ```

- **Parameters**   Returns an object of type **Node**, which is the current node assigned **LastNode**
- **Precondition**   None
- **Postcondition**   None
- **Exceptions**   None

An implementation of the **Last** property is as shown in the following code:

```
ReadOnly Property Last() As Node
  Get
    Return LastNode
  End Get
End Property
```

The PreviousNode Property

The **Previous** property is a custom property that returns the node currently assigned to **NodePrevious**.

The definition for the **PreviousNode** property is as follows:

- **Property Name: PreviousNode**   The property returns the **NodePrevious** object
- **Property Signatures**

  ```
  ReadOnly Property PreviousNode() As Node
  ```

- **Parameters**   Returns an object of type **Node**, which is the current node assigned **NodePrevious**
- **Precondition**   None
- **Postcondition**   None
- **Exceptions**   None

An implementation of the **PreviousNode** property is as shown in the following code:

```
Property PreviousNode() As Node
  Get
    Return NodePrevious
  End Get
  Set(ByVal Value As Node)
    NodePrevious = Value
  End Set
End Property
```

The Remove Method

Last of the tricky methods to implement are **IList.Remove** and **IList.RemoveAt**. The two methods are closely related, as you will see. The interface does not specify that you need to provide a location (an index value) in the list for the target of the **Remove** method. Instead, an additional **IList.RemoveAt** is defined for that. This method is simply passed an object representing the data in the **Node** to be removed.

Now, because the interface is a contract you can't simply change the signature willy-nilly. That means that we have to provide an implementation behind the interface that deals with the fact that the client is just going to send data to the interface and you are expected to find the first element or node holding that matches the data received. Then you remove the node returned on the first hit. It would have been much easier if the method accepted an object of type **Node** for removal because we could just remove the node assigned **CurrentNode,** instead of needing to go look for that first node containing the data to delete.

With the support we already have for searching and iterating over the list, finding the first instance of the node holding the specified data is not that difficult. There is a bit of jostling to do but the **Remove** method's jostling is similar to the jostling we needed to do in the **Add** method. Consider the following definition for **Remove:**

- **Method Name: Remove**   The method removes a node from the list container. The implementor can only remove the first node holding data destined for removal. If there are more nodes containing the same data you will have to recall the method to remove the remaining nodes.

- **Method Signature**

  ```
  Public Sub Remove(ByVal node As Object) Implements IList.Remove
  ```

- **Parameters**   The method takes an argument of type **Object** representing the data in the node that will be removed

- **Precondition**   The method checks the location of the first node representing the data to be removed

- **Postcondition**   No postcondition

- **Exceptions**   This method throws two exceptions. It will throw an exception of type **ArgumentOutOfRangeException** when the index specified does not exist in the list (it is thus outside the bounds of the structure—that is, less than zero and higher than **Count**). The **Catch** handler also writes the exception's message to the **exceptInfo** field, which is scoped to **BaseNodeCollection**. It will also throw an exception of type **NodeNotFoundException** if the index is –1, indicative of a search turning up negative and returning –1.

We can implement **Remove** as follows:

```
Public Sub Remove(ByVal node As Object) Implements IList.Remove
   Dim index As Integer = IndexOf(node)
   Try
     If (Count <= 0) Then
       Throw New ArgumentOutOfRangeException()
```

```
      ElseIf (index = -1) Then
        Throw New NodeNotFoundException()
      'what if the target is at the tail of the list
      ElseIf (index = Me.Count - 1) Then
        RemoveFirst
        Return
      'what if the target is at the head of the list
      ElseIf index = 0 Then
        RemoveLast()
        Return
      Else 'what if the target is anywhere in the list
        RemoveInBetween
        Return
      End If
    Catch ArgExcept As ArgumentOutOfRangeException
      exceptinfo = ArgExcept.Message
    Catch NodeExcept As NodeNotFoundException
      exceptinfo = NodeExcept.Message
    End Try
End Sub
```

There are three possible remove options. You can remove the node in the tail position, the so-called tail node. You can remove the node in the head position, the so-called head node (or **LastNode**). And you can remove a node from anywhere in between the tail and head positions.

Once the **Remove** method knows the location of the node to remove it can call one of three methods to perform the snip. These methods are listed as follows:

```
Private Function RemoveLast() As Object
  FindItem(0)
  Try
    If (CurrentNode Is Nothing) Then
      Throw New NodeNotFoundException()
    Else
      LastNode = CurrentNode.NodeNext
      CurrentNode = Nothing
      CurrentNode = LastNode
      num -= 1
    End If
  Catch NodeExcept As NodeNotFoundException
    exceptinfo = NodeExcept.Message
```

```
    End Try
End Function

Private Sub RemoveFirst()
  NodePrevious.NodeNext = Nothing
  num -= 1
End Function

Private Sub RemoveInBetween()
  NodePrevious.NodeNext = CurrentNode.NodeNext
  CurrentNode = NodePrevious
  NodePrevious = Nothing
  num -= 1
End Sub
```

As you can see from this code, the removal process is simply a matter of de-referencing the referenced node. Because **Nothing** cuts the node loose, the garbage collector can come around and reclaim the resources that the "dead" object consumed. Also notice that we need to decrement **num** or count will no longer be accurate.

Remove is typically used as follows:

```
List.Remove("Mr Noble")
```

The RemoveAt

The **IList.RemoveAt** method is a variation of the **IList.Remove** method that *can* take an **Integer** to represent the location in the list to remove the node from. This method simply chases up an iterator to land on the node to remove. It makes the target node the **CurrentNode** and then one of either **RemoveFirst**, **RemoveLast**, or **RemoveInBetween**.

Consider the following definition for **RemoveAt**:

- **Method Name: Remove**   The method removes a node from the list container at the specifed location.

- **Method Signature**
  ```
  Public Sub RemoveAt(ByVal index As Integer) Implements IList.RemoveAt
  ```

- **Parameters**   The method takes an argument of type **Object** representing the data in the node that will be removed

- **Precondition**   The method checks the location of the first node representing the data to be removed

- **Postcondition**   No postcondition

■ **Exceptions**   This method throws two exceptions. It will throw an exception of type **ArgumentOutOfRangeException** when the index specified does not exist in the list (it is thus outside the bounds of the structure—that is, below zero and higher than **Count**). The **Catch** handler also writes the exception's message to the **exceptInfo** field, which is scoped to **BaseNodeCollection**. It will also throw an exception of type **NodeNotFoundException** if the index is –1, indicative of a search turning up negative and returning –1.

We can implement **RemoveAt** as follows:

```
Public Sub RemoveAt(ByVal index As Integer)_
  Implements IList.RemoveAt
  If (index < 0 Or index >= Count) Then
    Throw New ArgumentOutOfRangeException()
  End If
  If (index = Me.Count - 1) Then
    RemoveFirst()
    Return
  'what if the target is at the end of the list
  ElseIf index = 0 Then
    RemoveLast()
    Return
  Else 'what if the target is somewhere between first and last
    Dim myIterator As System.Collections.IEnumerator = Me.GetEnumerator()
    Dim intI As Integer
    While intI < index
      myIterator.MoveNext()
    intI += 1
  End While
    RemoveInBetween()
  End If
  Catch ArgExcept As ArgumentOutOfRangeException
    exceptinfo = ArgExcept.Message
  Catch NodeExcept As NodeNotFoundException
    exceptinfo = NodeExcept.Message
  End Try
End Sub
```

RemoveAt is typically used as follows:

```
List.RemoveAt(0)
```

Implementing the Iterator

IEnumerator's implementation provides the base functionality needed for an *iterator*—a device that moves from one object to the next in a collection. **IEnumerable** is the proxy interface given the task—through exposing of a single member, a method—of returning an iterator (enumerator) for the target collection. The following list describes the interfaces' members and the utility derived from their implementation:

- **Reset**   Moves the iterator back to its starting position, just before the first node. Calling **MoveNext** places the iterator at the first position

- **Current**   A property that returns the current node (the one the iterator is positioned at). We can use this property to assign **CurrentNode**

- **MoveNext**   Moves the iterator to the next node in the list

While you can implement and work with **IEnumerator** alone—forgoing implementation of **IEnumerable**—implementing the **GetEnumerator** method in your collection is a convenient way to access an **IEnumerator** without having to permanently couple it to any particular collection object as you can see in the forthcoming sections. Incidentally, the enumerator interfaces are also used to create an iterator that can "walk" a collection of **XMLNode** objects.

The **Iterator** class can be composed in **BaseNodeCollection** but there is not much point to doing so. Unlike the **Node** class, which is part and parcel of a list or tree container, the iterator (or enumerator) is independent enough to stand on its own in a separate class that is implemented at the same level as the **BaseNodeCollection** class. This will allow you to target the iterator class at other collections because the methods of the **Iterator** class are simple enough to use with a variety of collection objects that employ **Node** objects as the elements of their collections.

The following represents the base **Iterator** class.

```
Imports Nodals.BaseNodeCollection
Imports Vb7cr
Public Class Iterator
  Implements IEnumerator

  Private Position As Node
  Private Previous As Node
  Private workList As BaseNodeCollection
  Private iteratorInfo As String

  Public Sub New(ByRef list As BaseNodeCollection)
    MyBase.New()
    workList = list
```

```
    Reset()
  End Sub

  Public Sub Reset() Implements IEnumerator.Reset
    workList.CurrentPosition = Nothing
  End Sub

  Function MoveNext() As Boolean Implements IEnumerator.MoveNext
    Try
      If workList.Last Is Nothing Then
        Throw New NodeNotFoundException()
      End If
      If (workList.CurrentPosition Is Nothing) Then
        workList.CurrentPosition = workList.Last
        Return True
      Else
        If (workList.CurrentPosition.NodeNext Is Nothing) Then
          Reset()
          Return False
        End If
        workList.PreviousNode = workList.CurrentPosition
        workList.CurrentPosition =_
        workList.CurrentPosition.NodeNext
        Return True
      End If
    Catch NExcept As NodeNotFoundException
      iteratorInfo = "No nodes exist in this container."
    End Try
  End Function

  Public ReadOnly Property Current() _
    As Object Implements IEnumerator.Current
    Get
      Return workList.CurrentPosition
    End Get
  End Property
End Class
```

The **MoveNext** method is the workhorse of this class. With its reference to an instance of **BaseNodeCollection**, which it receives upon instantiation via its **New** constructor, it traverses the list by shuffling the nodes into different positions—the previous node is assigned to the current position and the current node is assigned to the next position and so on.

The **Reset** method is implemented very simply. It just causes the iterator to lose its place in the list. The next time you make a call to **MoveNext**, the iterator is forced to start from the beginning again. The **IEnumerator** interface specifies that **IEnumerator** objects typically scroll in one direction. The iterator shown here starts at the head of the list and proceeds to the tail, going from the last node that was added to the list to the first node that was added—as if the list of nodes is a stack. The current version of the iterator does not support backward scrolling.

Reset is also called in the constructor so that the iterator is automatically reset whenever **New** is called.

The last member implemented here is the **Current** property. It simply returns the **Node** object assigned to the **CurrentPosition**. Note that **CurrentPosition** and **CurrentNode** both refer to the same thing, only **CurrentPosition** is the **BaseNodeCollection** property that accesses the data from the internal and private **CurrentNode** variable.

Note	*The formal Iterator pattern specifies a **CurrentItem** method as well as a **Next** method that is the equivalent of **MoveNext**. It also supports indexing, which can be easily implemented but is not really a necessity.*

The following code demonstrates the iterator at work. The method **PrintNodesDemo1** makes an iterator using the **BaseNodeCollection**'s **GetEnumerator** method, while **PrintNodeDemo2** does the same thing using the **For Each . . . Next** construct.

```
Module LinkedListDemo

  Dim List As New BaseNodeCollection()

  Sub Main()
    List.Add("I")
    List.Add("just")
    List.Add("love")
    List.Add("OOP")
    List.Add("with")
    List.Add("VB.NET")
    PrintNodesDemo1()
    PrintNodesDemo2()
  End Sub

  Public Sub PrintNodesDemo1()
    Dim myIterator As System.Collections.IEnumerator = _
    List.GetEnumerator()
    While myIterator.MoveNext()
       Console.WriteLine(myIterator.Current.Data.ToString)
    End While
```

```
      End Sub

      Public Sub PrintNodesDemo2()
        Dim element As BaseNodeCollection.Node
        For Each element In List
          Console.WriteLine(element.Data)
        Next
      End Sub
End Module
```

The printout to the console for both cases shown in the code is as follows:

```
I
just
love
OOP
with
VB.NET
```

Note *The code for the **BaseNodeCollection**, **Iterator**, and **Node** classes can be found in the Nodals project in the Vb7cr solution.*

Observations

This chapter extended our discussion of data structures and provided us with some interesting code. But most of all, it showed what's possible with a pure object-oriented language like Visual Basic .NET. We saw many scenarios creating linked lists wherein objects and their interfaces are aggregated into container classes after they have been first defined as composite classes. We also looked at how Visual Basic can adopt—and then run with—many of the formal patterns that have emerged to assist OO design and development over the years. Some of these patterns could be represented with classic VB. However, it is the native support for interfaces, polymorphism, encapsulation, and inheritance that makes all of the patterns adopted by languages such as Java and C++ more than applicable to Visual Basic .NET and the .NET Framework.

We are going to take this further in the next chapter, where we'll look at patterns for adapting interfaces, delegations, and delegates, as well as some advanced uses of interfaces.

CLASSES AND OBJECTS

The Complete Reference

Visual Basic .NET

Chapter 14

Advanced Interface Patterns: Adapters, Delegates, and Events

I have already devoted a significant portion of this book to the subject of implementation inheritance (genericity), composition, and bridging. In the last four chapters, I examined interface implementation extensively. Now I will concentrate on advanced interface patterns, which underpin the .NET **Delegate** construct and the .NET event model.

A number of years ago, I found that **Adapter** classes and interfaces, **Wrapper** interfaces, and **Delegates** were some of the hardest concepts to understand (for all OO students, especially Java and Visual J++ programmers). The .NET **Delegate** construct is vitally important to .NET programming, in particular, and OO, in general; yet, interfaces and **Delegates** cause more concern for .NET programmers than any other facet of this extensive framework. Therefore, it is critical for us to acquire a thorough understanding of this material.

Many who don't understand how **Delegates** work have incorrectly attributed a magical status to them. In truth, **Delegates** are a very simple construct that derives from well-conceived patterns that the OO industry has provided for more than half a decade. No Harry Potter analogy needs to be interjected into discussions of them, as you will see in this chapter. Once you master **Delegates**, they will come to represent your most powerful tool—alongside interfaces and inheritance—for programming polymorphism.

You know that interfaces and **Delegates** are now fully implemented in the Visual Basic language. But, if you can't use their sophisticated utility—regardless of your programming knowledge—you will not make it to the software-development majors. This chapter is probably the most important one to understand entirely—for beginning and experienced programmers alike. I hope you will ponder this information until you have completely absorbed it.

Interfaces have *nothing* to do with the implementation inheritance pattern, per se (the principal subject of Chapter 9), but they do have *everything* to do with polymorphism. .NET interfaces can be completely de-coupled from any of their implementations. Thus, the implementation can be varied on the back end, while the interfaces can be adapted on the front end—without the two ends being any the wiser. I talked about this de-coupling in earlier chapters, but I did not discuss adapting the interfaces of concrete classes. I will discuss this subject in the current chapter.

If you understood the concepts behind interfaces presented in the previous chapters, especially Chapter 10, and realized why the interface architecture of the .NET Framework is so important, then you'll quickly grasp the idea behind interface adaptation, delegation and the **Delegate** class, and events. **Delegates**, in fact, are the implementation of a fundamental design pattern that provides the highest form of class de-coupling and class cohesion in a framework. They allow highly sophisticated designs to be applied to .NET applications, and they underpin not only the .NET event model discussed here, but the entire framework itself.

This chapter may be somewhat controversial and is written in a style that evokes some emotion—a technique that I hope will not only inspire you to read through complex concepts, but also help you to retain them. I am also seeking to promote debate and further your thinking regarding design, code, and choice of constructs to suit your purpose.

However, to grasp how **Delegates** work, it is essential to have an unshakable foundation in interfaces, in general, and interface adaptation, in particular, as well as in the concept of wrapping. Thus, the subject of delegation is allied to the subject of adaptation—the technique whereby you adapt an interface so that another object can use it.

Wrapping is the part where an additional class may be needed to translate messages, marshal calls, or convert data-types between clients and servers. The formal pattern names are *"Adapter," "Wrapper,"* and *"Delegation."* The following short list places these terms in their relevant contexts:

- **Receiver** or **Server**   The object or class that contains the implementation and a domain-specific interface. It is the final destination (the implementation of a method) of the call message of a **Sender** or **Client** (unless an overriding method intervenes). The **Receiver** is shown in the following illustration, on the receiving end of the method call (from whence it came does not matter).

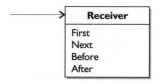

- **Sender** or **Client**   The object or class that has an interest in the services or implementation of the **Reciever** or **Server**. The **Sender** is represented here.

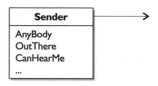

- **Adapter**   A concrete class or an interface that adapts the interface of a **Receiver**. Often it may be necessary to do more that adapt interfaces, and an **Adapter** may have to provide additional functionality to allow access to the **Receiver**. Often referred to as a **Wrapper**, it may need to contain code that marshals calls and converts data-types. Thus, it accomplishes much more than simply adapting interfaces. Inner classes, or derivatives of a **Receiver**, can also play the role of an **Adapter** or **Wrapper** (as shown in Figure 14-1). They may also redirect calls to overriding or varying implementation.

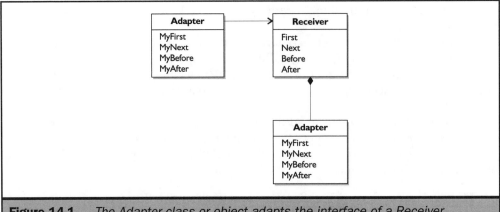

Figure 14-1.   *The Adapter class or object adapts the interface of a Receiver*

■ **Adaptee**   The interface to an **Adapter,** which is exposed to clients. An **Adapter** (or, less likely, a **Receiver)** may provide "pluggable" support by "implementing" an **Adaptee** interface (as shown in Figure 14-2). The implementation of interfaces such as **ICollection** and **IEnumerable**, discussed in the previous chapters, are examples of "pluggable" support.

■ **Delegate**   A sophisticated name for a sophisticated **Adaptee**, which is also a complex and specialized construct in the .NET Framework. However, on the surface it is really nothing more than a specialized interface pointing to a single method at the **Receiver**. The interrupted method calls from Sender to Delegate and from **Delegate** to **Receiver**—as illustrated in the illustration—indicate the

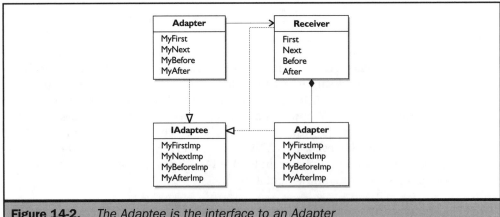

Figure 14-2.   *The Adaptee is the interface to an Adapter*

method call may arrive at the interface indirectly (perhaps from an event in the case of the **Delegate** interface, and from an **Adapter** in the case of the **Receiver**).

Sender	Delegate	Receiver
AnyBody OutThere CanHearMe ...	MeFirst	First Next Before After

Note   *We will add the event definitions to our list later, once we have sorted out these issues.*

The next two sections probe the **Adapter** and **Wrapper** patterns. You will learn along the way that **Adapter** interfaces and classes also provide a viable event model, which many programmers vociferously defend. In fact, adapters underpin the Java-Swing event model—one that can certainly be applied to .NET programming and especially to Visual Basic .NET.

Adapters and Wrappers

The *Adapter* pattern—which is also known as the *Wrapper* pattern—converts the interface of a class or an object, however coupled, into an interface that clients expect or can use. **Adapter** and **Wrapper** classes may make use of **Adaptee** interfaces to let otherwise incompatible classes and objects—including those written in different languages— work together or interoperate.

For the benefit of clients, you can adapt the interfaces of classes and objects written in the same language. It is the easiest level of adaptation you can implement. You can also adapt interfaces written in other languages that are part of a framework. It is very common in the .NET Framework to allow implementation to be "pluggable" into any language—a practice I will discuss shortly. This intermediate level is a little harder, but it will be something you might find yourself doing often.

Finally, you can adapt interfaces of classes that are neither written in the same language nor part of the same framework. These include the classes of independent software-development kits, those of libraries and components, and any class or object that was not otherwise intended for the class or consumer-objects for which they are being adapted. This third level of adaptation is the most complex and most difficult, requiring conversion of data-types and tricky call-marshaling. It necessitates the mettle of an experienced "wrapper" programmer who understands implicitly the source and target languages and the development environments.

A good example of the last level of adaptation is the wrapping of COM interfaces for access by .NET code. This is the interoperation support that provides access to the COM home world, which is still very much developer Prime in Microsoft's part of the galaxy. COM and .NET are as different from each other as coffee is from couscous.

COM code—COM objects and components—are written in unmanaged languages, such as VB 6, Delphi, Visual J++ (not Java), and (primarily) C++, and their interfaces are registered with the operating system. The .NET components, however, are written in the managed .NET languages like Visual Basic .NET, Visual C# .NET, or Visual J# .NET (pidgin Java for the .NET Framework). As you know, .NET interfaces are not registered with the operating system, and they are executed by the CLR, as directed by metadata.

Essentially, COM objects run in one reality while .NET objects run in another. The two realities are parallel in the Windows universe, so you need to connect them via a "wormhole." On each side of the wormhole, you need to adapt the star-gate or jump-gate interfaces, so that the other side can come through in one piece. On the COM side, you'll provide .NET-callable interfaces that .NET clients can understand; on the .NET side, you have COM-callable interfaces for COM clients.

With all the investment in COM code still very much at large, it was incumbent upon Microsoft to create adapter and/or wrapper layers for its valuable COM objects. After all, COM is still Microsoft's bread and butter, as Corolla is for Toyota. Regardless of the fanfare surrounding .NET, there are literally millions of COM objects afloat, which means we can't discount COM for a very long time.

Consider the ".NET" server technology the company sells. It is primarily composed of COM bits. A favorite example is Index Server, whose COM object is typically programmed against classic ASP pages and VBScript; however, the rapid adoption of Visual Basic .NET and ASP.NET requires that Index Server's objects be exposed to ASP.NET code—which is programmed in Visual Basic .NET (or any .NET language). This requires wrapper classes specifically aimed at the Index Server's COM interfaces. The next section demonstrates accessing Index Server from ASP.NET to illustrate the seamless integration and interoperation of .NET and the COM world.

Another good example is Commerce Server. By and large Commerce Server is nothing more than a comprehensive collection of COM objects. So without adaptation and wrapping of its COM interfaces, it is practically off limits to .NET. **Adapter** interfaces or **Wrapper**s thus allow Microsoft's flagship e-commerce product to be accessible to its .NET brainchildren. I'll discuss this interop next.

Interface Adaptation in Action—COM-.NET Interop

"COM-.NET interop" is accomplished via the .NET Framework's callable wrappers for achieving interoperability between COM servers and .NET clients, and COM clients and .NET servers.

The wrapper class that provides access to COM is called a *Runtime Callable Wrapper (RCW)*, and it allows your .NET objects to interoperate with COM servers as if they were .NET managed types. Adaptation is needed because .NET objects cannot call COM directly; they don't know how. The classes "wrap" the COM objects, which are activated (instantiated) in the standard way and programmed against in the manner I've outlined in the past chapters.

To expose a .NET object to a COM client, the CLR conversely provides a *COM Callable Wrapper (CCW)* that adapts the interface of a managed object. This adaptation in the other direction is necessary because COM objects do not know how to reference .NET objects directly. The COM clients and .NET clients thus use the wrappers as a proxy into each other's worlds as shown in Figure 14-3.

The primary function of the wrappers is to marshal calls between .NET and COM. Manual adaptation, as mentioned earlier, is not an easy task, even for the most accomplished programmer. In the mid-1990s, it took a solo programmer with experience many weeks to adapt ADO (Active Data Objects) interfaces for Borland's Delphi. The CLR adapts COM's ADO in about ten seconds (of course Microsoft took a lot longer to get this level of automatic adaptation down pat).

The CLR makes the adaptations for you by automatically generating the wrapper interfaces. It creates a single RCW for each COM object. And by being totally de-coupled, the interface can be referenced by a .NET class or object—irrespective of the number of references that may exist on the COM object.

The code on the following page uses the adaptation of Index Server's COM API, which goes by the unusual name of **Cisso** (meaning unknown). Essentially, the wrapper allows any number of .NET clients to instantiate the "**Interop.Cisso**" adapter interface. Your applications are unaware that the object behind the interface is really a COM object.

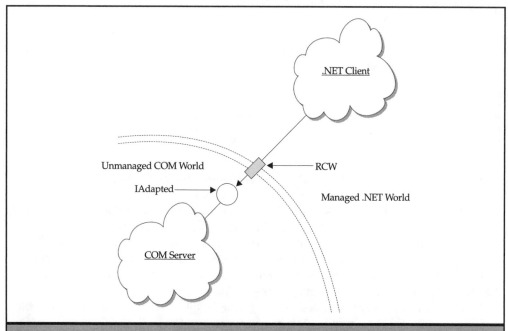

Figure 14-3. *Bridging the .NET (managed) reality to COM*

CLASSES AND OBJECTS

This ASP.NET code accesses the Index Server COM components and ADO components with very little effort (and brings the legacy database objects into the modern word of .NET data access):

```
Public Function SearchWithCisso(ByRef searchString As String, _
   ByRef rankBase As Integer, _
   ByRef catalog As String, _
   ByRef sortorder As String, _
   ByRef columns As String) As DataSet
   Try
     Dim myDA As OleDbDataAdapter = New OleDbDataAdapter()
     Dim myDS As DataSet = New DataSet()
     'This call passes the user's search string to a method
     'that prepares it for submission to Index Server
     cissoQuery.Query = PrepareSearchString(searchString)
     cissoQuery.Catalog = catalog
     cissoQuery.SortBy = sortorder
     cissoQuery.Columns = columns
     cissoQuery.MaxRecords = rankBase
     cissoQueryRS = cissoQuery.CreateRecordset("nonsequential")
     adoRS = cissoQueryRS
     myDA.Fill(myDS, adoRS, "Results")
     Return myDS
     'no need to close the recordset as required by ADO
     'because the GC does this for us
     'cissoQueryRS.Close()
     'adoRS.Close()
   Catch Except As Exception
     Console.WriteLine(Except.Message)
   End Try
End Function
```

Conversely, when you adapt a .NET server interface for a COM client, the runtime creates a single managed CCW for it. Any number of COM clients can reference this interface. As Figure 14-4 shows, multiple COM clients can hold a reference to the CCW that exposes the adapted (essentially new) interface. Figure 14-4 portrays how both COM and .NET clients can reference the same managed object simultaneously.

The primary purpose of these adapter interfaces (interfaced with **IAdaptee** in the figures) is to marshal calls between managed and unmanaged code. CCWs also control the identity and lifetime of the managed objects they wrap.

While .NET objects are allocated on the garbage-collected heap, which enables the runtime to move them around in memory as necessary, the CLR allocates memory for the CCW from a non-collected heap—as standard value-types do. This makes it possible

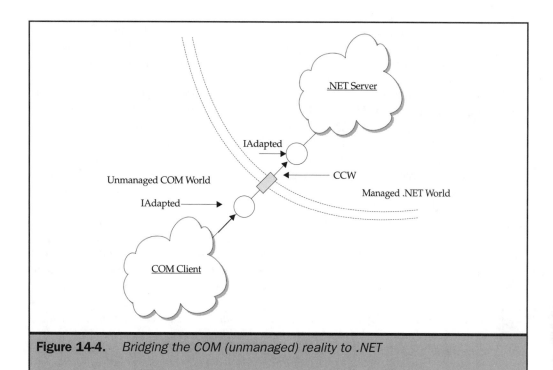

Figure 14-4.   *Bridging the COM (unmanaged) reality to .NET*

for COM clients to reference the wrapper interfaces as they do standard COM objects. Essentially, the COM clients can count the references they have on the CCW objects directly. Thus, when the COM client's count on the CCW reaches zero, it releases its reference on the wrapper, which de-references the managed object. The CLR disposes of the reference while the GC collects the object as part of its normal garbage-collection cycle.

From the .NET client's perspective in accessing a COM object, the CLR creates an assembly infused with metadata collected from the COM object's type library. The CLR thus instantiates the COM object being called and produces a wrapper interface for that object. The wrapper maintains a cache of interface pointers on its COM object and releases its reference to it when the RCW is no longer needed. At this point, the runtime invokes standard garbage collection on the wrapper.

These adapter constructs (the RCW and the CCW) marshal various things: the data between managed and unmanaged code, as well as method arguments and method return values. They also translate the data between the two worlds whenever differing representations are passed through their interfaces. For example, when a .NET client passes a **String** in an argument to the CCW, the wrapper converts the **String** to a **BSTR** type (a 32-bit pointer to the character data) that the COM object understands. **BSTR**s are thus converted to **String**s when the data comes back from the COM world. **String**-like data usually requires conversion while other types, such as a 4-byte **Integer**, require none.

The classes that wrap COM objects expose the COM interfaces to the .NET clients transparently and allow the COM objects to access components as if they were .NET objects. Wrapping takes into account all the HRESULTS, return values, reference counting, and other COM ingredients.

In the next chapter I examine another "wrap"—the File System Object for files and folders (otherwise known as **FSO**), and the Index Server COM object. These COM objects were cooked up long before the .NET Framework arrived on the menu of development options, yet they partner well with .NET. So, if you have any investment in unmanaged code exposed as COM objects, they are automatically available to .NET clients.

If you have an investment in unmanaged code that you want to expose to .NET, and the code is not exposed as COM objects, then you have three choices. First, you could rewrite your code in Visual Basic .NET, which would probably be too time-consuming and expensive. Second, you could create a new custom interop layer for your code, an alternative that is less expensive than the first option but still a complex undertaking. Third, you could create the necessary COM-type libraries for the code (with a tool like Visual J++). The latter would require the least effort and expense, and it is preferable to expose the unmanaged code with COM interfaces rather than rewrite it for .NET.

Note *We must remember that adding interoperability impacts performance, no matter how unnoticeable it may be. It is best to try to work with the classes in the .NET base-class library and leave COM interop to your "out-of-options" situations, if only to get used to using the native classes.*

Taking unmanaged code interface adaptation further is beyond the scope of this book. However, we do need to determine how to adapt classes within our operating framework. In other words, let's first ascertain what it means to adapt .NET interfaces for use by other .NET classes and objects. This will put us on the road to understanding **Delegate**s and events.

The Adapter Pattern in .NET

The Adapter pattern prescribes how an **Adapter** class or object adapts an interface that clients will be able to use and couples it with a **Receiver**'s interface that the clients do not know how to use. For the record, the original implementation in the **Receiver** does not need to be known by the clients and it can vary—which is polymorphism in all its magnificent glory (see the related Bridge and Strategy patterns in the last chapter).

Objects and classes can receive messages either directly or indirectly. The following illustration first shows the normal process of sending the call message directly to an object with which it knows how to communicate—by direct reference to a class or an object.

When a client object needs to call a method in the server object—but it cannot call the method directly, as it normally would in an association or instantiation context between the two objects—it makes the call by way of an **Adapter** or a proxy. The message may be sent to the **Adaptee** or **Delegate**, which provides an interface. In Figure 14-5, the **Sender** sends a method call to an interface and has no knowledge, or desire to have knowledge, of how that interface gets to the operative code—the code in the **Receiver**—behind that method call. The **Sender** typically *delegates* the actual call to the **Adaptee**, or **Delegate**.

The **Adapter** classes can, of course, do a lot more than just delegate method calls, as I discussed in the interop section. They can check arguments, throw exceptions, and include support from other [imported] classes. The **Adapter** class can be as sophisticated as it needs to be. Remember that the client need not know the **Adapter** exists.

When you implement the standard **Receiver** objects, you do not design or construct code to cater to the indirect arrival of call messages. But you can build in support for indirection with pluggable interfaces.

The level of adapting the **Adapter** class needs to provide can range from simply implementing a single interface to supporting a highly sophisticated set of operations in the **Receiver** class—possibly even re-implementing the methods of the **Receiver** so that the **Adaptee** can reference the new functionality. Also, the amount of work depends on the difference between the **Adapter**'s interface and the **Receiver**'s interface.

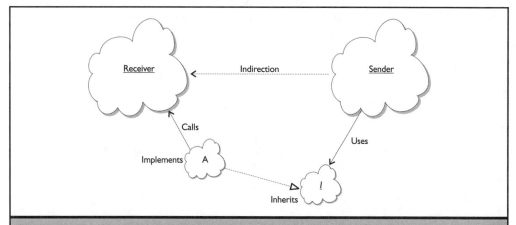

Figure 14-5.   *An **Adapter** is able to act as the interface to the **Receiver** object on behalf of a client that cannot call the **Receiver** object directly*

CLASSES AND OBJECTS

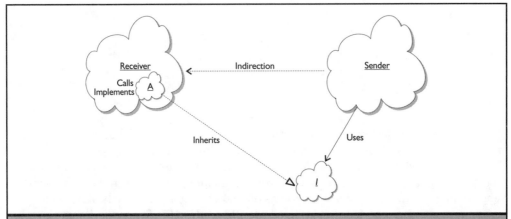

Figure 14-6. *The **Adapter** object is a subclass or inner (composite) class of the **Adaptee***

When adapting classes, the **Adapter** class may either inherit the implementation of the **Receiver** class, or it can be composed as an inner, composite, class of the **Receiver** via the Composite pattern. Figure 14-6 illustrates how this latter option differs from the adaptation scenario in Figure 14-5.

In other words, we say the **Adapter** class can commit to the **Adaptee** class by gaining full access to the **Receiver**'s operations through inheritance or by virtue of being a composite or inner class. This of course prevents the **Adapter** nested in the **Receiver** class from adapting child classes. Additional **Adapter** classes will be needed to cooperate with child classes and adapt them.

When inheriting from the **Receiver**, your **Adapter** class has the additional benefit of being able to override the parent implementation. An inner or nested class can also inherit from its parent and still implement the interface the client needs to access.

The Composite adapter implementation is illustrated in the following code:

```
Public Class Trajectory

  Private Rock As Asteroid
  Private RockLoc As Coordinates

  Private Shared Function CurrentRocLoc() As Coordinates
    'no one other than adapter can call this method
    Return RockLoc
  End Function


  Public Class TrajectoryAdapter
```

```
    Public Function RetrRocLoc() As Coordinates
      'calls the outer's private shared method
      Return CurrentRocLoc()
    End Function

  End Class

End Class
```

The following code in the **TrajectorConsole** (the **Sender**) can access the necessary data via the **Adapter**'s method.

```
Imports Vb7cr.Trajectory
Public Class TrajectoryConsole

  Dim FindRoc As TrajectoryAdapter
  Public Sub ObtainRocHeading()
    Plot(FindRoc.RetrRocLoc())
  End Sub

End Class
```

In the following example the de-coupling is turned up another notch with the adding of an **Adaptee** interface to the scenario (and a lot more code in the process).

```
Public Class Trajectory

    Private Rock As Asteroid
    Private RockLoc As Coordinates

    Private Shared Function CurrentRocLoc() As Coordinates
    'Only the adapter can call this method
      Return RockLoc
    End Function

  Public Class TrajectoryAdapter
    Implements IRocLoc

    Public Function RetrRocLoc() _
      As Integer Implements IRocLoc.RetrRocLoc
```

```
                'calls the outer's private shared method
                Return CurrentRocLoc()

        End Function
    End Class 'TrajectoryAdapter
End Class 'Trajectory
```

The Interface contains the singleton method reference.

```
Public Interface IRocLoc
    Function RetrRocLoc() As Coordinates
End Interface
```

And the **Sender** stays the same.

```
Inports Vb7cr.Trajectory
Public Class TrajectoryConsole
    Dim FindRoc As TrajectoryAdapter
    Dim GetRoc As IRocLoc = FindRoc
    Public Sub ObtainRocHeading()
        Plot(GetRoc.RetrRocLoc())
    End Sub
End Class
```

What does the **Adapter** pattern achieve?

- The **Sender** and the **Receiver** remain completely disinterested in each other's existence. It's not a matter of loose coupling; there is no coupling at all because the **Sender** has no way of accessing the private data and methods of the **Receiver**. In the above examples the **TrajectoryConsole** makes a reference to the **Adapter,** which it delegates to. If the **Adapter** implements an **Adaptee** interface then the de-coupling becomes more radical because only the implemented method of the **Adaptee** can be called at the **Adapter**. In both cases the **Adapter** makes a private, privileged call to the **Receiver**, where the ultimate implementation lies, which handles the call.

- Method indirection. The "contra-indication" for this loose coupling scenario is that more complexity is added to the application, and it thus becomes a lot more difficult to understand. So all good adaptation needs to be accompanied by clear documentation and diagrams.

- The ability to use an existing class or object whose interface is not suitable for the client—such as referencing COM from .NET applications.

- The ability to create a class that can be used by a wide number of clients local to the framework and even foreign to it. Providing good interface, **Adaptee** support, and pluggable interfaces will help your class become as widely distributed as possible.

- The ability to adapt the original interface of a parent through the multiple implementation of more than one interface. This lets you use any existing subclasses of the parent without having to create an adapter for each subclass.

- The ability to provide an event model in which one or multiple **Receiver** objects, given the alias of **Listener**, can receive the event communications initiated at the **Sender**.

The consequences of adapting an object differ from those of adapting a class. A single **Adapter** object can be engineered to collaborate with many **Adapter** objects, including the other **Adapter**s of subclasses of the parent **Receiver**.

The downside of adapting the object rather than the class is that you lose the ability to override easily. In order to override the **Receiver**'s methods, you will need to create a child-class of the **Receiver** and make this derived/composite class the **Adapter** instead. This also works around the issue of having to share (make static) the method in the **Receiver**, which may not always be convenient or desirable.

The following code now throws inheritance into the mix. It shows the **Sender** object calling the method via the **Adaptee**'s interface but it no longer needs to reference the outer **Receiver** method. With inheritance we now get more de-coupling with respect to the **Receiver**. The **Adapter** object, however, may then reference the parent **Receiver**'s operations, or it can decide to override the parent.

```
Public Class Trajectory

  Protected Overridable Function CurrentRocLoc() As Coordinates
    Return CurrentRocLoc
  End Function

Public Class TrajectoryAdapter
  Inherits Trajectory
  Implements IRocLoc
  Protected Overrides Function CurrentRocLoc() As Coordinates
    'extended method
    'or call to base method
    Return MyBase.CurrentRocLoc
  End Function


  Public Function NewRetrRocLoc() As Integer _
  Implements IRocLoc.RetrRocLoc
```

```
      'calls the overriden method
      Return CurrentRocLoc()
    End Function
  End Class
End Class
```

The **Adaptee** interface and the **Sender** do not need to change.

 *We can use the **MyClass** keyword in the **Adapter** to alternate between using the overridden method or using the original method in the parent class. The **MyBase** keyword also comes into the picture here.*

Its is also easy to add additional listeners to the picture by "registering" them with the sender. This can be done as follows:

```
Imports Vb7cr.Trajectory
Public Class TrajectoryConsole

  Dim GetRoc As IRocLoc = New TrajectoryAdapter()
  Dim GetRoc2 As IRocLoc2 = New TrajectoryAdapter()
ShuttleTrajectory.TrajectoryAdapter()

  Public Sub ObtainRocHeading()
    PlotNearSide(GetRoc.RetrRocLoc())
    PlotFarSide(GetRoc2.RetrRocLoc())
  End Sub

End Class
```

There are also various ways using the flexibility of interfaces and the **Adapter**s for the **Sender** to choose how the call should be handled. It can pass the reference from the **Receiver** to a quasi-constructor or initializer in the **Adaptee** or **Adapter** and the **Adapter** can make the decision (via a formal parameter list). The **Adapter** might also choose to implement additional methods. And in the case of newer or alternate versions of the **Adapter** methods the **Adaptee** interface can inherit another **Adaptee**. The latter example is shown in the following code:

```
Public Interface IRocLoc
  Function OldRetrRocLoc() As Coordinates
End Interface
```

```
Public Interface IRocLoc2
  Inherits IRocLoc
  Function RetrRocLoc() As Coordinates
End Interface

Public Class TrajectoryConsole
  Dim GetRoc As IRocLoc2 = New Trajectory.TrajectoryAdapter()
  Public Sub ObtainRocHeading()
    GetRoc.RetrRocLoc()
    GetRoc.OldRetrRocLoc()
  End Sub
End Class
```

The second method uses the Composite-class pattern in which the **Adapter** is nested in the **Receiver**. The **Adapter** can be automatically instantiated with the **Receiver** and exposed via its interface. The **Adapter** object is instantiated at the same time the **Receiver** is. This latter approach to delegation and adaptation is used by Java as its event-handling model, which we will now investigate.

The Adapter Pattern Event Model

This pattern is effective, but it is also the subject of much debate. It has also caused much attrition between Sun and Microsoft for a number of years. First, let's discuss the concept of an event model. No matter whether you use **Adapter** classes or a **Delegate**, the actual model follows similar processes. So this discussion will apply to the **Delegate** Event Model discussed later.

Events are triggered by occurrences in a **Sender** object—such as a user clicking a button, which is an event in a button object, or a message arriving via email, which is an event in an object that downloads email. When an event is *"fired"* or *"raised"* by the **Sender**, the **Sender** hopes that a single object, or many objects, which are called "listeners," will ultimately receive the notification.

Listening basically means that the objects have been provided the facility to be on the receiving end of an event message. That facility is afforded by the **Adapter**—and the possible intervention of an **Adaptee**, which the **Adapter** implements—or by a **Delegate**. Thus, the event model is no different from the communication processes described in the above section on **Adapter**s and portrayed in Figures 14-5 and 14-6 (and the earlier UML figures in this chapter).

When the **Listener** forwards the message, the **Receiver** is supposed to do something with it. Some receivers may make a sound in response to an event; others may change a background color; others may set in motion a highly complex chain of events that returns data—such as the result of a computation—back to the **Sender** at the "event horizon."

The architecture set up with **Adaptee**s and **Delegate**s dictates that the source of the event and the final place where it is handled are completely separate from each other. As explained, an event can be handled in several separate **Receiver** classes.

In the following example we simulate a simple event. (Trapping mouse clicks and keyboard events are a little too complex to show here, because they require getting into the message pumps of the Windows sub-system. That is handled automatically for us, as discussed later.) This code raises an event when a condition is met inside a loop; as soon as an asteroid moves into a zone that is being monitored by the space crafts' trajectory systems it sends a message to an event handler.

```
Public Class TrajectoryConsole

  Dim GetRoc As IRocLoc2 = New Trajectory.TrajectoryAdapter()
  Public Sub ObtainRocHeading()
    GetRoc.RetrRocLoc()
  End Sub

  Public Sub WatchForRock()
    While Trajectory.MaintenanceState = MaintenanceState.Enabled
      If Not GetRoc.RetrRocLoc > RocLocations.Collision Then
        OnRockRedAlert()
      End If
    End While
  End Sub

  Public Sub OnRockRedAlert()
    Navigation.AlterCourse(GetRoc.RetrRocLoc)
  End Sub
End Class
```

It is possible in the above model to allow more than one **Listener** and **Receiver** to respond to the event. We simply have to "register" additional listener interfaces with the event-handler method, or we can bridge the same interface to multiple adapter classes that implement the interface.

This is the **Adapter** Event Model, albeit a very simple version of it. For starters, registering the additional **Listener** in the event is a tedious process when done manually, as shown here. A better solution would be to create a special collection object that can maintain a list of **Adaptee** interfaces. (This is in fact what is done in Java implementations coupled to several other features of the language that exploit the Adapter/Interface model, such as the ability to declare anonymous inner classes.) Such an object would implement **Add** and **Remove** methods to handle the registration and de-registration of the listeners. The .NET **Delegate** provides such a facility, as we will see later.

Of course, you need formal event objects that are able to trap mouse clicks, keyboards events, and the events generated by various system services—such as closing a window, or changing the property of a form. Fortunately, we don't need to code our own event objects. The .NET Framework has provided the .NET **Event** construct for our event-raising needs.

Finally, this model uses the services of composite **Adapter**s (the listeners), via the proxy of **Adaptee** interfaces, to reference the functionality of the **Receiver** or **Respondent** object or class. Composite or inner classes are used because they have exclusive, privileged access to the methods of the **Receiver**; they may also override the **Receiver**'s methods and provide other means of sophisticated handling.

Delegates use the **AddressOf** operator or the **Delegate** class **Invoke** method to dynamically reference the **Receiver**'s method at runtime. The **Delegate** Event Model is discussed later in this chapter. **Delegate**s, **Adapter**s, and **Adaptee**s are not only useful with events or event-driven scenarios, but they also have their place in general delegation patterns, as the following section illustrates.

Delegation: Please Help Me!

We all suffer at work and at home because we fail to delegate. Frequently, we need to delegate because we have too much to do, but we should also delegate when someone else can do a better job than we can *at the present time*.

That's the human aspect of delegation, and many programmers need to learn how to delegate properly. But, they also need to know when to delegate operations to the methods of other objects. Many times a problem simply calls for a client class or object to delegate additional or alternative execution and processing to another method in another class. In order for the delegate to do its work properly and return the result, a client should never be coupled to the server. Inheritance has been so hyped over the years that many programmers write code as if they believed there were no alternative in object-oriented software engineering. But classes that inherit one-from-the-other are tightly coupled one-to-the-other. Inheritance, as we discussed in previous chapters, is used to build class hierarchies. But, there are many times when problem domains do not qualify for implementation inheritance, or the problems or limitations simply should not be addressed through inheritance.

If you were experimenting with a new breed of dog, the last thing you would think of doing is bringing a cat into the gene pool. But at the code level, thinking in terms of "dogs" and "cats" is not always possible, and often you're tempted to inherit or extend a class just to get some of the fur provided in the parent into your implementation.

While inheritance patterns promote reuse and extension of classes, delegation patterns promote using an uncoupled (not necessarily unrelated) object's functionality. In other words, the class or object that needs functionality calls the other object's method directly, or indirectly, rather than inherit that functionality.

CLASSES AND OBJECTS

You may now feel like saying "Hold it. First, what's the fuss about **Delegate**s and delegation? My classes can call the methods of other classes anyway. Second, what do interfaces have to do with any of this?" You are right to question the logic on both scores. However, **Delegate**s add a lot more spice to the recipe. This will become clearer as we progress.

Inheritance captures the *is-a-kind-of* relationships that couple classes. The relationships between the classes are static and rigid in nature—not to mention very niche or vertically oriented in scope. Delegation patterns instead capture the importance of the *is-a-role* played by relationships. Delegated objects can play multiple roles for other objects. Their methods can be used for multiple roles and called by any classes that need the functionality—even if indirect and especially if the client has no idea where the implementation actually resides. This is what we want in an event model, where event listeners remain disconnected from the objects that cause and raise events. Listeners can be delegated the task of responding to events—from more than one raucous object.

One of the most important differences between delegation and inheritance is that a **Delegate** or an interface is a means of accessing varying functionality at runtime, while inheritance is set up at design time. The same is true of the standard direct method call, the message sent from one object to another. Before we look at delegation in detail, let's first understand why inheritance is not always the panacea it is often thought to be.

The class **Canine** represents an object that contains properties representative of the genus Canidae. A good example of these properties is that all canines howl, especially at a full moon, so the **Canine** class would define a **Howl** method. From the **Canine** class, we can inherit the wild and domestic canines, **Wolves** and **Dogs.** From **Wolves,** we can derive **Foxes, Wolves,** and **Jackals,** because they all share common traits. From **Dogs** we can derive **Greyhound, Labrador, Akita,** and **Pomeranian** among others.

It thus seems logical that to create a new class derived from **Dogs** you can simply inherit from the parent. This serves the purpose of ensuring that all member classes in the **Dog** hierarchy gain access to common functionality. For example, all **Dog** classes inherit the **ClimbOnLap** method, even 150-pound Akitas. It's not usual for big dogs to activate the **ClimbOnLap** desire, but the inclination is still there.

So far so good, but what if your classes now need to perform different roles. What if your inherited class of **Dog** needs to instantiate a dog that leads the blind, rescues people in the mountains, tracks escaped convicts, watches over property, or does police work. There are so many roles that a dog can perform, that to represent them all by inheritance would require you to create hundreds if not thousands of subclasses. As in nature, it's not so simple to inherit what another has taken years to accomplish. As kids we delegate to our parents what we cannot yet achieve ourselves.

In the case of doggy software, you need to delegate the behavior and role (functionality) to another object. So, we create a class called **LeadBlind** and define methods in it that can be used by objects to process the color of traffic lights—**ProcessGreen, ProcessRed, ProcessYellow**.

And it doesn't stop there. While all dogs have an affinity for the human lap, all dogs can play different roles. The class **LeadBlind** may in fact be too specific. Many different breeds of dogs lead the blind, and the same breeds are often trained to perform cadaver work—looking for body parts—do rescue work, help with rehab, track animals, track people, or recover objects. It might then make sense to design an object called **MedServices** that encapsulates similar methods all dogs can use. The dogs that need to play roles that are medical in nature can then delegate to the methods in the **MedServices** class.

Inheritance is great if you need to makes sure that all your **Dog** objects can inherit the **Bark** method from the base class as shown in Figure 14-7.

Figure 14-11, however, represents different **Dog**s (classes) using medical-rescue classes. The **Dog**s delegate the medical-rescue operations to the **MedServices** class. The difference between nature and software programming is that we can make **MedServices** available to *any* **Dog** that needs it. Every **Dog** can play the role of a medical rescue **Dog** by simply accessing medical-rescue operations. In the flesh, dogs need to be trained to perform medical rescue; they don't just adapt overnight. In code, using the object *delegated* the job of providing the medical-services method allows each class of **Dog** to access the *delegate* **MedServices'** operations without having to inherit anything from the **MedServices** class. This is illustrated in Figure 14-8.

Delegation is thus simply a means of reusing or accessing a class' behavior by allowing clients to delegate to it—a technique often referred to as indirection, because the method call, or message as they say in Smalltalkville, bounces off redirecting constructs, such as event-raising methods. The client needing help is the *delegator*, and it calls to the *delegate* class for access to its methods, for a value. But only the delegate decides how it will process the request and how it returns data, if at all.

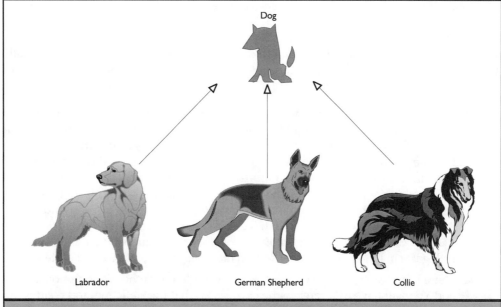

Dog

Labrador   German Shepherd   Collie

Figure 14-7.   *Class **Dog** begets subclasses **Labrador**, **GermanShepherd**, and **Collie**; all require the **BARK** method*

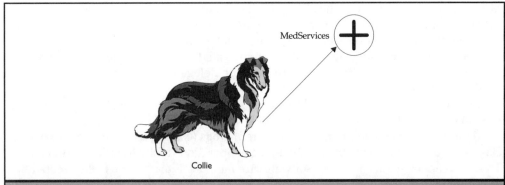

Figure 14-8. *Various subclasses of **Dog** can delegate to the **MedServices** class when they need operations that help them to play the roles of medical-rescue dogs*

The dividing line, thus, between inheritance and delegation takes us back to Chapter 1's discussion of coupling vs. uncoupling, and the relationships among classes, interfaces, and implementation. Inheritance and delegation both have their strengths and weaknesses. What we lose in one we make up in the other. In short, programming without one or the other is like trying to climb a ladder that has every alternate rung missing.

It takes practice and a keen eye for design to see how inheritance and delegation should evolve in your models at the design stage and in code at the code-construction stage. The dynamism of our software can easily be crippled, because the very dynamic access we require on the one hand becomes blocked or restricted by the OO foundation we want on the other hand.

What other problems cannot be (easily) solved by inheritance? We have seen over the past few chapters (especially Chapter 7) that method calls are made either statically to static (shared) methods, or dynamically to instance methods. These standard method calls have the following limitations:

- Methods complete synchronously. Method **A** calls method **B** and then waits for method **B** to complete. Method **B** completes and then returns to **A**, with or without a value. But there are many situations in which dynamism of software requires that the calling method continues to execute code while the called method **B** goes off and does its own thing, returning later with values for **A**, or returning with nothing at all. The problem with synchronous completion is that you can never invoke a method anonymously. And if you can't invoke anonymously, then you can't put your software at the control of the user. *Requirement: Asynchronous and anonymous methods calls for event handling*. We will demonstrate this ability of **Delegate**s in this chapter, in the section on "Delegates vs. Function Pointers."

- There is no way to obtain clean access to a singleton method, anonymously or not. You still have to reference the entire class that the static method resides in or instantiate the entire object and all its data just to call a single instance method.

The problem is exacerbated by certain interface implementation, because you cannot implement a single method—you are required to implement the entire interface. To look at it crudely, that's like having your nagging in-laws with you whenever you want to spend some time alone with your spouse. The so-called function pointer, or rather method pointer, has thus become a desirable construct in OO software. But function pointers are not object-oriented, nor can they be easily couched in OO terms. *Requirement: Function pointers—or, more correctly, method pointers—in acceptable object semantics.*

■ Private methods cannot be called from the external interface of the class, nor can private data be accessed. There are very good reasons to keep data, as well as certain methods and properties, private all the time. The problem is you can't expose and hide these members at will, so an implementation that may require access to a private method or data some of the time will force you to keep the method and data public all of the time. Clearly, that's not a desirable situation; public data is bad for reentrance, threading, maintenance, quality control, and security. *Requirement: Privileged* **(Friend)** *access to private data and methods.*

■ There is no way to easily change or vary the operations—the client calls to alternate functionality—that ensue after a method is called at runtime. A flexible architecture lets you change the implementation behind an interface or allows the **Receiver** and the **Sender** to be related indirectly by way of the **Delegate**—yet they remain totally disconnected at the same time. The polymorphism is also deterministic; the operation is chosen at the behest of the caller. *Requirement: Changing the method implementation at runtime.*

■ There is no way to asynchronously invoke multiple methods on the same method call—not only as a chain but also with each method call concurrent and disconnected from the next. This is clearly a requirement for event-driven programs, where a single event becomes the interest of numerous event-handling methods listening for that event. *Requirement: multicast method calls.*

Forget about inheritance helping you. You can't simply inherit from a parent just to access implementation. Every time you extend a class, you lose your only inheritance ticket for that class (and we will not go into the problem of multiple inheritance again here). Furthermore, you still do not gain access to the singleton method, nor are you able to easily vary its implementation at runtime. In fact, your problem is now much worse if you inherit implementation. You now have numerous methods you might not need cluttering up the class. There is nothing worse than a class full of overloaded and overridden methods you are not using. An example of code clutter is the following non-implemented class:

```
Public Overrides Sub PatheticMethod()
'...to be implemented when we have a reason
End Sub
```

So, you could consider the interface route and implement the method in the class that needs the operations. As fantastic as interfaces are, they have a major drawback: you are forced to implement every method and all the additional words that go with interface implementation. That's a lot of work in exchange for access to one method (even if all you do is re-declare the method without implementing it); and, if you just implement singleton-method interfaces, you end up with a lot of classes.

The **Adapter** route, while powerful, has one major drawback. It is coupled to the **Receiver.** This means that it is impossible to entice a class that implements a sophisticated method into the role of **Receiver.** If the source or ownership of the class in not within reach you have no way of infiltrating an **Adapter** into the class as a composite unless you are allowed to inherit from the intended **Receiver.**

So what are your options? Well, there are two design patterns that are possible in OO languages: **Adapter** classes and a special **Delegate** class that can directly reference the entry point of a method in the **Receiver.** The former is the prodigal child of the Java event model; the latter is the prodigal child of the Microsoft event model (which, it can be argued, is largely the Borland Delphi brainchild). Both patterns can be implemented in Visual Basic .NET, and that's exactly what we will do. We looked at the Interface/Adapter model. Now let's have a look at the Delegate model.

Delegates

What is a **Delegate**? *A **Delegate** is a class that maintains a reference to a single method in an Adapter or a Receiver class.*

Delegates are not new—many Visual J++ developers proved the architecture much to the displeasure of Sun. In fact, the **Delegate** architecture was a principal reason why Visual J++ developers became the seemingly cast-away orphans in the bitter Java custody battle between Sun and Microsoft.

Delegate implementation is now key to event-driven software in .NET, and you need an unshakable knowledge of **Delegate** modeling and construction to effectively program against the .NET event model. **Delegate**s are essential in many areas, especially in creating components and controls. You can program against various event models in a multitude of ways, but the **Delegate** architecture for event-driven software has proven to be one of the most powerful and elegant architectures you will work with in the .NET Framework.

Officially, .NET **Delegate**s have their roots in Microsoft Visual J++ 6.0 (circa 1998), and ultimately they are borrowed from the Object Pascal/Delphi bound method call architecture (circa 1994). The pattern provides a powerful software construct that many non-object-oriented languages—such as C, Pascal, and Modula—have achieved with function pointers. Unlike function pointers, **Delegate**s are couched in object-oriented semantics; in essence, they are reference types that can call shared and instance methods of other classes. The idea of pointers in an OO language conjures up the image in many minds of code that requires a greater than 160 IQ to master; yet, **Delegate**s are type-safe and secure. Also, function pointers can only reference static functions; standard include files or class operations. **Delegate**s can reference both static and instance methods.

In the same fashion in which the **Delegate** class is defined in the Visual J++ **com.ms .lang.Delegate** namespace, the .NET Framework defines its **Delegate** declaration in the **System.Delegate** namespace. As we discussed in the earlier section on the Adapter pattern, **Delegate**s are objects existing for the purpose of directly calling the methods of other objects.

The illustration shows how an instance of a **Delegate** binds to a method in the **Adapter** or **Receiver** class. To the **Delegate,** which is a sophisticated **Adaptee** that has been liberated from its surrogate **Receiver**, both an intervening **Adapter**'s and the **Receiver**'s interfaces and methods are callable entities.

How does the client invoke the **Delegate**? Earlier we saw how a **Client** or **Sender** communicates through the native interface that has an implementation relationship with the **Adapter** class. We also saw how the **Sender** can invoke varying implementations through the interface by passing arguments to the **Adapter**'s methods. Well, lo and behold—a **Delegate** works in much the same way. The big difference is that the **Delegate** class (the interface) and the **Adapter**'s call to the **Receiver** are represented in the same construct—the **Delegate** class.

Note   *In case you were wondering,* **Delegate***s are allocated on the heap as shown in Chapter 2, Figure 2-1. This brings their efficiency (as a type of method pointer) into question, as discussed later in this chapter.*

Like **Adapter** classes, in fact more so, **Delegate**s do not need to know or care about the classes or the objects they reference—the **Adapter** or **Receiver**. They can vary their calls to any object at runtime, which satisfies a desire we expressed earlier. What matters is that the signature of the **Adapter**'s method matches the signature of the method definition prescribed in the **Delegate**. As in the interface-implementation relationship, the **Delegate** definition must match the **Adapter**'s definition. This pattern renders **Delegate**s ideally suited for "anonymous" invocation. Furthermore, a **Delegate** is much more powerful than an inner-class **Adapter** because its construct is specialized to this task, while the interface is not (an argument that Sun claims is irrelevant).

While you can certainly use **Adapter** classes and interfaces for delegation and event invocation, **Delegate**s are the .NET (or rather Microsoft) way, and the following section explores their every aspect so you can work effectively with them.

Understanding Delegates

The best way to get up to speed with **Delegate**s is to understand how they are *declared*, *instantiated*, and *invoked*. Since we cannot instantiate anything before we declare it, let's start with **Delegate** declaration.

Declaring the Delegate

The **Delegate** is declared using the following syntax for **Sub** methods:

[*<attrlist>*] [**Public** | **Private** | **Protected** | **Friend** | **Protected Friend**] _
[**Shadows**] **Delegate** [**Sub**] *name* [([*arglist*])]

which results in the following code:

```
'double sniff action for tracking dogs
Delegate Sub Sniff(ByVal Cloth As Clothing, _
  ByVal Sock As Clothing)
```

and the following syntax for **Function** methods:

[*<attrlist>*] [**Public** | **Private** | **Protected** | **Friend** | **Protected Friend**] _
[**Shadows**] **Delegate** [**Function**] *name* [([*arglist*])]

which results in the following actions:

```
'mouse catching action
Delegate Function CatchMouse(ByVal Cheddar As Cheese) As Mouse
```

These lines can be placed in your class along with the standard type-declarations. You can also declare them deeper into your classes, nearer to the code that uses them.

As you can see, while the **Delegate** is a reference-type, it is not defined like a standard reference type, value type, or even like an interface. You can only define the **Delegate** and bind it (or point) to a single method signature in the **Receiver**. You cannot encapsulate the method between any **Delegate/End Delegate** construct, such as the **Interface/End Interface** keywords.

You should understand that you do not create a **Delegate** class in the way you create a standard class. You use it more like one of the built in types, albeit with the ability to specify the method signature you intend to invoke. Think of it like the **Double** value type that you can access for its **Epsilon** value, and so on.

While the **Delegate** class is the base-class for **Delegate** types, and multicast **Delegate**s, only Visual Basic can explicitly derive from it—in the same way it instantiates the built in types and **Array**s. In other words, is not permissible to derive a new type from a

Delegate type. The **Delegate** class itself is an abstract class; but only the system can use it as a type from which to derive **Delegate** types.

Early Bound Delegate Declares

There are two ways to instantiate the **Delegate** in your code: through early-bound or late-bound semantics. You can forward declare the **Delegate** (early-bound) in your code via its internal or protected instantiation semantics using **New** with the **AddressOf** operator. Or you can use the **CreateDelegate** method of the **System.Delegate** class (which is a late-bound construct). Lets first deal with the early bound syntax.

The following example revisits the earlier **Trajectory** example where we used **Adapter** classes to handle the method calls. In the following example we have the choice of preserving the hidden method in the **Receiver** or we can continue to reference an inner **Adapter** object. For the sake of simplicity let's forgo the inner **Adapter** class and make the **Receiver**'s method public.

```
Public Class Trajectory

   Private Rock As Asteroid
   Private RockLoc As Coordinates

   Public Function CurrentRocLoc() As Coordinates
      Return CurrentRocLoc
   End Function
End Class
```

Now we create our **Delegate** early as shown in the following code:

```
Delegate Function GetRocLoc() As Coordinates
```

This **Delegate** does not have to be declared in any class. It can stand on its own or it can be placed near the point of reference as shown in the following code along with a second **Delegate** that invokes a laser beam.

```
Public Class TrajectoryConsole

   Delegate Function GetRocLoc() As Coordinates
   Dim Traj As New Trajectory()
   Dim GetRocDel As GetRocLoc = AddressOf Traj.CurrentRocLoc
   Dim Plot As New CoordinateObject

   Public Sub ObtainRocHeading()
```

```
      Plot = GetRocDel()
    End Sub

    Public Sub WatchForRock()
      While Trajectory.MaintenanceState = MaintenanceState.Enabled
        ObtainRocHeading
        If Not GetRoc.RetrRocLoc > RocLocations.Collision Then
          OnRockRedAlert()
        End If
      End While
    End Sub

    Public Sub OnRockRedAlert()
      Navigation.AlterCourse(GetRoc.RetrRocLoc)
    End Sub
End Class
```

In this code the **TrajectoryConsole** declares **GetRocLoc**, which is used to delegate to the **Trajectory** class for navigation. The declaration is as follows:

```
Delegate Function GetRocLoc() As Coordinates
```

The **Delegate** is triggered in the **While** loop that keep checking for asteroid positions by simply calling the **GetRocDel**. That's really all there is to using the early bound **Delegate**. The alternative syntax for early bound declaration is as follows:

```
Dim GetRocDel As GetRocLoc
GetRocDel = New GetRocLoc(AddressOf Traj.CurrentRocLoc)
```

or

```
Dim GetRocDel As New GetRocLoc(AddressOf Traj.CurrentRocLoc)
```

which is the same thing as

```
Dim GetRocDel As GetRocLoc = AddressOf Traj.CurrentRocLoc
```

Late Bound Delegate Declares

With all early bound declaration (such as method referencing, object and type declarations, and variable referencing) the compiler has the advantage of being able to check that it can support the desired operations at runtime. You have the same advantage when declaring **Delegate**s early as well. The compiler checks that the **Delegate** has exposed the method reference legally (such as providing the correct return type), and that the method can be called.

When you declare the **Delegate** late you lose this advantage of apriori knowledge about the constructs that are going to be invoked. In particular you lose the advantage of knowing if the **Sender** method's arguments are going to be accepted by the **Receiver** method's parameter list. But late binding is important and would make many advanced programming needs difficult to cater to. In this regard the Framework also supports late declared or late bound **Delegate**s, which are supported by the Visual Basic .NET compiler.

Declaring a late bound **Delegate** requires you to declare the **Delegate** class as we did before. However, the reference variable of the **Delegate** when declared points to nothing and does nothing; it's gutless until runtime, when the variable's reference is cast up to the **Delegate**. After the cast we can invoke the **Delegate** as we do in the early bound semantics.

The late bound route is taken using the **CreateDelegate** method, which should be very familiar to programmers who have programmed against COM and ActiveX components. This syntax is as follows:

```
Function CreateDelegate( _
    ByVal type As Type, _
    ByVal method As MethodInfo _
) As Delegate
```

The method is overloaded to allow you the following options:

- **CreateDelegate(Type, MethodInfo)**   This method creates **Delegate**s for static or shared methods only. These are methods that belong to static classes rather than instances (objects). The **Type** parameter expects an argument identifying the type of the **Delegate** to create. The **MethodInfo** parameter expects an argument describing the method the **Delegate** encapsulates.

- **CreateDelegate(Type, Object, String)**   This method creates a **Delegate** of the specified type that represents the particular instance method to invoke on the specified class instance. The **Type** parameter represents the type of **Delegate** to create, the **Object** parameter represents the class instance on which the method is invoked, and the **String** parameter represents the name of the instance method that the **Delegate** is to represent.

- **CreateDelegate(Type, Type, String)**   This method creates a **Delegate** of the specified type that represents a static method in a specified class. The first **Type** parameter represents the type of **Delegate** to create, and the second **Type** parameter represents the type representing the class that implements the method. The **String** parameter represents the name of the static method that the **Delegate** is to represent.

■ **CreateDelegate(Type, Object, String, Boolean)** This method creates a **Delegate** of the specified type that represents the specified instance method to invoke on the specified class instance with the specified case-sensitivity. The **Type** parameter represents the type of **Delegate** to create, the **Object** parameter represents the **Receiver** class instance on which method is invoked, the **String** parameter represents the name of the instance method that the **Delegate** references, and the **Boolean** parameter represents **True** or **False,** indicating whether to ignore the case when comparing the name of the method.

The following version of the **TrajectoryConsole** application makes use of the late bound semantics. First we cook up the **Delegate** as we did before.

```
Delegate Function GetRocLoc(ByVal some As Integer) As Coordinates
```

Then we set up the late bound declarations in the **Sender** object as shown in the following code.

```
Public Class TrajectorConsole

  Dim Traj As New Trajectory()
  Dim GetRocDel As GetRocLoc
  Dim Traj As New Trajectory()

  Public Sub ObtainRocHeading(ByVal opt As Integer)
    Try
      Select Case Option
        Case 0
          GetRocDel = CType(CreateDelegate(GetType(GetRocLoc), _
          Traj, "CurrentRocLoc"), GetRocLoc)
          GetRocDel.Invoke(Asteroids.AlphaAsteroid)
        Case 1
          GetRocDel = CType(CreateDelegate(GetType(GetRocLoc), _
          Traj, "AltCurrentRocLoc"), GetRocLoc)
          GetRocDel.Invoke(Asteroids.BravoAsteroid)
        Case 2
          GetRocDel = CType(CreateDelegate(GetType(GetRocLoc), _
          Traj, "PortCurrentRocLoc"), GetRocLoc)
          GetRocDel.Invoke(Asteroid.CharlieAsteroid)
        Case Else
          GetRocDel = CType(CreateDelegate(GetType(GetRocLoc), _
          Traj, "StarboardCurrentRocLoc"), GetRocLoc)
```

```
        GetRocDel.Invoke(Asteroids.ZuluAsteroid)
    End Select
  End Try
End Sub
End Class
```

The utility you get from the late declares is evident in the example here where a **Select Case** statement block is used to upcast the **Delegate** variable at exactly the time it is needed. What's the beef? As you can see you can vary which method gets called in the **Trajectory** object.

When you go the early bound route you commit the **Delegate** to a method and you can't change that at runtime. While you get a lot of power by being able to vary method calls like this, which reminds us a lot of the Strategy pattern demonstrated in the last chapter, the technique is dangerous. Why? There is no way the compiler can know in advance if the method being referenced actually exists. If you make a mistake in your code a call to a non-existent method can do some serious damage. In the case of the **Trajectory** programmer, the spaceship would turn to port and collide with the asteroid (well, you will only make that mistake once).

Sorting Data with Delegates

Let's get down to business. The captain wants a sorted list of every asteroid that has passed us over the last few days. Not a problem: the last 50,000 asteroids we passed since moving to warp five were dumped to a huge XML file just this morning. So we only need to serialize that file into an array and then sort it. Looks like a fast partitioned bubble sort or a quicksort will do the trick.

Chapter 12 presented an example of a partitioned bubble sort algorithm in Visual Basic .NET. The idea was that bubble sort could be sped up by $n/2$ operations if we just chopped the array into partitions and then recursively sorted the partitions. We won't go into the specification again, but let's look at the code again.

```
Public Overloads BubbleSort(ByRef array() As Integer, _
  ByVal outerStart As Integer, _
  ByVal innerStart As Integer, _
  ByVal bound As Integer)
  If outerStart >= bound Then
    Exit Function
  End If
Dim outer, inner As Integer
  For outer = outerStart To bound
    For inner = innerStart To bound
```

```
        If (array(inner) > array(inner + 1)) Then
           Transpose(array, inner, inner + 1)
        End If
      Next inner
   Next outer
   BubbleSort(array, outer, inner, array.Length - 2)
End Sub
```

If you examine this method you'll see that the sort divides the array into two and then recursively sorts the two parts. On a big array this doubles the rate of **BubbleSort** sorts. The more you partition the array the more you speed up the sort. The big problem with this algorithm is that the recursion is very tricky. This is not a complex method but the more recursive calls we make the harder it is to factor the recursion. A complex method demanding recursion can take a long time to get right.

Also remember the **If …Then** conditional, which acts as the stopping condition for the recursion. Without it the method would recur until the arrow of time turns around and comes back because the recursive call (the last line in the method in bold) gets recalled repeatedly. So we need something to knock the continuing cycle, short of a huge exception when the method runs out of variables or flies out of the bounds of the array.

I would also hate to try and obviate the recursion using some iterative construct, like a **While** loop. You'll succeed only in pulling your hair out.

But we can easily and very elegantly replace the recursion and the iteration with two or more **Delegate**s with astonishing ease. Implementing this with **Delegate**s was achieved in a fraction of the time it took to factor out the recursive elements. And we get the benefit of dropping the stopping condition. Now look at the same method sans the recursion:

```
Public Overloads BubbleSort(ByRef array() As Integer, _
   ByVal outerStart As Integer, _
   ByVal innerStart As Integer, _
   ByVal bound As Integer)
   Dim outer, inner As Integer
   For outer = outerStart To bound
     For inner = innerStart To bound
       If (array(inner) > array(inner + 1)) Then
          Transpose(array, inner, inner + 1)
       End If
     Next inner
   Next outer
End Sub
```

There are no more recursive calls and no more stopping condition. But take note of the method that calls this **BubbleSort** method.

```
Public Class ArrayUtils

  Delegate Sub DoubleSortDel1(ByRef array() As Integer, _
    ByVal outer As Integer, _
    ByVal inner As Integer, _
    ByVal bound As Integer)
    Dim dblSort1 As DoubleSortDel1 = AddressOf Queuer.BubbleSort

  Public Sub PartitionSort(ByRef Array() As Integer)
    dblSort1(Array, 0, 0, Array.Length \ 2)
    dblSort1(Array, Array.Length \ 2 + 1, Array.Length \ 2 + 1, Array.Length - 2)
    Merge(mergearray)
  End Sub
End Class
```

The **PartitionSort** method almost concurrently sorts the two parts of the single array using the two **Delegate**s. The first **Delegate** sorts the first half and the second **Delegate** sorts the second half. Lastly, the independent call to the **Merge** method combines the partitions into one array.

The **QuickSort** method has a lot more potential for implementing **Delegate**s. First, the **QuickSort** with recursive calls and areas can be replaced with delegate calls called out in bold:

```
Public Overloads Sub QuickSort(ByRef Array() As Integer, _
  ByVal outerStart As Integer, _
  ByVal innerStart As Integer, _
  ByVal bound As Integer)
  Dim outer, inner As Integer
  If Not (outerStart >= Array.Length - 1) Then
    If (bound <= 0) Then
      bound = QuickPart(Array)
    End If
    For outer = outerStart To bound
      For inner = innerStart To bound
        If (Array(inner).CompareTo(Array(inner + 1))) > 0 Then
          Transpose(Array, inner, inner + 1)
        End If
      Next inner
    Next outer
      QuickSort(Array, outer, inner, Array.Length - 2)
  End If
End Sub
```

We can nix the first conditional and the call to partition the array via the **QuickPart** method. We can simply call **QuickPart** from the method asking for the sort because we are not dependent on variables and values to control a stopping condition or for arguments in the recursive calls.

There is also potential to make late bound method calls to different **Transpose** methods. I implemented the **Transpose** three different ways. The first uses simple variable shuffling, the second makes use of a **Stack** object, which is great for juggling objects, and a third makes use of the **XOr** operator to transpose numbers. Here a **Delegate** can be created for each choice of **Transpose** method.

But, most important, we can drop the recursion in this method as well. Have a look at the revised code now:

```
Public Overloads Sub QuickSort(ByRef Array() As Integer, _
  ByVal outerStart As Integer, _
  ByVal innerStart As Integer, _
  ByVal bound As Integer)
  Dim outer, inner As Integer
  For outer = outerStart To bound
    For inner = innerStart To bound
      If (Array(inner).CompareTo(Array(inner + 1))) > 0 Then
        Transpose(Array, inner, inner + 1)
      End If
    Next inner
  Next outer
End Sub
```

And the call to the **Delegates** is as follows:

```
Delegate Sub QSortDel(ByRef array() As Integer, _
  ByVal outer As Integer, _
  ByVal inner As Integer, _
  ByVal bound As Integer) _
Dim QSortD1 As QSortDel = AddressOf Queuer.QuickSortD

Public Sub KwikSortDel(ByRef Array() As Integer)
  Dim bound As Integer = QuickPart(Array)
  QSortD1(Array, 0, 0, bound)
  QSortD1(Array, bound, bound, Array.Length - 2)
End Sub
```

Remember, there are three simple steps in defining and using the **Delegate**:

1. **Declare the Delegate.** A **Delegate** is declared in the class that needs to use it as follows:

```
Public Delegate Compare(ByRef Obj1 As Integer, ByRef Obj2 as
Integer) As Integer
```

2. **Instantiate the Delegate**. **Delegate**s are created using **CreateDelegate** for late-binding as follows:

```
GetRocDel = CType(CreateDelegate(GetType(GetRocLoc), _
Traj, "CurrentRocLoc"), GetRocLoc)
```

And for early-binding as follows:

```
Dim QSortD1 As QSortDel = AddressOf Queuer.QuickSortD
```

3. **Invoke the Delegate**. **Delegate**s are invoked using the Invoke method as follows:

```
SorterDelegate.Invoke()
```

or simply calling the method.

```
IsGreaterThan.Invoke(IntArray(j),(MaxVal))
```

Remembering the three steps will help you successfully incorporate **Delegate**s (and **Adapter** classes for that matter) into your code. Let's now extend this and investigate how **Delegate**s underpin the .NET Framework event model.

Multicast Delegates

Delegates contain members that provide their necessary invocation services—the operations that call the method in the target classes or objects. A **Delegate** can call one method, in which case its invocation list stores only one method reference. This is known as a singlecast, unicast, or noncombinable **Delegate**.

A **Delegate** that invokes a list of method references is a multicast **Delegate**. A **Delegate** that invokes a collection of methods is known as a multicast **Delegate**; that is, the method calls or invocations are combinable. If a **Delegate** only has one method reference, one method to invoke, it is known as a singlecast, or noncombinable, **Delegate**. By combining we mean the operations invoked by the multicast calls are combined into a collection of operations. You combine **Delegate**s using the **Delegate.Combine** as shown in the following code:

```
QSortDeld3 = CType(System.Delegate.Combine_
(QSortDeld1, QSortDeld3), QSortDeld1)
```

The reason behind calling on the **CType** method is that the method that does the combining must be cast up to the same type of the **Delegate**s being combined. If you don't make the **CType** call a type-mismatch exception is thrown.

The entire invocation list is ordered like an array, and each element of the list contains exactly one of the methods invoked by the **Delegate**. There can be duplicate method references in the list, and each method is called once for each reference. The **Delegate** also invokes the methods in the order in which they appear in the list, and the **Delegate** will attempt the invocation each time it is activated.

To evaluate the invocation list at any time, you can call the **GetInvocationList** method on the **Delegate**. This method call returns an array which will either contain one method reference of a singlecast (noncombinable) **Delegate** or more than one method reference in an array representing a multicast (combinable) **Delegate**. The following code demonstrates the creation of the multicast **Delegate** that combines the two calls we made to the **QuickSort** method in the previous section.

> **Note**   *The internal structure of the invocation list is that of a linked list. But the method returns the list in an array for convenience.*

```
Sub Fire Twice
  Dim QSortDel1, QSortDel2, QSortDel3 As QSortDel
  QSortDel1 = AddressOf P1
  QSortDel2 = AddressOf P2

  'Now you create QSortDel3, a cast of QSortDel1 and QSortDel2
  QSortDel3 = CType(System.Delegate.Combine(QSortDel1, QSortDel2), QSortDel1)
  QSortDel3 'Invokes the method call from P1 and P2

End Sub
```

You can call the third **Delegate**'s **GetInvocationList** method, which returns an array of references to you. You can then inspect the array list of method references by simply iterating and displaying the contents of the array to the console.

Delegates are immutable, so once you create them and populate the invocation list, you can't change it. Changing invocation order can only be done by creating a new **Delegate**.

The **Delegate** class also contains methods for combining operations. In other words, you can take one **Delegate** and combine its invocation list with that of another. This action, performed with the **Combine** method, does not change the current **Delegate**. Instead, it returns a new **Delegate** with the combined operations of the two original ones. The **Remove** method performs the opposite of **Combine**; it returns a new **Delegate** with the invocation list of one of the **Delegate**s removed. **Combine** returns null if one of the **Delegate**'s lists is devoid of method references. In this case, the **Delegate** is returned unchanged when the combining or removing operation does not affect anything.

Delegates return values to their clients when the referenced method signature returns a value. For example, when the method to invoke is a function, or a result type, the **Delegate** returns the value it receives from the **Delegatee** or **Receiver** class.

Naturally, multicast methods cannot return values from multiple invocations of function methods; thus, multicast **Delegate**s are declared as **Sub Delegate**s. However, when the signature of a method includes a parameter that is passed by reference, its final value is the result of every method in the list executing sequentially and updating the parameter's value.

Any one of the methods in either the unicast or multicast **Delegate** can throw an exception. When an exception occurs, the method stops executing and the exception is passed back to the caller of the **Delegate**. The remaining methods in the list are not invoked, even if you catch and successfully handle the exception.

*.NET compilers provide two additional methods to the **Delegate** for asynchronous programming, and callback operations: **BeginInvoke** and **EndInvoke**.*

The .NET Framework Event Model: Delegates and Events

Using **Delegate**s in an event model is also not a new idea. Windows-bound Java programmers encountered them in the Windows Foundation Classes and used them to wire up events in applications created with Visual J++.

Delegates are used to bridge the listeners for events (the **Receiver** objects we have been discussing) to the events in the **Sender** object or client. As soon as something happens in the client the **Delegate** is invoked and it calls the method it is pointing to in the **Receiver** object. That's all there is to this event model. Besides several constructs that make wiring and plumbing the event system in your application easier, there is nothing more to the .NET event model than what we have already covered in this chapter. But let's look at the event constructs a little closer.

Suppose my **Trajectory** application needs to constantly monitor space for an asteroid threatening the ship and suddenly one comes into a critical proximity. The software can fire an event that collects the necessary data regarding the coordinates of the asteroid and can pass this information to the **Delegate**. The **Delegate** then invokes the method in the weapons systems represented by the **Weapons** class and fires a laser at the approaching asteroid. To cater to this algorithm, the application could expose an **AsteroidEnter** event or the applications could simply invoke the **Delegate** object.

The class that encapsulates the events maintains the current state of the application, possibly by implementing a state machine, as discussed in the previous chapter. The states provide key information about each event and the operating mode of the application. So in "scanning" or "sensing" mode the application watches for that pesky asteroid and as soon as the closest one returns threatening data the event is fired. The following code is doing exactly what I have just described:

```
Public Class Trajectory
```

```vbnet
   Dim TrajState As New TrajectoryState
   Dim aSensors As New AsteroidSensors()

   Public Function CurrentRocLoc(ByVal ast As Asteroids) As Coordinates
      CurrentRocLoc = aSensors.RetrieveAlpha()
      Return CurrentRocLoc
   End Function

   ReadOnly Property IsEnabled() As Boolean
      Get
         Return TrajState.CurrentState
      End Get
   End Property
End Class

Public Class WeaponsArray

   Public Sub FireAsteroidLaser(ByVal roc As Asteroid, _
      ByVal loc As Coordinates)
      'code not implemented until laser gun meets
      'universal standards
      Console.WriteLine("Firing Laser")
   End Sub

End Class

Delegate Function GetRocLoc(ByVal roc As Asteroids) As Coordinates

Public Module TrajectorConsole
   Dim Traj As New Trajectory()
   Dim Weps As New WeaponsArray()
   Dim RocLoc As New Coordinates()
   Dim Roc As New Asteroid()

   Dim GetRocDel As GetRocLoc = AddressOf Traj.CurrentRocLoc
   Delegate Sub FireLaser(ByVal roc As Asteroid, ByVal loc As Coordinates)
   Dim FireIt As FireLaser = AddressOf Weps.FireAsteroidLaser
   Public Event AsteroidEnter As FireLaser

   Public Function ObtainRocHeading() As Coordinates
      RocLoc = GetRocDel(Asteroids.AlphaAsteroid)
   End Function  Public Sub WatchForRock()
      While Traj.IsEnabled
         ObtainRocHeading()
            If Not (RocLoc.X And RocLoc.Y) > AlertEnum.StandDown Then
```

```
            'Or FireIt(Roc, RocLoc)
            RaiseEvent AsteroidEnter(Roc, RocLoc)
            'Or OnRockRedAlert
        End If
    End While
End Sub

Public Sub Main()
  WatchForRock()
  Console.ReadLine()
End Sub

Protected Sub OnRockRedAlert()
  RaiseEvent AsteroidEnter(Roc, RocLoc)
End Sub

End Module
```

Looking closely at this code, you will notice the constructs that provide the event functionality. Two **Delegate**s are created as follows:

```
Delegate Function GetRocLoc(ByVal roc As Asteroids) As Coordinates
Delegate Sub FireLaser(ByVal roc As Asteroid, ByVal loc As Coordinates)
```

The first **Delegate** you'll remember from our earlier discussion introducing **Delegate**s. It merely fires on a regular basis checking on the movement of asteroids. The second **Delegate** (**FireLaser**) will be triggered in the "event of" the **GetRocLoc Delegate** returning that dangerous information. The following method in the code is wired up to the two **Delegate**s as follows:

```
Public Sub WatchForRock()
    While Traj.IsEnabled
      ObtainRocHeading()
      If Not (RocLoc.X And RocLoc.Y) > AlertEnum.StandDown Then
        'Or FireIt(Roc, RocLoc)
        RaiseEvent AsteroidEnter(Roc, RocLoc)
        'Or OnRockRedAlert
      End If
  End While
End Sub
```

The call to **ObtainRocHeading** brings back data about the coordinates of the asteroid. It continues to check until the **IsEnabled** state of the **Trajectory** application is disabled. As long as the application is enabled it will continue to invoke the **Delegate** and determine if the current location of the asteroid calculates to a sum that is higher than the **StandDown** alert. As soon as it computes lower than **StandDown** the event will trigger the **Delegate**.

The event construct is declared as follows:

```
Public Event AsteroidEnter As FireLaser
```

All it does is bind to the **FireLaser** delegate. But where does it get the parameters needed by the **Delegate**—the asteroid it is aimed at (out of a list of millions) and its current coordinates. The parameter list is provided at the point the event is raised, using the RaiseEvent keyword. That code is as follows:

```
RaiseEvent AsteroidEnter(Roc, RocLoc)
```

You will also see from the earlier example that the above code does exactly the same thing as the following code:

```
FireIt(Roc, RocLoc)
```

As soon as **RaiseEvent** is invoked the **Delegate** calls the **Receiver**, passes in the coordinates and the name of the asteroid to zap and that rock is history.

There are a number of other classes that flesh out this event model. First, an information class is defined to hold any data you need to pass to the **Receiver**. This would be useful for the other users of the **Weapons** class, like the Weapons Officer or a database. This can be any class derived from **EventArgs**, a framework class you must inherit from. While you have no direct control over the **EventArgs** base-class, you can nevertheless override certain functionality from it. This code provides an example of such specialization in this class:

```
Public Class LaserEventArgs
    Inherits EventArgs
    Public ReadOnly Property Information () As String
      ' ...
    End Property
      ' ...
End Class
```

Second, you can also name the **Delegate** with event handling semantics—typically by suffixing the identifier with the words **EventHandler**, as in **AsteroidSightedEvent**

Handler. The so-called **EventHandler** works like any **Delegate** discussed earlier, so don't be confused when you see it littered all over your GUI applications. It can be unicast or multicast, and it encapsulates the reference (binds) to a method or methods in the **EventArgs** specialization. The following code provides an example of an event-handler **Delegate** for the **Trajectory** application:

```
Public Delegate Sub AsteroidEnterEventHandler(sender As Object, _
  e As LaserEventArgs)
```

If you do not need to provide data to the target of the **Delegate**, you can simply use the default event **Delegate** provided by the framework at **System.EventHandler** as follows:

```
Public Event NoDataEventHandler As EventHandler
```

This serves the purpose of simply binding the occurrence to the no-data event handler. Third, an event is defined in the client code using the **Event** keyword and this syntax:

[<attrlist>] [**Public** | **Private** | **Protected** | **Friend** | **Protected Friend**] _

[**Shadows**] **Event** *eventname*[(*arglist*)] _
[**Implements** *interfacename.interfaceeventname*]

Fourth, you should also provide a method—preferably prefixed with the word **On**, as in **OnAsteroidEnter**—that raises the event in your application. This makes it easier to understand what's going on in the application, although at times it seems to be a waste to move the **RaiseEvent** statement to another method, possibly far way from the point it was raised. Using **On** is not required, but this style helps distinguish event methods in your code and helps render your applications easier to follow and maintain. Calling the **OnAsteroidEnter** or **OnAsteroidExit** method (from the client class or an inner-state object) starts the "chain of events" by first invoking the **Delegate**. Here is an example:

```
Protected Sub OnRockRedAlert()
  RaiseEvent AsteroidEnter(Roc, RocLoc)
End Sub
```

Notice that the method raising the event is modified with the **Protected** keyword. Although not essential, I recommend this to allow derived classes to override the event without attaching a **Delegate** to it. When deriving from a parent class that implements the event, the derived class must always call the method in the parent class that raises it (**MyBase.OnEvent**). This ensures that **Delegate**s defined in the base-class receive the event.

Getting Ready to Wire-up: The Event Model in a Nutshell

Let's summarize the event model or pattern preferred for .NET applications:

1. An event **Delegate** is constructed in your client class (or a proxy) as follows:

```
Delegate Function GetRocLoc(ByVal roc As Asteroids) As Coordinates
```

or

```
Public Delegate Sub EventNameEventHandler(sender As Object, _
e As EventNameEventArgs)
```

If you simply need to make something happen and do not need to send data about the source or the event, you can use a simplified no-return **Delegate** as follows:

```
Public Delegate Sub EventNameEventHandler()
```

Remember, however, that the **Delegate**'s method signature and the signature of the target method must match.

2. Your client class (or a proxy) defines an event as follows:

```
Public Event AsteroidEnter As FireLases
```

or

```
Public Event EventName As EventNameEventHandler
```

which bridges the event to the **Delegate**.

3. Your client class (or a proxy) implements a method that is activated to raise the event. This method signature should use the **On** prefix as follows:

```
Public Sub OnAsteroidEnter()
```

4. The class or object that handles the event (the target object) derives from the **EventArgs** base-class. In this class, you will code methods that respond to the **Delegate** invocation. They will perform an action either with or without data (source of the event or event information or both), and they may even return data to the **Delegate**.

At this juncture, it makes sense to stop and ask if such an elaborate delegation construct is necessary, since .NET provides incredible native support for interfaces. This next section tackles the case of (**Adapter**) Interface vs. **Delegate**.

Delegate Events vs. Adapter Events

Delegates and interfaces are similar, because they both allow an interface to be completely separated from an implementation. Interfaces let you vary the implementation that can be accessed via a compatible de-coupled interface. A **Delegate** specifies the signature of a method in the same semantic terms as an interface. In this regard, programmers can write methods—that is, provide implementation—that can be seamlessly coupled with the **Delegate** interface.

If you think about it, interfaces and **Delegate**s do the same thing. Thus, if .NET has interfaces, why does it also need **Delegate**s? There has been bitter debate on the subject in OO circles for many years. Let's investigate the differences for ourselves, starting first with interfaces.

Interfaces may be limited in their utility for several reasons:

- Classes can only implement an interface once.

- Name collisions between interfaces can preclude a class from implementing multiple interfaces. This is one of the reasons multiple inheritance is not available in .NET.

- Interfaces are public, and their members are public. You cannot expose the members via any other access level. This is not a limiting factor for interfaces. If the members were not publicly visible, they would not be able to function as interfaces. However, it may be a limitation in a delegation or event-generating scenario.

To overcome these limitations and to allow a **Receiver**'s or **Target**'s methods to be accessed in a delegation arrangement, we nest an **Adapter** interface as an inner or composite interface class in a **Receiver**, or in a descendent of a **Receiver**. An **Adapter** composite provides a number of benefits in a delegation arrangement. However, often a container such as a form is the source of many events. A form may employ multiple controls and components. It may have many buttons, combo boxes, lists, timers, multiples text boxes, and multiple labels.

Thus, if you employ an interface-based event or interfaced- based delegation model, a typical form may require dozens of **Adapter** implementations— one for every event or delegation instance. The result is an explosion of **Adapter**s. This may have a negative impact on performance, though in most cases this would not be too noticeable. But the bigger issue is that it requires you to be doing a lot of implementation and interface management. In a lengthy application, this could mean managing hundreds of interfaces to accommodate an extensive event-driven solution.

Delegates are easier to manage for the following reasons:

- First, there is no such thing as a "name collision" in the employment of **Delegate**s. As long as a method's signature matches the signature in the **Delegate**, and a return type matches the return type of the **Delegate**, you can call its method anything you like.

- Second, while **Delegate**s can't invoke the private members of **Receiver** objects, it is still possible to invoke friends or the public methods of **Adapter**s.

- Third, classes can implement as many methods as needed, and the **Receiver** objects need no special constructs, such as composite adapter-interfaces, to

CLASSES AND OBJECTS

expose the methods to an event model. Wiring up the events to the **Receiver** becomes nothing more than pointing the **Delegate** to the address of the **Receiver**'s method.

- Fourth, a lot less code is required to implement **Delegate**s.

In addition, **Delegate**s tolerate unhandled events—which is a common occurrence—better than interfaces, because they wrap a single method. In an interface event-based system, a message is still sent to an interface that impacts the receiver, even if the event is unhandled. While **Delegate**s also set messages in motion, the speed and size penalty for the unhandled events is much less than it would be for sending a call to an interface.

To handle even one event, the **Receiver** must still implement the entire event-interface, and the Sender must still raise all of the events in an event interface, whether or not the **Receiver** has been equipped to handle them. **Delegate**s can't bind method calls if there are no methods in the **Receiver** to bind; thus, the case of the missing event handler is not possible in a **Delegate** event model. Even if a method is not implemented in the **Receiver**, there is still zero cost or impact upon the **Receiver**, because no adapter needs to be resident.

The **Delegate** event model and the delegation model are easier to implement, because it's easier to discover the facilities of **Receiver** objects and their inclination to handle events. And, most important, **Receiver** implementors, the programmers, need no extra effort and code in order to offer their classes and objects for event handling. A receiver also requires no special action to register listener status with the construct that marshals the event-handler calls, such as aggregation in an **Adaptee** class. **Delegate**s register listener interests implicitly in the method reference itself.

In this regard, **Delegate**s are able to intrinsically support multicast scenarios. Creating and managing multicast events requires little more than the combination of **Delegate** references, as described earlier. The same task in interface-based event systems is difficult, time-consuming, and error-prone. In short, **Delegate**s make event-wiring easy.

However, the Interface/**Adapter** event model has some advantages over the **Delegate**s, not only for events but to support general **Adapter** pattern algorithms. The following arguments against **Delegate**s have been offered up by the anti-**Delegate** community ever since they were introduced in Visual J++:

- Bound-method references add complexity to the type system. This is not really a complexity cost for the programmer but more of a concern for the type-system architects. However, the bound-method call wrap in the **Delegate** construct is a special case in what is otherwise a pure object-oriented framework, in which classes do everything and are everything. A **Delegate** is thus a new type that needs special treatment by the type system.

- While **Delegate**s are technically classes, the semantics and language needed to implement them is cryptic and complex, even though less code is required in comparison to **Adapter**-interface construction. While interface bridging and interface-member referencing are more difficult than simple object-member referencing, it is still easier to construct the interface reference code than the **Delegate** reference code.

■ **Delegate**s are not very expressive and do nothing else but reference a method call. They cannot implement groups of operations or contain state or be expanded in any way. In many respects, they are nothing but function pointers, which are undesirable in an OO framework.

The argument against **Delegate**s is that the reference to a single method can just as easily be provided in a more simple fashion using a single member **Adapter** object. **Adapter**s obviously require additional code and some incorporation into the **Receiver** code. As an example of the **Adapter** interface model, you can compare sorting with **Adapter**s pattern as I did with the **Delegate**s earlier in this chapter.

Having implemented both models in this chapter we can arrive at a conclusion that the .NET Framework is flexible enough to accommodate both event models. In some scenarios, adapter interfaces are a better fit, while in other instances **Delegate**s do a better job. Claiming that **Delegate**s detract from the OO'ness of .NET is a matter of personal conviction. **Delegate** syntax and semantics do not detract from the overall OO semantics of .NET programming at all.

An explosion of interfaces does not impact the application any more than an explosion of **Delegate**s does. There can be problems, however, with the overhead of the additional adapter classes in an extensive event-driven application. The additional code adds up—a situation that is alleviated with a method pointer, which doesn't impact the **Receiver** in any way.

Delegates, like **Adapter** classes, are more useful for event processing. For example, you might want an object that raises events to be able to call different event handlers under different circumstances. Unfortunately, the object-raising events cannot know ahead of time which event handler is managing a specific event. Visual Basic .NET lets you dynamically associate event handlers with events by creating a **Delegate** for you when you use the **AddHandler** statement. At runtime, the **Delegate** forwards calls to the appropriate event handler.

Although you can create your own **Delegate**s, in most cases Visual Basic .NET automatically generates the **Delegate** and takes care of the details for you. For example, an **Event** statement implicitly defines a **Delegate** class named **EventName .EventHandler** as a nested class of the class containing the **Event** statement—and with the same signature as the event. The **AddressOf** statement implicitly creates an instance of a **Delegate**.

Delegates vs. Function Pointers

Since **Delegate**s are a form of method pointer, it is useful to compare them to function pointers. It can be said that **Delegate**s address many of the scenarios addressed by function pointers. The latter do not belong in .NET, just as they do not belong in any true OO framework. The additional effort to protect the object-orientation, type safety, and security of the runtime would not be worth the effort. But for interest's sake, and to enable us to understand **Delegate**s more, let's see how **Delegate**s differ from C++-style function pointers.

- **Delegates are object-oriented**   **Delegate**s are classes, and while they wrap a call to a method they still behave like objects. C++ function pointers are not classes and have no relationship at all with the C++ object-oriented constructs.

- **Delegates are type safe**   The .NET type system and the CLR enforce type safety of **Delegate**s. To be encapsulated by a **Delegate**, the method reference must precisely match the **Delegate** in number of arguments, type of arguments, and return types. While the method names can differ, if the signatures do not coincide, the **Delegate** cannot be instantiated. Traditional function pointers on the other hand undergo no such safety checks. You can easily crash a system if you cast incorrectly. The power and flexibility you have with function pointers thus carries a price, as C/C++ programmers have discovered for years. Even the most experienced C++ programmers need to walk on eggshells when working with function pointers. In short, **Delegate**s do not let you "muck" with your code.

- **Delegates are secure**   The CLR and type system ensure both the safety of **Delegate**s and that they behave according to the requirements of the security system. In other words, **Delegate**s cannot gain access to code they are not entitled to mix with. C++-style function pointers do not work within a trust-based security system and cannot be adopted into a distributed software model like the .NET Framework, in which everything revolves around secure programming.

Observations

When it invented, or refined, the **Delegate** construct for VJ++, Microsoft proposed the **Delegate** solution not as an alternative to interfaces, but rather as an alternative in the Java event model and to promote the loose coupling between classes in event-handling scenarios, which also set the stage for an elegant anonymous invocation model. Sun refused to accept the proposal to include **Delegate**s in Java, but Microsoft went ahead anyway and built **Delegate** support into the Windows Foundation Classes (WFC)—the precursor to the .NET Framework class library—an issue that had the phones at Sun's lawyers ringing off the hook.

As a result, **Delegate**s could only be used in software that ran on Microsoft's JVM, which was unacceptable to Sun because it, essentially, violated the "write once, run everywhere"™ philosophy and many other "rules" Microsoft had apparently disobeyed. So now you have Visual J++ **Delegate**s in the .NET Framework, "write once, run on every Windows." I have been a Java fan for years, and still am, but I find **Delegate**s so powerful and elegant that it's difficult to see why Sun had such a nervous breakdown over them.

The beauty of .NET is that no matter what you believe, both **Event** models can be adopted with relative ease. While **Delegate**s will be the recommended route for wiring events, Visual Basic .NET's support for native interfaces and the relative ease with which you can construct adapters lets you work with both. That's an amazing amount of power, don't you think?

As for the Asteroid/Trajectory application you can inspect it further in the source code that comes with this book. It is included in the Vb7cr.Asteroids project.

The Complete Reference

Chapter 15

Data Processing and I/O

This chapter deals with Visual Basic .NET's and the .NET Framework's text, character, and binary data processing abilities, as well as the I/O support for streams. We also introduce the regular expression classes and file operations and get acquainted with the extensive support for XML. Data processing and I/O represents the largest chapter in this book (and in most programming books) because it represents the most common task any programmer will be required to perform, from simply reading a command-line argument to loading a data warehouse with a hundred million bytes of information.

The discussion of files and streams also provides extensive examples of managing files and folders, streaming data to and from objects (serialization), and more. Much of the code examples were extracted from a utility called Indexworks, which tests classes I built to work against Microsoft Index Server. These include examples that write noise words (words to strip out of search phrases that Web surfers submit) to a noise words file that is loaded into an array or a linked list in the objects that send queries to Index Server.

The last section in this chapter "Serialization with XML" demonstrates providing XML serialization support for the linked list and node objects we worked on in Chapter 13. It follows after a long discussion on file I/O and demonstrates how to serialize the entire linked list and its node out to a file on the hard disk. It will show how, when starting the application, the entire linked list object and its data nodes can be reconstituted back into the application for immediate use.

Data Processing

Many languages are judged by their ability to manipulate and manage text and characters. Visual Basic .NET is no exception. The reason is simple: Without this fundamental ability, we would be unable to process data and represent it to our users, store it in databases, or print it to documents. There is hardly an application or algorithm that does not require the facilities for some form of text or character manipulation. We write text to the console, to dialog boxes, to event logs, and to the Debug Output window. We capture text from user input, such as reading a character from the console. We break text apart, interpret it, clean it up, and send it back to the screen, to databases, to files, to printers, to e-mail and pagers, and to remote devices.

In today's highly distributed world, text is king. The days of jumping through hoops and eating fire to get binary objects from one point on a network to another have been put behind us with the advent of XML, a sophisticated metadata framework for describing individual elements represented as text. Nowadays, all forms of data, including data destined only for computer consumption, travels with the elements that describe it. This so-called metadata, couched in XML tags, has turned text into the universal language of computing. As long as a receiver can read the XML (using an XML parser or method that reads XML tags) and can support what the text requires, it will know what to do with it.

In the not too distant past, sending a simple string from a VB application to a Java application or a Delphi application (or vice versa) was akin to cracking a coconut with a crayon. Each language would encode and encapsulate its text in a form that other applications could not easily translate. Strings wrapped in various codes needed to be unwrapped or translated—a process akin to the translation of English between a Mississippi maiden out on a first date with a soccer freak from Liverpool. XML, the universal translator, changes all that.

The .NET Framework provides the power of text and character manipulation and processing in the form of several classes that have an exceptional assortment of features for you to use. In particular, we will look at the following namespaces and their respective classes:

- **System.String**   The class that represents an immutable series of characters represented in the value of the **String** reference object. This is the base **String** storage and manipulation object, a type that behaves and is constructed like a fixed array of characters. The **String**'s members provide you with the tools to operate on a series of characters in every conceivable way. Because the **String**'s value is immutable, changes to the **String** are stored in its clone or copy, which then becomes the new **String**.

- **System.Text**   A namespace that encapsulates classes like **StringBuilder**, which is a mutable series of characters. Unlike **String**, it lets you add to and change the original value, in chunks or one character at a time. The **StringBuilder** class is a powerful utility. You saw it in action in Chapter 5, in the "Shifting Bits" section. We discuss it in more detail in this chapter.

- **System.Text.RegularExpressions**   A namespace that represents classes for creating and processing regular expressions. Regular expressions provide a powerful, flexible, and efficient model for processing text.

- **System.IO**   An extensive namespace that encapsulates classes for all manner of file operations, IO, .NET's support for streams, and so on. It also caters to readers and writers, where methods such as **Read**, **Write**, **ReadLine**, and **WriteLine** originate.

- **System.Xml**   A namespace that represents the core XML processing classes. Specifically, we are going to discuss the XML classes that provide core XML text reading and writing functionality. The specifics of XML constructs and concepts such as documents, schemas, paths, and transformations are beyond the scope of this book (in fact, .NET's support for XML is so extensive that it is probably beyond the scope of any book).

Let's start with the construct we are probably the most familiar with, the **String** class.

Working with Strings

Instantiating and initializing a **String** object is easy in Visual Basic .NET. The Framework provides an immutable string-handling class, which is found at the **System.String** namespace. While **String** is a reference type, it behaves a lot like one of the fundamental data types, such as **Decimal** or **Integer**, common in the non-OOP environments. When you need an instance of **String**, you do not need to provide the **New** keyword because you do not have access to the constructor of the object.

There have been many examples of creating and initializing **String** objects in this book, so if you've been reading the chapters in sequence, no doubt you already know how to declare and use an instance of **String** with an initial value. The following code instantiates the **String** object and initializes its value field (**ToString**) with a string:

```
Dim Str As String = "TestString, TestString 1, 2, 3"
```

The **String** class is an immutable type, which means that any operations performed on the **String** return a new—seemly modified—version of the **String** rather than the original instance. By making **String** an immutable type, it can be very efficient to work with. We'll look at the **StringBuilder** class later in this chapter when we explore working with mutable string-like structures. You can also easily convert the **String** object to objects of other fundamental types, such as **Char** and **Byte**. (Refer to Chapter 4 for more information on conversion.)

Members of the String Class

Let's look at the members of the **String** class before we start using them in our example applications. Table 15-1 lists the important methods, minus most of the methods inherited from **Object**.

Clone

This member is inherited as it is in all the .NET types, but it is especially useful in the **String** class. It lets you declare a new object and then clone another object to it bit for bit. You then end up with two identical copies of the **String**. You can then work with the new object in place of the cloned one. The following code demonstrates the cloning of a **String** object:

```
Dim sText, sTextDisplay As String
Dim sClone As Object
sText = "hello world"
sClone = sText.Clone()
sTextDisplay = sClone.ToString()
Console.WriteLine("Result: {0}", sTextDisplay)
```

What You Need to Do	Method or Property to Use
Get the **Char** at a specific index in the **String**	**Char** (p)
Get the length of the **String**	**Length** (p)
Compare two **String**s	**Compare** (s), **CompareOrdinal** (s)
Compare a target **String** to a source **String**	**CompareTo**
Join source **String** to target **String**	**Concat** (s)
Copy source **String** object to target **String**	**Copy** (s)
Clone the source **String**	**Clone**
Copy characters into an array	**CopyTo**
Test the beginning and ends of **String**s	**EndsWith, StartsWith**
Format numeric **String**s	**Format** (s)
Get the index location of characters in a **String**	**IndexOf, LastIndexOf, LastIndexOfAny**
Insert sub-**String**s into a **String**	**Insert**
Obtain a reference to a **String**	**Intern** (s), **IsInterned** (s)
Manipulate sub-**String**s	**Join, Split** (s)
Pad **String**s with additional characters	**PadLeft, PadRight**
Remove characters from a **String**	**Remove**
Replace characters in a **String**	**Replace**
Isolate a sub-**String** from a **String**	**SubString**
Trim characters from the beginning and ends of **String**s	**Trim, TrimEnd, TrimStart**
Copy the characters in the **String** to a Unicode character array	**ToCharArray**
Covert all characters in the **String** to lowercase	**ToLower**
Return the value of the **String** object	**ToString**
Convert all the characters in the **String** to uppercase	**ToUpper**

Table 15-1. *String Manipulation Methods and Properties (Several are Static)*

CLASSES AND OBJECTS

Compare

The **Compare** method lets you compare two **String** object values to each other. This static method returns 0 for a match and –1 for no match, indicating the equality, or not, of the two values (see Table 15-1). The syntax is as follows:

```
String.Compare(StrA, StrB)
```

Consider the following code:

```
Dim sText, sNewText, sTextDisplay As String
Dim num As Integer
sNewText = "hello world"
sTextDisplay = "hello world"
num = sText.Compare(sNewText, sTextDisplay)
Console.WriteLine("Result: {0}", CStr(num))
```

The **String**s are equal and the output to the console is

```
Result: 0
```

You also do not always need to call an instance method because a lot of methods provided by the **String** class are static. Here's an example:

```
num = String.Compare(sNewText, sTextDisplay)
```

In Table 15-1 the static methods are denoted with the "(s)" symbol.

This fast method can tell you whether or not you have a match of values. You can ignore the reason for the mismatch. You can also use the **CompareTo** method to test for actual equality of the object's values. Table 15-2 lists the return values and their meanings for the Compare method.

If the Ordinal Returned Is	Then
Negative ordinal	**strS** is less than **strT**
0	**strS** and **strT** are equal
Positive ordinal	**strS** is greater than **strT**

Table 15-2. *Compare Method's Return Codes*

A similar method in the **String** object is **CompareOrdinal**. This member compares the **String** object without regard for language or culture. The following line

```
n = sText.CompareOrdinal(sNewText, sTextDisplay)
```

returns the same three result ordinals as the **Compare** method.

CompareTo

The **CompareTo** method is similar to the preceding comparison method, but instead of taking two **String** objects as parameters, the method compares the **String** parameter to the owner of the method. Consider the following code:

```
Dim sText1, sText2 As String
Dim num As Integer
sText1 = "hello human"
sText2 = "hello human"
num = sText1.CompareTo(sText2)
Console.WriteLine("Result: {0}", CStr(num))
```

The **String** objects are equal.

Concat

The **Concat** method concatenates (joins) two or more **String**s together. The result is a new, third **String** that is the combination of **String** values of the source and target objects and that contains the concatenated **String**s. The syntax is as follows:

```
ing1.Concat(ing2)
```

or

```
String.Concat(ing1, ing2)
```

which joins **ing1** and **ing2** to form a new **String**. However, the method can take up to three **String**s and has application in **Array** types. The following code shows how you can concat three **String** values:

```
Dim ing1, ing2, ing3 As String
ing1 = "Florida, "
ing2 = "we have a (voting) problem."
Console.WriteLine(String.Concat(ing1, ing2, ing3))
```

The output to the console is the **String** representation of **ing3**, which is the concatenation of **ing1** and **ing2**. Note that the original **String**s **ing1** and **ing2** are not modified in any way. The result to the console is as follows:

```
Florida, we have a (voting) problem.
```

Copy

The **Copy** method provides a simple means of copying one **String** object to another. The original value is left untouched. The **Copy** syntax is demonstrated in the following example:

```
Dim ing1, ing2 As String
ing1 = "Florida, we have a (voting) problem."
Console.WriteLine(ing2.Copy(ing1))
```

If you cannot guess what gets written to the console, then *you* have a problem. You do not need to forward declare a source **String** object to copy from, as the following example illustrates:

```
Dim orida As String
Console.WriteLine(orida.Copy("Florida, we have a (voting)
problem."))
```

CopyTo

The **CopyTo** method is a little more complex than the **Copy** method, but it works harder to give much more manipulation power. The **CopyTo** method takes a character at the source position of a **String**, at your selected index value, and then copies the character to a destination position in a character **Array**. The base syntax is as follows:

```
Str1.CopyTo(int1, myArray, int2, int3)
```

The character at **int1** is the starting point or source index in the source **String**—in the preceding example, the source is **Str1**. The parameter **myArray** is the destination **Array** you must provide. Finally, **Int2** is the starting index or destination index in the target **Array** and **Int3** is the number of characters to copy from the source **String**, as shown in the following example:

```
Dim intI As Integer
Dim str1 As String = "Houston, we have a problem."
```

```
Dim myArray(5) As Char
str1.CopyTo(0, myArray, 0, 4)
str1.CopyTo(10, myArray, 4, 1)
For intI = 0 To 4
  Console.WriteLine(myArray(intI))
Next I
```

In the preceding code example, we have declared an array (**myArray**) of type **Char** to hold five characters. Then we copy four characters into **myArray** starting at index 0 and ending at index 3. Next, using **str1**, we copy character "e" in position 10 in the **String** to the index position 5 in the **Array**. The characters copied into the **Array** are "h," "o," "u," "s," and "e."

Finally, to write the **Array** contents to the console, we used a **For . . . Next** loop (refer to Chapter 6), which loops four times to output the characters and display the following:

```
h
o
u
s
e
```

EndsWith, StartsWith

The **EndsWith** and **StartsWith** methods are useful for simple checks on whether certain **String**s or even single characters appear at the beginning or end of **String**s. You will receive **True** or **False** if the **String** you are hoping to find *is* or *is not* at the end or beginning of your **String**. Let's check out this useful method:

```
Str.EndsWith()
Str.StartsWith()
```

Have a look at the following example:

```
Dim str1 As String = "Houston, we have a problem."
If str1.EndsWith("problem") Then
  console.WriteLine("true")
End If
```

In the example, the output to the console can never happen because the period has been omitted from the **EndsWith** test and the statement is thus **False**.

Equals

The **Equals** method—inherited from **System.Object**—provides a means of determining, through the return of **True** or **False**, if a certain **String** is equal in value to another **String**. Thus, if we think **str1** is "X," the **Equals** method allows us to determine if it is indeed "X." This method is convenient for testing values of **Strings** to control flow in a method—a so-called sentinel construct. The syntax is as follows:

```
str1.Equals(str2)
```

Now consider the following code (note that case is important):

```
Dim s1 As String = "Florida, we are T-10 and counting."
If s1.Equals("Florida, we are T-10 and counting.") Then
  Console.WriteLine("True")
End If
```

Now you can also use the **Is** operator or the equal (=) operator to obtain the same results in the preceding code. We only need to change one line, as follows:

```
If s1 Is "Florida, we are T-10 and counting." Then
```

Note *It's a good idea to get into the habit of using the **Is** operator.*

Format

The .NET Framework contains a **String** formatting method that provides standard formatting of a **String**'s characters, or the specified sub-**String**. It works by replacing the target **String** with the textual equivalent of a numeric, date and time, or enumerator value. The legacy Visual Basic **Format** function has also been wrapped by the .NET Framework, as demonstrated later in this section. See also "String Formatting," later in this chapter.

Note *The {0} specifier is the placeholder for a string of characters to be inserted into a **String** object. It works like the C language's % specifier .*

The types are formatted through the **Format** function applicable to the data type being rendered. The basic syntax is as follows:

```
Str1.Format("The answer is {0:####}", answer)
```

Format is a static method, so the following syntax is also applicable:

```
Str1 = Format("The answer is {0:####}", answer)
```

The .NET formatting support also provides for custom formatting for more flexibility, which is illustrated later in the section "String Formatting."

IndexOf, LastIndexOf

The **IndexOf** and **LastIndexOf** methods provide a facility for locating a character or a set of characters in a **String** object. In a word processing application, for example, you will want to provide your users with the facility of searching for and replacing strings. Consider the following code snippet:

```
Dim str1 As String
str1 = "I waste a lot of time playing with my xbox."
Console.WriteLine(str1.IndexOf("x"))
```

It is rather easy to work out in your head the output to the console. It is the integer 38 of course—being the last character in the above **String** object. If the character is not present in the **String**, a return value of –1 is reported.

The method **LastIndexOf** provides a slightly different facility. It reports the last occurrence of a particular character in the **String**. In the preceding example, there are two occurrences of "x" so the return value is 41. But if we searched for "o" we could get 17 as the return value because there are two occurrences of "o" in the **String**, and we are looking for the last one.

Insert

The **Insert** method inserts a **String** into another **String** in a location specified in the method. Consider the following code:

```
Dim str1 As String
str1 = "The little black xbox"
Console.WriteLine(str1.Insert(4, "very expensive "))
```

The **String** argument "very expensive" is inserted at integer 4 in the **String** s1 to display to the console the following:

```
The very expensive little black xbox
```

Intern, IsInterned

Often, **String** objects can get quite large, and the task of comparing them can become quite slow in computing terms. The **Intern** method provides a facility for obtaining a reference to a **String** that speeds up comparison operations by an order of magnitude. The **Intern** method is also useful for creating **Strings** on-the-fly and then providing an immediate facility for using the **String** in a number of operations.

When you invoke the **Intern** method of different **String** objects that have the same content as the original **String** object, you will obtain a reference to the first object. For every object instantiated that is the same as the original object, you will obtain multiple references to the same object by interning each new **String** object. Interned **Strings** can be compared with the = operator (equals) instead of calling the more resource-intensive **equals** operator, which literally has to compare each character in the corresponding **String**.

The following code demonstrates the interning of **String** objects:

```
Public Sub TestIntern
Dim s1, s2, s3, s4 As String
s1 = "The small brown fox"
s2 = "The small brown fox"
s3.Intern(s1)
s4.Intern(s2)
  If s3 = s4 Then
    Console.WriteLine("Jeez that was quick")
  End If
End Sub
```

The **String** object also provides the method **IsInterned**, which when called provides a reference to the **String** if it has already been interned. Otherwise, it returns null and you can proceed to call **Intern** or handle the null return value as an exception.

Join, Split

The **Join** and **Split** methods are used with arrays. The **Split** method can be used to chop up a **String** at the characters in the **String** you designate as separators. The pieces of **Strings** can then be slotted into a **String** array. The **Join** method copies the **String** elements occupying an array of type **String** and connects them with separators or characters to assemble a **String**.

The following code first designates a separator character. In this example, we designate the blank character (" ") as the separator (**str1**). The code shows that **str1** is passed as a char into an array of type char. We then use the element of the array as the specifier for chopping up the **String str2** (**str2** is *split* at the blanks in the lines). At this point in the execution, **sArray** holds a **String** (each word in the sentence) in each element or index position in the array.

```
Dim intI As Integer
Dim str1, str2 As String
```

```
Dim seps(1) As Char
Dim sArray(6) As String
str1 = "   "
str2 = "The cow jumped over the moon"
str1.CopyTo(0, seps, 0, 1)
sArray = str2.Split(seps)
For I = 0 To 5
    Console.WriteLine(sArray(I))
Next I
Console.WriteLine(s2.Join("*", sArray))
```

The first console output is derived from a loop that copies each word from the array and displays it on the console. The second console output joins copies of all the elements of the first array into a sentence, using the star or asterisk (*) character as the separator. The console's output is as follows for the first call to the **WriteLine** method:

```
The
cow
jumped
over
the
moon
```

The console's next output is as follows for the second call to **WriteLine**:

```
The*cow*jumped*over*the*moon
```

PadLeft, PadRight

The padding method either left or right aligns a **String** in its field and then pads the other end of the **String** with spaces or a specified character to fill up the specified length of the field. The following code works for both left and right padding of **Strings**:

```
Dim s1 As String = "Holy cow"
Dim dot As Char = Convert.ToChar(".")
Console.WriteLine(s1.PadLeft(20, dot)) 'or
Console.WriteLine(s1.PadRight(20, dot))
```

The output to the console is as follows:

```
Holy cow.........
...........Holy cow
```

*Observe the **Convert.ToChar** method used in the preceding code to change a character literal to a char value. There is no character literal that forces conversion to type char.*

Remove

Remove lets you remove a designated number of characters from a particular start index in a **String**. The following code demonstrates this:

```
Dim s1 As String = "Holly cow"
Dim s2 As String = s1.Remove(3, 1)
Console.WriteLine(s2)
```

Replace

Replace lets you replace a character in a **String** with a new character. Consider the following code:

```
Dim str As String = "Holy cow"
Dim charc As Char = Convert.ToChar("w")
Dim charc1 As Char = Convert.ToChar("p")
str = str.Replace(charc, charc1)
Console.WriteLine(str)
```

The console output is as follows:

```
Holy cop
```

SubString

The **SubString** method lets you split a **String** into two **Strings** at the index location in the **String** and then return the sub-**String** including the character at the index location. In the example provided, we want to return just the sub-**String** and not the blank or space character at the location we obtain for the start of the sub-**String**. The following code adds 1 to the location of the blank or space between the two words. We used the **IndexOf** method to find the blank:

```
Dim str As String = "Holy cow"
Dim intI As Integer = str.LastIndexOf(" ")
str = str.SubString(int + 1)
Console.WriteLine(str)
```

This returns just the word "cow" to the console.

ToCharArray

The **ToCharArray** method lets you copy a **String** to a character array. You can easily reference the character array as follows:

```
Dim str As String = "Holy cow"
Console.WriteLine(str.ToCharArray(0, 2))
```

The console output is as follows:

```
ho
```

ToLower, ToUpper

Often, you might need to convert characters to either upper- or lowercase. The methods **ToLower** and **ToUpper** allow you to toggle text as lower- or uppercase. For example, the code

```
Dim str As String = "holy cow"
str = str.ToUpper()
Console.WriteLine(str)
```

writes HOLY COW to the console. **ToLower** converts uppercase to lowercase. Incidentally, the method does not take an argument.

Trim, TrimEnd, TrimStart

The trim functions let you trim white spaces from the beginning and end of **String**s. **Trim** lets you trim the start and end of **String**s with one call.

Classic Visual Basic String Functions

In addition to the **String** object's methods, the legacy-style VB functions listed in Table 15-3 are also supported by Visual Basic .NET. These are accessible via the **Microsoft.VisualBasic.Strings** namespace.

These **String** manipulation functions are just as useful in Visual Basic .NET as they are in classic VB. If you can easily solve your problems using the native **String** manipulation methods, then you should prefer those so that you lessen the burden of and reliance on legacy code. On the other hand, if one of these functions does the job, don't hesitate to use it. I have used several of these functions in .NET applications to reduce the amount of code I needed to write to achieve a certain result and I found no noticeable problems or overhead.

What You Need to Do	Function to Use
Compares two **String**s	**StrComp**
Converts **String**s according to constants supplied to the function	**StrConv**
Returns a **String** or object consisting of the specified character repeated the specified number of times	**StrDup**
Returns a **String** in which the character order of a specified **String** is reversed	**StrReverse, InStrRev**
Converts **String**s from uppercase to lowercase and vice versa	**LCase, UCase**
Inserts spaces in **String**s	**Space**
Determines the length of a **String**	**Len**
Reformats **String**s	**Format, FormatCurrency, FormatDateTime, FormatNumber, FormatPercent**
Retrieves the sub-**String** the specified number of characters from the left or right	**Left, Right**
Retrieves a **String** left- or right-aligned to a specified number of characters	**LSet, RSet**
Retrieves sub-**String**s	**Mid**
Strips spaces from **String**s	**LTrim, RTrim, Trim**
Finds a sub-**String** in a **String**	**InStr, InStrRev**
Retrieves the **Integer** values associated with ANSI and ASCII characters	**Asc, AscW**
Retrieves the character associated with the specified character code	**Chr, ChrW**
Returns a **Char** value representing the character from the specified index in the supplied **String**	**GetChar**
Replaces one **String** with another	**Replace**

Table 15-3. *Classic Functions Wrapped by the **Microsoft.VisualBasic.Strings** Class*

What You Need to Do	Function to Use
Retrieves subsets (as arrays) of **String**s from a filter applied to an array	**Filter**
Retrieves an array containing the result of splitting a **String**	**Split**
Retrieves the result of a join of two **String**s	**Join**

Table 15-3. *Classic Functions Wrapped by the **Microsoft.VisualBasic.Strings** Class* (continued)

To use these functions, you need to reference the Visual Basic Run-Time Library.

String Formatting

As mentioned earlier, the .NET Framework provides three types of format providers. These provide formatting of numeric **String**s, data and time **String**s, and **Enumeration String**s. These "formatters" are wired into the **ToString** methods of the fundamental data types that implement the **IFormattable** interface, such as **Int32** (**Integer**), **Int64** (**Long**), **Single**s, **Double**s, **DateTime**, **Enumerator**, and the like.

As demonstrated earlier in this chapter and in various places in this book, these formatters are also present in the workings of the **Console** and **String** classes and other classes, such as those in the **System.IO** namespace, that process text. See the "Format" section earlier in this chapter.

Classes that provide the formatter "masks" or "patterns, such as {00:00} and separator tokens and decimal point tokens, are known as format providers. These classes implement the **IFormatProvider** interface.

The format provider is typically passed to an overloaded **ToString** method as defined by the **IFormattable** interface. If no provider is passed, then the method can be coded to use a default format provider against the arguments processed to it. In such situations where no providers are passed, the formatting is implicit to the method, which obtains the mask and its tokens from one of the standard framework format providers. However, **ToString** methods typically implement **IFormattable** to provide the support in one of their overloaded variations (such as **Console.WriteLine**).

The key format providers that implement the **IFormatProvider** interface are listed as follows:

- **NumberFormatInfo**   Formatting information for numeric data types
- **DateTimeFormatInfo**   Formatting information for **DateTime** objects
- **CultureInfo**   Formatting information for different cultures

In cases where formatting information is needed but no **IFormatProvider** is supplied, the **CultureInfo** object associated with the current thread is usually used.

NumberFormatInfo

The standard **NumberFormatInfo String** comprises a character that represents the format, such as *currency* or *decimal,* followed by digits that represent the precision. Table 15-4 lists the standard formats supported by the **Format** method.

Currency

The **Currency** formatter is used to convert the given numerical value to a currency value. The currency value can contain a locale-specific currency amount. The format information is determined by the current locale, but you can override this by passing in the **NumberFormatInfo** object as an argument. The default in the United States is, of course, USD. For example:

```
Console.WriteLine("{0:c}", 1250.99)
Console.WriteLine("{0:c}", -1250.99)
```

 *The **Console.WriteLine** method automatically calls **String.Format** as demonstrated in the preceding and following examples (as does **ToString** if the argument can be formatted as defined by the **IFormattable** interface).*

Format Specifier	Output
C, c	**Currency**
D, d	**Decimal**
E, e	**Exponential** (scientific)
F, f	**Fixed-point**
G, g	**General**
N, n	**Number**
R, r	**Roundtrip.** This format ensures that numbers converted to **String**s will get the same value when they are converted back to numbers.
X, x	**Hexadecimal**

Table 15-4.   *The Built-in Formatters, or Format Providers, that Implement **IFormatProvider***

The output to the console is the following:

```
$1,250.99
($1,250.99)
```

Decimal

The **Decimal** formatter can be used to convert the numerical value to an **Integer** value. For example:

```
Console.WriteLine("{0:D}", 125099)
```

writes 125099 to the console, but

```
Console.WriteLine("{0:D10}", 125099)
```

writes 00000125099 to the console, representing ten digits (five as passed by the parameter and five zeros for left-padding).

Exponential

The **Exponential** formatter (scientific) formats the value passed to the **String** in the form of

```
m.dddE+xxx
```

As indicated, the decimal point is always preceded by one digit. The number of decimal places is specified by the precision specifier (six places is the default). You can use the format specifier to determine the case of the "E" in the output, as illustrated in the following examples:

```
Console.WriteLine("{0:E}", 125.8)
Console.WriteLine("{0:E10}", 125.88)
Console.WriteLine("{0:E5}", 125.88))
```

This example writes the following to the console:

```
1.258000E+002
1.2580000000E+002
1.25880e+002
```

Fixed-Point

The **Fixed-Point** formatter is used to convert the value provided in the argument to a **String** and then specify the number of places after the decimal point to round the number. For example, the following code:

```
Console.WriteLine("{0:F}", 125.88)
Console.WriteLine("{0:F10}", 125.88)
Console.WriteLine("{0:F0}", 125.88)
```

provides this output:

```
125.88
125.8800000000
126
```

General

The **General** formatter is used to convert the **String** to a numerical value of either fixed-point format or scientific format. This is often used in calculator software to write to the format that provides a more compact representation. For example, the following code:

```
Console.WriteLine("{0:G}", 12345.67)
Console.WriteLine("{0:G4}", 12345.67)
Console.WriteLine("{0:G6}", 12345.67)
```

provides the following output to the console:

```
12345.67
1.2345E4
12345.7
```

Number

The **Number** format allows you to convert a large number that has a decimal point to a number that can be better read with commas. For example, the following code:

```
Console.WriteLine("{0:N}", 12345.67)
Console.WriteLine("{0:N3}", 12345.67)
```

displays the following on the console:

```
12,345.67
12,345.678
```

The default is two decimal places, while in the second example, we explicitly specified three decimal places.

Round-trip

Round-trip is an implicit format provider that ensures that data converted from number **String**s will get the same value when converted back.

Hexadecimal

If you need to convert a **String** value to hexadecimal, you can use the **Hexadecimal** formatter. In the following example, the uppercase *X* gives you uppercase letters, and the lowercase *x* gives you lowercase letters. The minimum number of digits to display is set by the precision specifier. If the number is smaller than the precision specifier, it will be padded to the width specified. The following code provides examples (note the case differentiation, emphasized by the author):

```
Console.WriteLine("{0:x}", 123)
Console.WriteLine("{0:X3}", 123)
```

The output is as follows:

```
7b
07B
```

DateTimeFormatInfo

The **DateType** data type also implements **IFormattable**, which allows date and time information to be formatted as a **String**, like the numeric types, in the overloaded **DateTime.ToString** method. The format provider for **DateTime** formatting is the **DateTimeFormatInfo** class.

Again, both standard format **String**s and custom format **String**s and the output are influenced by the culture context associated with the current thread or a **CultureInfo** object passed to the **ToString** method (see also Chapter 4). Custom format **String**s allow you to be more flexible and are useful in the rare occasions that the standard formatters are insufficient.

Table 15-5 provides the list of standard **DateTime** format **String**s. These **String**s are interpreted as standard format specifiers if they contain only one of the single format specifiers listed here. Some of the formatters have specific nuances that may require escape characters and certain treatment to obtain the desired result. Be sure to consult the .NET Framework SDK for specifics.

The formatters will throw **ArgumentException** if the specified format characters are not expected by the receiving method. As long as you stick to the characters in the table, you will not have a problem.

Format Specifier	Output
d	Short date pattern displays a pattern defined by **DateTimeFormatInfo.ShortDatePattern** property
D	Long date pattern displays a pattern defined by the **DateTimeFormatInfo.LongDatePattern** property
t	Short time pattern displays a pattern defined by the **DateTimeFormatInfo.ShortTimePattern** property
T	Long time pattern displays a pattern defined by the **DateTimeFormatInfo.LongTimePattern** property
f	Full date/time pattern (short time) displays a combination of the long date and short time patterns, separated by a space
F	Full date/time pattern (long time) displays a pattern defined by the **DateTimeFormatInfo.FullDateTimePattern** property
g	General date/time pattern (short time) displays a combination of the short date and short time patterns, separated by a space
G	General date/time pattern (long time) displays a combination of the short date and long time patterns, separated by a space
M or m	Month day pattern displays a pattern defined by **DateTimeFormatInfo.MonthDayPattern** property
R or r	RFC1123 pattern displays a pattern defined by the **DateTimeFormatInfo.RFC1123Pattern** property
s	Sortable date/time pattern that conforms to ISO 8601. It displays a pattern defined by the **DateTimeFormatInfo.SortableDateTimePattern** property. The property references the **CultureInfo.InvariantCulture** property, and the format follows the custom pattern "yyyy-MM-ddTHH:mm:ss."

Table 15-5. *The Standard **DateTime** Formatters and property/patterns associated with the current thread or by a specified format provider*

u	Universal sortable date/time pattern displays a pattern defined by the **DateTimeFormatInfo.UniversalSortableDateTime Pattern** property. Because it is a defined standard and the property is read-only, the pattern is always the same regardless of culture or format provider. The format follows the custom pattern "yyyy-MM-dd HH:mm:ssZ."
U	Universal sortable date/time pattern displays a pattern defined by the **DateTimeFormatInfo.FullDateTimePattern** property. Note that the time displayed is for the universal time, rather than local time.
Y or y	Year month pattern displays a pattern defined by the **DateTimeFormatInfo.YearMonthPattern** property
Any other single character	Regarded as an unknown specifier

Table 15-5. *The Standard **DateTime** Formatters and property/patterns associated with the current thread or by a specified format provider* (continued)

However, be aware that adding a single character to the formatter, even a white space, such as {"u"} will cause the format **String** to be interpreted as a custom formatter. You also need to take into account that formatters are influenced by the settings in the Regional Options control panel. This means that computers with different cultures or different date and time settings will cause different patterns to be displayed.

Table 15-6 displays the standard format strings for formatting **DateTime** objects. Date and time separators displayed by formatters are defined by the **DateSeparator** and **TimeSeparator** characters associated with the **DateTimeFormat** property of the current culture.

While using the formatters specified in Table 15-6 is straightforward, keep in mind that, in cases where the **InvariantCulture** is referenced by the "r", "s", and "u" specifiers, the characters associated with the **DateSeparator** and **TimeSeparator** characters do not change based on the current culture.

Custom Formatters

As mentioned earlier, custom formatters can be used to control the output format of your values. When you use the **Custom** format option, special characters are used as a template to shape the output. Characters that are not recognized are simply copied to the output. Here are some examples of custom formatters for numerical data.

Format Specifier	Culture Information	Output
d en	US	4/10/2001
d en	NZ	10/04/2001
d de	DE	10.04.2001
D en	US	Tuesday, April 10, 2001
T en	US	3:51:24 PM
T es	ES	15:51:24
f en	US	Tuesday, April 10, 2001 3:51 PM
f fr	FR	Mardi 10 avril 2001 15:51
r en	US	Tue, 10 Apr 2001 15:51:24 GMT
r zh	SG	Tue, 10 Apr 2001 15:51:24 GMT
s en	US	2001 0410T15:51:24
s pt	BR	20010410T15:51:24
u en	US	20010410 15:51:24Z
u sv	FI	20010410 15:51:24Z
m en	US	April 10
m ms	MY	10 April
y en	US	April, 2001
y af	ZA	April 2001
L en	UZ	Unrecognized format specifier; a format exception is thrown

Table 15-6.   *Formatters for the **DateTime** Object*

Digit or Zero for a Placeholder

The following code formats the output to the designated number of digits using a zero as the placeholder. If there are more placeholders than digits passed in the argument, the output is left-padded with the placeholder zeros. For example:

```
Console.WriteLine("{0:111}", 1234)
Console.WriteLine("{0:00}", 12)
Console.WriteLine("{0:0000}", 123)
Console.WriteLine("{0:0000}", 1234)
```

provides the following output

```
111
12
0123
1234
```

In the preceding output, the first line generates three of digit "1" because this placeholder is not recognized by the method and is thus simply copied to the output, and the number (1234) as the argument is ignored. The second line shows output limited to two digits. The third line shows output limited to four digits, but because we only provide a three-digit **String** as the argument, the number is left-padded with a zero. The fourth line shows four numbers formatted to a **String** of four digits.

Using a Digit or Pound for a Placeholder

The pound (or hash) character can be used as the digit or space placeholder. This placeholder works just like the zero except that a space or blank is inserted into the output if no digit is used in the specified position. For example:

```
Console.WriteLine("{0:####}", 123)
Console.WriteLine("{0:####}", 1234)
Console.WriteLine("{0:##}", 123456)
```

writes the following output to the console:

```
123
1234
123456
```

Custom Positioning of the Decimal Point

You can determine the position of the decimal point in a **String** of numerals by specifying the position of the period (.) character in the format **String**. You can also customize the character used as a decimal point in the **NumberFormatInfo** class. Here is an example:

```
Console.WriteLine("{0:####.000}", 123456.7)
Console.WriteLine("{0:##.000}", 12345.67)
Console.WriteLine("{0:#.000}", 1.234567)
```

The following code writes the following **Strings** to the console:

```
123456.700
12345.670
1.235
```

Using the Group Separator

The group separator is a comma (,) and can be used to format large numbers to make them easier to read. You typically add the comma three places after the decimal point to specify a number such as 1,000.00 or higher. The character used as the specifier can also be customized in the **NumberFormatInfo** class. The following example illustrates placement of the group separator:

```
Console.WriteLine("{0:##,###}", 123456.7)
Console.WriteLine("{0:##,###,000.000}", 1234567.1234567)
Console.WriteLine("{0:#,#.000}", 1234567.1234567)
```

The output to console looks like this:

```
123,457
1,234,567.123
1,234,567.123
```

Using Percent Notation

You can use the percent (%) specifier to denote that a number be displayed as a percentage. The number will be multiplied by 100 before formatting. In the following example:

```
Console.WriteLine("{0:##,000%}", 123.45)
Console.WriteLine("{0:00%}", 0.123)
```

you get the following percentages displayed in the console:

```
12,345%
12%
```

Building Strings with StringBuilder

The efficiency of the **String** object as an immutable type has its downside. Every time you change the **String**, you create a new **String** object that requires its own memory location. If you need to repetitively work with a **String**, shaping it for a particular task, you have the additional overhead of the constant creation of new **String** objects every time you need to cut, add, and move characters around in the **String**.

When you need to constantly work with a **String**, such as an algorithm that takes UNC paths and converts them to HTML paths, or when you need a storage location to shove characters into, like a stack, then you need to turn to the **StringBuilder** class. This class can be found on the **System.Text.StringBuilder** namespace and allows you to keep working with a **String** of characters represented by the same objects for as long as it is needed. The great feature of the object is that you get to reference the collection of characters as a single **String**—far less code than that "soda-fountain" **Stack** that requires extensive "popping."

 *In the BitShifters code in Chapter 5, we used the **StringBuilder** object, albeit in C# garb, as a place to stuff bits.*

The **StringBuilder** class is created similarly to the **String** object, as follows:

```
Dim MyStringBuilder As New StringBuilder("Hello Ariel!")
```

Naturally, you have access to this object's **ToString** method, so I won't go into it. The members of the **StringBuilder** class are listed in Table 15-7.

Capacity

Once you have declared a variable of **StringBuilder**, it's easy to work with. This property ensures that the capacity of this instance of **StringBuilder** is at least the specified value. To set the capacity in the declaration, first initialize the object and pass in the capacity value—in this case 25—as the second argument to the constructor as follows:

```
Dim MyStringBuilder As New StringBuilder("Hello Ariel!", 85)
```

Meanwhile, the **MaxCapacity** property, as listed in Table 15-7, gets the maximum capacity of the object.

Append

The **Append** method can be used to add text or a collection of characters to the end of the object's collection of characters. The following code example initializes a **StringBuilder** object to "To be or not to be" and then appends some text to the end of the **StringBuilder** object. Space is allocated automatically as needed.

```
Dim MyStringBuilder As New StringBuilder_
("To be or not to be . . . ")
MyStringBuilder.Append("that is the question")
Console.WriteLine(MyStringBuilder)
```

Member	Purpose
New	Creates a new instance of the **StringBuilder** class
Capacity (p)	Allocates the maximum number of characters that can be contained in the memory allocated by the object
Chars (p)	Retrieves or returns the character at the specified character position in the object
Length (p)	Retrieves or returns the length of the object's value
MaxCapacity (p)	Retrieves the maximum capacity of the object
Append	Appends characters onto the end of the **String** representation in the object
AppendFormat	Works like **Append** but the **StringBuilder** object can take a formatted **String**, as we discussed in the previous section. Each format specification is replaced by the **String** representation of a corresponding object argument
EnsureCapacity	Used to make sure that the capacity of the object you are referencing is at least a specified value
Insert	Inserts the collection of characters of a specified object into the referenced object, at a specified character position
Remove	Kicks out individual characters or a range from the object. Use **Remove** to flush the object
Replace	Lets you replace all occurrences of a specified character or a collection of characters in the object with other specified characters

Table 15-7. *Members of the **StringBuilder** Class*

As you can imagine, this method is heavily overloaded so that you can append the full gamut of data types into your object.

The following example chews through the long date and time **String** pushed out by Index Server to inform you of the last time a file it is stalking was modified:

```
For intI = 0 To pRow(4).ToString.LastIndexOf("/") + 4
'4 for the year xx/xx/2XXX
  sBuilder.Append(pRow(4).ToString.Chars(intI))
Next
```

So the value "02/02/2002 14:26:47 PM" is reduced to "02/02/2002." You might first grasp for a **String** manipulator method, but the **For Next** loop chews down this particular **String** like a wolf on lamb ribs.

AppendFormat

The **AppendFormat** method adds text to the end of the **StringBuilder** object, but also implements the **IFormattable** interface and therefore accepts the standard format Strings described in the formatting section. You can use this method to customize the format of variables and append those values to a **StringBuilder** object. The following code example uses the **AppendFormat** method to place an integer value formatted as a currency value at the end of a **StringBuilder** object:

```
Dim intI As Integer = 1450
Dim sBuilder As New StringBuilder()
sBuilder.Append("Total remaining is ")
SBuilder.AppendFormat("{0:C}", intI)
Console.WriteLine(sBuilder)
```

The preceding code snippet writes the following to the console:

```
Total remaining is $1,450.00
```

Insert

The **Insert** method adds a **String** or object to a specified position in your **StringBuilder** object. The following code snippet uses this method to insert a word into the sixth position of a **StringBuilder** class:

```
Dim sBuilder As New StringBuilder("Hello Ariel!")
sBuilder.Insert(6, "Beautiful ")
Console.WriteLine(sBuilder)
```

Remove

You can use the **Remove** method to remove a specified number of characters from the current **StringBuilder** object, beginning at a specified zero-based index. The following code example uses the **Remove** method to shorten a **StringBuilder**'s value:

```
Dim sBuilder As New StringBuilder("Hello Ariel!")
sBuilder.Remove(5, 7)
Console.WriteLine(sBuilder)
```

CLASSES AND OBJECTS

Replace

Use the **Replace** method to replace characters within the **StringBuilder** object with other specified characters. This example uses the **Replace** method to search a **StringBuilder** object for all instances of the exclamation point character (!) and replace them with the question mark character (?):

```
Dim sBuilder As New StringBuilder("Hello Ariel!")
sBuilder.Replace("!"c, "?"c)
Console.WriteLine(sBuilder)
```

See anything you like in the preceding methods? In the following code for an Index Server application, I used a **StringBuilder** object inside a **While** loop (this was later implemented with a regular expression). I extracted the date information as previously described and then flushed the builder for the next iteration of the loop. Once the entire table is built, the structure is dispatched, lock, stock, and barrel, to an awaiting Web client.

```
While row <= rows
  rownum += 1 'this comes first because we use it in the HTML table
  pRow = CType(rowIterator.Current, DataRow) 'get the row
  TABLE1.Rows(row).Cells(0).InnerText = CStr(rownum) & "."
  TABLE1.Rows(row).Cells(1).InnerText = pRow(2).ToString
  TABLE1.Rows(row).Cells(2).InnerText = pRow(3).ToString
  'extract a short date from the spaghetti _
  'date sent by the index server
  For intI = 0 To pRow(4).ToString.LastIndexOf("/") + 4
    '4 for the year xx/xx/2001
    sbuilder.Append(pRow(4).ToString.Chars(intI))
  Next
  TABLE1.Rows(row).Cells(3).InnerText = sBuilder.ToString
  'clear the builder for the next record
  sBuilder.Remove(0, intI)
  intI = 0
  TABLE1.Rows(row).Cells(1).InnerHtml = "<A HREF='/Searchfiles/" & _
    Row(2).ToString & "'>" & pRow(2).ToString & "</A>"
  row += 1
  'we need this test because we don't want to advance
  'the cursor when paging backwards
  cursor += 1
  If Not rowIterator.MoveNext() Then
```

```
    Exit While
  End If
End While
```

Regular Expressions

The .NET Framework equips you with probably the most sophisticated and advanced regular expression engine in existence today. If you don't know what regular expressions are, then consider the definition provided by this book:

"A regular expression is a character or a combination of characters (which form a pattern) used to find a matching character, **String**, or combination of characters in a sample. The expression can be a simple wildcard, such as the "?" (question mark) or "*" (star or asterisk)—which matches to anything—to a complex combination of characters that can find a match according to a simple or complex matching rule. The characters that form the matching "rule" are known as metacharacters. And the regular expression language is called a metalanguage."

Once you have found a match (or not) you can simply act on the success or failure result or perform some operation on the match, such as replace it with other strings or copy it somewhere.

If you remember DOS or the command line (I hear from many programmers who don't remember what a command line or DOS looks like any more), then you'll remember the command **Copy *.Doc** or **Dir *.Txt**. The * on the command is a metacharacter that instructs the file system to copy or list "all" files in a target folder with the .doc or .txt extension. The * is the metacharacter that means "all" in this case. The regular language provides this facility with a metalanguage enabling you not only to find matches according to the most sophisticated and extreme of rules, but with the ability to replace, edit, delete, or otherwise manipulate the **String**s and characters at the same time.

This chapter will provide some examples of regular expressions at work, but an extensive treatment of the subject is far beyond the scope of this book. Several books are dedicated to the subject and are worth reading cover to cover. I must warn you, though—and a description of the "regex" facilities in .NET coming up will bear me out—regular expressions are not for the faint of heart. The preceding code illustrates the simplest and most basic use. But the metalanguage is extremely cryptic. Designing a sophisticated match expression combined with actions requires lots of patience and time. If you need a good match expression and your clock is ticking, make a call to a guru and pay whatever he or she is asking.

The **System.Text.RegularExpressions** namespace contains the classes that access the .NET Framework regular expression engine. The functionality is accessible in the **RegularExpressions** namespace members listed in Table 15-8.

Class Member	Purpose
Capture	Represents the results obtained from a single subexpression capture. **Capture** also represents one sub-**String** for a single successful capture
CaptureCollection	Represents a sequence of capture sub-**String**s. **CaptureCollection** returns the set of captures from a single capturing group
Group	Represents the results from a single capturing group. A capturing group can capture zero, one, or more **String**s in a single match with the use of quantifiers. The **Group** supplies a collection of **Capture** objects
GroupCollection	Represents a collection of captured groups. **GroupCollection** returns the set of captured groups in a single match
Match	Represents the results from a single regular expression match
MatchCollection	Represents the set of successful matches found by recursively applying a regular expression pattern to the input **String**
Regex	Represents an immutable regular expression
RegexCompilationInfo	Provides information that the compiler uses to compile a regular expression to a stand-alone assembly
MatchEvaluator (d)	The delegate that is called each time a regular expression match is found during a **Replace** operation
RegexOptions (e)	Provides enumerated values to use to set regular expression options

Table 15-8.   *Members of the **RegularExpressions** Class*

The regular expression classes are part of the base class library and can be used with any language or tool that targets the Common Language Runtime, including ASP.NET and Visual Studio .NET.

The regex support in .NET is also designed to be compatible with the Perl 5 regex framework (which, before .NET, was considered the mother of all regex frameworks). Now the .NET Framework regular expressions include features not yet seen in other implementations. These include right-to-left matching and on-the-fly compilation where the CLR compiles the regex into an assembly.

The .NET Framework Regex Metalanguage

This section introduces you to the important sections in the .NET Framework regular expression metalanguage. The constructs are extensive and this section thus only provides an introduction, a very short one at that. For a detailed listing of the constructs, visit the .NET Framework SDK.

■ **Character escape symbols**   These represent the most important regular expression language operators, escaped single characters. For example, the escape character \ (a single backslash) signals to the regular expression parser that the character following the backslash is not an operator. For example, the parser treats an asterisk (*) as a repeating quantifier and treats a backslash followed by an asterisk (*) as the Unicode character 002A. See the SDK for the list of character escapes.

■ **Substitution symbols**   Substitutions are allowed only within replacement patterns. For similar functionality within regular expressions, use a backreference (for example, \1), described later in this list. Character escapes and substitutions are the only special constructs recognized in a replacement pattern. All the syntactic constructs described in the following items are allowed only in regular expression matching patterns as opposed to replacement patterns.

■ **Regex character symbols**   You can find the Unicode category that a character belongs to with the method **GetUnicodeCategory**. For more information on Unicode character categories, see the document "Unicode Data File Format," available on the Unicode Technical Committee's (UTC) Web site at www.unicode.org/Public/UNIDATA/UnicodeData.html.

■ **Atomic zero width assertions**   These represent metacharacters that do not cause the engine to advance through the string or consume characters. They simply cause a match to succeed or fail depending on the current position in the **String**. For instance, ^ specifies that the current position is at the beginning of a line or string. Thus, the regular expression ^FTP returns only those occurrences of the character string "FTP" that occur at the beginning of a line.

■ **Quantifiers**   Quantifiers add optional quantity data to a regular expression. A quantifier expression applies to the character, group, or character class that immediately precedes it. The .NET Framework regular expressions support minimal matching (lazy) quantifiers. See the SDK for the metacharacters that affect matching quantity.

■ **Groupings**   These constructs allow you to capture groups of subexpressions and to increase the efficiency of regular expressions with noncapturing lookahead and lookbehind modifiers. For example, (?<name>) captures the matched substring into a group name or number name. The string used for name must not contain any punctuation and it cannot begin with a number. You can use single quotes instead of angle brackets; for example, (?'name').

■ **Backreference**   These constructs represent the optional parameters that add backreference modifiers to a regular expression. For example, \<name> can provide the (\w)\1 construct to find doubled word characters.

■ **Alternations**   These special characters modify a regular expression to allow either/or matching. These match any one of the terms separated by the Or | (vertical bar) character; for example, cat | dog | tiger. The leftmost successful match wins.

■ **Miscellaneous**   There are a few miscellaneous constructs that represent sub-expressions that modify a regular expression. For example, (?imnsx-imnsx) sets or disables options such as case insensitivity to be turned on or off in the middle of a pattern.

The following sections present some examples of how the classes and constructs are used.

Capture

The **Capture** class contains the results from a single subexpression capture. The following example loops through a **Group** collection, extracts the **Capture** collection from each member of **Group**, and assigns the variables **pos** and **len** to the character position in the original **String** where each **String** or character was found and the length of each **String**, respectively:

```
Public Sub MatEx(ByVal source As String)
  Dim intI As Integer
  Dim intJ As Integer
  Dim aRegex As Regex
  Dim aMatch As Match
  Dim aCapCollection As CaptureCollection
  Dim pos, len As Integer
  ARegex = New Regex("{0}", source)
  aMatch = Regex.Match("{0}", source)
  While aMatch.Groups(intI).Value <> ""
    aCapCollection = aMatch.Groups(intI).Captures
    For intJ = 0 To aCapCollection.Count - 1
      pos = aCapCollection(intJ).Index
      len = aCapCollection(intJ).Length
    Next intJ
    intI += 1
  End While
End Sub
```

Group

The **Group** class represents the results from a single capturing group. Because Group can capture zero, one, or more strings in a single match (using quantifiers), it contains a collection of **Capture** objects. Because Group inherits from **Capture**, the last substring captured can be accessed directly (the Group instance itself is equivalent to the last item of the collection returned by the **Captures** property).

Instances of Group are returned by the property **Match.Groups(groupnum)**, or **Match.Groups("groupname")** if the "(?<groupname>)" grouping construct is used. The following code example uses nested grouping constructs to capture substrings into groups:

```
Public DoMatchGroups(ByVal source As String, ByVal rsource As Regex)
Dim matchPos(20) As Integer
Dim matchResults(20) As String
Dim aRegex As New Regex(rsource)
Dim aMatch As Match = aRegex.Match(source)
Dim intI As Integer
  While Not (aMatch.Groups(intI).Value = "")
    matchResults(intI) = aMatch.Groups(intI).Value
    matchPosition(intI) = aMatch.Groups(intI).Index
    intI += 1
  End While
End Sub
```

The **Match** class represents the results of a regular expression matching operation.

Regex

This simple example shows how to use the **Regex.Replace** method when a match is found in the target that is being parsed. The **StripNoise** method looks in a **String** for all instances of words provided in the array of samples and then deletes the matches from the target **String**:

```
Private Function StripNoise(ByVal sentence As String) As String
  While x <= UBound(noiseArray)
    sentence = Regex.Replace(sentence, noiseArray(x), "")
    x += 1
  End While
    Return sentence
End Function
```

The method then returns the new **String** minus the matched words. Trying to use one of the **String** manipulation methods or functions in an extensive block of text or a stream of characters would be extremely difficult, and in many cases not at all possible.

You would also use regular expressions to parse complex TCP/IP headers to locate and remedy malformed URLs. You know how complex some of these headers can be. If you need to look for misplaced periods, white spaces, illegal characters, duplication of @ ("at") symbols, and so on, nothing other than a regular expression can do the job for you. I also use it to "scrub" data and "prepare" complex search **String**s supplied against the likes of the Microsoft Index Server search engine, which chokes on a comma or a period or misplaced white space.

File, Stream, and Text IO Operations

The .NET Framework provides an impressive range of IO namespaces that contain dozens of classes used for writing, reading, and streaming all manner of text, characters, and binary data, as well as file, folder, and path support. Many of them, such as those represented by the **System.IO**, **System.Text**, and **System.XML** namespaces, let you code asynchronous and synchronous reading and writing of data to streams and files. All these namespaces are currently partitioned across the **mscorlib**, **System**, **System.Text**, and **System.XML** assemblies.

The files you work with in your programs are typically ordered collections of bytes, representing characters on a file system. Files are static; they squat on your hard disks like chickens hatching eggs. Streams, on the other hand, are continuous "rivers" of data, writing to and reading from various devices. Streams are constantly on the move.

Streams typically originate from files on devices like hard disks, CDs, and DVDs, and other devices for persistent storage such as tape drives and optical disks. Streaming data moves across processes and workspaces on your workstation, and between computers on the vast networks of the world. They move from persistent memory into volatile memory and back again in a constant ebb and flow of data. Eventually, streams of data get fed to printers for physical representation like annual reports or user manuals (after some time, the pages can be fashioned into paper airplanes and tossed out of windows or shredded when the FBI comes knocking).

The following is a list of the key sections we will discuss that facilitate basic I/O for the .NET Framework:

- **File and Directories**   This section presents the classes that encapsulate the functionality of all known file and directory processing operations. Files are opened, closed, and manipulated using the classes in this section. This section also covers the key file operation classes, such as file access enumerations, file mode enumerations, file information classes, directory information classes, and so on. The principal classes discussed here are **File**, **FileInfo**, **Directory**, **DirectoryInfo**, and **Path**. **File**, **Directory**, and **Path** descend directly from **System.Object** while **FileInfo** and **DirectoryInfo** are descendants of **FileSystemInfo**. We also look at **BinaryReader** and **BinaryWriter**, which also derive from **System.Object**.

For the nostalgic, I will discuss briefly .NET's support for the classic **FileSystemObject**, aka **FSO**, which has been the mainstay API of classic VB file system programming for some time now.

■ **Streams**   This section discusses the classes that support data streaming, reading and writing data to objects and devices, and so on. The principal class discussed here is **FileStream.** Most of the stream-utility classes derive from **System.IO.Stream.**

■ **Readers and Writers**   This section covers the text readers and writers that are available to you. They derive from **System.IO.TextWriter** and **System.IO.TextReader**. We will also discuss how these readers and writers can be bridged to various classes and objects like **File** and **StringBuilder**.

Let's begin our sojourn into .NET data processing by discussing basic file operations first. You also need a good understanding of how file processing works before working with the **Stream** objects, because streams objects are bridged to file operations.

Files and Directories

An application devoid of support for files and directories is like a vehicle without wheels or a boat without a propeller. Simply put, it's not going anywhere. There are a lot of cool things in .NET in general and Visual Basic .NET in particular that you don't need to have an initial grounding in. A thorough understanding of the core elements and concepts discussed in this book will help you get up to speed on them quickly. But I deem it essential that you become totally immersed in .NET's file handling and I/O support before the opening bell (before you start a .NET paying project), or you'll be declared a TKO by the end of round 1.

There are two approaches to coding against the file and directory libraries that ship with the .NET Framework. You can reference static operations classes (**File**, **Directory**, and **Path**), or you can create file and directory objects using the **FileInfo** and **DirectoryInfo** classes. (Refer to Chapter 9 if you are unsure of the difference between an operations class and a class that can be instantiated—that is, activated as an object).

For many operations, you can simply use the static or shared classes, but there will be many reasons to work with file and folder objects. For starters, if you herald from the world-wide sister-brotherhood of classic VB programmer you'll probably be very familiar with the **File System Object (FSO)**. Most established VB programmers use the **FSO** all the time. Both **FileInfo** and **DirectoryInfo** let you code against a similar and thus familiar object model as the **FSO**.

If you are not familiar with file and directory object models, consider the objects as objects that represent files or directories, or abstractions thereof. An operations class is somewhat disconnected from the file or directory you intend to work on, but a file or directory object is more like a programmable file or directory object, with a layer you can code against.

 The .NET Framework and the CLR obviate the need for loading and reading files for application initialization (refer to the section "Working with Configuration Files" in Chapter 17).

The File Class

The **File** class provides the .NET Framework's support for all manner of file handling. With this class, you can create, copy, delete, move, and open files and much more. **File** is a static or shared "operations" class and not a class for objects. You cannot instantiate **File** and it has no constructor. To use **File**, simply reference it as follows:

```
File.Copy("c:\doh.txt", "c:\ray.txt")
```

If you need to use file objects to do your file operations, use the **FileInfo** class, which contains instance methods that work like the methods of the **File** class but live in objects. Static methods, being shared, incur more security overhead, whereas instance methods do not always require security checks. Table 15-9 lists the static (s) members of **File**.

 See "Basic File Class Operations" at the end of this section for a discussion of the methods most frequently used for standard file I/O operations.

You have the potential to raise exceptions if you provide malformed filenames and path information. The following examples of paths will get processed by the **File** methods, but you should consider using the **Path** class, discussed next, to help reduce path errors:

```
"c:\doh\ray.txt"
"c:\doh"
"doh\ray.txt" 'a relative path and file name
"\\doh\ray\" 'A UNC path for a server and share name.
```

Path

Programming against the file and directory classes is not rocket science, but the potential for problems in your code is increased because you need to pass complex arguments (such as the various mode and access constants discussed in the next section). One parameter that can be a minefield represents the path information argument you need to pass to the various methods of the file and directory classes.

The other stickler in file and directory operations is having to deal with the differences between the various file systems on the Windows platform—FAT, FAT32, and the mighty NTFS. The current file system on the platform you are targeting your

Member	Purpose
AppendText	Bridges to a **StreamWriter** that appends UTF-8 encoded text to an existing file
Copy	Copies a source file to a new target file
Create	Creates a file on a given fully qualified path
CreateText	Creates or opens a new file for writing UTF-8 encoded text
Delete	Deletes the file on the given fully qualified path. An exception is not thrown if the specified file does not exist
Exists	Checks if a specific file exists
GetAttributes	Retrieves the **FileAttributes** on the file on a given fully qualified path
GetCreationTime	Retrieves the creation date and time of the specified file or directory
GetLastAccessTime	Retrieves the date and time that the file or directory was last accessed
GetLastWriteTime	Retrieves the date and time that the file or directory was last written to
Move	Moves the source file to a new folder. It also provides the option of a new filename
Open	Opens a **FileStream** on the given path
OpenRead	Opens an existing file for reading
OpenText	Opens an existing UTF-8 encoded text file for reading
OpenWrite	Opens an existing file for writing
SetAttributes	Sets the specified **FileAttributes** on the file on the given path
SetCreationTime	Sets the date and time that the file was created
SetLastAccessTime	Sets the date and time that the given file was last accessed
SetLastWriteTime	Sets the date and time that the given file was last written to

Table 15-9.   *The Static Methods of **File***

application to determines the exact format of a path. You might not always have the pleasure of working with one file system, or even accessing a file or directory on a system other than a version of FAT or NTFS. You thus need to come up with a flexible design to accommodate changing file system conditions.

Some paths start with drive or volume letters, while others do not. Some file systems maintain file extensions, and some do not. Some systems maintain a three-character extension; others let you maintain extensions of more than three characters. The separator characters of path namespaces also differ from platform to platform. And you probably know that various TCP/IP path elements are separated with forward slashes instead of the backslashes of the UNC.

Paths can also contain absolute or relative location information. Absolute paths specify physical locations that can be uniquely identified. Relative paths specify a partial location that still requires additional resolution.

File systems on the various platforms in use today are as different as humming birds are from fruit beetles. To cater to these differences (remember we are living in the era of the Internet and distributed functionality), .NET provides a class you can use to process path strings as platform independently as possible.

The members of the **Path** class are not used to physically operate on files and folders. You will use the aforementioned file and directory classes and objects for that. But **Path**'s members are used to verify and modify path strings before you submit them as arguments to methods that do manipulate file systems objects.

When you use **Path** to verify a path string, it will throw an **ArgumentException** if your path string characters do not evaluate correctly. You decide what is or is not correct. The invalid characters get defined in an **InvalidPathChars** array, which gets looked at when you request verification.

Here's an example: Invalid path characters on some platforms include quote ("), less than (<), greater than (>), pipe (|), backspace (\b), null (\0), and Unicode characters 16 through 18 and 20 through 25. You'll thus insert these characters into the **InvalidPathChars** array and then use this construct to filter out bad path strings.

The **Path** class is also very useful for other path operations, such as enabling you to quickly and easily perform common operations like determining whether a filename extension is part of a path, or the combining of two strings to make one pathname. Table 15-10 lists the members of the **Path** class.

The following example uses several members of the **Path** class to work files and path names and to determine if the paths passed to various file and directory methods are acceptable. Please note that these properties have been extracted from a class that encapsulates the contructs of the **Path** class. The first example calls the **Combine** method to make a full path name out of the directory and file names:

```
'Make a path
Public ReadOnly Property FilePath() As String
   Get
      Return PathChecker.Combine(pName, fName)
```

```
   End Get
End Property
```

This **FilePath** property information returned is

```
C:\indexworks\noisefile.txt
```

Member	Purpose
AltDirectorySeparatorChar	Provides a platform-specific alternate character used to separate directory levels in a path string that reflects a hierarchical file system organization
DirectorySeparatorChar	Provides a platform-specific character used to separate directory levels in a path string that reflects a hierarchical file system organization
InvalidPathChars	Provides a platform-specific array of characters that cannot be specified in path string arguments passed to members of the **Path** class
PathSeparator	A platform-specific separator character used to separate path strings in environment variables
VolumeSeparatorChar	Provides a platform-specific volume separator character
ChangeExtension	Changes the extension of a path string
Combine	Combines two path strings
GetDirectoryName	Retrieves the directory information for the specified path string
GetExtension	Retrieves the extension of the specified path string
GetFileName	Retrieves the filename and extension of the specified path string

Table 15-10.   *Members of the **Path** Operations Class*

Member	Purpose
GetFileNameWithoutExtension	Retrieves the filename of the specified path string without the extension
GetFullPath	Retrieves the absolute path for the specified path string
GetPathRoot	Retrieves the root directory information of the specified path
GetTempFileName	Retrieves a unique temporary filename and creates a zero-byte file by that name on disk
GetTempPath	Retrieves the path of the current system's temporary folder
HasExtension	Determines whether a path includes a filename extension
IsPathRooted	Retrieves a value indicating whether the specified path string contains absolute or relative path information

Table 15-10. *Members of the **Path** Operations Class* (continued)

The following example extracts the root from the above-specified full path and file name:

```
Public ReadOnly Property PathRoot() As String
  Get
    Return PathChecker.GetPathRoot(FilePath)
  End Get
End Property
```

The **PathRoot** information returned is

```
C:\
```

The following example tests to see if a logical root exists in a path string. It returns **False** when the **FilePath** property passes "indexwork\noisefile.txt" to the **IsPathRooted** method.

```
Public ReadOnly Property CheckRooted() As Boolean
  Get
    Return PathChecker.IsPathRooted(FilePath)
```

```
   End Get
End Property
```

Remember that **Path** is not privy to exactly what's cooking on the hard disks or devices, volatile or built of silicone and metal. Just because a drive and file path check though the **Path**'s string gauntlet does not mean the actual drive, computer, and network actually exist at the time the path checks out.

File Enumerations

Among the parameters required by various methods for file operations are certain values that are represented by a collection of enumeration classes. These classes include constants for file access, synchronous or asynchronous processing, and file attributes. Table 15-11 lists the file enumeration classes.

Note   *These enumerations can apply to* **FileInfo** *and* **FileStream** *classes as well, so get used to them now.*

FileAccess

Various file-handling methods require you to specify the level of file access enjoyed by the user or process accessing the file. The default file access level is full *read* and *write* capability on a file. A **FlagsAttribute** attribute decorates the class (refer to Chapter 8) so that the CLR can evaluate bitwise combinations of the members of the enumeration. Table 15-12 lists the three **FileAccess** attributes.

Here is an example that grants read-only access to a file. This allows it to be opened by the **File** operation while someone else is using the file, but only allows the other, latter users to read the file. They cannot write to it until they get the chance to open the file with write access, as demonstrated in the following code:

```
Dim noisefile As New FileStream(filePath, FileMode.Open, _
    FileAccess.Read, FileShare.Read)
```

Enumeration	Purpose
FileAccess	Read and write access to a file
FileShare	Level of access permitted for a file that is already in use
FileMode	Synchronous or asynchronous access to the file in use

Table 15-11.   *File Enumeration Classes*

Member	Purpose
Read	Read access to the file. Data can be read from the file. Combine with **Write** for read/write access
ReadWrite	Read and write access to the file. Data can be written to and read from the file
Write	Write access to the file. Data can be written to the file. Combine with **Read** for read/write access

Table 15-12.   *Constants for the **FileAccess** Attributes Parameter*

FileAttributes

This enumeration class provides additional attributes for files and directories. A **FlagsAttribute** attribute also decorates the file. Table 15-13 lists the file and directory attributes that permeate up from the WinNT.h wrapper. The table also indicates where the attributes are applicable to files and where they are applicable to directories. The asterisk (*) denotes that the facility may not be supported by all file systems.

Not all attributes can be accommodated by every file system in existence. For example, reparse points and support for mounted folders and encryption only arrived with the Windows 2000 operating system.

FileMode

The **FileMode** parameter lets you specify the treatment of a file as it is accessed. For example, you can specify if the file should be opened in **Append** mode, which causes the opening object supporting a **Seek** method to seek to the end of the file, where the new data gets appended. **OpenCreate**, for example, lets the opening object create and open the file in the same pass.

These attributes can be specified in **File's** (and **FileInfo's**) **Open** methods and the constructors of **FileStream** and **IsolatedStorageFileStream**. They control whether the file can be overwritten, created, or opened, or open in some combination modes. Table 15-14 lists the **FileMode** enumeration's constants.

Member	Purpose
Archive	Use this attribute to mark a file for backup or removal.
Compressed	Indicates the object is compressed.*
Device	Reserved for future use.
Directory	Indicates the object is a directory.
Encrypted	Indicates the object encrypted. At the file object level, all data in the file is encrypted. At the directory level, this attribute indicates that all newly created files and files in subdirectories get encrypted.*
Hidden	The file is marked as hidden so that the file system does not allow it to be shown in a directory listing. The user can usually change this at the directory level to show hidden files.
Normal	Normal here means no other attributes, other than "normal," are set.
NotContentIndexed	Files that are marked with this attribute do not get indexed by Index Server or some other content indexing service.
Offline	When a file is marked offline, it means that its data is not immediately available.
ReadOnly	The file is read-only. See also the file access attributes.
ReparsePoint	This means the file contains a reparse point, which is a block of user-defined data associated with a file or a directory. *
SparseFile	A sparse file is typically a large file whose data is mostly zeros.
System	This means your file is part of the operating system or it is used exclusively by the operating system.
Temporary	A temporary file is usually a placeholder for a file currently in volatile memory. Your application should delete temporary files as soon as they are no longer needed.

* The asterisk denotes that the facility may not be supported by all file systems.

Table 15-13.   *Constants for the **FileAttributes** Parameter*

Member	Description
Append	Seeks to the end of the existing file when it is opened; if the file does not exist, the file system creates a new file
Create	Forces the creation of a new file
CreateNew	Requests the file system to create a new file with the given name
Open	Requests that the file system should open an existing file
OpenOrCreate	Requests that the file system should open a file if it exists; otherwise, a new file should be created
Truncate	Requests that the file system should open an existing file

Table 15-14.   *Constants for the **FileMode** Parameter*

The following list demonstrates the use of these attributes in the **File.Open** methods:

■ **Append**   This attribute can only be used in conjunction with **FileAccess.Write**. Any attempt to read in the same pass gets rebuked with **ArgumentException**. The following code demonstrates **FileMode.Append**:

```
Dim noisefile As New FileStream(filePath, FileMode.Append, _
FileAccess.Read, FileShare.Read)
```

■ **Create**   If the file already exists, it will be overwritten. This requires **PermissionAccess.Write** and **FileIOPermissionAccess.Append**. **FileMode.Create** is the equivalent of requesting that if the file does not exist, use **CreateNew**; otherwise, use **Truncate**. The following code checks use **File**'s **Exist** method to choose either **Create** or **CreateNew**. There are various techniques you can use to prevent inadvertent deletion of a file when trying to create a new one. The following **If. . .Then** condition is one example:

```
If Not (File.Exists(FilePath)) Then
  Dim noisefile As New FileStream(FilePath, FileMode.Create, _
  FileAccess.Read, FileShare.Read)
End If
```

■ **CreateNew**   This attribute requires **FileIOPermissionAccess.Read** and **FileIOPermissionAccess.Append**. This attribute provides better protection of existing files than the **Create** attribute discussed earlier, because it will cause an **IOException** that prevents damage to the existing file. The following examples illustrates its usage.

```
Dim noiseFile As New FileStream(filePath, FileMode.CreateNew, _
FileAccess.Read, FileShare.Read)
```

■ **Open** This attribute also requires **FileIOPermissionAccess.Read**. It will cause a **FileNotFoundException** if the file does not exist. The following examples demonstrates opening the file in **Read** mode:

```
Dim noiseFile As New FileStream(filePath, FileMode.Open, _
FileAccess.Read, FileShare.Read)
```

■ **OpenOrCreate** A useful attribute if you are creating a number of files. Use this attribute with **FileAccess.Read** and **FileIOPermissionAccess.Read**. When you use **FileAccess.ReadWrite** and the file exists, **FileIOPermissionAccess.Write** is required at the same time. But if the file does not exist, **FileIOPermissionAccess.Append** is required in addition to **Read** and **Write**. The following example shows this happening:

```
Dim noiseFile As New FileStream(filePath, FileMode.OpenOrCreate, _
FileAccess.Read, FileShare.Read)
```

■ **Truncate** This attribute will cause an existing file to be opened and cleared or flushed in one pass. In other words, as soon as it is opened, the file size of the file is zero bytes. This operation requires **FileIOPermissionAccess.Write**. Naturally, any attempts to read from a truncated file will result in an exception. The following method opens a file and specifies truncation:

```
Dim noiseFile As New FileStream(filePath, FileMode.Truncate, _
FileAccess.Read, FileShare.Read)
```

 *If a file is already open when you try to open it using one of the **Read**, **Write**, or **None** flags, the operation will fail. You can only gain access to the file once the current owner has closed it. And even if the file is closed and you pass one of the above flags, you may still need additional permissions to access it.*

FileShare

The constants exposed in the **FileShare** enumeration map to constants that let you specify to the file system exactly how a file should be opened when it opens it. These constants are typically passed to the **Open** methods of **File** and **FileInfo** and in the constructors of **FileStream** (discussed later in this chapter) and the **IsolateStorageFileStream**. Table 15-15 lists the constants of this enumeration.

Basic File Class Operations

This section demonstrates how to create and work with files. In the example code, I have created a class with various methods that call the **File** class's static methods. I then allow other objects to delegate to this wrapper or bridge the objects for file operations.

Member	Purpose
Inheritable	Allows the file handle to be inherited by child processes. This feature is apparently not directly supported by the Win32 API.
None	Rebukes attempts to share access to a file. Any request to open the file by the current process or any another process fails until the file is closed.
Read	Allows subsequent opening of the file for reading
ReadWrite	Allows subsequent opening of the file for reading or writing
Write	Allows subsequent opening of the file for writing

Table 15-15. *Constants for the **FileShare** Parameter*

How to Create a File

The **Create** and **CreateText** methods let you create a file at the end of the fully qualified path. You can choose to call the **Create** method that returns a reference to the created file, or you can call **CreateText** to open a file for writing in UTF-8 encoded data. The following code demonstrates calling **CreateText**. (See the examples for using **Create** earlier in the chapter.) Note also that the following code calls for a **Boolean** result from the **Exists** method to prevent an existing file from being deleted as a result of a create process.

```
If Not (File.Exists(FilePath)) Then
   If FileFile.CreateText(FilePath)
End If
```

How to Copy a File

The following code demonstrates the copying of an existing file to a new file:

```
File.Copy(SourceFile, TargetFile)
```

The arguments **SourceFile** and **TargetFile** provide the **Copy** method with source and target path and file names. If you omit directory information **Copy** sources and targets the folder of the application it is executed from.

How to Delete a File

The following code demonstrates the call to delete a file. Delete will throw an exception if it is unable to delete the target file for any reason.

```
File.Delete(TargetFile)
```

The method also traps the exception that will be inevitable if you attempt to delete a file that is not on the fully qualified path, or that simply does not exist.

Getting and Setting File Attributes and Access Information on Files

You will always have cause to peek at file attributes and use them in various file-handling scenarios. The following example demonstrates retrieving the attributes that adorn a given file with the **GetAttributes** method.

```
Public Function GetFileAtts(ByVal fileandpath As String) _
   As System.IO.FileAttributes
   'FilePath = c:\indexworks\noisefile.txt
   Debug.WriteLine(File.GetAttributes(FilePath))
End Function
```

With the list of attributes in hand, we can write the code that sets and changes certain attributes. This is achieved using the **SetAttributes** method in the following code:

```
File.SetAttributes(FilePath, FileAttributes.Hidden)
```

To report on the time a file was created, last accessed, and last written to, and to set these attributes, you can use the methods **GetCreationTime**, **GetLastAccessTime**, **GetLastWriteTime**, **SetCreationTime**, **SetLastAccessTime**, and **SetLastWriteTime**, respectively. The following code extracts this information from all the files in a directory and writes the information to a file that is stored in a directory. Then a process checks the last time the file directory activity status file was written to and, if a certain number of hours have passed, re-creates the status file and then resets its creation time (see the section "FileSystemWatcher," later in the chapter).

Moving Files Around

The **Move** method moves a file to a new location. The method also provides the option of changing the filename, as demonstrated in the following code:

```
File.Move(SourceFile, TargetFile)
```

CLASSES AND OBJECTS

The arguments **SourceFile** and **TargetFile** provide **File.Move** with source and target path and file names. The **Move** method throws exceptions if it cannot source the file or the destination already contains a file of the same name as the one being moved.

Directory

The **Directory** class contains static methods exposed for the purpose of creating, moving, and enumerating through directories and subdirectories. As is the case with the **File** class, **Directory** is a shared operations class. If you need to perform folder operations via an object, then you can use the **DirectoryInfo** class, discussed shortly. Table 15-16 lists the members of the **Directory** class.

 Malformed path strings will cause exceptions. Refer to "The File Class" and "Path" earlier in this chapter. Both sections provide specifics to ensure you pass well-formed path strings to these methods.

The static methods of **Directory** are straightforward, so I am not going to cover each method with its own example. The following code, however, parses a given directory and then reports what it finds to the console:

```
Public Shared Sub ProcessDirectory(ByVal targetDir As String)
  Dim subdirectory As String
  Dim fileName As String
  Dim subdirectories As String() = Directory.GetDirectories(targetDir)
  Dim files As String() = Directory.GetFiles(targetDir)
  For Each fileName In files
    PrintFileInfo(fileName)
  Next fileName
  For Each subdirectory In subdirectories
    ProcessDirectory(subdirectory)
  Next subdirectory
End Sub
```

The **ProcessDirectory** method starts off taking the path of a target directory passed to it and then it recursively enumerates all subdirectories in the target directory. The full path is then written to the console using the **PrintFileInfo** method in the following code:

```
Public Shared Sub PrintFileInfo(ByVal path As String)
  Console.WriteLine("Found: {0}", path)
End Sub
```

Member	Purpose
CreateDirectory	Creates directories and subdirectories on a given path
Delete	Deletes directory contents
Exists	Checks if given paths exist
GetCreationTime	Retrieves creation dates and times of directories
GetCurrentDirectory	Retrieves current working directories of the applications
GetDirectories	Retrieves names of subdirectories in specified directories
GetDirectoryRoot	Retrieves volume information, root information, or both for the specified paths
GetFiles	Retrieves the names of files in the specified directories
GetFileSystem Entries	Retrieves the names of all files and subdirectories in the specified directory
GetLastAccessTime	Retrieves the date and time the specified file or directory was last accessed
GetLastWriteTime	Retrieves the date and time the specified file or directory was last written to
GetLogicalDrives	Retrieves the names of the logical drives on this computer; for example, "c:\"
GetParent	Retrieves the parent directory of the specified path, including both absolute and relative paths
Move	Moves files or folders and directory contents to a new location
SetCreationTime	Lets you set the creation date and time for files or directories
SetCurrentDirectory	Lets you create the current working directory
SetLastAccessTime	Lets you set the date and time the specified file or directory was last accessed
SetLastWriteTime	Lets you set the date and time a directory was last written to

Table 15-16.   *The Static Members of the **Directory** Class*

The FileInfo Class

This class contains methods that provide the same service as the **File** class. The main difference between the two classes is that **FileInfo**'s methods are instance methods and the class contains a constructor that lets you create it as an object. What you get is a reference variable to an object that represents or abstracts a file. The class also provides a handful of properties that make reporting on a file easier. The members of **FileInfo** (sans methods inherited from **Object**) are listed in Table 15-17.

Member	Purpose
Attributes (p)	Gets or sets the **FileAttributes** of the current **FileSystemInfo** object
CreationTime (p)	Gets or sets the creation time of the current **FileSystemInfo** object
Directory (p)	Gets an instance of the parent directory
DirectoryName (p)	Gets a string representing the directory's full path
Exists (p)	Gets a value indicating whether a file exists
Extension (p)	Gets the string representing the extension part of the file
FullName (p)	Gets the full path of the directory or file
LastAccessTime (p)	Gets or sets the time the current file or directory was last accessed
LastWriteTime (p)	Gets or sets the time when the current file or directory was last written to
Length (p)	Gets the size of the current file or directory
Name (p)	Gets the name of the file
AppendText	Creates a **StreamWriter** that appends text to the file represented by this instance of the **FileInfo**

Table 15-17.   *The Members of the **FileInfo** Class*

Member	Purpose
CopyTo	Copies an existing file to a new file
Create	Creates a file
CreateText	Creates a **StreamWriter** that writes a new text file
Delete	Permanently deletes a file
MoveTo	Moves a specified file to a new location, providing the option to specify a new filename
Open	Opens a file with various read/write and sharing privileges
OpenRead	Creates a read-only **FileStream**
OpenText	Creates a **StreamReader** with UTF8 encoding that reads from an existing text file
OpenWrite	Creates a write-only **FileStream**
Refresh	Refreshes the state of the object

Table 15-17.   *The Members of the **FileInfo** Class* (continued)

Apart from the semantic differences, the reduction in security checks, and a few additional members like **Refresh** and **Length**, this class provides the same operations on files as the **File** class. As I said, if you get more utility out of a file system object and prefer to stick with a .NET file handling class, then use **FileInfo** over the legacy FSO.

Also, the same exception raised for **File** problems applies to **FileInfo** problems, especially malformed paths and file information.

DirectoryInfo

Table 15-18 lists the methods and properties of the **DirectoryInfo** class. This class can be instantiated and its members are instance members. Instantiation gets you access to a useful collection of properties that provide information such as file extensions, parent directory names, root folders, and so on.

Member	Purpose
Attributes (p)	Retrieves or changes the **FileAttributes** of the current resource
CreationTime (p)	Retrieves or changes the creation time of the current resource
Exists (p)	Retrieves or changes a value indicating whether the directory exists
Extension (p)	Retrieves or changes the string representing the extension part of the file
FullName (p)	Retrieves the full path of the directory or file
LastAccessTime (p)	Retrieves or changes the time the current file or directory was last accessed
LastWriteTime (p)	Retrieves or changes the time when the current file or directory was last written to
Name Overridden (p)	Retrieves the name of this **DirectoryInfo** instance
Parent (p)	Retrieves the parent directory of a specified subdirectory
Root (p)	Retrieves the root portion of a path
Create	Creates a directory
CreateSubdirectory	Creates a subdirectory or subdirectories on the given path. The path can be relative to this instance
Delete	Deletes the resource directory and its contents from a path
GetDirectories	Retrieves the subdirectories of the current directory
GetFiles	Retrieves a file list from the current directory
GetFileSystemInfos	Retrieves an array of strongly typed **FileSystemInfo** objects
MoveTo	Moves a directory and its contents to a new path
Refresh	Refreshes the state of the object

Table 15-18.   *The Instance Members of the **DirectoryInfo** Object*

Instantiate a **DirectoryInfo** object passing in the directory path string (**pName**) to the method as follows:

```
Dim dirinfo As New DirectoryInfo("pName")
```

You can then code against the object, as demonstrated in the following example, which maintains a reference to a **DirectoryInfo** object for folder management:

```
Dim dirifo As New DirectoryInfo("pName")
If dirinfo.Exists = False Then
   'create the directory
   dirinfo.Create()
End If
```

Creating a file and opening it are also quite simple with the **DirectoryInfo** class. Here is an example:

```
Dim folders As New DirectoryInfo("C:\indexworks")
folders.CreateSubdirectory("noisefiles")
```

Notice in the above example the **CreateSubdirectory** method only needs the name of the subdirectory. It will throw an exception if you try to pass it path information.

Using the Classic File System Object

The .NET Framework can wrap the classic File System Object (**FSO**) that many VB programmers are familiar with. Bringing the **FSO** into .NET is a process that happens in less than ten mouse clicks, so the only difficulty you may have in using it is deciding if you want to or have to. If you know your way around the **FSO** model, you can continue to program against it, because the interop layer that wraps this legacy object provides seamless access to the original objects in its COM DLL (the Microsoft Scripting Runtime). If this support helps you with migration or porting, then you need to consider it until you are ready to adopt the **FileInfo** and **DirectoryInfo** classes.

If, however, you do not care for the **FSO** or are not moving code from VB to Visual Basic .NET, then stick with the "native" classes that don't need the additional overhead of the interop layers (the **FSO** is still very fast, even in .NET).

For those of you who do not know about the **FSO** object model, it encapsulates the following objects:

- **Drive** Lets you extract information about drives attached to the local computer or a remote computer on the network. With it, you can determine how much space is available on the drive, what share names it has, and so on. The **Drive** object lets you access other devices as well, such as a CD-ROM drive, a RAM disk, and a DVD.

- **Drives**   Exposes **Count** and **Item** properties
- **Folder**   Lets you create, delete, or move folders. It also supports the ability to research folder names, paths, and more
- **File**   Lets you create, delete, or move files. It also supports the ability to research filenames, paths, and other information.
- **TextStream**   Lets you read and write text files

Note   *The **FSO** is particularly weak against binary streams.*

To use the **FSO** in your application, you need to create a reference to the **Scripting** type library (Scrrun.dll) in which it resides. This is a COM object that typically lives in the operating system's folders (such as C:\Winnt\System32). But you can access and reference it in your project by adding the reference to it from the References Folder, Add Reference option, or from your project's menus. The low-down on adding interop references can be found in Chapters 3 and 4.

Click the COM tab in the Add Reference dialog box and scroll down to the item that reads Microsoft Scripting Runtime. Double-click the item to select it and click OK. Presto, an interop wrapper is spun around this legacy DLL, and you can start using it (just don't go "interopping" every legacy DLL you've been using in your VB apps for the past ten years, or your apps will start crawling to a halt in no time).

At the top of your class that you are going to use to code against the **FSO** add an **Imports** statement and point it to the **Scripting** namespace created in the interop wrapper. You'll see it the second you type **Imports**. You can now start using the facilities in this namespace immediately.

The following code demonstrates how to instantiate a new **FSO**:

```
Dim fso As New FileSystemObject
```

Or you can call old faithful, the **CreateObject** method, and pass the FQNS (the legacy type library and the object it encapsulates) to the **FSO** as an argument. This affects the bridge as well. The latter option is demonstrated as follows:

```
Dim fso = CreateObject("Scripting.FileSystemObject")
```

Once you have referenced the Scripting DLL, you can browse the **interop.Scripting** assembly in the Object Browser. You will notice that most of the objects, classes, and methods do not offer anything special or different from the native **File** and **FileInfo** classes (we will also be covering .NET's **Directory** and **Path** classes shortly, so sit tight). However, the **Drive** and **Drives** classes are worth looking at.

Drive provides you with a neat collection of methods for accessing volume information, available space, drive letters, share names, and so on. What I like about **Drive** is its ability to access drive information on both local computers and remote computers on the network. The properties listed in Table 15-19 provide disk and volume information.

Property	Purpose
TotalSize	Retrieves the total size of the drive, in bytes
AvailableSpace, FreeSpace	Retrieves the amount of space available on the drive, in bytes
DriveLetter, Letter	Retrieves the drive letters assigned to the drive
DriveType	Retrieves the type of drive (removable, fixed, network, CD-ROM, or RAM disk)
SerialNumber	Retrieves the drive's serial number
FileSystem	Retrieves the type of file system on the drive (FAT, FAT32, or NTFS)
IsReady	Used to determine if the drive is available for use
ShareName, VolumeName	Provides the name of the share and/or volume
Path, RootFolder	Provides the path or root folder of the drive

Table 15-19. *The Properties of the **Drive** Class in the File System Object*

A **Drives** object that comes packaged into the FSO model also exposes a **Count** property and an **Item** property. The following code demonstrates how to instantiate the object via the FSO interface and access its members.

```
Dim fso As New FileSystemObject()
DriveInfo.Add(fso.Drives.Count())
```

FileSystemWatcher

Objects of the **FileSystemWatcher** class watch the file system and report to you the moment a file or folder changes. There are so many uses for this class that it would be pointless to try and list them all. I have used it to trigger events that tell my data processing applications that it's time to go to work on a folder and process files that have changed.

The **FileSystemWatcher** class lets you also watch for changes in a specified directory on a network drive, or a remote computer. But before you get caught up in the "novelty" of this class, remember that the "watcher" is platform-dependent. **FileSystemWatcher** only works on Windows XP, .NET Server, Windows 2000, and Windows NT 4.0. Your remote computers must have one of these platforms installed for the component to function properly. You cannot watch a remote Windows NT 4.0 computer from a Windows NT 4.0 computer.

FileSystemWatcher does not attempt to watch CDs and DVDs, which don't change. Its members are listed in Table 15-20.

Member	Description
Container (p)	Retrieves the **IContainer** that contains the component
EnableRaisingEvents (p)	Retrieves or changes a value indicating whether the component is enabled
Filter (p)	Retrieves or changes the filter string, used to determine what files are monitored in a directory
IncludeSubdirectories (p)	Retrieves or changes a value indicating whether subdirectories within the specified path should be monitored
InternalBufferSize (p)	Retrieves or changes the size of the internal buffer
NotifyFilter (p)	Retrieves or changes the type of changes to watch for
Path (p)	Retrieves or changes the path of the directory to watch
Site (p)	See **Component.Site** of the **Component** class
SynchronizingObject (p)	Retrieves or changes the object used to marshal the event handler calls issued as a result of a directory change
BeginInit	Begins the initialization of a **FileSystemWatcher** used on a form or used by another component. The initialization occurs at run time.
EndInit	Ends the initialization of a **FileSystemWatcher** used on a form or used by another component. The initialization occurs at run time.
Equals (inherited from **Object**)	Determines whether two **Object** instances are equal

Table 15-20. *The Members of the **FileSystemWatcher** Class*

Member	Description
WaitForChanged	A synchronous method that returns a structure that contains specific information on the change that occurred
Changed (e)	Occurs when a file or directory in the specified Path is changed
Created (e)	Occurs when a file or directory in the specified Path is created
Deleted (e)	Occurs when a file or directory in the specified Path is deleted
Disposed (e) (inherited from **Component**)	Adds an event handler to listen to the **Disposed** event on the component
Error (e)	Occurs when the internal buffer overflows
Renamed (e)	Occurs when a file or directory in the specified Path is renamed

Table 15-20.   *The Members of the **FileSystemWatcher** Class* (continued)

The following example watches a folder for changes in files that will trigger the need to re-create the files and folder status report. It creates a **FileSystemWatcher** to watch the directory specified at run time. The component is set to watch for changes in **LastWrite** and **LastAccess** time, and the creation, deletion, or renaming of text files in the directory. If a file is changed, created, or deleted, the path to the file prints to the console. When a file is renamed, the old and new paths print to the console.

```
Public Sub Watching()
  'declare a watcher
  Dim Watcher As New FileSystemWatcher()
  'specify a path
  Watcher.Path = "c:\indexworks"
  'specify the notify filters
  Watcher.NotifyFilter = (NotifyFilters.LastAccess _
  Or NotifyFilters.LastWrite _
  Or NotifyFilters.FileName _
  Or NotifyFilters.DirectoryName)
  'the file to watch
  Watcher.Filter = "noisefile.txt"
```

```
    'Specify event handlers.
    AddHandler watcher.Changed, AddressOf OnChanged
    'Start
    Watcher.EnableRaisingEvents = True
End Sub

'implement the event handler.
Public Shared Sub OnChanged(ByVal source As Object, _
    ByVal eArgs As FileSystemEventArgs)
    'Reload the noisewords file after it has been changed
    Indexworks.Reload(FilePath)
End Sub
```

The following ingredients in this code should be noted.

NotifyFilters

Changes to watch for in a file or folder are specified by constants of the **NotifyFilters** enumeration and set to the **NotifyFilter** property. Like the constants of the file mode, access, and attributes enumerations, this enumeration has a **FlagsAttribute** attribute that allows a bitwise combination of its member values. In other words, you can combine constants to watch for more than one kind of change. For example, you can watch for changes in the size of a file *or* a folder, *and* for changes in security settings. The combination raises an event anytime there is a change in size or security settings of a file or folder.

Table 15-21 lists the constants of the **NotifyFilters** enumeration.

Use these filter constants to specify the constant or constant combinations to watch. To watch for changes in all files, set the **Filter** property in the object to an empty string (""). If you are watching for a specific file, then set the **Filter** property to the filename as follows:

```
Watcher.Filter = "noisefile.txt"
```

To watch for changes in all text files, simply set the **Filter** property as follows:

```
Watcher.Filter = "*.txt"
```

By the way, hidden files are not ignored.

WatcherChangeTypes

Changes to watch for that may occur to a file or folder are specified by constants of the **WatcherChangeTypes** enumeration and set to the event hanlder. This enumeration

Member	Purpose
Attributes	Represents the attributes of the file or folder
CreationTime	Represents the time the file or folder was created
DirectoryName	Represents the name of the directory
FileName	Represents the name of the file
LastAccess	Represents the date the file or folder was last opened
LastWrite	Represents the date the file or folder last had anything written to it
Security	Represents the security settings of the file or folder
Size	Represents the size of the file or folder

Table 15-21.   *Members of the **NotifyFilters** Enumeration*

also has a **FlagsAttribute** attribute decorating it that allows the CLR to reference bitwise combinations of its member values. Each of the **WatcherChangeTypes** constants is associated with an event in **FileSystemWatcher**. The constant members of this enumeration are listed in Table 15-22.

Member	Description
All	Fires on the creation, deletion, change, or renaming of a file or folder
Changed	Fires on the change of a file or folder. The types of changes include: changes to size, attributes, security settings, last write, and last access time.
Created	Fires on the creation of a file or folder
Deleted	Fires on the deletion of a file or folder
Renamed	Fires on the renaming of a file or folder

Table 15-22.   *The Constants of the **FileSystemWatcher** Enumeration*

You also need to be careful not to create too many events in the **FileSystemWatcher** object, a problem that can arise when a file you are watching is moved to another folder you are also watching. You'll get events for the "departing files" as well as the "arrival files." For example, moving a file from one location to another generates a delete event, **OnDelete**, when the file departs. Then you get an **OnCreated** event when the file arrives at its new location.

You also need to be cognizant of the changes other applications make on your files. Backup software changes the attributes of files. Virus software also has a stake in the file system because it opens files, inspects them, and then closes them. Products like Open File Manager, which lets backup software back up open files, may also conflict.

Too many changes in a short time may also cause the object's buffer to overflow. This will cause the object to lose track of changes in the directory. Memory used by the object is also expensive, because it comes from nonpaged memory that cannot be swapped out to disk. The key is to keep the buffer as small as possible and avoid a buffer overflow by refining your operations. This means dropping unnecessary or redundant filters and subdirectories.

Streams

The previous section covered how we can manage files and folders. Now we will cover the support .NET provides for getting data into files and getting it out again. This is the crux of I/O, and .NET accomplishes it with streams.

The .NET Framework defines a base class called **Stream** that supports the reading and writing of bytes. Any time that you implement stream I/O functionality, you will inherit, or directly instantiate, objects from the classes inherited from **Stream**. The derivatives of **Stream** can be found in **Sytem.IO**, **System.Net**, **System.Security**, and **System.XML**.

Stream is an abstract class and has been extended in a variety of specialized child classes. You can derive from **Stream** and build your own classes to support streaming. But you would be hard-pressed to come up with something that isn't already supported in the base class library (other than soda streams), or that isn't already earmarked for the next release of the .NET Framework.

The **Stream** class and its children provide a facility for handling data, blocks of bytes, without having to care about what happens down in the basement of the operating system. There is no need for you to burden yourself with the myriad details of how data flows down to metal and across the wire. The various layers beyond your method calls are dealt with by the CLR and the file system. So perfectly aligned are these classes with the platform that writing and reading to streams makes you feel guilty for what programmers in the "Wild West" days of C and Assembly had to go through.

The following classes derive from **Stream**:

- **BufferedStream** Reads and writes to other **Stream** objects. This class can be derived from and instantiated.

- **FileStream**   Bridges a **Stream** object to a file for synchronous and asynchronous read and write operations. This class can be derived from and instantiated.

- **MemoryStream**   Creates a **Stream** in memory that can read a block of bytes from a current stream and write the data to a buffer. This class can be derived from and instantiated.

- **CrytoStream**   Defines a **Stream** that bridges data objects to cryptographic services. This class can be derived from and instantiated.

- **NetworkStream**   Defines a **Stream** that bridges data objects to network services. This class can be derived from and instantiated.

The preceding classes provide data streaming operations. This data may be persisted by bridging certain objects to various backing stores. However, the **Stream** objects do not necessarily need to be saved. Your objects might stream volatile information, resident only in memory. For algorithms not requiring backing stores and other output or input devices, you can simply use **MemoryStream** objects.

MemoryStream objects support access to a nonbuffered stream that encapsulates data directly accessible in memory. The object has no backing store and can thus be used as a temporary buffer. On the other hand, when you need to write data to the network, you'll use classes like **NetworkStream**. Your standard text or binary streams can also be managed using the **FileStream** class. **Stream** objects enable you to obtain random access to files through the use of a **Seek** method, discussed shortly.

Another **Stream** derivative you will find yourself using on many occasions is the **CryptoStream** class. We'll go over it briefly later in this chapter. This class is also not included in the **System.IO** namespace but has been added to the **System.Security.Cryptography** namespace.

BufferedStream objects provide a buffering bridge for other **Stream** objects, such as the **NetworkStream** object. The **BufferedStream** object stores the stream data in memory in a special byte cache, which cuts down on the number of calls the object needs to be made to the OS.

FileStream

FileStream objects can be used to implement all of the standard input, output, and error stream functionality. With these objects, you can read and write to file objects on the file system. With it you can also bridge to various file-related operating system handles, such as pipes, standard input, and standard output. The input and output of data is buffered to facilitate performance.

The **File** class, discussed earlier in this chapter, is typically used to create and bridge **FileStream** objects to files based on file paths and the standard input, standard output, and standard error devices. **MemoryStream** similarly bridges to a byte array.

The principal method in a **FileStream** object is **Seek**. It supports random access to files and allows the read/write position to be moved to any position within a file. The location is obtained using byte offset reference point parameters. The following code demonstrates the creation and opening of a file and the subsequent bridge to the **FileStream** object used to write to the file:

```
Dim aFile As New FileStream(source, IO.FileMode.Create)
```

In the preceding code, a file is opened, or created if it does not already exist, and information is appended to the end of the file. The contents of the file are then written to standard output for display.

Byte offsets are relative to a seek reference point. A seek reference point can be the beginning of the file, a position in the file, or the end of the file. The three **SeekOrigin** constructs are the properties of the **SeekOrigin** class.

Disk files always support random access. At the time of construction, the **CanSeek** property is set to true or false depending on the underlying file type. Specifically, if the underlying file type is FILE_TYPE_DISK, as defined in winbase.h, the **CanSeek** property is true. Otherwise, the **CanSeek** property is false.

Table 15-23 lists the members of the **FileStream** class.

Member	Purpose
CanRead (p)	Retrieves a value indicating whether the current stream supports reading
CanSeek (p)	Retrieves a value indicating whether the current stream supports seeking
CanWrite (p)	Retrieves a value indicating whether the current stream supports writing
Handle (p)	Retrieves the operating system file handle for the file that the current **FileStream** object encapsulates
IsAsync (p)	Retrieves a value indicating whether the **FileStream** was opened asynchronously or synchronously
Length (p)	Retrieves the length, in bytes, of the stream
Name (p)	Retrieves the name of the **FileStream** that was passed to the constructor
Position (p)	Retrieves or changes the current position of this stream
BeginRead	Begins an asynchronous read
BeginWrite	Begins an asynchronous write

Table 15-23. *The Members of **FileStream***

Member	Purpose
Close	Closes the file and releases any resources associated with the current file stream
EndRead	Waits for the pending asynchronous read to complete
EndWrite	Ends an asynchronous write, blocking until the I/O operation has completed
Flush	Clears all buffers for this stream and causes any buffered data to be written to the underlying device
Lock	Prevents access by other processes to all or part of a file
Read	Reads a block of bytes from the stream and writes the data in a given buffer
ReadByte	Reads a byte from the file and advances the read position one byte
Seek	Changes the current position of this stream to the given value
SetLength	Changes the length of this stream to the given value
ToString	Returns a **String** that represents the current **Object**
Unlock	Allows access by other processes to all or part of a file that was previously locked
Write	Overridden. Writes a block of bytes to this stream using data from a buffer.
WriteByte	Overridden. Writes a byte to the current position in the file stream

Table 15-23.   *The Members of **FileStream*** (continued)

BeginRead, BeginWrite

When you get ready to open a file object using **FileStream**, you need to specify either synchronous or asynchronous mode. The read and write methods support both modes but, depending on your data and the algorithm, the modes provide significant performance consequences for the synchronous methods (**Read** and **Write**) and the asynchronous methods (**BeginRead** and **BeginWrite**).

Both sets of methods will work in either mode; however, the mode will affect the performance of these methods. **FileStream** defaults to opening files synchronously, but the constructor is overloaded and provides a version of **New** to open files asynchronously.

While either can be used, the underlying file system determines which resources might allow access in only one of these modes. While **FileStream** opens the operating system handle synchronously, this impacts asynchronous method calls, which are made independently of the file systems. To use asynchronous methods, construct the object with a constructor that allows you to specify an **isAsync** argument.

The signature of this **BeginRead** method is as follows:

```
Overrides Public Function BeginRead(ByVal array() As Byte, _
   ByVal offset As Integer, _
   ByVal numBytes As Integer, _
   ByVal userCallback As AsyncCallback, _
   ByVal stateObject As Object _
) As IAsyncResult
```

The following list describes its parameters:

- **array**   A buffer to read data into
- **offset**   The byte offset in the array at which to begin reading
- **numBytes**   The maximum number of bytes to read
- **userCallback**   The method to be called when the asynchronous read operation is completed
- **stateObject**   A user-provided object that distinguishes this particular asynchronous read request from other requests

Before you call **BeginRead**, issue a condition check on the **CanRead** property. This will let you determine whether your object has the all-clear to move into high gear. **BeginRead** will also choke on invalid arguments and throws out exceptions immediately. Wrapping up the method calls in exception handling code is thus critical. Exceptions are also raised during asynchronous read requests. For example, a read may fail if the file reference dies through disk failure, corruption, or some other file catastrophe.

By default, streams smaller than 64KB complete synchronously for better performance. The additional effort required for asynchronous I/O on such small streams negates the advantages of asynchronous I/O. Also, you need to call **EndRead** with **IAsyncResult** to find out how many bytes were read.

Table 15-24 lists the possible exceptions that can result from good read requests that go bad.

Exception	Condition
ArgumentException	The **array** variable's length minus offset is less than **numBytes**
ArgumentNullException	The **array** variable references **Nothing**
ArgumentOutOfRangeException	The **offset** or **numBytes** is negative
IOException	An asynchronous read was attempted past the end of the file

Table 15-24.   *Exceptions That Can Be Generated on a **BeginRead** Operation*

Seek

The **Seek** method changes the current position in the stream to the value passed as the argument. Its signature is as follows:

```
Overrides Public Function Seek( _
  ByVal offset As Long, _
  ByVal origin As SeekOrigin _
) As Long
```

The following list describes its parameters:

- **offset**   A point relative to the origin from which to begin seeking.
- **origin**   A value that specifies the beginning, the end, or the current position as a reference point for **origin**, using a value of type **SeekOrigin**.
- **Return Value**   You get back the new position in the stream.

Seek can cause the exceptions listed in Table 15-25.

You can use the **CanSeek** property to determine whether the current instance supports seeking. Also note that seeking to any location beyond the length of the stream is supported. Set the position to one byte beyond the end of the stream, as recommended by the SDK documentation to open a new file and write to it. This lets you append to the file. Just remember that the position cannot be set to more than one byte beyond the end of the stream.

Exception	Type Condition
IOException	An I/O error occurred
NotSupportedException	The stream does not support seeking. This can happen if the **FileStream** is constructed from a pipe or console output.
ArgumentException	Attempted seeking before the beginning of the stream or more than one byte past the end of the stream
ObjectDisposedException	Methods were called after the stream was closed

Table 15-25.   *Exceptions That Can Be Generated on a **Seek** Operation*

One of the classes you will find especially interesting is **IsolatedStorageFileStream**. This class supports the streaming of data to isolated storage units, which are a form of private file systems that can contain files and that can only be accessed by an owner, an application, or user.

Writing to a file stream object can be performed like the following examples which add words to the top of the noisewords files. Existing words are pushed down:

```
Public Sub AddWords(ByVal fileandpath As String, ByVal neword As String)
  Dim aFile As New FileStream(source, IO.FileMode.OpenOrCreate, _
  FileAccess.Write)
  Dim wordadder As StreamWriter = New StreamWriter(aFile)
  'Gets new words to add to the file.
  wordadder.WriteLine("neword)
  wordadder.Close()
End Sub
```

After the words are added, the file stream is closed and the information is automatically saved. The following example appends to a file. Instead of the words inserted at the top of the file, they are appended at the end of the text in the file:

```
Public Sub AddWords(ByVal source As String, ByVal neword As String)
  Dim aFile As New FileStream(source, IO.FileMode.OpenOrCreate, _
  FileAccess.Write)
  Dim wordadder As StreamWriter = New StreamWriter(aFile)
  'Gets new words to append to the end of the file.
```

```
      wordadder.BaseStream.Seek(0, SeekOrigin.End)
      wordadder.WriteLine("neword)
      wordadder.Close()
End Sub
```

In the preceding examples, there is a slight difference at the **Seek** calls. The change is the **BaseStream.Seek** method of the **StreamWriter** object that we created. I did a **SeekOrigin.End** on the **StreamWriter** object, and since the mode that we opened the file in was **FileMode.OpenOrCreate**, it opened the existing file that we created earlier. This means that the subsequent executions of the second example will append the data to the file. You can easily change the position by changing the **SeekOrigin** enumeration. This is demonstrated as follows:

```
Public Sub AddWords(ByVal source As String, ByVal neword As String)
  Dim aFile As New FileStream(source, IO.FileMode.OpenOrCreate, _
  FileAccess.Write)
  Dim wordadder As StreamWriter = New StreamWriter(aFile)
  'Gets new words to append to the end of the file.
  wordadder.BaseStream.Seek(0, SeekOrigin.Begin)
  wordadder.WriteLine("neword")
  wordadder.Close()
End Sub
```

If I were to rerun the earlier example, the file would get overwritten, because I am not moving the pointer to the end of the file; I am just writing as soon as I open the file.

SeekOrigin Enumeration

The **SeekOrigin** construct is used by the **Seek** methods of the **Stream** and "writer" classes described in this chapter. **Seek** methods take an offset parameter that is relative to the position specified by **SeekOrigin**. Table 15-26 lists the **SeekOrigin** constants.

Member	Purpose
Begin	Specifies the beginning of a stream
Current	Specifies the current position within a stream
End	Specifies the end of a stream

Table 15-26. *Constants of the **SeekOrigin** Enumeration*

This following example shows a use of **SeekOrigin** with **BaseStream** and **Seek** to set the file pointer of the underlying stream to the beginning:

```
Dim aFile As New FileStream(source, FileMode.OpenOrCreate,_
FileAccess.Read)
Dim wordReader As New StreamReader(aFile)
'Position the file StreamReader file pointer at the beginning.
wordReader.BaseStream.Seek(0, SeekOrigin.Begin)
```

The following example demonstrates the **Current** constant of the **SeekOrigin** enumeration. First it creates a **FileStream** object with the file access option set to write. Then it creates a **StreamWriter** object to write the data into the file (with full path) passed to the method's **source** parameter. The word to write to the file is passed to the **noiseword** parameter.

```
Public Sub AddNoises(ByVal source As String, _
  ByVal noiseword As String)
  Dim fStream As New FileStream(source, FileMode.OpenOrCreate, _
  FileAccess.Write)
  ' Create a 'StreamWriter' to write the data into the file.
  Dim sWriter As New StreamWriter(fStream)
  sWriter.WriteLine(noiseword)
  ' Update the 'StreamWriter'.
  sWriter.Flush()
  ' Close the 'StreamWriter' and FileStream.
  sWriter.Close()
  fStream.Close()
End Sub
```

The following method now reads the contents of the file into an array as follows:

```
Public Sub ReadNoises(ByVal source As String)
  Dim fStream As New FileStream(source, FileMode.OpenOrCreate, _
    FileAccess.Read)
  'Place the cursor at the beginnig of the file.
  fStream.Seek(0, SeekOrigin.Begin)
  'Get a byte array
  Dim byteArray(20) As Byte
  'Read the first twenty characters into the byte array.
  fStream.Read(byteArray, 0, 20)
  Dim Encoder As New ASCIIEncoding()
  Console.WriteLine("The Contents of the array are {0}: ", _
```

```
   Encoder.GetString(byteArray))
Console.WriteLine(Encoder.GetString(byteArray))
'Increment the file pointer from CurrentPosition by one character.
fStream.Seek(1, SeekOrigin.Current)
'Read the next five characters.
fStream.Read(byteArray, 0, 20)
Console.WriteLine("The rest of the array are {0}: ", _
   Encoder.GetString(byteArray))
'Close the FileStream.
fStream.Close()
End Sub
```

BufferedStream

A buffered stream's purpose in life is to read and write to another stream. **BufferedStream** is essentially a block of bytes in memory used to cache data, thereby reducing the number of calls to the operating system. You will use your buffers to improve read and write performance, but you cannot use a buffer to read and write at the same time. Objects of the **BufferedStream** work like the **FileStream** object, but the **Read** and **Write** methods of **BufferedStream** are used to automatically maintain the buffer. I liken it to overdraft protection for a stream.

If you always read and write for sizes greater than the internal buffer size, then **BufferedStream** might not even allocate the internal buffer. **BufferedStream** also buffers reads and writes in a shared buffer. Usually, you do a series of reads or writes, but rarely alternate between reading and writing.

The following method example demonstrates the creation of a **BufferedStream** object bridged to the earlier declared standard **FileStream** object:

```
Public Sub AddNoises(ByVal source As String, _
ByVal noiseword As String)
   Dim fStream As New FileStream(source, FileMode.OpenOrCreate, _
      FileAccess.Write)
   Dim bStream As New BufferedStream(fStream)
   'Create a 'StreamWriter' to write the data into the file.
   Dim sWriter As New StreamWriter(bStream)
   sWriter.WriteLine(noiseword)
   ' Update the 'StreamWriter'.
   sWriter.Flush()
   ' Close the 'StreamWriter' and FileStream.
   sWriter.Close()
   fStream.Close()
End Sub
```

NetworkStream

A **NetworkStream** object provides the underlying stream of data for network access. **NetworkStream** implements the standard .NET Framework stream mechanism to send and receive data through network sockets. It also supports both synchronous and asynchronous access to the network data stream.

CryptoStream

The CLR also uses a streams model for reading and writing encrypted data. This service is provided by the **CryptoStream** object. Any cryptographic objects that implement **CryptoStream** can be chained together with any objects that implement **Stream**, so the streamed output from one object can be bridged into the input of another object. The intermediate result (the output from the first object) does not need to be stored separately.

MemoryStream

MemoryStream is no different from the previously mentioned streams except that volatile memory is used as the so-called backing store rather than a disk or network sockets. This class encapsulates data stored as an unsigned byte array that gets initialized upon the instantiation of the **MemoryStream** object. However, the array can also be created empty. The encapsulated data in the object is thus directly accessible in memory. **Memory** streams can reduce the need for temporary buffers and files in an application, which can improve performance by an order of magnitude.

GetBuffer

To create a **MemoryStream** object with a publicly visible buffer, simply call the default constructor. A stream can be declared resizable, which resizes the array, but in that respect, multiple calls to **GetBuffer** might not return the same array. You can also use the **Capacity** property, which retrieves or changes the number of bytes allocated to the stream. This ensures consistent results. **GetBuffer** also works when the **MemoryStream** is closed.

ToArray

The **ToArray** method is useful for translocating the contents of the **MemoryStream** to a formal **Byte** array. If the current object was instantiated on a **Byte** array, then a copy of the section of the array to which this instance has access is returned. **MemoryStream** also supports a **WriteTo** method that lets you write the entire contents of the memory stream to another stream—one that has a persistent backing store, for example.

Readers and Writers

So far we have looked at classes that let you work with **Strings** that also provide a facility for you to retrieve or supply the **String**. We have also gone from manipulating **String** data to constructing **Strings** and using them in various display fields. While capturing the values provided by the various **ToString** methods is possible, the classes and utilities discussed earlier don't provide much in the way of features that get data on the road. **StringReader** and **StringWriter** provide the basic facilities for character I/O.

The .NET Framework's data streaming (I/O) support inherits from the abstract **TextReader** and **TextWriter** classes that live in the **System.IO** namespace. These classes form the basis of support for internationally viable and highly distributed software because they support Unicode character streams.

Text Encoding

Before we look at the reader and writer classes, understand that methods are provided to convert **Arrays** and **Strings** of Unicode characters to and from **Arrays** of **Bytes** encoded for a target code page. A number of encoding implementations are thus provided in the **System.Text** namespace. The following list presents these encoding classes:

- **ASCIIEncoding class**   Encodes Unicode characters as single 7-bit ASCII characters. It only supports character values between U+0000 and U+007F.

- **UnicodeEncoding**   Encodes each Unicode character as two consecutive **Bytes**. Both little-endian (code page 1200) and big-endian (code page 1201) **Byte** orders are supported.

- **UTF7Encoding**   Encodes Unicode characters using the UTF-7 encoding (UTF-7 stands for UCS Transformation Format, 7-bit form). This encoding supports all Unicode character values, and can also be accessed as code page 65000.

- **UTF8Encoding**   Encodes Unicode characters using the UTF-8 encoding (UTF-8 stands for UCS Transformation Format, 8-bit form). This encoding supports all Unicode character values, and can also be accessed as code page 65001.

Other encoding can be accessed using the **GetEncoding** method that passes a code page or name argument.

When the data to be converted is only available in sequential blocks (such as data read from a stream), an application can use a decoder or an encoder to perform the conversion. This is also useful when the amount of data is so large that it needs to be divided into smaller blocks. Decoders and encoders are obtained using the **GetDecoder** and **GetEncoder** methods. An application can use the properties of this class, such as **ASCII**, **Default**, **Unicode**, **UTF7**, and **UTF8**, to obtain encodings.

CLASSES AND OBJECTS

Applications can initialize new instances of encoding objects through the **ASCIIEncoding,** **UnicodeEncoding, UTF7Encoding,** and **UTF8Encoding** classes.

Through an encoding, the **GetBytes** method is used to convert arrays of **Unicode** characters to **Array**s of **Bytes**, and the **GetChars** method is used to convert **Array**s of **Byte**s to **Array**s of Unicode characters. The **GetBytes** and **GetChars** methods maintain no state between conversions.

The core **GetBytes** and **GetChars** methods require you to provide the destination buffer and ensure that the buffer is large enough to hold the entire result of the conversion. An application can use one of the following methods to calculate the required size of the destination buffer.

The **GetByteCount** and **GetCharCount** methods can be used to compute the exact size of the result of a particular conversion, and an appropriately sized buffer for that conversion can then be allocated.

The **GetMaxByteCount** and **GetMaxCharCount** methods can be used to compute the maximum possible size of a conversion of a given number of bytes or characters, and a buffer of that size can then be reused for multiple conversions.

The **GetMaxByteCount** method generally uses less memory, whereas the second method **GetMaxCharCount** generally executes faster. See the .NET Framework SDK documentation for the various encoding and decoding methods.

StringReader/StringWriter

Besides the standard methods of the **StringBuilder** class, which make it useful on its own, the framework bridges **StringBuilder** to both the **StringWriter** and **StringReader** classes. This cooperation between the "builder" classes and the "transport" classes lets you stream characters into and out of **StringBuilder** objects as a type of staging area where **String**s get to go to be manipulated. You can think of these classes as the instruments you can use to write and read characters to the **StringBuilder** object.

Despite being the **StringBuilder**'s apprentices, these classes are located in the **System.IO** namespace (while **StringBuilder** lives in **System.Text**), which has a lot to do with the fact that **StringWriter** derives from **TextWriter** (discussed in this section). Table 15-27 presents the important members of the **StringReader** class.

The syntax for creating a **StringReader** class is as follows:

```
Dim s as new StringReader("C:\MyFile.txt")
```

Table 15-28 lists the members of the **StringWriter** class.

*If these methods look familiar, they should. The **Console** class uses synchronized (thread-safe) instances of **TextWriter** and **TextReader** to write to and read from the console. Later, we take a look at the support for streaming and how all these classes connect.*

Member	Purpose
Close	Closes the **StringReader**
Peek	Returns the next available character but does not consume it
Read	Reads the next character or next set of characters from the input string
ReadBlock	Reads a maximum of counted characters from the current stream and writes the data to the buffer, beginning at a specified location
ReadLine	Reads a line from the underlying string
ReadToEnd	Reads to the end of the text stream

Table 15-27.   *The Members of the **StringReader** Class*

Member	Purpose
Encoding (p)	Retrieves the encoding in which the output is written
FormatProvider (p)	Retrieves an object that controls formatting
NewLine (p)	Retrieves or changes the line terminator string used by the current **TextWriter**
Close	Closes the current **StringWriter** and the underlying stream
CreateObjRef	Creates an object that contains all the relevant information required to generate a proxy used to communicate with a remote object
Flush	Clears all buffers for the current writer and causes any buffered data to be written to the underlying device
GetLifetimeService	Retrieves the current lifetime service object that controls the lifetime policy for this instance
GetStringBuilder	Returns the underlying **StringBuilder** object
Write	Writes to this instance of the **StringWriter**
WriteLine	Writes some data as specified by the overloaded parameters, followed by a line terminator

Table 15-28.   *The Members of the **StringWriter** Class*

Write

User the **Write** method to write data to an object that can receive a text input stream, such as **StringBuilder**. The following code illustrates writing to a **StringBuilder** object:

```
Public Sub AddWords(ByVal source As String, ByVal newword As String)
  Dim sBuilder As New StringBuilder()
  Dim strWriter As New StringWriter(sBuilder)
  strWriter.Write(newword)
  'check if write worked
  Console.WriteLine(sBuilder)
End Sub
```

Write does not force a new line, and new text is either appended to the existing text or, depending on the object, overwrites it.

WriteLine

The **WriteLine** method works exactly like **Write**, but adds a line terminator to the end of the **String**, which forces a new line. This is demonstrated as follows:

```
Console.WriteLine(sBuilder)
```

GetStringBuilder

The **GetStringBuilder** method will return an instance of **StringBuilder** that you can write to. Append and insert your characters to the object as demonstrated in the earlier "Building Strings with StringBuilder" section and then simply write the object to a line.

```
Public Sub AddChars()
  'Create a StringBuilder with 20 characters capacity and capped at 20
  Dim sBuilder As New StringBuilder(20, 20)
  'Create a character array to hold characters that will be
  'fed into the StringBuilder.
  Dim charArray As Char() = {"I"c, " "c, "l"c, "o"c, "v"c, "e"c, _
    " "c, "V"c, "B"c, " "c, "."c, "N"c, "E"c, "T"c, "."c}
  'Create a StringWriter...
   Dim strWriter As New StringWriter()
  'and bridge it to the StringBuilder object
   sBuilder = strWriter.GetStringBuilder()
  'Write a bunch of characters from the array to the StringBuilder.
  strWriter.Write(charArray, 0, 15)
   Console.WriteLine(sBuilder)
End Sub
```

The code writes "I Love VB .NET" to the console. The technique shown here is useful for building **Strings** that you can then simply write to a text output stream. The receiver picks up the object and simply writes to the console or similar device.

Flush

Flush can also be used to write to the output device. But the method clears the writer's buffer in the process. The following example demonstrates flushing to a **StringBuilder** object:

```
sBuilder = strWriter.GetStringBuilder()
'Write a bunch of characters from the array to the StringBuilder.
strWriter.Write(charArray, 0, 15)
strWriter.Flush(charArray, 0, 15)
Console.WriteLine(sBuilder)
```

Close

The **Close** method simply shuts down the writer and its underlying stream as follows:

```
strWriter.Close()
```

StreamReader/StreamWriter

While derivatives of the **Stream** class are intended for **Byte** I/O, the **StreamReader** and **StreamWriter** classes are intended for writing to and reading from a standard text file. The **StreamReader** and **StreamWriter** classes default to UTF-8 encoding unless specified otherwise, instead of defaulting to the ANSI code page for the current system. UTF-8 handles Unicode characters correctly and provides consistent results on localized versions of the operating system. See the earlier "Text Encoding" discussion.

Table 15-29 lists the members of the **StreamReader** class; Table 15-30 lists the members of the **StreamWriter** class.

The **Read** and **Write** methods read and write the number of characters specified by their **Count** parameter. These are to be distinguished from **BufferedStream.Read** and **BufferedStream.Write**, which read and write the number of bytes specified by a **count** parameter. Use the **BufferedStream** methods only for reading and writing an integral number of byte array elements. For example:

```
Dim sReader As New StreamReader(FilePath)
```

The optional arguments are as follows:

- **encoding** Specified character encoding to use
- **BufferSize** Suggested minimum buffer size
- **DetectEncodingFromByteOrderMarks** Encoding type indicator

Member	Purpose
Null (p)	A **StreamReader** around an empty stream
BaseStream (p)	Returns the underlying stream
CurrentEncoding (p)	Retrieves the current character encoding that the current **StreamReader** is using
Close	Closes the **StreamReader** and releases any system resources associated with the reader
CreateObjRef	Creates an object that contains all the relevant information required to generate a proxy used to communicate with a remote object
DiscardBufferedData	Allows a **StreamReader** to discard its current data
Peek	Returns the next available character but does not consume it
Read	Reads the next character or next set of characters from the input stream
ReadBlock	Reads a maximum of counted characters from the current stream and writes the data to a buffer, beginning at a specified index
ReadLine	Reads a line of characters from the current stream and returns the data as a string
ReadToEnd	Reads the stream from the current position to the end of the stream

Table 15-29.   *The Members of the **StreamReader** Class*

When you read data from the **StreamReader** for the first time, you can change the encoding by changing the **encoding** flag.

The **DetectEndcodingFromByteOrderMarks** detects the encoding from the first three bytes of the stream. The big-endian, little-endian, and UTF-8 Unicode text is automatically recognized. If the encoding cannot be determined, the user-defined encoding is implemented.

StreamWriter defaults to using an instance of the **UTF8Encoding** object unless specified otherwise. This instance of **UTF8Encoding** is constructed such that the **Encoding.GetPreamble** method returns the Unicode byte order mark written in UTF-8.

Member	Purpose
Null (Nothing) (p)	Provides a **StreamWriter** with a backing store that can be written to, but not read from
AutoFlush (p)	Retrieves or changes a value indicating whether the **StreamWriter** will flush its buffer to the underlying stream after every call to **Console.Write** or **Console.WriteLine**
BaseStream (p)	Retrieves the underlying stream that interfaces with a backing store
Encoding (p)	Retrieves the encoding in which the output is written
FormatProvider (p)	Retrieves an object that controls formatting
NewLine (p)	Retrieves or changes the line terminator string used by the current **TextWriter**
Close	Closes the current **StreamWriter** and the underlying stream
Flush	Clears all buffers for the current writer and causes any buffered data to be written to the underlying stream
Write	Writes to the stream
WriteLine	Writes some data as specified by the overloaded parameters, followed by a line terminator

Table 15-30.   *The Pertinent Members of **StreamWriter***

The preamble of the encoding is added to a stream when you are not appending to an existing stream. This means any text file you create with **StreamWriter** will have three byte order marks at its beginning. UTF-8 handles all Unicode characters correctly and gives consistent results on localized versions of the operating system. If we now create a **StreamReader** class, we can figure out what we wrote to the **StreamWriter** with the following code:

```
Dim sReader As StreamReader =  New StreamReader(fStream)
sReader.BaseStream.Seek(0, SeekOrigin.Begin)
For intX = 0 to 25
  Console.Write cstr(rReader.Read)
Next intX
```

CLASSES AND OBJECTS

BinaryReader/BinaryWriter

The **BinaryReader** and **BinaryWriter** classes read and write primitive data types as binary values in a specific encoding. The primary methods in these classes are **Read** and **Write**, which come in a different flavor for every data type supported in the framework.

XML I/O

The .NET XML namespaces remind me of the Amazon jungle. So vast, so thick, and so chock-full of functionality that you need a dedicated platoon of experts to decipher them—in a book dedicated to the subject of .NET XML support. Still, two classes in the XML realm belong in our inner circle of I/O support because they represent the fundamental ability to read and write: **XMLTextReader** and the **XMLTextWriter**.

Reading XML Files

The **XmlTextReader** object provides forward-only, read-only access to a stream of XML data. You can gain programmatic access to the current node in the text by being able to reference the node on which the reader is positioned. The reader advances through the data by being able to use any of the read methods and properties to reflect the value of the current node.

The **XmlTextReader** class implements the abstract **XmlReader,** which has been designed to conform to W3C Extensible Markup Language (XML) 1.0 and the Namespaces in XML recommendations. **XmlTextReader** provides us with the functionality listed in Table 15-31.

The **XmlTextReader** class provides the parsing and tokenizing functionality we need to read XML files. The XML Document Object Model (DOM) provides great flexibility for loading XML files as documents, but there is still the need to read XML as a file-based stream and perform basic element manipulation. Since loading XML via the services of the DOM does require some overhead, loading XML files through the **XmlTextReader** is normally faster and more efficient.

To read an XML file, declare an instance of the **XmlTextReader** in the same way you declare a standard text reader, and then call the **Read** method until you reach the end of the XML file. Here is a simple implementation of this example, where the **"xmlfilepath"** parameter expects the path to a valid XML file:

```
Public Sub RdzXML(ByVal xmlfilepath As String)
  Dim xmlRdr As XmlTextReader = New XmlTextReader(xmlfilepath)
  Do While xmlRdr.Read()
    'Do something x-rated
  Loop
End Sub
```

Member	Purpose
AttributeCount (p)	Retrieves the number of attributes on the current node
BaseURI (p)	Retrieves the base URI of the current node
CanResolveEntity (p)	Retrieves a value indicating whether this reader can parse and resolve entities
Depth (p)	Retrieves the depth of the current node in the XML document
Encoding (p)	Retrieves the encoding of the document
EOF (p)	Retrieves a value indicating whether the reader is positioned at the end of the stream
HasAttributes (p)	Retrieves a value indicating whether the current node has any attributes
HasValue (p)	Retrieves a value indicating whether the current node can have a Value
IsDefault (p)	Retrieves a value indicating whether the current node is an attribute that was generated from the default value defined in the DTD or schema
IsEmptyElement (p)	Retrieves a value indicating whether the current node is an empty element (for example, **<MyElement/>**)
Item (p)	Retrieves the value of the attribute
LineNumber (p)	Retrieves the current line number
LinePosition (p)	Retrieves the current line position
LocalName (p)	Retrieves the local name of the current node
Name (p)	Retrieves the qualified name of the current node
Namespaces (p)	Retrieves or changes a value indicating whether to do namespace support
NamespaceURI (p)	Retrieves the namespace URI (as defined in the W3C Namespace specification) of the node on which the reader is positioned
NameTable (p)	Retrieves the **XmlNameTable** associated with this implementation

Table 15-31.   *The Members of the **XMLTextReader** Class*

Member	Purpose
NodeType (p)	Retrieves the type of the current node
Normalization (p)	Retrieves or changes a value indicating whether to normalize white space and attribute values
Prefix (p)	Retrieves the namespace prefix associated with the current node
QuoteChar (p)	Retrieves the quotation mark character used to enclose the value of an attribute node
ReadState (p)	Retrieves the state of the reader
Value (p)	Retrieves the text value of the current node
WhitespaceHandling (p)	Retrieves or changes a value that specifies how white space is handled
XmlLang (p)	Retrieves the current xml:lang scope
XmlResolver (p)	Changes the **XmlResolver** used for resolving DTD references
XmlSpace (p)	Retrieves the current xml:space scope
Close	Changes the **ReadState** to **Closed**
Equals (inherited from Object)	Determines whether two **Object** instances are equal
GetAttribute	Retrieves the value of an attribute
GetRemainder	Retrieves the remainder of the buffered XML
IsStartElement	Tests if the current content node is a start tag
LookupNamespace	Resolves a namespace prefix in the current element's scope
MoveToAttribute	Moves to the specified attribute
MoveToContent	Checks whether the current node is a content (non–white space text, CDATA, Element, EndElement, EntityReference, or EndEntity) node. If the node is not a content node, the reader skips ahead to the next content node or end of file. It skips over nodes of the following types: **ProcessingInstruction**, **DocumentType**, **Comment**, **Whitespace**, or **SignificantWhitespace**.

Table 15-31.   *The Members of the **XMLTextReader** Class* (continued)

Member	Purpose
MoveToElement	Moves to the element that contains the current attribute node
MoveToFirstAttribute	Moves to the first attribute
MoveToNextAttribute	Moves to the next attribute
Read Overridden	Reads the next node from the stream
ReadAttributeValue	Parses the attribute value into one or more **Text**, **EntityReference**, or **EndEntity** nodes
ReadBase64	Decodes Base64 and returns the decoded binary bytes
ReadBinHex	Decodes BinHex and returns the decoded binary bytes
ReadChars	Reads the text contents of an element into a character buffer. This method is designed to read large streams of embedded text by calling it successively.
ReadElementString	This is a helper method for reading simple text-only elements
ReadEndElement	Checks that the current content node is an end tag and advances the reader to the next node
ReadInnerXml	Reads all the content, including markup, as a string
ReadOuterXml	Reads the content, including markup, representing this node and all its children
ReadStartElement	Checks that the current node is an element and advances the reader to the next node
ReadString	Reads the contents of an element or a text node as a string
ResetState	Resets the state of the reader to **ReadState.Initial**
ResolveEntity	Resolves the entity reference for **EntityReference** nodes
Skip	Skips the children of the current node

Table 15-31. *The Members of the **XMLTextReader** Class* (continued)

CLASSES AND OBJECTS

Note *The **XmlTextReader** class is located in System.Xml.*

When we read the file, the **XmlTextReader** class that we create maintains a **nodetype** property used to return the type of node currently being read. The **Name** property retrieves element and attribute names, and the **Value** property retrieves the text value that the node contains. Consider the following example of reading the XML file, and returning the **Name** and **Value** property:

```
Public Sub RdzXML(ByVal xmlfilepath As String)
  Dim xmlRdr As XmlTextReader = New XmlTextReader(xmlfilepath)
  Do While xmlRdr.Read()
    Console.WriteLine(xmlRdr.Name & xmlRdr.Value)
  Loop
End Sub
```

Table 15-32 describes the node types and their equivalent in the W3C DOM. The types are further explained in the list that follows the table.

- **Attribute** nodes can have the following child node types: **Text** and **EntityReference**. The **Attribute** node does not appear as the child node of any other node type. It is not considered a child node of an **Element**.

- **CDATA** sections are used to escape blocks of text that would otherwise be recognized as markup. A **CDATA** node cannot have any child nodes. It can appear as the child of the **DocumentFragment**, **EntityReference**, and **Element** nodes.

- **Comment** nodes cannot have any child nodes. They can appear as the child of the **Document**, **DocumentFragment**, **Element**, and **EntityReference** nodes.

- **Document** nodes can have the following child node types: **XmlDeclaration**, **Element** (maximum of one), **ProcessingInstruction**, **Comment**, and **DocumentType**. Document nodes cannot appear as the child of any node types.

- **DocumentFragment** nodes associate a node or subtree with a document without actually being contained within the document. A **DocumentFragment** node can have the following child node types: **Element**, **ProcessingInstruction**, **Comment**, **Text**, **CDATA**, and **EntityReference**. **DocumentFragment** nodes cannot appear as the child of any node types.

- **DocumentType** nodes can have the following child node types: **Notation** and **Entity**. They can appear as the child of the **Document** node.

- **Element** nodes can have the following child node types: **Element**, **Text**, **Comment**, **ProcessingInstruction**, **CDATA**, and **EntityReference**. The **Element** can be the child of the **Document**, **DocumentFragment**, **EntityReference**, and **Element** nodes.

- **Entity** nodes can have child nodes that represent the expanded entity (for example, **Text** and **EntityReference** nodes). The **Entity** can appear as the child of the **DocumentType** node.

Node Type	XML	Value
None		0
Element	<name>	1
Attribute	Id='123'	2
Text	'123'	3
CDATA	<![CDATA[...]]>	4
EntityReference	&foo;	5
Entity	<!ENTITY...>	6
ProcessingInstruction	<?pi test?>	7
Comment	<!—comment—>	8
Document		9
DocumentType	<!DOCTYPE...>	10
DocumentFragment		11
Notation	<!NOTATION...>	12
Whitespace	Whitespace	13
SignificantWhiteSpace	Whitespace between markup in a mixed content model	14
EndTag	</foo>	15
EndEntity	Returned when the reader is at the end of the entity replacement as a result of a call to **ExpendEntry**	16
CharacterEntity	Returned when the reader has been told to report character entities	17

Table 15-32.   *XML Node Types*

- **EntityReference** nodes can have the following child node types: **Element**, **ProcessingInstruction**, **Comment**, **Text**, **CDATA**, and **EntityReference**. An **EntityReference** node can appear as the child of the **Attribute**, **DocumentFragment**, **Element**, and **EntityReference** nodes.

- **Notation** nodes cannot have any child nodes. A **Notation** node can appear as the child of the **DocumentType** node.

- **ProcessingInstruction** nodes cannot have any child nodes. Such a node can appear as the child of the **Document**, **DocumentFragment**, **Element**, and **EntityReference** nodes.

- **Text** nodes cannot have any child nodes. The **Text** node can appear as the child node of the **Attribute**, **DocumentFragment**, **Element**, and **EntityReference** nodes.

- **XmlDeclaration** nodes must be the first node in the document. This node cannot have children. It is a child of the **Document** node. It can have attributes that provide version and encoding information.

Using the **XmlTextReader** is no different to using the earlier reader and writer classes discussed, so we don't need any elaborate examples here to show how it works. The same goes for the **XmlTextWriter** class coming up.

Writing XML Files with XMLTextWriter

The **XMLTextWriter** represents a writer that provides a fast, noncached, forward-only way of generating streams or files containing XML data that conforms to the W3C Extensible Markup Language (XML) 1.0 and the namespaces in XML recommendations.

The **XmlTextWriter** maintains a namespace stack corresponding to all the namespaces defined in the current element stack. Using **XmlTextWriter** you can declare namespaces manually. Table 15-33 lists the pertinent members of **XmlTextWriter**.

The following example writes data to represent a data set:

```
Public Sub rytzXml(ByVal target As String)
  Dim xmlRyter As XmlTextWriter = New XmlTextWriter(target, _
    System.Text.Encoding.ASCII)
  xmlRyter.WriteStartElement("Body")
  xmlRyter.WriteAttributeString("xmlns", "noo", Nothing, "urn:1")
  xmlRyter.WriteStartElement("oyvey", "urn:1")
  xmlRyter.WriteEndElement()
  xmlRyter.WriteStartElement("oyvey", "urn:1")
  xmlRyter.WriteEndElement()
  xmlRyter.WriteEndElement()
  xmlRyter.Close()
End Sub
```

Member	Purpose
BaseStream (p)	Retrieves the underlying stream object
Formatting (p)	Indicates how the output is formatted
Indentation (p)	Retrieves or changes how many **IndentChars** to write for each level in the hierarchy when **Formatting** is set to **Formatting.Indented**
IndentChar (p)	Retrieves or changes the character to use for indenting when **Formatting** is set to **Formatting.Indented**
Namespaces (p)	Retrieves or changes a value indicating whether to do namespace support
QuoteChar (p)	Retrieves or changes the character to use to quote attribute values
WriteState (p)	Retrieves the state of the write
XmlLang (p)	Retrieves the current xml:lang scope
XmlSpace (p)	Retrieves an **XmlSpace** representing the current xml:space scope
Close	Closes this stream and the underlying stream
Flush	Flushes whatever is in the buffer to the underlying streams and also flushes the underlying stream
LookupPrefix	Returns the closest prefix defined in the current namespace scope for the namespace URI
WriteAttributes	When overridden in a derived class, writes out all the attributes found at the current position in the **XmlReader**
WriteAttributeString	When overridden in a derived class, writes an attribute with the specified value
WriteBase64	Encodes the specified binary bytes as Base64 and writes out the resulting text
WriteBinHex	Encodes the specified binary bytes as BinHex and writes out the resulting text

Table 15-33.   *The Pertinent Members of the **XmlTextWriter** Class*

Member	Purpose
WriteCData	Writes out a <![CDATA[...]]> block containing the specified text
WriteCharEntity	Forces the generation of a character entity for the specified Unicode character value
WriteChars	Writes text a buffer at a time
WriteComment	Writes out a comment <!--...--> containing the specified text
WriteDocType	Writes the DOCTYPE declaration with the specified name and optional attributes
WriteElementString	When overridden in a derived class, writes an element containing a string value
WriteEndAttribute	Closes the previous **WriteStartAttribute** call
WriteEndDocument	Closes any open elements or attributes and puts the writer back in the **Start** state
WriteEndElement	Closes one element and pops the corresponding namespace scope
WriteEntityRef	Writes out an entity reference as follows: & name
WriteFullEndElement	Closes one element and pops the corresponding namespace scope
WriteName	Writes out the specified name, ensuring it is a valid name according to the W3C XML 1.0 recommendation (www.w3.org/TR/1998/REC-xml-19980210#NT-Name)
WriteNmToken	Writes out the specified name, ensuring it is a valid **NmToken** according to the W3C XML 1.0 recommendation (www.w3.org/TR/1998/REC-xml-19980210#NT-Name)
WriteNode	When overridden in a derived class, copies everything from the reader to the writer and moves the reader to the start of the next sibling

Table 15-33.   *The Pertinent Members of the **XmlTextWriter** Class* (continued)

Member	Purpose
WriteProcessingInstruction	Writes out a processing instruction with a space between the name and text as follows: <?name text?>
WriteQualifiedName	Writes out the namespace-qualified name. This method looks up the prefix that is in scope for the given namespace.
WriteRaw	Writes raw markup manually
WriteStartAttribute	Writes the start of an attribute
WriteStartDocument	Writes the XML declaration with the version "1.0"
WriteStartElement	Writes the specified start tag
WriteString	Writes the given text content
WriteSurrogateCharEntity	Generates and writes the surrogate character entity for the surrogate character pair
WriteWhitespace	Writes out the given white space

Table 15-33. *The Pertinent Members of the **XmlTextWriter** Class* (continued)

CLASSES AND OBJECTS

The preceding code produces the following output (noo and oyvey are Yiddish XML):

```
<Body xmlns:noo="urn:1">
  <noo:oyvey />
  <noo:oyvey />
</Body>
```

The writer promotes the namespace declaration to the root element to avoid having it duplicated on the two child elements. The child elements pick up the prefix from the namespace declaration. **XmlTextWriter** also allows you to override the current namespace declaration. In the following example, the namespace URI "foo" is overridden by "bar" to produce the XML element **<q:node xmlns:q="bar"/>**.

```
xmlRyter.WriteStartElement("q", "node", "foo")
xmlRyter.WriteAttributeString("xmlns", "q", Nothing, "bar")
```

The **Write** methods can take a prefix as an argument to let you specify which prefix to use. Also, if there are multiple namespace declarations mapping different prefixes to the same namespace URI, **XmlTextWriter** walks the stack of namespace declarations backward and picks the closest one. When the **WriteAttributeString** call does not specify a prefix, the writer uses the last prefix pushed onto the namespace stack.

If namespace conflicts occur, **XmlTextWriter** resolves them by generating alternate prefixes. For example, if an attribute and element have the same prefix but different namespaces, **XmlTextWriter** generates an alternate prefix for the attribute. The generated prefixes are named n{i}, where i is a number beginning at 1. The number is reset to 1 for each element.

Attributes that are associated with a namespace URI must have a prefix (default namespaces do not apply to attributes). This conforms to section 5.2 of the "W3C Namespaces in XML" recommendation. If an attribute references a namespace URI, but does not specify a prefix, the writer generates a prefix for the attribute.

When writing an empty element, an additional space is added between the tag name and the closing tag: for example, **<item />**. This provides compatibility with older browsers.

When a **String** is used as a method parameter, a reference to **Nothing** and **String.Empty** is equivalent. **String.Empty** follows the W3C rules.

You can also write strongly typed data by using the **XmlConvert** class which works just like the standard **Convert** class. For example, the following line of code converts **String** data to **Double** data:

```
Dim total As Double = XmlConvert.ToDouble(reader.ReadInnerXml())
```

There is a ton of XML specific information that would be terrific to cover but much of it belongs in a book dedicated to the subject. However, there is one more I/O facility we need to look at in this book before we can close the long chapter: serialization.

Serialization with XML

Serialization support in .NET is extensive. The base implementations and interfaces are derived from **System.Runtime.Serialization**. The **System.Runtime.Serialization.Formatters** namespace provides enumeration support and the base classes for the serialization formatting. Then we have access to two namespaces that provide the actual implementation and formatting. One class provides binary formatting (**Formatters.Binary**) and the other, which we are going to use, provides text formatting in SOAP format (**Formatters.Soap**).

The **Soap** class is very useful for serializing across and through network boundaries, because the data, XML, is encapsulated in a SOAP envelope. The framework also provides a namespace specializing in pure XML serialization streams, essentially serializing into and out of XML documents.

Serialization is very useful for persisting data stored in various data structures. It's also very lightweight and efficient to use, especially for applications running on Web servers, database servers, and various facilities that you may need to scale. One scenario where serialization comes in handy is loading data into an application at start up. The data can be easily piped into an object that is created on the fly at runtime. The Indexworks application introduced at the beginning of the chapter is one such application.

The outmoded way of loading data into the application at runtime would have you create an array or some other data structure, initialize the structure, open a flat text file, read the data into the array, and then position the array for access by the application's various components. The modern approach instead lets you suck in (serialize) the XML file into the application's processing space, creating and initializing the object that holds the data all at the same time.

The lattter sophisticated approach cuts out the step of having to read in the data and add it to the elements of an array or the nodes of a linked list one element or node at a time. It's like having the entire object and all its data sitting on the disk ready for loading at a moment's notice (in fact it's exactly that).

Let's make the linked list class we constructed in Chapter 13 work with serialization. This will allow a consumer of the linked list class not only to persist the data while an application works on the list, but every time the application starts up, the object and data can be automatically reconstituted inside the application ready for use.

Before we can use the serialization classes, we have to decorate the classes we want to serialize as being serializable. Let's apply this to our linked list class (**BaseNodeContainer**). This entails providing serialization attributes for the base class. This is done with the following code, part of which has been set in bold, so that you can easily see the changes from the class constructed earlier:

```
Option Explicit On
Option Strict On

Imports System
Imports System.Runtime.Serialization

<Serializable()> Public Class BaseNodeCollection
```

What's now different about the preceding class compared to the classes shown throughout the book? For starters, the class makes a reference to the **Serialization** classes by importing the **System.Runtime.Serialization** namespace. This is defined using the Visual Basic .NET attributes indicators, <>.

But remember that the **BaseNodeContainer** class also contains a composite **Node** class so we need to decorate that class with the same attribute as follows:

```
<Serializable()> Public Class Node
```

You next need to provide a method in the base class that performs the actual serialization. But before you can do that, you need to build the file and stream support into the class to get the data in the object to the file system, and store it in a folder somewhere. This can now be easily accomplished with the extensive I/O facilities we have covered in earlier parts of this chapter, which by now we should have mastered.

To do the object serializing and persist the data, you will need to create a method that walks the graph, serializes the data in the SOAP/XML format, and then saves the stream into a file. The following method achieves that objective:

```
Public Sub PlayOutList(ByVal target As String)
  Dim meData As New SoapFormatter()
  Try
    If File.Exists(target) Then
      File.Delete(target)
    ElseIf (Not File.Exists(target)) Then
      Dim fileForObject As New FileStream(target, IO.FileMode.Create)
      meData.Serialize(fileForObject, Me)
      fileForObject.Close()
    End If
  Catch e As Exception
    Me.exceptinfo = e.Message
  End Try
End Sub
```

The first step in actually implementing serialization using the SOAP format is to create a new **SoapFormatter** object to process the SOAP stream, and this was done using the following line:

```
Dim meData As New SoapFormatter()
```

However, to instantiate **SoapFormatter** as **meData**, we need to reference the **SoapFormatter** class. This should be done using an **Imports** directive as follows:

```
Imports System.Runtime.Serialization.Formatters.Soap
```

Next it would be a good idea to create the stream and file support for our object or it will be going nowhere in a hurry. This is achieved using the following code:

```
If File.Exists(target) Then
  File.Delete(target)
ElseIf (Not File.Exists(target)) Then
  Dim fileForObject As New FileStream(target, IO.FileMode.Create)
...
```

So, what have we done here so far? In the **SerializeOut** method, we created a **SoapFormatting** object that provides the necessary transport to move the data from the object's location in memory to storage. We could have used TCP or some other transport mechanism, but SOAP is an excellent protocol to use and allows us to support the serialization of the object across machine and even process boundaries.

Notice the **target** parameter in the **PlayOutList** signature. This variable gives us a unique string containing path and filename as the target that will receive the current object to be serialized.

Finally, we call the **Serialize** method on the **FileStream** object and reference the current object's data via the **Me** keyword. Here's the code that achieves this:

```
meData.Serialize(fileForObject, Me)
fileForObject.Close()
```

To recap: first, we created a new file to receive the SOAP stream. Then, we called the **Serialize** method on **Me** and bridged it to the target file. After the job is done, it is a good idea to close down the **FileStream** object with a simple call to its **Close** method. You can check the serialized data in the file. If everything worked according to plan, the saved file will contain data that looks like this (very much abridged with the data in the linked list shown in bold):

```
<SOAP-ENV:Envelope
xmlns:xsi="http://www.w3.org/2001/XMLSchema-instance"
xmlns:xsd="http://www.w3.org/2001/XMLSchema"
xmlns:SOAP-ENC="http://schemas.xmlsoap.org/soap/encoding/"
xmlns:SOAP-ENV="http://schemas.xmlsoap.org/soap/envelope/"
SOAP-ENV:encodingStyle="http://schemas.xmlsoap.org/soap/encoding/"
. . .

<Data id="ref-6" xsi:type="SOAP-ENC:string">I</Data>
<Data id="ref-7" xsi:type="SOAP-ENC:string">love</Data>
<Data id="ref-10" xsi:type="SOAP-ENC:string">VB</Data>
<Data id="ref-12" xsi:type="SOAP-ENC:string"> </Data>
<Data id="ref-14" xsi:type="SOAP-ENC:string">.</Data>
<Data id="ref-16" xsi:type="SOAP-ENC:string">NET</Data>
. . .

</SOAP-ENV:Body>
</SOAP-ENV:Envelope>
```

That's all there is to serializing object data out to some persistent storage location. Instantiating the class automatically provides the serialization support.

Activating Serialization at Run Time

There is no code in the **BaseNodeContainer** class that fires serialization events (that automatically calls the **SerializeOut** method), so at first we will have to do it manually from the application user interface, which we will create with many of the resources we will learn about in the next chapter. And, we could easily add a timed interval event that calls the **PlayOutList** method every few seconds or minutes.

In the meantime, the following line of code triggers the serialization manually:

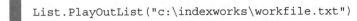

```
List.PlayOutList("c:\indexworks\workfile.txt")
```

We simply call the method and pass it the target file information. This method then invokes the serialization process in the class, and that's all there is to it.

Now what happens if the application is shut down (or the machine shuts down abnormally while we are in the middle of a read (a power failure or something))? How do we get back the data we had when we first started up or last wrote to the **List** object? Reconstituting the object is as easy as spewing out to the file. We need to create a method to implements the deserialization. Follow these steps to provide this:

1. Check if an object was serialized to disk. This could be as simple as checking for the target file.

2. Create a holding object in the application of the type to receive the data from the file.

3. Create a SOAP formatter to recover the data from the file.

4. Open the file.

5. Deserialize into the holding object.

This is demonstrated in the followed deserializer method, which can be provided by an external facility, like the application's startup object or the user interface:

```
Public Sub PlayInList(ByVal source As String)
  Try
    If File.Exists(source) Then
      Dim fileForRecover As Stream = File.OpenRead(source)
      Dim aClone As New BaseNodeCollection()
      Dim meData As New SoapFormatter()
      aClone = CType(meData.Deserialize(fileForRecover), _
      BaseNodeCollection)
      fileForRecover.Close()
      List = aClone
    End If
  Catch E As Exception
    Me.exceptinfo = E.Message
  End Try
End Sub
```

If all works well the linked list gets sucked off the hard disk and is streamed into the application, just in time to service the first Web surfer's hit on the search page. What's cooking in the **PlayInList** method? First, we needed to create a new **Stream** to open the file in the **source** folder. The code that achieves this can be written as follows:

```
Dim fileForRecover As Stream = File.OpenRead(source)
```

*Notice how we can simply call **File.OpenRead** and feed it to the stream.*

Next, we have to create a new **SoapFormatter** just as we did earlier. The code that achieved this is as follows:

```
Dim meData As New SoapFormatter()
```

Finally, we call the **Deserialize** method and close the file when we are done. Notice that we use **CType** to explicitly convert the holder type to the type represented in deserialized data.

```
aClone = CType(meData.Deserialize(fileForRecover), _
BaseNodeCollection)
fileForRecover.Close()
```

At this point, our job is not yet done. We got the data back, but it is in an object that is not currently being referenced by our application. However, all that's left to do is to copy the data in one object to the other. There are several different ways to recover the data, but just assigning the new object to the old object's reference variable (**List**) is the easiest (as long as the old object is not yet holding active data that will be lost when you cut its lifeline).

To call the deserializer method at run time is not difficult to achieve. You could call it shortly after startup, as demonstrated in the following code, to enhance the console application:

```
Public Sub New
  MyBase.New
  List.PlayListIn()
End Sub
```

That's all there is to the serialization. Incidentally, for local applications that do not need to serialize across network streams, it would be faster and more secure to use the binary formatter class.

Observations

While this chapter might be big enough to be called a book, it still represents a tiny portion of the I/O and data processing ability of .NET. This chapter demonstrated the design and creation of several business objects that are useful in a variety of data processing scenarios. We used a variety of facilities in the .NET Framework to achieve the results. These included the exhaustive **String**, character and text manipulation classes, the file I/O and directory management classes, classes that empower us to read and write to streams of text and binary data, and finally, that critical requirement all businesses now harp after, XML support.

In the next chapter, we'll complete the mission by providing smart user interface elements to all of this functionality.

The Complete Reference

Visual
Basic
.NET

Part IV

Writing Software with VB .NET

Chapter 16

Interfacing with the End User

We have come a long way from Chapter 1, which discussed how important it is to separate application logic, business logic, functionality, operations, and services from the user interface and its logic. Recall Figure 1-2, which illustrated a bunch of related file transfer operations that operate in the background or behind the UI components on a form. Most of this book is devoted to everything you need to know to build the logic in first-class applications—the code behind. Now we have to put an interface on the application, so that our users find the application useful, productive, and worth all the money you invested creating the product.

The reason I have delayed our study of Windows forms, visual controls, and UI components to the second-to-last chapter is to stress how important this way of thinking (separation of business and user interface logic) is. If you did not pick up on this theme in the opening chapters and throughout the book, then it should become very clear to you in this chapter. It is the only way you can write software in the modern age of distributed computing and component, widget-based, breakfast factory, software development. In fact, it is the only way you should write software.

Waiting until this point in the book to get into forms and UI stuff is very different from how past VB books were written, which typically launched into the subject from the get go. I read many of those book years ago, and I always felt the authors were trying to get the readers up and running as quickly as possible (in some cases, the franchise, the target readers, of the book merited this approach) before presenting a solid foundation for writing code. Often, too much emphasis was placed on creating applications centered on forms that were nowhere near those used in the real world—"dragging and dropping" your way to a finished product in what seemed akin to painting by numbers.

> **Note**
> *Another big payoff of first learning all you can about the .NET object model in the earlier chapters is that you will be able to navigate around the forms and control classes like a pro. Visual controls and components, such as forms and menus, are all objects, so you'll have an insider's understanding of how their properties, identifiers, modifiers, and so on are defined, specified, and set.*

I believe that the only thing this so-called rapid application development achieved was rapid application frustration, because keen developers would lose interest due to the frustration of not learning what it takes to write good software. Here is a good example from an e-mail I received while writing this chapter:

> "I am depressed. I have made two classes. The first has the input fields and the second accesses a table. But I don't know the way to link them and pass the data from the first class to the second. I don't know how to create the container object that will contain the data. In the first class I have created a table. Please help."

The problem with many developers (like this one) is that they spend too much time looking at cute UIs and not enough time implementing the application.

It was also amazing to me, circa 1995, how completely different Delphi and VB books were from the new Java books that were taking the world by storm. They hardly covered the UI subject, partly because Java's UI technology was so bad in the first years that seven-day-old roadkill looked better on your desktop.

The world of software development has changed dramatically in the past few years. Before the advent of the Web and distributed computing (which has your objects potentially spread all around the network), programmers typically engineered *heavy forms,* forms in which most of the logic and functionality is packed into the form's module or class itself. Much of the business logic—such as database connections, algorithms that managed data structures, events, file operations, I/O, network connections, error handling, and so on—were programmed in functions and procedures in one single form file (or at least encapsulated into it).

This model sufficed in the years before objects, because most applications, especially the ones written by Delphi and Visual Basic programmers, centered around a heavy user interface, comprising a bunch of heavy forms, that squatted on a user's computer. That was acceptable for the era because nothing but the form itself was able to use the functionality built into it. This is illustrated in Figure 16-1, showing a fat form interacting with the user and doing most of the application processing itself.

At the same time, packing all that functionality and data into a single form, or a collection of forms, did little good for application design, maintenance, reusability, quality assurance, and so much more that object-orientation brought.

Sure, by version 6 of classic VB, we had some semblance of OOP and could delegate specialized operations and functionality to VB 6 classes. But inheritance and native

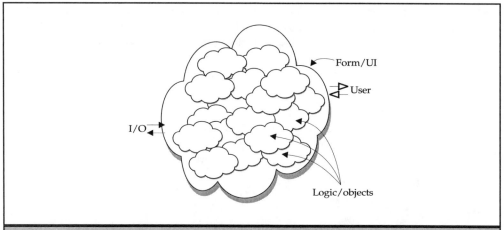

Figure 16-1. *The fat form's logic is hard to maintain, reuse, extend, and debug*

interfaces were lacking, and thus it was not as easy to decouple UI logic from business or core logic like you can with Java.

As we have discussed in the past 15 chapters, you have all the power you need in a pure object-oriented framework to delegate UI logic—interacting with the user, getting data from the user, presenting data and information to the user—to the form. Behind the scenes, objects are delegated the tasks of getting information from the components on the forms, processing and computing that information, and returning it to the form so that the form can present it to the user. This is illustrated (similarly to Figure 1-2) in Figure 16-2, where objects are created behind the form, and the form sits in the middle as the intermediary between business logic on the back end and the end user on the front end.

Light forms that interact with decoupled code in objects provide you another important benefit. With objects, shared classes, delegates, and interfaces completely disconnected from the UI, the UI can change in any way it needs to, to accommodate the user, without affecting a single line of code in the objects (where the action happens). In other words, your UI can be located on a watch, a PDA, a telephone, a server, a workstation, a tablet, on the other side of the galaxy, on a console, or in another reality, without affecting the business logic in any way whatsoever.

This disconnection is exactly how ASP.NET applications and rich-client applications will work as we move into mainstream .NET development. All it takes to move a desktop application to the Internet is to drop the form-based UI running on the client, and replace it with a Web form running on Internet Explorer.

The separation of the two application "domains" allows an effective development team to keep its best UI people working on the front end while the logic and objects in the operational side of the application can be worked on by the best class and object designers and code construction workers. As long as the "back-end" developers understand that they are creating classes and objects that clients' code will "hook" into, you can achieve a highly cohesive and productive software development workforce that lets developers that have an artistic flair do a lot more that just screen painting.

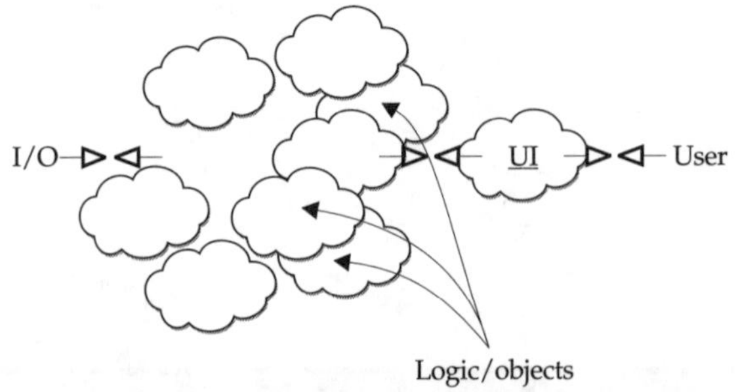

Figure 16-2.   *The light form and its objects are easier to maintain, reuse, extend, and debug*

There is no longer an excuse not to delegate properly with Visual Basic .NET and the power of the .NET Framework. There is no excuse not to extend specialized and generic collections of classes with inheritance, and there is no excuse not to delegate and use the power of polymorphism with native interfaces and delegates.

A Windows forms program can be a stand-alone executable or exist as the client portion of a multitiered system. There are various ways of connecting to the back-end logic, and the most cutting-edge method is via Web services technology over HTTP. The server typically can be connected to a database, a mail server, or any other collection of objects you care to call "server." The Windows forms technology is such that your new featherweight classes can act as the UI to a powerful, data-enabled system that leverages the rich UI of a client application with the advanced processing of an application server. To encapsulate this is a single utterance: "The Web is dead, long live the Web."

Windows Forms

The Windows Forms technology is the new UI solution for the .NET Framework. All UI elements, such as forms and visual input, output, and presentation components, extend a hierarchy of classes found in the **System.Windows.Forms** namespace. You can use the forms classes and controls classes as is, or derive from them to create your own UI and visual controls and components. The Windows forms are an ideal OOP solution for creating rich UIs for local workstation clients, or as thin UIs developed for multitier distributed solutions.

Windows-based UIs are typically cast in the following three styles:

- **Single document interface (SDI)**   This is the UI that only opens a single document, such as Notepad or WordPad or Outlook, which opens e-mails. You first have to close the current document before you can open a new one. You can use the SDI application for simple document editors, various utilities, and applications that do not need to work with multiple open forms.

- **Multiple document interface (MDI)**   This UI contains numerous forms that encapsulate documents, database input fields, grids, drawing areas, and various layouts and components. You can open new forms in the UI as you need them. You do not need to close forms before opening new ones. Forms inside the main form are enumerated into the Window menu for easy management and access. A good example of the MDI application is Microsoft Word.

- **Explorer-style interface**   This UI is an SDI application that is split into two panes inside a single parent form. The left pane provides access to a tree of items, such as the so-called "cool" bar or some other type of collection. The right pane provides the details of the node selected from the tree. A good example of this type of interface is Microsoft Outlook or Windows Explorer.

A form is your application's little claim of screen space that you will use to communicate with users. Your form will occupy either a portion of the screen or all of it. Forms are typically rectangular in shape and can be made to shrink or grow to any size—from the size of a dime or less, to the size of the screen when the form is fully maximized. Forms can be solid, opaque, or invisible. With advanced support of the Windows XP and .NET Server operating systems, forms can also now be any shape.

You use the form to present information to the user and to accept input from the user. This is achieved by placing familiar objects on the form, with which the user interacts to send and receive information to and from the application.

UI developers arrange the controls on the form in an aesthetic and productive manner by exposing the various properties of the input/output controls placed on the form. The properties of the controls define their behavior and affect how the user interacts with the application.

As the interface developer, you will also spend a substantial amount of your time behind the form's UI, implementing its code. Controls do not magically hook into existing functionality you have written; you still have to "wire up" the UI to the back end and business logic and hook up the events to the event handlers and event listeners. This wiring involves capturing events generated by the controls on the form, such as text being entered, mouse clicks, button clicks, scrolling through lists, collapsing and expanding trees, and so on. The events communicate with interested objects that monitor the form for services they need to perform, such as sending data to a database and retrieving data from the database.

A Form Is an Object

As previously stated many times, a class is a template or a blueprint for an object. The .NET Form class is such a blueprint for the form object that you instantiate. **Form** classes can also be extended by you. This means you can easily inherit from existing framework or custom forms to add functionality or modify existing behavior. In other words, when you add a form to your project, you can choose to inherit from the standard **Form** class or from a custom base **Form** class you may have already developed. The form hierarchy of classes is a perfect example of how inheritance is used as the foundation for all specializations of classes in an OO framework. **Form** objects are also controls, because the standard form provided by the framework ultimately inherits from its parent **Control** class.

Chapter 9 presented a concise introduction to the **Form** class in the discussion of inheritance and aggregation. We saw then how a form can be created entirely in the Code Editor. But Visual Studio makes it far easier to use the Windows Forms Designer to create and modify forms. Later in this section, we will discuss the steps to take to kick off a UI project with the creation of your main form, and any collateral forms used by your application.

The System.Windows.Forms Namespace

The **System.Windows.Forms** namespace contains the collection of classes used for creating Windows-based UI applications. The classes in this namespace can be grouped as follows:

- Control
- UserControl
- Form
- Controls
- Components
- Common Dialog Boxes

Most of the classes within the **System.Windows.Forms** namespace are specializations of the base **Control** class, which provides the base functionality for all controls that are displayed on a **Form**. You will derive from the **Form** class or a specialization of it to represent a window component of your application. Windows can be manipulated interactively through their properties to play the roles of dialog boxes, modeless windows, message boxes, and MDI clients. One form, the parent, becomes the form that represents the application.

The *controls* of an application are familiar objects the user will interact with on a form. Controls typically refer to text boxes, labels, check boxes, radio buttons, list boxes, buttons, and so on. A control can be a small graphical enhancer, such as a slider gauge, or something much more complex, such as a grid or spreadsheet-like control that binds to a data source and displays the contents of a table in the cells of the grid.

The **System.Windows.Forms** namespace encapsulates an impressive collection of control classes that we can use to create the elegant and very functional user interfaces. For example, if we need to build a text editor, the namespace provides us with **TextBox** controls we can use for editing comments and writing documentation, and **ComboBox** controls for choosing section details in the documentation, such as headers, footers, and labels for specifications. We'll use other controls, such as **Label** and **ToolTip**, to display information.

The representation of the project folders, class files, and class members can be provided with the **TreeView** control and the **ListView** control. We'll also use buttons and the **ToolBar** control. We are not attaching to any databases, so we don't need to worry about **DataGrid** controls and other databound controls in our initial exploration of UI elements.

The *components* of an application are often synonymous with controls, but it helps to discern or group nonvisual controls by referring to them as components. These components typically include help items, menu items, help constructs, and tooltips.

Common dialog boxes provide the interface to common operations, such as saving files, opening files, printing and print setup, and so on. These forms are prefabricated, so we can simply "plug" them into our application with less than a full line of code. In the early days of programming for the Windows OS, we had to code these reusable constructs ourselves.

Good examples of these "pluggable" dialog boxes are the interfaces to the printing facilities, like **PageSetupDialog**, **PrintPreviewDialog**, and **PrintDialog**. These objects will be useful for controlling various actions required in the printing of our documents.

Various enumerations in the **System.Windows.Forms** namespace provide various constants that control the look and feel of the UI components and controls.

There are also a number of information controls at our disposal that do not derive from the **Control** class but still provide visual components of the UI. These include **ToolTip**, **ErrorProvider**, and several classes we have already explored, such as **Menu** and **MenuItem**. There is also a **ContextMenu** control that enables you to display menus in the context used to invoke the menu within an application. **Help** and **HelpProvider** are two other classes that enable us to communicate with the user and enrich their experience with our applications.

The **System.Windows.Forms** namespace also encapsulates the **MessageBox** class that lets us display a message box to the user, lets the user click certain buttons, and may also prompt the user for certain information.

*To support Windows XP visual styles, you can set the **FlatStyle** property of some of your visual controls to **System**.*

Automatically Generated Code

While you can easily construct a Windows application in code from scratch, as demonstrated in Chapter 9, it is much easier and makes much more sense to let Visual Studio generate the initial application shell for you.

When you select Windows Application from the New Project dialog box, Visual Studio creates a solution (if one is not open for the new application) and places your new project in it. This project contains various references to core assemblies, namespaces, and so on, and one class, which is named **Form1** by default.

To see the namespaces imported by default, open the Project Properties dialog box. To access this, right-click the project in Solution Explorer, choose Properties, and then choose Imports from the panel on the left side.

The default code generated when you create a form is as follows:

```
Public Class Form1
    Inherits System.Windows.Forms.Form
```

```
Note   The following code is contained within a region by default.
#Region " Windows Forms Designer generated code "
    Public Sub New()
        MyBase.New()
        ' This call is required by the Windows Forms Designer.
        InitializeComponent()
        ' Add any initialization after the InitializeComponent() call.
    End Sub

    ' Form overrides dispose to clean up the component list.
    Protected Overloads Overrides Sub Dispose(ByVal disposing As Boolean)
        If disposing Then
            If Not (components Is Nothing) Then
                components.Dispose()
            End If
        End If
        MyBase.Dispose(disposing)
    End Sub

    ' Required by the Windows Forms Designer.
    Private components As System.ComponentModel.Container

    ' NOTE: The following procedure is required by the Windows Forms Designer.
    ' It can be modified using the Windows Forms Designer.
    ' Do not modify it using the Code Editor.
    <System.Diagnostics.DebuggerStepThrough()> Private Sub InitializeComponent()
        components = New System.ComponentModel.Container()
        Me.Text = "Form1"
    End Sub
#End Region

End Class
```

The **InitializeComponent** section is of interest to you because it is used by the IDE to hold the property values that you visually set in the Windows Forms Designer. These properties persist in the application and are required by the main form.

Introduction to Threading

User interfaces and forms applications often present an opportunity to engage additional threads to help keep the application responsive and enrich the user experience. Applications that perform extensive processing and limit themselves to single threads can cause the UI and access to controls and components to be locked out while the main application thread waits for the process attached to the end of it to complete. In simple terms, locking a user out of an application, even intermittently, is akin to putting a gun to your head and squeezing the trigger.

Lengthy processes, such as long downloads, backing up data, loading data to databases, extensive searching, sorts, virus checking, and the like, could and should be allocated to new threads. An application will fast lose the support of its users if every time it needs to perform a hefty service the user has to take a walk around the block or do something else to kill some time, like looking for King Solomon's mines.

While there are various techniques that can help increase the responsiveness of the application while it processes the data necessary to get the job done, nothing is as effective as invoking multiple threads, especially on computers with only one processor. These threads are fondly known as "workers." You give them a task to perform and then send them off to do the work, while you continue with the other chores.

The .NET Framework's threading model is equipped to take advantage of the small slices of time between user-driven events to process data in the background. For example, a user can continue developing, designing, or configuring an application while the thread recalculates the data in the background within the same application space.

If your user needs to download an extensive document, search and replace some phrases in a document, or sort a big array, they can still keep working while another thread performs the computations or tasks that would normally lock the user out of the application.

Your single application domain of a .NET application can use multiple threads where high-priority threads can manage time-critical tasks and low-priority threads can cater to ad-hoc access required by the user. Having multiple threads on the back end, in a server application, also allows more clients to connect to the service simultaneously. And if the system has multiple processors, multiple threads can be executed on the additional processing stack in true parallel concurrent processing wizardry.

The downside to threading is that it is much more difficult than single threading to design and implement, as you will see in the following code. Threads process independently of each other and, by and large, the order of execution of the threads is nondeterministic. The management of the different threads, controlling the lifetime of the threads, sharing resources between threads, thread cooperation and interoperation, and so on constitute a complicated and complex process.

Threading is also resource intensive. The more threads you throw at an application, the more OS and platform resources you consume. You are still limited by available memory and still have to share hard disks, network connections, ports, the file system, and, of course, the processor. The .NET Framework's thread model also involves the instantiation and support of **AppDomain** objects, which also need to be managed.

In the application design arena, you need to manage threads carefully. If you have too many threads running the opposite of what you were looking to achieve, application response will suffer. Poorly designed and implemented threading architecture can bring an application to a halt and cause it to crash.

Thread termination and destruction needs also need to be addressed, and you need to manage and monitor the thread operations and processing, which can be a potential source of bugs in the application.

To share resources on any machine or in the application, you need to synchronize the access of the threads. Not doing so can cause thread deadlocks and various other conditions that can make your code horrendously difficult to construct, manage, and maintain. Typically, multiple threads need to be synchronized to share ports, file systems, global static (shared) fields, reentrance, access priority, and so on.

In extensive systems, like the send and receive engines of a mail server, or the service engine of a telephony application or automatic call distributor, threading support can be an all-consuming expedition into extensive program design and implementation, involving transaction monitoring, managing critical sections, and prioritizing.

It is for these latter reasons that I considered an extensive treatment of concurrent program design and threading with the .NET Thread Model beyond the scope of this book. So, what I present here should be seen as little more than an introduction to the threading model in .NET, and something to get you started for simple threading algorithms in UIs.

Nevertheless, implementing basic threading support for scenarios such as sorting data and maintaining UI responsiveness is important.

Note *For an in-depth discussion on how Windows operating systems implement threading, concurrency, and parallel processing, and the differences between preemptive and nonpreemptive multitasking, log on to www.sdamag.com and download the white paper, "Concurrent Programming on Windows NT," by Jeffrey R. Shapiro (Jacaranda Communications, Inc, 1987, 2002).*

The User Interface and Thread Design

Generally speaking, providing an application with support for multiple threads and threading is not a task akin to dropping controls onto forms or wiring up visual elements and event handlers to application logic. It requires careful planning and design, because your UI will make use of the threads through which to run the wires that connect the UI logic to the business and application logic of your product.

You can think of the threading and wiring up of the application as akin to flying a jetliner that is controlled by numerous wires, which are accessed and controlled by the pilot and other flight engineers from their cockpit controls. The UI is like a cockpit, and all the controls and gadgets that make the jet fly are the controls and components that give your application its flight ability.

On the back end are the engines that push the craft and the controls that alter the pitch of wing flaps that allow the pilot to steer the craft in a certain heading, to land, and to take off. Connecting the two ends are the wires, the threads. If the threads snap or collide and get entangled, the passengers and the flight crew are doomed to certain death.

So is it with threading an application, especially one with a complex UI and some advanced business and application logic down in the engine room. To get us taxiing on the runway, however, the easiest way to handle a multithread requirement to keep a UI responsive is with the aid of an additional thread devoted to background tasks that can relieve the interface and keep the user working. Before we get into the implementation of a thread, and pop the hood to yank at the wires, let's first have a brief look at the .NET Framework's thread model.

The .NET Framework's Thread Model

The .NET Framework's thread model is represented by the **System.Threading** namespace, which is partitioned between the System (classes for thread delegates) and mscorlib assemblies. The classes and constructs in this namespace contain all the support for threads, thread synchronization, thread events, critical sections, thread prioritizing, locking, and monitoring.

We learned in Chapter 2 the relevance of application domains and how they are applied to the .NET Framework execution environment. These subprocesses provide the operation context and environment that our managed .NET applications run in. When you start an application, the CLR implicitly provides a single thread for it and allocates it to the application domain that represents your program. The single thread (and any future threads) wires up your application to the base OS, in unmanaged space.

However, you can spawn additional threads from your application to handle concurrent operations, and the CLR also gives programmatic opportunity and ability to create additional application domains.

Managed threads are allowed to operate freely within your application process in its domain, and they are allowed to move freely between application domains. It is also possible to maintain only one thread in your application domain and move it between several application domains. This is essentially what the .NET Framework refers to as its "free-threading model." It is precisely this model, and the power of its implementation, that requires you to devote a significant effort to a sound threading architecture for critical concurrent processing applications that need it. In a nutshell, so powerful is the model that "given enough thread, you can easily hang yourself."

Getting Started with Basic Threading

The central character in the threading model story is the **System.Threading.Thread** class. **Thread** objects extend **System.Object** but they cannot be further extended by you or me. The instantiation of multiple **Thread** objects is demonstrated in

Figure 16-3. You can instantiate and put into service as many **Thread**s as you need to execute any methods in any objects or classes referenced in your application. The threads run concurrently so any objects that are the target of the threads are processed concurrently with the objects accessed by other threads. Naturally, if there is only one thread in an application the only object that can be processing is the one that is the target of the thread.

The **Thread** object controls the thread, sets its priority, and monitors its execution status. Think of it as nothing more than the "worker" I mentioned earlier that you summon and have "run a method" while you go off and do something else.

Table 16-1 lists the basic members of the **System.Threading** namespace we will encounter in this chapter. Of course, there are loads more classes and constructs in the namespace, but they will be tackled in the advanced threading treatise.

To start a new thread in the application, we must first create a delegate to represent the method to execute. Then, we pass that delegate to a new instance of the **Thread** object. That's really all there is to adding multithreading to your application.

The following code added to an application creates a new **Thread** object and receives a reference to a method that fires the maintance run. The thread then takes off concurrent to the main application thread and works in the background.

```
Public Sub StartMaintenance()
   'Create and instance of the object that encapsulates
   'the IndexOps maintenance methods
   Dim IdxMaintenance As New IndexOpsMaintenance()
   Dim idxM As New ThreadStart(AddressOf IdxMaintenance.StartMaintenance)
   Dim IdxThread As New Thread(idxM)
   IdxThread.Start
End Sub
```

This code employs the **ThreadStart** delegate, which is used to point to the program code executed by a **Thread** (remember from Chapter 14 that delegates underpin the entire .NET Framework). It is very similar to an event that gets fired, and the delegate

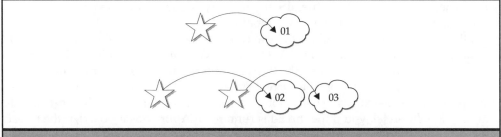

Figure 16-3.   *Multiple **Thread** objects means concurrent processing*

Classes	Purpose
IsAlive (p)	A property that retrieves a value indicating the execution status of the current thread
ThreadState (p)	A property that retrieves the state of the referenced **Thread** object
Thread	The class for creating, controlling, and managing threads
ThreadAbortException	The exception that is thrown when a call is made to the **Thread.Abort** method
ThreadExceptionEventArgs	The data for the **ThreadException** event
ThreadStart (d)	The delegate that represents the method that will handle the **Start** event of a **Thread**
ThreadStateException	The exception that is thrown when a **Thread** is in an invalid **ThreadState** for the method call

Table 16-1. *Abridged Listing of Classes in the **System.Threading** Namespace*

is simply used to "wrap" (in other words, specify the interface) the method signature to be executed. The **AddressOf** operator is used to bind to the method in the class it is implemented in.

After the delegation is complete, the **Thread** object's **Start** method is invoked. If you call **Start** more than once on the same working thread, a **ThreadStateException** will be raised. Naturally, it's good programming practice to always enclose threading operations in **Try . . . Catch. . . Finally** blocks.

Start's job is to make an asynchronous request to the OS for a thread. **Start** completes immediately, and if the system gives the "go" the thread goes to work. At this point, you can access the data in the **ThreadState** property. This information provides you with the ability to check in on your worker at will.

If the **Thread** runs into trouble, you can call its **Abort** method, which shuts it down and raises a **ThreadAbortException**. At this point, you can also peek at the **IsAlive** property, which will return **True** if the thread is still running or **False** if it is dead.

ThreadState can also report the current state of the **Thread** object at any time. This property provides an extensive collection of constants encapsulated in the **ThreadState** enumeration. It can tell you if the thread is running, if **Abort** was invoked, if the thread is sleeping, if the thread is stopped, and so on.

You can gain a significant performance boost by using an additional thread to cater to the request of a user to engage in an operation that may require some lengthy processing time. Using the extra thread in this fashion is pretty straightforward. Rather than putting the single application thread allocated to every application to work on such a task, simply create the **Thread** object as shown in the preceding code and delegate it to the job of managing the thread.

You also do not have to hard-code the thread creation code into any of your forms. Simply delegate to one of the business objects referenced from the form. The object and its thread go off and do their work and the user can continue without being any the wiser.

It looks simple enough. The difficulties arise when you need to create more threads that potentially go off and collide with each other. You can imagine the problems if more than one maintenance **Thread** object was created in the preceding code and they all tried to access the same files. One thread might start serializing a file out to disk while another may be trying to serialize it back to the application. That's where the advanced features provided by locks, monitors, thread pools, waits, and critical sections come into play. Reaching that level is a thread for another day.

MDI Applications

The MDI application comprises a single containing parent form and a collection of MDI child windows. The child windows, known as the "subwindows," present various interaction opportunities for the user as he or she works with the application. An MDI parent form is not difficult to create. You can create the form using the Windows Forms Designer, in a visual style, or nonvisually in code.

Creating the MDI Parent

A form is made into an MDI parent form at design time by setting its **IsMDIContainer** property to **True**. This can be done from the form's property editor or in code. Once this property is set to **True**, the form becomes the MDI container and all other windows become its so-called children.

To get started with an MDI application, perform the following steps:

1. Create a Windows Application project from the File, New menu or from the Add, New Project menu accessible from the Solution Explorer.

2. When the new form appears in the designer, click its body and select the **IsMDIContainer** property from the Properties window. Set the property to **True**. The main body of the window disappears, leaving a white canvas that serves as the backdrop for the interaction with the child windows. Child windows can be expanded to fill this inner frame, and the menus of the child window can be merged with the parent.

You can set the **IsMDIContainer** property in code as follows:

1. Switch to code view by right-clicking the form's icon in Solution Explorer and choosing View Code from the form's context menus.

2. In the **InitializeComponent** method, add the following line of code:

```
Me.IsMDIContainer = True
```

You can also set the following properties while in this method, or from the Properties window:

```
Me.Name = "MainForm"
Me.Text = "Indexworks"
Me.WindowState = FormWindowState.Maximized
```

At this point, it makes life easier if you rename the actual source code file to something more meaningful than Form1.vb. I changed the name to MForm (for main form), which tells me that the form contains the source for the parent form. I also renamed the class file for the form to **MainForm**, which is more useful than **Class1**. The **Text** property shown in the preceding code is the caption at the top of the parent form, which you reserve for the name of the application.

It is easier to work with MDI child windows when the parent form is maximized. You will also notice that the edges of the MDI parent form will be the same as the system color, which you set in the Windows System control panel. This property is not affected by the back color set using the **Control.BackColor** property. At this juncture, if the form is too small in the designer, you can make it bigger by dragging with the mouse, or you can set the height and width with the following code in the **InitializeComponent** method:

```
Me.ClientSize = New System.Drawing.Size(600, 400)
```

Once this is done, you can add the first menu resources to the parent form as follows:

1. Switch to visual mode and click the form so that the Toolbox becomes active.

2. Drag or double-click a **MainMenu** component from the Toolbox palette to the form. The first thing you'll notice is that the menu hides as soon as it hits the form. You can get it back from the drop-down list at the top of the Properties window.

3. Click the menu component's top-level menu item and set the property to **&File**. You can also create sub-submenu items like **&New**, **&Close**, and **&Exit** in the same manner. And you can also create top-level menu items called **&Window** and **&Help**, although a Help menu may be a long way off at this stage from

being implemented (nothing wrong with starting the Help system at the beginning of the development; after all, if you followed my advice in the past chapters, most of the application—the code behind—has already been built). The File menu items are where you write the code to create, and open windows, and the Close menu will be used to close down the application. The Window menu will be used to keep track of open MDI child windows that are enumerated. The menus and the form built at this point are illustrated in Figure 16-4.

Tip   *Rename the menus from the default identifiers, like MenuItem2, that Visual Studio assigns. This will make it easier for you to find and set properties in the correct menu item later when the number of menus listed in the Properties window grows. You also need more intuitive menu names for the event wiring that comes later when you connect the click on a menu item to an event that causes something to happen in the application.*

4. Save and build the form, which, at this point, is nothing more than an empty MDI application that consists of nothing more than the main form. Build the form by selecting the project in Solution Explorer, right-click to expose the context menus, and select Debug | Start New Instance. The application will now run maximized as we had earlier set. The menus will not work, because we have not wired up any code under them. But, you can close the application from the Close facility ("x" or "Close Alt + F4") in the top-right or top-left corner, respectively.

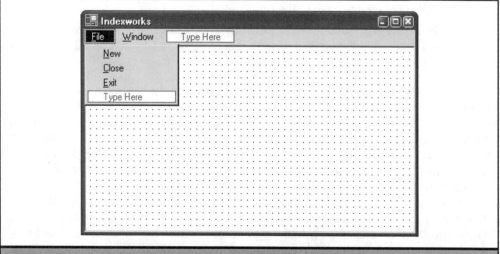

Figure 16-4.   *The new MDI parent form and initial menus*

*You may get a build error stating that the compiler could not find the entry point to the application. That will happen if you change the class name in code from **Class1** to something else (VS is not updated when you change the name manually). It's an easy fix from the Properties window, where you select the new name as the so-called WinMain entry point.*

Creating the MDI Children

An MDI application would not be an MDI application without child forms, so you need to create the template object that instantiates them. To do this, we will add a child form class to the MDI parent, which already has a Window top-level menu item, as well as New and Close to create, close, and enumerate the child form objects, respectively. Return to the drop-down list at the top of the Properties window and select the &Window menu item. You can set its **MDIList** property to **True**.

This property provides the facility to enumerate the "handles" of open or created child windows, essentially instantiated form objects, and maintain the list in the Window menu. You can also place a check mark next to the active child window in this menu. To set this up, go to Solution Explorer, right-click the project name, select Add, and then select Windows Form. This form serves as the template for all MDI child forms. In other words, every time your user selects New from the menu, an instance of this form object will be created. To create the child form in the designer, do as follows:

1. In Solution Explorer, select the name of the project, right-click, and select Add New Item. The Add New Item dialog box appears.

2. Now select Local Project Items from the Categories pane and Windows Form from the Templates pane to the right.

3. In the Name box, name the form **Child.vb** and click the Open button to add the form to the project. The Windows Forms Designer adds another tab to the work area and displays "child" on the canvas.

You can now change the name of the class and its various properties, as we did earlier with the parent. I named the class **ChildForm** (try to avoid giving the class the same name as the file—such as dittoname.vb).You can then also drag whatever controls and components you need onto the child form, thereby aggregating these controls and components to the child class. You do not need to explicitly make the child class a child class, because by default its **IsMDIContainer** property is set to **False**. After all, you can only have one parent MDI container, and it's already been created.

But we do need to wire up the child class to the MDI parent. We can start the ball rolling by creating an event handler under the New menu item we created earlier. To do that, simply double-click New in the parent form. An event handler, just like the ones we studied in Chapter 14, is created and defined in the MDI parent class with all the necessary event constructs.

Now we need to add some code to the event handler, which will create new MDI child forms whenever the user clicks the New menu item. The following code handles the job of instantiating new child window objects. As you write the method, you'll easily spot the correct class in the object browser that IntelliSense pops up under your fingertips. It's a good thing we renamed it from **Form1**, because we can be sure we are referencing the correct class.

```
Private Sub NewMenu_Click(ByVal sender As System.Object, ByVal e As _
System.EventArgs) Handles NewMenu.Click
  Dim AnMDIChild As New ChildForm()
  AnMDIChild.MdiParent = Me
  AnMDIChild.Show()
End Sub
```

Build your application (from the Project menu's Debug, Start New Instance menu item). If your method is implemented as shown in the above code, you'll be able to create new MDI child forms. By setting the **MDIlist** property to **True**, we can see the enumeration of child windows in the Window menu, as illustrated in Figure 16-5.

As mentioned earlier, if you place menus on the child form, they will be merged automatically with the menu items of the parent, provided you have set the

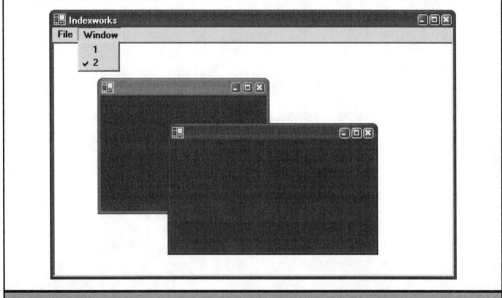

Figure 16-5.   *An MDI application with child windows*

MergeType property of the main menu to **MergeItems**. Additionally, you can also set the **MergeOrder** property so that the menu items from both menus appear in the order you specify.

The Active Child

When you implement child forms in MDI applications, you need a way to reference the active form from other forms and from the parent form. Seldom do you ever work with a child form in total isolation from the rest of the application and its sibling forms. For example, how would you be able to copy text from one child form's text editor to another child form's text editor without having access to the handles of source and target objects?

You can obtain a reference on the active form by using the facility of the parent's **ActiveMDIChild** property. The property returns to you the child form that currently has the focus, or the form that was the most recently active.

In addition, you also need to have information about which control on a child form is active. This information comes to you by way of the **ActiveControl** property. So, if we have more than one control active on a form, this property lets us know which control is currently in focus, or being referenced.

The following code demonstrates the referencing of these properties, and thus of the various properties exposed to the form objects:

```
Public Sub IndexCopy_Click(ByVal sender As Object, _
    ByVal e As System.EventArgs) Handles IndexCopy.Click

    ' Get the active child form.
    Dim activeChild As Form = Me.ActiveMDIChild

    ' If there is an active child form, find the active control, which
    ' in this example should be a RichTextBox.
    If (Not activeChild Is Nothing) Then
        Try
            Dim textBox As TextBox = _
            Ctype(activeChild.ActiveControl, RichTextBox)
            If (Not textBox Is Nothing) Then
                ' Put selected text on Clipboard.
                Clipboard.SetDataObject(textBox.SelectedText)
            End If
        Catch
            MessageBox.Show("Please select TextBox.")
        End Try
    End If
End Sub
```

Arranging the Forms

If you provide the user with the ability to open more than one form, you'll want to provide the ability to arrange the forms automatically. The built-in options you have for arranging all the forms as a collection are Tile, Cascade, and Arrange.

You can provide the arranging facility by reference any one of the **MDILayout** enumeration values that cause the child forms to arrange as you specify. The enumeration values let you arrange the child forms as cascading, as horizontally or vertically tiled, or as child form icons that are fanned out along the lower portion of the MDI form in a minimized state.

You can also use constructs such as the event handlers called by a menu item's **Click** event. This lets you create a menu item, such as Cascade Windows, that provides the effect of cascading child MDI child windows.

To arrange child forms, create a method to set the **MDILayout** enumeration for the parent. The following code demonstrates referencing the **Cascade** constant of the **MDILayout** enumeration for the child windows of the MDI parent form. You will typically use the enumeration in your code as follows:

```
Protected Sub CascadeWindows_Click(ByVal sender As System.Object, _
  ByVal e As System.EventArgs)
  MainForm.LayoutMDI(System.Windows.Forms.MDILayout.Cascade)
End Sub
```

That's about as far as I need to take you with MDI applications. The rest of the chapter explores the various UI elements you can use for building out your MDI application.

Delegating Application Startup and Shutdown

The life of your application typically begins and ends with the parent or main form. When you close the main form, you terminate the life of the application. However, your main form does not have to become the controlling object in the life of your application. You can relocate the entry point and delegate the application's start up and shut down code to other objects. This can be achieved by moving the startup logic into a separate object that only you know exists somewhere in the vast expanse of memory called the heap. You can then start the application from this object and control the arrival and visibility of the forms of your application from the new startup location. The application only ends when you close down the startup/shutdown object by sending it a particular message.

We can add the startup/shutdown class to the project from our Project menus, or we can create a singleton class from scratch as we did in Chapter 13. Within the new

WRITING SOFTWARE WITH VB .NET

class, simply provide a method that controls the appearance and visibility of the main form. This is demonstrated in the following code:

```
Sub Main()
  Dim idxWorks as New IndexWorksMainForm()
  'make a whole lot more of this for here
  idxWorks.Show()
End Sub
```

You still need to change the startup object for the project to be the "hidden" object instead of **Form1** as discussed earlier. Build the application. Now when the application runs, the code within the hidden object executes before you do anything with the instance of **Form1**. You can now do whatever you like with your forms in the background without the user's knowledge. For example, you can set up your form's visibility via its **Visible** property and thus delay its initial arrival into the world.

Keeping a Form on Top

The **TopMost** property of a form specifies whether the form is a topmost form. On the Windows 2000 operating systems and later, the topmost form is always on top of all windows in a given application. On Windows 98, the topmost form is always on top of all windows in all applications.

The **TopMost** property is useful to keep toolbar windows in front of your application's main window so that the user always has access to frequently used items. The topmost form will float above other, non–topmost forms, even when it is not active.

Making a form topmost requires you to set the **TopMost** property to **True**. You can set it interactively in the Properties window, or in code as shown here:

```
Public Sub SetFormTopMost()
  ToolbarForm.TopMost = True
End Sub
```

Form Transparency

The form opacity value allows you to control the opacity of the windows that are displayed in your application. To make a form more transparent, you need only vary the value in its **Opacity** property. Transparent forms are only supported on Windows 2000 or later. Your transparent forms will be completely opaque when run on older OSs, such as Windows 98, and the value set for the **Opacity** property is ignored.

You can set the opacity interactively in the Properties window. The values (of type **Double**) lie between the ranges 0.0 (complete transparency) and 1.0 (complete opacity). The following code shows how to control the opacity programmatically:

```
Public Sub GetThinner()
  FadeForm.Opacity = 0.5
End Sub
```

Modality

Another very important property of forms and dialog boxes is the modality property, which specifies whether a form is either modal or modeless. Modal forms or dialog boxes prevent you from working with the rest of the application until you close them. They are very useful to control user input and to make sure a user is presented with a message in a dialog box or acknowledges and reacts to the requirements of the modal dialog box. Only after clicking OK will the dialog box close and allow the user to continue. A modal dialog box prompting a user to save information or do something next before anything else is the common use for the modality property.

Modeless forms, on the other hand, let you move between forms in the application freely. Open child forms, such as text editors, are modeless. You can switch between the forms with no restrictions and you can continue to work anywhere in the application while the modeless forms are displayed.

You should avoid modeless forms in situations where you do not want your user to access forms and parts of the application in an unpredictable order. A typical reason to provide the modality is to prevent your user from working on something in one window and then opening another window and doing something unpredictable that affects what they were doing in the other window, such as changing data in one window that was edited in another.

Tool windows, for example, can be shown modeless, because the target of the tools and buttons is the form that is currently in focus. A find, search, and replace dialog box is a good example, as is a dialog box for setting document properties such as fonts and margins. The common dialog boxes are modal, because you don't want to open the print facility over one form to print and then inadvertently change out the focus of the target form.

The following code displays a form as a modal dialog box:

```
Public Sub ShowFormsModal(ByRef aForm As Form)
  aForm.ShowDialog()
End Sub
```

WRITING SOFTWARE WITH VB .NET

The **ShowFormsModal** method here takes an argument that can be used to show a form in modal or dialog state. In the following code, we establish your main form as the owner:

```
Private Sub mnuAbout_Click(ByVal sender As Object, _
   ByVal e As System.EventArgs) Handles mnuAbout.Click
   Dim orm As New Form()
   orm.ShowDialog(Me)
End Sub
```

To display a form as a modeless dialog box, call the **Show** method as follows:

```
Dim orm As New Form()
orm.Show()
```

Remember that if a form is shown modal, any code following the **ShowDialog** call is not executed until the dialog box is closed. When a form is shown as modeless, any code following the call to **Show** is executed immediately.

Changing Borders

We can determine the look and feel of our forms by setting various border properties. This is done by changing the **FormBorderStyle** property. The property also lets you control the resizing behavior of the form, how the caption bar is displayed, and what buttons might appear on the form. Table 16-2 lists the property settings for changing borders.

All the border styles listed in Table 16-2, with the exception of **None**, provide the Close box on the right side of the title bar. You can set the border style of the form interactively with the **FormBorderStyle** property.

The border style of the form is set using the **FormBorderStyle** enumeration, so you can also easily set the border style programmatically by setting the **FormBorderStyle** property to one of the values of the enumeration. The following code provides an example:

```
SearchDlgBx.FormBorderStyle = FormBorderStyle.FixedDialog
```

This code sets the form to a border style that lets the form have Minimize and Maximize buttons. You can also specify whether you would like either or both of these to be functional; however, the Minimize and Maximize buttons are enabled by default, and their functionality is manipulated through property settings as well.

Setting	Purpose
None	The form contains no border or border-related elements. It is used for startup forms.
Fixed 3D Not resizable	For 3-D border effects. You can include control-menu box, title bar, Maximize and Minimize buttons on the title bar. Provides a raised border relative to the body of the form.
Fixed Dialog Not resizable	For dialog boxes. It can include control-menu box, title bar, Maximize and Minimize buttons on the title bar. Provides a recessed border relative to the body of the form.
Fixed Single Not resizable	Can include control-menu box, title bar, Maximize button, and Minimize button. Resizable only using Maximize and Minimize buttons. Creates a single line border.
Fixed Tool	For tool windows. It displays a nonsizable window with a Close button and title bar text in a reduced font size. This form does not appear in the Windows taskbar.
Sizable (Default)	Use as main window and child windows. The form is resizable and can include control-menu box, title bar, Maximize button, and Minimize button. It can be resized using the control-menu box, Maximize button, and Minimize button on the title bar, or by using the mouse pointer on any edge.
Sizable Tool	A sizable tool window displays sizable with a Close button and title bar text in a reduced font size. The form does not appear in the Windows taskbar.

Table 16-2.   *Border Styles for Forms*

To disable the Minimize and Maximize buttons set the **MinimizeBox** or **MaximizeBox** properties to **False** (properties such as this are inherited, and it is thus easier to set them interactively in the Properties editor). Changing these properties does not always remove the box, but it may simply disable it.

Changing the Size of Forms

A form can be easily resized by accessing its sizing properties in code or interactively from the Windows Forms Designer. To resize a form in the Windows Forms Designer, simply click it and drag one of the sizing handles that hover at the borders of the form. These handles are the small white boxes on the borders that change the mouse pointer into a double-headed arrow when you touch them.

 For more control in resizing the form, press the arrow keys while holding down the SHIFT *key.*

Entering the values for the width and height, separated by a comma, in the Properties window will change the size, but you can also drill down into the **Size** properties to enter individual **Width** and **Height** values.

You can resize the forms programmatically at run time as demonstrated in the following example, which shows the form size set to 100 by 100 pixels:

```
MainForm.Size = New System.Drawing.Size(100, 100)
```

Changing the **Width** and **Height** properties can be done individually as follows:

```
MainForm.Width = 300
```

In the preceding code, the height of the form remains unchanged. You can also change **Width** or **Height** by setting the **Size** property in the following style:

```
MainForm.Size = New Size(300, Form1.Size.Height)
```

Form size can also be changed in increments programmatically as demonstrated in the following line:

```
MainForm.Width += 200
```

This code sets the width of the form to 200 pixels wider than the current setting. You should always use the **Height** or **Width** property to change the size of a form, unless you're setting both at the same time. The following code, for example, will not change the form size:

```
Dim orm As New Form()
orm.Size.X += 100
```

The **Size** property only returns the **Size** structure containing a copy of the form's height and width, and the X member of this structure is incremented by 100. You would then use the X value somewhere else, but it does not act on the original form size.

Screen Location

You can specify exactly where a form is to be located at startup or at any time during the application's lifetime. This is done by entering values in the form's **Location** property. The position is specified, in pixels, a number of pixels away from the top of the screen and from the left corner of the screen.

I would, however, set the **StartPosition** of the application to the **WindowsDefaultLocation** constant. This tells the OS to compute the best location for the form at startup, based on the current hardware and user preferences. You really have no way of knowing at design time what the user's environment might be. Some people like to chain monitors together and you are thus never certain just how much screen real estate the user really has.

Screen size and resolution are also important, and you will often find your application installed to the lowest resolution in an environment that requires it. I have a client, for example, that has no choice but to set the screen resolution of workers to 600×400 pixels, because a commercial application does not render well in anything higher (so all other UIs suffer).

You can, however, use the Properties window to set the **StartPosition** property to **Manual**. Then, you can type the values for the **Location** property, separated by a comma, as you did earlier with the **Size** values. The first number (X) is the distance from the left border of the display area, and the second number (Y) is the distance from the upper border of the display area. You can also expand the **Location** property to enter the X and Y subproperty values individually.

To position forms programmatically in code, set the **Location** property values by using a **Point** object, as shown in the following example:

```
Form1.Location = New Point (100, 100)
```

You can change the X or Y coordinates of the form's location using the **Left** subproperty for the X coordinate and the **Top** subproperty for the Y coordinate. In the following example we adjust the form's X coordinate to the 300-pixel point:

```
Form1.Left = 300
```

Form position can also be changed in increments programmatically, as demonstrated in the following line:

```
Form1.Left += 200
```

Tip   *The **Location** property can be used to set the X and Y positions simultaneously. But they can also be set individually. To do this, first set the form's **Left** (X) or **Top** (Y) subproperty. The **Point** structure or value type itself only represents the form's location, which is merely a copy of the form's current coordinates.*

WRITING SOFTWARE WITH VB .NET

Also, in light of the fact that a small percentage of users work upside down or lying horizontally, the taskbar may not always be on the bottom default location of the desktop. It would thus be a good idea to use the **DesktopLocation** property to factor in the startup location of your form. It sets the location of your form relative to the taskbar. Docking the taskbar to the left or top obscures the desktop's 0-based X and Y coordinates (0,0). Thus, a form with the **DesktopLocation** property set to (0, 0) will always appear in the upper-left corner of the primary monitor, but a taskbar, if present, will not obscure it.

To set the **DesktopLocation** property programmatically, set it as you would any other property as follows:

```
Dim idxNoiseLst As New Form()
idxNoiseLst.DesktopLocation = New Point (100,100)
```

By the way, if you are looking for the **DesktopLocation** property in the Properties window (as I first did), you will not have any luck. It can only be set programmatically as described here.

Components and Controls

Now that you've become the master of the form, the hard work begins. For a UI to be useful and to gain the trust and support of the user, it needs to be well thought out, well scoped, and intelligently constructed. Of course, it also needs to be aesthetic and pleasing to the eye. Your users should not find themselves struggling to navigate the application as if they had just parachuted into the deepest South China jungle.

User interface design, however, is beyond the scope of this book. Besides, another task that is even more demanding on the programmer, is adding controls and components to the forms and connecting the UI logic to the business and functional logic of the application.

A term that adequately sums up the effort involved in working with visual controls and components is "wiring up the application." The remainder of this chapter is dedicated to doing exactly that, as we review the important characteristics of the standard components and controls that Visual Studio provides.

Adding Components and Controls to Forms

Adding components and controls to forms at design time is easy. You simply double-click the item to add it, or drag it from the Toolbox (as shown in Chapter 3) to the form. The control is added to the form with the specified location and size, which are easy to set in the Properties window or in code. However, you may have a need to add controls and components at run time. This is easy to do because, as you know, controls and components are objects that can simply be instantiated at run time and aggregated to the **Form** object.

The following example adds a **TextBox** control to the form whenever a certain **Button** control is clicked. You provide the method that handles the **Click** event and then programmatically adds the control, as show here:

```
Private Sub Button1_Click(ByVal sender As System.Object, ByVal e As
System.EventArgs) Handles Button1.Click
    Dim MyText As New TextBox()
    MyText.Location = New Point(25, 25)
    Me.Controls.Add(MyText)
End Sub
```

Nonvisual controls can be added at design time and run time, as previously shown. Some controls, however, do not have a visual element or any visual properties, so you cannot see them on the grid when they are aggregated to the form. In the past, OCX, VBX, and VCL nonvisual components were typically represented by a button on the form that becomes invisible at compile time. This is no longer the case with the Visual Studio .NET form designer. Instead, nonvisual controls and components, such as menus, are placed into a tray that is anchored at the bottom of the designer.

Once a nonvisual control has been added to the component tray, you can select the component and set its properties as you would any other control on the form. This is demonstrated in Figure 16-6, which shows the addition of a **Timer** control to the form.

 *Components often have control-specific properties that must be set. In the case of the **Timer** control, you need to enable it via its **Enabled** property. The interval of the timer also defaults to 100 milliseconds.*

To add such a component to a Windows Form programmatically, you would write code like this:

```
Dim MainFormTimer As New Timer()
```

You can also add the control to a component collection by adding the following elements in your declaration:

```
Dim MainFormTimer As New Timer(Me.components)
```

Layout and Grouping

The Toolbox provides several controls or components that you can use for layout and to group controls in the UI. For example, you would use a **GroupBox** as a container in

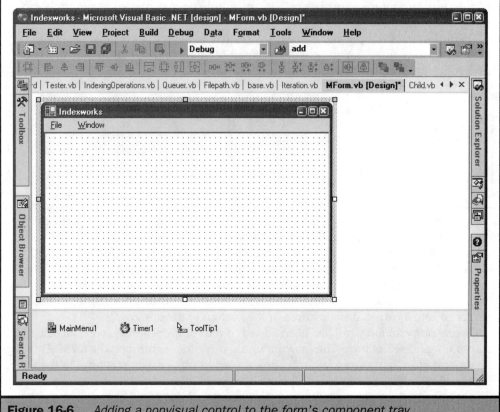

Figure 16-6. *Adding a nonvisual control to the form's component tray*

which to group a collection of **EditBox** controls that serve a common purpose, such as representing the fields of an Address table in a database.

The layout and grouping controls provided are as follows:

- **Panels** Panels cordon off a portion of form real estate to identify a collection of controls that belong together.

- **GroupBoxes** Like panels, group boxes also collect together a number of controls that serve a common task.

- **Tabs** Tabs are used to group controls onto separate pages and hide the controls on a tab that is not in focus. The analogy is a tabbed notebook or a tabbed folder in a filing cabinet.

- **ScrollBars** These are used to group controls, but the canvas is made scrollable so that you can hide controls in a space that is longer or wider than the current form or screen's bounds. Scroll bars are typical in text editors in which you scroll down from page to page rather than tabbing from page to page.

- **Splitters** These elements let you change the width or height of panels relative to other panels or windows they are docked up against.

Panels

Panels not only give the user information about a collection of controls on a form—a visual cue—they are also useful as a design-time tool. Once you have aggregated a collection of controls to a **Panel** object, you can simply move the panel, and all contents of the panel move with it. This is essentially aggregation cranked up several notches: the **Panel** object is aggregated to the **Form** object and the controls are aggregated to the **Panel** object.

The **Panel** control and the **GroupBox** control are used for the same purpose, but **Panel**s can be given scroll bars, which allows them to hold a large number of controls while the dimensions remain the same. **Panel**s also do not have captions, which **GroupBox** controls do. To display the scroll bars of a **Panel**, you need to set its **AutoScroll** property to **True**.

Panels can also be easily customized by setting the **BackColor**, **BackgroundImage**, and **BorderStyle** properties. The **BorderStyle** property enhances the visual element of the panel. It can be set to show no visible border (its default), in which case the user does not see the panel at all, or it can be given plain borders (**FixedSingle**) or a shadowed border (**Fixed3D**).

You can also use a **Panel** to group collections of controls, such as a group of **RadioButton** controls. The **Panel** control's **Enabled** property can also be used to enable or disable all the controls that it contains, which is a useful utility for referencing the entire collection of controls at the same time.

The following code adds a **Panel** control to the **IdxSearchForm** and adds a **Label** and a **TextBox** control to the **Panel**. The **Panel** control's borders are set to display three-dimensionally so that you can distinguish where the **Panel** control is located on the form in relation to other objects.

```
Me.Panel1.Controls.AddRange(New System.Windows.Forms.Control() _
{Me.Label1, Me.TextBox1})
Me.Panel1.Location = New System.Drawing.Point(16, 24)
Me.Panel1.Name = "Panel1"
Me.Panel1.Size = New System.Drawing.Size(296, 160)
Me.Panel1.TabIndex = 2
Me.Panel1.BorderStyle = BorderStyle.Fixed3
```

Figure 16-7 shows the provision of the **Panel** in the **IdxSearchForm**.

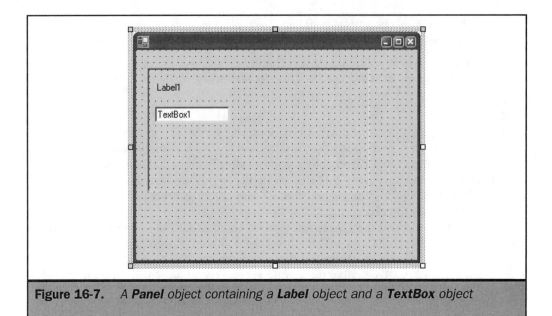

Figure 16-7. A *Panel* object containing a *Label* object and a *TextBox* object

GroupBox

The **GroupBox** controls are also used to provide an identifiable grouping for other controls. **GroupBox** controls are used to collect controls in a group by function, such as all the text entry fields of a particular collection of columns in a table. Like the **Panel** control, if you move the **GroupBox** control, all its contained controls move, too.

The **GroupBox** also displays a frame around a group of controls with or without the caption. The useful property of the **GroupBox** is that the controls within it operate exclusively from other controls on the form or other **GroupBox** components. At the class or object level, the components are simply nested or inner classes of the **GroupBox** class, so they do not see the controls of other **GroupBox** classes that are composed at the same level on the form (see Chapter 9, "Aggregation and Composition: Reuse by Containment"). In other words, if you contain a logical group of **RadioButton** controls, changing their toggle values has no effect on the **RadioButton**s of other **GroupBox**es.

You can add controls to the **GroupBox** with the **Add** method, but you cannot reference a **GroupBox** control to receive focus. Use the Properties window to inspect the properties of the **GroupBox**. The **GroupBox** is shown in Figure 16-8.

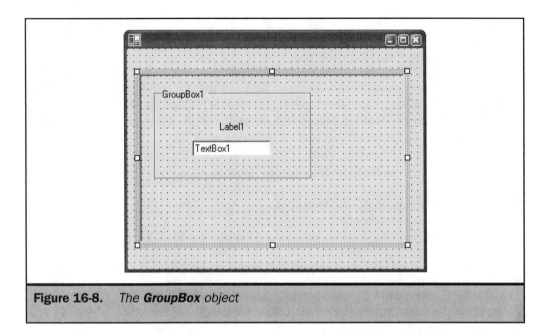

Figure 16-8. *The GroupBox object*

The following example instantiates a **GroupBox** and two **RadioButtons**. The **RadioButton** objects are aggregated to the **GroupBox**, which is in turn aggregated to the **Form** object's **Controls** collection.

```
Private Sub AddInitializeMyGroupBox()
  Dim grpBox1 As New GroupBox()
  Dim rdoButton1 As New RadioButton()
  Dim rdoButton2 As New RadioButton()
  grpBox1.FlatStyle = FlatStyle.System
  grpBox1.Controls.Add(rdoButton1)
  grpBox1.Controls.Add(rdoButton2)
  Me.Controls.Add(grpBox1)
End Sub
```

TabControl

TabControl objects display multiple tabs, like the dividers in a notebook or the folders in a filing cabinet. The tabs themselves are objects, so they can contain pictures and even other controls. You typically use the **Tab** control to simulate a multiple-page dialog box that appears many places in the Windows OS, such as the Connection Status dialog box of your networking resources.

The most important property of the **TabControl**, however, is its **TabPages**, which contain the individual tabs. Each individual tab is a **TabPage** object and, when clicked, the **Click** event is raised in the **TabPage** object. Adding a **TabPage** can be done interactively as demonstrated in Figure 16-9, or as shown programatically by the code that follows.

```
Me.TabControl1.Controls.AddRange(New System.Windows.Forms.Control() _
{Me.TabPage1})
Me.TabControl1.Name = "TabControl1"
Me.TabControl1.SelectedIndex = 0
Me.TabControl1.Size = New System.Drawing.Size(352, 248)
Me.TabControl1.TabIndex = 0
Me.TabPage1.Location = New System.Drawing.Point(4, 22)
Me.TabPage1.Name = "TabPage1"
Me.TabPage1.Size = New System.Drawing.Size(344, 222)
Me.TabPage1.TabIndex = 0
Me.TabPage1.Text = "TabPage1"
```

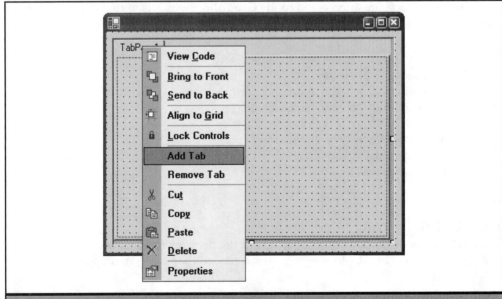

Figure 16-9.   *Adding **TabControl** and **TabPage** objects*

ScrollBar

ScrollBar objects are a little different from the objects discussed earlier, which derive from various base objects when you declare them. To create your own scroll bar class, you first need to inherit from either the **VScrollBar** or **HScrollBar** class (representing vertical or horizontal scrolling actions, respectively).

You can adjust the scroll range of the scroll bar control by setting its **Minimum** and **Maximum** properties. You can also adjust the distance the **ScrollBar** scrolls with each click of its scroll buttons, by setting its **SmallChange** and **LargeChange** properties. To adjust the starting point of your **ScrollBar**, set its **Value** property when the control is initially displayed.

The following code adds a vertical scrollbar to the **Panel** object.

```
Me.Panel1.Controls.AddRange(New System.Windows.Forms.Control() _
{Me.VScrollBar1, Me.Label1, Me.TextBox1})
```

By the way, before you rush to add scroll bars everywhere, check first if the controls are not automatically composed of them. This is the case with many controls, and thus the **ScrollBar**'s interface and properties are simply merged with the interface of its container.

Splitter

A **Splitter** control lets you resize docked controls at run time. For example, if you have two panels docked against each other and to all sides, the **Splitter** lets you resize the controls that are docked to the edges of the **Splitter**. When you hover the mouse pointer over the **Splitter** control, your cursor changes to indicate that the controls docked to the **Splitter** control can be resized. So, if **PanelA**'s width decreases by 10 pixels, **PanelB**'s width increases by 10 pixels.

We will use a **Splitter** to resize the **Panel**s in the workspace. To do this, create a form, add the **Panel** controls to the form, and set the **Dock** property to **DockStyle.Left**. Add a **Splitter** control to the form and set its **Dock** property to **DockStyle.Left** as well. Then add another **Panel** to the form and set its **Dock** property to **DockStyle.Right**. When you are done the **Splitter** arrangement will resemble the example shown in Figure 16-10.

The code behind the **Splitter** is as follows:

```
Me.RightPanel.Dock = System.Windows.Forms.DockStyle.Right
Me.RightPanel.Location = New System.Drawing.Point(156, 0)
Me.RightPanel.Name = "Details"
Me.RightPanel.Size = New System.Drawing.Size(200, 252)
Me.RightPanel.TabIndex = 2
Me.Splitter.Location = New System.Drawing.Point(136, 0)
```

```
Me.Splitter.Name = "Splitter"
Me.Splitter.Size = New System.Drawing.Size(3, 252)
Me.Splitter.TabIndex = 1
Me.Splitter.TabStop = False
Me.LeftPanel.Dock = System.Windows.Forms.DockStyle.Left
Me.LeftPanel.Name = "Tree"
Me.LeftPanel.Size = New System.Drawing.Size(136, 252)
Me.LeftPanel.TabIndex = 0
```

Note *Resizing a control using the **Splitter** control can only be done using the mouse. It is not possible to access the **Splitter** control using the keyboard.*

Positioning Controls

Positioning a control on the canvas of the form is simple enough to do with the mouse. For more control, you can use the arrow keys. You can also position a control via its properties interactively in the Properties window or in code.

To set the properties interactively, type values for the **Location** property, separated by a comma, to the location within its container. The first number (X) is the distance from the left border of the container area; the second number (Y) is the distance from the upper border of the container area. The measurements are all in pixels. You can also expand the **Location** property to type the X and Y values individually.

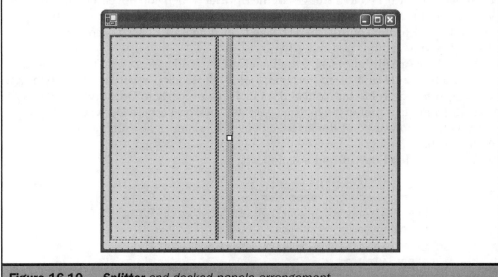

Figure 16-10. *Splitter* and docked panels arrangement

Setting the location in code can be done as follows:

```
OpenButton.Location = New Point (100, 100)
```

As discussed for earlier controls that aggregate **Point** objects, do not try to implicitly set the X and Y coordinates of the **Point** type, because it only represents the control's location; it does not affect the location of the control.

Setting a Single Property for Multiple Controls

You can select more than one type of control and specify the same value for all the controls. This technique can be useful, for example, if you add several **Button** controls to a form and you want to make sure they are all the same size, or all aligned left or right, and so on. You can select multiple controls of different types, but the Properties window displays only the properties that are common to all the selected controls, such as **Width** and **Height**.

To select all the controls at the same time, hold down the CTRL key and click each control once. You can also click the left mouse button and drag it over the group of controls, as you do when selecting files in an Explorer window.

Complex Property Pages

Some controls, like HTML tables, are complex and require the services of advanced property pages for interactive manipulation. Some maintain collections of objects, such as **ListBox**es. The property pages are represented in custom dialog boxes. To access the property page for a control, select the control whose property page you want to access. Then, in the Properties window, click the button of the Property that indicates a Property Pages button. The Property Pages dialog box for the control is displayed.

You can, however, still provide the data in code, and for complex property pages, I prefer to set my own properties in code. For example, providing a large collection of values for a **DropDown** list is much easier and quicker to do in code. Setting up an HTML table, for the most part, is far too complex and buggy to set up via its property pages. The following code shows how to generate a search results HTML table in code, a task that is very frustrating to do interactively. (Frankly, the property pages for HTML controls are nearly useless in my opinion, and you need to just get down to typing it all out, as the following example demonstrates.)

```
Public Sub CreateTable(ByVal cursor As Integer, _
  ByVal rows As Integer)
  Dim numCells As Integer
  Dim rowNum As Integer
  Try
    While rowNum <= rows - 1
```

WRITING SOFTWARE WITH VB .NET

```
      Dim newRow As New HtmlTableRow()
      While numCells <= maxCells - 1
        Dim newCell As New HtmlTableCell()
        newRow.Cells.Add(newCell)
        numCells += 1
      End While
      TABLE1.Rows.Add(newRow)
      numCells = 0
      rowNum += 1
    End While
      AddData(cursor, rows)
  Catch Except As Exception
    exceptInfo = Except.Message
  End Try
End Sub
```

Using The Property Grid

The property grid that is shown in the Properties window is itself an object of the type **PropertyGrid**, and you can create a new instance of it at will. It can be placed on the parent control, and you set its **SelectedObject** to the object to display the properties for. The information displayed in the grid is a once-only retrieval of the properties at the time the object is assigned to the grid. So, if a property value of the object specified by the **SelectedObject** is changed in code at run time, the new value is not displayed in the grid until it is refreshed, which can be done by reselecting the object to reference or by simply dereferencing the grid and instantiating a new one.

The property tabs within the property grid appear as buttons on the toolbar at the top of the **PropertyGrid**. They vary in scope, as defined in the **PropertyTabScope** enumeration. To use the **PropertyGrid**, you need to add it to the Toolbox in the IDE because it is not one of the default controls. Once you add a **PropertyGrid** to the Toolbox, you can drag and drop it onto the form like any other control. Of course, you can bypass the Toolbox work and declare an instance of the **PropertyGrid** class in your code.

The following example illustrates creating a **PropertyGrid** and setting its location on a form. This example assumes a form with a **TextBox** on it.

```
Public Sub New()
  Dim propGrid As New PropertyGrid()
  propGrid.CommandsVisibleIfAvailable = True
  propGrid.Location = New Point(10, 20)
  propGrid.Size = New System.Drawing.Size(400, 300)
```

```
    propGrid.TabIndex = 1
    propGrid.Text = "Property Grid"
    Me.Controls.Add(propGrid)
    propGrid.SelectedObject = seachEdit
End Sub
```

Note   *Refer to Chapter 3 for specific information about the Toolbox window.*

Menus and Toolbars

Adding and working with shortcut menus, status bars, and toolbars, either interactively
or programmatically, is not difficult at all. Menus typically provide commands, grouped
by a common theme such as file operations, to your users. Toolbars use buttons to
expose the same functionality in the menus or any frequently required operations.
Context menus "pop up" in response to a right-click of a mouse and present options in
the context in which they were requested. Status bars are used to indicate the application
state or to provide information about processing in the application, such as a document
that is printing or data that is being transmitted or received.

Adding Menus and Menu Items Programmatically

To add a menu to a Windows **Form** programmatically, define a method that includes
the code to add the menu to your form:

```
Public Sub AddMenu()
  Dim mnuFile As New MainMenu()
  Me.Menu = mnuFile
End Sub
```

Once you have added the code for the menu to your form, you need to add child or
submenu items to it. Menu contents are kept within a collection, so you can add menu
items to a menu at run time by simply adding **MenuItem** objects to the collection.

Within the method, you create the child menus to the **MainMenu** object's collection
as follows:

```
Dim menuItemFile As New MenuItem("&File")
Dim menuItemNew As New MenuItem("&New")
```

A **MainMenu** object contains no menu items, so once you add the first menu item
to the object, it becomes the menu's heading. This is why the **Text** property of

menuItemFile in the example is set to **&File**. Within the method, assign the top-level menu item and add subsequent menu items to it as shown here:

```
menuItemFile.MenuItems.Add(menuItemNew)
menuItemNew.MenuItems.Add(menuItemProject)
```

To create submenus, you can simply add **MenuItem** objects to the **MenuItems** collection of the parent **MenuItem**. So, to add a third menu item (**menuItemOpen**) as a submenu of the second menu item (**menuItemNew**) shown here, just add the following line of code:

```
menuItemNew.MenuItems.Add(menuItemOpen)
```

Menu items can also be dynamically added to the collection in the same code that creates them. The following example shows you how to add another menu item to the preceding collection:

```
menuItemFile.MenuItems.Add("Save &As")
```

As demonstrated earlier in this chapter, in the section "MDI Applications," you provide functionality for the menu items through an event handler that is provided under the **MenuItem**'s.**Click** event.

Context-Changing Menus

The following example shows how to create a menu arrangement that changes state according to the activities of the user. When the application starts, it will have only a traditional File menu with New, Open, and Exit commands. But as soon as the user selects either the New or Open menu item, the application state changes and the menu items change accordingly.

To do this for your application, create a multicast event handler called **GetMenu** for the New and Open menu items. This is a multicast delegate that will respond to the **Click** events of both menu items. Enter the following code in the **GetMenu** event handler:

```
Private Sub GetMenu(ByVal sender As Object, _
ByVal e As System.EventArgs) Handles MenuItem1.Click
    LoadAlternateMenu()
End Sub
```

Now we can switch focus to the second menu on the response of the click handler with the following code:

```
Private Sub LoadAlternateMenu()
   Me.Menu = MainMenu1
End Sub
```

You can make a copy of the top-level menu item and all of its submenu items by simply dragging another **MainMenu** component from the Toolbox to the form. Then, in the Menu Designer, right-click the "Type Here" area and choose Paste. The menu items you previously selected from the first **MainMenu** component are pasted into the second.

To test the application, run the debugger. The form first shows a menu that contains File, New, Open, and Exit menu items. But as soon as you click New or Open, an event is raised by which the **GetMenu** event handler (among others) processes the code related to the event. The application state changes and the new menus are swapped in.

Moving menu items between menus or within menus is made possible because the item objects are maintained in a collection. At design time, you can move entire menu structures around within the Menu Designer. But at run time, menu items can be moved between **MainMenu** objects or **MenuItem** objects, which allows for some measure of customization.

To move a menu item programmatically, at run time, simply change the index position of the **MenuIitem** object as shown here:

```
Public Sub ChangeMenuItem ()
   Me.Menu.MenuItems(0).MenuItems(0).Index += 1
End Sub
```

Menus can also be copied, cut, and pasted from the designer, which automatically takes care of referencing issues for you. In code, however, it can get a bit tricky because the menu operations are often duplicated in context menus, or toolbar buttons and shortcuts. You can, however, use the **CloneMenu** method of the **MenuItem** class to make a copy of the menu in code, and then work with its members as a separate class.

Copying menu items preserves property settings and event handlers you have established with the original menu items, so that the new menu items you have created use these same event handlers. This occurs because the entire **MenuItem** object is cloned, along with everything connected to it.

You can also enable and disable menu items to channel a user's activities or limit and broaden them as they progress with the application. All menu items are enabled by default when created, but you can disable them by setting the **Enabled** property to **False**. You can also access the property interactively in the Properties window.

To disable a menu item programmatically in code, the following line is all you need:

```
MenuItem1.Enabled = False
```

However, if you disable the first or top-level menu item in a menu (for example, the File menu item in a traditional File menu), you end up disabling all the menu items contained within the menu because you are in effect disabling the collection. This is the proper behavior, and disabling a submenu item that has sub-submenu items disables all the sub-submenu items as well.

But rather than hiding menu commands that are unavailable to the user by setting the **Visible** property to **False,** you can hide the entire menu tree by setting the topmost menu item **Visible** property to **False**. This not only obviates the need to enable and disable menu items, and the effort involved in tracking the state, but it is better to hide and disable the entire menu because this keeps the UI clean and free of clutter. Besides, users often click a disabled menu item; I have seen this done numerous times. If you decide to hide a menu chain, you must also disable the menu, because hiding does not prevent access to a menu command via other routes, such as a shortcut key.

To hide a menu item programmatically, you can use the following line of code:

```
MenuItem1.Visible = False
```

You can also merge menu items programmatically, which is common in MDI applications where the menus of the children are merged with the parent form's menus. The following example shows how this is done in code:

```
Public Sub MergeMenus()
   childMenu.MergeMenu(parentMenu)
End Sub
```

As mentioned earlier in the section "MDI Applications," two properties, **MergeType** and **MergeOrder**, are used to determine how individual menu items are handled during the merge and the order of their placement relative to the other **MenuItem** in the newly merged menu. You can set these properties on **MenuItems** individually or collectively to determine the items' presence and location within a menu merge. The following example sets these two properties for a menu item, **MenuItemMain**:

```
Public Sub MainMenuMergeProperties()
   MenuItemMain.MergeType = MenuMerge.Add
   MenuItemMain.MergeOrder = 1
End Sub
```

Enhancing Menus

There are four built-in enhancements that can dress up menus in a way that conveys more information to users:

- **Check marks** These can be used to designate whether a feature on a menu is turned on or off, such as whether certain toolbars in an application are visible, or to indicate which of a list of files or windows is visible to the user or available.

- **Shortcut keys** These are keyboard commands that let you access menu items within an application. The access keys allow direct access to keyboard commands usually by way of combining the ALT key and the underlined access key that is hooked to the desired menu or menu item. A good example is the ALT-F4 combination used to close the window or application.

- **Separator bars** These are used to group related commands within a menu, which makes the menus easier to follow.

- **RadioChecks** When a property of a menu item is set to **True**, it displays a small dot (•) next to the item—which indicates that the item is selected.

To add a check mark to a menu item programmatically, reference the menu item in code and set the **Checked** property to **True** as follows:

```
MenuItemMain.Checked = True
```

To add a shortcut key to a menu item programmatically, add the following code to set the **Shortcut** property to one of the values of the **Shortcut** enumeration:

```
MenuItemMain.Shortcut = System.Windows.Forms.Shortcut.F4
```

Adding an access key is done when you set the **Text** property (in the Properties window, in the Menu Designer, or in code), by prefixing the letter that will stand as the key with an ampersand (&). This underlines the letter to signify that it is the key. For example, typing **F&ile** as the **Text** property of a menu item causes the text label to be written as File. To navigate to this menu item, press ALT-I. Alternatively, you can also provide an access key to the superior level, which would obviate the need to press ALT in the sublevel. For example, if under the File menu we provided a Close label on a menu item (**Cl&ose**), all the user would need to do is press ALT-I-O to select the Close menu item. This is standard Windows navigation stuff that has been around since the 16-bit era.

To add a separator bar as a menu item, right-click the location where you want a separator bar, and choose New Separator. Or when setting the **Text** property interactively or in code, providing a dash (–) makes the menu item a separator bar.

Besides the preceding four enhancements, you can also designate one of the items as the default item. This is done by simply setting its **DefaultItem** property to **True**. The default item then appears in bold text.

WRITING SOFTWARE WITH VB .NET

A menu item's **Checked** property can also be set to either **True** or **False**, which indicates whether or not the menu item is selected. If its **RadioCheck** property is set to **True**, a radio button appears next to the item.

Adding a check mark to a menu item at design time involves nothing more than clicking the area to the left of the menu item. This sets the **Checked** property to **True** without the need to select the property in the Properties window. Naturally, all of these properties can be set in code.

Finally, just as with earlier versions of Visual Studio and Visual Basic, you can indicate to the compiler that your code will undertake to draw the menu item. This is done by setting the **OwnerDraw** property to **True**. Use **OwnerDraw** to provide your own code to render the menu item. With some time and dedication, you can perform some magic with the menus, such as adding icons, changing colors and fonts, and more.

 To set these dynamic properties interactively, navigate to the DynamicProperties option on the menu's items properties and click the Property Pages button to open the Dynamic Properties dialog box.

The Menu Class

This class is the base class for the **MainMenu**, **MenuItem**, and **ContextMenu** classes. You cannot create an instance of this class, but you can extend it as in the preceding classes. The menus for an application are comprised of aggregated or composite **MenuItem** objects. The **MenuItem** objects are contained in the **MainMenu** and presented as an entire menu structure for a form or a **ContextMenu** that is used to list shortcuts and context-sensitive options.

Unlike many base classes, the **Menu** base class delegates to its derived classes to define its properties. In addition to the properties that are provided for all of the derived menu classes, the **Menu** class also provides methods, such as **CloneMenu** and **MergeMenu**, that provide the implementation to create new menus from existing menus, or to merge two menu structures together, and the like.

The **Menu** class also exposes the composite class **Menu.MenuItemCollection**. This class defines the collection of **MenuItem** objects used by the **MenuItems** property. You can use the methods of the **Menu.MenuItemCollection** class to add and remove menu items from a **MainMenu**, **ContextMenu**, or **MenuItem**, as shown earlier.

Responding to User Input

As we learned in Chapter 14, an event handler is a method that is bound to an event. When the event is triggered, usually in response to a message from the Windows subsystem, such as a keypress or a mouse click, the code within the event handler is executed.

Each event handler lists two parameters that are used in the handle of the event. The following example shows an event handler for a **Button** control's **Click** event:

```
Private Sub button1_Click(ByVal sender As System.Object, _
  ByVal e As System.EventArgs) Handles button1.Click
  'And . . .
End Sub
```

The first parameter expects an argument that passes a reference to the object that raised the event. The second parameter (**e** in the preceding example) passes an object specific to the event that is being handled, which connects the event to information relative to the event. By obtaining a reference to the sender in this fashion, you can provide the facility to gain access to the sender's properties and public methods. This can be used to obtain information such as the location of the mouse for mouse events or data being transferred in drag-and-drop events.

UI events comprise the bulk of your interface logic and are thus the most complex code constructs you will need to concern yourself with in the UI. Everything else involves little more than setting and getting properties.

To create a UI event handler, switch to View Code mode and from the Class Name drop-down box (refer to Chapter 3) above your code to the left (under the Editor tab), select the control that you want to add a specific event handler to (remember, controls are classes). From the Method Name drop-down box on the right, select the event for which you want to add a specific handler (when you select the control's class in the left drop-down box, all events in that class, if any, are listed in the Method Name drop-down box to the right). Choose the event, and the Code Editor automatically inserts the appropriate event handler into your code and positions the insertion point within the method. The following example provides the **Click** event for the **Button** control:

```
Private Sub Button1_Click(ByVal sender As System.Object, ByVal e As
System.EventArgs) Handles Button1.Click
  'Add Event Handler Code Here
End Sub
```

You can also generate the handler by double-clicking the control on the form. There will come a time when you have done this enough times to know how to wire up the event code manually. I find that I can wire up events faster in the Code Editor than by switching between windows, modes, and drop-down list boxes.

Binding Events Dynamically

In line with what I just said about wiring up an application manually, you can provide code to create event handlers at run time. This practice serves to wire up the events at run time, which lets you control which event handlers are activated depending on the condition or state of the application at a certain time. Similar to late binding, you can think of this as "late wiring."

Hot Spots

Hot spots are regions in your application that can be referenced by a cursor's tracking position. By default, the hot spot is set to the upper-left corner of the cursor (coordinates 0,0). So, as soon as the cursor hits the coordinates specified in the hot spot, an event can be raised. To set a cursor's hot spot you use Visual Studio's Image Editor toolbar, which is accessed from the Tools, Customize menu. Select the Set Hotspot tool and then click the pixels you want to designate as the cursor's hot spot. The **Hotspot** property in the Properties window displays the new coordinates.

 Tooltips can be made to appear when you hover your cursor over a toolbar button. These tips can help you identify the function of each button.

Mouse and Keyboard Events

Mice can do a lot more than nibble cheese. In a Windows UI, they can let you know when one of their buttons has been clicked or released, or when the mouse pointer leaves or enters some part of the application. This information is provided in the form of **MouseDown**, **MouseUp**, **MouseMove**, **MouseEnter**, **MouseLeave**, and **MouseHover** events.

KeyPress events also bubble up from the OS and are made available to you in **KeyPress**, **KeyDown**, and **KeyUp** events. Mouse event handlers receive an argument of type **EventArgs** containing data related to their events; however, key-press event handlers receive an argument of type **KeyEventArgs** (a derivative of **EventArgs**) containing data specific to the keypress or key release events.

When wiring up mouse events, you can also change the mouse cursor. You typically marry the ability to change the cursor to the **MouseEnter** and **MouseLeave** events. These are used to provide feedback to the user that something is happening, not happening, or that certain areas are offlimits or welcome to the explorative nature of your cursor. The event is exposed in the following code example:

```
Public Event MouseDown As MouseEventHandler
```

Table 16-3 lists the **MouseEventArgs** properties to provide information specific to the mouse event.

Mouse events occur in the following order:

1. MouseEnter
2. MouseMove
3. MouseHover/MouseDown/MouseWheel
4. MouseUp
5. MouseLeave

Property	Purpose
Button	Tells you which mouse button was pressed
Clicks	Tells you how many times the mouse button was pressed and released
Delta	Retrieves a signed count of the number of *detents* the mouse wheel has rotated. A detent is one notch of the mouse wheel.
X	Retrieves the X coordinate of a mouse click
Y	Retrieves the Y coordinate of a mouse click

Table 16-3.   *MouseEventArgs Properties*

Keyboard Events

Keyboard events are fired when a key is pressed in a control that has the focus. The code for a keyboard event looks like this:

```
Public Event KeyPress As KeyPressEventHandler
```

The key event handler receives an argument of type **KeyPressEventArgs** containing data related to this keypress event. Table 16-4 lists the **KeyPressEventArgs** properties that provide information related to the event received.

Property	Purpose
Handled	Retrieves or returns a value to the property indicating whether the **KeyPress** event was handled
KeyChar	Retrieves the **KeyChar** (character pressed) value corresponding to the key pressed

Table 16-4.   *KeyPressEvenArgs Properties*

Key events occur in the following order:

1. KeyDown
2. KeyPress
3. KeyUp

Using a Timer to Fire Events

A timer can also be used to raise events at regular intervals. The component discussed here is designed for UIs, but the server-based timer is also available in the .NET Framework (see the SDK documentation).

The timer is switched on when you set its **Enabled** property to **True**, and the default interval of 100 milliseconds can be changed in the **Interval** property. Each **Tick** event is raised at every interval, which is where you add the code you want executed.

A **Timer** control is started and stopped by calling its **Start** and **Stop** methods, respectively. Stopping a timer has the effect of pausing it. Timers on forms are typically used for single-threaded algorithms, where the UI threads are used to perform some processing. The timer thus requires that you maintain the UI message pump and always operate from the same thread, or marshal the call onto another thread.

Collecting User Input

Many controls and components are designed to collect information from the user or to prompt the user to generate actions and events in the UI. These include the controls listed in Table 16-5.

Buttons

The most common control used to elicit a user response is a **Button** control. Button press events let you place code in the **Click** event handler to perform any action defined in the button event. The following example instantiates a **Button**, sets its **DialogResult** property to **DialogResult.OK**, and adds it to a **Form**:

```
Private Sub AddAButton()
  Dim button1 As New Button()
  button1.DialogResult = DialogResult.OK
  Me.Controls.Add(button1)
End Sub
```

Edit Text Boxes

The **TextBox** control lets your user provide text input to an application. The control provided by .NET includes additional functionality not found in the standard

Control	Purpose
Buttons	Button press events let you place code in the **Click** event handler to perform any action defined in the button event. The analogy is clicking a physical VCR button.
Text Edit boxes	Lets the user enter text in a field-like container
Check boxes	Lets the user choose items on a check list
Radio buttons	Provide a toggle facility (only one may be on at any time)
Combo boxes	Provide a list of items to choose from
DomainUpDownBox	A combination of a text box and a pair of buttons for moving up or down through a list without having to expand it
NumericUpDownBox	A combination of a text box and a pair of buttons for moving up or down through a list of numbers
DateAndTimePicker	A control for interactively selecting a single item from a list of dates or times
Calendar	A control of some graphical proportions that allows a user to view and set date information. The analogy is a calendar hanging on the wall.
Palette	A preconfigured dialog box that allows the user to select a color from a palette and to add custom colors to that palette
List Box	A control that displays a list of items from which the user can choose
CheckedListBox	A control that displays a list of items the user can check to signify a selection
ListView	A list of items in a container, such as the list of files in a folder
TreeView	A collection of items organized in a hierarchical fashion, with roots, branches, and leaf nodes
TrackBar	A control that lets you set positions on a notched scale
ToolBar	A form-like object that contains and enumerates buttons representing menu options and events

Table 16-5.   *User Interface Controls for Soliciting and Obtaining Input*

Windows **TextBox** control. For example, it provides multiline editing and password character masking combined into a single control. In other words, the framework has combined the functions of a classic edit box with a text box (which is why you will not find a **TextBox** control in the Toolbox).

However, the **TextBox** is mainly used to display, or accept, a single line of text. The **Multiline** and **ScrollBars** properties are used to enable multiple lines of text to be displayed or entered. Setting the **AcceptsTab** and **AcceptsReturn** properties to **True** allows enhanced text manipulation and turns the control into a multiline **TextBox**, as shown in Figure 16-11.

The code for the **TextBox** control shown in Figure 16-11 is as follows:

```
Me.TextBox1.Location = New System.Drawing.Point(8, 8)
Me.TextBox1.Multiline = True
Me.TextBox1.Name = "TextBox1"
Me.TextBox1.ScrollBars = System.Windows.Forms.ScrollBars.Vertical
Me.TextBox1.Size = New System.Drawing.Size(344, 240)
Me.TextBox1.TabIndex = 0
Me.TextBox1.Text = "TextBox1"
```

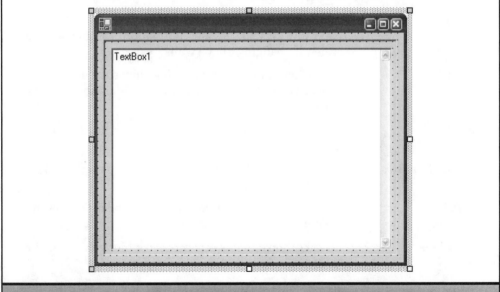

Figure 16-11. *The **TextBox** control configured as a multiline "text editor" with scroll bars*

You can also limit the amount of text entered into the **TextBox** control by setting its **MaxLength** property to a specific number of characters. Masking features let the **TextBox** control be used for passwords and other user-defined information. Use the **PasswordChar** property to mask characters entered in a single-line version of the control, as demonstrated in the following code. Regardless of what the user enters, it is displayed as a star (asterisk) on Windows versions prior to Windows XP and .NET Server (the latter displays a blob instead of the asterisk).

```
Private Sub InitializeTextBox ()
  'Add text into the control at startup.
    TextBox1.Text = "Add noise word."
End Sub
```

You also have the option of setting the insertion point in a **TextBox** control by setting the **SelectionStart** property to the desired value. Zero places the insertion point immediately to the left of the first character. If you set the **SelectionLength** property to the length of the text you want to select, the control cannot be written to. The following code always returns the insertion point to 0. The **TextBox1_Enter** event handler must be bound to the control.

```
Private Sub TextBox1_Enter(ByVal sender As Object, ByVal e As
System.EventArgs) Handles TextBox1.Enter
    TextBox1.SelectionStart = 0
    TextBox1.SelectionLength = 0
End Sub
```

You can also use the **TextBox** control as a read-only control. For example, the **TextBox** may display a value that is typically editable, but the control can be set to prevent the user from changing the value, until the read-only state changes. To create a read-only text box, simply set the **TextBox** control's **ReadOnly** property to **True**. With the property set to **True**, users can still scroll and highlight text in a text box. They just can't make changes. Copying is also possible from a text box, but cutting and pasting are not. You would typically use the **RichEdit** control for cut-and-paste operations, as shown later in this chapter.

Incidentally, the **ReadOnly** property only affects user input. You can still change the text box text at run time by changing the **Text** property.

When you need to show quotation marks (" ") in the text, as in this example:

```
Examples: "&, (, #, %, $"
```

insert two quotation marks in a row as an embedded quotation mark, as follows:

```
Private Sub InsertQuote()
  TextBox1.Text = "Examples: ""&,(,*,%,$"" "
End Sub
```

Alternatively, you can insert the ASCII or Unicode character for a quotation mark, as shown in the following example:

```
Private Sub InsertAscii()
  TextBox1.Text = "Examples: " & Chr(34) & "&,(,*,%,$" & Chr(34)
End Sub
```

You can also define a constant for the character, and use it where needed:

```
Const OpenQuote As String = """"
Const CloseQuote As String = """"
TextBox1.Text = "Examples: " & OpenQuote & "&,(,*,%,$" & CloseQuote
```

You can also write code to select text in the **TextBox** control. You write code that searches the text value for a particular **String**, or use a string-manipulation method to alert the user to the string's position in the box. Then, you can write code to select the text by setting the **SelectionStart** property to the beginning of the text string found. The **SelectionStart** property is an ordinal value that indicates the insertion point in the text, with 0 being the leftmost position, and the length of the string after the last character being the rightmost position. If the **SelectionStart** property is set to a value equal to or greater than the number of characters in the text box, the insertion point is placed after the last character.

You can also set the **SelectionLength** property to the length of the text to be selected. The **SelectionLength** property is also an ordinal value that sets the width of the insertion point. If you set the **SelectionLength** to a number greater than 0, it will cause that number of characters to be selected—and the selection starts from the current insertion point.

The following code selects the contents of a text box when the control's **Enter** event occurs:

```
Private Sub TextBox1_Enter(ByVal sender As Object, ByVal e As
System.EventArgs) Handles TextBox1.Enter
  TextBox1.SelectionStart = 0
  TextBox1.SelectionLength = TextBox1.Text.Length
End Sub
```

Check Boxes

The **CheckBox** control indicates whether or not a particular item is selected. It is commonly used to present multiple choice (Yes/No or True/False) selections to a user. You can use **CheckBox** controls in groups to display multiple choices from which the user can select one or more.

Radio Buttons

The **RadioButton** controls present a set of two or more mutually exclusive choices to your user. A radio button is like an on/off toggle switch. When one button is on, all others that are part of the same container are off. Radio buttons in separate containers, such as a group in a panel, are isolated from the condition of the other group because their scope of visibility in the container is blocked by the bounding class.

Combo Boxes

The **ComboBox** control is used to display data in a drop-down combo box. By default, the **ComboBox** control appears in two parts: the top part is a text box that allows the user to type a list item; the second part is a list box that displays a list of items from which the user can select one item.

DomainUpDown

The **DomainUpDown** control looks like a combination of a text box and a pair of buttons for iterating up or down through a list. This control displays and sets the current text from the list of choices in the control. The user can select the string by clicking the Up and Down buttons to move through the list, by pressing the UP ARROW and DOWN ARROW keys, or by typing a string that matches an item in the list. You might consider using this control for selecting items from an alphabetically sorted list of names, and you can sort the list by setting its **Sorted** property to **True**. This control is very similar to the **ListBox** or **ComboBox** controls and is a lot simpler to use, as shown in Figure 16-12.

NumericUpDown

The **NumericUpDown** control works like the **DomainUpDown** control. The **NumericUpDown** control displays and sets a single numeric value from its list of choices. Your user can increment and decrement the number by pressing Up and Down buttons, by pressing the UP ARROW and DOWN ARROW keys, or by typing a number. Pressing the UP ARROW key moves the value toward the maximum; pressing the DOWN ARROW key moves the value toward the minimum. **NumericUpDown** controls are used in many Windows Control Panel applications. The numbers displayed may be in a variety of formats, including hexadecimal.

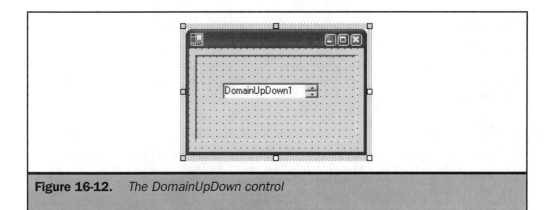

Figure 16-12.   *The DomainUpDown control*

Date and Time Picker

The **DateTimePicker** control lets the user select a single item from a list of dates or times. When used to represent a date, it appears in two parts: a drop-down list with a date represented in text, and a grid that appears when you click the down arrow next to the list. The grid looks like the **MonthCalendar** control, which can be used for selecting multiple dates. An alternative to the grid, useful for editing times instead of dates, are the **Up** and **Down** buttons that appear when the **ShowUpDown** property is set to **True**.

Calendar

The **MonthCalendar** provides an intuitive graphical interface in the form of a calendar to allow you to view and set date information. The control displays a calendar that contains the numbered days of the month, arranged in columns underneath the days of the week, with the selected range of dates highlighted. The control is illustrated in Figure 16-13.

The user can select a different month by clicking the arrow buttons that appear on either side of the month caption. This control lets the user select more than one date, whereas the **DateTimeControl** does not.

You might consider using a **DateTimePicker** control instead of a **MonthCalendar** if you need custom and possibly programmatic date formatting or need to enforce a single selection for input.

A Palette

The **ColorDialog** component is a preconfigured dialog box containing a palette that lets the user select a color from the palette and to add custom colors to that palette. This

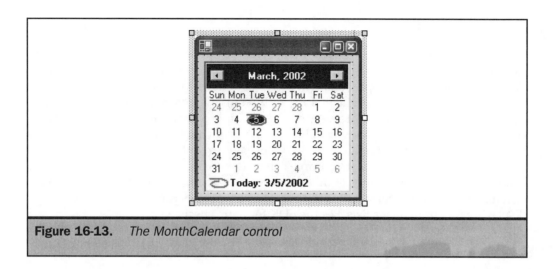

Figure 16-13. *The MonthCalendar control*

is a common dialog box that you see in all other Windows applications that offer color selection, including Visual Studio. It makes sense to use this palette instead of configuring a new palette.

Like the other common dialog boxes, this control has certain read/write properties that will be set to default values. You can, however, change these values in the dialog box's constructor.

List Boxes

The **ListBox** control is an old favorite in Windows applications. It displays a list of items to your users and allows them to select one or more items. This control has an embedded vertical scroll box that is displayed if the total number of items exceeds the number that can be displayed. The control can also show multiple columns when you set its **MultiColumn** property to **True**. If you set the **ScrollAlwaysVisible** to **True**, the scroll bars appear regardless of the number of items or columns. You can also code against the **SelectionMode** property to determine the number of list items that can be selected at a time.

CheckedListBox

The **CheckedListBox** control extends the **ListBox** control with the ability to check off items in the lists. The checked list boxes can only have one item, but a selected item is not the same thing as a checked item. These controls can also be data bound, like list boxes, by programming against the **DataSource** property. They can also obtain their items from a collection, using the **Items** property.

ListView

The **ListView** control displays a list of items with the option of including an icon with each item. The typical use of the **ListView** control is to create the details facility in a Windows Explorer–style application. There are four modes to use with the basic version of this control: LargeIcon, SmallIcon, List, and Details. LargeIcon mode displays large icons next to the item text; the items appear in multiple columns if the control is large enough. SmallIcon mode is just a small-icon version of LargeIcon mode.

List mode displays the small icons, and the list is presented as a single column. Details mode shows the items in multiple columns with details represented in the columns. You can add columns to this control in your code. You also have the option of setting the **View** property in this control. The view modes provide the ability to display images from image lists. See the SDK for more specifics.

Trackbars (Sliders)

TrackBar controls, often known as "slider" controls, are used mostly for adjusting a numeric value. The **TrackBar** control has two parts: the slider, or thumb, and the notches. The slider is the part that can be adjusted by sliding from side to side or up and down. Its position on the control provides the facility to return the **Value** property. The notches indicate a range of values placed at evenly spaced position on the scale.

Toolbars

The **ToolBar** control is used as a staging area for displaying a row of drop-down menus and bitmapped buttons. Toolbar buttons may be mapped to menu item commands and can be configured to appear and behave as push buttons, drop-down menus, or separators. Typically, a toolbar provides quick access to the application's most frequently used facilities.

A **ToolBar** control may be "docked" along the top of its parent window, which is its usual place. It may also be docked to any side of the window, or it may float. You can also change the size of the **ToolBar** and drag it. The toolbar can display tooltips. To display **ToolTips**, the **ShowToolTips** property of the control must be set to **True** (see "ToolTip" later in this chapter).

TreeView

The **TreeView** control displays a hierarchy of tree nodes exactly like the hierarchy of classes in the Object Browser. Each node can contain child nodes and parent nodes, and child nodes can themselves be parent nodes. The tree can also be expanded or collapsed.

The **TreeView** control also provides the ability to display check boxes next to the nodes. This can be done by programming against the tree view's **CheckBoxes** property.

Selecting or clearing nodes is achieved by setting the node's **Checked** property to **True** or **False**.

Presentation and Informational Controls

Some controls and components are designed to present information to users. These include the controls listed in Table 16-6.

Labeling

Labels are used to display text or images that cannot be edited. They are used to identify objects on a form. They provide descriptions of what certain controls do, provide instruction, and simply identify controls for the user. Labels are used to describe text boxes, list boxes, combo boxes, and more.

Labels can also be manipulated at run time to respond to event and application state. For example, if your application takes a few minutes to process a change, you can display a processing-status message in a label and then change it when the job is done.

Control	Purpose
Label	Displays text or images that cannot be edited
LinkLabel	Allows you to add Web-style links to **Forms** applications
StatusBar	Used on forms to display status information
NotifyIcon	Typically used to display icons for processes that run in the background and do not show a UI much of the time
PictureBox	Used to display bitmaps, GIFs, JPEGs, metafiles, or icons
ImageList	Provides a container to store images
ProgressBar	Visually indicates the progress of a lengthy operation
Grids	Displays data in a series of rows and columns
ToolTip	Displays text when the user points at certain controls
ErrorProvider	Alerts the user in a nonintrusive way to errors
HelpProvider	Used to display help information

Table 16-6. *Informational Controls*

To set the text displayed by a control programmatically, set the **Text** property to a string. To create an underlined access key like those shown in the earlier menu examples, simply include an ampersand (&) before the access letter designated as the access key. You can also set the **Font** property by assigning the font to an object of type **System.Drawing.Font**, as shown here:

```
Button1.Font = New Font("Arial", 10, FontStyle.Bold,
GraphicsUnit.Point)
```

LinkLabel

This control is used like a label but it doubles as a hyperlink that can connect the user to other applications or a Web page. You can change the control's link color and set the part of the link that activates the jump. The **LinkColor**, **VisitedLinkColor**, and **ActiveLinkColor** properties let you set the colors of the link so that it behaves just like an HTML link. It even has a **LinkClicked** event that enables you to wire up an event handler when the link text is selected.

The following example creates a **LinkLabel** control that displays a link, and displays the Microsoft Web site in the default browser when the link defined in the control's text is clicked. The example defines a method that initializes the **LinkLabel** control as well as a method that will handle the **LinkClicked** event of the control. The event handler of the **LinkClicked** event uses the **LinkData** property of the **LinkLabel.Link** class to determine the URL to display in the default browser. This example assumes that it is located within a **Form** class.

Status Bar

StatusBar controls belong in every UI. They are a marvelous facility for keeping the user regularly informed on the state of things in the application. You typically dock it to the bottom of your application's main window.

The **StatusBar** control acts as a container for status bar panels that are aggregated into the bar. These panels display text, icons, and various objects to indicate state and so on. You can also embed animation icons in the panels to indicate a process churning away in the background. You are no doubt familiar with Internet Explorer's status bar, which publishes the URL of a page when the mouse rolls over the hyperlink. To see a status bar in action, have a look at the one in Visual Studio.

Icons

The **NotifyIcon** component is typically used to display icons for processes that run in the background. An example of such a process is a backup facility that can be accessed by clicking its icon in the status notification area of a taskbar.

Each **NotifyIcon** component displays a single icon in the status area. If you have three background processes and wish to display an icon for each, you must add three

NotifyIcon components to the form. The key properties of the **NotifyIcon** component are **Icon** and **Visible**. The **Icon** property sets the icon that appears in the status area. In order for the icon to appear, the **Visible** property must be set to **True**. Icons can have associated ToolTips and context menus.

PictureBox

PictureBox controls are used to display graphics in bitmap, GIF, JPEG, metafile, or icon formats. The picture that is displayed is determined by the **Image** property, which you can set at run time or design time. The **SizeMode** property controls how the image and control fit with each other.

ImageList

The **ImageList** component is used to store the aforementioned images in a structure that provides a controlled access for controls that use images. For example, you can create a control that alternates the display of various images by iterating through the collection at certain intervals.

One **ImageList** control can be associated with multiple controls. For example, your **ListView** icons and **TreeView** icons access the same list of icons in the image.

The **ImageList** uses a handle to manage the list of images. The **Handle** is not created until certain operations, including getting the **Image**s, getting the **Handle**, and calling **Draw**, are performed on the image list.

Progress Bars

A **ProgressBar** control provides information about how a lengthy progress is proceeding. The control shows a bar that fills in from left to right like a thermometer or a barometer gauge. The progress bar can be set to show in a system highlight color as an operation progresses. It can also display a label showing the percentage complete.

The benefit of the progress bar is that it keeps your users informed of how an application is progressing with a particular task. Otherwise, the user might think the application has crashed or frozen. A good example is downloading Visual Studio .NET from MSDN. You can watch the progress bar as the download progresses over a 72+ hour operation.

Grids

Grids display data in a series of rows and columns. The available **DataGrid** displays information from a table in a database it is bound to. Data from the table fills the rows and columns, in the same fashion that it appears in the table.

The **DataGrid** can be bound to data with multiple related tables, and if navigation is enabled on the grid, the grid will display expanders in each row. An expander allows navigation from a parent table to a child table. Clicking a node displays the child table, and clicking the Back button displays the original parent table. In this fashion, the grid displays the hierarchical or referential relationships between tables. The **DataGrid** also provides a UI for a dataset, navigation between related tables, and rich formatting and editing capabilities.

The display and manipulation of data have been separated into two function domains: the control handles the UI to present the data, whereas the data updates are handled by the data-binding architecture and the ADO.NET data providers.

ToolTip

ToolTips are useful components that display text when you point to a control or element in the UI. **ToolTip**s are applicable to any control on your form. The control is very useful as a screen real-estate saver. In older versions of Windows, we would add a label to further explain the purpose of a button or a similar control. The label would take up a lot of space, and in a UI with an extensive toolbar, the excessive use of labels under buttons became a management burden. With tooltips, you can display a small icon on a button and use a **ToolTip** to explain the button's function.

To use the **ToolTip** component, you can code against its **ToolTip** property, which can be applied to multiple controls on a **Form** or some other container. In other words, one **ToolTip** control is sufficient for a **TextBox** control and a nearby button.

The ErrorProvider Control

ErrorProvider control lets you show the user in a nonintrusive way that something is wrong somewhere. You would use this control when validating user input on a form, or displaying errors within a dataset. The error provider is a better alternative than displaying an error message in a message box, because it is easy to forget about the error after the OK button on the message box has been clicked. With this control, you can keep the error message visible until the user has cleared the error. It is also far better than a message box to connect the user to the exact element causing a problem, such as a missing value in a text box that must collect a value from the user, like a **LastName** edit box.

You can also wire a **ToolTip** to the error so that when the user positions the mouse pointer over the error icon, the **ToolTip** will appear and provide more information about what needs to be done to clear the error.

ErrorProviders are invaluable when used in tandem with data-bound controls. When using **ErrorProvider** with data-bound controls, you need to specify the **ContainerControl**, either in the constructor or by setting the **ContainerControl** property.

Help Provider

HelpProvider components are used to associate an HTML Help 1.x Help file (CHM files, produced with the HTML Help Workshop, or HTM files) with your application. You can provide help resources in the following ways:

- **Context-sensitive Help**   This help would be applied to controls on your forms.
- **Dialog box context-sensitive Help**   This type of help is associated with a particular dialog box or specific controls on a dialog box.
- **Open Help files**   Classic help that lets you open to a location in a help file, or to the help system's Table of Contents, Index, or Search facility.

Printing Support

For simple printing support, you can use the built-in **PrintDialog** component, which is a preconfigured dialog box that your user can use to select a printer, choose the pages to print, and determine other print-related settings in Windows applications.

This standard control can be used to let your users print selected pages, print all pages, print selected ranges, or print selections. In short, it lets your users print via a facility they are probably familiar with, because this dialog box is used by almost all applications that provide printing support.

Drag and Drop

Drag-and-drop operations are often required in your applications. This facility is achieved by programming against events, such as **DragEnter**, **DragLeave**, and **DragDrop**. You can easily wire up a drag-drop facility in your application by accessing and evaluating the information provided in the event arguments of the aforementioned events.

Dragging Data

You begin drag-and-drop routines by dragging. It all starts with the implementation provided in the **DoDragDrop** method of your control. In the following example, the **MouseDown** starts the drag operation (any event can be used to initiate the drag-and-drop procedure):

```
Private Sub Button1_MouseDown(ByVal sender As Object, _
ByVal e As System.Windows.Forms.MouseEventArgs) _
```

WRITING SOFTWARE WITH VB .NET

```
Handles Button1.MouseDown
   Button1.DoDragDrop(Button1.Text, DragDropEffects.Copy _
   Or DragDropEffects.Move)
End Sub
```

The results of the drag are determined by the arguments provided to the **DoDragDrop** method. This method interoperates with the **DataEventArgs.Data** property and the **DataEventArgs.AllowedEffect** Property to facilitate the event handling.

Any data can be used as a parameter in the **DoDragDrop** method. In the preceding example, the **Text** property of the **Button** control is used (rather than hard-coding a value or retrieving data from a dataset) because the property is related to the location being dragged from (the **Button** control).

While a drag operation is underway, you can work with the **QueryContinueDrag** event, which queries the system for permission to continue dragging. When handling this method, it is also the appropriate point for you to call methods that will have an effect on the drag operation, such as expanding a **TreeNode** in a **TreeView** control when the cursor lands on it.

Dropping Data

Dragging operations usually end with the data being dropped somewhere, such as a location on the form or on a control. You can change the cursor when it crosses into an area of the form or when it hovers over a region occupied by a control that is correctly configured for dropping data. Any area on a form or control can be configured to accept dropped data by setting the **AllowDrop** property. You then handle **DragEnter** and **DragDrop** events on the destination. Adding drop support to the target begins with setting the **AllowDrop** property to **True**.

To do this, access the **DragEnter** event for the control where the drop will occur, and use an **If** statement to do type-checking to ensure the data being dragged is of an acceptable data type for the target. The code then sets the effect that will happen when the drop occurs to a value in the **DragDropEffects** enumeration. This is shown in the following code:

```
Private Sub TextBox1_DragEnter(ByVal sender As Object, _
  ByVal e As System.Windows.Forms.DragEventArgs) _
  Handles TextBox1.DragEnter
   If (e.Data.GetDataPresent(DataFormats.Text)) Then
     e.Effect = DragDropEffects.Copy
   Else
     e.Effect = DragDropEffects.None
```

```
    End If
End Sub
```

You can also define your own **DataFormats**. This is as simple as specifying your own object as the **Object** parameter of the **SetData** method. The object must be specified as serializable, which you can do with **Serializable** attributes. The **DragDrop** event also lets you access the data dragged using the **GetData** method. In the following example, the target of the drag is a **TextBox** control. The code sets the **Text** property of the **TextBox** control equal to the data being dragged.

```
Private Sub TextBox1_DragDrop(ByVal sender As Object, _
  ByVal e As System.Windows.Forms.DragEventArgs) _
  Handles TextBox1.DragDrop
  TextBox1.Text = e.Data.GetData(DataFormats.Text).ToString
End Sub
```

You can also code the **DragDrop** facility to the **KeyState** property, so that you can make certain things happen during the drag-and-drop operation based on what CTRL key is pressed.

Note   *Dragging and dropping between applications is no different than drag-drop between the controls in an application. You just need to make sure the applications on either side of the drag-drop behave according to the "contract" established between the **AllowedEffect** and **Effect** properties as shown in the above code.*

Using the Clipboard

To store data in the Clipboard facility, you can use the **SetDataObject** method to send the data to the **Clipboard** object. The following sends the text of a **TextBox** control to the Clipboard:

```
Private Sub Button1_Click(ByVal sender As System.Object, _
  ByVal e As System.EventArgs) Handles Button1.Click
  Clipboard.SetDataObject(TextBox1.Text)
End Sub
```

To retrieve information from the Clipboard simply drag a **TextBox** control and a **Button** control to the form. Double-click the **Button** to create the **Click** event handler where you will write your code.

You still need to write code to get the data from the Clipboard using the **GetDataObject** method. You can also test the data using the **GetDataPresent** method. This will tell you what **DataFormats** object is being used. The last step will be to set the **Text** property of the **TextBox** control to the string represented in the data. This you will do using the **GetData** method. Here's an example of how this is done:

```
Private Sub Button1_Click(ByVal sender As System.Object, _
  ByVal e As System.EventArgs) Handles Button1.Click
  Dim aDataObj As IDataObject = Clipboard.GetDataObject()
  If (aDataObj.GetDataPresent(DataFormats.Text)) Then
    TextBox1.Text = aDataObj.GetData(DataFormats.Text).ToString()
  End If
End Sub
```

Observation

Putting together a sophisticated UI is not an easy task. I have developed several extensive UIs in the past decade and the job does not seem to get easier. This is due in large to the sophisticated technology available to us, which keeps getting more and more advanced. Still, the advice I offered in this book's introduction and in several other places stands: You should separate application and business logic from the UI logic.

You also need to get up to speed on the foundations of the language and the data structures before tackling UI logic. Of course, if you are part of an experienced team, the responsibilities of the UI can be delegated to people who have experience putting together sophisticated UIs.

Finally, a word about OCX controls. These components are easily wrapped but they tend to be heavy. All .NET controls can replace the legacy OCX controls, and where charting is needed, such as in the utility of the **MSChart** OCX, continue to use the OCX until you have managed to replace it with native .NET controls, which will always be faster and easier to use, especially for applications that require scalability.

The
Complete
Reference

Visual
Basic
.NET

Chapter 17

Getting Ready to Release

For the most part, our investigation into the core programming facilities and software constructs of Visual Basic .NET and the .NET Framework are behind us. Now it's time for you to dig into the subjects of enterprise-level programming with Visual Basic .NET, quality control and assurance, debugging, application deployment, and security. These are all extensive subjects and I would not be able to do them justice in this book if I tried.

For now, you may be getting ready to rapidly move applications out of your development environments and into the hands of beta testers, those QA/QC engineers and end users who knowingly or contractually have committed to being your guinea pigs. This chapter gives you the know-how for preparing your code for this next critical level.

Chapter 16 investigated the user interface, but it also "coupled" the functionality in the unseen critical code with the human user. At this point, we must be aware of an important fact: No matter how well-designed or well "coded" an application, you will lose customers when your applications consistently crash or lose the user's data.

Over the past few decades, much has been said about how to write quality software. This book has nothing new to add to discussions and debates on testing, quality control, and quality assurance. If you are starting to study developing, I recommend that you get up to speed on debugging concepts and techniques before tackling the Visual Studio .NET debugging tools. Still, this chapter is designed to acquaint you with the variety of debugging aids in the .NET Framework and Visual Studio that can be used with Visual Basic .NET.

We have discussed themes and concepts for defensive programming throughout this book. These include conditional constructs, exception handling, documentation, pseudocode, modeling, iterative design, private variables, and protected methods. We have discussed the code construction business as if the possibility of bugs were as remote as Saturn's moons. To conserve space, the code examples in this book have not been littered with debug symbols, debug statements, and comments. But we all know that software can never be bug-free.

A computer science professor once told me that in every million lines of code there were sufficient errors in logic, design, and semantics to require 30 million years of revision before the software could be considered "defect-free." I am not sure how the professor came up with this theory, but the point is that software can never be defect-free. However, you should approach quality control and assurance without fear and understand that a well-written application means achieving certain levels of usability and reliability. Those levels are the goals you set for making an acceptable product. Once you have objectives for a stable product, how do you ensure that your software lives up to its promise? The question cannot be answered fully in this book. Nothing in the .NET Framework or Visual Studio .NET can magically ensure software is usable and meets a certain standard. Only you and your programming team can ensure that your software is as error-free as possible beginning with the first class diagram you create.

A development environment would not be worth its hype if it did not provide a sophisticated set of tools that helps you find errors when things do go wrong. This chapter introduces two facilities to help you find defects as quickly as possible: the **System.Diagnostics** namespace and Visual Studio .NET's symbolic debugger.

The chapter will also introduce you to tracing, compiling release builds, and setting up configuration files. First, let's investigate the resources we have at our disposal when somewhere, sometime, someone screams, "It doesn't work!"

Thinking in Debug Terms

Before you can debug a .NET Framework application, the compiler and the run-time environment must be configured for the debug "state of mind." Visual Studio does this for you automatically when you place your application in Debug mode, as described shortly. This configuration is essential to enable a debugger to attach to the application for the purpose of producing symbols and line maps for your source code and the Microsoft Intermediate Language (MSIL) that presents it to the CLR.

Released software, which is debugged for release candidate builds, can then be profiled to boost performance. The job of the profiler, a software tool, is to evaluate and describe the lines of source code that generate the most frequently executed code, and then estimate how much time it takes to execute them.

In addition to Visual Studio's debugging utilities, you can examine and improve the performance of .NET Framework applications using the following resources:

- **Classes in the Systems.Diagnostics namespace**   This chapter investigates the **Debug** and **Trace** classes in this namespace in some depth.

- **Runtime Debugger (Cordbg.exe)**   This is Microsoft's standard .NET command-line debugger, which is not covered in this book.

- **Microsoft Common Language Runtime Debugger (DbgCLR.exe)**   This debugger ships with the .NET SDK and is not covered in this book.

You can use the **System.Diagnostics** classes for tracing execution flow, and you can use the **Process**, **EventLog**, and **PerformanceCounter** classes for profiling code. You can also use the Cordbg.exe command-line debugger to debug managed code from the command-line interpreter. If you prefer not to labor on the command line, the DbgCLR.exe can be accessed in a familiar Windows interface. Both compilers are used for debugging managed code. The latter is located in the %\FrameworkSDK\ GuiDebug folder, while the former can be found in the Microsoft Visual Studio .NET\ FrameworkSDK\Bin folder.

The System.Diagnostics Namespace

To get you on the road to proving that your code works, the .NET Framework provides a namespace jam-packed with classes and various components specifically designed to allow you to interact with system processes, event logs, performance counters, and other run-time elements. This namespace also includes a collection of services used with thread management (see Chapter 16) and a special class—**Debug**—specifically used to help debug your code on a line-by-line basis. The **Debug** class is further discussed later in this section.

Tables 17-1 and 17-2 list the resources in this namespace and briefly describe the services they provide.

Class *	Description
BooleanSwitch	A **Boolean** construct that you can use for conditional elements in your code. It provides conditions logic for control debugging and tracing output.
ConditionalAttribute	An attribute that indicates to compilers that a method is callable only if a specified preprocessing identifier is applied to it. This attribute is thus especially useful for ensuring the compiler keeps certain debug information in the assembly during run time, because debug information is typically stripped out in the release build.
CounterCreationData	Used to define and create custom counter objects. With this class, you can specify the counter type, name, and help string for a custom counter.
CounterCreationDataCollection	Used to create strongly typed collections of **CounterCreationData** objects
CounterSampleCalculator	Contains a single static method for computing raw performance counter data
Debug	The main debug class that provides a set of methods and properties that you will use as an aid in debugging code
DebuggableAttribute	An attribute that modifies code generation for run-time just-in-time (JIT) debugging. This attribute can be used to specify how the CLR gathers debug information at run time.

Table 17-1. *Base and Final Classes in the **System.Diagnostics** Namespace*

Class *	Description
Debugger	Allows you to communicate directly with the debugger. For example, it contains a method called **Launch** that fires up the debugger from within your code.
DebuggerHiddenAttribute	Specifies the **DebuggerHiddenAttribute**
DebuggerStepThroughAttribute	Specifies the **DebuggerStepThroughAttribute**
DefaultTraceListener	The main class that provides the default output methods and behavior for tracing (see "Tracing and the Trace Class" later in this chapter)
EntryWrittenEventArgs	The event data target for the **EntryWritten** event
EventLog	Provides the interaction with Windows event logs
EventLogEntry	Encapsulates a single record in the event log
EventLogEntryCollection	Defines size and enumerators for a collection of **EventLogEntry** instances
EventLogInstaller	Used for installing and configuring an event log that your application reads from or writes to when running. This class can be used by an installation utility (for example, InstallUtil.exe) when installing an event log
EventLogPermission	Allows control of code access permissions for event logging
EventLogPermissionAttribute	Contains the attribute for allowing declarative permission checks for event logging
EventLogPermissionEntry	Defines the smallest unit of a code access security permission that is set for an **EventLog**
EventLogPermissionEntryCollection	Contains a strongly typed collection of **EventLogPermissionEntry** objects
EventLogTraceListener	Provides a simple listener that directs tracing or debugging output to an **EventLog**
FileVersionInfo	Used to access version information for a file on disk
InstanceData.	Holds instance data associated with a performance counter sample

Table 17-1.   *Base and Final Classes in the **System.Diagnostics** Namespace* (continued)

WRITING SOFTWARE
WITH VB .NET

Class *	Description
InstanceDataCollection	Provides a strongly typed collection of **InstanceData** objects
InstanceDataCollectionCollection	Provides a strongly typed collection of **InstanceDataCollection** objects
MonitoringDescriptionAttribute	Contains an attribute that specifies a description for a property or event
PerformanceCounter	Represents a Windows NT performance counter component
PerformanceCounterCategory	Represents a performance object, which defines a category of performance counters
PerformanceCounterInstaller	Specifies an installer for the **PerformanceCounter** component
PerformanceCounterPermission	Allows control of code access permissions for a **PerformanceCounter**
PerformanceCounterPermission-Attribute	Allows declarative performance counter permission checks
PerformanceCounterPermissionEntry	Defines the smallest unit of a code access security permission that is set for a **PerformanceCounter**
PerformanceCounterPermissionEntry Collection	Contains a strongly typed collection of **PerformanceCounterPermissionEntry** objects
Process	Provides access to local and remote processes and enables you to start and stop local system processes
ProcessModule	Represents a DLL or EXE file that is loaded into a particular process
ProcessModuleCollection	Provides a strongly typed collection of **ProcessModule** objects

Table 17-1. *Base and Final Classes in the **System.Diagnostics** Namespace* (continued)

Class [*]	Description
ProcessStartInfo	Specifies a set of values used when starting a process
ProcessThread	Represents an operating system process thread
ProcessThreadCollection	Provides a strongly typed collection of **ProcessThread** objects
StackFrame	Provides information about a **StackFrame**
StackTrace	Acquires a stack trace
Switch (a)	A base class for creating new debugging and tracing switches
TextWriterTraceListener	Directs tracing or debugging output to a **TextWriter** or to a **Stream** object
Trace (fi)	Provides a set of methods and properties that help you trace the execution of your code
TraceListener (a)	A base class for the listeners who monitor trace and debug output
TraceListenerCollection (abstract)	A base class that provides a thread-safe list of **TraceListener** objects
TraceSwitch	Provides a multilevel switch to control tracing and debug output without recompiling your code
CounterSample (struct)	A class that defines a structure holding the raw data for a performance counter
EntryWrittenEventHandler (d)	An event handler (**Delegate**) that represents the method that will handle the **EntryWritten** event of an **EventLog**

[*] These classes are split between System and mscorlib assemblies.

Table 17-1.   *Base and Final Classes in the **System.Diagnostics** Namespace* (continued)

Enumerations	Description
EventLogEntryType	Specifies the event type of an event log entry
EventLogPermissionAccess	Defines access levels used by **EventLog** permission classes
PerformanceCounterPermissionAccess	Defines access levels used by **PerformanceCounter** permission classes
PerformanceCounterType	Specifies the formula used to calculate the **NextValue** method for a **PerformanceCounter** instance
ProcessPriorityClass	Indicates the priority that the system associates with a process. This value, together with the priority value of each thread of the process, determines each thread's base priority level.
ProcessWindowStyle	Specifies how a new window should appear when the system starts a process
ThreadPriorityLevel	Specifies the priority level of a thread
ThreadState	Specifies the current execution state of the thread
ThreadWaitReason	Specifies the reason a thread is waiting
TraceLevel	Specifies what messages to output for the **Debug**, **Trace**, and **TraceSwitch** classes

Table 17-2. *Enumerations Available to the **System.Diagnostics** Namespace*

The **Debug** class is one of the most important classes in this namespace, and we have seen it in action in several places in this book. You will use the method and properties of the **Debug** class to print debugging information and check your logic with assertions. One of the best features of this class is that it can help you track errors and assure quality without having to bloat a file with all manner of debug information that will only impact the performance and code size of your final version.

Note *When you use the **Trace** facility to debug applications, no additional code is generated and inserted into your classes, so you can compile **Trace** support directly into release builds.*

The **BooleanSwitch** and **TraceSwitch** classes are used to provide a means to dynamically control tracing output. You also have the ability to modify the values of these switches in a configuration file that is instantly loaded at run time. So, you don't have to recompile your application to change a value from **False** to **True**. More information about these facilities is presented in the "Run-time Configuration Files" section later in this chapter.

The section "Tracing and the Trace Class" will also show you how to customize the tracing output's target with **TraceListener** instances or remove instances from the **Listeners** collection. As described in Table 17-1, the **DefaultTraceListener** class emits trace output it collects from your trace statements.

Enabling Debugging

Before you can test or debug software in Visual Studio—in fact, before you can write software at all—you need to place the development environment into a debug mode. There are two modes that Visual Studio .NET (and most IDEs) supports: *Debug mode* for debug builds, and *Release mode* for release builds. These two fundamental modes can be specified in Visual Studio, in your code, at the command line, or in configuration files.

Before we examine these alternative locations for debug specifications, consider what it means to be in "Debug mode." When you compile and execute applications or build libraries, you and the development environment place myriad elements and symbols into your code and into your assemblies as debugging aids. These elements comprise switches, conditional constructs, asserts, compiler directives, and the like that add to the final footprint of the application or library.

You will also provide elements in your code that materialize at run time, such as information written to event logs, performance monitors, and dialog boxes. These are certainly elements you would not want to have compiled into your final release. It's especially damaging for an error that could have passed harmlessly to a log file to pop in front of your paying customer's face with all manner of obscene language (it's amazing how often that happens).

Unless an end user explicitly opts into being a guinea pig for you as a beta tester or a release candidate user, you will want to strip the debug elements from the final deliverables without affecting how it runs. Not only will the *release build* footprint of the final versions be much lighter than the *debug build,* the application will load a lot faster, run a lot faster, and, most important, won't risk offending anyone. It will also be more secure, because many horror stories have surfaced over the years that relate how a hacker cracked some code by getting in through a debug element that left the door open.

Also, you cannot use the debugging aids that are included in the IDE if the application is not in Debug mode. For example, you can't set breakpoints at lines in the code and step through or over statements.

To switch modes from Visual Studio, go to the Build menu and select Configuration Manager. The dialog box in Figure 17-1 loads.

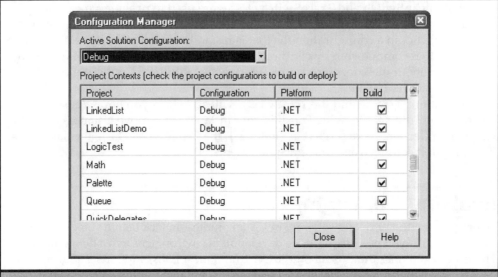

Figure 17-1. *Configuration Manager is used to set Debug mode or Release mode in the application's configuration.*

The shortcut to switching configurations and accessing Configuration Manager is via the Solution Configuration drop-down box on the standard toolbar (it's usually positioned between the Window and Help menus).

To enable debugging from the command line, add the **/d:DEBUG=True** flag to the compiler command line.

You can also enclose segments of your code in Debug mode. The following example uses the **Debug** class to indicate the beginning and ending of a program's execution. The example also uses **Indent** and **Unindent** to distinguish the tracing output.

```
Public Function Main(args() As String) As Integer
  Debug.Listeners.Add(New TextWriterTraceListener(Console.Out))
  Debug.AutoFlush = True
  Debug.Indent()
  Debug.WriteLine("Entering Main")
  Console.WriteLine("Working...")
  Debug.WriteLine("Exiting Main")
  Debug.Unindent()
  Return 0
End Function 'Main
```

Configuration Manager essentially places Debug mode or Release mode information into the configuration file that accompanies your deliverables. We'll cover the configuration files in the following section.

For the most part, you can simply choose the mode from Configuration Manager. If you are working through the examples in this book, you will not need to concern yourself with tailoring the configuration files or building complex command-line compiler solution files, as we will discuss shortly. (In other words, you do not need to freak out about these configurations just to get cracking writing debug build code as soon as possible or just to learn Visual Basic .NET.)

When you start programming and use Visual Studio to create projects with the variety of wizards and templates that come with the product, the IDE automatically creates separate debug and release configurations and sets them up with appropriate default options and sundry other settings as follows:

- **Debug configuration** Specifies that you will compile your code with full symbolic debug information in Microsoft format and without optimization (optimization complicates debugging, since the relationship between the source code and debugger-generated instructions is more complex).

- **Release configuration** Specifies that your release code will be fully optimized and contains no symbolic debug information. Debug information, however, may still be generated in the separate PDB (Program Debug Database) files, which are stored in your project's debug folders (refer to Chapter 3).

You can also change the settings for a configuration using the Solution Property Pages dialog box (Configuration folder).

Run-time Configuration Files

A small collection of CLR-loaded XML-based configuration files can be used to change settings that influence application processing without the need to recompile applications. Your applications will run even if these files are not included because the CLR does not depend on them to bootstrap your assemblies, but they are extremely lightweight and their loading does not impact the CLR or your resources in any way. These files are listed as follows:

- **Machine configuration files** These files (**Machine.config**) contain settings that apply to a specific computer.

- **Application configuration files** These files contain settings specific to an application.

- **Security configuration files** These files contain information about the code group hierarchy and permission sets associated with a policy level (see Chapter 2).

WRITING SOFTWARE WITH VB .NET

Machine Configuration File

The machine configuration files are located in the %runtime install path%\Config directory of the computer. They contain configuration settings for machine-wide assembly binding, built-in remoting channels, and ASP.NET-specific information. System administrators deploying and maintaining .NET Framework environments will usually manage these files under the guidance of your oh so wonderfully written documentation.

The configuration system of the CLR will first look in the machine configuration file for any **<appSettings>** elements and other configuration sections you might consider defining. Then it goes to the application configuration file.

While you can place application-specific information in this file, it is suggested you keep the machine configuration file small and manageable and stick the application-specific settings in the application configuration file.

However, it may make more sense to place application-specific information that more than one application needs into the machine configuration file. Think of this file as the return of your long-lost INI file in the days of DOS and Windows 3.X—and you're probably also thinking, "Gee, we've come so far to be back where we started."

If you have a number of applications that require the same settings, the machine configuration file obviates the need to have these settings in more than one location.

Application Configuration File

This file contains all the configuration settings that the CLR reads (such as assembly binding policy, remoting objects, and so on) in order to "manage" your application. It also provides the settings that the application needs to read.

Where you place this file and what you name it depends on the name of the application using it and the location and host of the actual application. As we discussed in Chapter 2, the host can be one of the following:

- **Standard managed executable**   The configuration file location for an application hosted by the standard executable host of a machine is the same directory as the application. You will also name the configuration file with the same name as the application and give it the .config extension. For example, the ShuttleInjectorUI.exe application discussed in Chapter 9 is associated with ShuttleInjectorUI.exe.config. If you are like most normal developers and are reading this chapter last, doing a machine-wide search for configuration files will turn up several dozen (along with all the Java ones that belong to that "other" run-time environment).

- **ASP.NET-hosted application**   The ASP.NET configuration files are called Web.config; ASP.NET applications inherit the settings of configuration files in the URL path. For example, if you are given the URL www.sdamag

.com/netbooks/netb, where /netb is the Web application, the configuration file associated with the application is located at the /netb path.

- **Internet Explorer-hosted application**   Applications hosted in Internet Explorer also have a configuration file. Its location is specified in a **<link>** tag with the following syntax:

```
<link rel="ConfigurationFileName" href="location">
```

In this tag, **location** is a URL to the configuration file. This sets the application base. The configuration file must be located on the same Web site as the application.

Security Configuration File

This file contains important security information. You should use the .NET Framework Configuration tool (Mscorcfg.msc), which is installed into the Control Panel's Administrative Tools folder, or the Code Access Security Policy tool (Caspol.exe) to modify security policy. This ensures that policy changes do not corrupt the security configuration files, which could lead to a breakdown in security or a collapse in run-time integrity.

Working with Configuration Files

The .NET Framework provides the necessary facilities for reading configuration files directly from your applications in the **System.Configuration** namespace. The CLR and your applications can read from these files but you cannot write to them from this API. Writing to configuration files is not difficult, especially if you have a flair for all things XML.

The configuration files contain XML format elements, which are the logical data structures that encapsulate your configuration information. The tags are used to mark the beginning and ending of configuration segments. You can use a standard XML editor (such as the popular XML Spy) or Visual Studio's XML Designer, which was introduced in Chapter 15, "XML I/O," to edit the files and check their integrity.

An example of a configuration file tag is the **<runtime>** element, which consists of the **<runtime>child elements</runtime>** fields. As with all XML files, empty elements have a start tag, but no end tag.

You specify configuration settings using predefined attributes, which are name/value pairs inside an element's **<start>** tag. The following example specifies two attributes (**version** and **href**) for the **<codeBase>** element, which specifies where the runtime can locate an assembly

```
<codeBase version="2.0.0.0"
href="http://www.sdamag.com/myAssembly.dll"/>
```

Note *Configuration files are case-sensitive.*

The following XML code is an example extracted for the Debug mode directives in the application configuration file:

```
<configuration>
  <system.diagnostics>
  <debug autoflush="true" indentsize="7" />
  </system.diagnostics>
</configuration>
```

The full compliment of configuration file tags is available in the .NET Framework SDK.

Working with the Debug Class

The **System.Diagnostics.Debug** class provides a collection of useful methods and properties that help you track and eliminate errors and logic problems in your code. To use the class, simply import it into your class (as described in many places in this book). Most of the time, simply placing your projects into Debug mode implicitly provides access to the **System.Diagnostics** namespace.

The **Debug** class is obviously static or shared and, of course, provides a consolidated collection of static operations. You thus don't need to do much (such as instantiation) to use the class and its methods.

The Debug Write Methods

One of the first methods seen in various places in this book is the **WriteLine** method, which is a similar construct to the **DebugPrint** method in classic VB. **WriteLine** simply writes debug information to the Output window as described in Chapter 4.

You will use this method most often with assertion and conditional logic used in testing, as you have seen in many places in this book. It has no measurable performance impact in your code. It also does little harm to leave **Debug** statements in your code, because they are not accessible in the release version of your software. When you compile in Release mode Visual Studio strips out the **Debug** statements.

Other **Write** methods include the following:

- **Write**   An overloaded method that overwrites to the current line information about the debug to the trace listeners in the **Listeners** collection.

- **WriteLine**   An overloaded method that writes to a new line information about the debug to the trace listeners in the **Listeners** collection.

- **WriteIf** An overloaded method that overwrites to the current line information about the debug to the trace listeners in the **Listeners** collection but only if a condition is true.

- **WriteLineIf** An overloaded method that writes information to a new line about the debug to the Output window or to a trace listener if a condition is true.

Note *The **Write** methods are discussed throughout Chapter 15.*

The **Debug** class also provides an assert method to display an Assert dialog box and emit an assertion that will always activate on **False**. Before we discuss this further, let's review what we know about an assert construct (experienced programmers may skip this next part).

Assertion

Assertions have been used in routines long before the OOP rave, even before the structured programming years took root. An "assertion" is a method used as a programming aid to test if certain assumptions about the program's state, condition, and data are true at a certain point in its execution.

The assertion, or **Assert** statement, tests a condition, which you specify as an argument to the **Assert** method. If the condition evaluates to **True**, no action occurs. If the condition evaluates to **False**, the assertion fails and the assertion logic is processed. If you are running under the debugger, your program enters Break mode on failure. The overloaded signatures for the **Debug.Assert** are as follows:

- **Public Shared Sub Assert(Boolean)** Checks for a condition and outputs the call stack if the condition is **False**.

- **Public Shared Sub Assert(Boolean, String)** Checks for a condition and displays a message if the condition is **False**.

- **Public Shared Sub Assert(Boolean, String, String)** Checks for a condition and displays both specified messages if the condition is **False**.

Note *You can use the **Assert** method from either the **Debug** class or the **Trace** class (both of which are included in the **System.Diagnostics** namespace). **Debug** class methods are not included in a release version of your program, so they do not increase the size or reduce the speed of your release code.*

In the preceding methods, the first argument, which is mandatory, represents the condition that you want to check. If you call **Assert** with only one argument, as described in the preceding list, the method will check the condition and, if it turns out to be **False**, transmit the contents of the call stack to the Assert message box. The following example demonstrates calling **Assert** and passing one argument to the single-parameter version:

```
Debug.Assert(index < 0)
```

In this case the **index** value was greater than 0 and the message box shown in the illustration is displayed.

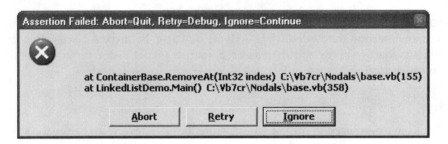

You can see the **Assert** at work in the following code snippet at a location that might make sense as an exception throw point:

```
Public Sub RemoveAt(ByVal index As Integer) Implements IList.RemoveAt
   Try
     Debug.Assert(index <= 0)
       If (index < 0 Or index >= Count) Then
         Throw New ArgumentOutOfRangeException()
       End If
'...
End Sub
```

>
>
> *If you prefer a less obnoxious failure notification than the **Assert** message box there are a few things you can do. The **DefaultTraceListener** (see the "Tracing and the Trace Class" section coming up) controls the output for the **Assert** method so you can turn off the message box (see the "Setting Assertions in Configuration Files" towards the end of this section. The output can be directed to the Debug Output window, other listeners, log files, and so on. You can also control the listeners directly in your code (see the section "Tracing and the Trace Class" coming up).*

As you can see from the following examples, both second and third parameters take **String** arguments. Calling **Assert** with two or three arguments forces **Assert** to check the condition and, if the result is **False**, output one or two **String**s to the Output window. The following examples demonstrate calling **Assert** and passing in two or three arguments:

```
Debug.Assert(index < 0, "Index points to nothing at the tail.")
Debug.Assert(index > count - 1), "Index points to nothing at the _
  head.", Format(size, "G"))
```

You will use the **Debug.Assert** method to test conditions that should hold true if your code is correct. In the following example, I used **Assert** to debug the Singleton pattern implementation:

```
Shared Function GetInstance() As Singleton
  Singleton = New Singleton()
  Singleton.Number += 1
  Debug.Assert(Singleton.Number > 1)
  If (Singleton.Number > 1) Then
    'I have no exception to use here yet
  End If
    Return Singleton
  End If
End Function
```

When you run this code under the watchful eye of the debugger, the assertion method is activated. But in the release version it is not, so there is no additional overhead. However, while debugging the code it's convenient to abort out of the method if no exception handler is present, or you don't want the overhead of handling the exception. Exception handling during debugging often involves having to traipse through the exception handler stack, which can be a tedious process.

Since **Debug** methods vanish when you compile to the release build of your code, you should replace **Debug.Assert** methods with **Trace.Assert** methods, which persist in the release version. In other words, **Debug.Assert** is not applicable for error checking that may respond to exceptions in release software. If you want to create an assertion method you can include in your code, create a new class and encapsulate your own release **Assert** method in that class. The compiler could not care less about your custom code (if it's all right).

It's rather easy to code asserts that do pretty much the same thing as the asserts in the **System.Diagnostics** namespace. The only reason really to create your own is in the event you want to provide some specialized functionality because the **Debug** and **Trace** classes are sealed and you have no means of overriding anything. To create your own assert, create a static class and toss the static collection of overloaded static assert methods into the file.

Here is an example of an assert method implementation:

```
Public Sub Assert(ByVal assertion As Boolean, message As String)
  If Not assertion Then
```

```
      Beep()
      Debug.WriteLine(message)
      End
   End If
End Sub
```

Okay, so **Assert** fails. Now what? You can do a number of things on the **False** condition. You can, for example, display a message box or write something to the file system, a log file, or a database. You can program the **Assert** to write results to a console window, which provides you a window into the world of the method you are checking, you can have it write to the operating system's standard event log or you can have it write to a log file. See the section "Tracing and the Trace Class" for more information on these features.

Using a log file for **Assert** output is useful because it allows you to examine persistent data. You can easily add time and date information as well as source object and method identifiers to guide your way through the log file.

When you use **Debug.Assert**, make sure that any code inside the **Assert** does not change the results of the program if the **Assert** is removed. Otherwise, you may accidentally introduce a bug that only shows up in the release build of your application. Handle **Assert** statements that contain method calls with care.

Be careful of writing an **Assert** method that, for example, results in an incrementing of a variable your algorithm depends on. In Debug mode, the **Assert** is harmless, but when you build the release version, you end up with a bug in the code because the **Assert** is eliminated. To avoid such problems, avoid using **Assert** as a substitute for the formal conditional structures discussed in Chapter 6. It's a debugging aid, no more and no less.

You may even be tempted to use **Trace.Assert**, which, unlike **Debug.Assert**, does not go AWOL in the release code. While **Trace.Assert** is safe, you should not fall into the habit of using this construct in this manner. After all, the transition to **Debug** and disaster is only a class identifier away.

Assert can be called to run in a so-called User Interface mode to display the Assertion Failed message box when the condition fails. The actions that occur when an assertion fails are controlled by the **Debug.Listeners** or **Trace.Listeners** property.

The output behavior can be customized by adding a **TraceListener** object to the **Listeners** collection, by removing a **TraceListener** from the **Listeners** collection, or by overriding the **Fail** method of an existing **TraceListener**. For example, **Fail** can be overridden in a specialized implementation and programmed to write to an event log or a file instead of displaying the Assertion Failed dialog box.

Setting Assertions in Configuration Files

If you prefer, you can set an assertion in your program configuration file instead of in your code. The **Assert** method's metadata must be in the configuration file corresponding to the name of your application. The metadata in the file can be used to enable and disable the **Assert** method and even set the name of its log file. The following is an example of the configuration file **Assert** method set for User Interface mode (uienabled):

```
<configuration>
  <system.diagnostics>
    <switches>
      <assert assertuienabled="true" logfilename="c:\\myFile.log" />
    </switches>
  </system.diagnostics>
</configuration>
```

Fail

The **Debug.Fail** method simply transmits an error message of your choosing. The method signature is overloaded as follows:

- **Public Shared Sub Fail(String)**   Transmits a single error message.
- **Public Shared Sub Fail(String, String)**   Transmits two error messages. The first is typically the base error message, while the second string can be used to provide additional information.

The following example uses the **Fail** method to print a message during exception handling:

```
Catch e As Exception
  Debug.Fail("Invalid data: " + Data.ToString(), _
  "Failed in BaseNodeCollections.Insert method.")
End Try
```

You can also use the **Fail** method in a conditional statement:

```
Public Function Encrypt(ByVal level As Integer, ByVal obj As Object) As Object
  Select Case level
    Case 0
      Encrypt = Cipher.EncryptLowBit(obj)
    Case 1
      Encrypt = Cipher.EncryptMediumBit(obj)
    Case 2
      Encrypt = Cipher.EncryptHighBit(obj)
    Case Else
      Debug.Fail("level arg not provided " & level, _
      "in class Encipher")
  End Select
End Function
```

WRITING SOFTWARE
WITH VB .NET

Tracing and the Trace Class

The .NET Framework's **System.Diagnostics** namespace provides a sophisticated API that lets you monitor the execution and performance of your applications while they are running, in both debug and release builds. This facility is called *tracing* and it is underpinned by the **Trace** and **Debug** classes.

As we just discussed, the **Debug** class provides access to constructs that are only available to the debug builds of your software. The compiler automatically strips the debug statements out when you compile the release build. If you want to build tracing support into releasable software, then you need to implement the tracing facility via the **System.Diagnostics.Trace** class.

The **Trace** class, and the tracing support, lets you record and monitor information while a released application is running. Information trapped by the special listening objects can "pipe" the information out to log files, text files, databases, and consoles and monitor windows for real-time and archival analysis.

The members of the **Trace** class are identical to the members of the **Debug** class, so we don't need to go into them in any detail. Even the **Assert** works the same. The only difference, as mentioned, is that **Trace** code survives release build compilation.

The fact that tracing and instrumentation are also available to ASP.NET applications opens up a whole new host of opportunities for building highly scaleable and reliable Web and e-commerce applications.

Instrumentation

The .NET Framework uses the term *instrumentation* to refer to the ability to monitor or measure the level of an application's or algorithm's performance and for diagnostics. Instrumentation thus gives you the ability to incorporate the following support in your deliverables:

- **Code tracing** The ability to receive information about the execution of an application during run time.

- **Performance counters** These are objects or components that are used to collect information about the performance of your applications.

- **Event logs** These are log files, both custom and operating system, that receive and organize any events in the execution of your application that you need to persist for analysis, archival, and documentation purposes.

If you have been developing Web applications you know that getting real-time data from the application (such as number of connections) is extremely difficult and complex. The tracing and diagnostics support in .NET changes everything to a point where migration from classic VB and ASP is taken for granted simply because so much more power and control are available to both developers and system administrators.

In a distributed applications environment, for example, you will find tracing invaluable under circumstances where it is almost impossible to test and monitor the application in the field. How often have you had to guess at how an application will perform in the field, and how often have you had to enlist the services of your customer to volunteer or expose itself to situations that will allow you to monitor your code?

It is not always possible to monitor how a distributed application will respond to high volumes, different setups, and unique end-user behaviors. Also, much software today has no user interface or console that can provide a window to an application's internals. This is very much in line with the software development philosophy I have expounded in this book, whereby much of the operational and business logic of a complex application is disconnected or decoupled from the user interface; it operates "behind the scenes." This is very much the case with Web and distributed applications and thin clients (not browser-based clients) that access so-called "Web-services" over HTTP.

By *instrumenting* the application—that is, by placing trace statements at strategic locations in your code—the objects that do all the hard work in the background can publish information about their operations to system administrators, QA/QC staff, testers, and developers. Location, as previously mentioned, is not an issue because the trace information can be sent wherever the network takes you, with sufficient bandwidth.

Trace statements make it so that you don't have to worry about loading the original source code on site, or try to modify it, recompile it, and otherwise attempt to reproduce errors within the debugging environment, which is usually not accurate, and does not represent the real operating circumstances.

Placing trace statements in your code is usually facilitated by the incorporation of trace switches. These conditional elements let you control whether tracing occurs and how extensive it is. In a production environment, using configuration files as discussed earlier lets you control how the switches are used in the field or at the customer's location.

Understanding the Phases of Code Tracing

Typically, three phases are involved in supporting tracing in your application:

- **Instrumentation** This is the phase where you add tracing code to your application; that is, methods that will activate **Trace** class operations.

- **Tracing** This is the phase where the tracing code pipes information to specified "listeners."

- **Analysis** This is the phase where you evaluate the tracing information to identify and understand problems in the application or how it is performing.

The default output mechanism during the development stages is the Output window in Visual Studio .NET. In a deployed application, you'll switch the output of the methods to the target listeners you specify.

*Like the placing of **Debug** statements, placing **Trace** statements requires care and common sense.*

Listening to Your Code

The output from **Trace** statements is collected in objects called *listeners.* Listeners derive from the base **TraceListener** class, which we will investigate shortly. The **System.Diagnostics** namespace provides pluggable listeners you can use (discussed very briefly in the class tables near the beginning of this chapter). Listeners receive the trace output and write it to an output device. The output devices can be windows, consoles, logs, text files, the network, and so on.

When you create a trace listener, you can add it to the **Trace.Listeners** collection, allowing the listener to receive all trace output from any trace statement sending output to the collection. You can also manage the collection as you would any collection that implements the **ICollections** interface, as discussed in Chapter 13.

All listeners in the **Listeners** collection receive the messages described in Table 17-1, but how they play out the inbound messages depends on the listener and the device it implements. For example, the **DefaultTraceListener** displays the **Assert** dialog box when it receives a **Fail** notification, or a failed **Assert** notification, while the **TextWriterTraceListener** writes the output to a **TextWriter** object or a stream.

The three predefined listeners are described as follows:

- **TextWriterTraceListener**   Directs output to an instance of the **TextWriter** class or to anything that is a derivative or specialization of the **Stream** class. It can also write to the console or to a file, because these are specialized **Stream** classes. (Refer to Chapter 15 for a full discussion of streams and the **Stream** class.)

- **EventLogTraceListener**   Redirects output to an event log.

- **DefaultTraceListener**   Sends **Write** and **WriteLine** messages to the **OutputDebugString** and to the **Debugger.Log** facility. Visual Studio picks up these messages and sends them to the Output window, as you may have already noticed.

If you want any listener besides the **DefaultTraceListener** to receive **Debug** and **Trace** output, you must add it to the **Listeners** collection described shortly.

A **DefaultTraceListener** is also provided as a means of giving you at least one listener to write to. It's useful in situations where other listeners are no longer receiving output or have gone offline for some reason. If for some reason you nix the **DefaultTraceListener** and are left with no listeners in the collection, the output is simply lost. You won't crash your application, because trace output is backing up inside somewhere with nowhere to go.

However, **Fail** and failed **Assert** messages are also delivered to the **OutputDebugString** facility (the Windows API) and the **Debugger.Log** facility. They also pop up a message box. This behavior is the default behavior for **Debug** and **Trace** messages, because

DefaultTraceListener is automatically included in every **Listeners** collection and is the only listener automatically included. (See the section "Adding Listeners to a Collection" later in this chapter.)

The following code listing shows you how to send output to the **Listeners** collection:

```
Debug.WriteLine("Number of nodes = " & List.Count)
'Use this example when tracing.
Trace.WriteLine("Item inserted is: " & CurrentNode.Data)
```

Debug and *Trace* share the same **Listeners** collection. Adding a listener object to a *Debug.Listeners* collection in your application means both classes get the benefit of the trace.

The following code redirects trace information to a console:

```
'First get rid of left-overs
Trace.Listeners.Clear()
'and then send new data to the console
Trace.Listeners.Add(New TextWriterTraceListener(Console.Out))
```

Adding Listeners to a Collection

Adding listeners is simply a matter of referencing the **Trace.Listeners** collection and calling its **Add** method. This is demonstrated in the following code:

```
Trace.Listeners.Add(New TextWriterTraceListener(Console.Out))
```

Any listener in the **Listeners** collection gets the same messages from the trace output methods. For example, you can set up two listeners, such as a **TextWriterTraceListener** and an **EventLogTraceListener**. Both these listeners receive the same message. However, the **TextWriterTraceListener** directs its output to a stream, while **EventLogTraceListener** directs its output to an event log.

Whenever tracing or debugging is enabled, the **DefaultTraceListener** is automatically created and initialized. But to direct to more than the default source, you must create and initialize additional trace listeners.

The listeners you create should reflect your individual needs. For example, you might want a text record of all trace output. In this case, you would create a listener that writes all output to a new text file when enabled. On the other hand, you might only want to view output during application execution. In that case, you might create a listener that directs all output to a console window.

Creating and initializing your trace listener is simple. First you declare your trace listener. Then, if the particular listener you are creating requires any other objects, you declare them as well. The following example shows how to create a listener that writes to a text file:

```
' Visual Basic
' Creates the text file that the trace listener will write to.
Dim WarpLog as New System.IO.FileStream("C:\warplog.txt", _
    IO.FileMode.OpenOrCreate)
' Creates the new trace listener
Dim warpLogListener As New TextWriterTraceListener(WarpLog)
```

If you want your listener to receive all trace output, add your trace listener to the **Listeners** collection. The following example shows how to do this:

```
Trace.Listeners.Add(warpLogListener)
```

If you do not want your listener to receive trace output, do not add it to the **Listeners** collection. You can make sure that output is transmitted through a listener independent of the **Listeners** collection. This is achieved by simply calling the listener's own output methods. The following example shows how to write a line to a listener that is not in the **Listeners** collection:

```
warpLogListener.WriteLine("Warp Log Started.")
```

If your listener is not a member of the **Listeners** collection, it may be necessary to call the **Flush** method to record your output by flushing the buffers of all listeners in the **Listeners** collection:

```
Trace.Flush()
warpLogListener.Flush()
```

Adding a Listener to the Configuration File

To set the level of your listener, edit the configuration file that corresponds to the name of your application. Within this file, you can add a listener and set its type and its parameter, remove a listener, or clear all the listeners previously set by the application. The configuration file should be formatted similar to the following example:

```
<configuration>
  <system.diagnostics>
   <switches>
    <add name="MagicTraceSwitch" value="3" />
   </switches>
```

```
 <trace autoflush="false" indentsize="4">
  <listeners>
   <add name="myListener"
    type= "System.Diagnostics.TextWriterTraceListener,System"
    initializeData="c:\myListener.log" />
   <remove type="System.Diagnostics.DefaultTraceListener,System"/>
  </listeners>
 </trace>
</system.diagnostics>
</configuration>
```

Developer-Defined Listeners

You can define your own listeners by inheriting from the **TraceListener** base class and overriding its methods with your customized methods. Table 17-3 lists the members of this class.

Member	Description
IndentLevel	Provides or retrieves the indent level
IndentSize	Provides or retrieves the number of spaces in an indent
Name	Provides or retrieves a name for this **TraceListener**
Close	When overridden in a derived class, closes the output stream so it no longer receives tracing or debugging output
Dispose	Releases the resources used by the **TraceListener**
Fail	Emits error messages to the listener you create when you implement the **TraceListener** class
Flush	When overridden in a derived class, flushes the output buffer
Write	Writes a message, category name, or the value of an object's **ToString** method to the listener you create when you implement the **TraceListener** class.
WriteLine	Writes a message, category name, or the value of an object's **ToString** method to the listener you create when you implement the **TraceListener** class, followed by a line terminator.

Table 17-3.   *Members of the **TraceListener** Class*

Member	Description
NeedIndent	Provides or retrieves a value indicating whether to indent the output
WriteIndent	Writes the indent to the listener you create when you implement this class, and resets the **NeedIndent** property to false

Table 17-3. *Members of the **TraceListener** Class* (continued)

You can also customize your tracing environment by implementing your own listener objects. Your custom trace listener might, for example, choose a database server as its output device and add messages to a table, or it could package up the trace data and e-mail it somewhere (remember to throw an exception if your boss is on the e-mail list). Your custom listeners should support the six overridable methods listed in Table 17-3.

Trace Switches

To filter tracing output or filter based on certain conditions in your code, you use objects called *trace switches.* With these switches, you can enable, disable, and filter tracing output as you need. Without these switches, your applications would transmit trace information until the cows come home. Switches do not have to litter your code, either; they can be configured externally in the application configuration file.

The .NET Framework provides two types of trace switches, which work together as a team: **BooleanSwitch** and **TraceSwitch**. The **BooleanSwitch** class is like a toggle switch (on/off) that you use as a gate to enter regions of your code that will transmit the trace information. The **TraceSwitch** class lets you enable the trace switch for a particular tracing level. All trace messages specified for or below the level will be transmitted to the listener. (You can also implement your own switches by deriving from the abstract class **Switch**.)

How would you use the trace switches? The following example lets you receive all the trace data in the **TraceTest** method as well as any error messages in the rest of the application:

```
Dim warpTraceSwitch as New TraceSwitch("Warp Trace Switch", _
    "Class: BaseInjector")
warpTraceSwitch.Level = TraceLevel.Info
MessageBox.Show(warpTraceSwitch.TraceWarning.ToString())
MessageBox.Show(warpTraceSwitch.TraceVerbose.ToString())
```

As you can see, we are using one trace switch for the **TestTrace** method and one switch for the rest of the code. Using the CONFIG file to configure the switches to the appropriate settings is not difficult and provides you the facility to achieve the same result with the flexibility of a CONFIG file.

With switches, you can leave trace directives in your code without fear that trace information will be streamed out until every hard disk in the universe is full. It will also be a good idea to deploy an application with tracing disabled and then enable the tracing with switches in the configuration file when you need to get information centered around an application running at a customer's site. Tracing is switched on by simply stopping the application, changing the information in the configuration file, and then restarting the application.

Trace Levels

A **TraceSwitch** object contains four properties that return **Boolean** values to indicate the level that a certain switch is set at. The properties are listed as follows:

- **TraceSwitch.TraceError**
- **TraceSwitch.TraceWarning**
- **TraceSwitch.TraceInfo**
- **TraceSwitch.TraceVerbose**

These levels allow you to tailor tracing information and limit the output to the information you need for the problem at hand. As you can see, the level of detail you want is achieved by merely setting the trace switches to the appropriate trace level of tracing output. You can also opt not to "hear" messages at all.

The properties in the preceding list correspond to the values 1 through 4 of the **TraceLevel** enumeration that is provided in Table 17-4.

Enumeration	Description
Off, 0	Trace is off
Error, 1	Send only error messages
Warning, 2	Send warning messages and error messages only
Info, 3	Send informational messages, warning messages, and error messages only
Verbose, 4	Send verbose messages, informational messages, warning messages, and error messages only

Table 17-4.   *TraceLevel Enumeration and Its Values*

WRITING SOFTWARE WITH VB .NET

The **TraceSwitch** properties are cumulative and thus direct the maximum trace level for a switch. For example, if you set **TraceInfo** to **True**, then **TraceError** and **TraceWarning** are automatically **True**. **TraceVerbose** will, however, be **False**.

Debugging with Visual Studio .NET

This section is not intended to be a definitive guide to debugging with Visual Studio .NET but rather a short guide to get you started. This book does not have the scope to cover the "art" of debugging with Visual Studio. I emphasize the word "art" because often debugging is just that. It is also a discipline. It is well known that debugging is not the strongest point of many programmers. In fact, research has shown that perhaps only 10 percent of gainfully employed programmers can effectively debug an application.

Debugging .NET applications for the most part is no different from debugging applications written in other languages, unmanaged code, other virtual-machine runtimes, and even midrange and mainframe computing environments. There is also a large school of thought that debugging should be an exercise of last resort because programs should be well thought out and modeled *completely*.

There is also a school of thought that believes the best debugging tool you have is your mind. This school believes that, based on good design, good programmers can mentally "debug" their applications line for line and "trace" their thoughts to the origin of the bug—without debugging aids. I very much believe that your mind is the best debugger, and in many cases the only one. But mentally stepping through code without debugging tools? I don't think so.

Visual Studio .NET provides a rich collection of debugging aids that can help you find the errors and defects in your code. Errors are inevitable in every application, and the tools you have at your disposal will help you connect your thoughts and understanding about your code, with the actual lines of code in the IDE (as opposed to the lines of code you "see" in your mind).

What Species Is Your Bug

Bugs come in three species: syntax, semantic, and logic. The most common type of bug you are likely to encounter is the syntax one. These bugs are not too dangerous, because they are common, seen a lot, and can be squished very easily. They occur when the code you write does not conform to the so-called "rules of grammar" of the language you have chosen to write in.

Syntax bugs are the easiest to find and fix, and the compiler, which checks your code as you write it and tells you what's wrong, can mostly knock out and automatically fry these critters as they show up. So powerful is Visual Basic .NET's background compiler that syntax bugs are for all intents and purposes eliminated as they appear. You can change that power, however, so that you learn by your mistakes. Just try to type 50 lines of code in "Visual Notepad .NET" and see how far you get.

Visual Studio pumps syntax error messages to the Output window. And the ones it does not automatically correct are flagged with the location of a syntax error (line number and file) and a terse description of the problem. Sometimes the compiler is not accurate and only gives you enough bait to go fishing with. At that point, you need to fish in your mind and mentally trace your way to the location of the error that is causing the bug.

Semantic bugs are more subtle and thus more difficult to find. These errors occur even when the syntax of your code is correct, but the semantics or meaning leads to results that were not exactly intended (to put it mildly). Because they are unrelated to syntax errors, they are not caught by the compiler, so it can't tell you where they are.

It is important to remember that compilers and interpreters concern themselves only with the structure of the code you write, not the semantics or meaning. Semantic errors can be very subtle and go unnoticed for many full moons. Others are more dangerous and can create disaster for everyone concerned.

The third type of bug, which no debugger can catch, is the logic bug. It's a killer that can bring down an elephant of an application. And the reason is simple: Not even the full resources of the U.S. Government will be able to invent a debugger that steps through the lines of code in your mind.

Logic errors occur when the code is syntactically and semantically correct but the logic of the program performs certain operations that you did not intend or expect. The simplest, and most dangerous, logic errors occur when variables do not represent valid data. Your program continues to process normally, but the eventual outcome may be (at the least) incorrect data or (at the worst) system or process failure.

You can only eliminate logic errors with the model or specification in one hand, the debugging aids in the other hand, and your mind at peak concentration levels.

The only way to detect logic errors is to test your program. This can be done manually by you or independent testers, or automatically with testing software that can be scripted to "test drive" your code from every possible angle until something goes wrong. Testing is best done by people independent of the programmers, because the programmers generally are not objective enough or are not sufficiently disconnected from the source code in the source files and the source code in their minds.

Testing should be an integral part of your software development process, but it also has its limitations. Testing may turn up errors, or it may even cause system failure, but finding the error that caused the failure or detected the fault while the software was undergoing testing isn't easy. Testing coupled with tracing can help you find the source of the error. You then need a debugging aid to find the offending variable, statement, or expression and change it. You will then use your debugging tools—and their amazing ability to step through the actual code—in a controlled execution, to determine if the changes you made were the correct ones to make.

Debugging Aids

Debugging aids are tools that allow you to observe the run-time behavior of your program, to determine the location of errors, and to monitor what an application is doing at any given point in its running time.

Most new programmers learn to debug by first injecting standard programming constructs into their code, such as writes to the console or to message boxes (my favorite is to sound one beep if code went into the **If**, and two beeps if did not). While this works, removing these elements at run time is a drag, which is why we have the **Debug** and **Trace** classes to make such efforts easier to manage. Not removing them can also cause unexpected results.

Debugging aids let you examine the content of variable fields, insert a breakpoint in your code to stop execution at a point of interest, step over statements, step through statements, and so on. When a program is stopped at a line in your code, you are afforded the opportunity to examine local variables and other relevant data while the application is in a frozen state. Computers process data fast, and without the ability to freeze them at any point or trace the results of their execution and examine the state the software and its data are in, it would be impossible to find the cause of even the most simple errors.

Breakpoints

The most common means of examining the state and behavior of your application is by setting breakpoints. These are typically set in a Visual Studio source window. You can also choose to set them in the debugger's Disassembly window. You can also use the **Stop** keyword to halt execution in Debug mode. However, setting breakpoints does not add anything to your code, and thus it is a cleaner means of halting execution at any appropriate line in the code.

The Disassembly window collects and presents the instructions created from your source code while the application is running. It is useful for examining how your source code is translated into the intermediate code that will eventually be converted to machine-readable code. You will use the Disassembly to see how your source code translates into resource-intensive instructions, such as how certain statements can result in too much boxing and unboxing activity (refer to Chapter 8).

The following list provides descriptions of the various debugger features and utilities:

- **Autos Window**   This window automatically shows you the variables used in the current statement, in the three statements before the current statement and in the three statements after the current statement.

- **Execution control**   Visual Studio provides you with the ability to control execution of your program. The debugger lets you start (or continue) execution, break execution, stop execution, step through your code, run to a specified location in your code, and set execution points.

■ **Attach to a running program or multiple programs**   Visual Studio provides the ability to attach to programs that are running in processes outside of Visual Studio. You can use this attach capability to debug a program that was not created in Visual Studio. You can also debug multiple programs simultaneously, debug programs running on remote machines, or debug programs in separate processes (such as DLLs) that cannot easily be started from Visual Studio. You can also use this ability to start the debugger automatically when a program crashes while running outside of the development environment, even on another machine.

■ **Just-in-time debugging**   Visual Studio provides the ability to perform JIT debugging (a technique for debugging a program that is started outside of Visual Studio). JIT debugging can also be implemented from a remote machine.

■ **Automatic launching**   Visual Studio provides the ability to start it when you start the application from Windows. The IDE loads your application in Debug mode, ready for your command to start execution. This facility is useful for debugging services and COM out-of-process servers.

■ **Dumps**   Visual Studio provides the ability to dump to disk files that include instructions. Dumps are used to test a program on a machine or location that does not have access to the IDE or source code, such as your customer's site. When a crash occurs, you can save a dump file and debug it later on the machine that has the source files and the IDE.

■ **Breakpoints**   Visual Studio provides the full range of breakpoint options, such as setting, disabling, removing, and editing breakpoints in various debugger windows.

■ **Call Stack window**   This window lets you view the calls current on the call stack, byte offsets and other call related information.

■ **Exception handling**   Visual Studio provides the ability to debug exception handlers. You have the ability to change the handling and to see where the exception occurred and then examine the variable contents.

■ **Disassembly window**   This window in Visual Studio displays the basic instructions that represent your source code. A disassembler takes machine code and coverts it back to an assembly-language form, the step between source code and machine or CLR-readable code.

■ **Locals window**   This windows displays variables local to the current context.

■ **Me window**   This window displays the data members of the current object containing the method the code is currently executing.

■ **Memory windows**   These windows (there are four of them) can be used to view large buffers, strings, and other data that does not display well in the Watch or Variables window.

■ **Modules window**   This window provides information about the DLL files and EXE used by the current application.

- **Registers window**   The Registers window displays the contents of a register. It is useful to keep the Registers window open as you step through your code because it lets you see register values change as your code executes.

- **Running Documents window**   This window provides information related to any script files used by the current application.

- **Threads window**   This window lets you access the threads that are currently running in your application.

- **Watch window**   The Watch window is used to evaluate variables and expressions and keep the results. The Watch window can also be used to edit the value of a variable or register.

- **QuickWatch dialog box**   The QuickWatch dialog box can be used to quickly evaluate a variable or expression. It is simpler to use than the Watch window.

Note   *Edit and Continue is a feature of Visual Studio that lets you change your source code while your program is in Break mode and then apply those changes without having to end the debug session and rebuild your program. This feature was available to Visual Studio 6 and was made available to Visual Basic 6 programmers. Unfortunately, it is a feature only available to C++ programmers as of the first release of Visual Studio .NET, and we pray it will return to the Visual Basic language side of the house as soon as possible.*

Getting Started

Your first debugging activity will likely be to set breakpoints in your code and step through your application. The following is the order of the steps you will take through your code:

1. Start execution.
2. Break execution (halt execution).
3. Continue (resume execution).
4. Stop execution.
5. Step through the application.
6. Run to a specified location.
7. Set the execution point.

To set a breakpoint in your code, place your cursor at a valid line for a breakpoint and then double-click in the left margin of the source code editor. A breakpoint, represented by a large round blob, is inserted, as illusrated here.

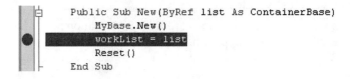

Alternatively, if you don't have the source code file open in front of you, you can set a breakpoint in the New Breakpoint dialog box. As illustrated in Figure 17-2, this dialog box can be opened by selecting the Debug menu and choosing New Breakpoint.

As stated earlier, you can also set a breakpoint in the Disassembly window after the application has been started and is in Break mode. This window, shown in Figure 17-3, can be accessed by selecting from the Debug, Windows, Disassembly menu item.

As soon as the application breaks, you can start debugging from the options presented on the Debug menu. These include Step Into, Step Over, and Step Out. You can also right-click in the source window and choose various options in the shortcut/context-sensitive menu.

When you choose Start, your application starts and runs until it reaches the breakpoint your have set. But if you then choose Step Into or Step Over, your application starts, executes, and then breaks on the first breakpoint.

If you choose Run To Cursor, your application will start as usual and then it will run until it reaches either the breakpoint or the cursor location, whichever comes first. You can set the cursor location in a source window, which is the easiest method. When a break fails to occur, it could mean that execution never reached the code where the cursor was set.

Your solution may contain more than one project, and you can choose the startup project that will be launched by the Debug menu execution commands. You can also

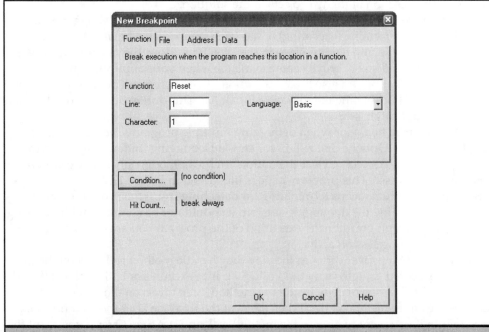

Figure 17-2. *The New Breakpoint dialog box*

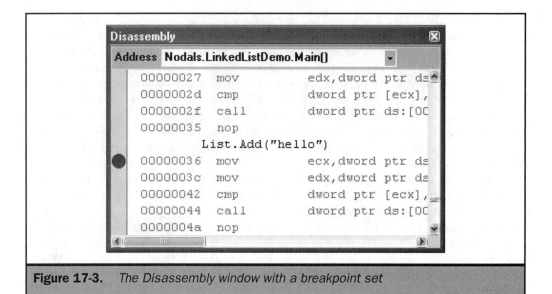

Figure 17-3. *The Disassembly window with a breakpoint set*

set the default startup application from your project folders in Solution Explorer and build one of a collection of many projects in the solution.

When you are debugging an application with the Visual Studio debugger, your application is either running (executing) or has been stopped on a break. Many debugger features, such as evaluating expressions in the Watch window, the memory windows, the Disassembly, and so on, only become available when your application has been stopped on a break. You can also break execution of your program manually from the Debug menu by choosing the menu option Break All. This option becomes disabled as soon as your application stops.

To change break behavior when debugging multiple programs, you can choose Tools, Options. The Options dialog box contains a Debugging folder. Drill down to the General page and select or clear the option "In break mode, only stop execution of the current process." This property page is illustrated in Figure 17-4.

Stopping execution means terminating (or detaching from) the program you are debugging and ending the debugging session. It should not be confused with breaking execution, which temporarily halts execution of the program you are debugging but leaves the debugging session active.

Step Into and Step Over differ in the way they handle method calls. When the line about to be executed contains a method call, Step Into executes only the call itself, and then halts at the first line of code inside the method. Step Over, on the other hand, processes the entire method code. It then stops at the first line after the method call. Use Step Into if you want to go into the method call, and use Step Over if you want to avoid stepping into the methods.

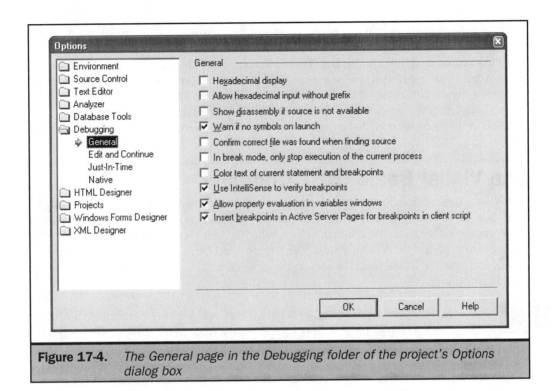

Figure 17-4. *The General page in the Debugging folder of the project's Options dialog box*

On a nested method call, Step Into steps into the most deeply nested function. If you use Step Into on a call like **Method1(Method2())**, the debugger steps into the method **Method2**. Use Step Out when you are inside the method and want to return to the calling method. Step Out resumes execution of your code until the method returns. It then breaks at the return point in the calling method.

You will learn that there are times when you should not (or need not) set a breakpoint. The Visual Studio debugger provides specific commands to run to the cursor location or to a specified method. You can also move the execution point to set the next statement of code (or assembly-language instruction) to be executed.

A yellow arrowhead in the margin of a source or Disassembly window identifies the current location of the execution point in the source code or disassembled code. You can move the execution point, and thus skip over a portion of code to execute. You can also return to a line that was previously executed. You can use this feature to skip a section of code, such as a sector that contains a known bug, and continue debugging elsewhere.

Note *In managed code, you cannot change the execution point after an exception has occurred.*

To set the next statement to execute, perform the following: In a source window or Disassembly window, right-click the statement or assembly language instruction you want to execute next and choose Set Next Statement from the shortcut menu. If the current execution point is in the same source file as the statement you want to set, you can move the execution point by dragging the marker arrow. Or you can go to the source code, click the execution point marker (yellow arrowhead), and drag it to a location in the same source file where you want to set the next statement to be executed.

The Visual Basic .NET Compiler

The Visual Basic .NET Compiler compiles your class files to an intermediate language or IL (see the Microsoft Intermediate Language discussion is Chapter 2). You can invoke the compiler either from the command line, which is what we are going to kick off with here, or from within the Visual Studio .NET Integrated Development Environment (IDE), as discussed in the final section on the compiler, "Using the Visual Studio Build Commands."

As we discussed earlier, the compiler is named VBC and is a single executable file that resides in the folders of the .NET Framework—usually at C:\Windows\ Microsoft.Net\ Framework\ v1.0.3512\VBC.EXE.

To invoke the compiler, simply reference the path to it in a DOS batch file or from the command line as VBC, as described earlier in the "Getting Started" section. The command-line directives of the VBC are described in Table 17-5.

Directives	Purpose	VS .NET	Example/Usage
@	Use to specify a response file, which obviates the need for a complex DOS batch file.	N/A	See the section "Using a Response File for Compilation" after this table
/?	Displays compiler command-line options in the console and short-circuits compilation.	N/A	c:\..\vbc /?

Table 17-5.   *The VBC Command-Line Compiler Directives*

Directives	Purpose	VS .NET	Example/Usage
| /addmodule | Lets you compile a class into a module, which contains no metadata about the class the module contains. You can then add the module to the project you are currently compiling. | No | ```
Vbc
/addmodule:t1.
netmodule t2.vb
``` |
| /baseaddress | Lets you specify the base address of a DLL. | Yes (in Property Pages) | Set programmatically |
| /bugreport | Use to produce a file that contains bug report information. | No | ```
vbc /bugreport:
bugs.txt
nodals.vb
``` |
| /debug | Use to produce debugging information. | Yes (in Property Pages) | ```
vbc /debug /out:
Nodals.txt
Nodals.vb
``` |
| /define | Lets you define constants that can be used for conditional compilation. | No, use #Const | ```
Vbc /define:
DEBUGMODE=True,TR
APERRORS=False
test.vb
``` |
| /delaysign | Allows you to decide later if your assembly will be fully or partially signed. | N/A (use Strong Name Tool) | Set programmatically |
| /help | Displays compiler command-line options in the console and short-circuits compilation. See the ? directive in this table. | N/A | ```
c:\..\vbc /help
``` |

Table 17-5. *The VBC Command-Line Compiler Directives* (continued)
```

Directives	Purpose	VS .NET	Example/Usage
/imports	Use for referencing classes in a namespace from a specified assembly.	Same as using Imports in your code, or settings in Project Properties Dialog Box	Set programmatically
/keycontainer	Lets you specify the key container for a key pair to give an assembly a strong name.	See /delaysign	`vbc/keycontainer: key1 nodals.vb`
/keyfile	Lets you specify the key file containing a key or key pair to give an assembly a strong name.	See /delaysign	`vbc /keyfile: myfile.sn nodals.vb`
/libpath	Lets you specify the location of assemblies referenced via the /reference option.	Yes. See Project Properties Dialog Box	`vbc /libpath:c:\ /reference:nodes. dll nodals.vb`
/linkresource	Lets you create a link to a managed resource.	N/A	`vbc /linkresource: rf.resource uiapp.vb`
/main	Lets you specify the class that contains the Sub Main required at startup. See the section on assemblies in this chapter.	Yes. See Project Properties Dialog Box	`vbc nodals.vb list.vb /main:nodals`

Table 17-5. *The VBC Command-Line Compiler Directives* (continued)

Directives	Purpose	VS .NET	Example/Usage
/nologo	Lets you switch off the Microsoft copyright information.	N/A	vbc /nologo nodals.vb
/nowarn	Lets you switch off the compiler's warnings generator.	Yes. See Project Properties Dialog Box	vbc /nowarn nodals.vb
/optimize	Toggles code optimization.	Yes, See Project Properties Dialog Box	Optimize or optimize+ to enable, or optimize- to suppress
/optioncompare	Lets you specify whether string comparisons in your classes should be binary or should use locale-specific text semantics.	Yes, See Project Properties Dialog Box	See Chapter 4, for Options Directives
/optionexplicit	Lets you specify that code requires explicit declaration of variables.	Yes. See Project Properties Dialog Box	See Chapter 4, Option Directives
/optionstrict	Lets you specify that strict language semantics are enforced in your code.	Yes. See Project Properties Dialog Box	See Chapter 4, Option Directives
/out	Lets you specify the output file.	Yes. See Project Properties Dialog Box	vbc nodals.vb /out:demo.exe

Table 17-5.   *The VBC Command-Line Compiler Directives* (continued)

Directives	Purpose	VS .NET	Example/Usage
/quite	The compiler will not display syntax-related errors and warnings.	N/A	```vbc /quiet nodals.vb```
/recurse	Lets you specify subfolders to search for source files to compile.	N/A	```/recurse:Test\ABC *.vb```
/reference	Lets you import metadata from an assembly.	Yes. See Add Referencs dialog box	```vbc /reference: metad1.dll```
/removechecks	Lets you disable integer overflow checking.	Yes. See Project Properties Dialog Box	```vbc /remove intchecks+ nodals.vb```
/resource	Lets you embed a managed resource in an assembly.	Yes	```vbc /res: rf.resource node.vb```
/rootnamespace	Lets you specify a namespace for all type declarations.	Yes. See Add References dialog box	See the Namespaces section in Chapter 4 and the Assemblies section in Chapters 2 and 3
/target	Lets you specify the format of the output file using one of four options: /target:exe /target:library /target:module /target:winexe	Yes. See Project Properties Dialog Box	exe = console app library = class library module = no manifest winexe = Win app

Table 17-5. *The VBC Command-Line Compiler Directives* (continued)

Directives	Purpose	VS .NET	Example/Usage
/utf8output	Lets you display compiler output using UTF-8 encoding.	N/A	`vbc /utf8output nodes.vb`
/verbose	Lets you specify to display all information generated during compilation.	N/A	`vbc /verbose nodes.vb`
/warnaserror	Lets you promote warnings to errors.	Yes. See Project Properties Dialog Box	`vbc /warnaserror nodes.vb`
/win32icon	Lets you insert a ICO file (icon) into the output file.	Yes. See Project Properties Dialog Box	`vbc /win32icon: rf.ico in.vb`
/win32resource	Lets you insert a Win32 resource into the output file.	N/A	`vbc /win32 resource:rf.res injui.vb`

Table 17-5. *The VBC Command-Line Compiler Directives* (continued)

Compiling from the command line can be very useful, especially when you make changes to a collection of files you are maintaining in a library. A number of options from the command line are not available in Visual Studio using the "visual compiler" and are explained further in this chapter.

Using a Response File for Compilation

A response file (RSP) is essential for compiling from the command line with a number of compiler options or to specify a collection of files. The response file obviates the need to concoct a complex DOS batch file to send commands to the compiler. It lets you specify input, output, and conditional directives for the compiler. You can also place more than one response file on the command line, or type a list into a batch file.

Command-line commands for the compiler must be placed on a single line in the response file. You can specify multiple files and options on the line, but your best bet is to keep the lines short, because complex lines are hard to maintain.

Response files can also be documented using the pound sign (#) to signify the comment line the compiler must ignore. The following code example demonstrates compiling the welcome.vb source files from a response file:

```
#the first file compiled for the comp ref.
/target:exe
/out:e:\VB7CR\Ch2\welcome.exe
#**********The file/s to compile**********
e:\VB7cr\Welcome\welcome.vb
```

The preceding code in the response file specifies that the target is a standard executable (EXE) that is a console application. This is specified on the **/target** line. It also specifies the output folder on the **/out** line.

Tip   *The VBC does not like spaces and complex paths like "e:\All my vb files\chapter 2." So, save yourself the aggravation and stick with simple spaceless paths, as demonstrated in the preceding code. Spaces after the options (such as /out: c:\path) also cause the VBC problems. I have found it best to forgo the fancy folder VS sets up under Documents and Settings and create a stand-alone folder system of simple names and structure. See also the discussion of the /libpath compiler directive in the next section.*

Managing a Class Library from the Command Line

Using the response file system previously discussed can make it easier for you to place all of your class files into their respective namespaces and then specify the assembly name to package everything. In this section, we will go through the steps to create such a library with a weak name (strong naming is further discussed in Chapter 19).

The following collection of class files were developed for *Visual Basic .NET Developer's Headstart* (McGraw-Hill/Osborne, 2001), the precursor to *Visual Basic .NET Complete Reference*:

- Crew.vb
- Engineer.vb
- IcrewSecurity.vb

These files can thus be placed into their own namespace, called **Vb7hs.Ch5**. The files are maintained in a folder called VB7HS.Ch5, which mirrors the namespace on the file system. This is not required; it is just a convenient method of organizing class files on the file system hierarchy as they should appear in the namespace. The assembly name for the classes is called **Vb7hscode.dll**.

Now the response file includes the root /namespace for the files and is thus constructed as follows:

```
#the demo assembly for the Visual Basic.NET Headstart.
/target:library
/out:c:\VB7HS\Ch5\Vb7hscode.dll
/rootnamespace:Vb7hs.Ch5
#**********The file/s to compile**********
c:\VB7HS\Ch5\Crew.vb
c:\VB7HS\Ch5\Engineer.vb
c:\VB7HS\Ch5\ICrewSecurity.vb
```

That's all there is to creating a class library for distribution from the command line.

Conditional Compilation Directives

You can use conditional compilation to choose certain sections of code to compile over other sections. For example, you may want to compile versions of your software for Windows 98 and other versions for Windows 2000 and Windows XP. You may also want to compile regions of code over other regions (say, to test how one method implementation performs over another), or you may want to localize an application for multiple languages or cultures. Conditional compilation statements run during compile time, but remain sterile at run time.

To declare a conditional compiler constant in code, use the **#Const** directive around the regions of code to be conditionally compiled. The conditional statement to use is the **#If...Then...#Else** directive.

Here's an example to create U.S. and U.K. versions of the same application from the same source code with alternative messages for each culture. Simply embed platform-specific code segments in **#If...Then** statements using the predefined constants **USVersion** and **UKVersion**. The following example demonstrates how to do this:

```
#If USVersion Then
  ' <code specific to the French language version>.
#ElseIf UKVersion Then
  ' <code specific to the German language version>.
#Else
  ' <code specific to other versions>.
#End If
```

Now when you set the value of the **USVersion** constant to **True** at compile time, the conditional code for the **USVersion** version is compiled. But if you set the value of the **UKVersion** constant to **True** (and leave **USVersion** to **False**), the compiler uses the **UKVersion**. Setting neither to **True** forces the code in the last **Else** block to be compiled.

You can set conditional compilation constants in one of three ways:

- In the Property Pages dialog box
- At the command line when using the command-line compiler
- In your code

Conditional compilation constants have a special scope that cannot be accessed from standard code in any way. The scope of a conditional compilation constant is dependent on the way it is set. To set constants in the Property Pages dialog box, do so before creating your executable file.

To set constants at the command line, use the **/d** switch to enter conditional compilation constants, as in the following example:

```
vbc Engineer.vb /d:USVersion=-1:conANSI=0
```

No space is required between the **/d** switch and the first constant.

Make a note that command-line declarations override declarations entered in the Property Pages dialog box, but they do not cancel or reset them. In other words, the arguments set in the Property Pages dialog box remain in effect for subsequent compilations but are quashed as long as you issue directives at the command line.

When writing constants in the code itself, there are no strict rules as to their placement, since their scope is the entire module in which they are declared. To set constants in your code, place the constants in the declaration block of the module or class in which they are used. This helps keep your code organized and easier to read.

Observations

This chapter focused on the art of debugging, and described how the **Debug** and **Trace** classes can be used for defect management and quality control. We also discussed how to use the classes in debug versions and release versions of your code.

Looking back, you may now think that this discussion would have been better earlier in the book, especially if you are new to the concepts of debugging. But I felt it would have detracted from the lessons at hand, and injecting debug statements in the example code would have been distracting. As a result, I also removed most debug statements from the code in this book and replaced many **Debug.Write** and **Debug .WriteLine** calls with the **Console** class and **Trace** class equivalents of these methods.

We also briefly discussed using the Visual Studio .NET debugging tools. But our discussion was just a small taste of what is a very complex and comprehensive discussion.

We have come a long way after all these pages. As you have seen, this book focuses mostly on the core programming concepts and constructs. If you have read every chapter and have gone over the source code examples, you will be ready to start writing your own applications and tackle more complex subjects like creating enterprise applications with ASP.NET and ADO.NET, employing advanced graphics applications using the GDI+ libraries, and discovering distributed computing solutions using the .NET Remoting classes, Web Services, and network libraries.

Index

D

M

INTERNATIONAL CONTACT INFORMATION

AUSTRALIA
McGraw-Hill Book Company Australia Pty. Ltd.
TEL +61-2-9417-9899
FAX +61-2-9417-5687
http://www.mcgraw-hill.com.au
books-it_sydney@mcgraw-hill.com

CANADA
McGraw-Hill Ryerson Ltd.
TEL +905-430-5000
FAX +905-430-5020
http://www.mcgrawhill.ca

GREECE, MIDDLE EAST,
NORTHERN AFRICA
McGraw-Hill Hellas
TEL +30-1-656-0990-3-4
FAX +30-1-654-5525

MEXICO (Also serving Latin America)
McGraw-Hill Interamericana Editores S.A. de C.V.
TEL +525-117-1583
FAX +525-117-1589
http://www.mcgraw-hill.com.mx
fernando_castellanos@mcgraw-hill.com

SINGAPORE (Serving Asia)
McGraw-Hill Book Company
TEL +65-863-1580
FAX +65-862-3354
http://www.mcgraw-hill.com.sg
mghasia@mcgraw-hill.com

SOUTH AFRICA
McGraw-Hill South Africa
TEL +27-11-622-7512
FAX +27-11-622-9045
robyn_swanepoel@mcgraw-hill.com

UNITED KINGDOM & EUROPE
(Excluding Southern Europe)
McGraw-Hill Education Europe
TEL +44-1-628-502500
FAX +44-1-628-770224
http://www.mcgraw-hill.co.uk
computing_neurope@mcgraw-hill.com

ALL OTHER INQUIRIES Contact:
Osborne/McGraw-Hill
TEL +1-510-549-6600
FAX +1-510-883-7600
http://www.osborne.com
omg_international@mcgraw-hill.com